Environment, Land Use and Urban Policy

Environmental Analysis and Economic Policy

Series Editors: Kenneth Button
Professor of Public Policy
The Institute of Public Policy, George Mason University, USA

Peter Nijkamp
Professor in Regional, Urban and Environmental Economics
Free University, Amsterdam, The Netherlands

Wherever possible, the articles in these volumes have been reproduced as originally published using facsimile reproduction, inclusive of footnotes and pagination to facilitate ease of reference.

For a list of all Edward Elgar published titles visit our site on the World Wide Web at
http://www.e-elgar.co.uk

Environment, Land Use and Urban Policy

Edited by

David Banister

Professor of Transport Planning, University College London, UK

Kenneth Button

Professor of Public Policy, The Institute of Public Policy, George Mason University, USA

and

Peter Nijkamp

Professor in Regional, Urban and Environmental Economics, Free University, Amsterdam, The Netherlands

ENVIRONMENTAL ANALYSIS AND ECONOMIC POLICY

An Elgar Reference Collection
Cheltenham, UK • Northampton, MA, USA

Published by
Edward Elgar Publishing Ltd
Glensanda House
Montpellier Parade
Cheltenham
Glos GL50 1UA
UK

Edward Elgar Publishing, Inc.
136 West Street
Suite 202
Northampton
Massachusetts 01060
USA

A catalogue record for this book is available from the British Library.

Library of Congress Cataloguing in Publication Data

Environment, land use and urban policy / edited by David Banister, Kenneth Button,
    and Peter Nijkamp.
        (Environmental analysis and economic policy: 2)
        Includes index.
        1. Land-use—Environmental aspects. 2. Urban Policy. 3. Sustainable
    development. I. Banister, David. II. Button, Kenneth. III. Nijkamp, Peter.
    IV. Series: An Elgar reference collection.
    HD108.3.E58   1999
    333.77—dc21   99–21909
                                                                              CIP

ISBN 1 85898 722 9

Printed and bound in Great Britain by Biddles Ltd, Guildford and King's Lynn

Contents

Acknowledgements

The editors and publishers wish to thank the authors and the following publishers who have kindly given permission for the use of copyright material.

American Planning Association for articles: John Friedmann and Barclay Hudson (1974), 'Knowledge and Action: A Guide to Planning Theory', *Journal of the American Institute of Planners*, **40** (1), January, 2–16; Peter Hall (1989), 'The Turbulent Eighth Decade: Challenges to American City Planning', *Journal of the American Planning Association*, **55** (3), Summer, 275, 277–82; John Friedmann (1989), 'Planning, Politics, and the Environment', Benjamin Chinitz, 'Growth Management from an Economist's Perspective' and Hilda Blanco and Michael Neuman, 'The Environment as Common Ground: Learning from Practice', *Journal of the American Planning Association*, **55** (3), Summer, 334–41; Robert Cervero (1994), 'Rail Transit and Joint Development: Land Market Impacts in Washington, D.C. and Atlanta', *Journal of the American Planning Association*, **60** (1), Winter, 83–94; Scott Campbell (1996), 'Green Cities, Growing Cities, Just Cities? Urban Planning and the Contradictions of Sustainable Development', *Journal of the American Planning Association*, **62** (3), Summer, 296–312; Peter Gordon and Harry W. Richardson (1997), 'Are Compact Cities a Desirable Planning Goal?', *Journal of the American Planning Association*, **63** (1), Winter, 95–106.

Beech Tree Publishing for article: N. Lee and F. Walsh (1992), 'Strategic Environmental Assessment: An Overview', *Project Appraisal*, **7** (3), September, 126–36.

Blackwell Publishers for article: Richard F. Muth (1985), 'Models of Land-Use, Housing, and Rent: An Evaluation', *Journal of Regional Science*, **25** (4), November, 593–606.

Blackwell Publishers Ltd for article and excerpt: Manuel Castells (1980), 'Cities and Regions beyond the Crisis: Invitation to a Debate', *International Journal of Urban and Regional Research*, **4** (1), March, 127–9; Michael Batty (1989), 'Urban Modelling and Planning: Reflections, Retrodictions and Prescriptions', in Bill Macmillan (ed.), *Remodelling Geography*, Chapter 10, 147–69, references.

Carfax Publishing Ltd for articles: Nathaniel Lichfield (1970), 'Evaluation Methodology of Urban and Regional Plans: A Review', *Regional Studies*, **4** (2), August, 151–65; Andreas Faludi (1983), 'Critical Rationalism and Planning Methodology', *Urban Studies*, **20** (3), August, 265–78; Andrew Blowers (1993), 'Environmental Policy: The Quest for Sustainable Development', *Urban Studies*, **30** (4/5), May, 775–96; William P. Anderson, Pavlos S. Kanaroglou and Eric J. Miller (1996), 'Urban Form, Energy and the Environment: A Review of Issues, Evidence and Policy', *Urban Studies*, **33** (1), February, 7–35; David Satterthwaite

(1997), 'Sustainable Cities or Cities that Contribute to Sustainable Development?', *Urban Studies*, **34** (10), October, 1667–91.

Daedalus, Journal of the American Academy of Arts and Sciences for article and excerpt: Kevin Lynch (1961), 'The Patterns of the Metropolis', *Daedalus*, **90**, Winter, 79–98; William Alonso (1966), 'Cities, Planners, and Urban Renewal', in James Q. Wilson (ed.), *Urban Renewal: The Record and the Controversy*, 437–53.

Earthscan Publications Ltd/Kogan Page Ltd for excerpt: Michael Breheny and Ralph Rookwood (1993), 'Planning the Sustainable City Region', in Andrew Blowers (ed.), *Planning for a Sustainable Environment: A Report by the Town and Country Planning Association*, Chapter 9, 150–89, 223–4.

Elsevier Science Ltd for articles: R. Andrew Sayer (1976), 'A Critique of Urban Modelling: From Regional Science to Urban and Regional Political Economy', *Progress in Planning*, **6** (3), 187–9, 191–253; Robert Cervero and John Landis (1997), 'Twenty Years of the Bay Area Rapid Transit System: Land Use and Development Impacts', *Transportation Research A*, **31** (4), 309–33.

Johns Hopkins University Press for excerpt: Melvin M. Webber (1963), 'Order in Diversity: Community Without Propinquity', in Lowdon Wingo, Jr. (ed.), *Cities and Space: The Future Use of Urban Land*, 23–54.

Liverpool University Press for articles: Colin Clark (1958), 'Transport – Maker and Breaker of Cities', *Town Planning Review*, **28** (4), January, 237–50; Richard E. Klosterman (1985), 'Arguments For and Against Planning', *Town Planning Review*, **56** (1), January, 5–20.

Pion Ltd for article: D. Banister, S. Watson and C. Wood (1997), 'Sustainable Cities: Transport, Energy and Urban Form', *Environment and Planning B*, **24** (1), 125–43.

Policy and Politics for article: R.H. Williams (1986), 'EC Environment Policy, Land Use Planning and Pollution Control', *Policy and Politics*, **14** (1), January, 93–106.

Routledge and Herbert Girardet for excerpt: Herbert Girardet (1990), 'The Metabolism of Cities', in David Cadman and Geoffrey Payne (eds), *The Living City: Towards a Sustainable Future*, Chapter 8, 170–80.

Rutgers – The State University of New Jersey, Center for Urban Policy Research for excerpt: David Harvey (1978), 'On Planning the Ideology of Planning', in Robert W. Burchell and George Sternlieb (eds), *Planning Theory in the 1980's: A Search for Future Directions*, 213–33.

Taylor and Francis for article: Peter W.G. Newman and Jeffrey R. Kenworthy (1991), 'Transport and Urban Form in Thirty-Two of the World's Principal Cities', *Transport Reviews*, **11** (3), 249–70.

University of Wisconsin Press for article: Michael A. Toman (1994), 'Economics and "Sustainability": Balancing Trade-offs and Imperatives', *Land Economics*, **70** (4), November, 399–413.

Every effort has been made to trace all the copyright holders but if any have been inadvertently overlooked the publishers will be pleased to make the necessary arrangement at the first opportunity.

In addition the publishers wish to thank the Library of the London School of Economics and Political Science, the Marshall Library of Economics, Cambridge University and B & N Microfilm, London for their assistance in obtaining these articles.

Series Preface

Kenneth Button and Peter Nijkamp

The environment has been a dominant theme for research and public policy during the latter part of the twentieth century and there is no sign that this will change as we move to the new millennium. The global interest in environmental matters in part stems from the increased pressures that a mounting population and increased production puts on the planet's natural resource base. Additionally, as personal incomes rise and leisure time becomes more freely available in the developed world, concern with more immediate human needs give way to an interest in preservation and conservation for future generations and for others. Science has also contributed by both highlighting emerging environmental problems and discovering the importance of many components of the natural environment for medical and other uses.

Historically, the interest in the environment can be traced through several phases, each with its own particular emphasis. The interest is also far from new and in antiquity there were often laws governing such things as the removal of night soil and the use of noisy wagons into towns. Traditionally, also the natural environment was seen as a source of the necessities of life and was controlled through farming techniques to ensure that food was adequate to maintain the population. Land use was controlled and water resources were often regulated at the local and regional levels.

With the Industrial Revolution came population growth, urbanization and the accelerated exploitation of natural resources. Malthus advanced ideas of over population while others, such as Jevons, became concerned about the finite nature of such resources as coal. The new technologies contaminated water courses and the widespread use of carbon fuels led to atmospheric pollution. In cities, dirt, noise and urban decay led to new ideas of town planning and ideal cities.

Much of the interest in the latter part of the last century centred around public health. As knowledge of how disease was spread – urban authorities in particular sought to improve the local environment by such measures as sewage control and clean water supply to reduce the spread of germs and infection. This trend, much later, spread to policies embodied in various pieces of clean air legislation to reduce local atmospheric pollution that causes smog and other harmful effects.

Wealthy societies, and the better off within poorer societies, with the time and resources to expand, became concerned with the built environment and in shaping nature in ways they found aesthetically pleasing. Over the centuries this has led to landscaping of the countryside and the provision of parks and gardens in urban areas.

The twentieth century has seen many of these trends continue although some of the problems, such as depletion of natural resources, initially appeared less severe as new sources were found in Africa, South America and Asia. Difficulties in feeding and otherwise sustaining the burgeoning populations of these regions, however, resurrected Malthusian concerns over whether the planet could sustain itself. Increasing reliance on fossil fuels for energy and the geographical concentration of the main reserves of oil in politically unstable areas resurrected concern over natural resource reserves in the post Second World War period.

More fundamental to modern debates has been the global orientation of recent concerns. This has been accompanied by a much more popular interest in the state of the natural environment. Kenneth Boulding's development of the idea of 'spaceship earth' attracted much attention, as did the rather doom ladened prophesies of the Club of Rome, but this was subsequently overshadowed by the publication of the Brundtland Report, *Our Common Future*, with its emphasis on the need to maintain resources for future generations. With the report came the much touted, but universally ambiguous, concept of sustainable development.

Just as the academic interest in the environment has evolved so has the institutional setting in which the topic is debated and researched. In a very general way as our understanding of the environment has progressed and as technology has developed so there has been a movement out from micro-policy making in the hands of city councils, lords of the manor and the like to macro-policy making, involving global agencies such as the United Nations and World Bank. Indeed, one of the pressing issues of contemporary environmental debate is the appropriate jurisdiction for different levels of government.

For those interested in researching environmental topics, either from the standpoint of the beginner or of that of an expert wishing to expand an established basis of knowledge, there are practical problems. Environmental analysis extends across virtually all academic disciplines although many such as economics and engineering have specific sub-areas of interest specifically devoted to environmental issues. The multidisciplinary and transdisciplinary nature of environmental research makes it difficult to keep track of the key literature. To those new to the field there is the added problem of tracing back to find classic papers or research results. There are now a large number of specialist journals that deal with environmental topics but this is often adding to the problem of collecting information rather than reducing it. While these journals and periodicals provide explicitly environmental research findings, other general journals in economics, sociology, geography, engineering, medicine, biology and so on still continue to publish important findings.

The aim of this series of edited books is to provide both a set of reference volumes for those already in the field and to facilitate newcomers with accessible core material. The aim is not to offer readings on the purely scientific issues but rather to limit the papers to those concerned with social science aspects of the environment. This does not mean that we have excluded papers with a natural science orientation but rather the focus is on the softer debates and research. There are seven volumes in the series. The papers have all been previously published but do not constitute a set of traditional classics. While many of the articles have an established pedigree, equally there are less often referenced pieces. The aim of each volume is to paint a picture of how a topic area has developed, provide an indication as to some of the key contributions to this development but also look at some of the more recent literature that covers policy considerations.

The books cover a wide range of topic areas. At one extreme there are the macro-oriented volumes edited with Bob Ayres looking at the *Global Aspects of the Environment* while, in conjunction with Kerry Turner, there is a collection concerned with *Ecosystems and Nature*. Also at the aggregate level, edited with Hans Opschoor, there is a volume which focuses on *Environmental Economics and Development*. At the other extreme there are volumes concerned with micro-issues such as that along with Ken Willis that deals with *Environmental*

Valuation and with David Banister on *The Environment, Land Use and Urban Policy*. Transport's impact on the environment is multifaceted and can be severe hence there is a volume edited with Yoshi Hayashi, *The Environment and Transport* dealing exclusively with that subject. Finally, edited with Tom Tietenberg there is a collection that looks more generally at *Environmental Instruments and Institutions*.

We accept that there are many omissions from the collections and that others may have made different selections or have structured the material differently. Space limits what can be included and there is much more that could have been justified in a larger exercise (although this would add further to deforestation). We have also had to omit work by many eminent and important scholars for the same reason. As for structuring the material, a number of possible cuts are possible, the ones selected here just seem logical to us and would seem to fit with the needs of both researchers and, possibly, teachers.

Introduction

David Banister, Kenneth Button and Peter Nijkamp

Introduction

Modern urban planning developed as a response to the social and economic problems created by the Industrial Revolution over 200 years ago. There was a mass exodus of people from the countryside seeking work, new opportunities and greater wealth. The social structure of the new and growing cities was not able to meet the needs for shelter, for public services (like water and waste disposal), or for the treatment of health. The public health requirements formed the original focus for action in the cities, particularly as a result of the cholera epidemics which swept, for example, Britain in 1832, 1848 and 1866, and the high infant mortality rates. A series of Public Health Acts (1848 and 1875) set up the administrative and financial arrangements, which together with the Local Government Acts of 1888 and 1894 formed the statutory basis for planning in Britain (Hall, 1992).

Since that time, urban planning has continuously struggled for its own identity as it has interfaces with so many aspects of society. Early in the century it was grappling with market forces that were transforming the city into a more complex entity. This was replaced later with the decline of the central city and the decentralization of people and activities to the suburbs. Various problems such as housing and the homeless, the unemployed and the underclass, and the construction of new infrastructure and urban renewal have repeatedly been central to the concerns of planning, but often in different guises. Urban planning in the US has evolved from city planning and social science, but in Europe the tradition is based more on physical design, whilst in the UK there is a mixed approach (Alonso, Chapter 1). The nature of planning is also different to many other disciplines as the methods and processes are eclectic, often being borrowed from other disciplines. Similarly, there is a strong desire for action, not just knowledge.

More recently, the environment has become a new focus for land use and urban policy. This is not the slum improvement of the nineteenth century which sought to provide housing, clean water and sewage for the burgeoning industrial cities, but a new concern over the quality of the environment. People and businesses are now leaving the city as the perceived quality of life has deteriorated, and as modern lifestyles and activities no longer require such close proximity of homes, workplaces and other activities. Transport, particularly suburban rail and the car, has had an instrumental role in this decentralization process.

The city is thus a source of concern. From the viewpoint of urban economists the city is involved in a permanent struggle between economies of scale and scope (localization advantages, economies of density and so on) and agglomeration diseconomies (congestion, pollution, criminality and so on). Urban land use is reflecting this structural conflict of interest through the patterns of residential and locational ramifications (Fujita, 1989). As a result the city is faced with a dynamic movement where compact ways of living and working on the one hand and dispersed patterns of living and working on the other hand (such as urban sprawl, the edge city) are in turn advocated. This has in the past decade also provoked new debates on optimal city size (such as Abdel-Rahman and Fujita, 1990; Anas, 1990; Gordon and Richardson, Chapter 27). This new urban economic discussion on the optimal pattern and size of urban activities is directly and indirectly playing a major role in the current debate on sustainable cities. An excellent recent review of the methods used by economists to explain the evolution of urban spatial structure is given by Anas, Arnott and Small (1998).

The arguments about sustainable development have defined a new role for land use and urban policy as the city is seen as being the most sustainable form of urban development (Banister, 1997; Ewing, 1997). The most appropriate means to make the built environment compatible with the wider natural environment is to seek to provide facilities and services in close proximity to where people live, preferably within walking or cycling distance, or a short journey by public transport. This is the principal means by which a high quality urban environment can be created, which has low levels of pollution and congestion, and maintains quality through secure, safe and attractive local environments. This means further development of the mixture of existing medium and large cities which already have a high quality urban environment (such as many historical cities), and at the same time creating new urban forms based on agglomerations of smaller urban centres linked by high quality public transport.

Context of Contributions

The papers selected for this book have tried to reflect the thinking behind the varied history of urban planning thought, together with the continued search for environmental quality. Over 100 years ago, the development of modern urban planning was dependent upon policy concerns about basic public health and the survival of the city. It is ironic that at the present time, public health is again the focus of much urban policy, but the environment has a very different meaning. We start with a series of classic papers on land use and urban policy, which are followed by a group of key papers on planning theory and modelling approaches. This provides the main theoretical elements of the land use and urban policy debates which have been central to the development of the subject area. We then introduce the environment into the picture. As noted above, this has been a relatively recent addition as it reflects the renewed interest in both the local and global environmental issues. The final group of papers describe the most recent debates over the nature of the sustainable city and how urban policy can help achieve a new vision of a high quality city life.

Classic Papers

Part I focuses on the recent contributions of the leading researchers on land use and urban policy. Two basic phases in thinking on urban policy and planning can be identified. Much of the early research has been examining urban policy as a physical design process that is based on master plans and innovative thinking on urban form (for example, new town developments and Radburn). This started from simple zoning, but soon produced wonderful plans on how the city should develop (Hall, Chapter 3). It was in the 1950s that views changed, partly as a result of the new agenda for cities, but also because there was a strong desire for systems analysis and the use of quantification to establish clear relationships between land use, land value, rents and movements, based primarily in the paradigm of rationality (Batty, Chapter 10). Since that time, the analysis has become far more sophisticated as methods and data have developed, and as the focus of urban policy has switched from the primary concern over physical relationships towards more social and ecological analysis. So urban planning and policy have moved from simple zoning, through utopian visions, to the quantified city, the enterprise city and now the ecological city (Girardet, Chapter 19).

This process has not been a smooth one. In the 1970s the ideological critique of planning, particularly from the Marxists, severely undermined the rationale for planning which was to achieve a 'successful' ordering of the built environment (Harvey, Chapter 4). Cities existed for the production, circulation, exchange and consumption of goods and services, and the accumulation of capital. Provided that urban policy continued to promote the dominance of capital over labour, it was doomed to frustration and eventual failure. Other urban theorists (Webber, Chapter 5; Clark, Chapter 2) examined the city more from the economic rather than the political perspective. The essential rationale for urbanism was the agglomeration benefits reflected in the specializations and range of activities that people could participate in within cities. The city is efficient as it allows agglomeration, but it is also a failure as the quality of the environment has been substantially reduced.

Different views emanate on how this dilemma can be resolved. In Chapter 2 Clark argues that the city will disintegrate as transport has become so much more efficient and permits a dispersal of population. He concludes that this is one of the few examples in economics where the unchecked operation of the free market does not produce the most socially desirable results. He goes on to argue for compactness and medium sized settlements (150 000 inhabitants) where people can relate to the affairs of their local community and get involved. A contrary view is promoted by Webber in Chapter 5 where spatial separation (propinquity) no longer accurately reflects function relationships within cities. Policy should be directed at diversity in settlement and land use patterns, and not some ideal. Each city is likely to develop its own patterns of land uses that best serves its social structure.

Planning Theory

Although these classic papers have given a positive view of the nature and role of planning in society, that position has not been uncontroversial. Planning has been criticized as being of limited relevance to a modern democratic free market society (Klosterman, Chapter 9). Economic arguments have been based on the advantage and deficiencies of competitive markets; pluralist arguments are based on the benefits and limitations of interest group interactions; the traditionalists have returned to the golden era of planned cities and design; and the neo-Marxists' arguments attempt to demolish planning by labelling it as the mechanism to ensure the dominance of capital over labour (Castells, Chapter 6). Different defences have been provided. Faludi (1973, Chapter 7, 1985) and Friend and Jessop (1969) urge the continuation of rationality in planning even though there are substantial sources of uncertainty. Responsible decision making means defining decision situations and the key element must be that those decisions are accountable. However, if this is the case, then decision making processes need to be set against some normative standard, but this in turn maybe dangerous as the process can become technocratic and positivistic. This is one of the basic dilemmas of planning theory that seeks to be logical, impartial and democratic, yet is seen to be illogical, biased and autocratic – hence the attractiveness of more modest theories such as Lindblom's disjointed incrementalism or mutual adjustment (1959).

Scott and Roweis (1977) attempt to place the contemporary urbanization process within the capitalist mode of production and they see planning as an ever-changing historical process. Planning theory should therefore also be continually shaped by reference to special tensions. The notion of rationality is rejected. Their conclusion is that urban planning is in an impossible position as the social and property relations of a capitalist society creates an urban process which rejects collective action in the form of urban planning. So urban planning tends to be restricted to amelioration of the negative outcomes of this contradictory process of urban land development. The resolution to this dilemma is that planning itself must become more political. The rationalist and the social organization (or human) perspectives have formed the two opposing foundations of planning theory, but in between there have been many variants (Friedmann and Hudson, Chapter 8).

This pluralist perspective addresses issues such as the need within competitive markets to provide public or collective consumption goods such as a healthy and pleasant environment. It reflects the instability of markets to deal with social costs and benefits of production and consumption which are not reflected in market prices or revenues. It covers the need for improved understanding of the long term effects of location decisions so that decisions can be fully informed. It reflects the fact that market competition cannot resolve distributional questions in a socially acceptable manner. As Klosterman concludes in Chapter 9, planning must accept this challenge and realize its potential through expanded conceptions of the public interest, information and political action.

Modelling Approaches and Evaluation

One of the great contributions of planning to urban policy has been the development and application of models which in turn became institutionalized and professionalized (Batty, Chapter 10). In particular, the systems approach requires the city to be represented as a series of quantifiable relationships, not as explanations about how cities work. Although the methods and techniques of urban systems analysis are widely used, they have been attacked for their lack of theory (Sayer, Chapter 14). Temporal change and causality are not seen as part of the process of urban development (Harvey, 1973), as the focus is on the extrapolation of the present patterns of functioning. The Lowry models, for example, do not attempt to describe the development process of land acquisition, financing and development, but extrapolate the existing relationships between different types of employment through a series of spatial interaction models. In Chapter 14 Sayer criticizes this approach as a restrictive conception of 'science' that is typified in the preoccupation of regional science with mathematical form – the dominant positivistic concept of science.

The use of models in urban planning has become more mature and it is now seen as one form of communication and understanding, including the presentation of data and analysis to decision makers (Batty, Chapter 10). Yet, substantial research still continues (for example, Muth, Chapter 13) on simple monocentric models of employment, transport land use and households which are then elaborated upon through multi-centre developments and the clustering of land uses. In parallel with the modelling of urban systems, the evaluation of plans has advanced, both at the individual project level, but also at the strategic policy level (Lee and Walsh, Chapter 11; Williams, Chapter 15). Environmental assessment extends the scope of planning control through the pursuit of higher standards and the acceptance of responsibility. But it also provides a major preventative measure through the application of land use planning methods at the city, national and EU levels to reduce environmental degradation. Central to most planning analysis is the necessity to make choices between alternatives, both in terms of the well established economic methods (such as cost benefit analysis and financial analysis) and in terms of community welfare (such as goals achievement, planning balance sheet and multi criteria analysis). There are a wide range of evaluation methods (Lichfield cites 20 such methods in Chapter 12), and these are now being augmented by new requirements for strategic environmental assessment, pollution measurement and monitoring, distributional analysis and compensation assessment.

Urban Policy and the Environment

Urban policy, the spatial configuration of cities and their relationship to the urban environment now form the focus of much research. In Chapter 16 Anderson *et al.* provide a synthesis about the links between urban form, energy and the environment, with a particular focus on the question of transport. It illustrates the change in urban planning from the quest for theories of the city towards problem solving within the city and the necessity to move away from single sector solutions towards more holistic explanations. There are fundamental questions such as whether land use changes actually make any difference to behavioural patterns, whether policy interventions have a significant impact on the prosperity of the city, or whether environmental policy can achieve sustainable development (Blowers, Chapter 17). Here we focus on two major issues. One relates to the future of the city in an environmentally concerned world, and the other concentrates on the nature of the sustainable city. In the last ten years, there has been a substantial growth in concern over the environment and sustainable development. For the economist (for example, Toman, Chapter 21), the key issue is intergenerational equity and the social capital that should be passed on to future generations. There is a trade off between equity and welfare maximization, where safe minimum standards might be set so that future generations are no worse off than the present. This is a modified Rawlsian view of justice (Rawls, 1971).

Nevertheless, the implications of a modified growth principle means that priorities in the city must be adapted to accommodate the environment. In Chapter 18 Friedmann makes a series of propositions on how cities should develop under growth management through reductions in consumption and uneven development. The process envisaged is overtly political, and includes the mobilization of social activities so that decentralized planning takes place within strong central guidance. This vision of the city environmental and political, contrasts with the city ecological (Girardet, Chapter 19). At present the city transforms environmental resources into waste, but the ecological city must become more circular where resources are recycled and waste is minimized. This means a reorganization of the metabolism of cities, where the throughput of raw materials, energy, consumer goods, and the generation and treatment of waste are all assessed in terms of their long-term ecological viability.

One of the basic questions, still unresolved, is the effect that land use changes can have in reshaping cities. In terms of its physical structure Lynch (Chapter 20) identifies three groups of vital factors for each city of a given size – the magnitude and the pattern of the structural density and its condition; the capacity, type and pattern of facilities for all types of circulation; and the location of fixed activities. The most significant features of the composite pattern are the grain (the degree of intimacy between facilities and homes), the focal organization (the interrelation of the nodes of concentration and interchange), and the accessibility (the general proximity in terms of time). Even though there are many problems of congestion, quality and environment, the city still has tremendous economic and social advantages which must make it the focus for sustainable living. Lynch proposes different types of urban form, but concludes that spatial form might not affect the quality of the environment, more the social well-being of the city.

Sustainable Cities

The most appropriate nature of urban form is central to the sustainable development debate. There are three main goals of planning (environment, economic development and social equity) and the role of planning is to work within the tensions that these three fundamental aims produce. It is like a triangle with sustainable development at the centre, but the only way to reach the centre is through confronting and resolving the conflicts by means of the integration of social theory with environmental thinking (Campbell, Chapter 24). Planners have to decide whether to remain outside the conflict and act as mediators or to jump into the struggle and promote their own visions of ecological and economic development.

This debate has been most active with respect to the crucial role that transport has in achieving sustainable development. The catalyst for the debate was the study of 32 major world cities (Newman and Kenworthy, Chapter 28) which demonstrated clear links between transport and urban form, at least at the city level. It was suggested that economic factors, such as petrol prices and income levels were less important than direct interventions from planners through location strategies and investment in public transport. The reaction from the USA was strong, both on criticizing the quality of the empirical analysis and on questioning the implications for urban policy. The basic disagreement is whether the promotion of compact cities is an appropriate planning goal (Gordon and Richardson, Chapter 27; Ewing, 1997). On the one hand there are those (principally Gordon and Richardson) who are strongly in favour of market forces for the allocation of land for development, for the decisions on residential densities, for the achievement of energy resource savings, for the promotion of city centre development, for the maintenance of competition between cities, for the examination of the equity implications of compactness, and for the balancing of the impacts of suburbanization. On the other hand, there are those (Ewing, 1997; Cervero and Landis, Chapter 26; and Banister, 1997) who take a less extreme position and focus on the means to reduce trip lengths, encourage moderate concentration, the provision of local facilities, and mixed land uses.

The empirical evidence is complex. There does seem to be some limited impact on land markets from joint developments at rail transit stations (Cervero, Chapter 25), mainly in the form of slightly higher rents and lower vacancy rates. But in the most comprehensive study over 20 years of the Bay Area Rapid Transit (BART) in San Francisco, Cervero and Landis

(Chapter 26) have not found compact, orderly growth with a multi-centred settlement pattern. Even in the longer term, the land use changes associated with BART have been localized and limited to down town San Francisco and Oakland, together with a few suburban stations. Most of the growth in the region has been linked to the freeway system, not the rail system. At the city level in the UK, the links between travel patterns, energy use and urban form in terms of its physical, economic and social structure have been examined (Banister *et al.*, Chapter 22). It is the physical characteristics that link most closely with energy use in transport through density, size and amount of open space. Yet, even here data limitations make comparison difficult, and this is further complicated by the social and economic structures of cities which are so different.

The sustainable city needs to be examined within its region, to encompass its labour market area and its wider sphere of influence. This is what Breheny and Rookwood (Chapter 23) call the social city region, which in turn is an adaptation of the terminology used by Ebenezer Howard, one of the early generations of great planning thinkers. Howard (1898) published his seminal text *To-morrow: A Peaceful Path to Real Reform* exactly one hundred years ago and advocated the polycentred social city. It has taken a century to come full circle. There is no single solution to the sustainable city, but there must be a range of policies linked to the different current situations found in the diversity of the cities around the world – 'The Multiple City' approach to sustainability.

The same basic issues are being addressed in all world cities (Satterthwaite, Chapter 29), as environmental performance goals have be set against the social, economic and political goals of sustainable development. Yet progress towards sustainability has been slow amongst the nations in the 'North' and this discourages progress among the nations of the 'South' where three-quarters of the population live. Even though consumption, use of resources, waste generation and pollution are all increasing in the 'southern cities', they can still legitimately argue that the current levels in the 'northern cities' are much higher and have been so historically. There is a lot of catching up to do and the responsibility for action lies in the affluent cities. Cities have to improve their own environmental quality without transferring those costs to other people, other ecosystems, or into the future.

Though well established on the policy agenda, the environment has not yet secured an equal role with economic management. Indeed, the close interdependency between economic prosperity and environmental prosperity is not really recognized, and its integration at all levels of decision making is embryonic. The new focus on sustainable development and a high quality of life within the city seems to be the next step towards the ultimate integration of urban policy, land use and the environment.

References

Abdel-Rahman, H. and Fujita, M. (1990), 'Product variety, Marshallian externalities, and city size', *Journal of Regional Science*, **30** (2), 165–83.

Anas, A. (1990), 'Taste heterogenerity and urban spatial structure', *Journal of Urban Economics*, **28** (3), 318–35.

Anas, A., Arnott, R., and Small, K.A. (1998), 'Urban Spatial Structure', *Journal of Economic Literature*, **36**, September, 1426–64.

Banister, D. (1997), 'Reducing the need to travel', *Environment and Planning B*, **24** (3), 437–49.

Ewing, R. (1997), 'Is Los Angeles style sprawl desirable?', *Journal of the American Planning Association*, **63** (1), 107–26.
Faludi, A. (1973), *Planning Theory*, Oxford: Pergamon Press.
Faludi, A. (1985), 'The return of rationality', in M. Breheny and A. Hooper (eds), *Rationality in Planning: Critical Essays on the Role of Rationality in Urban and Regional Planning*, London: Pion, 27–47.
Friend, J.K. and Jessop, W.N. (1969), *Local Government and Strategic Choice*, London: Tavistock Publications.
Fujita, M. (1989), *Urban Economic Theory*, Cambridge: Cambridge University Press.
Hall, P. (1992), *Urban and Regional Planning*, London: Routledge.
Harvey, D. (1973), *Social Justice and the City*, London: Edward Arnold.
Howard, E. (1898), *To-morrow: A Peaceful Path to Real Reform*, London: Swan Sonnenschein.
Lindblom, C.E. (1959), 'The science of muddling through', *Public Administration Review*, **19** (1), 79–88.
Rawls, J. (1971), *Theory of Justice*, Baltimore: Johns Hopkins University Press.
Scott, A.J. and Roweis, S.T. (1977), 'Urban planning in theory and practise: An appraisal', *Environment and Planning A*, **9**, 1097–119.

Part I
Classic Papers

[1]
Cities, Planners, and Urban Renewal*

WILLIAM ALONSO

The city planning profession, like most adolescents, is self-conscious. It worries about its appearance, it strikes poses, it adopts and discards heroes, it revolts against its parents while depending on them. It tries, in short, to establish its own identity. This identity is the product of its intellectual ancestry and of its early development, of its current situation and, perhaps to a greater extent than other professions, of the appearances and realities of the object of its concern, which is the city. It is a profession in rapid change, full of contradictions and given to excesses. Such a subject cannot be portrayed at rest and separately from its object, and so we will consider some of the forces that have made it what it is, but principally we will consider some of the issues that confront it and how it is coping with them, for it is in action that the importance and the weaknesses of the profession can be seen.

City planning in the United States stems from several roots, of which the earliest is architectural. The 1893 Columbian Exposition in Chicago dazzled Americans with the classic magnificence of the fairgrounds, and many visitors returned to their communities eager

* Reprinted by permission from *Daedalus*, published by the American Academy of Arts and Sciences, Brookline, Massachusetts, Vol. 92, No. 4 (Fall 1963), *The Professions*, pp. 824–839, where it appeared under the title "Cities and City Planners."

to ennoble their appearance in a movement called City Beautiful. The common manifestation of this movement was a superficial playing with boulevards, waterfronts and neoclassical architecture, but some of the writings of the period show a sensitive awareness of the society and the economy to be housed in this splendid container. The City Beautiful faded gradually out of American planning. Aesthetic concern for three-dimensional design returned with vigor only after World War II, and then largely as a result of European influences such as the Congrès International de l'Architecture Moderne (CIAM), of which Le Corbusier was the principal figure. However, those who now practice in this vein owe their first allegiance to architecture rather than to city planning, and they often call themselves urban designers.

Other seminal influences are harder to differentiate from one another. The muckrakers and other early reformers focused interest on the housing of workers, considering finances, family life and social organization as well as design. The development of urban sociology, mostly in Chicago in the 1920's and 1930's, served to document the conditions of urban living and shifted attention from the aesthetic of urban form to an analytic geography concerned with the social and economic landscape of the city. The New Deal provided funds and a national program for reform, emphasizing slum clearance and public housing. The naive social darwinism popularized by Herbert Spencer had held that poverty and slum conditions were the just deserts of the inferior and necessary conditions for social progress. It now became an article of faith that slums and bad housing were the cause of ill health, criminality, illegitimacy and other social evils. Consequently there was as much effort directed to tearing down slums as to providing new housing for those displaced. Today this seems a gallant charge against windmills. We have learned, for instance, that the slum is often a tightly knit social fabric that provides security and gradual acculturation to urban life, and that moving its inhabitants to antiseptic piles of brick can be cruel. We have learned that slums are often manifestations of racial as well as of class inequality, but we have not learned much about solving this thornier problem. This does not mean that nothing need be done about slums, but that the brave solutions that had seemed so evident have proved inadequate, and that learning advances slowly and painfully.

Advocates of city planning, as most urban reformers, were deeply suspicious of corrupt municipal governments, and they advocated the use of appointed commissions that could keep their hands clean of the filth of politics. From the 1920's to World War II untold planning commissions were organized, and each would hire a planner to produce a Master Plan. This consisted of proposals for parkways, a waterfront improvement, a new city hall and other items, and, always, a zoning ordinance. Public works, for obvious reasons, could often be sold by the commission to the city government. The zoning ordinance, stating what land could be used for what purposes, was often adopted, but it tended to degenerate. Seldom prepared with sufficient understanding of structural relationships, its administration consisted of a joyful or reluctant granting of variances and exceptions, so that it soon became riddled with holes. The planning commission in a social sense, and the zoning ordinance in a real estate sense, represented middle and upper class values and were too often holding operations against the forces of change. Since zoning combined conservatism with the planning advocated by the progressives, it often enjoyed considerable support together with indifferent success.

Faith that technical analysis is superior to the political process as a means of arriving at decisions has been another fountainhead of planning, at least since Hoover's 1920's. Techniques have improved by leaps and bounds in recent years in such areas as the estimation of the demand for housing, offices and highways and the calculation of the impact of particular measures. Many questions have thus been validly removed from the politician to the analyst, and this has given strength to the apolitical view of planning.

But there is a strong counter-current, and in many cases planning is moving closer to politics with the realization that what is needed is not so much a plan as a planning process. That is to say, the Master Plan, reflecting its architectural ancestry, presented a picture of an ideal final stage, much as the plans for a building represent the completed building, and the only question was how to carry it out. Today it is clear that in the nature of things every plan is tentative, both because information is imperfect and because there is no final stage: there is always a future beyond the stage projected. What is needed is continuing planning, which produces every year a plan for the next few years, and every few years a plan for the next two or three decades, so that the next steps and the distant goals are known at all times. With this concept, plans have become the companions of policy and the planner has moved inside government into a position similar to that of a general staff in an army. When plans are statements of policies the emphasis shifts from the solution of particular problems through particular projects to a view of the city as a complicated system to be guided as well as corrected.

These are the architectural, the reformist and the technocratic roots of planning. Other influences might be mentioned, such as the utopian movements with their long and colorful history, or the paradoxical importance of the romantic anti-urban attitudes in England and America, of which Lewis Mumford is a representative. There is also the British version of city planning, which is called town planning, and the continental versions, which are often called urbanism. Suffice it to say that they are closer to physical design and further from the social sciences than is American city planning.

Training for the profession is offered in the United States and Canada at some three dozen accredited schools of planning, almost all offering postgraduate programs only, two to three years long and leading to the degree of Master of City Planning. People are attracted into the profession from many fields. Students from an architectural background are now only a modest plurality. Most of the others come from liberal arts and the social sciences, some from law and the natural sciences. Their motives for entering planning are mixed. Because of the great shortage of planners, good wages and rapid promotion are certain to attract people. But altruistic motives are also important: a desire to improve our environment, to help make the good life possible in cities. Some people, although very few now, are dedicated to particular ideologies, from New Deal liberalism to several forms of socialism. The majority are apparently not interested in political ideas. Rather they feel good will toward their fellow man and, in a general way, they wish to improve his lot.

In recent years doctoral programs have gained in importance. These are offered by half a dozen universities, and they direct their training to research and teaching rather than to professional practice. Their development has raised again the question of whether the field has a valid body of knowledge or of expertness. No clear answer emerges. Certain topics interest planners principally, and others fall within traditional academic disciplines. Perhaps the answer is that the planner brings a point of view, an area of concern or a set of questions that he must answer as best he can because of the urgent problems of cities. The approach is eclectic in that it takes much from others, but the pressure of responsibility for action rather than of knowledge for its own sake forces a shifting synthesis which, whatever its intellectual inadequacies, goes to the issues and does not trouble itself with the territorial rights that tradition has established between, let us say, economics and geography. Had city planning the self-confidence, it might paraphrase the well-known definition that mathematics is what mathematicians do.

The situation of planners in this respect is very similar to that of medicine some time ago. Medicine is also a goal-oriented activity that makes use of other academic fields such as chemistry and biology. It uses their tools and findings and raises questions which may be explored by people in the field itself or in related fields. In the same way, in recent years, planning has produced a great deal of research activity under a variety of labels, including that of planning. There has resulted an explosion of knowledge and, unfortunately, a greater flood of literature with which no one person can hope to keep up, leading to the paradox of specialization in a profession that a decade ago prided itself in producing generalists in an age of specialists.

The naming of the planning association, which was founded in 1917, stimulated a revealing debate in choosing between American Institute of Planners or American Institute of Planning. The issue at stake was whether the organization should represent the activity of planning, in which anyone can participate by thinking intelligently about the future, or whether it should represent a particular body of men who labeled themselves city planners. The second alternative was chosen, and today the American Institute of Planners follows a policy of professional closure. It has persuaded agencies to write into their job specifications educational and experience requirements, and it has been discussing the establishment of registration examinations. The British Town Planning Institute, unconcerned with the semantics of its name, has had such examinations for years.

This is the profession that is trying to meet the challenge of urban change. By and large, it is right and sensible to train people to deal with urban problems and to permit them to advise the public and the authorities on these matters. It is true that our knowledge of urban phenomena is rudimentary, comparable perhaps to the knowledge of the human body at the time of Harvey's discovery of the circulation of blood. That is to say, we know a great deal, not nearly enough and much of it wrong. Still, the problems are there and decisions must be made. The advice of a good planner is probably the best available, but it is likely that in ten or fifteen years our understanding will have advanced through research and experience to where the advice of the average planner will be better than that of the best today, just as today's planners are better than those of one or two decades ago.

Knowledge is inadequate and solutions shallow, and to improve this situation it is right to be impatient with the profession. It has attracted as yet relatively few first-rate minds, and these must be prodded to produce their best. The apostolic zeal of the aesthetic and reformist heritages and many years of frustration still manifest themselves in a crusading attitude of yea-saying and a distrust of criticism. City planners are more influential than ever before, and there is a danger that power may corrupt, that mistakes will be repeated and justified rather than teach how things may be better done. Success can too easily be measured by activity and expenditure.

Perhaps these dangers to the profession can best be made clear by considering the urban situation today and by showing the inadequacy of the more popular solutions. A modern city is the most complex social and economic system that has ever existed, and, to keep from getting lost, we will focus on the interplay between size and structure of cities as the background for current planning practice.

When things change in size, they tend to change in structure. A grown man is not, at least physically, merely a very large baby. Science fiction to the contrary, being a fly implies being neither bigger nor smaller than the usual size of flies. A mutant the size of a freight car is impossible: it could not fly, its legs would buckle if it tried to walk, and, anyway, it would die of asphyxiation, since its breathing mechanism can serve only bodies a fraction of an inch in diameter. Size and structure depend upon each other. The critical relation between size and structure applies as well to social organisms such as nations and cities. But while the relation is easily accepted by most people in the biological realm, for some reason we seem to have difficulty in understanding it in the social realm, and this often leads to trouble. The fact is that, with economic development, cities and countries tend to grow, and as their size increases, their structure changes.

Looking at it from the other side, a change in structure tends to demand a change in size. Economic development is a continuing change in the structure of a society. With economic development the size of cities has changed. In the eighteenth century, a city of a few tens of thousands was a large and important city, and a few hundred thousands made a very large city in the nineteenth. In the twentieth century we have seen the city of a few millions emerge as the dominant form. Of course, this many people simply do not fit into the municipal boundaries which had been established for the earlier, smaller cities. The population has spilled over, and the urban mass covers a number of municipal units, in many cases in the United States straddling two and even three states. This urban mass, which we call by the awkward names of metropolitan area or metropolis, is the true city of today. We still refer to parts of the metropolis as "cities" or "towns," and these parts maintain their existence as municipal corporations, but they are no longer true cities in the sense of a geographic community of work and home. The facts have changed, but our thinking—much less our system of government—has not kept up with them.

But the metropolis is no mere large-scale model of the older city any more than the *Queen Mary* is a large-scale model of the *Santa María*. It is well known that economic development has brought specialization to the work of men. It has also brought about the specialization of space for men's activities. Work, home, shopping and recreation are more separated than they have ever been. Vast areas of homes specialize by race, income, family, size, age and tastes of residents. Shops cluster and separate according to price, style, variety and type of goods offered, and according to whether they are reached on foot, by car or by mass transit. Factories and offices gather and separate in complicated rhythms of their own. The great variety of indoor and outdoor amusements distribute themselves in this space according to the markets they serve.

Those who disparage the monotony of our metropolitan areas see only half the picture. There are in fact more things under the sun than there used to be, but these things are usually grouped together rather than mixed. There is therefore little variety in any one place, although there is more variety to the whole. Curiously, those who complain of monotony often also complain of the chaos of our urban areas. This apparent contradiction disappears if we think of these critics as on foot in the first instance and in a car in the second. If one is walking, the immediate area seems large and unchanging. But if one is in a car, one travels much faster and sees more things in a short time, and then the great variety of the city may become bewildering.

Bewildering, yes; but is it chaos? Chaos is only the absence of order, and order is nothing but the understanding of structure. There can be no question that our metropolitan areas have a structure, and that serious students of cities understand it fairly well, know how it got to be that way, and how it is likely to develop. The chaos of which the critics complain, then, refers not to the lack of structure but to the difficulty of perceiving it; and the problem is not one of restructuring but one of making understanding easier. A person moving through a city must be given visual clues and explanations of where he is and where he is going, of what these places are and of how they are related to each other. Many suburban residential areas should be given a more intense focus and clearer edges. Adjacent areas, such as the financial and the commercial in most downtowns, should be differentiated and articulated. People must be given a clearer image of the structure of urban areas while preserving variety and surprise within the elements of that structure. This is a very recent way of looking at urban design, but it should have considerable impact, taking the aesthetics of city planning beyond the architectural consideration of groups of buildings to the treatment of urban form as such.

The bigger pieces making up the mosaic of the metropolitan structure have also been criticized on grounds other than aesthetic. That side of sociology that used to be called social philosophy has attacked the social monotony of the suburbs, and most planners have concurred. The organization man, the member of the lonely crowd, seeks status in the endless urban sprawl by living in a house with a picture window which is usually cracked. These critics deplore the anonymity, the dullness, the conformism and the shallowness of suburban living, and they point out how short the suburbs fall of that pastoral ideal which they question in the first instance. Children brought up in this synthetic environment know nothing of the real world outside, meet only children of families exactly like their own, and grow up to be intolerant, uninteresting, ignorant conformists. The meeting place for men is the town dump, which is lacking in dignity. The women lead lives of intolerable loneliness and boredom or of frantic activity as charwomen, chairwomen, nursemaids, or hostesses, according to whom one reads.

These portraits or caricatures have proliferated recently. Some of the strokes in these portraits may be questioned, such as the relative ranges of experience of central city and suburban children, but the distaste of the authors for this suburban way of life is what is important. These critics are not just reporting on a way of life: they are judging it. By the skillful use of language they are criticizing and trying to change the tastes of their readers to have them see the suburban way of life in a new and most unflattering light. The fact, the evidence shows, is that this way of life is what most Americans want, that they are getting it and that they feel, and are supported by any reasonable comparison, that they never had it so good. Whether these people are instances of ensnared *Boobus americanus* or latter-day Candides happily tending their gardens depends on one's viewpoint. In my opinion, they are achieving their ideal, however imperfectly. Various city planners have proposed alternative modes of considerable merit and ingenuity, but their schemes have had only local and partial success. If there is to be any fundamental change, it will have to be by an extraordinary innovation in the field of taste, offering an alternative type of housing and manner of living which is as deeply rooted in the traditions and feelings of our society as is the present suburban house. What this alternative may be, if there is one, we will not know until it succeeds.

The changes in size, and therefore in structure, of cities have affected their centers as well as their edges. While the suburbs have continued to grow very fast, virtually every central city has lost population in the last decade. This has brought about a strange alliance between the intellectual—usually liberal—critics of the suburbs and those businessmen—usually conservative—with an interest in central city real estate. Their combined argument runs: the city (the central city is meant) is dying; the city is the focus of our economy and the center of our culture; therefore, unless something is done, our economy is endangered and our culture is weakened. This, of course, is nonsense. The city today is the metropolitan area, and it is growing lustily. As it grows it is developing and changing in structure, redistributing people and activities. What is in fact happening is that, as a result of this redistribution, businesses and people are shifting out from the center. This hurts some downtown businesses, though it benefits business at other locations, where new centers are forming. Like all transitions, it has its costs and dangers, but to argue that it imperils the economy as a whole would be like arguing that the development of the automobile hurt the horseshoe and buggywhip industries, and that therefore it imperiled the economy. On the cultural side as well, the argument is weak. People can move about very rapidly (this is what has made the suburbs possible), and can attend lectures, concerts, museums or the theater regardless of where they live. It may be that the suburbanite prefers to watch television, but that is a fundamental problem of our culture's tastes and attitudes, not of geographic location. If he were somehow dragged back, kicking and screaming, to the central city, once he quieted down a bit he would presumably turn on his television set.

In the past few years there has been a great deal of effort to put new life into the central cities, spearheaded by the federal Urban Renewal Program and generally endorsed by city planners. This program has much good in it, but the obsolete fractioning of our metropolitan areas into many different tax units has perverted local motives and has resulted in many futile and very expensive projects. Suppose, for instance, that a central city has a slum area. It is a well-documented fact that slum areas cost a city, in terms of police and fire protection, welfare payments, schools and other expenses, much more than they pay in taxes. On the other hand, an area of wealthy residents in apartments pays into the city much more than it takes out in municipal services. A city is, in legal terms, a municipal corporation, and like any other corporation it will be anxious to exchange a losing line for a profitable one. In other words, any municipality will gladly trade its poor for some other municipality's rich.

Under the Urban Renewal Program, a city may do just that. It may acquire a slum area under eminent domain, clear it of its buildings and sell it to a developer. No one today can afford to build for the poor without subsidy. On expensive central land it is nearly impossible to build at all except for the rich, and even that must be done at high density by means of apartment towers. On central land, the city can be quite certain that it is exchanging the poor slum-dwellers for wealthy apartment-dwellers. The cost of this operation to the city is one third of the difference between what it paid for the area to its previous owners and what the developer pays the city for it. The federal government pays the other two thirds. The profits to the city will be the increased tax revenue resulting from newer and more expensive property plus the savings in city services. This is likely to prove profitable to the municipal corporation. For instance, one large recent project cleared an area where the average income of families was $234 per month and built there apartments with an average rent of $200 per month. Only families with a monthly income of $1000 or more would normally pay such rents.

But if this type of renewal eliminates slums in an area and improves municipal finances, what is wrong with it? The answer is simple. One must look not at areas but at people; not at the finances of one tax unit but at the finances of the metropolitan area. The poor who lived in the slum have simply moved elsewhere, and the municipality hopes that they have moved to some nearby municipality, which will then be obliged to contend with their money-losing presence. Usually, the poor not only receive no direct benefit, but the clearing of the slum may reduce the housing supply for their income group, making higher rents and more crowding likely in the low-rent housing market. The high-income groups could have had housing, new or old, elsewhere, probably in the suburbs. What has happened is that the various tax units in the metropolitan area are playing an expensive game of musical chairs with the poor and the rich for tax dollars. The poor that one city has got rid of go to another city; the expensive housing that one city has gained has been gained at the expense of another city, and there is no net gain for the metropolitan area.

The federal government is playing an equivocal role with respect to metropolitan structure. With its right hand, the Urban Renewal Program, it is trying to breathe new life into the centers of metropolitan areas, counter to the ongoing structural trends. With its left, however, it is reinforcing these trends and weakening the center. It does this with its F.H.A. mortgage insurance policies and its income tax policies, which permit the homeowner to deduct the interest on his mortgage and the property tax on his home, while the renter can deduct no part of his rent. This makes owning much more attractive financially than renting and provides a powerful extra push to the suburbs. Suburbanization is the basic trend of large cities, deeply rooted in taste and the economics of land. It would take government intervention and controls of a different order of magnitude than the current Urban Renewal Program to reverse these trends, even without contradictory policies.

Meanwhile, preserving the fiction that the metropolis is composed of independent parts makes the process of growth more painful for the suburbs as well as for the center. While central cities worry because they are losing the middle and upper classes and are left only with the poor, who tend to be minorities such as Negroes, Puerto Ricans, or Mexicans, the suburbs pretend that these poor are not *their* poor, and that the suburban population is not made up of stockbrokers, professionals and insurance men but rather of home-steaders and Jeffersonian farmers conducting their affairs in a small, self-contained community not affected by the problems in the central cities. But the suburbs have their problems too, both social and financial. Because they are composed of families with children, one third to one half of their population is in the public schools; because they are absorbing most of the population growth of the nation, they need new streets, sewers and other facilities; and much of their energy is spent in anxious battle to keep out people with incomes lower than their own as well as others who would not "fit." Every part of the metropolis is encouraged to beggar its neighbor, and the egoism and short-sightedness of fictional independence serve only to create new problems.

Business and industry as well as population are also being redistributed, and Urban Renewal is also trying to preserve these activities in the central city. But again, the geographic fragmentation of an obsolete governmental structure tends to distort and pervert the renewal decisions. A recent federal publication, trying to show that the renewal of commercial and industrial areas makes economic sense, presented approvingly the case of a central city in which renewal had resulted in $180,000,000 of new construction and an increase of $200,000 in yearly property taxes to the city. This makes no economic sense to me: the increased tax revenue is only about one tenth of 1 per cent of the total investment, not big enough to be a justifying factor. Furthermore, from the point of view of the private investor, taxes are an expense, not a profit. When we look at the public share of the investment we can understand what has happened. The federal government contributed $8,000,000 and the city, $4,000,000. The new taxes represent 5 per cent on the city's investment. This is a reasonable return on the city's investment of $4,000,000; but to base the economic sense of an investment forty-five times as big on a reasonable return to the city is akin to basing the decision to have a major operation on the attractiveness of his fees to the surgeon. Such things happen, but they are not often considered desirable. They are, in fact, unethical and immoral.

The important questions are whether the total private and public investments are an efficient use of capital, profitable by ordinary business standards; and whether the total public investment to have the development take place in the central city is productive when compared with the efficiency of development elsewhere or of no development at all. This is a difficult question, but it is seldom asked by city planners, let alone answered. It may be that such an investment is wise, but we do not know that it is.

The ordinary investment criteria are not the only ones that apply in such cases. There are important qualitative changes which do not appear in any balance sheet, but which nonetheless may benefit every inhabitant of the metropolis. Without positive action the urban center may wither, and the metropolis may become a vast, amorphous, headless amoeba. A strong center is needed socially, economically and psychologically, for it is here that urban life is lived in full, and virtually all activities in the metropolitan area focus towards it. Here is the center of power, where a new enterprise may be conceived over lunch; here a woman may shop at a department store, look at expensive merchandise in exclusive shops, have dinner in a fine restaurant, and then go to the theater; here one may find a shop that specializes in stringed instruments or clothing for six-foot women, a man who can repair jade or ivory, someone who is an expert in importing from Hong Kong, an agency that can supply the names and addresses of a few thousand street railway enthusiasts or likely opponents of the death penalty. But this variety and

450 / WILLIAM ALONSO

richness is possible only because there are enough things and enough people downtown to attract more things and more people. Let the size of the downtown area drop below the necessary critical mass, and dissolution will follow. There will not be enough six-foot girls coming downtown for there to be a shop especially for them. There will not be enough lunch-time demand to keep a fine restaurant going, and if there are no restaurants, the theaters will suffer. Unless downtown is big enough, there will be no downtown. Some activities will move to the suburbs, but many will die or will never come into existence. Life will become much duller and more homogenized.

But why, if metropolitan areas are getting bigger, should the downtown area be in any danger? Once again, it is a matter of critical size. The suburbs have grown enough, and are far enough away from the old center, for there to be enough local demand to justify local department stores, lawyers and architects, fashion and furniture stores, and other services. Of course, these do not have the variety and size of their downtown equivalents, but they have grown largely at the expense of the downtown area. Industry has been shifting from railroads to trucks, and increasingly it prefers one-story buildings with ample parking, leading, of course, to suburban locations; and industry pulls related activities along with it. Even some large offices have tried moving to the suburbs, but with indifferent success.

These changes in metropolitan structure have indeed placed the downtown area in danger, for each move reduces its size and its attractiveness. But is this a short-run danger or a long-run destiny? Consider the trends that favor downtown. The employment composition of every country, as it develops, shifts increasingly to white collar jobs, and these are typically downtown jobs. Automation and rapid communication not only increase the proportion of "head" over "hand" workers; they permit their spatial separation. As physical production is automated and depersonalized, and as communications improve, managers and supervisors can send impersonal orders to a more distant production line and still be downtown for the advantages of personal contact with other decision-makers. Therefore, although the physical production part of industry may continue to become suburban, the management of that production may become more centralized. And as our population becomes richer and better educated, it seeks the luxurious, the sophisticated and the specialized, which are the major attractions of downtown. In short, then, there are very powerful forces which in the long run will mean a resurgence of the downtown area. It will be a different downtown in that it will be a more purely distilled essence of what we have today; but it will be all the better for that.

Is Urban Renewal in the downtown area a holding operation to counteract the short-run forces which are endangering the urban center until these long-run trends establish themselves? The answer is yes and no. Urban Renewal is for the preservation of the downtown area, but it uses short-run arguments and short-run thinking. It uses subsidies to create new and glamorous buildings without asking how these buildings will be used in thirty years. For instance, most of our important metropolitan areas were founded next to water, and downtown was based on proximity to the port on the edge of the urban area. But, as the port decreases in relative importance (which it almost universally has), and the urban area increases in size, downtown tends to seek the center of the urban mass. It creeps away from the water, at a rate of perhaps one-half mile every twenty years. Are not many of today's projects in the older parts of downtown trying to recreate a center on land that is fated to be an edge? Are they not trying to bring an old center back to life, rather than being midwives to the birth of a new and more viable center?

It makes excellent sense to subsidize the center if the danger to its critical size is a temporary one and a return to health is likely in the long run. But it is less than wise to pour money into glamorous architectural groupings looking with admiration and civic pride only to the size of the capital investment, the increased tax base and the added floor space. If the urban centers are shrinking, their immediate problem is overcapacity, and adding floor space will not solve it; if rents at the center are too high, so that suburban locations are more attractive by comparison, expensive buildings, strongly assessed and paying high taxes, are unlikely to be the solution. It cannot be denied that new and well-designed buildings have a glamor that attracts businesses and customers, and that they may give the downtown area a feeling of effervescence and restore confidence. But new buildings get old very quickly.

To save the downtown area, what is needed is a downtown that works well. Many of the new downtown projects are composed mostly of free-standing buildings, handsomely set about in open space, designed as sculpture on a grandiose scale. The emphasis is put on the project as such, not on the downtown area as a part of the urban system. Not enough attention is paid to the way one element relates to another. For instance, most downtowns have evolved with buildings standing side by side, filling up the blocks, with the streets as channels between them. According to their economic strength and ability to pay rent, activities take locations on the main street, on the side streets, or on the back streets, all close to each other and dependent on each other. Most of the new developments place their buildings standing free *within* the block, and little or no provision is made for those businesses that would go on side and back streets because they cannot pay prime rents. Yet many of these smaller businesses are the lubrication and the ball bearings needed for the smooth operation of the larger businesses, and many of them, such as restaurants, bars and book and specialty stores, make downtown interesting and human. The downtown area is the brain tissue of the metropolis, a complex, evolving, and little understood organ. If it is sick, it may require surgery, but this surgery should be done with sensitive fingers, with the finest surgical instruments, and with the closest attention to what is in fact being done.

In the past half-century our cities have outgrown our concepts and our tools, and I have tried to show how the lagging understanding of the changes in kind that go with changes in size has led us to try remedies which are unsuited to the ills of our urban areas. In this sense, I have been writing mostly about the past and present. What about the future? For the past few years there has been growing professional and popular interest in the step beyond the metropolis, even though we have yet to digest the present reality. The words *megapolis* and *megalopolis* are being heard with increasing frequency, usually applied to an almost continuous string of cities running from Washington, D.C. to Boston. And once this idea is launched, similar patterns are seen emerging on the West and Gulf Coasts, in Argentina and Venezuela, in Indonesia and in Europe.

The pattern does not consist of a string of metropolitan areas standing shoulder to shoulder, fighting for space like a crowd in a subway, but of metropolitan areas in a functioning group, interacting with each other. In the same manner that economic development has made the size of the typical nation inadequate and has called for super-nations, it seems that soon—at least in historical time—urban units will go beyond the scale of the metropolis to the scale of the megapolis. And just as the metropolitan area is not made up of an accumulation of little cities complete in themselves but on a system of specialized and therefore dissimilar areas, the various metropolitan units of megapolis will specialize and become more different from each other than they are today. No one knows with any certainty what the fields of economic specialization will be, or how the social specialization which occurs in metropolitan areas will reappear at the megapolitan scale, though comparisons between Washington, New York, Boston, and other cities are quite suggestive. It does seem likely that history may continue to outpace our ability to grasp and deal with our urban problems, and that, like generals, city planners may be fated always to fight the day's battles with the outworn ideas of their last war.

But even today, at the level of metropolitan development, perhaps the ultimate question is who is to be the planner's client. Is it the commission, the mayor, the council or the voters? Is it only the residents of the city, or future residents, or those who work there but live elsewhere? Should consideration be given to the interests of the region and the nation when they run counter to the city's? When we say a plan is good and desirable, who will benefit and who wants it? I have emphasized the effects of the municipal fragmentation of urban areas. Most city planners are in favor of metropolitan government but work for a particular municipality. What is their responsibility and who is their public? Questions of goals and clients are particularly difficult for city planners, but ultimately it is these questions of ethics and responsibility that distinguish a profession from other occupations.

[2]

TRANSPORT—
MAKER AND BREAKER OF CITIES

by COLIN CLARK

WE sometimes ask ourselves what are the really basic needs of man, even under the most primitive conditions. Answering this question from our own intuition, from the fertile imaginations of archaeologists, or from the conflicting reports of anthropologists, we generally reach some conclusions about food, clothing and shelter, though our primitive ancestors seem to have made do with the minimum, at any rate in the two latter respects.

A little further reflection or research however shows us that these are only end-products, and that man cannot live, as man, at all without possessing, not merely one or two, but a considerable variety of implements which are absolutely necessary before he can obtain or prepare his food, or materials for shelter or clothing. So our attention becomes diverted to a remarkable variety of implements for various productive purposes. We reflect all too little on man's need for a less tangible implement, namely transport. A system of transport is a necessity which, like the respiratory system of the body, we take entirely for granted as long as it is working well—our imagination just fails to tell us what would happen if it broke down. Without some form of transport indeed it is hard to conceive human life at all. The most primitive people known, in Central Africa or the Australian aborigines, weave themselves baskets or bags in which to carry a few necessary tools on their perpetual wanderings.

For a nomadic life is the only one open to such people. As changes in weather and ecology altered the distribution of fish and game, they roamed the earth in pursuit of them, and when the wild life of one district had been depleted, they moved on to another. Before the advent of agriculture, life in a settled village was only possible for those who had access to unusually abundant supplies of natural food, as for instance the dwellers by the fishing rivers by the Pacific coast of North America.[1] Under such conditions, people may be able to begin to live together in groups not larger than six to twelve families, hunting and fishing over an area of 80-100 square kilometres, with a permanent central camp site. So began, it is held, life in settled communities, and with it the possibility of specialization of economic function, which is the necessary condition for any form of civilization. But why were these first settlements so limited in size? Simply from considerations of transport. A primitive village trying to collect food over any greater area than that would involve itself in an altogether uneconomic amount of travelling to and fro.

It was no doubt in such villages that the first forms of agriculture (which may have preceded the domestication of animals) were tried. Under these circumstances[2] much higher densities became possible. The crudest type of agriculture involved (as it does in some districts in Africa now) the recurrent burning of forests, and then leaving the land fallow for long periods. The estimated land requirement per person fell steadily from 1 square kilometre to half a square kilometre when domestic animals had been introduced, down to one-sixth of a square kilometre (30-40 acres) under the conditions under which our ancestors were probably living, say, about the time of Julius Caesar.

The introduction of agriculture was a technical change (the greatest technical change in human history) which very much increased the density at which any area of good land could be settled, and in that sense *reduced* the amount of transport needed to support any given number of people. What then happened was that our ancestors, depending perhaps upon an inspiration originally received from the East, and when there was sufficiently firm political order to make it possible, began taking advantage of the economic resources set free by agricultural improvement in order to construct the first cities.

It is a mistake to regard the objects of the city as solely economic. This is an error of latter-day barbarians from which primitive barbarians were free; for they thought of the objects of cities as military, political, cultural and religious, as well as economic. The exchange of goods, and also the prevention of crime, Aristotle wrote, were conditions without which the city could not exist; but they did not define its object, which was ' the sharing of the good life ' by as many families as possible.

The existence of a city, by its nature, creates a demand for transport of food, fuel and building materials, as well as persons, into the city, and of a considerably smaller quantity of manufactured goods out of it.

We have now reached the stage where we can make some of our reasoning quantitative and not merely qualitative. People living on the plainest diets, with little meat, dairy produce or beverages, and depending therefore mainly upon grain, apart from a few vegetables which they may grow for themselves, will need about a quarter of a ton of grain per head per year. Instead of trying to express transport costs in money or money equivalent, we can get much simpler and clearer results by expressing the number of kilogrammes (1,000 kilogrammes to the ton) of grain required to pay for 1 ton/kilometre of transport. For the cost of transport by simple river boat under these conditions, we can use data from present-day India or China, or from the Ancient World as recorded by the Edict of Diocletian. In each case we get a roughly similar result, that a ton/kilometre of transport costs about 1 kilogramme of grain i.e. that a ton of grain could be carried for 1,000 kilometres (620 miles) in a river boat before its price was doubled.

This was, and is, cheap transport. Where human porterage has to be used, even in China, where labour is very cheap, costs rise to $4\frac{1}{2}$ kilogrammes per ton/kilometre. In Africa and India, where labour is not so cheap, these costs rise to 6 or more. There are indeed some remote and mountainous districts in present-day Italy where human porterage is still used; but at a cost of nearly ten kilogrammes of grain per ton/kilometre (i.e. a journey of 65 miles would double the price of grain).

Where pack animals are available these costs can be considerably reduced. But it is only by the use of ox-wagons, after the building of a really satisfactory network of roads, that costs as low as 2 kilogrammes per ton/kilometre (twice the cost of water haulage) can be obtained.

These facts should bring home the great importance of water transport to ancient and medieval cities, and indeed to many cities still in the modern world.

Early urban civilizations which lacked water transport, and in some cases even lacked pack animals, were in difficult circumstances. Professor Gourou, the French geographer, attributes the downfall of the Maya civilization (about the sixth century A.D.) to this cause. From accounts of the remains of houses it has been concluded that their population density in some districts was as high as sixty to the square kilometre (4 acres per head); indeed, without such a population density they could hardly have constructed such magnificent buildings. We also know that their civilization suddenly came to an end. Hypotheses about a climatic change which might have caused this, fly in the face of all other available evidence on this subject, and there is nothing to indicate war, epidemic, earthquake or similar disaster. While some historians, admittedly proceeding by analogy, hypothecate some internal decay of the social structure, Professor Gourou firmly places the responsibility on transport and agriculture. A maize-eating people, like most of the indigenous population of America, their method of cultivation was precisely the same as that of their distant descendants in the same spot today, periodically to fell and burn a stretch of forest, and then to cultivate maize by hand among the ashes. This method gives a high immediate yield, rapidly falling off after a few years, necessitating then the clearing of a further stretch of forest. In a soil leached by tropical rains, and therefore somewhat poor, the roots of forest trees can bring up minerals from the sub-soil, and these minerals remain in the ash when they are burnt. So this method of cultivation, in effect, met the lack of chemical fertilizers, by concentrating the minerals of many years' forest growth into the soil for two or three years' cropping.

This method is certainly very demanding of land. In this territory at the present day[3] it is found that a density of ten persons per square kilometre is more than can be supported permanently in one place; such a village, formed only fifty years ago, is already showing signs of disintegration; people are beginning to leave it and to cultivate plots outside.[4] It is true that, of the maize grown, only about 45 per cent. is consumed in the village, and the remainder transported away for sale. But it remains true that a dense population would be unable to support itself under these circumstances, without chemical fertilizers. Were transport available, a city would be able to support itself in such a world by collecting small surpluses from growers over a wide distance. But lacking navigable rivers, or even beasts of burden, when all loads had to be carried on men's heads, this was not possible.

The Inca and Aztec civilizations, which did build large cities and survive, likewise lacked beasts of burden. The fact that the Aztec capital was situated on a lake however must have facilitated its transport considerably. Both these civilizations grew up in much drier climates than the Maya, applying irrigation water to rich unleached soils, and so were probably able to obtain continuous high yields of maize on much more limited areas of land. Nevertheless, they appeared to have had to devote an abnormal proportion of their economic resources to transport of grain by human porterage.

Geographers have much to tell us about the origin of cities; about the military, administrative and religious functions which they performed, as well as economic. With some differences in emphasis, every city probably performs all four of these functions. But to understand the origins—and sometimes the decay—of cities, we must take into account the necessary limiting factors, often forgotten, of agriculture and transport; namely that any city, and *a fortiori* a large city, is only possible in proximity to land which can give steadily high yields of grain, and also with good transport. These conditions are best fulfilled where we have a large navigable fresh water river flowing through arid but fertile land which can be irrigated for agriculture—conditions fulfilled alike by the Indus Valley civilization, the Sumerian civilization in Irak, the Nile Valley and the legendary city of Timbuctoo.

Unlike the various forms of land transport, where cost is approximately proportionate to distance (save that a greater allowance to meet the cost of returning empty may have to be made in the case of longer distances) the cost of sea transport by sailing ship varies much less with distance. The principal costs incurred are in providing the ship and the crew and in getting the goods loaded and unloaded; once these have been met, the additional costs incurred in adding a few hundred miles to the voyage are comparatively slight. Whether we take data from the ancient world, from the Middle Ages or from the eighteenth century we get much the same result, namely that to transport a ton by sea involves a cost equivalent to 200-300 kilograms of grain, almost irrespective of distance (this charge represents a 20-30 per cent. addition to price if the cargo is grain, less if it is a more valuable commodity). Professor Postan[5] gives a number of examples to show that transport in the Middle Ages was a great deal cheaper than was generally supposed. He claims indeed that *relative to cost of manufacture* costs of transport were lower in the Middle Ages than in the early nineteenth century. So as soon as the Middle Ages could establish a degree of political order comparable with that of the ancient world, commerce and quickly growing cities, some of them reaching considerable size, again became possible, but still subject to the limiting condition that they must have access to good water transport.

Under medieval conditions, commerce however was still only possible in commodities whose value was high in relation to their weight. Among agricultural products, commerce in wool, hides and wine took place over long distances. There was some commerce in grain, but it was not a general rule. Between regions lacking water transport there was little commerce in grain, as can be shown by the great local variability of prices. There was some commerce in timber to regions lacking it, such as the Netherlands, and even in coal. But, generally speaking, an agricultural village in the Middle Ages still had to practice a high degree of self-sufficiency, supplying its own building material and handicraft products, as well as all its farm produce.

Is it worth our while to examine so intimately the economics and transport of our ancestors in the Middle Ages? It is, for the reason that these conditions still prevail in the modern world. Just as really primitive transport, relying on head porterage, can still be found in some parts of Africa, so many more advanced countries in the modern world, such as Yugoslavia, Thailand and many regions of India, though possessing a railway system, nevertheless have to depend on a truly medieval system of transport, of ox-wagons moving over muddy tracks, once you get more than a few miles away from the railways and main roads. In many of these countries transport is the real limiting factor preventing further economic growth and urbanization—a fact to which economists have paid all too little attention. It must be tantalizing for the villager in such a country to think (and he probably does so think) that perhaps twenty miles away there is a railway capable of bringing all the resources of civilization to his door, but that the cost of transporting any substantial quantity of his farm produce to the market to exchange for them is almost prohibitive. So the village remains medieval in its economic structure, producing for itself all the necessities of life, and often doing the job very badly; and this lack of economic specialization, in its turn, causes the village's agriculture to be very much less productive than it might otherwise have been.

What we have called ' medieval transport ' prevailed in Britain until quite late in the eighteenth century. The cost of transporting goods by wagon was much the same as it always had been, in those districts where wagon roads were available; many parts of England still had to rely on pack horses. A really substantial change was brought about by canals, a device first used in China, Holland and France, actively taken up in the late eighteenth century in Britain and Ireland. At the same time, there was a considerable improvement of the roads, perhaps designed predominantly to improve passenger and mail transport by stage coaches, which were still rather primitive in the mid-eighteenth century, and only reached their best speed and highest development just before they were displaced by railways. But this improvement in the roads must have benefited wagon transport too.

These improvements in transport were a necessary condition for the beginnings of heavy industry, iron and steel, pottery, chemicals and the like. It is true that such goods had been made before, but usually only for local markets, or transported at such great expense that no real growth of demand was possible. Once these industries really began to grow, we then had the nuclei of what were to become important industrial cities in the nineteenth century. It is true that Birmingham and Sheffield had originally distributed their products (consisting in those days of light metal goods) by pack-horse; but their growth became very rapid as transport improved. The cotton industry in its first stages was dependent upon the construction of good wagon roads, to distribute the raw cotton from Liverpool throughout Lancashire, and to take away the finished product. The dependence of the manufacturer, particularly in heavy industry, upon transport to assemble bulky materials for him and to distribute his products so that he can reach a large market, is absolute and unqualified. Without a growth in the size of the market, handicrafts cannot transform themselves into industries.

While the modern world can still exhibit to us examples of primitive and medieval transport it cannot, unfortunately, show us any example now of a country still in the canal-boat and stage-coach stage of transport. It is a pity that we cannot see a working model of it because under this system in Britain (it lasted until the 1830's) the growth of some quite large cities, both industrial and trading, became possible. But it is important for us to realize that the growth of these cities was still held in check, as it had been throughout previous ages, by transport requirements. Arthur Young has left information from which it is possible to draw a series of price-contour rings around London, with the price of food rapidly rising as you move towards the centre, simply because of the transport costs incurred in carrying it there. This checked the growth of the city in two ways. In the first place, all those with a fixed income hesitated to live in London, if they could live in the country, where food was so much cheaper; and secondly, London employers had to pay a much higher money wage (not necessarily a higher real wage) than country employers in order to attract labour. As a result, London-made goods, even if they were highly fabricated, with value high in proportion to their weight, and costing relatively little to transport, nevertheless had incurred higher labour costs, and therefore found it more difficult to compete in distant markets.

Railway transport overthrew, for the first time in history, the natural barriers which had hitherto prevented too great a concentration of industry in any urban centre. The great cities of the world up to that date indeed had been still built up primarily for their political, military or religious importance rather than their commercial or industrial functions; from 1830 onwards the latter were to predominate.

We have got so used to thinking of the cost of living (except perhaps for rents) in the country being much the same as in London, or indeed in a few respects higher, that we fail to realize that these late eighteenth century conditions still prevail in some countries in the modern world. In a country which has railways, but where other transport facilities are very poor and where distances are great—India is the best example—the price of food in the industrial cities is much higher than in the villages; wages there have to be higher too, and the ability of industrial goods to compete in rural markets is thereby limited. If and when India's transport improves, further urbanization and centralization of manufacture are to be expected.

The great effect of railway transport was to bring to inland places economic facilities which had hitherto only been available to sea, river and canal ports. The effectiveness of the railway also depended upon the construction of a comparatively dense network. While all transport to and from the railway still had to be by wagon, a distance of twenty miles could constitute an overwhelming economic burden.

In Britain, a great deal of capital (too much, in the opinion of many economists) was invested in railway building in the 1840's and 1850's, and by the end of the latter decade we had practically the railway network which we have now. The first effects upon agriculture were probably even more marked and immediate than the effects upon industry. Railway transport quickly broke up the old self-sufficient village with its handicraftsmen and traders, by making possible the sale of much cheaper industrially-produced goods. But at the same time it brought about the far-reaching re-arrangement of agricultural production on the basis of regional specialization (although the long-distance transport of liquid milk did not become general until about the turn of the century). This regional specialization, particularly the diversion of livestock and dairy farming to the hillier and wetter counties in the west, and concentration of grain production in the drier counties, released a great deal of latent productivity, from which both producers and consumers benefited. The effect of the re-organization of agriculture and of the displacement of the village handicraftsmen was to set free a large volume of labour which was drawn (or, it might be more accurate to say, driven by poverty) into urban employment, thereby making possible a further large expansion of industry.

The English agriculturist welcomed this geographical specialization of agricultural production, which benefited him as well as the country as a whole, up till about 1870. But he did not like it when the process was carried a stage further. By that date, American and Canadian railways and steam ships were opening up new grain-growing lands which could produce cheaper still. The British exporter could produce plenty of goods to exchange for imported grain, so the result was a further contraction of British agriculture.

Apart from their effects on agriculture, the most immediate and striking consequence of the railways was to make possible a further rapid development of heavy industry, whose main function was to supply the world with the capital goods then needed for further industrial and transport development.

But, once again, need we take such a detailed interest in what was happening a hundred years ago? Unfortunately we must. Our educational and intellectual processes are so slow that a great number of people, including many in influential positions, have still got their minds firmly fixed on the problems of a hundred years ago. This is particularly the case with the Marxian socialists. The economic development of Russia was controlled by a man who suffered from what can be only described as a psychological obsession with steel works (when he changed his name he called himself after them) which in fact greatly slowed down Russia's economic development, because of the inordinate attention given to this one commodity. A leading official of one very poor country once explained to me that he was going to build a steel works, even if he had to import every ounce of ore and every ounce of fuel, because steel was 'a psychological necessity.' This mild form of lunacy (for these are really the correct terms in which to describe it) has affected geographers, most of whom still go on writing text books to explain that the industrial development of different regions of the world depends upon the availability of coal and mineral resources. More seriously, it affects economists, who continue to write that the location of industry depends upon the relative advantages and disadvantages of each site for the transport of fuel and heavy materials. These views may have contained some element of truth some hundred years ago, but they are almost completely irrelevant now.

It is the aberrations of the economists which have done more harm than those of the geographers. Erroneous statements in geographical text books are read and forgotten again. But the erroneous doctrines of economists have influenced statesmen and legislators to believe that whatever location industrialists chose was in fact necessarily dictated by transport costs, and that it was therefore out of the question to interfere with it. These views were not even challenged until the time of the Barlow Report in 1940, by which date, in England, it was rather late to do anything about it.

It would take too much space and involve too much economic reasoning to attempt to describe here the considerations which do in fact determine the location of industry. The old idea about transport costs is hopelessly inapplicable because, except for a few ' heavy industries ' which are now of quite small relative importance, transport costs represent only a trivial proportion of costs of production. In enumerating the reasons which determine the choice of location by the individual manufacturer we soon find that it is not safe here to assume, as is assumed in many other branches of economics, that whatever choice benefits the individual manufacturer will also prove to be the most advantageous choice for society as a whole.

For what does happen in fact is that we get a cumulative process of ' to him that hath shall more be given,' whereby districts which already have abundant manufactures tend to attract still more, creating extreme congestion in some regions, and poverty and depopulation in others. When we look at the map of the world, we find that what can be described as successful manufacturing regions i.e. those whose industries are capable of selling new products competitively on the world market, apart from old-established but declining industries, or industries enjoying artificial production, are very limited. Lösch, the German economist who has probably made the best study of this subject, concluded that the regions in Western Europe which have a high concentration of successful manufactures now were in fact those which had already succeeded in achieving a dense population, under the conditions of agriculture and transport prevailing at the time, in the eighteenth century. The good markets, transport facilities, reserves of skilled labour, and ancillary business services which a dense pop-ulation made possible, attracted new industries to the same regions; and the same processes have been going on (with exceptions) cumulatively for two centuries.

What recent world history has shown however is that a really forceful newcomer can succeed in establishing a successful new industrial region. Sometimes this is due to a wealthy and populous new market springing up, arising in the first instance out of agricultural and mineral development. Examples of this are the new industrial regions growing up in California and Texas in the United States. Alternatively, regions with good transport and dense population, but lacking other industrial facilities, can nevertheless get started and can sell their products on the world market. The outstanding examples of this, during the last half century, have been Japan and the textile exporting region of India.

In order to break into the world market these new regions have had to be willing to work for much lower money wages than their competitors. (The cost of living in these countries is lower too, and their real wages are not so far below the level of other industrial countries as are their money wages).

So we pass from the railway age to the age of road transport. The railways immeasurably cheapened long-distance transport. But once the goods had been unloaded from the train or ship on to a horse-dray their costs of transport were very high. The inevitable consequence of this was that industry was concentrated in compact and densely populated industrial towns, or directly along the waterfront in sea ports. Motor transport unfroze this concentration. Costs are incurred inevitably, in getting goods off ship or rail on to a motor truck; but once this has been done, unlike a horse vehicle, it makes little difference whether you carry them two or twenty miles. It was motor transport which provided the economic basis without which the present-day 'sprawl' of industrial towns would have been impossible.

On a railway, the principal element in costs (which may or may not be reflected in the freight rates charged) is incurred in getting the goods on and off the train, getting the train made up and started, and shunting it through junctions. Once this has been done the additional or marginal cost of running the railway wagon an extra hundred miles or so is small. So a railway, by its nature, has high terminal and low marginal costs. A road vehicle has lower terminal and higher marginal costs; although year by year terminal costs tend to increase, as the growing volume of traffic calls for more elaborate organization. But, in general, it is clearly more advantageous to use road vehicles for short journeys and rail for longer. There is a point, which can be fairly precisely measured, at which the railways' lower marginal costs offset their higher terminal costs. In the 1920's, when road transport was in its infancy, this critical distance was only about 75 miles—any transport for a greater distance than that was more cheaply done by rail. But development has been swift. The lower marginal costs of the railway now only give it the advantage over road transport in journeys over 200 miles in length in British conditions (300 miles in American conditions). In a country as small as Britain, and with most of the population and industry concentrated in a fairly narrow industrial belt, most journeys in fact are below 200 miles in length. Economists therefore should not have been surprised when a complete statistical survey, undertaken for the first time in 1954, showed that, apart from mineral traffic, threequarters of all the transport of the country (measured by ton-mileage) is now carried by road.

It seems safe to predict that road transport will go on improving further, and that industry will make still more use of it in the future. (The simple discovery of articulated vehicles, whereby the engine is uncoupled from the body and goes straight to work on another load without waiting for the unloading of the old one, has by itself effected great economies in road transport costs). Industrialization in the future, relying upon road transport, will be spread out, we may perhaps predict, over fairly wide zones. But we can also predict that remote districts, over 100 miles distant from the principal industrial centres, will, under these conditions, probably continue to deteriorate economically.

The effects of road transport on industry have been so interesting that we tend to ignore their equally interesting effects upon agriculture. In the first place—this consideration does not apply in Britain, where the railway network is unusually dense, but applies very much in some other countries—road transport has made agriculture possible in many regions where it was formerly uneconomic. Much of what is now good wheat-growing land in Canada and the United States of America was, until as late as the 1920's, used for grazing only because it was fifty or more miles from a railway, and the cost of carrying the entire harvest over that distance by horse-power made wheat growing unremunerative.

Apart from grain, wool and the like, much agricultural produce benefits from quick transport, and agriculturists therefore have been even more interested than industrialists in road transport. In any country with good roads, agriculturists now only make a minimum use of the railways for transport of milk, fruit, vegetables, livestock and meat. In the United States, when the goods are perishable, road consignments, often in refrigerated vehicles, for distances over two thousand miles, are quite common.

The result of this development has been that geographical specialization in agriculture has further greatly increased. It seems almost incredible, but it is in fact the case that most of the potatoes for the whole of the United States market are grown in three highly specialized small regions. Though less striking, increased agricultural specialization is visible in Britain. The mixed farm is declining in favour of the specialized dairy or cattle farm in the West and grain or potato farm in the East.

The road transport age which followed the railway age has set the manufacturer and trader free from the close confines of industrial cities, within which they had previously been held. But by the same token it began setting the people free too. With transport more readily available, homes no longer had to be cramped within a narrow circle around the industrial centre, any more than did workshops.

The result has been what planners generally apostrophise as ' sprawl.' The precise extent of sprawl can be seen from the attached diagram of densities in the various zones of London, at different dates from 1801 to 1951. Within the innermost three miles, where most of the population used to live, densities are

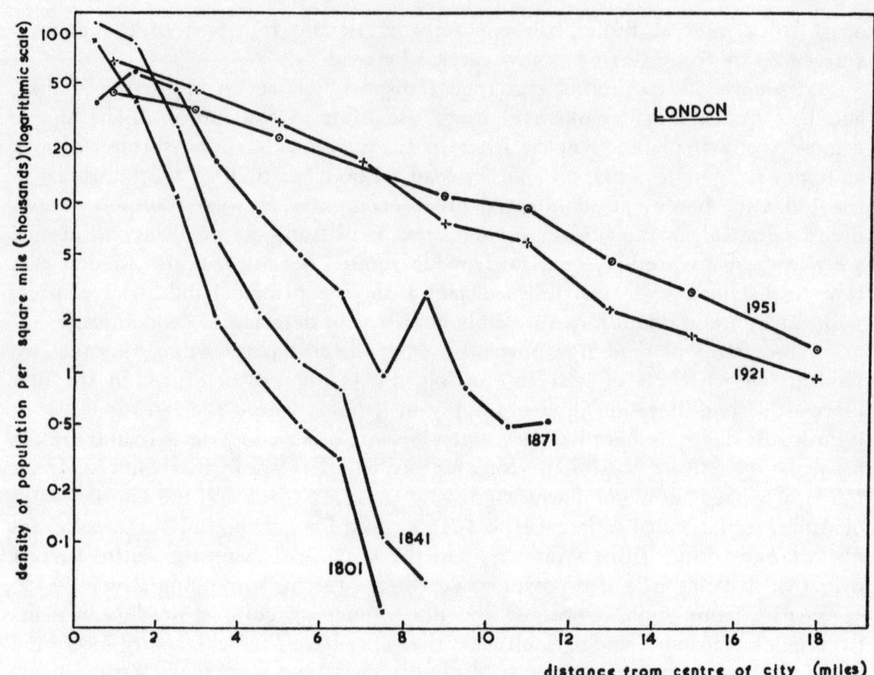

Fig. 1
Changes in population density in London, 1801–1951. The diagram shows that within
the innermost three miles, where most of the population used to live, densities are much
lower than they were a century ago. Within a radius of seven miles, densities are lower
now than they were in 1921. It is in the more distant suburbs that densities continue
to increase.

now much lower than they were a century ago. Within a radius of 7 miles, densities are lower now than they were in 1921. It is in the more and more distant suburbs that densities continue to increase.

In 1801, only the richest people, who could afford horses or carriages, were able to live more than 3 or 4 miles away from the centre of the city. There were no buses, and the average man had to rely upon walking for his transport, whether proceeding to work or to recreation. By 1841 the population had greatly increased. There were by then a few buses, expensive in relation to wages at the time, and the great majority of Londoners were still dependent on walking for their transport. Under these circumstances, it was hardly possible for the expansion of the city to take it any further out. The line on the density diagram remained at about the same slope as it had been in 1801, with just more people packed into each zone of the city.

It is interesting to find cities in present-day India which, although they may have a few trams or buses, nevertheless price them beyond the means of most of the citizens, who are still dependent upon walking for their transport. Under these circumstances, even where population is very large, we find compact cities of extraordinary density being built up.

In London, we can see the pattern of settlement beginning to loosen by 1871. Some horse-bus and horse-tramway services had been developed by then; but the principal factor had been the provision of reasonably cheap workmen's tickets on the railways. (This concession had been enforced by Parliament, against the wishes of the railway companies). Moreover, an underground service of steam trains was just coming into operation (for travellers who did not mind soot and fumes). Before the end of the century, this was to be electrified, and supplemented by a service of electric trams and motor buses.

The implement which really chiselled apart the compact Victorian city was the electric tram. We can reach this conclusion in an interesting indirect manner. There is an ingenious method (worked out by Dr. Hans Singer) of computing what the economist calls the annual value of pure urban site rents, which can best be defined as the estimated annual gross rent obtainable from each built-up site, less maintenance and interest on the estimated replacement cost (less appropriate depreciation) of the building in its present state. The annual value of these rents, relative to the national income as a whole, was rising all through the nineteenth century, thereby indicating an increasing urgency in the demand for urban space. But with the turn of the century this series also turned and began to decline. The electric tram, and other transport facilities, were, it is true, creating new site values in the suburbs; but at the same time they were destroying old site values faster, or at any rate fast enough, to make the aggregate site rent rise less rapidly than national income in general.

It is impossible to give a precise estimate of the situation at present, because for so many years all urban property, both residential and commercial, has stood at artificial values because of rent restriction. But, judging by the experience of other countries, this fall in the relative level of site rents has always most certainly continued.

The pattern of ' sprawl ' shown for London has been fairly closely followed by other big cities with electric railway (underground or surface) transport— New York, Chicago, Sydney, Manchester, and, less expectedly, Tokyo and Osaka too. But, without electric railways, a similar pattern also develops in modern cities dependent upon private car transport, supplemented by a few buses, such as Los Angeles.

But, the reader may say, must there not be an end to this process? We can understand people living 15 or 20 miles away from their work, perhaps even 30 or 40 miles away if they work in a city as big as New York, and are rich enough to pay for expensive transport. But that surely must be the limit. Is not ' sprawl ' coming to an end?

But—for better or for worse—it is not. There is a defect, a simple defect, in the above argument. A man's work-place need not be in the centre of the city. To an increasing degree now, the work-places are moving out with the people. When there is widespread unemployment, as in the 1930's, employers can expect people to travel considerable distances in search of jobs. In a time of labour shortage, they find it necessary to bring the jobs much nearer to the people, particularly those employers who want to employ women.

So work-places have begun to move out, and also, to an increasing degree, centres of shopping, recreation, education and the like. We can see this process more clearly in the United States and Canada where it has begun earlier and proceeded faster, than here. But there can be no doubt that it is coming. Until virtually every family, as in Canada and the United States, is able to afford a car, we will not get a situation such as is developing in big American cities, where nearly all the new department store development is now in the suburbs, particularly in 'controlled regional shopping centres,' where a group of traders combine to provide a shopping centre with acres of car parking. At our present rate of economic progress, we will take some time to reach this objective, especially as our fiscal policy is designed to place heavy taxes on the petrol and cars which people do want, in order to subsidise the building of houses more expensive than people are willing to pay for. But universal car ownership will come sooner or later, and the prudent planner must make his plans accordingly.

By the same token, people living near the centre of a big congested industrial city, be it London or New York, find it hardly worth while running a car, even when they can well afford to do so, because of the lack of parking space and the extremely high costs of garaging. In an age when all their friends have cars, this will be an additional factor helping to pull population out to the suburbs.

This flight of population to the suburbs is a source of dismay to many—to city councils about the loss of rateable value, to insurance companies and other important property owners who are frightened of a decline in real estate values, to town planners who find the problem of suburban planning beyond them and who would prefer to go back two or three centuries and redesign a nice compact Wren-like city, and, in the Federal Housing Administration in the United States (our own civil servants mostly have more sense) bureaucrats whose actions seem to be based on no rational criteria at all, and who just seem to like tall, and extremely expensive, blocks of flats on congested sites for their own sake.

With us, there are a number of City Councils who have made up their minds (for good reasons or bad) not to export population across the City border if they can help it, and the differential subsidies on expensive high density buildings have enabled them to persist in this policy. Also a good many architects (who have thought little about this problem) and some town-planners (who should have thought about it) have favoured high-density residential development.

But even this formidable combination of forces will not be able permanently to withstand the pressure of popular opinion, for the ordinary family really does prefer a house in comparatively spacious surroundings, and certainly resents paying taxation to finance obviously uneconomic blocks of flats.

While in this matter we must move with the current of popular opinion, we should nevertheless realize the destination towards which it is leading us. It is nothing less than the complete disintegration of the city, even of the conurbation, as we know it. Transport has indeed done its work all too well. The final result, if we go on the way we are now going, will be an ugly and planless dispersal of population spreading almost uniformly over a whole industrial zone— perhaps in England an almost continuous built-up area from Liverpool to Dover, with most of the rest of the country impoverished and depopulated. This is undoubtedly one of the examples, perhaps one of the few examples in economics, where the unchecked operation of the free market certainly does not produce the most socially desirable results. For reasons which should be clear, though it is impossible here to state them at length, it is desirable that people should be grouped into communities of manageable size, in which citizens are capable of understanding the affairs of their local community, and taking some part in its government and other activities. Such communities need a certain degree of compactness, so that their citizens do not have to travel too far to reach each other; while at the same time they need to be clearly separated from other communities by an intervening zone of unbuilt agricultural land; for it is another important social principle that town dwellers should have easy access to open country, just as agriculturists do not want to be too far from towns. For economic, social and political reasons alike[6] we should take (to the best of our present knowledge) communities sized about 150,000 as our objective. A community of this size is large enough to give its inhabitants, and those of the neighbouring rural areas, a full range of economic and administrative services. But we should not allow our community to become any larger if we want its citizens to retain civic pride and interest in their local affairs, if we want its traffic to remain reasonably free from congestion, and if we want to prevent local administration from becoming both expensive and bureaucratic.

NOTES AND REFERENCES

1 See Professor Karl Sauer, Geographical Review, January 1947.

2 A convenient summary of the economics of primitive populations, with citation of authorities, is given by Taylor, Canadian Journal of Economics and Political Science, August 1950.

3 Study of the village of Chan Kom, in Yucatan, by Redfield and Villa (quoted by Professor Gourou).

4 Of the land available to the village, only 5 per cent. is cleared each year. Land is usually cultivated for two years and then fallowed for seven years. A considerable proportion of the land is not considered worth cultivating at all.

5 Cambridge Economic History of Europe.

6 For more detailed evidence see my article in Econometrica, April 1945.

[3]

The Turbulent Eighth Decade
Challenges to American City Planning

Peter Hall

Hall is professor of city and regional planning and director of the Institute of Urban and Regional Development at the University of California, Berkeley. This article is based loosely on his *Cities of Tomorrow: An Intellectual History of Urban Planning and Design in the Twentieth Century* (Basil Blackwell, New York, 1989). He is currently working with Ann Markusen, Scott Campbell, and Sabina Deitrick on *The Rise of the Gunbelt*, a study of the military remapping of America in the post-World War II era, for publication in mid-1990.

City planning in America has no official certificate of birth. But, if a date has to be chosen, it is surely 1909: the year of the First National Conference on City Planning and Congestion and the publication of Burnham's Chicago Plan. American planning is 80 years old this summer. It celebrates other anniversaries too: it is 60 years since the appearance of the New York Regional Plan, 50 years since the Futurama Exhibit and the screening of *The City* at the New York World's Fair, and 40 years since the passage of the Housing and Slum Clearance Act. It is surely a year for celebration.

And also for reflection. In these eight decades, city planning in America has come a long way. It has established itself as an institutional force across the nation, as a part of the social and political fabric. And never was the need for planning so evident, as witness the stream of media reports that tell on the one hand of crack wars tearing the last remaining life out of inner city areas, of an urban underclass becoming ever more economically, socially, and geographically separated from the mainstream and, on the other, of unparalleled suburban growth pressures, of spreading freeway traffic gridlock, of resulting NIMBY-style conflicts. Thus, the problems that brought planning forth have not gone away. Some of them, indeed, show a frightening persistence. And planning—even using that term in the widest possible sense, to embrace a whole range of economic and social planning initiatives—has not yet come close to solving them.

The history of planning shows that these problems, and these responses, are not unique to the United States—though often, America is the bellwether that warns the rest of the world of coming urban storms. To an extraordinary degree, the international planning movement was born in reaction to a set of common problems in the world's great cities at the close of the nineteenth century. Early in the new century, the movement evolved to grapple with market forces that were transforming that city into a different kind of urban entity. Later, faced with the decline of the central city, it evolved yet new responses to that problem. There are intriguing parallels between one country and another, as there are between one historical period and another: the urban underclass is perceived as a central problem today, as it was at the turn of the century.

But the historical comparisons are not precise, and neither are the geographical ones. The underclass of 1989 is not the same phenomenon as the underclass of 1890. Urban renewal in 1989 is again a major issue, but it is not the same as renewal in 1949. And planning in the United States has evolved differently from planning in Great Britain, France, Germany, and Scandinavia. The reasons for these differences, both over time and across place, are a mixture of economic forces, political traditions, and cultural ideologies. Issues recycle and come uppermost again, but the responses are subtly different in every era and every country. Why that should be is a central topic for the planning historian.

THE TURBULENT EIGHTH DECADE

Without too much historic-poetic license, we can distinguish ten periods in the brief history of planning, both here in the United States and elsewhere in the world.

The City Pathological, 1890–1901

Quite suddenly, between 1880 and 1890, the respectable bourgeois urban world discovered the slum city that festered underneath it. Two remarkable pieces of journalism—Andrew Mearns' *The Bitter Cry of Outcast London*, in 1883, and Jacob Riis' *How the Other Half Lives*, in New York in 1890—provided the trigger. The reaction was a mixture of fear and guilt. In London, Beatrice Webb wrote of "a new consciousness of sin . . . a collective or class consciousness, amounting to a conviction, that the industrial organism, which had yielded rent, interest and profit on a stupendous scale, had failed to provide a decent livelihood and tolerable conditions for a majority of the inhabitants"; while H. M. Hyndman, leader of the Social Democratic Foundation, wrote that "[e]ven among the useless men and women who dub themselves 'society' . . . [t]he dread word 'Revolution' is sometimes spoken aloud in jest." And in New York, Jacob Riis evoked the same fear: the tenement dwellers, he wrote, "hold within their clutch the wealth and business of New York, hold them at their mercy in the day of mob-rule and wrath. The bullet-proof shelters, the stacks of hand-grenades, and the Gatling guns of the sub-Treasury are tacit admissions of the fact and of the quality of the mercy expected."

The origin, then, was precisely the same: it was the discovery of the urban underclass, numbering—according to both Riis and the Tenement House Commission of 1894—three in five of the New York population. The motive, in the words of the commission, was "[t]he redemption of the tenement classes," which lay "partly in the redemption of the family, the most conservative unit in civilization, to its proper share of space, natural light and air, and the cultivation of the domestic arts, one of which is cleanliness." And, in New York and Chicago and a dozen other cities, it was the socialization of the new immigrants who were so overrepresented in the tenement population. That was the principal motive behind Jane Addams' settlement house movement at Hull House in Chicago, itself modeled faithfully on Toynbee Hall in London's East End; it was likewise the major concern of the sociologist-planner Clarence Perry, who devised the concept of neighborhood unit at the Russell Sage Foundation between 1909 and 1929; it was also the obsessional subject-matter of Robert E. Park and his co-researchers in the Chicago School of Sociology during the 1920s. But neither Addams, nor Perry, nor Park found an effective answer: an immigrant later confessed that he went to Hull House "for an occasional shower, that was all"; Park, in 1925, concluded a paper on community organization and juvenile delinquency by apologizing that his paper lacked a moral, confessing that "the problem of juvenile delinquency seems to have its sources in conditions over which, in our present knowledge, we have very little control."

There was, however, one key feature of the American response that sharply marked it off from that of the Europeans. There, in Britain, France, and Germany alike, the answer was government support for social housing programs. Here, the New York Tenement House Commission report of 1900, principally authored by Lawrence Veiller, decisively rejected public intervention; private benevolence could do the job, the commission held, provided a framework of physical regulation was put in place. As Catherine Bauer bemoaned in the 1930s, that one report put back the cause of public housing in America for decades. Peter Marcuse has suggested that this unique divorce occurred because of the three issues that then emerged—fire and disease dangers, fear of disorder, protection of real estate values. The first two issues soon faded, leaving the infant art of planning to an alliance of real estate interests and middle class home-buyers.

The City Beautiful, 1901–1915

Whatever the explanation, the fact is that almost from the start, and for at least two decades, American city planning was almost entirely removed from the kind of social concern that drove the movement in Europe. In the first decade of the new century, the City Beautiful movement represented a deliberate and conscious attempt to impose on America's greatest cities the kind of heavily formalistic urban reconstruction that Haussmann had carried through in Paris, and Cerda in Barcelona, between 1850 and 1870. The irony was that virtually all those attempts were made by patrons of an autocratic regal or imperial regime, while here—in Cleveland, in San Francisco, in Chicago above all—the agency was an alliance of downtown merchants. Burnham shamelessly appealed to their base motives: "No one has estimated the number of millions of money made in Chicago and expended elsewhere," he suggested, "but the sum must be a large one. What would be the effect upon our retail business at home if this money were circulated here? What would be the effect upon our prosperity if the town were so delightful that most of the men who grow independent financially in the Mississippi Valley, or west of it, were to come to Chicago to live?" Pericles' investment in ancient Athens, he argued, was still paying for itself in tourist revenue. He may, of course, have had tongue in cheek. But he knew his audience; rather remarkably, most of the plan got completed.

Not elsewhere, though. The plan contained a built-in contradiction, in that it favored centralization but then tried to control it. Already, at that crucial first National

Conference on City Planning and Congestion in 1909, other planners and their business backers were seeing that this solution—a kind of aristocratic city for merchant princes, as Mel Scott once put it—was going to cost more than the backers were willing to pay. The result, hastened perhaps by Burnham's death in 1912, was an abrupt switch from the City Beautiful to the City Functional.

The City Functional, 1916–1939

The new solution was far more down-to-earth. It included zoning of land uses accompanied by advisory city planning commissions. It proved instantly and hugely successful. Starting with New York City's historic Zoning Ordinance of 1916, zoning had been adopted by more than 750 communities by the end of the 1920s. The reason was that everyone could see that it was good for business. So, of course, was the City Beautiful, or so its proponents had claimed; but everyone could see that zoning came much cheaper.

What was good for business was the right kind of people: the right customers downtown, the right neighbors in the new streetcar suburbs. In New York, the Fifth Avenue merchants backed zoning because they were concerned that floods of immigrant garment workers would compromise their exclusive stores. Edward Bassett, father of the New York scheme, later wrote that one of the major purposes of zoning was to prevent the "premature depreciation of settled localities." Out in the suburbs, it was the same story: the first-known use of zoning, in Modesto, California, in the 1880s, was to keep Chinese laundries out of residential areas. In the historic 1926 Supreme Court case of *Euclid v. Ambler*, the great planner-lawyer Alfred Bettman argued that zoning served the public welfare by enhancing the community's property values; the Court's decision gave the inhabitants of Euclid, a middle class bedroom community next door to Cleveland, a guarantee that their investments would not be compromised by industrial development.

In practice, as one later observer succinctly put it, the notion was to preserve real estate values in settled neighborhoods, while imposing only nominal restrictions in areas that held out the possibility of profit. One of the basic city planning texts of the 1920s, from the husband-and-wife team Hubbard and Hubbard, italicized the point: *"Zoning and plat control divide honors in being reported the most profitable results of city planning."* As the Hubbards succinctly put it in a chapter heading: "IT PAYS TO PLAN." Thus, far from being a device to speed the transition of the immigrant poor from the tenements to the streetcar suburbs, zoning in practice became a way of keeping them where they were. And, despite rare exceptions like Bettman's Cincinnati, zoning was usually divorced from city planning: the first was legally based, mandatory, and invariable, the second voluntary, advisory, nonmandatory, and irregular. In practical terms, the City Functional was—and is—without doubt the dominant American contribution to the planning movement; but it is a curiously low-key, unidealistic one. It is

driven hard by the demands of profit from land development. And it is almost totally bereft of vision.

The City Visionary, 1923–1936

There was a massive exception to all this, of course: the small band of visionaries—including Lewis Mumford, Henry Wright, Clarence Stein, Stuart Chase, Benton MacKaye, and Catherine Bauer—who constituted the Regional Planning Association of America from 1923 on. Dedicated followers and interpreters of Ebenezer Howard and Patrick Geddes, they blended the ideas of their British masters with skeins of distinctively American thought—Harvard physiography, Thoreau's ideas on self-sufficiency, and southern regionalism—to produce something much more than the sum of its parts. The basis, for both Howard and Geddes, was a Kropotkinesque anarchism: a vision of small, largely self-sufficient rural communities in ecological balance with their rich natural resources. Because of this, they went far beyond even Howard's blueprint for garden cities as the solution for the ills of the congested metropolis: they wanted nothing less than a reconstruction of the whole foundation of American life, based on what they saw as the liberating effect of the automobile and the electric power plant.

It did not, and perhaps could not ever, come to pass; the vision was too utopian, the forces lined up against them were too strong. Their main practical experiment, the garden city of Radburn, soon came to grief in the Depression and is today swallowed up in the amorphous suburban sprawl of northern New Jersey. What might have been the truest realizations of their vision, the greenbelt towns of Rexford Tugwell's Resettlement Administration and the regional plan for the Tennessee Valley, alike foundered, as Congress halted the first, and as personal feuding and ideological differences drained the second of meaning.

The New Deal represented a unique chance for American planning to go a European road, a decade before Europe itself did so; but by 1936, with FDR in political retreat, the battle was lost and it fell to Britain, Sweden, and France to implement the RPAA's ideas. Writing to Frederic Osborn after publication of Abercrombie's 1944 Greater London Plan, Mumford said that it was "the best single document on planning, in every respect, that has come out since Howard's book itself. ... The original job of making the idea credible has been performed," he went on, "and the main task now is to master the political methods that will most effectively translate it into a reality. We have not yet reached that stage here," he prophetically concluded, "and I fear the results of our immaturity will show once the post-war building boom . . . gets under way."

He proved right: the British Labour government of 1945 essentially did what Tugwell had failed to do, and what Howard had thought no government anywhere would ever do, successfully launching a national program that eventually resulted in 30 new towns; America had to rest content with a series of isolated commercial ini-

THE TURBULENT EIGHTH DECADE

tiatives, some of which, such as James Rouse's Columbia, had superficial similarities to their British cousins, but none of which represented the core of the Howard-Mumford-Osborn vision.

There was a rare paradox here, as Mumford would have been the first to emphasize. Because the United States was so far ahead of Europe in technological diffusion, in the 1920s and 1930s it was already possible to see the implications in a way that would have been impossible elsewhere. Clarence Stein's contribution to the 1925 RPAA manifesto, *Dinosaur Cities*, uncannily predicts the outmovement of industry from the cities and the resulting inner city problem that would actually take place more than 40 years later. Benton MacKaye's essay of 1930, *The Townless Highway*, similarly anticipates the freeway and the dispersed settlement form of the 1950s and 1960s. So, in a different way, did Frank Lloyd Wright's personal manifesto *Broadacre City*, a few years later, though he always held aloof from the RPAA group. After World War II, the irony was that they all lived to see their vision, but as a shell without the substance: bedroom suburbs instead of garden cities, white-collar commuters instead of farmer-artisans. All of these planners were visionaries, and the forces of reality—embodied in the City Functional tradition—proved too strong.

The tragic irony was already evident, for those who could foresee what was coming, in the epic intellectual battle of 1930–1931 between Lewis Mumford and Thomas Adams, author of the Regional Plan of New York, over what the RPAA saw as the failings of that plan. For Mumford, it was a pernicious document, whose implementation would result in a multiplication of the failings it purported to condemn: congestion, overcentralization, uncontrolled growth. The plan, in essence, was the City Functional at the regional scale. For Adams, who had begun his career as Howard's lieutenant at Letchworth, the issue was "whether we stand still and talk ideals or move forward and get as much realization of our idea as possible in a necessarily imperfect society, capable only of imperfect solutions to its problems." They parted ways; and much of the plan became reality, largely because of the energies of Robert Moses, who provided the needed arterial connections, while the remarkable vision of the RPAA remained forever on paper.

The City Renewable, 1937–1964

There was but one historical thread connecting the RPAA with postwar America, and a curious one at that: it was the role that Catherine Bauer, perhaps the group's most effective political advocate, played as proponent of affordable housing. Her first attempt to achieve this, which culminated in the creation of the Federal Housing Association in 1934, had perverse effects: very soon, the agency was redlining the inner cities and effectively denying mortgages in predominantly black areas. The second attempt, which resulted in the historic Wagner Act of 1937, represented an uneasy compromise between Bauer and the construction unions, who wanted public

housing, and the real estate interests who had backed the 1934 Act, and who wanted anything but. Public housing was to be seen as a temporary expedient for the deserving poor, who would soon be out of it and into FHA-supported mortgages; it would exclude the predominantly black urban underclass. The means to that end was the federal government's support of the construction but not the subsequent running costs. When at the end of the 1940s that barrier was reached, and poor welfare families at last entered the projects, the resulting financial contradictions proved catastrophic: they were symbolized, a quarter-century later, by the demolition of the Pruitt-Igoe apartments in St. Louis, which had been allowed to deteriorate until they became uninhabitable.

But in 1949 and 1954, Congress again grappled with the issue. And this time, as Catherine Bauer memorably put it, "seldom had such a diverse group of would-be angels tried to dance on the same small pin." Once again, though, it was the real estate lobby that emerged right in the center. They wanted, not public housing, but federally aided commercial development at the edge of downtown. The public housers went along with them in the hope of getting something, but were largely thwarted; in city after city—Philadelphia, Pittsburgh, Hartford, New Haven, Boston, San Francisco—the developers sought "the blight that's right," as Charles Abrams inimitably put it. So it was the low-income black sections close to the CBD that went, while the promised public housing failed to materialize.

The truly amazing feature of those years, in retrospect, is the way in which it happened. True, the real estate interests proved as powerful as they had before. But they marshaled wide-ranging growth coalitions that embraced liberal-technocratic mayors like New Haven's Lee and Chicago's Daley, labor councils, construction-trade representatives, good-government groups, professional planners and others; at first, even the public housing lobby. It took a long time to appreciate that, as in Boston's West End, they were actually destroying entire stable neighborhoods.

That was because of the prevailing intellectual ethos. The fashionable buzzwords of the late 1950s and early 1960s were comprehensive renewal, systems analysis in planning, and integrated land use-transportation planning. Planning was invaded by a battery of computer-based techniques derived from the transportation engineers, and by a related philosophy derived from the aerospace program and ultimately embodied in Robert McNamara's Pentagon. Planning, it was argued, could be based on rational choice among alternatives, using quantified techniques. Anything that could not be expressed in numbers was inherently suspect. The result was a heavy bias in favor of efficiency, which could be measured in terms of time and money, and against equity and intangibles, which could not: the City Functional approach, plus computer models. Given that bias, the destruction of old neighborhoods for new freeways and new commercial development was not merely inevitable; it came to have a scientific validity.

PETER HALL

Finally, the break came. To appreciate the force of the change, it is only necessary to compare the content of the Journal in, say, 1959 and in 1969. The furor broke in the early 1960s, with publication of devastating criticisms like Herbert Gans's *The Urban Villagers* and Martin Anderson's *The Federal Bulldozer*. It happened also to be the time of the first revolt against urban freeways, which stopped San Francisco's Embarcadero freeway in mid-air. Within an astonishingly short time, it caused an almost complete inversion of almost every basic value in American planning practice and planning education. And not merely in the United States: the same revolution stopped freeways in London, the Covent Garden redevelopment, and renewal in central Stockholm, as well as producing paralysis over the Les Halles redevelopment in Paris.

The City Grassrooted, 1965–1980

By the end of the 1960s, all was changed. The civil rights movement had been followed by the free speech movement; the riots had torn through the newly renewed cities, revealing just how little the process had done for the underclass; opposition to Vietnam, and with it the whole Pentagon style of planning, was at its peak. Almost every value that planners had cherished was now stood on its head. Instead of a belief in top-down planning by benign value-free experts, there was now a deep distrust of professional expertise and a demand for advocacy planning based on grassroots involvement. But, paradoxically, in one vital respect there was little change: the planners would now perform many of the functions of the elected officials, and it was by no means clear how they could avoid the charge that they were still controlling and manipulating the action.

Within a few years, the new skein of radical planning unraveled into a number of incompatible threads: the social learning or new humanist school, the neo-anarchism of Friedmann, and finally the ascendant Marxists, who made common cause for only a very short while until they too splintered in debate. They were however united on one point: their agreement that the planner had not got much power, and deserved to have less. Planners, in the version that came to dominate in the late 1970s, were mere agents of the capitalist local state, seeking palliatives to stave off crisis in the system; but in the process, they would sidestep one problem only to face another. Because traditional theories of planning had ignored this essential fact, the Marxists argued, they were essentially vacuous, and worse: in seeking to define an ideal mode of planning, devoid of social and political content, they aimed to depoliticize planning and thus to legitimate it and better serve the system.

The City Theoretical, 1975–1989

It was the most disturbing critique of planning that had emerged in the profession's seven decades of life, particularly since so much of it was coming from within the nation's—and the world's—most prestigious planning schools. But it was more notable for what it destroyed than for what it put in its place. If planning had been a mere tool of the system, how then to create something that was not? At this point, many of the radical critics fell silent. Some flatly denied that, given continuance of the system, any positive theory of planning action was necessary or desirable. Others retreated to bold but largely vacuous rhetoric. By the end of the 1970s, planning theory had become divorced from planning practice. And the top products of the nation's top planning schools were becoming increasingly uninterested in the day-to-day activity of planning.

In the 1980s, some continued to argue at these rarified levels of theory. In a revealing special issue of *Society* (November/December 1988), eight professors from the nation's top schools debate the question of planning, power, and politics. The truly amazing point about this discussion is that hardly anywhere, in nearly 40 pages of close print, is there any mention of the kinds of things planners actually do, the kinds of issues they confront in their working lives. (To be fair, Charles Hoch devotes two paragraphs to homelessness.) Now, no one would deny that it is vitally important for student planners to understand why planners do what they do, particularly if and when they act irrationally. But one would have thought it also vital to relate this to the subject of what they do.

Other top theorists have sought various ways out of the impasse. Some, like Allen Scott and Manuel Castells, have moved away from questions of the relation between theory and action, and into heavily empirical investigations of changing economic and social structures—a movement, in other words, from urban planning to urban political economy. Others, like Ann Markusen, Barry Bluestone and Bennett Harrison, have sought to combine this style of analysis with active regional policy prescription for older industrial regions. Yet others, like John Friedmann and John Forester, have continued to grapple with the problem of connecting theory with action—in Forester's case, by drawing on German critical theory. But, stripped of the dense Teutonic undergrowth, the resulting prescriptions sound uncannily like those of the advocacy planners of 15 years earlier: cultivate community networks, listen carefully to the people, go out to those who are least well organized, educate the citizenry, supply plenty of information, and ensure that people know how to use it. It is essentially a theory of practice.

Numerous other members of academe, both faculty and students, seem to have tired of the debate, preferring to get back to hands-on planning. The big growth areas of the 1980s have included economic development planning for distressed regions and communities, the understanding of project finance as the key to urban development and redevelopment, the achievement of affordable housing, and the use of the personal computer, coupled with geographic information systems, to help solve these and other problems.

The result, not unique to the United States, but ex-

THE TURBULENT EIGHTH DECADE

ceptionally evident here, has been the emergence of several kinds of disjunctures: between planning theory and planning practice; between what is taught in the top schools and in the more run-of-the-mill institutions; and, within the former, between theoretical and practical streams. As a result, these top schools now turn out two types of students. One type flourishes in a great variety of special situations: research for distressed cities and regions, community leadership, heroic efforts with slum-dwellers in third-world cities. The other are academic theorists—professorial clones. The more mundane institutions still turn out conventional planners, that is, land use planners, the people the outside world still recognizes by the term.

The City Enterprising, 1980–1989

Meanwhile, outside the ivory tower, life goes on. Planning practice, as ever, relates to the challenges and opportunities before it. The most distinctive feature of the 1980s is what could be called planning-as-project, or planning-as-real-estate-development. The models are Baltimore's Inner Harbor, Boston's Quincy Market and Waterfront, San Diego's Horton Plaza, and a score of imitators. (In Europe, the same phenomenon is visible on an even grander scale, in London's Docklands and in the Parisian Eurodisneyland.) Each consists of the mega-development of a huge site, through the cooperation of public and private capital, and involving major injections of money from government—huge public works, subsidies linked to private leverage, and tax exemptions in the form of enterprise zones—as well as new institutional forms. Some might say that this is urban renewal all over again. Indeed, in Boston and Baltimore the development follows a straight line, but the scale is grander and the stakes are bigger—no less than the transformation of decayed industrial and port cities into leading centers of the new nodal-service economy, through a new combination of producer services, theme-park entertainment, leisure shopping and street theater. No wonder the students in the schools are studying project finance.

The radical critics can, of course, have a field day once again. As has occurred so often in twentieth-century American urban history, public planning and public money are being harnessed to the pursuit of private profit: the City Functional lives. As in the era of urban renewal, powerful growth coalitions back the enterprise. While the new service jobs may be dead-end and low-paying—no adequate substitute for the lost opportunities in the steel mills and the docks—the fact is that, in many cities of the industrial heartland, this is the only game in town.

The service sector may also be the most potent source of jobs, perhaps the only source of jobs, to bring the unemployed, unskilled underclass of the surrounding inner city back into the mainstream economy. That particular bundle of concerns—the transition to a service economy, the sharp division within that economy between the white collar providers of producer services and the pink collar providers of consumer services (and,

within the white collars, between top managers/professionals and keyboard punchers), the mismatch between demand and supply in the job market, the increasing marginalization of the underclass—constitutes one of the great challenges to American city planning at the end of the 1980s. Do you join in meeting it, or catcall from the sidelines? This is the dilemma that faces many in the profession and the schools today.

The City of Ecologically Conscious NIMBYism, 1980–1989

In yet other places, there is a different set of challenges: the growth of the suburbs, the development within them of entirely new service nodes (Tyson's Corner, I-680, Irvine) and the transformation of older rural centers, the rapid spread of suburban gridlock as the infrastructure of the 1960s is overwhelmed, the problems of water supply and waste management and air quality, the loss of open space and rural qualities in huge swathes of land around the major metropolitan areas. Hand in hand with these trends, inevitably, goes the multiplication of special interest groups devoted to maintaining and enhancing the quality of environment, but also to stopping further development—the arrival of NIMBYism as the populist political philosophy of the 1980s. Everywhere from New Hampshire and Virginia to the San Francisco Bay and the Central Valley, these problems of growth and spread now dominate the lives of many, perhaps most, Americans. And planning, as yet, has no clear and consistent set of answers.

Further, the two bundles of concerns may have a common basis. The Rousification of the cities really represents a desperate attempt to find an answer to a question that many cannot bring themselves to say out loud: in the new urban landscape of technology-led deconcentration, what exactly is the role of the traditional city? Even if some places manage to survive on the basis of their special qualities—New York, Chicago, and Los Angeles as major world centers; Boston and San Francisco, as centers of education, technology, culture, and tourism; and Atlanta, Dallas, and Denver as regional nodes—can all of America's cities survive? Or do they represent some historic anomaly, destined to disappear like the ghost towns of the West? Or will they be reconstructed as Disney-style parodies of the places they once were, living museums of the urban past? Is it possible again to create *integrated* downtowns, as Jonathan Barnett suggests in the Spring 1989 *Journal*?

The City Pathological Revisited, 1890–1989

Tied to these concerns is another: the rediscovery of the original obsession, the one that gave rise to planning's birth. To tell the truth, the urban underclass never went away; that much is clear from a succession of fine empirical studies, from DuBois at the end of the nineteenth century, through Park and his colleagues in the 1920s,

PETER HALL

Frazier in the 1930s and again in the 1950s, Myrdal in the 1940s and Moynihan in the 1960s, to Wilson in the 1970s and 1980s. What is uncanny is that all tell essentially the same story: of traditional preindustrial cultures overwhelmed by the transition to urban life, of the particular stress on the first urban-born generation, of the collapse of the family and the destruction of traditional parental authority, of the resulting problems in the schools and the courts.

There is perhaps one difference, underlined by Wilson: the sharp division of the black community, since the 1960s, into a middle class mainstream group and an ever-more-segregated underclass. But, as DuBois clearly shows, the same division was present in Philadelphia in 1899; it was just not as sharply etched in the geography of the city. Because the black community was always so ghettoized—a fact missed by the Chicago pioneers, and only discovered through recent research—mainstream and underclass lived cheek by jowl. Now they do not, and the child of the underclass grows up in a community where only very poor people live, where only very poor children go to school. Donna Shalala and Julia Vitullo-Martin gave us the figures in the Winter 1989 *Journal*: nearly two-thirds of all poor blacks, in 1980, lived in areas where the great majority of people are poor. The possibility of escape is virtually zero, and the clear threat is the one broached by Park as long ago as 1924: "In the great city the poor, the vicious, and the delinquent, crushed in an unhealthful and contagious intimacy, breed in and in, soul and body." As the media report the horrendous trends—three out of five black births are illegitimate, three in five poor black families are female-headed, the leading cause of death for black teenage males is homicide—what is clearly at stake, as Park long ago foresaw and has now come true, is nothing less than the future of urban life in America.

Given a challenge of that order, there is not much justification for continuing to stand on the academic sidelines. America needs its best brains, its most fertile imaginations, in its urban planning profession. It needs a new generation of Mumfords, Steins, Bauers, Tugwells, Perloffs. And its planning schools need to focus their efforts on feasible solutions. To be sure, they will not be achieved by unaided local action; they will need policy initiatives in state capitols and in HUD, backed by the planning profession.

Shalala and Vitullo-Martin provide a preliminary six-part list: a federal borrowing authority to rebuild urban capital stocks; a regenerated HUD to grapple with the housing problems of the poor; a national rescue corporation for distressed cities; powerful education training job programs targeted at children and teenagers; criminalization of addictive drugs; and a national campaign to deal with AIDS. Others may have different lists; they should be debated through successive issues of this *Journal*. Once the debating and the lobbying is over, and a program is adopted, it will need dedicated and imaginative application. In planning's 80 years, there never was a more vital job to do.

AUTHOR'S NOTE

I wish to thank Michael Teitz for valuable comments on a first draft of this essay.

[4]

On Planning the Ideology of Planning

David Harvey

It is a truism to say that we all plan. But planning as a profession has a much more restricted domain. Fight as they might for some other rationale for their existence, professional planners find themselves confined, for the most part, to the task of defining and attempting to achieve a "successful" ordering of the built environment. In the ultimate instance the planner is concerned with the "proper" location, the appropriate mix of activities in space of all the diverse elements which make up the totality of physical structures—the houses, roads, factories, offices, water and sewage disposal facilities, hospitals, schools, and the like—which comprise the built environment. From time to time the spatial ordering of the built environment is treated as an end sufficient unto itself and some form of environmental determinism takes hold. At other times this ordering is seen as a reflection rather than a determinant of social relations and planning is seen as a process rather than as a plan—and so the planner heaves himself away from the drawing board to attend meetings with bankers, community groups, land developers, and the like, in the hope that a timely intervention here or a preventive measure there may achieve a "better" overall result. But "better" assumes some purpose which is easy enough to specify in general but more difficult to particularize about. As a physical resource complex created out of human labor and ingenuity, the built environment must primarily function to be useful for production, circulation, exchange and consumption. It is the job of the planner to intervene in the production of this complex composite commodity and to ensure its proper management and maintenance. But this poses immediately the question, useful or better for what and to whom?

Planning and the Reproduction of the Social Order

It would be easy to jump from these initial questions straight away into some pluralistic model of society in which the planner acts either as an arbitrator or as a corrective weight in the conflicts amongst a diversity of interest groups, each of which strives to get a piece of the pie. Such a jump leaves out a crucial step. Society works, after all, on the basic principle that the most important activity is that which contributes to its own reproduction. We do not have to enquire far to find out what this activity entails. Consider, for example, the various conceptions of the city as "workshops of industrial civilization," as "nerve centers for the economic, social,

213

cultural and political life" of society, as centers for innovation, exchange and communication and as living environments for people.[1] All of these—and more—are common enough conceptions. And if we accept one or all of them, then the role of the planner can simply be defined as ensuring that the built environment comprises those necessary physical infrastructures which serve the processes we have in mind. If the "workshop" dissolves into a chaos of disorganization, if the "nerve center" loses its coherence, if innovation is stymied, if communication and exchange processes become garbled, if the living conditions become intolerable, then the reproduction of the social order is in doubt.

We can push this argument further. We live, after all, in a society which, for want of a better phrase, is founded on capitalist principles of private property and market exchange, a society which presupposes certain basic social relationships with respect to production, distribution and consumption which themselves must be reproduced if the social order is to survive. And so we arrive at what may appear a rather cosmic question: what is the role of the urban-regional planner in the context of these overall processes of social reproduction? Critical analysis should reveal the answers. Yet it is a measure of the failings of contemporary social science (from which the planning literature draws much of its inspiration) that we have to approach answers with circumspection as well as tact should we dare to depart from the traditional canons as to what may or may not be said. For this reason I shall begin with a brief digression in order to open up new vistas for discussion.

When we consider the economic system, most of us feel at home with analyses based on the categories of land, labor and capital as "factors" of production. We recognize that social reproduction depends upon the perpetual combination of these elements and that growth requires the recombination of these factors into new configurations which are in some sense more productive. These categories, we often admit, are rather too abstract and from time to time we break them down to take account of the fact that neither land nor labor are homogeneous and that capital can take productive (physical) or liquid (money) form. Nevertheless, we seem prepared to accept a high level of abstraction, without too much questioning as to the validity or efficacy of the concepts employed. Yet most of us blanch when faced with a sociological description of society which appeals to the concept of class relations between landlords, laborers and capitalists. If we write in such terms we will likely be dismissed as too simplistic or as engaging in levels of abstraction which make no sense. At worst, such concepts will be regarded as offensive and ideological compared to the supposedly non-ideological concepts of land, labor and capital. Why and on what grounds, philosophical, practical or otherwise, was it decided that one form of abstraction made sense and was appropriate while the other was out of order? Does it not make reasonable sense to connect our sociological thinking with our economics, albeit in a rather simplistic and primitive way? Does it make sense, even, to tell the inner city tenant that the rent paid to the landlord is not really a payment to that man who drives a big car and lives in the suburbs, but a payment to a scarce factor of production? The "scientization" of social science seems to have been accomplished by masking real social relationships—by representing the social relations between people and groups of people as relations between things. The reification implied by this tactic is plain enough to see and the dangers of reification are well-known. Yet we seem to be at ease with the reifications and to accept them uncritically even though the possibility exists that in so doing we destroy our capacity to understand, manage, control and alter the social order in ways favorable to our individual or collective purposes. In this paper, therefore, I will seek to place the planner in the context of a sociological description of society which sees class relations as fundamental.

Class Relations and the Built Environment

In any society the actual class relations which exist are bound to be complex and fluid. This is particularly true in a society such as ours. The class categories which we use are not regarded as immutable. And in the same way that we can disaggregate land, labor and capital as factors of production so we can produce a finer mesh of categories to describe the class structure. We know that land and property ownership comprises residual feudal institutions (the church, for example), large property companies, part-time landlords, homeowners, and so on. We know also that the interests of rentier "money capitalists" may diverge substantially from the interests of producers in industry and agriculture and that the laboring class is not homogeneous because of the stratifications and differentials generated according to the hierarchical division of labor and various wage rates. But in a short paper of this sort I must perforce stick to the simplest categories which help us to understand the planner's role within the social structure. So let us proceed with the simplest conception we can devise and consider, in turn, how each class or fraction of a class relates to the built environment which is the primary concern of the planner.

1. The class of laborers is made up of all of those individuals who sell a commodity—labor power—on the market in return for a wage or salary. The consumption requirements of labor—which are in practice highly differentiated—will in part be met by work within the household and in part be procured by exchanges of wages earned against commodities produced. The commodity requirements of labor depend upon the balance between domestic economy products and market purchases as well as upon

the environmental, historical and cultural considerations which fix the
standard of living of labor. Labor looks to the built environment as a
means of consumption and as a means for its own reproduction and, perhaps, expansion. Labor is sensitive to both the cost and the spatial disposition (access) of the various items in the built environment—housing,
educational and recreational facilities, services of all kinds, etc.—which
facilitate survival and reproduction at a given standard of living.

2. We can define capitalists as all those who engage in entrepreneurial
functions of any kind with the intent of obtaining a profit. As a class,
capitalists are primarily concerned with accumulation and their activities
form, in our kind of society, the primary engine for economic development
and growth. Capital "in general"—which we will use as a handy term for
the capitalist class as a whole—looks to the built environment for two
reasons. Firstly, the built environment functions as a set of use values
for enhancing the production and accumulation of capital. The physical
infrastructures form a kind of fixed capital—much of which is collectively
provided and used—which can be used as a means of production, of exchange or of circulation. Secondly, the production of the built environment
forms a substantial market for commodities (such as structural steel) and
services (such as legal and administrative services) and therefore contributes to the total effective demand for the products which capitalists
themselves produce. On occasion, the built environment can become a
kind of "dumping ground" for surplus money capital or idle productive
capacity (sometimes by design as in the public works programs of the
1930's) with the result that there are periodic bouts of overproduction and
subsequent devaluation of the assets embedded in the built environment
itself. The "wave-like" pattern of investment in the built environment is
a very noticeable feature in the economic history of capitalist societies.[2]

3. A particular faction of capital seeks a rate of return on its capital by
building new elements in the built environment. This faction—the construction interest—engages in a particular kind of commodity production
under rather peculiar conditions. Much of what happens in the way of
construction activity has to be understood in terms of the technical, economic and political organization of the construction interest.

4. We can define landlords as those who, by virtue of their ownership
of land and property, can extract a rent (actual or imputed) for the use
of the resources they control. In societies dominated by feudal residuals,
the landlord interest may be quite distinct from that of capital, but in
the United States ownership in land and property became a very important
form of investment from the eighteenth century onwards. Under these
conditions the "land and property interest" is simply reduced to a faction
of capital (usually the money capitalists and the rentiers) investing in
the appropriation of rent. This brings us to consider the important role

of property companies, developers, banks and other financial intermediaries (insurance companies, pension funds, savings and loan associations, etc.) in the land and property market. And we should also add that "home-ownership" does not quite mean what it says because most homeowners actually share equity with a financial institution and do not possess title to the property. In the United States, therefore, we have to think of the land and property interest primarily as a faction of capital investing in rental appropriation.

I shall assume for purposes of analytic convenience that a clear distinction exists between these classes and factions and that each pursues its own interests single-mindedly. In a capitalist society, of course, the whole structure of social relations is founded on the domination of capitalists over laborers. To put it this way is simply to acknowledge that the capitalists make the investment decisions, create the jobs and the commodities, and function as the catalytic agents in capitalist growth. We cannot hold, on the one hand, that America was created by the efforts of private entrepreneurs and deny on the other that capital dominates labor. Labor is not passive, of course, but its actions are defensive and at best confined to gaining a reasonable share of the national product. But if labor controlled the investment decisions then we would not be justified any longer in describing our society as capitalist. Our interest here is not so much to focus on this primary antagonism but to examine the myriad secondary forms of conflict which can spin off from it to weave a complex web of arguments over the production and use of the built environment. Appropriators (landlords and property owners) may be in conflict with construction interests, capitalists may be dissatisfied with the activities of both factions, while labor may be at odds with all of the others. And if the transport system or the sewage system does not work then both labor and capital will be equally put out. Let us consider two examples which, in spite of their hypothetical nature, illustrate the complex alliances which can form and shed some light on the kinds of problems which urban planners typically face.

We will start with the proposition that the price of existing resources in the built environment—and, hence, the rate of rental appropriation—is highly sensitive to the costs and rate of new construction. Suppose the construction interests are badly organized, in a slump or unable to gain easy access to cheap land and that the rate of new construction is low and the costs high. Under these conditions those seeking the appropriation of rent possess the power to increase their rate of return by raising rental on, say, housing. Labor may resist, tenant organizations may spring up and seek to control the rate of rental appropriation and to keep the cost of living down. If they succeed, tenant organizations may even drive the rate of return on existing resources downwards to the point where investment withdraws entirely (perhaps producing abandonment). If labor lacks organization and power in the community but is well-organized and powerful in the work place, a rising rate of appropriation may result in the pursuit of higher wages which, if granted, may lower the rate of profit and accumulation. A rational response of the capitalist class under these conditions is to seek an alliance with labor to curb excessive rental appropriations, to free land for new construction and to see to it that cheap (perhaps even subsidized) housing is built for the laboring class. We can see this sort of coalition in action when large corporate interests in suburban locations join with civil rights groups in trying to break suburban zoning restrictions which exclude low-wage populations from the suburbs. An exploration of this dimension to conflict can tell us much about the structure of contemporary urban problems.

The second case we will consider arises out of the general dynamic of capitalist accumulation which, from time to time, produces chronic overproduction, surplus real productive capacity and idle money capital desperately in need of productive outlets. In such a situation, money is easily come by to produce long-term investments in the built environment and a vast investment wave flows into the production of the built environment which serves as a vent for surplus capital—such was the boom experienced from 1970 to 1973. But at some point the existence of overproduction becomes plain to see—be it office space in Manhattan or of housing in Detroit—and the property boom collapses in a wave of bankruptcies and "refinancings" (consider, for example, the fall of the secondary banks associated with the London property market in 1973 and the dismal performance of the Real Estate Investment Trusts in the United States with some $11 billion in assets, half of which are currently earning no rate of return at all). What becomes evident in this case is that excessive investment brings in its wake disinvestment and devaluation of capital for at least some segment of "the landed interest." The construction interest is also faced with an extremely difficult pattern of booms and slumps which militates against the creation of a viable long-term organization for the coherent production of the built environment. If labor sinks part of its equity into the property market then it, too, may find its savings devalued by such processes and, through community organization and political action, it may seek to protect itself as well as it can. In this case also, we can discern a structure to our urban problems which is explicable in terms of the conflicting requirements of the various classes and factions as they face up to the problems created by the use of built environment as a vent for surplus capital in a period of overaccumulation.

These dimensions of conflict are cut across, however, by a completely different set of considerations which arise out of the fact that the built environment is comprised of assets which are typically both long-lived and fixed and immobile in space. This means that we are dealing with commodities which must be produced and used under conditions of "natural monopoly" in space. It also happens that since the built environment is to be conceived of as a complex composite commodity, the individual elements have strong "externality" effects on other elements. We thus find that competition for use of resources is monopolistic competition in space, that capitalists can compete with capitalists for advantageously positioned resources, that laborers can compete with laborers for survival chances, access, and the like, while land and property owners seek to influence the positioning of new elements in the built environment (particularly transport facilities) so as to gain indirect benefits. The basic structure of class and factional conflicts is therefore modified and in some instances totally transformed into a structure of geographical conflict which pits laborers in the suburbs against laborers in the city, capitalists in the industrial northeast against capitalists in the sunbelt, and so on.

The distinctive role and task of the planner has to be understood against the background of the strong currents of both interclass and factional conflict, on the one hand, and the geographical competition which natural monopolies in space inevitably generate, on the other.

The Production, Maintenance and Management of the Built Environment

The built environment must incorporate the necessary use values to facilitate social reproduction and growth. Its overall efficiency and rationality can be tested and measured in terms of how well it functions in relationship to these tasks. The sophisticated model builders within the planning fraternity have long sought to translate this conception into a search for some idealized *optimum optimorum* for the city or for regional structure. Such a search can be entertaining and it can generate insights into certain typical characteristics of urban structure, but as an enterprise it is utopian, idealized and fruitless. A more down-to-earth analysis suggests that the indications of failure of the built environment to provide the necessary use values are not too hard to spot. The evidence of *crisis* and of failure to reproduce effectively or to grow at a steady rate of accumulation, is a clear indicator of a lack of balance which requires some kind of corrective action.

Unfortunately, "crisis" is a much overused word. Anybody who wants anything in this society is forced to shout "crisis" as loudly as possible in order to get anything done. For the underprivileged and the poor, the "crisis" is permanent and endemic. We will take a narrower view and define a crisis as a particular conjuncture in which the reproduction of capitalist society is in jeopardy. The main signals are falling rates of profit, soaring unemployment and inflation, idle productive capacity and idle money capital lacking profitable employment, financial, institutional and political chaos and civil strife. And we can identify three wellsprings out of which crises in capitalist society typically flow. First, an imbalanced outcome of the struggle between the classes or factions of classes acquires so much power that it can force the wage rate up and the accumulation rate down; finance capital dominates and engages in speculative binges which de-stabilize the system, etc.). Second, accumulation pushes growth beyond the capacity of the sustaining natural resource base at the same time as technological innovation slackens. Third, a tendency towards overaccumulation and overproduction is omnipresent in capitalist societies because individual entrepreneurs, pursuing their own individual self-interest, collectively push the dynamic of aggregative accumulation away from a balanced growth path.

The particular role of the built environment in all of this is complex in its details but simple in principle. Failure to invest in those elements in the built environment which contribute to accumulation is no different in principle than the failure of entrepreneurs to invest and reinvest in fixed capital equipment. The problem with the built environment is that much of it functions as *collective* fixed capital (transport, sewage and disposal systems, etc.). Some way has to be found, therefore, to ensure a flow of investment into the built environment and to ensure that individual investment decisions are coordinated in both time and space so that the aggregative needs of capitalist producers are met. By the same token, failure to invest in the means of consumption for labor may raise the wage rate, generate civil strife or (in the worst kind of eventuality) physically diminish the supply of labor. In both cases failure to invest in the right quantities, at the right times and in the right places can be a progenitor of a crisis of accumulation and growth. Overinvestment in the built environment is, on the other hand, simply a devaluation of capital which nobody, surely, welcomes. And so we arrive at the general conception of the *potential* for a harmonious, balanced investment process in the built environment. Any departure from this path will entail either underinvestment (and a constraint upon accumulation) or overinvestment (and the devaluation of capital). The problem is to find some way to ensure that such a potentiality for balanced growth is realized under the conditions of a capitalist investment process.

The built environment is long-lived, fixed and immobile in space and a complex composite commodity the individual elements of which may be produced, maintained, managed and owned by quite diverse interests. Plainly, there is a problem of coordination because mistakes are very difficult to recoup and individual producers may not always act to produce the proper mix of elements in space. The time stream of benefits to be derived also poses some peculiar problems. The physical landscape created at one point in time may be suited to the needs of society at that point but become antagonistic later as the dynamics of accumulation and societal growth alter the use value requirements of both capital and labor. Tensions may then arise because the long-lived use values embedded in the built environment cannot easily be altered on a grand scale—witness the problems endemic to many of the older industrial and commercial cities in the industrial northeast of the United States at the present time.

Investment in the built environment can be coordinated with general social requirements in one, or a mix of three ways:

1. Allocations can be arrived at through market mechanisms. Elements which can be privately appropriated under the legal relations of private property—houses, factories, offices, stores, warehouses, etc.—can be rented and traded. This sets up the price signals which, under pure competitive bidding, will allocate land and plant to the best-paying uses. The price signals also make it possible to calculate a rate of return on new investments which usually generates a flow of new investment to wherever the rate of return is above that to be had given similar risks in other sectors of the capital market. But the innumerable externality effects and the importance of "public good" items which cannot be privately appropriated —streets, sidewalks, etc.—generate frequent market failures and imperfections so that in no country is investment in the built environment left entirely to competitive market mechanisms.

2. Allocations may be arrived at under the auspices of some hegemonic controlling interest—a land or developer monopoly, controlling financial interests, and the like.[3] This is not an irrational move because a large scale enterprise coordinating investments of many different types can "internalize the externalities" and thereby make more rational decisions from the investor standpoint—the land grant railroads provide an excellent historical example of such monopolistic control, while Rouse's Columbia provides a contemporary example. The trouble with monopolization and hegemonic control is that the pricing system becomes artificial (and this can lead to misallocations) while there is nothing to ensure that monopoly power is not abused.

3. State intervention is an omnipresent feature in the production, maintenance and management of the built environment.[4] The transport system —prime example of a "natural monopoly" in space—has always posed the problem of private gain versus public social benefit, private property rights versus aggregative social needs. The abuse of monopoly power (which it is all too easy to accumulate in spatial terms) has ever brought forth state regulation as a response. The pervasive externality effects have in all countries led to state regulation of the spatial order to reduce the risks which attach to long-term investment decisions. And the "public goods"

elements in the built environment—the streets, sidewalks, sewers and drainage systems, etc.—which cannot feasibly be privately appropriated have always been created by direct investment on the part of the agencies of the state. The theme of "public improvement" has been writ large in the history of all American cities.

The exact mix of private market, monopolistic control and state intervention and provision has varied with time as well as from place to place. Which mix is chosen or, more likely, arrived at by a complex historical process, is not that important. What is important, is that it should ensure the creation of a built environment which serves the purpose of social reproduction and that it should do so in such a manner that crises are avoided as far as is possible.

Urban Planning as Part of the Instrumentalities of State

The proper conception of the role of the state in capitalist society is controversial.[5] I shall simply take the view that the institutions of state and the processes whereby state powers are exercised must be so fashioned that they, too, contribute, insofar as they can, to the reproduction and growth of the social system. Under this conception we can derive certain basic functions of the capitalist state. It should:

1. help to stabilize an otherwise rather erratic economic and social system by acting as a "crisis-manager,"

2. strive to create the conditions for "balanced growth" and a smooth process of accumulation,

3. contain civil strife and factional struggles by repression (police power), cooptation (buying off politically or economically) or integration (trying to harmonize the demands of warring classes or factions).

The State can effectively perform all of these functions only if it succeeds in internalizing within its processes the conflicting interests of classes, factions, diverse geographical groupings, etc. A state which is entirely controlled by one and only one faction, which can operate only repressively and never through integration or cooptation, will likely be unstable and will likely survive only under conditions which are, in any case, chronically unstable. The social democratic State is one which can internalize diverse conflicting interests and which, by means of the checks and balances it contains, can prevent any one faction or class from seizing direct control of all of the instrumentalities of government and putting them to its own direct use. Yet the social democratic State is still a capitalist state in the sense that it is a capitalist social order which it is helping to reproduce. If the instrumentalities of state power are turned against the existing social order, then we see a crisis of the State, the outcome of which will determine whether the social order changes or whether the organization of the State reverts to its basic role of serving societal reproduction.

The urban planner occupies just one niche within the total complex of of the instrumentalities of state power. The internalization of conflicting interests and needs within the State typically puts one branch of the bureaucracy at loggerheads with another, one level or branch of government against another, and even different departments at odds with each other within the same bureaucracy. In what follows, however, we will lay aside these diverse crosscurrents of conflict and seek to abstract some sense of the real limitations placed upon the urban planner by virtue of his or her role and thereby come to identify more clearly the nature of the role itself. To hasten the argument along, I shall simply suggest that the planner's task is to contribute to the processes of social reproduction and that in so doing the planner is equipped with powers vis-à-vis the production, maintenance and management of the built environment which permit him or her to intervene in order to stabilize, to create the conditions for "balanced growth," to contain civil strife and factional struggles by repression, cooptation or integration. And to fulfill these goals successfully, the planning process as a whole (in which the planner fulfills only one set of tasks) must be relatively open. This conception may appear unduly simplistic but a down-to-earth analysis of what planners actually do as opposed to what they or the mandarins of the planning fraternity think they do, suggests that the conception is not far from the mark. And the history of those who seek to depart radically from this fairly circumscribed path suggests that they either encounter frustration or else give up the role of planner entirely.[6]

The Knowledge of the Planner and Its Implied "World View"

In order to perform the necessary tasks effectively, the planner needs to acquire an understanding of how the built environment works in relationship to social reproduction and how the various facets of competitive, monopolistic and state production of the built environment relate to each other in the context of often conflicting class and factional requirements. Planners are therefore taught to appreciate how everything relates to everything else in an urban system, to think in terms of costs and benefits (although they may not necessarily resort to techniques of cost-benefit analysis) and to have some sympathetic understanding of the problems which face the private producers of the built environment, the landlord interest, the urban poor, the managers of financial institutions, the downtown business interests, and so on. The accumulation of planning knowledge arises through incremental understandings of what would be the "best" configuration of investment (both spatial and in terms of quantitative balance) to facilitate social reproduction. But the most important shifts in understanding come in the course of those crises in which something obviously must be done because social reproduction is in jeopardy.

The planner requires something else as well as a basic understanding of how the system works from a purely technical standpoint. In resorting to tools of repression, cooptation and integration, the planner requires justification and legitimation, a set of powerful arguments with which to confront warring factional interests and class antagonisms. In striving to affect reconciliation, the planner must perforce resort to the idea of the potentiality for harmonious balance in society. And it is on this fundamental notion of social harmony that the ideology of planning is built. The planner seeks to intervene to restore "balance" but the "balance" implied is that which is necessary to reduce civil strife and to maintain the requisite conditions for the steady accumulation of capital. From time to time, of course, planners may be "captured" (by corruption, political patronage or even by "radical" arguments) by one class/faction or another and thereby lose the capacity to act as stabilizers and harmonizers—but such a condition, though endemic, is inherently unstable and the inevitable reform movement will most probably sweep it away when it is no longer consistent with the requirements of the social order as a whole. The role of the planner, then, ultimately derives its justification and legitimacy from intervening to restore that balance which perpetuates the existing social order. And the planner fashions an ideology appropriate to the role.

This does not necessarily mean that the planner is a mere defender of the status quo. The dynamics of accumulation and of societal growth are such as to create endemic tensions between the built environment as is and as it should be, while the evils which stem from the abuse of spatial monopoly can quickly become widespread and dangerous for social reproduction. Part of the planner's task is to spot both present and future dangers and to head off, if possible, an incipient "crisis of the built environment". In fact the whole tradition of planning is progressive in the sense that the planner's commitment to the ideology of social harmony— unless it is perverted or corrupted in some way—always puts the planner in the role of "righter of wrongs", "corrector of imbalances" and "defender of the public interest". The limits to this progressive stance are clearly set, however, by the fact that the definitions of the public interest, of imbalance and of inequity are set according to the requirements for the reproduction of the social order which is, whether we like the term or not, a distinctively capitalistic social order.

The planner's knowledge of the world cannot be separated from this necessary ideological commitment. Existing and planned orderings to the built environment are evaluated against some notion of a "rational" sociospatial ordering. But it is the capitalistic definition of rationality to which we appeal.[7] The principle of "rationality" is an ideal—the central core to a pervasive ideology—which itself depends upon the notion of harmonious processes of social reproduction under capitalism. The limits to the planner's understanding of the world are set by this underlying ideological commitment. In the reverse direction, the planner's knowledge is used ideologically, as both legitimation and justification for certain forms of action. Political struggles and arguments may, under the planner's influence, be reduced to technical arguments for which a "rational" solution can easily be found. Those who do not accept such a solution are then open to attack as "unreasonable" and "irrational". In this manner both the real understanding of the world and the prevailing ideology fuse into a world view. I do not mean to imply that all planners subscribe to the same world view—they manifestly do not and it would be disfunctional were they to do so. Some planners are very technocratic and seek to translate all political issues into technical problems while other planners take a much more political stance. But whatever their position, the fusion of technical understandings with a necessary ideology produces a complex mix within the planning fraternity of capacity to understand and to intervene in a realistic and advantageous way and capacity to repress, coopt and integrate in a way that appears justifiable and legitimate.

Civil Strife, Crises of Accumulation and Shifts in the Planner's World View

The planner's world view, defined as the necessary knowledge for appropriate intervention and the necessary ideology to justify and legitimate action, has altered with changing circumstances. But knowledge and ideology do not change overnight. The concepts, categories, relationships and images through which we interpret the world are, so to speak, the fixed capital of our intellectual world and are no more easily transformed than the physical infrastructures of the city itself. It usually takes a crisis, a rush of ideas pouring forth under the pressure of events, radically to change the planner's world view and even then radical change comes but slowly. And while the fundamentals of ideology—the notion of social harmony—may stay intact, the meanings attached must change according to whatever it is that is out of balance. The history of capitalist societies these last two hundred years suggests, however, that certain problems are endemic, problems that simply will not go away no matter how hard we try. Consequently we find that the shifting world view of the planner exhibits an accumulation of technical understandings combined with a mere swaying from side to side in ideological stance from which the planner appears to learn little or nothing, let us illustrate.

The capitalist growth process has been punctuated, at quite regular intervals, by phases of acute social tension and civil strife. These phases are not historical accidents but can be traced back to the fundamental characteristics of capitalist societies and the growth processes entailed. We have not space to elaborate on this theme here, but it is important to note that the organization of work under capitalism is predicated on a separation between "working" and "living," on control of work by the capitalist and alienated labor for the employee, and on a dynamic relation between the wage rate and the rate of profit which is founded on the social necessity for a surplus of labor which may vary quantitatively according to time and place. Generally speaking it is the concentration of low-wage populations and unemployment in either time or space which sets the stage for civil strife.

The response is some mixture of repression, cooptation and integration. The urban planner's role in all of this is to define policies which facilitate social control and which serve to reestablish social harmony through cooptation and integration. Consider, for example, the spatial distribution of the population, particularly of the unemployed and low-wage earners. The revolutions of 1848, the Paris Commune of 1871, the urban violence which accompanied the great railroad strikes of 1877 in the United States and Chicago's celebrated "Haymarket affair" of 1886 demonstrated the revolutionary dangers associated with high concentrations of what Charles Loring Brace called, in the 1870's, "the dangerous classes" of society.[8] The problem could be dealt with by a policy of dispersal which meant that ways had to be found to permit the poor and the unemployed to escape their chronic entrapment in space. The urban working class had to be dispersed and subjected to what reformers on both sides of the the Atlantic called "the moral influence" of the suburbs.[9] Suburbanization facilitated by cheap communication was seen as part of the solution. The urban planners and reformers of the time pressed hard for policies of dispersal via mass transit facilities such as those provided under the Cheap Trains Act of 1882 in Britain and the streetcars in the United States, while the search for cheap housing and means to promote social stability through working class home-ownership began in earnest. In much the same way, planners in the 1960's responded to the urban riots by seeking ways to disperse the ghetto by improved transport relations, promoting homeownership, opening up housing opportunities in the suburbs (although this time round the Victorian rhetoric of "moral influence" was replaced by the more "rational" appeal of "social stability"). In the process, the laboring classes undoubtedly gain in real living standards while the planner acts as advocate for the poor and the underprivileged, raises the cry of social justice and equity, expresses moral outrage at the conditions of life of the urban poor and reaches for ways to restore social harmony.

The alternative to dispersal is what we now call "gilding the ghetto" and this, too, is a well-tried tactic in the struggle to control civil strife in urban areas. As early as 1812, the Reverend Thomas Chalmers raised the specter of a tide of revolutionary violence sweeping Britain as working class popula-

tions steadily concentrated in large urban areas. Chalmers saw "the principle of community" as the main bulwark of defense against this revolutionary
tide—a principle which sought to establish harmony between the classes
around the basic institutions of community.[10] The principle entailed also
a commitment to community improvement, the attempt to instill some sense
of civic or community pride capable of transgressing class boundaries. The
church was then the most important institution, but we now think of other
instrumentalities also—political inclusion, citizen participation, community
commitment to educational, recreational and other services as well as the
sense of pride in neighborhood which inevitably means a "better" quality
to the built environment. From Chalmers through Octavia Hill and Jane
Addams, to Model Cities and citizen participation, we have a continuous
thread of an argument which suggests that social stability can be restored
in periods of social unrest by an active pursuit of "the principle of community" and all that this means in the way of community betterment and
social improvement—and again, the planner typically acts as advocate, as
catalyst in promoting the spirit of community improvement.

One dimension to this idea of "improvement" is that of environmental
quality. Olmstead was perhaps the first fully to recognize that the efficiency
of labor might be enhanced by providing a compensatory sense of harmony
with nature in the living place, although it is important to recognize that
Olmstead was building on a rather older tradition.[11] At issue here is the
relation to nature in a most fundamental sense. Industrial capitalism,
armed with the factory system, organized a work process which transformed
the relation between the worker and nature into a travesty of its older
artisan self. Reduced to a thing, a commodity, a mere "factor" of production, the worker became alienated from the product of work, the process
of production and ultimately from nature itself, particularly in the industrial
city where, as Dickens puts it, "Nature was as strongly bricked out as killing
airs and gases were bricked in." [12] The romantic reaction against the new
industrial order ultimately led in the practice of urban design and planning
to the attempt to counter in the sphere of consumption for what had been
lost in the sphere of production.[13] The attempt to "bring nature back into
the living environments" within the city has been a consistent theme in
planning since Olmstead's time onwards. Yet it is, in the final analysis, an
attempt based in what Raymond Williams calls "an effective and imposing
mystification" for there is something in the relation to nature in the work
process which can never be compensated for in the consumption sphere.[14]
The planner, armed with concepts of ecological balance and the notion of
harmony with nature, acts once more as advocate and brings real gains.
But the real solutions to these problems lie elsewhere, in the work process
itself.

Civil strife and social discontent provide only one set of problems which the planner must address. The dynamic of accumulation with its periodic crises of overaccumulation pose an entirely different set. The crises are not accidental. They are to be viewed, rather, as major periods of "rationalization," of "shake-outs and shake-downs" which restore balance to an economic system temporarily gone mad. The fact that crises perform this rationalizing function is no comfort to those caught in their midst. And at such conjunctures planners must either simply administer the budget cuts and plan the shrinkage according to the strict requirements of an externally imposed fiscal logic of the sort now being applied to New York, or seek to head up a movement for a forced rationalization of the urban system. The pursuit of the city beautiful is replaced by the search for the city efficient, the cry of social justice is replaced by the slogan "efficiency in government" and those planners armed with a ruthless cost-benefit calculus, a rational and technocratic commitment to efficiency for efficiency's sake, come into their own.

"Rationalization" means, of course, doing whatever must be done to reestablish the conditions for a positive rate of accumulation. When economic growth goes negative—as it did, for example, in 1893, the early 1930's or in 1970 and 1974, then the reproduction of the social order is plainly in doubt. The task at such conjunctures is to find out what is wrong and right it. The physical infrastructure of the city may be congested, inefficient and too costly to use for purposes of production and exchange. Such barriers (which were obvious to all in the progressive era, for example) must be removed and if the planner does not willingly help to do so, then the escalating competition between jurisdictions for "development" at times of general decline will force the planner into action if he or she values the tax base (this kind of competitive pressure often leads communities to subsidize profits). If the problem lies in the consumption sphere—underconsumption or erratic movements in aggregate personal behaviors—then the state may seek to manage consumption either by fiscal devices or through collectivization. The management of collective consumption by means of the built environment at such points becomes a crucial part of the planner's task.[15] If the problem lies in lack or excess of investment in the built environment then the planner must perforce set to work to stimulate investment or to manage and "rationalize" devaluation with techniques of "planned shrinkage," urban renewal and even the production of "planning blight" (which amounts to nothing more than earmarking certain areas for devaluation).

I list these various possibilities because it is not always self-evident as to what must be done in the heat of a crisis of accumulation. At such conjunctures our knowledge of the system and how it works is crucial for action, unless we are to be led dangerously near the precipice of quite cataclysmic depression. And it is exactly at such points that the world view of the planner, restricted as it is by an ideological commitment, appears most defective, while the ideological stance of the planner may have to shift under the pressure of events from advocacy for the urban poor to one dedicated to business rationality and efficiency in government.

But ideologies, we have argued, do not change that easily, nor does our knowledge of the world. And so we find at each of the major turning points in our history, a *crisis of ideology*.[16] Past commitments must obviously be abandoned because they hinder our power to understand and most certainly lose their power to legitimate and justify (imagine trying to justify what is happening currently in New York by appealing to concepts of social justice). And as the pillars to the planner's world view slowly crumble, so the search begins for a new scaffolding for the future. At such a juncture, it becomes necessary to plan the ideology of planning.

Planning the Ideology of Planning—1978 Style

The organizers of this conference suggested in their invitation that the planning inspirations of the 1960's had faded and that our main task here was to define new horizons for planning the 1970's—new technologies, new instrumentalities, new goals . . . new everything in fact *except* a new ideology. Yet if my analysis is correct the real task here is to plan the ideology of planning to fit the economic realities of the 1970's rather than to meet the social unrest and civil strife of the 1960's.

Since many of those who inspired us in the 1960's are still with us and even participating in this conference, it is useful to ask what, if anything, went wrong? The crucial problem of the 1960's was civil strife and in particular the concentrated form of it associated with the urban riots in central city areas. That strife had to be contained by repression, cooptation and integration. In this the planner, armed with diverse ideologies and a variety of world views, played a crucial role. The dissidents were encouraged to go through "channels," to adhere to "procedures laid down" and somewhere down that path the planner laid in wait with a seemingly sophisticated technology, an intricate understanding of the world, through which political questions could be translated into technical questions which the mass of the population found hard to understand. But discontent cannot so easily be controlled and so the other string to the planner's bow was to find ways to disperse the urban poor, to divide and control them and to ameliorate their conditions of life.[17] The management of this process fell very much within the domain of urban planning and it generated conflicting ideological stances and world views within the planning profession itself. At first sight (and indeed at the time) it seemed as if planning theory was fragmented in the 1960's as different segments of the planning fraternity moved according to their position or inclination to one or other pole of the ideological spectrum. With the benefit of hindsight we can see that this process was nothing more than the internalization within the planning apparatus of conflicting social pressures and positions. And this internalization and the oppositions which it provoked proved functional, no matter what individuals thought or did. The technocrats helped to define the outer bounds of what could be done at the same time as they sought for new instrumentalities to accomplish dispersal and to establish social control. The advocates for the urban poor and the instrumentalities which they devised, provided the channels for cooptation and integration at the same time as they pushed the system to provide whatever could be provided, being careful to stop short at the boundaries which the technocrats and "fiscal conservatives" helped to define. Those who pushed advocacy too far were either forced out or deserted planning altogether and became activists and political organizers.

Judged in terms of their own ideological rhetoric, the pursuers of social justice failed, much as they did in the Progressive era, to accomplish what they set out to do, although the position of the "dangerous classes" in society undoubtedly improved somewhat in the late 1960's. But judged in relation to the reduction of civil strife, the reestablishment of social control and the "saving" of the capitalist social order, the planning techniques and ideologies of the 1960's were highly successful. Those who inspired us in the 1960's can congratulate themselves on a job well done.

But conditions changed quite radically in 1969-70. Stagflation emerged as the most serious problem and the negative growth rate of 1970 indicated that the fundamental processes of accumulation were in deep trouble. A loose monetary policy—the most potent tool in the management of the "political business cycle"—saw us through the election of 1972. But the boom was speculative and heavily dependent upon a massive overinvestment in the land, property and construction sectors which easy money typically encourages. By the end of 1973 it was plain that the built environment could absorb no more in the way of surplus capital and the rapid decline in property and construction, together with financial instability, triggered the subsequent depression. Unemployment doubled, real wages began to move downwards under the impact of severe "labor-disciplining" policies, social programs began to be savagely cut and all of the gains made after a decade of struggle in the 1960's by the poor and underprivileged were rolled back almost within the space of a year. The underlying logic of capitalist accumulation asserts itself in the form of a crisis in which real wages must diminish in order that inflation be stabilized and that accumulation (growth) can resume through reinvestment.

The pressure from this underlying logic is felt in all spheres. Local budgets have to shift towards fiscal conservatism and have to alter priorities from social programs to programs to stimulate and encourage development (often by subsidies and tax benefits). Planners talk grimly of the "hard tough decisions" that lie ahead. Those that sought social justice as an end in itself in the 1960's gradually shift their ground as they begin to argue that social justice can best be achieved by ensuring efficiency in government. Those that sought ecological balance and conservation in its own right in the 1960's begin to appeal to principles of rational and efficient management of our resources. The technocrats begin the search for ways to define more rational patterns of investment in the built environment, calculate costs and benefits more finely than ever. The gospel of efficiency comes to reign supreme.

All or this presupposes the capacity to accomplish a transformation of ideological balance within the planning fraternity—a transformation which turns out to be almost identical to that which was successfully accomplished during the progressive era. It can, of course, be done. But it takes effort and fairly sophisticated argument, of the sort which this conference will undoubtedly produce, to do it. And the transformation is made that much easier because the fundamentals of ideology remain intact. The commitment to the ideology of harmony within the capitalist social order remains the still point upon which the gyrations of planning ideology turn.

But if we step aside and reflect awhile upon the tortuous twists and turns in our history, a shadow of doubt might cross our minds. Perhaps the most imposing and effective mystification of all lies in the presupposition of harmony at the still point of the turning capitalist world. Perhaps there lies at the fulcrum of capitalist history not harmony but a social relation of domination of capital over labor. And if we pursue this possibility, we might come to understand why the planner seems doomed to a life of perpetual frustration, why the high-sounding ideals of planning theory are so frequently translated into grubby practices on the ground, how the shifts in world view and in ideological stance are social products rather than freely chosen. And we might even come to see that it is the commitment to an alien ideology which chains our thought and understanding in order to legitimate a social practice that preserves, in a deep sense, the domination of capital over labor. Should we reach *that* conclusion, then we would surely witness a markedly different reconstruction of the planner's world view than we are currently seeing. We might even begin to plan the reconstruction of society, instead of merely planning the ideology of planning.

NOTES

1. These various conceptions of the city can be found in, for example, L. Mumford, *The City in History* (New York, 1961); J. Jacobs, *The Economy of Cities* (New York, 1969); L. Wirth, *On Cities and Social Life* (edited by A.J. Reiss;

Chicago, 1964 ed.); National Resources Committee (of the United States), *Our Cities: Their Role in the National Economy* (Washington, D.C., 1937); R. Meier, *A Communications Theory of Urban Growth* (Cambridge, Mass., 1962).

2. The "long-waves" in economic development and in particular those associated with investment in the various components of the built environment are discussed in B. Thomas, *Migration and Economic Growth* (London, 1973 ed.); M. Abramovitz, *Evidences of Long Swings in Aggregate Construction Since the Civil War* (NBER, New York, 1964); S. Kuznets, *Capital in the American Economy* (Princeton, N.J., 1961); E. Mandel, *Late Capitalism* (London, 1975).

3. Some idea of the extent of hegemonic control exercised by finance capital over the land and property market can be gained from L. Downie, *Mortgage on America* (New York, 1974); G. Barker, J. Penney, and W. Seccombe, *Highrise and Superprofits* (Kitchener, Ontario, 1973); P. Ambrose, and R. Colenutt, *The Property Machine* (Harmondsworth, Middlesex, 1975); D. Harvey, "Class-Monopoly Rent, Finance Capital and the Urban Revolution," *Regional Studies,* 8 (1974): 239-55.

4. The French urbanists have worked on this aspect most carefully as in M. Castells and F. Godard, *Monopolville—l'Enterprise, l'Etat, l'Urbain* (1973), and C.G. Pickvance, ed., *Urban Sociology; Critical Essays* (London, 1976). See also the various essays in *Antipode*, Vol. 7, No. 4,—a special issue devoted to "The Political Economy of Urbanism" and D. Harvey, "The Political Economy of Urbanization in Advanced Capitalist Societies: the Case of the United States," (1975), in G. Gappert and H. Rose, eds., *The Social Economy of Cities* (Urban Affairs Annual, No. 9, Beverly Hills, California).

5. See, for example, E. Altvater, "Notes on Some Problems of State Interventionism", *Kapitalistate*, 1 (1973): 96-108 and 3, pp. 76-83; R. Miliband, *The State in Capitalist Society* (London, 1968); N. Poulantzas, *Political Power and Social Classes* (London, 1973); J. O'Connor, *The Fiscal Crisis of the State* (New York, 1973).

6. A good example of how planners might move down such a path is written up in R. Goodman, *After the Planners* (New York, 1971).

7. The meaning of the concept of "rationality" has been very thoroughly discussed in M. Godelier, *Rationality and Irrationality in Economics* (London, 1972).

8. C.L. Brace, *The Dangerous Classes of New York* (New York, 1889 ed.).

9. J.A. Tarr, "From City to Suburb: the "moral" influence of transportation technology," in A.B. Callow, ed. *American Urban History* (New York, 1973).

10. Reverend Thomas Chalmers, *The Christian and Civic Economy of Large Towns,* 3 Volumes (Glasgow, 1821-26).

11. See, for example, T. Bender, *Towards an Urban Vision* (Kentucky, 1975) and R.A. Walker, *Urban Reform Movements and the Suburban Solution* (Doctoral Dissertation, Department of Geography and Environmental Engineering, The Johns Hopkins University).

12. The phrase can be found in Charles Dickens, *Hard Times,* chapter 10.

13. I have examined this theme in much greater detail in D. Harvey, (forthcoming), "Class Conflict Under the Capitalist Form of Urbanization: Labour, Capital and Conflict over the Built Environment," *Politics and Society.*

14. R. Williams, *The Country and the City* (London, 1973).

15. Again, the French urbanists have discussed this idea at length in, for example, E. Preteceille, *Equipements Collectifs, Structures Urbaines et Consommation Sociale* (Paris, 1975) and M. Castells, "Collective Consumption and Urban Condtarictions in Advanced Capitalist Societies," in L. Lindberg, ed., *Patterns of Advanced Societies* (New York, 1975).

16. There is an important connection between crises in ideology and legitimation—see, for example, J. Habermas, *Legitimation Crisis* (Boston, 1975); for a history of shifting ideology in urban development see R.A. Walker, *Urban Reform Movements*.

17. See F. Piven, and R. Cloward, *Regulating the Poor* (New York, 1971) and R. Cloward and F. Piven, *The Politics of Turmoil* (New York, 1974).

[5]

ORDER IN DIVERSITY: COMMUNITY WITHOUT PROPINQUITY

MELVIN M. WEBBER

THE SPATIAL PATTERNS OF AMERICAN URBAN SETTLEMENTS are going to be considerably more dispersed, varied, and space-consuming than they ever were in the past—whatever metropolitan planners or anyone else may try to do about it. It is quite likely that most of the professional commentators will look upon this development with considerable disfavor, since these patterns will differ so markedly from our ideological precepts. But disparate spatial dispersion seems to be a built-in feature of the future—the complement of the increasing diversity that is coming to mark the processes of the nation's economy, its politics, and its social life. In addition, it seems to be the counterpart of a chain of technological developments that permit spatial separation of closely related people.

At this stage in the development of our thinking, students of the city are still unable to agree even on the nature of the phenomena they are dealing with. But it should surprise no one. For the plain fact of the matter is that, now, when the last rural threads of American society are being woven into the national urban fabric, the idea of city is becoming indistinguishable from the idea of society. If we lack consensus on an organizing conceptual structure of the city, it is mainly because we lack such a

24   *Order in Diversity*

structure for society as a whole. The burden, then, rests upon all
the arts, the humanities, and the sciences; and the task grows
increasingly difficult as the complexity of contemporary society
itself increases and as rapidly accumulating knowledge deprives
us of what we had thought to be stable pillars of understanding.

In previous eras, when the goals, the beliefs, the behavior, and
the roles of city folk were clearly distinguishable from those
of their rural brethren, and when urban settlements were
spatially discrete and physically bounded, schoolboy common
sense was sufficient to identify the marks of "urbanness." Now
all Americans are coming to share very similar cultural traits;
the physical boundaries of settlements are disappearing; and the
networks of interdependence among various groups are becoming functionally intricate and spatially widespread. With it all,
the old symbols of order are giving way to the signs of newly
emerging systems of organization that, in turn, are sapping the
usefulness of our established concepts of order.

Especially during the last fifteen years, the rapid expansion
of the large metropolitan settlements has been paralleled by a
rising flood of commentary, reporting and evaluating this remarkable event; and we have developed a new language for
dealing with it. Although the scholarly contributions to this
new literature tend to be appropriately restrained and the
journalistic and polemic contributions characteristically vitu-
perative, the emerging patterns of settlement are typically
greeted by both with disapproval if not frantic dismay. By now
almost everyone knows that the low-density developments on
the growing edge of the metropolis are a form of "cancerous
growth," scornfully dubbed with the most denunciatory of our
new lexicon's titles, "urban sprawl," "scatteration," "subtopia,"
and now "slurbs"—a pattern of development that "threatens
our national heritage of open space" while "decaying blight
rots out the city's heart" and a "demonic addiction to automobiles" threatens to "choke the life out of our cities." Clearly,
"our most cherished values" are imperiled by what is synop-
tically termed "urban chaos." However, such analysis by cliché

is likely to be helpful only as incitement to action; and action guided by obsolescent truths is likely to be effective only as reaffirmation of ideology.

We have often erred, I believe, in taking the visual symbols of urbanization to be marks of the important qualities of urban society; we have compared these symbols with our ideological precepts of order and found that they do not conform; and so we have mistaken for "urban chaos" what is more likely to be a newly emerging order whose signal qualities are complexity and diversity.

These changes now taking place in American society may well be compatible with—and perhaps call forth—metropolitan forms that are neither concentrated nor concentric nor contained. Sympathetic acceptance of this proposition might then lead us to new ways of seeing the metropolis, ways that are more sensitive to the environmental qualities that really matter. We might find new criteria for evaluating the changes in metropolitan spatial structure, suggesting that these changes are not as bad as we had thought. In turn, our approach to metropolitan spatial planning would be likely to shift from an ideological campaign to reconstruct the preconceived city forms that matched the social structures of past eras. Instead, we might see the emergence of a pragmatic, problem-solving approach in which the spatial aspects of the metropolis are viewed as continuous with and defined by the processes of urban society— in which space is distinguished from place, in which human interaction rather than land is seen as the fruitful focus of attention, and in which plans limited to the physical form of the urban settlement are no longer put forth as synoptic statements of our goals.

Metropolitan planning, then, would become the task of mutually accommodating changes in the spatial environment and changes in the social environment. And, because so much of the future is both unknowable and uncontrollable, the orientation of our efforts would shift from the inherently frustrating attempt to build the past in the future to the more realistic

26   *Order in Diversity*

strategy of guiding change in desired directions—from a seeking after predesigned end-states to a continuing and much more complex struggle with processes of becoming.

So radical a revision of our thoughtways is not likely to come easily, for we are firmly devoted to the a priori values that we associate with land (especially with open land), with urban centers (especially with the more concentrated and culturally rich centers), and with certain visual attributes of the urban settlement (especially those features that result from the clean boundary line and the physical separation of different types of objects). And, above all, we are devoted to a unitary conception of order that finds expression in the separation of land uses, the classifiable hierarchy of centers, and the visual scene that conforms to classical canons.

So, let us briefly reconsider the idea of city and review some of the current and impending changes to see what their consequences are likely to be for future urbanization in the United States. We can then re-examine the idea of urban space to see how we might allocate it with some greater degree of rationality.

THE QUALITIES OF "CITYNESS"

In the literature and in the popular mind, the idea of city is imprecise: the terms "city," "urban," "metropolitan," and the various other synonyms are applied to a wide variety of phenomena. Sometimes we speak of the city as though it were simply an artifact—an agglomeration of buildings, roads, and interstitial spaces that marks the settlements of large numbers of people. On other occasions we refer not to physical buildings but to concentrations of physical bodies of humans, as they accumulate in nodal concentrations at higher densities than in "nonurban" places. At other times we refer to the spatial concentration of the places at which human activities are conducted. At still other times we mean a particular set of institutions that mark urban systems of human organization, where we mean to identify the organizational arrangements through which human activities are related to each other—the formal and the informal role allocating systems and the authority systems controlling human behavior. In turn, we sometimes refer to patterns of behavior, and sometimes we mean to distinguish the social value systems of those people and groups that are "urban" from those that are "nonurban."

The values, the ways of life, the institutional arrangements, and the kinds of activities that characterize people living in high-density clusters amidst large concentrations of buildings have been traditionally quite different from those of people living on farms or in small settlements. The large American city has been distinguished by a particular set of these characteristics, and yet, depending upon the specific purposes of our examination, not all these characteristics are necessary conditions of urbanness.

Large numbers of the people concentrated at the centers of New York, Chicago, and most other large metropolitan areas are recent migrants from "rural" areas. Their values, their life styles, their occupational skills, and their social institutions are certainly undergoing rapid change, but, nonetheless, these people are still rural villagers and are likely to retain many of their ways through at least another generation. After an intensive study of the residents of Boston's West End, Herbert Gans could best typify these second- and third-generation descendants of Italian immigrants as "urban villagers," whose way of life in the geographic center of a large metropolitan settlement has retained strong similarities to the patterns inherited from the villages of Italy.[1] The cultural diversity typified by the West Enders living adjacent to Beacon Hill residents—rather than any particular social pattern—is one of the distinctive marks of the city.

The city also is frequently equated with the greatest variety of economic activities; modern urbanization is often conceived as the counterpart of industrialization. Industrialization carries with it an increasingly fine division of labor and, hence, an in-

---

[1] Herbert J. Gans, *The Urban Villagers* (New York: The Free Press of Glencoe, Inc., 1962).

28　　*Order in Diversity*

creasing interdependence among men having specialized skills, who exchange many types of goods and services with one another. As the industrial development process evolves, increasing varieties of goods and services are produced; purchasing power and hence consumer demands rise; and the economy moves ever further from the self-sufficiency of nonurban primitive societies.

Relatively few products and occupations are exclusively associated with urbanization. At an early date in history we might have been able to distinguish nonurban production from urban production by separating the extractive industries (agriculture, forestry, fishing, and mining) and their related occupations from all others. But this is no longer clear. When the skills of farmers and miners are so closely approximating those of men who work in factories and executive suites, the distinction is hard to retain. And when fishermen live on San Francisco's Telegraph Hill, when oilworkers are an industrial elite, and when farmers and foresters hold university degrees and maintain laboratories and research plots, it becomes very difficult indeed to avoid the conclusion that these men are more firmly integrated into the urban society than are Boston's West Enders.

To say this is not to extend the proposition that the amalgamation of the once-rural and once-urban societies is accompanying a movement to an "other-directed" "mass society.' The opportunities for a diversity of choices are clearly much greater in the United States today than they were 150 years ago when industrialization and the opportunities for social mobility were just beginning to stir new ideas and new ways into a poorly educated and unskilled population. Despite some gloomy predictions of the impending impacts of the mass communications media and of the pressures for conformity, the American population is realizing expanding opportunities for learning new ways, participating in more diverse types of activities, cultivating a wider variety of interests and tastes, developing greater capacities for understanding, and savoring richer experiences.

In the next fifty years it is likely that the rate at which the opportunities for learning and for social mobility expand will be even greater than in the last sixty years, when millions of uneducated immigrants from all over the world were integrated into every stratum of American society. Urban life, the communications media, and the public education systems are not likely to reduce all to a lowest common mediocrity. They are more likely to open doors to new ideas, to increased opportunities for being different from one's parents and others in the subculture in which one was reared—as those who have enjoyed these benefits already know and as the American Negroes are coming to know. Rather than a "mass culture" in a "mass society" the long-term prospect is for a maze of subcultures within an amazingly diverse society organized upon a broadly shared cultural base. This is the important meaning that the American brand of urbanization holds for human welfare.

During the past half-century the benefits of urbanization have been extended to an ever-growing proportion of the population: differentials in income distribution have narrowed; formal and informal educational opportunities have spread; Americans have flooded into the middle class. Access to information and ideas has thereby been extended to larger and larger percentages of the population, and this has been greatly abetted by the increasing ease of communication and transportation, *across* space, bringing books, periodicals, lectures, music, and personal observation to more and more people. As the individual's interests develop, he is better able to find others who share these interests and with whom he can associate. The communities with which he associates and to which he "belongs" are no longer only the communities of place to which his ancestors were restricted; Americans are becoming more closely tied to various interest communities than to place communities, whether the interest be based on occupational activities, leisure pastimes, social relationships, or intellectual pursuits. Members of interest communities within a freely communicating society need not be spatially concentrated (except, perhaps, during the formative stages of the interest community's development), for they are increasingly able to interact with each other wherever they may be located. This striking feature of contemporary urbanization is making it increasingly possible for men of all occupations

30   *Order in Diversity*

to participate in the national urban life, and, thereby, it is destroying the once-valid dichotomies that distinguished the rural
from the urban, the small town from the metropolis, the city
from the suburb.

THE SPATIAL CITY

Nothing that I have just said depends upon any specific assumption about the spatial patterns in which urbanites distribute themselves. I am contending that the essential qualities
of urbanness are cultural in character, not territorial, that these
qualities are not necessarily tied to the conceptions that see the
city as a spatial phenomenon. But throughout all of human
history these nonspatial qualities have indeed been typically associated with populations concentrated in high-density urban
settlements.

Although, as some have suggested, there may be certain psychological propensities that induce people to occupy the same
place, there seems to be almost universal agreement among
urban theorists that population agglomeration is a direct reflection of the specialization of occupations and interests that is at
the crux of urbanism and that makes individuals so dependent
upon others. Dependency gets expressed as human interaction—
whether through direct tactile or visual contact, face-to-face
conversation, the transmission of information and ideas via
written or electrical means, the exchange of money, or through
the exchange of goods or services. In the nature of things, all
types of interaction must occur through space, the scale of which
depends upon the locations of the parties to the transaction. It
is also in the nature of things that there are energy and time
costs in moving messages or physical objects through space; and
people who interact frequently with certain others seek to
reduce the costs of overcoming space by reducing the spatial distances separating them. Population clusterings are the direct expression of this drive to reduce the costs of interaction among

people who depend upon, and therefore communicate with, each other.

As the large metropolitan areas in the United States have grown ever larger, they have simultaneously become the places at which the widest varieties of specialists offer the widest varieties of specialized services, thus further increasing their attractiveness to other specialists in self-propelling waves. Here a person is best able to afford the costs of maintaining the web of communications that he relies upon and that, in turn, lies at the heart of complex social systems. Here the individual has an opportunity to engage in diverse kinds of activities, to enjoy the affluence that comes with diversity of specialized offerings; here cultural richness is not withheld simply because it is too costly to get to the place where it can be had.

The spatial city, with its high-density concentrations of people and buildings and its clustering of activity places, appears, then, as the derivative of the communications patterns of the individuals and groups that inhabit it. They have come here to gain accessibility to others and at a cost that they are willing and can afford to pay. The larger the number of people who are accessible to each other, the larger is the likely number of contacts among pairs, and the greater is the opportunity for the individual to accumulate the economic and cultural wealth that he seeks.

Having come to the urban settlement in an effort to lower its costs of communication, the household or the business establishment must then find that location within the settlement which is suitable to it. The competition for space within the settlement results in high land rents near the center, where communication costs are low, and low land rents near the edge of the settlement, where communication costs are high. The individual locator must therefore allocate some portion of his location budget to communication costs and some portion to rents. By choosing an outlying location with its typically larger space he substitutes communication costs (expended in out-of-pocket transportation payments, time, inconvenience, and lost oppor-

32   *Order in Diversity*

tunities for communication with others) for rents. And, since
rent levels decline slowly as one leaves the built-up portions of
the urban settlement and enters the agricultural areas, while
communication costs continue to rise as an almost direct function of distance, very few have been wont to move very far out
from the center of the urban settlement. The effect has traditionally been a compact settlement pattern, having very high
population and employment densities at the center where rents
are also highest, and having a fairly sharp boundary at the
settlement's margin.

It is this distinctive form of urban settlements throughout
history that has led us to equate urbanness with agglomerations
of population. Some architects, some city planners, and some
geographers would carry it still further, insisting that the essential qualities of the city are population agglomerations and
the accompanying building agglomerations themselves; and
they argue that the configurations and qualities of spatial forms
are themselves objects of value. The city, as artifact or as locational pattern of activity places, has thus become the city
planner's specific object of professional attention throughout
the world; and certain canons have evolved that are held as
guides for designers of spatial cities.

Sensitive to the cultural and economic productivity of populations residing in large and highly centralized urban settlements,
some city planners have deduced that the productivity is caused
by the spatial form; and plans for future growth of the settlement have therefore been geared to perpetuating or accentuat-
ing large, high-density concentrations. Other city planners, alert
to a different body of evidence, have viewed the large, high-
density city as the locus of filth, depravity, and the range of social pathologies that many of its residents are heir to. With a
similar hypothesis of spatial environmental determinism and
looking back with envy upon an idealization of the small-town
life that predominated in the eighteenth and early nineteenth
centuries, this group of planners has proposed that the large
settlements be dismantled, that their populations and industries

be redistributed to new small towns, and that all future settlements be prevented from growing beyond some predetermined, limited size.

Others have offered still other ideal forms. The metropolitan plan for the San Francisco Bay Area and Washington's Year 2000 plan propose star-like configurations surrounding a dominant center, with major subcenters along each of the radials.[2] The Greater London Plan calls for a somewhat similar pattern of subcenters surrounding central London, but these are to be spatially free-standing towns at the outer edge of a permanent greenbelt. Alert to the external economies that accompany large agglomerations, while sensitive to the problems that accompany high density and large size, Catherine Bauer Wurster has eschewed both the British New Towns doctrine and the American metropolitan growth patterns. She urges instead that major new settlements be separated from one another and limited to some half-million inhabitants each.[3] Others have proposed slightly different modifications of the Bay Area–Washington, the Greater London, and the Wurster schemes in the official plans prepared for Detroit, Atlanta, and Denver.

Despite some important differences among these proposals, however, they all conform to two underlying conceptions from which they stem:

1. The settlement is conceived as a spatial *unit,* almost as though it were an independent artifact—an independent object separable from others of its kind. The unit is spatially delineated by a surrounding band of land which, in contrast to the unit, has foliage but few people or buildings. In some of the schemes subunits are similarly delineated by green-

<hr>

[2] Parsons, Brinckerhoff, Hall, and Macdonald, *Regional Rapid Transit: Report to the San Francisco Bay Area Rapid Transit Commission* (San Francisco and New York: Parsons, Brinckerhoff, Hall, and Macdonald, 1956). National Capital Planning Commission and the National Capital Regional Planning Council, *Policies Plan for the Year 2000* (Washington: U.S. Government Printing Office, 1961).

[3] Catherine Bauer Wurster, "Framework for an Urban Society," in *Goals for Americans: The Report of the President's Commission on National Goals* (New York: Prentice-Hall, 1960).

34   *Order in Diversity*

belts; in others they are defined as subcenters, as subsidiary density peaks of resident and/or employed populations; but the unitary conception holds for all.

2. Whether the desired population size within the unit is to be large or small, whether subunits are to be fostered either as subsettlements within greenbelts or as subcenters within continuously built-up areas, the territorial extent of the "urbanized area" is to be deliberately contained, and a surrounding permanent greenbelt is to be maintained. The doctrine calls for distinct separation of land that is "urbanized" and land that is not. The editors of *Architectural Review* stated the contention with effective force, in "Outrage" and "Counter Attack," when they pleaded for sharply bounded separation of city, suburb, and country:

The crime of subtopia is that it blurs the distinction between places. It does so by smoothing down the differences between types of environment—town and country, country and suburb, suburb and wild—rather than directly between one town and another. It doesn't deliberately set out to make Glen Shiel look like Helvellyn; it does so in fact by introducing the same overpowering alien elements—in this case blanket afforestation and the wire that surrounds it—into both. The job of this issue [of the magazine] is to get straight the basic divisions between types of environment, and to suggest a framework for keeping each true to itself and distinct from its neighbors.[4]

Behind both ideas are the more fundamental beliefs that urban and rural comprise a dualism that should be clearly expressed in the physical and spatial form of the city, that orderliness depends upon boundedness, and that boundaries are in some way barriers. I have already indicated that the social and economic distinctions between urban and rural are weakening, and it is now appropriate that we examine the spatial counterparts of this blurring nonspatial boundary. I believe that the unitary conceptions of urban places are also fast becoming anachronistic, for the physical boundaries are rapidly collapsing;

[4] "Counter Attack," *Architectural Review*, 1955, pp. 355–56.

and, even where they are imposed by legal restraints, social intercourse, which has never respected physical boundaries anyway, is increasingly able to ignore them.

EMERGING SETTLEMENT PATTERNS

It is a striking feature of current, physical urbanization patterns that rapid growth is still occurring at the sites of the largest settlements and that these large settlements are to be found at widely scattered places on the continent. The westward population movement from the Atlantic Seaboard has not been a spatially homogeneous spread, but has leapfrogged over vast spaces to coagulate at such separated spots as the sites of Denver, Houston, Omaha, Los Angeles, San Francisco, and Seattle.

This is a very remarkable event. Los Angeles, San Francisco, San Diego, and Seattle, as examples, have been able to grow to their present proportions very largely as the result of a rapid expansion of industries that are located far from both their raw materials and their customers. The most obvious of these, of course, are the producers of aircraft, missiles, and electronic equipment which use materials manufactured in the East, in Canada, and throughout the world, and then sell most of their product to firms and governments that are also spatially dispersed. They seem to have been attracted to the West by its climate, its natural amenities, and by a regional style of life that their employees seem to find attractive. Once there, they are highly dependent upon good long-distance transportation. And, since successful management of these industries depends upon good access to information about technical processes, about markets, and about finance, they are equally dependent upon good long-distance communication.

It seems clear that the scale of growth there would not have been possible without first the railroad, ocean freighters, and the telegraph and then the telephone, the highways, and the airlines. All of these changes, we must remember, are very recent occurrences in the history of urban man. (The centennial of the

36   *Order in Diversity*

Pony Express was celebrated in 1961, and the Panama Canal is scarcely two generations old.) These technological changes have made it possible for individual establishments to operate efficiently thousands of miles away from the national business center at New York, the government center at Washington, and the industrial belt between Boston and Chicago, to which they are very intimately linked. At least at this territorial scale, it is apparent that economic and social propinquity is not dependent upon spatial propinquity.

These distant metropolitan areas continue to attract a wide variety of specialized firms and individuals, and most of them still prefer to locate *inside* these metropolitan settlements. It is impressive that the television industry, which requires such intricate co-ordination and split-second timing, has chosen to operate primarily out of two metropolitan areas at opposite ends of a continent, yet its establishments are located within the midst of each. Similarly, the financial institutions and administrative offices of corporations which also rely upon quick access to accurate information are attracted to locations within the midst of these settlements. The reasons are apparent.

Just as certain businesses must maintain rapid communications with linked establishments in other metropolitan areas throughout the nation and throughout the world, so too must they maintain easy communication with the vast numbers of local establishments that serve them and that in turn are served by them. The web of communication lines among interdependent establishments within the large urban settlements is extremely strong. Today it is possible to break off large chunks of urban America and place them at considerable distances from the national urban center in the East, but it does not yet seem possible for these chunks to be broken into smaller pieces and distributed over the countryside.

Nevertheless, the events that have marked the growth of widely separated metropolitan settlements force us to ask whether the same kinds of processes that induced their spatial dispersion might not also come to influence the spatial patterns of individual metropolitan settlements as well. A business firm can now move from Philadelphia to Los Angeles and retain close contact with the business world in the East while enjoying the natural amenities of the West; yet it has little choice but to locate within the Los Angeles Basin where it would be readily accessible to a large labor force, to suppliers, and to service establishments. It is attracted to the metropolitan settlement rather than the more pleasant Sierra Nevada foothills because here the costs of overcoming distance to linked establishments are lower. *The unique commodity that the metropolitan settlement has to offer is lower communication costs.* This is the paramount attraction for establishments and, hence, the dominant reason for high-density agglomeration.

The validity of this proposition would be apparent if we were to imagine a mythical world in which people or goods or messages could almost instantaneously be transported between any two establishments—say, in one minute of time and without other costs of any sort. One could then place his home on whichever mountaintop or lakeside he preferred and get to work, school, or shops anywhere in the world. Goods could be distributed to factories or homes without concern for their distances from the point of shipment. Decision-makers in industry and government could have immediate access to any available information and could come into almost immediate face-to-face contact with each other irrespective of where their offices were located, just as friends and relatives could visit in each other's livingrooms, wherever each might live. With transport costs between establishments reduced to nearly zero, few would be willing to suffer the costs of high density and high rent that are associated with high accessibility to the center of the metropolitan settlements. And yet, accessibility to all other establishments would be almost maximized, subject only to the one-minute travel time and to restraints of social distance. Under these assumptions, urban agglomerations would nearly disappear. Were it not that the immobility of certain landscape and climatic features would induce many household and business establishments to seek locations at places of high natural amenity, that some people may have attitudinal preferences for spa-

38   *Order in Diversity*

tial propinquity to others, and that some industrial processes cannot tolerate even one-minute travel times between industrial establishments, we would expect a virtually homogeneous dispersion across the face of the globe.

Of course, zero communication costs are an impossibility, but the history of civilization has been marked by a continuous decline in the effective costs of communication. Time costs and the costs of inconvenience between any given pair of geographic points have declined consistently; and the financial capacity to bear high dollar-costs has tended to counterbalance the high expenses attached to high speed and high comfort. The concomitant effect of very high speeds between distant points and slower speeds between nearby points has been nearly to equate the travel times between pairs of points on the surface of the earth. Certain improvements in transportation equipment that are now becoming possible could gradually reduce differential time costs of travel to nearly zero. The effects of this potential change on the spatial patterns of settlements would be dramatic.

SOME POTENTIAL CHANGES IN TRANSPORTATION AND COMMUNICATION TECHNOLOGY

We are all aware of the fact that, within metropolitan areas in the United States, the widespread use of the automobile has freed the family's residence from the fixed transit lines that had induced the familiar star-like form of settlement. The pattern of residential scatteration at the growing edges of most metropolitan areas would clearly not have happened without the private car; indeed, this pattern was not apparent until the auto induced the suburban developments of the twenties. The telephone, the motor truck, and transportable water, fuels, and electricity have further abetted this lacy settlement boundary. And, of course, all these trends have been further nurtured by a rising level of average family income and by credit arrangements that have made it possible for the average family to choose—and get—one or more autos, telephones, and houses.

Similarly the new communication devices, higher corporate incomes, and federal financial encouragement have made it possible for some foot-loose manufacturers and certain types of commercial establishments to locate in relatively outlying portions of metropolitan settlements.

To date, however, very few of these families and business establishments have chosen to locate very far from the metropolitan center, because the costs of maintaining the web of communications that are essential to their cultural and their economic well-being would simply be too high. Even though they might like to locate in a mountain setting, the benefits that would accrue from so pleasant a habitat seem to be far outweighed by the difficulties of maintaining contact with the various specialists they rely upon.

But today a great many of them are much farther away from the metropolitan center, in mileage distance, than they were even fifteen years ago, not to mention the differences that have occurred since the beginning of the century. Even so, a great many have chosen outlying locations without increasing their time distances to the center. Increased mileage distance carries a necessary increase in dollar costs, but the more sensitive component of communications costs in the locator's calculus seems to be the time costs, as the recent traffic studies and the phenomenal rise in long-distance telephone usage indicate.

Increases in travel speeds within most of the metropolitan settlements have been relatively modest as compared to the changing speeds of intermetropolitan travel that the airlines have brought. In part because the potentials of the new freeway systems have been so severely restrained by the countereffects of congestion and in part because the improvements in transit systems have been rare indeed, peak-hour travel speeds have not increased appreciably. But off-peak increases have been great in some places, and some changes are imminent that are likely to cause an emphatic change.

Where the urban freeway systems are uncongested, they have induced at least a doubling in speed and in some places a quadrupling—and the freeways do run freely in off-peak hours

40   *Order in Diversity*

As the urban freeway systems that are now under construction are extended farther out and connected to one another, an unprecedented degree of freedom and flexibility will be open to the traveler for moving among widely separated establishments in conducting his affairs. A network of freeways, such as that planned for the Los Angeles area, will make many points highly accessible, in direct contrast to the single high-access point that resulted from the traditional radial transit net. Even if new or improved high-speed fixed-route transit systems were to be superimposed on freeway networks, the freeway's leveling effect on accessibility would still be felt. And the positive advantages of automobiles over transit systems—affording, at their best, door-to-door, no-wait, no-transfer, private, and flexible-route service—make it inconceivable that they will be abandoned for a great part of intrametropolitan travel or that the expansion of the freeway systems on which they depend will taper off. We would do well, then, to accept the private vehicle as an indispensable medium of metropolitan interaction—more, as an important instrument of personal freedom.

There has been a great deal of speculation about characteristics of the evolutionary successor to the automobile, but it is probably too early to predict the exact form it will take. I would hazard some confident guesses, though, that it will not be a free-flight personal vehicle because the air-traffic control problems appear to be insoluble, that it will be automatically guided when on freeways and hence capable of traveling safely at much higher speeds, but that it will continue to be adaptable to use on local streets. If bumper-to-bumper movement at speeds of 150 miles per hour or more were to be attained, as current research-and-development work suggest is possible, greater per lane capacities and greater speeds would be realized than any rapid transit proposals now foresee for traditional train systems. When these on-route operating characteristics are coupled with the door-to-door, no-wait, no-transfer, privacy, and flexible route-end service of the personal vehicle, such a system would appear to be more than competitive with any type of rapid transit service now planned—with two important qualifications.

The costs would have to be reasonable, and the land use patterns would have to be compatible with the operating characteristics of the transportation system.

A system that would be capable of moving large numbers of cars into a small area within a short period of time would face the parking dilemma in compounded form. Although unpublished reports of the engineers at The RAND Corporation suggest that it would be mechanically possible and perhaps even economically feasible to build sufficient underground parking facilities on Manhattan to store private cars for all employees and shoppers who arrive there daily, the problem of moving large numbers of cars into and out of the garages during brief periods would call for so elaborate and costly a maze of access ramps as to discourage any serious effort to satisfy a parking demand of such magnitude. Before such an all-out effort is made to accommodate the traditional central business district to the private motor car, the summary effect of thousands of locational decisions by individual entrepreneurs would probably have been to evolve a land use pattern that more readily conforms to the auto's operating characteristics. With further increases in mass auto usage—especially if it could attain bumper-to-bumper, 150 mph movement—we are bound to experience a dispersion of many traditionally central activities to outlying but highly accessible locations. The dispersed developments accompanying the current freeways suggest the type of pattern that seems probable. Here, again, Los Angeles offers the best prototype available.

IN WHAT SENSE IS URBAN SPACE A RESOURCE?

I have been suggesting that the quintessence of urbanization is not population density or agglomeration but specialization, the concomitant interdependence, and the human interactions by which interdependencies are satisfied. Viewed from this orientation, the urban settlement is the spatial adaptation to demands of dependent activities and specialists for low com-

42   *Order in Diversity*

munication costs. It is helpful, therefore, to view the spatial city as a communications system, as a vastly complex switchboard through which messages and goods of various sorts are routed.

Information, ideas, and goods are the very stuff of civilization. The degree to which they are distributed to all individuals within a population stands as an important indicator of human welfare levels—as a measure of cultural and economic income. Of course, the distribution of this income is determined predominantly by institutional rather than spatial factors—only the rare Utopian has even suggested that the way to "the good society" is through the redesign of the spatial city. And yet, space intervenes as a friction against all types of communication. Surely, salvation does not lie in the remodeled spatial city; but, just as surely, levels of cultural and economic wealth could be increased if the spatial frictions that now limit the freedom to interact were reduced. This is the important justification for city planning's traditional concern with space.

In the very nature of Euclidean geometry, the space immediately surrounding an urban settlement is limited. Given a transportation-communication technology and its accompanying cost structure, close-in space has greater value than distant space, since nearby inhabitants have greater opportunities to interact with others in the settlement.

But as the transportation-communication technologies change to permit interaction over greater distances at constant or even at falling costs, more and more outlying space is thereby brought into the market, and the relative value of space adjacent to large settlements falls. Urban space, as it has been associated with the economies of localization and agglomeration, is thus a peculiar resource, characterized by increasing supply and by ever-declining value.

These cost-reducing and space-expanding effects of transportation-communication changes are being reinforced by most of the technological and social changes we have recently seen. The patterns of social stratification and of occupations, the organizational structures of businesses and of governments, the goods and the ideas that are being produced, and the average individual's ranges of interests and opportunities are steadily becoming more varied and less tradition-bound. In a similar way, the repercussions of these social changes and the direct impacts of some major technological changes have made for increasing diversity in the spatial structures of urban settlements.

Projections of future change, and especially changes in the technologies of transportation and communication, suggest that much greater variation will be possible in the next few decades. It is becoming difficult to avoid the parallel prediction that totally new spatial forms are in the offing.

To date, very few observers have gone so far as to predict that the nodally concentric form, that has marked every spatial city throughout history, could give way to nearly homogeneous dispersion of the nation's population across the continent; but the hesitancy may stem mainly from the fact that a non-nodal city of this sort would represent such a huge break with the past. Yet, never before in human history has it been so easy to communicate across long distances. Never before have men been able to maintain intimate and continuing contact with others across thousands of miles; never has intimacy been so independent of spatial propinquity. Never before has it seemed possible to build an array of specialized transportation equipment that would permit speed of travel to increase directly with mileage length of trip, thus having the capability of uniting all places within a continent with almost-equal time distance. And never before has it seemed economically feasible for the nodally cohesive spatial form that marks the contemporary large settlement to be replaced by drastically different forms, while the pattern of internal centering itself changes or, perhaps, dissolves.

A number of informed students have read the same evidence and have drawn different conclusions. Observing that the consequences of ongoing technological changes are spatially neutral, they suggest that increased ease of intercourse makes it all the more possible for households and business establishments to locate in the midst of high-density settlements. This was essentially the conclusion that Haig drew when he wrote, ". . . Instead of explaining why so large a portion of the popu-

44   *Order in Diversity*

lation is found in urban areas, one must give reasons why that portion is not even greater. The question is changed from 'Why live in the city?' to 'Why not live in the city?' " [5]

I am quick to agree that many of the recent and the imminent developments are ambiguous with respect to space. They could push urban spatial structure toward greater concentricity, toward greater dispersion, or, what I believe to be most likely, toward a very heterogeneous pattern. Since administrative and executive activities are so sensitive to the availability and immediacy of accurate information—and hence of good communications—they may be the bellwether of future spatial adjustments of other activities as well, and they therefore warrant our special attention.

The new electronic data-processing equipment and the accompanying procedures permit much more intensive use of downtown space than was ever possible with nonautomated office processes; but they can operate quite as effectively from an outlying location, far removed from the executive offices they serve. The sites adjacent to the central telephone exchange may offer competitive advantages over all others, and establishments relying upon computers, that in turn are tied to the long-distance telephone lines, seem to be clustering about the hub of those radial lines in much the manner that they once clustered about the hub of the radial trolley lines. At the same time we can already observe that outlying computer centers are attracting establishments that use their services.

The recent history of office construction in midtown New York, northwest Washington, and in the centers of most large metropolitan areas is frequently cited as clear evidence of the role that face-to-face contacts play in decision-making and of the importance of spatial propinquity in facilitating face-to-face contact. And yet, simultaneously, large numbers of executive offices have followed their production units to suburban locations, and some have established themselves in outlying spots,

[5] Robert M. Haig, "Toward an Understanding of the Metropolis," *New York Regional Survey, Regional Survey of New York and Its Environs,* Vol. 1 (New York: Regional Plan Association, Inc., 1927).

spatially separated from their production units and from all other establishments. The predominant movement in the New York area has been to the business center, but the fact that many have been able to move outside the built-up area suggests that a new degree of locational freedom is being added.

The patterns in Washington, Detroit, and Los Angeles clearly suggest that the walking-precinct type of central business district (CBD), with its restricted radius, compactness, and fixed-route transit service, is not the only effective spatial pattern for face-to-face communication. Washington's governmental and private offices are dispersed over so wide an area that few are within easy walking distance of each other. Meetings typically call for a short auto trip, either by taxi or private car. In Detroit and especially in Los Angeles, establishment types that have traditionally been CBD-oriented are much more dispersed throughout the settled area. Relying heavily upon the automobile, Los Angelenos seem to be able to conduct their business face-to-face, perhaps as frequently as do New Yorkers. Highly specialized firms employing highly specialized personnel are located in all parts of the Los Angeles Basin—in some places within fairly compact subcenters, in other places in quite scattered patterns. But the significant feature is this: few linked establishments are within walking distances of each other, and an auto trip is thus an adjunct to a face-to-face meeting.

Even with a moderate speed of automotive travel, considerable mileage can be covered within a short time. At door-to-door average speeds of only 15 mph, it takes but four minutes to get to another's office a mile away; and, especially for long-distance trips, average travel speeds are considerably higher, probably exceeding 50 mph door-to-door off-peak in Los Angeles. Although I know of no measurements of this sort having been made, I would guess that (after adjusting for the total number of establishments within the metropolitan area) an establishment on Wilshire Boulevard in Los Angeles has as many linked establishments within a given time-distance as does a similar establishment at Rockefeller Center.

Comparable studies of traffic patterns in New York and Los

46   *Order in Diversity*

Angeles will be completed within a few years, and it will then be possible to compare travel-time costs to commuters and shoppers, as well as to men who need to transact business face-to-face. I think it is safe to predict, however, that large differences will not be found, that Los Angelenos are just about as accessible to their work places and to the various urban service establishments as are New Yorkers, and perhaps even more accessible. Moreover, I would expect to find that Los Angeles residents maintain as diverse a range of contacts, that they interact with others as frequently and as intensively, that they are participants in as broad and as rich a range of communications as the resident of any other metropolitan area. I believe the popular notion among outsiders that Los Angeles is a cultural desert, is a myth whose basis lies in the ideology of metropolitan form. We have equated cultural wealth and urbanity with high-density cities; since Los Angeles is not spatially structured in the image of the culturally rich cities we have known, some have therefore inferred that life there must be empty and deprived of opportunity. It is strikingly apparent, however, that nearly seven million people and their employers seem to find this an amiable habitat and that Easterners continue to arrive at a rapid rate. It is also apparent that a considerable part of its attractiveness has been the natural setting and the opportunities to engage in activities outside the urban settlement itself.

If most of the social and technological changes I have mentioned were in fact neutral in their spatial impacts, this itself would represent a powerful new factor at work on the spatial organization of cities. Prior dominant modes of transportation and communication, traditional forms of organization of business and government, the older and more rigid patterns of economic and social stratification, and prior educational and occupational levels and opportunities all exerted positive pressures to population agglomeration around dominant high-density business-industrial-residential centers. If these pressures for concentration and concentricity are ebbing, the effects of counter processes will be increasingly manifest.

THE ASCENT OF AMENITY
AS LOCATIONAL DETERMINANT

Throughout our history, the locations and the internal arrangements of our cities have been predominantly shaped by the efforts of individual establishments to lower the costs of transporting goods, information, and people. If our speculations concerning the secular declines in these costs should prove to be valid, we can expect that the nontransportable on-site amenities will come to predominate as locational determinants.

Population growth in California, Arizona, Florida, and other naturally favored places can be largely attributed to the favorable climate and landscape. At smaller scale, in turn, new residential accommodations and new industrial establishments are being developed at those sites whose natural conditions are most favored by groups of various types. This is a very remarkable development; the luxury of locational choice is now being extended to ever-increasing numbers within an increasingly diverse population.

During the past sixty years the work week of American manufacturing workers has fallen from about 59 hours to something under 40, while wages have risen from an average of about $450 per year to about $4,700 (in constant 1947–49 dollars from about $1,250 to about $4,000 per year). The prospects are for a continuing reduction in working hours and for a continuing rise in disposable income, perhaps accompanied by a narrowing of the extremes in income distribution. When compounded by the availability of credit, higher levels of education, lowering ages of retirement, and a further dispersion of middle-class ways to larger proportions of the population, the range of choice open to most people—including the range of locational choice—is certain to increase greatly.

Although it is undoubtedly true that the success of recent suburban developments to some extent reflects rather limited

48 *Order in Diversity*

choices available within the contemporary metropolitan housing markets, it is also apparent that for most of their inhabitants these developments represent marked improvements in living standards. Most suburbanites in the upper-income brackets have made free locational choices, since they could afford more central sites. Even a recent disenchantment with suburban life has not refuted the compatibility of low-density housing developments with middle-class preferences for spaciousness, with middle-class attitudes about distance, with current status criteria, and with child-oriented family life.

Among certain professional groups that have recently been in high demand (most notably those specialists associated with research and development in the electronics, missiles, and petrochemical industries) the preferences for suburban-type residential environments within pleasant natural settings seem to have been so strong as to have affected the locations of these industries in California, Long Island, and the suburbs of Boston. To attract these skilled persons, whole industries have moved. Very few have chosen locations very far removed from the universities and the business complexes to which they are closely linked, but it is significant that they have tended to select outlying spots With increasing leisure time, increasing mobility via automobiles, and increased spending power, we can expect the average family to take much greater advantage of outdoor recreational activities available in the countryside accessible to his home. As transportation facilities are improved and week-ends lengthen, families will be able to travel longer distances than before. Some will prefer to locate their homes near recreational facilities, and the recreation place might even replace the work place as the major determinant of residential locations.

The range of locational choice is broadening at the same time that changing characteristics of the national population are breeding increasing diversity in people's locational preferences. Simultaneously, all segments of the national population are being woven into an increasingly complex social, political, and economic web, such that no person and no group is entirely independent of all other persons and all other groups.

The growing pluralism in American society is more than a growing multiplicity of types of people and institutions. Each person, each group bound by a community of interests, is integrally related to each other person and group, such that each is defined by its relations to all others and that a change in one induces a change in all others.

The kinds of information that can be read from maps showing urbanized areas or land use patterns are therefore likely to be misleading. Suggesting that settlements of one size or another are in some way independent units, in some way separated from each other and from the spatial field in which they lie, maps of this sort miss the essential meaning of urbanization. Whether the maps represent existing patterns or plans for future patterns, they present static snapshots of locational patterns of people or buildings or activity places and say nothing (except as the reader may interpolate) about the human interaction patterns that are at the heart of complex social processes. When people can interact with others across great distances and when they can readily move themselves into face-to-face positions as the need to do so arises, it scarcely matters whether a greenbelt intervenes or whether the space between them and their associates is used for houses and factories. Surely Los Angeles is an integral part of the national urban system, despite the 2,500-mile-wide greenbelt that separates it from New York. Surely Bakersfield is as integral a part of the southern California urban system as is Pasadena, despite the intervention of the Tehachapi Mountains and some 90 miles. Surely the researchers in Los Alamos are as much a part of the world-wide community of atomic physicists, as if they happened to be at Brookhaven or Berkeley or Argonne.

Spatial separation or propinquity is no longer an accurate indicator of functional relations; and, hence, mere locational pattern is no longer an adequate symbol of order. The task of the spatial planner is therefore considerably more difficult than we have traditionally thought. The normative guides that we have used have been oriented primarily to the form aspects that can be represented on maps and have applied static and simplistic

50   *Order in Diversity*

concepts of order that are not consonant with the processes of growing and complex urban systems.

It is a fairly simple matter to prepare a land use plan for a territory, if its spatial organization is to follow any one of the simple universal models that city planners have promulgated. Sites for "self-contained and balanced" new towns are readily found, and site plans are readily made. It is quite another matter to get the townspeople to behave as though they comprised a "self-contained and balanced community"—nor would many of us really want them to be deprived of the enriched lives that come with free communication with the "outside world." Plans for increased centrality and higher density can also be portrayed readily within the traditional idiom of land use planning; but, again, it is hard to believe that the advocates would be willing to deprive the residents of the opportunities to choose outlying locations. Nevertheless, whether small town or large concentration, the rules are clear and simple; the variables to be accounted are limited in number and in complexity; and the solution is determined before the problem is attacked.

It is considerably more difficult, however, to plan for diversity in settlement and land use patterns, for here the formal rules of urban form are not very helpful. No single scheme can be taken as a rule to be applied to all establishments and to all places. Rather, the locational requirements of the many diverse groups of establishments must establish the rules, and the optimum pattern would then resemble none of the doctrinal models.

The optimum land use pattern of the future metropolis is likely to be highly diversified. Since transportation costs will never fall to zero, the external economies associated with clusterings of similar and dissimilar establishments will continue to induce certain types of establishments to seek centers and sub-centers of many types. Some of these will be of the familiar employment and shopping-center types, whether in the CBD or in the unitary "regional center" molds. Other establishments, mutually linked to a third type of establishment, will undoubtedly continue to cluster about it wherever it may be, whether it be a stock exchange, a major university, an airport, or a large manufacturer or retailer. Other establishments will form sub-centers, largely as a result of their mutual desire to occupy a particularly pleasant site, although such growth inducements are self-limiting, of course. Those establishments that depend upon good access to information will undoubtedly continue to seek locations that best facilitate easy communication. For some, formal meeting places that accommodate scheduled encounters will suffice, and for many of these the airports and the convention halls are already serving a large part of their requirements. Others, such as the ladies' garment industry and the securities exchanges, may be so sensitive to changes in styles and/or market conditions as to induce even more intensive business concentrations of the sort that Manhattan typifies.

Simultaneously, the optimum patterns would include scattered developments for a great variety of establishments in a great variety of land use mixes and density patterns. For those manufacturers who prefer to locate factories and workers' housing near mountain skiing and hiking areas, for those lone wolves who prefer solitude and possibly a part-time farm, and for all those for whom a high-speed auto drive is no commuting deterrent, we can expect (and should encourage) scattered developments of the type now becoming common east of Boston and north of New York.

The future land use pattern will certainly not be one of homogeneous dispersion. Transportation and communication costs will never permit that, and the very uneven distribution of favored climates and landscapes would strongly discourage it. But a much greater degree of dispersion is both likely and desirable, while centers and subcenters of various compositions and densities persist and grow in a range of sizes spanning the whole spectrum from "center" to "sprawl."

If we are willing to accept the idea that the optimum urban settlement and land use patterns are likely to be as pluralistic as society itself, then the conceptions of spatial order will follow from our conceptions of social order. Our spatial plans, then, will be plans for diversity, designed to accommodate the dis-

52   *Order in Diversity*

parate demands upon land and space made by disparate individuals and groups that are bound up in the organized complexity of urban society.

PLANNED ALLOCATION OF URBAN SPACE

One of the planner's major tasks is to delineate the probable range of real future choice—the envelope within which goal-directed actions are likely to pay off. I read the evidence concerning the qualities and magnitudes of some uncontrollable aspects of future change to say that many of the spatial forms to which we have aspired are no longer within that envelope.

Moreover, I contend that we have been searching for the wrong grail, that the values associated with the desired urban structure do not reside in the spatial structure per se. One pattern of settlement and its internal land use form is superior to another only as it better serves to accommodate ongoing social processes and to further the nonspatial ends of the political community. I am flatly rejecting the contention that there is an overriding universal spatial or physical aesthetic of urban form.

Throughout this essay I have laid heavy emphasis upon the communication patterns that bring people into contact with others and that have created our traditional settlement patterns. I have done so because communication is a very powerful influence that has scarcely been studied. But it is not my view that this is the only important factor affecting urban spatial structure, or that the criteria for planning the spatial structure for complex urban communities stem from this relationship alone. No simple cause-and-effect relationships are likely to be uncovered in this field, for the maze of relationships within such complex open systems as urban societies are such that a change in one part of the web will reverberate to induce changes throughout all parts of the web. The problem of planning for the optimum utilization of urban space is far more complex than our present understanding permits us to even realize.

No attempt will be made here to catalogue the kinds of criteria that a rigorously conducted planning effort would need to weigh. I leave this omission not from modesty—only ignorance. But a few considerations can be mentioned, if only to suggest that my ignorance may not be complete.

I have chosen to deal with space, not with land, because, for the paramount purposes of men who engage in nonextractive industries, the surface of the earth has meaning as representation of communication distance rather than as inherent characteristics of the soil. I have contended that all space is urban space, since interaction among urbanites takes place through, or is inhibited by, all space. Space has significance for the urban planner primarily because of the implications that locational patterns have for fruitful interaction, hence for social welfare.

For some purposes, however, the surface of the earth does have meaning as soil or as minerals or as water storage; and in this context planners are indeed concerned with allocating *land* judiciously. With the prospect of increasing space utilization by urban activities, a growing conflict is inevitable between land users and space users. Fortunately the rate of increase in agricultural productivity continues to outpace the rate of population increase in the United States; and, in the face of embarrassing agricultural surpluses, the conflict is likely to thrive only in ideological disputes rather than in market competition.

Largely, I suspect, as vestige of our agrarian ancestry, many city planners and others hold to a rather fundamentalist belief in land. Land is seen as a scarce and sacred resource to be saved against those who would "encroach" upon and "desecrate" its natural features. To use good soils for housing is frequently decried as wasteful of a valuable natural resource, all the more objectionable because these changes are effectively irreversible. But the answer is surely not that simple. There may indeed be areas that would most profitably be retained in crops rather than in houses and factories, but in the places where the question arises the balance is probably more often in favor of the houses and factories. The values inherent in accessibility, that make those places attractive to the house buyer, are quite likely

54   *Order in Diversity*

to weigh more heavily than the values to be derived from crops. But no answers can be found a priori. Each site must be evaluated for the relative costs and benefits implicit in the alternative purposes for which it might be used.

Similarly, lands that might provide the recreational opportunities that are increasingly in demand might also be used for other purposes. But, again, no doctrinaire answers are likely to be found supportable. Again, each site must be subjected to an analysis of the welfare implications implicit in the substitutable uses. The benefits from recreational use are quite as real as those deriving from farms and houses. Within the total spatial field, places for recreational activity need to be developed. But no ready solutions are in hand; certainly the greenbelt doctrine in itself is insufficient basis for the investments that are required.

· · · · · ·

Within any given territory at any given time, space is finite. Present and future demands for it are highly diverse in their requirements, but we can surely learn enough about the characteristics of each type of user to equip ourselves to make more rational allocations than would occur under unguided market conditions. The task is not to "protect our natural heritage of open space" just because it is natural, or a heritage, or open, or because we see ourselves as Galahads defending the good form against the evils of urban sprawl. This is a mission of evangelists, not planners.

Rather, and as the barest minimum, the task is to seek that spatial distribution of urban populations and urban activities that will permit greater freedom for human interaction while, simultaneously, providing freer access to natural amenities and effective management of the landscape and of mineral resources.

This is no mean task. And probably the meanest part of the task will be to disabuse ourselves of some deep-seated doctrine that seeks order in simple mappable patterns, when it is really hiding in extremely complex social organization, instead.

Part II
Planning Theory

[6]

Cities and regions beyond the crisis:

invitation to a debate

In recent years urban and regional research has made considerable progress in addressing itself to the real world, employing intellectual tools which are able to come to grips with the problems experienced in people's everyday life. The real improvement is *not* that this new type of research employs a marxist framework or a class analysis perspective. Academic marxism can be as formalistic and useless as functionalism was in the past. The value of this new work is its ability to treat reality—which is never in a condition of social integration—in terms of social conflict. The point is to understand the interplay between the state, capital and space, to study the new forms of land rent in highly urbanized society, to research on the conditions of development of community protests, and so on, rather than, for example, playing games with mathematical models of 'the urban system'. In other words the attempt is to find concepts and methods which cast light on the real world, instead of codifying it into the obsolete categories of the academic establishment.

But such an intellectual perspective is a very demanding one. This is because it has to adapt continuously to the changing patterns of space and society. I have the feeling that we are all now far behind in our understanding of what *is* actually happening in cities and regions. At best the talk is of 'the current economic crisis', but we are no longer in the midst of such a crisis. We have already entered a new stage of development of the world capitalist

128 *Cities and regions beyond the crisis: invitation to a debate*

system which will be at least as different in comparison with the last 30 years as the post-second world war period was in respect to the pre-1929 period.

We are experiencing new international and interregional patterns of division of labour. We are also witnessing a counter-urbanization process, in the US more than in China. We are observing the disintegration of the suburban dream and an astonishing set of cross-cutting patterns in the central cities, parts of which have been abandoned at the same time as other parts have been gentrified. Furthermore, we can be sure that a low rate of growth in gross national product is going to be the rule rather than the exception in most advanced capitalist countries. In this situation austerity policies will be the main characteristic of government action, although major differences will occur on the basis of the governments' political complexion.

This new tough economic scene will be accompanied by three major social processes. First, a shift in cultural patterns, so that, increasingly, use values rather than exchange values will be emphasized. Second, an increasing incapacity of the political left (old or new) to adapt to the new conditions, given its attachment to a somewhat narrow working-class perspective. And, third, as a consequence of the limits of collective political alternatives, growing trends of social disintegration and individual violence, so that large sectors of the big cities will live in a state which will be dominated by defensive tribal organizations and a barbarian mood.

Hitherto all thinking about cities and regions, whether by Conservatives or progressives, has been dominated by the experience of the long period of sustained economic growth that has occurred in the postwar period. Conservatives dreamt of the construction of a giant technological landscape, while the left concentrated on trying to redistribute public goods and exercise social control of the over-heated machine of capital accumulation. Very few people gave much thought to the new situation of scarcity. The ecologists were among this minority, but they either missed the point (for example, by using the 'social structure' as a 'fixed variable' in the famous MIT model), or their work was stamped with the ideological bias of middle-class values, trying to mobilize the world in helping them keep non-degradable plastic rubbish out of their suburban backyards.

As the Italian urbanist Campos Venuti said in one of the most penetrating essays on this topic, '. . . in the current situation capitalist societies are proposing alternative policies based upon an austerity strategy. Carter and Giscard d'Estaing propose sacrifices in the name of a new model of economic growth. It is obviously "austerity for the benefit of capital" but their proposals are based on the real issues which national societies as well as the world will have to confront one day, in one way or in another' (Campos Venuti, 1978, 13).

So here is the new and important frontier for researchers who, in common with the editors of this journal, are concerned with life and death, work and pleasure, violence and justice, people and nature. We have to use whatever skills we have to try to understand the new urban and regional world we are now entering upon. We have never been through such a historical period before and we are, whether we like it or not, forced to consider new ideas and new ways of grasping what is going on. We wish to initiate an, albeit modest, but systematic and open debate on the issues raised in this note. All contributions will be welcome, although it is our belief that our readers will not be interested in sterile dogmatism or mere demagogy, both these being inimical to the intellectual and political values which have helped to form this publication.

The time is over, if ever it existed, when a single theory or a holy book could provide the 'right answer'. So the pages of the journal will be open to new ideas, however disturbing or dubious these may appear at first sight. This is not, however, an appeal to those who would contribute polemic rather than intellectual rigour. If anything we now need more of the latter than ever before in dealing with the crucial changes which are presently occurring in our world. We need to take more consideration, rather than less, of the complexity and variation of the processes that we face and seek to understand.

Ray Pahl's provocative contribution to this issue marks the opening of the new debate that we hope to stimulate. This contribution will certainly give rise to many criticisms. For example, I do not agree with the main conclusions about employment policy that could be drawn from the analysis. But the kind of questions that Pahl raises, and the style of work he proposes to develop are of central importance. In forthcoming issues of the journal there will be major contributions to this discussion by Campos Venuti, Chris Paris and others. We hope that the argument and discussion will develop through articles, shorter notes, reports on research findings and comments. Our aim, as always, is to develop the journal step by step as a more effective instrument to understand reality in order to change it.

Department of City and Regional Planning,   *Manuel Castells*
 University of California, Berkeley.

Campos Venuti, G. 1978: *Urbanistica e austerità*. Milan: Feltrinelli.

[7]

Critical Rationalism and Planning Methodology[1]

Andreas Faludi

[*First received Nov. 1981; revised version April 1982*]

Summary. This paper studies the implications of critical rationalism for planning and planning methodology. Centreing on planning as decision-making, a Popperian approach to decision-making in planning is formulated, with a view to throwing light on an old planning problem: the meaning of rationality.

Two important debates in planning in recent years have been, firstly about the proposition that the step from knowledge to action involves important problems of its own, (e.g. Reade, 1976) and secondly, whether rationality is a methodological proposition for decision-making on a par with falsification for empirical hypotheses (Faludi, 1978(a) & 1978(b)). Essentially, it concerns the question of whether it is appropriate to stick to rationality in the light of the manifest failure of planning practice to approximate this ideal, or whether it should be discarded as having been invalidated by practice. Of particular relevance here is Popper's reply to Lakatos' question *Under what conditions would you give up your demarcation criterion?*

> '*A question that I am almost regularly asked by intelligent students on their acquaintance with my work is the following: But is your own theory of falsifiability (and of scientific method in general) falsifiable? Now while this is a very natural question, it should not be asked by anybody familiar with my work. For the answer is that my theory is not empirical, but methodological or philosophical, and it need not therefore be falsifiable.*' (Popper, in Schilpp, 1974, p. 1010).

As yet, no planning methodology in the vein of critical rationalism exists. Least of all is there one to be found in the work of Popper himself.[2] Although the latter has written a great deal about planning, he seems to have had in mind planning as the central guidance of society. This is not the same as the view of planning as guiding practical decision-making developed below. As regards this, however, Popper's work is somewhat lacking in insight in the situations and the problems of decision-makers. When challenged on this point by Settle, he had few answers, pointing to some of the elements of his work referred to below (see Settle in Schilpp, 1974, p. 697–749, and Popper's *Replies to my critics*, p. 1117/1118, in the same work). But developing planning methodology further in the spirit of critical rationalism seems both possible and desirable nevertheless.

This paper is strictly limited in scope. Only Popper's own works are considered, and it marks only

Professor Faludi is at the Universiteit van Amsterdam, in the Subfakulteit planologie en demografie, Jodenbreestrat 23, 1011 NH Amsterdam.

[1] Based on a paper given at the Theory Workshop of the Education for Planning Association held at Manchester, 11th and 12th September, 1981; see: *Werkstukken van het Planologisch en Demografisch Instituut*, Nr. 40, University of Amsterdam.

[2] Unfortunately, Popper himself treats the rationality principle much less rigourously than the falsificationist rule, sometimes describing it even as an empirical truth. This has given rise to a critical essay by Koertge (1979) suggesting that it is bad methodological practice to protect it from refutation — as Popper seems to do. If Popper had described the rationality principle unambigously as a methodological rule on *a par* with the falsificationist one, this criticism could not have arisen.

the beginning of research work on this topic: the vast secondary literature, in particular from Germany, has been left out of consideration. For the time being anyway. With few exceptions this article limits itself to the field of urban and regional planning.

Popper in the planning literature

The Open Society and its Enemies (1966, 1st edition, 1945) and *The Poverty of Historicism* (1961, first published 1944/45) are contributions to what might be termed the classic planning debate. Other contributors were Lippmann (1939), Hayek (1944) and Mannheim (1940), to name but a few. The debate had been sparked off by the historic example of Soviet and Fascist planning and concerned the merits of classical liberal democracy as against societal planning from the centre.

The modern planning debate is different — though, to be sure it sometimes returns to the themes of the acceptability and the sheer possibility of central planning. Whereas the classic debate had largely been conducted by refugees from Nazi Germany, the modern one originated in the United States. There, societal planning had become anathema after World War II, and planners who had been involved in such attempts at it as setting up the National Resources Planning Board during the New Deal turned to less controversial fields like city and regional planning instead. In it, a fruitful research tradition on planning theory emerged. Also, many links were forged with another activity beyond suspicion, business planning.

Popper has never participated in this modern planning debate. In the *Foreword* to a recent German text book on environmental planning (Moewes, 1980) he professes himself a layman as regards urban planning. Still, it is interesting to note what he thinks the most relevant parts of this work are. He begins by pointing out that plans are rarely being implemented and that most of them are partly mistaken, pleading for what the literature describes as process planning. He holds up the approach of the engineer as providing an example of searching for, and learning from, mistakes. He recognises the difficulties faced by planners who cannot experiment, and whose mistakes will only emerge in the future. They must try and anticipate the future, yet their expectations can never be scientifically based.

He finishes this foreword by philosophising on the tradition of criticism in the arts and sciences and by dwelling somewhat further on the theme of learning from mistakes. It is clear that he regards the two books mentioned above as being the most relevant for planning.

This is echoed by the earlier references to his work. Probably, Braybrooke and Lindblom (1963, p. 46) are the first in the modern planning literature to refer to Popper. Their work does not concern urban and regional planning as such, but it is so widely referred to that we cannot ignore it. They relay Popper's emphasis on the limitations of man's intellectual capacities and of his available knowledge together with his argument that both preclude comprehensiveness in analysis. They conclude that a decision-making system, according to Popper, must be adapted to the experimental nature of social reform, in which ends are as much adjusted to means as means to ends. Also, they emulate his argument that one should concentrate on eliminating evil instead of pursuing goals (p. 82). As will be seen, this *'negative utilitarianism'* has attracted the attention of planning theorists.

These same points are referred to by Etzioni (1968, p. 268), who fails to answer the interesting question as to whether his alternative to incrementalism, *'mixing scanning'*, would get Popper's approval. Needham (1971, p. 318), in particular, picks up the theme of negative utilitarianism arguing that

'*... planning should generally try to solve problems rather than achieve goals'*.

but Faludi (1971) has denied the usefulness of this point: goals and problems may be seen as standing in a symmetric relationship to each other. In a joint paper, Needham and Faludi (1973) agree that the central issue is not that between goals and problems as starting points but that between collectivism and individualism.

The next spate of works raises the debate onto a different level. They tend to refer less to Popper's contribution to the classic planning debate and more to his works on the methodology of science, trying to establish a methodology of planning by way of analogy.

Thus, Chadwick (1970, p. 66) begins with an account of Popper's theory of objective knowledge as proceeding from problems to tentative solutions, error-elimination and so on. This process, he argues, must be adapted to applied research by introducing modelling culminating in a '*rational model of systemic planning, derived from scientific method*' (figure 4.3., p. 68; for criticisms see Camhis, 1979, pp. 51–52). Also, Chadwick introduces Popper's distinction between logical probability and verisimilitude (p. 155).

In his chapter on '*Satisfaction or Optimisation?*', Chadwick then puts forward a 'rational incrementalism'. In so doing, he refers to *The Poverty of Historicism*. Apparently, its strictures against utopian engineering, and the argument for a piecemeal approach, leave him uneasy:

> '*There may be situations in which the existing state of affairs is very undesirable, small changes will not achieve desired goals, and scientific methods have not confirmed the probable consequences of large incremental changes; here any change, even the continuation of existing policies, is a risk, and calculated risk becomes the most rational action.*' (p. 319).

Now, whereas this might be taken as a criticism of Popper — similar to criticisms sometimes made against piecemeal social engineering, and disjointed incrementalism as well — as being conservative (e.g. Etzioni, 1968, p. 220), Chadwick continues by criticising utopianism in turn. It has '*... a place in the setting of goals for society ...*', but utopias '*... are not a substitute for rational methods ...*' (p. 320). Further down, he is even more cautious as regards the utopian tradition in planning, relegating civic design to '*... the realm of aesthetics and art-criticism and appreciation only, not as an* essential *part of town planning as a social decision process*' (p. 353), thereby referring to Popper's argument '*... against the Platonic politician who composes cities for (political) beauty's sake.*' (see Popper, 1966, Vol. I., p. 145). In his usual, undecided manner, he adds: '*The point, at least, is worth debating.*'[3]

A few years later, both Hart (1973, 1976) and Gillingwater (1975) adopt a view of the planning process based on Popper's notion of the way in which organisms solve problems (see: '*Of clouds and clocks*', in: Popper, 1972). In both, the elimination of error plays a central part. Also, like Chadwick, whilst taking a leaf out of Popper's book, they do not wholly emulate disjointed incrementalism:

> '*... it is possible to reject both the fluid approach implicit in disjointed incrementalism and the cast-iron approach symbolized by the unitary Master Plan, and assert that there is at least one other way ... The third logically possible mode of planning ... views iterative planning as a spiral which seeks to serially and reciprocally relate image to reality within the context of induced, anticipated and unexpected change. Plans are necessarily probabilistic from this viewpoint because they have limited actual control over their environments and also because they are chronically short of reliable information ...*" (Hart, 1976, p. 23).

Furthermore, both Hart and Gillingwater develop the theme of '*plastic controls*' in organisms. It seems that it has a great deal of affinity with Etzioni's ideas on types of control and decision-making (see Faludi, 1973, chapter 15). Finally, Gillingwater adds to these ideas by identifying what he terms '*the ideology of rational planning*', not with Popper's stance (which he describes as deductive-indeterminism), but with inductive-determinism, and thus positivism.

Camhis (1979) does the same using different terms. His claim is that verificationism and logical positivism have their equivalent in rational-comprehensive planning, and falsificationism in disjointed incrementalism. However he only succeeds in showing that Braybrooke and Lindblom (1963) view Popper's piecemeal engineering as a forerunner of their strategy of disjointed incrementalism which is of course true. But nowhere do the latter refer to falsificationism. Camhis seems to confuse fallibility of human knowledge generally with falsificationism as a rule for obtaining the most reliable universal statements about reality.

Although it seems plausible that this analogy between falsificationism and disjointed incrementalism should exist, these two concepts relate to different problems. Falsificationism concerns the methodological problem of how to distinguish between scientific and other statements, whereas disjointed incrementalism suggests how problem solvers or

---

[3] It seems surprising that Camhis (1979, p. 51) could still label Chadwick an utopian. Surely, he expresses enough doubts about utopianism to escape that verdict!

decision-makers should proceed, given their limitations: it does not concern this demarcation problem at all. As we shall try to demonstrate below, the 'rational model' (Gillingwater) which Camhis describes as rational-comprehensive planning (i.e., *all* alternatives must be considered in the light of *all* consequences) can usefully be interpreted as a demarcation-criterion analogous to the falsification-ist rule, but applied to decisions. As such, it is not incompatible with disjointed incrementalism.

Whilst developing an interesting argument about the need for philosophical analysis of planning (particularly noteworthy are the references to utilitarianism) and raising relevant questions about the methodological status of Faludis work, Taylor (1980) is quite conventional as to his appreciation of the importance of Popper. Of course, it is useful to point out that the Geddesian doctrine of '*Survey-Analysis-Plan*' represents a crudely positivistic view of scientific method. In his paper on the *Three paradigms of Planning* Faludi, (1982), describes this as the object-centred view of planning and points out that its positivistic stance is no accident. Geddes explicitly emulates Comte.[4] Also we agree whole-heartedly with the conclusion drawn:

> '... *that planners should* not *seek to gain knowledge by first doing surveys in the hope of discovering empirical proofs (as the method of "survey — analysis — plan" suggests), but rather they should begin by formulating their ideas and assumptions about the given problem situation ...*' (p. 168).

It is the implication which one must take exception to as being, at best, only metaphorically true. Taylor says that ideas and assumptions should be formulated '*in the form of testable hypotheses*' and subjected to tests by '*empirical surveys in an endeavour to show how false these hypotheses are*', observing finally that '*this method could also be adopted as a means of critically examining planning proposals themselves*'. The author certainly does not want to take issue with the critical method, but in criticising a planning proposal, one must resort to methods which are *entirely different* from those used in criticising and perhaps falsifying empirical hypotheses.

The same point arises when discussing the work of McConnell (1981). Like Taylor, McConnell identifies two areas of philosophical inquiry most relevant to planning: methodology of science, and ethics. As regards the former, he takes his measure from Popper, as regards the latter from Rawls (1971). Our main criticism of McConnell (as with Taylor and others before him) is that, in arguing that plans should be made testable, he is imprecise. At the outset, he begins with the quite unexceptional position that '... *even the most ethically and politically derived statements used in planning should be expressed in specific relationships to particular groups, locations and periods of time if they are to be meaningful*' (p. 22). One would not take exception to the following argument:

> '... *the statements on which planning is based have to be testable in some sense — that is, there must be criteria, social and practical, against which to compare performance with expectation*' (p. 23).

In the discussion which follows however, he slips into talking about plans, or policies, rather than the statements on which they are based, giving the reader the distinctive impression that they are the same as theories, at least as far as the need for 'testing' them is concerned. This is confirmed when McConnell discusses the tests applicable to plans or policies:

> '... *all conjectures relating to planning should be tested for* justice *and for* responsiveness; *and that action based on such theories be tested for* effectiveness ... *There is however a theoretically more fundamental and thus prior test,* falsifiability, *which is based on Popper's approach, as explained* ... *If planning statements are not specific in terms of what is meant or intended they will not be testable ... In short, unless a theoretical statement is expressed in such terms that it can be falsified, it is too imprecise to be classed as an acceptable theory.*' (pp. 54/55).

Now, it is quite wrong to identify planning statements with theoretical statements and to argue that both should be made falsifiable. Since McConnell draws on Popper, we must take 'theoretical statements' to mean hypothetical universal statements. It

---

[4] At the same time, the author emphatically denies that — as Taylor seems to think — his talking about developing a 'positive' theory of planning would imply the same stance. As an adjective to theory, 'positive' merely denotes the desire to explain planning as it is. Nothing is said about the method of arriving at such theories.

CRITICAL RATIONALISM AND PLANNING METHODOLOGY   269

is just because they are universal statements that they can be falsified, i.e. such statements rule out a whole range of singular statements. If one is forced then to accept any one of these as being true — provisionally, that is, because there is no eternal truth —, then the hypothesis is falsified. This is the only meaning that should be attached to falsification by anyone drawing on Popper. As will be argued below, it is thus quite inappropriate to talk about plans, planning statements and the like being falsified.

All planning statements are singular statements: site X ought to be developed in 1988 by building three-storey blocks of flats housing Y number of people etc. etc. The point is not that these statements should not be as specific as possible — which is all that McConnell really seems to argue — but that it is misleading to refer to them being rendered specific as making them falsifiable. As it stands, then there is nothing specifically Popperian in McConnell's approach to planning, although, to be sure, he gives useful accounts of Popper's methodology of science on the way. That is with the exception of one short reference to Popper's *'negative utilitarianism'* in a section devoted to *'Ethical theories'*. There, McConnell rightly observes that '... *there remains the unsurmountable problem of comparative assessments — of suffering in this case*' (p. 148). He seems to forget at this point that he himself (on p. 45) has already emulated the conclusion on this issue reached by Needham and Faludi (1973), i.e. that goals and problems '... *represent different sides of the same coin*'. This should have led him to reject the idea that *'negative utilitarianism'* is any different from the usual form of (positive) utilitarianism.

Friedmann (1977) is the only planning theorist so far to refer to a concept drawn from late-Popperian philosophy, i.e. that of knowledge forming a world of its own, *'World 3'*[5]. His vicious attack on it as supporting a bureaucratic and technocratic view of planning is quite unwarranted. Even if this link existed, it would be quite besides the point to introduce it as an objection to this concept. Popper's argument must be seen against the backcloth of the problems in the theory of knowledge which he attempts to solve. If knowledge is objective in Popper's sense, forming a world apart from material things (World 1) and subjective emotions (World 2),

then so be it. One cannot reject this view merely because it does not complement some of our predilections in the field of political philosophy.

In fact Friedmann's understanding of Popper's concept of objective knowledge seems rather limited. As will be seen below, Popper's meaning is that, as soon as we part with them, the products of our minds acquire an existence of their own. No pretense of them being objectively true is involved, as Friedmann seems to assume. Contrary to Friedmann's belief, Popper's World 3 does not only include scientific theories either, as we shall see below in the section devoted to discussing Popper's ideas.

This review of the links between the planning literature and Popper's work reveals an increasing tendency to rely more on his philosophy of science than on his political views, developed under the threat of Nazi Germany — though, of course, the two are closely related. The present author finds himself in agreement with this. To be sure, Popper's arguments against central planning remain powerful, especially where they refer to man's limited intellectual capacities. But the crux of the matter is that their main punch is directed against a naive and thus dangerous form of planning. Little can be gleaned from these arguments as to the methodology of a modest form of planning, the need for which Popper would probably accept.

Where Popper's philosophy of science, rather than his social philosophy, is concerned, the literature at best reveals a rather superficial acceptance of fairly general ideas like 'error-elimination'. At worst, terms with a technical meaning, like falsification, are applied inappropriately to plans and policy statements. Clearly, a more thorough examination is needed of what a Popperian approach to the formulation of planning methodology really involves. In the main body of argument of this paper, therefore, planning will be located in the context of policy-making where accountability of decisions is a first requirement. The same requirement also exists in science, and the original solution offered by critical rationalism to the problem of accountability in science will be introduced. A similar solution to the problem of accountability will be shown to exist for policy-making in the form of the well-known requirement that decisions should be rational.

---

[5] In the area of management science though, Majone (1980) has applied the same concept in a way very similar to the present author's ideas presented below.

Planning as decision-making

The various meanings of planning range from the central guidance of society via forecasting the future, to a technocratic mode of decision-making. Bringing order into these meanings is a task of its own (See Faludi, 1982). In this paper, the definition of planning starts and ends with decision-making. Urban development can be viewed as an on-going stream of decisions. Developers decide to acquire land: land owners decide to throw it onto the market; investors decide to provide capital, architects decide on the shape of buildings, and the authorities decide to grant subsidies and to give planning permissions. The authorities, too, have to make investment decisions: sewage and road works; schools, etc. Buyers and tenants decide to take up residence in new development, vacating some other development, and so on.

Decisions become a matter of policy when they are the subject of some form of public announcement. Then, and only then, can they be criticised *before* they have taken effect. In this way, decisions are drawn into the context of argument, and standards may be applied to them. Decisions that are up for public discussion require extra consideration. The ensuing argument may raise questions concerning the relations of the decisions in question with other decisions, past, present and possible. Does the public authority's decision to build some road works still allow it to fulfil its promise to build a swimming pool? Clearly, much calculation is needed before such questions can be answered, if, indeed, they *can* be answered, for many of them are surrounded by considerable *uncertainty*. Planning is simply the attempt to do this figuring in systematic fashion, and mostly results in some form of statement concerning the overall context within which policy decisions are being taken. A public authority is under an obligation to demonstrate that it has attended to these matters and knows what it is doing. Public authorities thus formulate and adopt budgets, land use plans and other documents from which their overall policy may be gleaned.

Sometimes, these announcements become the subject of critical argument, exactly as announcements of individual policy decisions can. The standards are no different, though the uncertainties will generally be greater. Issues about the overall direction of policy are simply more difficult to define, let alone to resolve. The temptation to escape into wishful thinking is great. This is a danger because, if planning has no tangible effects in terms of guidance given to day to day policy decisions, then it is not worth the paper plans are written on. This is why it is claimed that the starting and end points of planning are decisions. Planning arises out of the requirement of accountability of policy decisions, and it results in guidance given to policy decisions. Add to this, that planning itself also involves the taking of decisions, i.e. about the form of plans, and it will be appreciated that decisions are simply crucial to the view of planning advocated in this paper.

A Popperian approach to decision-making[6]

Since decisions are crucial to this view of planning, they should also form the central concern of planning methodology. As in the methodology of science, a demarcation problem exists: how to distinguish responsible statements from those which cannot be defended? As far as the empirical sciences are concerned, the answer seems simple: responsible scientific statements are those which correspond with the facts, which can thus be verified. Popper's solution to the demarcation problem is different. Hypotheses can never be verified, but we can formulate them in such a way as to maximise their chances of being falsified, i.e. as boldly and as precisely as possible. The reward for submitting hypotheses to cruel testing in the pursuit of this aim is that the remaining hypotheses, those which have as yet not been falsified, are rich in information and surprise.

This falsificationist principle rests on a view of human knowledge as being fallible, and thus always open to improvement. But it cannot solve our problem of providing a standard for *decisions*. It has been formulated with a view to quite a specific demarcation problem concerning lawlike (universal) statements in the empirical sciences. Decisions are not such statements, and therefore cannot be proved wrong in the same way as hypotheses can be falsified. Of course, decisions can *go* wrong by having

---

[6] This section and the next are based on the author's Amsterdam inaugural lecture (Faludi, 1978-a; for a short account in English, see Faludi, 1978-b).

consequences which are different from those anticipated. Even then, the decision as such cannot always be criticised. Unforeseen consequences could have been genuinely unforeseeable at the time of taking them. This is a fundamental difference as against hypotheses. Hypotheses are universal statements. They can therefore fail everywhere and at any time.

Decisions relate to specific actors and what they intend to do at specific times. Thus, they are singular statements and cannot be rejected on grounds that other actors decide differently.

Even when the same actor decides differently at another moment in time, this cannot always be said to falsify the first decision. Our actor may simply take a fresh decision based on a new perception of the situation. Perhaps his predilections have changed, or maybe he has obtained better information. The statement with which he announces the reversal of his original decision will thus in fact relay a new decision. This does not invalidate the original one, it revokes it. Decisions can therefore not be falsified in the same sense that hypotheses can, nor would one think of falsifying them after they have been taken.

The time to argue about decisions is *before* taking them. The demarcation problem concerning responsible decisions must be approached in quite a different way from that concerning statements in the empirical sciences. It is still legitimate, though, to search for a solution to this problem in the spirit of critical rationalism. Critical rationalists reach out beyond the philosophy of the empirical sciences. They have a view of human knowledge as being fallible, but hold the capacity of human beings to solve their problems in high regard, nevertheless. Above all, they advocate an attitude, not just to science, but to life generally. According to them, the unity of method extends beyond the empirical sciences to practical affairs.

Reading Popper helps little in solving our demarcation problem. He refers to decisions frequently, in particular in *The Open Society and its Enemies*, but he deals only with their ethical aspects. The acceptance or rejection of moral criteria or standards involves decisions, and practical decisions in urban policy-making and planning rest on many such standards. But more is involved. Think alone of a road proposal, where empirical knowledge is also involved. Apart from the fact that the form of a road proposal is different from a statement proposing a standard, a practical proposal is not simply a matter of pronouncing on what is to be considered as morally good or bad: it is also a question of relating general moral principles and available knowledge to a specific situation, resulting in a statement of what ought to be done there and then.

When discussing the reasons for accepting 'rationalism', Popper ultimately sees this as a matter of taking a moral decision, and then he proceeds to describe what the consequences are of opting for the alternative, i.e. irrationalism. From this it seems reasonable to assume that Popper would agree to the following:

(a) Not only moral, but practical decisions as well, should be taken with a view to their consequence;
(b) Where there are alternatives, their consequences also need to be taken into consideration.

Based on this, a decision rule can be formulated which one may surmise would have Popper's agreement. It says that practical decisions should be taken by evaluating the consequences of the alternatives that offer themselves to the decision maker. To be more precise, *all* consequences of *all* alternatives need to be considered. In this way, the chances of a decision being criticised, and possibly rejected, are maximised in the spirit of critical rationalism. After all, every time a real alternative is being advanced and/or real consequences of decisions are being pointed out, neither of which have been considered by the decision maker, the decision needs to be reconsidered.

Now, this rule is exactly what is described in the literature as the rational planning process, or some such designation. We find it in Simon's classic book on *Administrative Behavior* (Simon, 1976, 1st edition 1945). It is the object of criticism by Lindblom attacking it as the synoptic ideal. The present author, amongst others, has defended it (Faludi, 1973-a, -b), and conclude that rationalism does for decisions what the falsificationist principle does for empirical hypotheses: i.e., it provides a standard for distinguishing responsible statements from those which cannot be defended.

Note that this standard says nothing whatsoever about the effectiveness of decisions, about whether they meet the situation, whether they are realistic, etc. All these issues, though important, concern the formulation of alternatives and the identification of their consequences, not the way they need to be related to each other in arriving at a decision. One may also say that the application of the decision rule as outlined above presupposes a *definition of the decision situation*, and that many intriguing problems in decision-making and planning have to do with this definition of the decision situation, not with the rationality rule as such. It is this definition of the decision situation that we turn to in the light of Popperian philosophy.

The definition of the decision situations: three Popperian building blocks

Popper seems to offer three building blocks for the methodology of planning as regards the definition of the decision situation: situational analysis, critical dualism and the application of empirical laws in their technological form.

To give an account of a decision implies giving a description of the decision situation. The problem of giving such a description is similar to that of historians describing situations in the past. Over history Popper says the following:

> '... *undoubtedly there can be no history without a point of view; like the natural sciences, history must be selective unless it is to be choked by a flood of poor and unrelated material ...*
> *The way out of this difficulty is, I believe, consciously to introduce a* preconcieved *selective point of view into one's history; ... this does not mean that we may twist the facts until they fit into a framework of preconceived ideas, nor that we may neglect the fact that does not fit ... But it means that we need not worry about all those facts and aspects which have no bearing upon our point of view and which therefore do not interest us*'. (Popper, 1961, p. 150).

This form of analysis starting from an explicitly chosen point of view depending on the situation concerned Popper describes as a situational analysis. In his autobiography, he gives the following account:

> '*By a situational analysis I mean a certain kind of tentative explanation of human action which appeals to the situation in which the agent finds himself ... we can try ... to give an idealized reconstruction of the* problem situation *in which the agent found himself, and to that extent make the action "understandable" ... that is to say,* adequate to his situation as he saw it' (Popper's '*Intellectual Autobiography*', in: Schilpp, 1974, p. 179).

The argument also applies to decision makers. Without a selective point of view they obtain too much information. This is *the* shortcoming of doctrine of '*Survey — Analysis — Plan*'. The choice of a point of view must be made *in advance* of conducting research, instead of the other way round.

But how can we be sure that actions are adequate to the situation in which the actor finds himself, as Popper demands? In deciding upon this question, values as well as factual knowledge will play their part. Two further elements of critical rationalism recommend themselves as additional building blocks at this point.

Critical dualism comes down to the impossibility of deriving value-choices from factual information. The adjective critical points to the fact that this makes it easier to criticise factual as well as value statements. It is therefore certainly *not* Popper's intention to suggest that any odd value-statement would do, simply because it cannot be derived from factual statements. On the contrary, the possibility of criticising value-statements is one of the features of critical dualism. It builds on the analogy which Popper draws between empirical and value-statements on the one hand, on the relations which critical rationalists see between facts and values on the other. The analogy between empirical and value statements is based on the fact that, in both cases, a normative ideal exists which forms the basis of criticism:

> '... *both proposals and propositions are alike in that we can discuss them, criticize them, and come to some decision about them. Secondly, there is some kind of regulative idea about both. In the realm of facts it is the idea of correspondence between statements and propositions and the facts; that is to say, the idea of truth. In the realm of standards and proposals, the regulative idea may be described in many ways ..., for example by the term right or good.*' (Popper, 1966, p. 384–385).

As to criticising value-statements, various possibilities exist.

Value-statements can prove untenable in the light of changing factual information or in relationship with other value-statements. Think alone of changing conceptions or urban renewal which have been influenced, amongst others, by the awareness of the social consequences of large-scale demolition. Another possibility for criticism arises when new ethical ideas emerge which make current proposals, and the value positions on which they are based, seem rather doubtful. Think of the rise of the philosophy of no-growth.

Critical dualism is thus imbued with the awareness of the interwovenness of facts and values. But how does this inter-wovenness work? What conclusions can we draw from knowledge in the form of empirical laws? The essence of Popper's ideas on this is that laws *exclude* certain expectations. The negative formulation of empirical laws is described as their technological form. This is

> '... *expressed by sentences of the form: "You cannot achieve such and such result", or perhaps, "You cannot achieve such and such ends without such and such concomitant effects"'*. (Popper, 1961, p. 61).

In other words, empirical knowledge excludes certain decisions, but it can never indicate which decisions ought to be taken. Thus, knowledge indicates the limits of freedom within which decision makers can make their choices.

These are the building blocks for dealing with the definition of decision situations in a methodologically responsible way.

Can they be combined into a theory of decision-making which is both acceptable, methodologically speaking, and a useful guide to practical decision makers? One would like to think that this is so and that those working on strategic choice in the tradition of Friend and Jessop (1977, 1st edition: 1969) are actually groping towards it. Further work on the interpretation of strategic choice in the light of critical rationalism is needed before we can be sure though. Meanwhile, we may put the concept of a definition of the decision situation into the wider context of Popper's theory of knowledge.

The definition of the decision situation and Popper's theory of knowledge

In this final section, the concept of a definition of the decision situation will be interpreted in the light of Popper's theory of knowledge as developed during the last twenty years, in the hope that it might be fruitful for the further development of planning methodology.

The following considerations comprise a vain effort to eliminate the concept of a planning subject from planning methodology. The reason for attempting it has been the difficulty of finding examples in planning practise of agents planning and acting accordingly. Of course, it is easy to identify a formal planning subject. But who is the real planning subject? The council adopting a budget, the Minister issuing guidelines? We *know* that, behind these terms, complex processes hide, and that their results are often a far cry from a coherent plan of action.

Looking at planning in the real world, it therefore seems attractive to let go the idea of a planning subject. In this way, planning methodology might draw a little closer to the chaotic impression we have of planning practice. When talking about networks and reticulists, Friend, Power and Yewlett (1974) seem to be driven by similar thoughts.

Now, it is possible that an analogy might be drawn between Popper's theory of knowledge and planning methodology. At first glance, the existence of a knowing subject is as equally self-evident an assumption for any theory of knowledge as that of a planning subject is for planning methodology. Yet, in his essay on *Epistemology without a knowing subject*, Popper (1972) does away with it. Perhaps one could equally well think of planning as a collective enterprise, without there being a central focus. Clearly, Lindblom's *mutual adjustment* would thus be vindicated (Lindblom 1965).

In the *Foreword* of *Objective Knowledge* (1972) which also includes the aforementioned essay on *Epistemology without a knowing subject* — Popper writes as follows:

> '*The essays in this book break with a tradition that can be traced back to Aristotle — the tradition of the common sense theory of knowledge as a subjectivist blunder. This blunder has dominated Western philosophy. I have made an attempt to eradicate it, and to replace it by an objective theory of essentially conjectural knowledge.*'

This rests on two propositions, i.e. that knowledge is objective on the one hand and hypothetical on the other. Whilst the second reflects Popper's well-known anti-positivistic stance and results in his falsificationist methodology discussed above, it is with the first proposition that we are here concerned.

When describing knowledge as objective, Popper does not, of course, mean to say that it is true, certain, reliable. His fallibilism would not allow him to do so. Rather, his meaning is that, as soon as we have parted with them, the products of our thought acquire an existence of their own. The most extensive discussion of this is to be found in his joint book with Eccles (1977), *The Self and its Brain*. There we find the key to the concept of knowledge as having an existence of its own. In the chapter *'Materialism transcends itself'*, Popper asks the question as to when we would regard something as *'real'*. His answer is:

'... that the entities which we conjecture to be real should be able to exert a causal effect upon the prima facie real things; that is, upon material things of an ordinary size ...' (Popper and Eccles, 1977, p. 9).

This applies to concepts like atom, force, force-field, etc., These

'... may be described as highly abstract theoretical entities; yet as they interact in a direct or indirect way with ordinary things, we accept them as real ...' (op. cit., p. 10).

Of course, the hypothetical character of knowledge remains. Because of this, our view of what is real can change. For instance:

'... having learned about physical forces, events, and processes, we may discover that material things, especially solids, are to be interpreted as very special physical processes, in which molecular forces play a dominant role ...' (op. cit.).

It is in this sense that Popper says knowledge is real. To appreciate this, his concept of a *World 3* must be introduced.

'First, there is the physical world — the universe of physical entities — ...; this I will call "World 1". Second, there is the world of mental states; including states of consciousness and psychological dispositions and unconscious states; this I will call "World 2". But there is also a third such world, the world of the contents of thought, and, indeed, of the products of the human mind; this I will call "World 3" ...' (op. cit., p. 38).

As examples of World 3-objects, Popper names: stories, explanatory myths, tools, scientific theories (whether true or false ones), scientific problems, social institutions and works of art. Many of these exist in the form of material (World 1) objects. But what is significant is what these express. To this content, Popper ascribes an existence of its own, because it meets the criteria as formulated above:

'One of my main theses is that World 3-objects can be real ... not only in their World 1 materializations ... but also in their World 3-aspects. As World 3-objects, they may induce men to produce other World 3-objects and, thereby, to act on World 1; an interaction with World 1 — even indirect interaction — I regard as a decisive argument for calling a thing real' (op. cit., p. 40).

With the help of his worlds, Popper attacks a number of philosophical problems, the *'common sense theory of knowledge'* being one of them. Knowledge does not require the assumption of a knowing subject, as this theory — a 'subjectivist blunder' — says. Rather, knowledge is the product of a collective effort. This applies to scientific knowledge in particular. Think alone of the inter-subjective nature of this knowledge and the role of the community of scientists. It is with respect to scientific knowledge that the preconditions of refining knowledge — of attaining verisimilitude — are particularly good. What is meant is, of course, the falsificationist principle — which takes us back to the hypothetical character of knowledge. Popper therefore ascribes a prominent role to scientific knowledge as laid down in one or the other accessible form: books, articles, etc. — in World 3.

Turning to the relationship between Popper's theory of knowledge and the definition of the decision situation, the latter may now be firmly located in World 3. The reason is that such a definition will be expressed in a form accessible to others, otherwise no argument could develop about the decision in question. In this way, it acquires an existence of its own, similarily to any other product of our thought, once it is expressed. Also, a definition of a decision situation — being a relatively complex statement, consists of other World 3-objects: descriptions of possible courses of action in specific situations, together with their expected consequences. Descriptions are expressed in one or the other language: diagrams, scientific concepts, ordinary English, mathematical symbols, etc. For the sake of defining a decision situation, these building blocks must be ordered in such a way that an understanding is generated of the situation under consideration.

Now, to distinguish such a definition of a decision situation from Popper's all-embracing World 3, one might describe it as a problem-specific world 3.[7]

In his essay 'On the theory of the objective mind' (Popper, 1972, pp. 153–90) Popper relates his more recent theory of knowledge to his earlier concept of situational analysis in a way which is very similar to the one here proposed. He writes about the problem situation as a problem focussing relevant segments of World 3 on the explanation of specific situations. In this way he extends his concept of World 3 to include not only knowledge itself, but also its application.

But what about the planning subject, i.e. the concept it all started from? World 3 knows no knowing subject. In expressing our ideas in a form which is accessible to others, they become common property. Ideas, problems, theories, etc. belong to all of us. Also, everybody's thought-products are admitted to World 3. Does the same apply to the problem-specific World 3, i.e. to definitions of decision situations? If so, then we could truly eliminate the planning subject as a concept from planning methodology.

At first glance, the same degree of openness applies as is the case with World 3. But all things know an infinite number of aspects, and thus an infinite number of statements can be made about everything. Naturally, this also applies to decision situations. Thus, the potential offer of building blocks for the definition of any decision situation is infinite. On the other hand, nobody has the capacity to deal with more than a limited amount of information at once. This means that it is impossible ever to complete the job of defining even the simplest decision situation. Still, such a definition remains a precondition of making any considered choice at all. Of course, what it all comes down to is that decision makers, even where they have the disposal of the most advanced information systems, must be *selec-*

tive as regards the aspects of any decision situation they attend to. Therefore, the distinction between what is and what is not *relevant* is what distinguishes a problem-specific World 3 from Popper's all-embracing one. In that world there is no need for selectivity other than by discarding elements which have outlived their usefulness. (Even then, they seem to remain in Popper's World 3, forming a sort of sediment on which the living World 3-objects prosper. For the rest, all utterances about the real world form legitimate World 3-objects).

As against this, the construction of a problem-specific World 3 requires the application of criteria of *relevance*.

Now, relevance points at what we were seeking to eliminate from planning methodology. Criteria of relevance cannot be formulated *in general*. Something is always relevant to *somebody*, and not to others. *This somebody is the planning subject*. Just because planning is concerned with what to do in *specific* situations, *the existence of a planning subject forms a necessary assumption in planning*.

This does not change the fact that planning practice shows little resemblance with decision-making by an agent who knows his mind and acts accordingly. Planning in practice often reminds us more of an uncontrolled stream of events with many participants, each pursuing his own ends. Nobody seems to be in command. But then, the planning subject need not be something tangible. It is a construct of our mind, and a necessary one at that. Every time we chose to look at two or more decision areas in relation to each other, we cannot but think about them *as if* they concerned one and the same subject. This is so because to think in this way is exactly what we mean by looking at them in relation to each other. By the same token, to look at several decisions as if they concerned one and the same subject can have *no other* meaning than to attend to their inter-relations. There is no other interpretation conceivable for any form of integrated policy making.

The assumption of a planning subject becomes particularly important when attending to what it means to understand a plan. It seems useful to attend to Popper's views on the way we grasp World 3-objects. In his view, the contact with the material

---

[7] Majone (1980, p. 158) refers to it as the 'policy space', i.e. 'a subset of Popper's World 3'.

manifestation of a World 3-object is far less important than the mental process of reconstructing it:

> '*According to my view, we may understand the grasping of a World 3-object as an active process. We have to explain it as the making, the re-creation, of that object. In order to understand a difficult Latin sentence, we have to construe it: to see how it is made, and to re-make it. In order to understand a problem, we have to try at least some of the more obvious solutions, and to discover that they fail; then we discover that there is a difficulty — a problem. In order to understand a theory, we have first to understand the problem which the theory was designed to solve, ...*
>
> *... In all these cases the understanding becomes "intuitive" when we have acquired the feeling that we can do the work of reconstruction at will, at any time*' (Popper and Eccles, 1977, p. 44).

Now, how can we reconstruct a definition of a decision situation, i.e. the World 3-object we are here concerned with? Only by assuming that there is a planning subject, and by looking at the situation through his presumed eyes! Another way does not seem to exist.

The author would like to think that this is a fruitful line of inquiry. In any case, the considerations above demonstrate what it means to give others insight into a decision situation — which is a precondition, like nothing else, of democractic procedures. It means to give them the opportunity to reconstruct that decision situation for themselves. It also shows what democratic procedures demand of politicians and the participating members of the public: the mental effort to do the reconstruction job, and to do it *well* from the point of view of the assumed planning subject. Of course, this does not mean that they have to accept that point of view. Indeed, nothing at all is said about which point of view should prevail, about who and what the planning subject should be. The purpose of this argument has only been to show that its introduction as a theoretical construct is necessary, every time we think about, talk about, and strive for any kind of planned action.[8]

Where does this leave planning practice in all its disorderliness? Do coalitions not split up frequently?

How often does it happen that a carefully built consensus breaks down when it comes to the crunch during implementation? But, from a methodological point of view, there is no problem. The unstructured stream of events simply has the upper hand. To be sure, individual actors may still plan for their own ends. They define *their* decision situations against the backcloth of their appreciation of this ongoing stream of events.

Why, then, does this image of an ongoing stream of events worry us at all? The reason is twofold. Firstly, we wrongly think that methodological assumptions, like that of the existence of a planning subject, must somehow meet the test of reality. When we then find that no such thing as a planning subject exists in fact, we are inclined to think that the concept is useless, or somehow based on the wrong analysis. But we can also draw another conclusion which is equally plausible, i.e. that there is very little planning in practice, simply *because* there are no planning subjects endowed with the capacity (cognitive as well as political) to plan. In this way, the concept of a planning subject becomes a criterion against which to measure practice, instead of practice becoming the criterion against which to measure the value of methodological concepts.

Another reason why the unstructured stream of events forms a source of disquiet is perhaps the following:- Maybe we can discover some actors here and there who show some capacity to plan and act accordingly, but it is only under very restricted circumstances that we can conceive of *societal action* as such as being planned? However, this is what we often understand planning to be. Seen in this light, it is a condition of planning that somebody (the state, the government, the leader, the party, etc.) should have on overview, should guide and plan. It is this assumption which makes us think that there is something wrong when we cannot discover any over-arching planning, nor the concommitant planning subject for that matter.

But nowhere did we make the assumption that the planning subject must be of this kind. We only refer to a planning subject where, in actual fact, planning in the sense of some coordinated attack on a number of inter-related decisions takes place.

---

[8] Low (forthcoming) puts personal construct theory forward as a way of understanding current planning practice. There is some affinity with the approach taken in this paper.

The effort to eliminate the planning subject from planning methodology has thus failed. It seems perfectly consistent with a Popperian point of view to retain it in the sense of the argument above: every effort at planning implies a definition of the decision situation from the point of view of the subject concerned. This definition may be seen as a problem-specific World 3. To the extent that planning as an activity means constructing such a world, we may also say that planning is the manipulation of World 3-objects, or symbols. It also results in new World 3-objects being formulated: rules, programmes, statements of intent, maps, etc., etc. That it should ultimately have an effect on the material world (World 1), *via* the operational decisions which are taken on the basis of plans is the point from which we have started.

Concluding comments

Popper's contribution to the classic planning debate, though significant, does not exhaust the importance of his philosophy for planning methodology. His theory of scientific method and theory of knowledge may prove more important. However, no ready-made Popperian planning methodology exists as yet. Clearly, there is some way to go before one can be developed. Once it exists, it may prove to have more antecedents than Popper alone. Lately, analytical philosophy has been paying attention to the theory of action. Planning being a form of action, this may prove another fruitful lead to follow. But will the results be any different? Popper is often identified with logical positivism and the Vienna Circle. He himself denies this and talks about a 'Popper-legend' (see Popper's *Replies to my critics*, in: Schilpp, 1974). But the points of difference concern problems which are central to the philosophy of the empirical sciences. Would a critical-rationalist differ from a logical-positivist as regards planning methodology?

It is our view that this is not so. Although in its early days, the Vienna Circle dismissed value judgements as meaningless, according to Kraft's authoritative history, this position quickly changed (Kraft, 1953). Next to Schlick, it was Kraft himself who concerned himself prominently with the problems of values. His views do not conflict in any obvious way with critical rationalism nor is there any obvious conflict with Simon's views as developed in his seminal *Administrative Behavior* (1976), his emulation of logical positivism notwithstanding.

Clearly, rooting planning methodology in the philosophy of science would require careful study of more than one school of thought. Perhaps the planning methodologist would then find that he need not get involved in all the disputes between the different camps simply because there is consensus as regards the issues which interest him most.

References

BRAYBOOKE, D. and LINDBLOM, C. E. (1963) *A Strategy of Decision*, The Free Press of Glencoe, Glencoe, Ill.

CHADWICK, G. (1978) *A Systems View of Planning*, Pergamon Oxford.

CAMHIS, M. (1979) *Planning Theory and Philosophy*, Tavistock, London.

ETZIONI, A. (1968) *The Active Society*, The Free Press, New York.

FALUDI, A. (1971) Problems with 'problem-solving', *Journal of the Royal Town Planning Institute*, vol. 57, p. 415.

FALUDI, A. (1973-a) *A Reader in Planning Theory*, Pergamon, Oxford.

FALUDI, A. (1973-b) *Planning Theory*, Pergamon, Oxford.

FALUDI, A. (1978-a) *Planologie en wetenschapsbeoefening* (inaugural lecture) published as a special issue of *Rooilijn*, a monthly journal of the Institute of Planning and Demography of the University of Amsterdam.

FALUDI, A. (1978-b) Beyond 'Planning Theory', *Werkstukken van het Planologisch en Demografisch Instituut*, no. 8, University of Amsterdam.

FALUDI, A. (1982) Three paradigms of planning theory, in: HEALEY, P. *et. al.* (eds.) *Planning Theory — Prospects for the 1980's.* Pergamon, Oxford.

FRIEDMANN, J. (1977) *The Epistemology of Social Practice: A Critique of Objective Knowledge*, mimeo published by the School of Architecture and Urban Planning of the University of California at Los Angeles; see also *Theory and Society*, vol. 6, pp. 75–92.

FRIEND, J. K., and JESSOP, W. N. (1977) *Local Government and Strategic Choice*, Pergamon, Oxford.

FRIEND, J. K., POWER, J., and YEWLETT, C. J. L. (1974) *Public Planning: the Inter-corporate Dimension*, Tavistock, London.

GILLINGWATER, D. (1975) *Regional Planning and Social Change*, Saxon House, Westmead, Farnborough, Hants.

HART, D. A. (1973) Ordering change and changing order, *Policy and Politics*, vol. 2, pp. 24–41.

HART, D. A. (1976) *Strategic Planning in London*, Pergamon, Oxford.

HAYEK, F. A. (1962) *The Road to Serfdom*, Routledge & Kegan Paul, London.

KOERTGE, N. (1979) The methodological status of Popper's rationality principle, *Theory and Decision*, vol. 10, pp. 83–95.

KRAFT, V. (1953) *The Vienna Circle*, Greenwood Press, New York.

LINDBLOM, C. E. (1965) *The Intelligence of Democracy*, The Free Press, New York.

LIPPMANN, W. (1937) *The Good Society*, Little, Brown and Co., Boston.

LOS, N. (1981) Some reflexions on epistemology, design and planning theory, in: DEAR, M., and SCOTT, A. J. (ed.) *Urbanism* and Urban Planning in Capitalist Society, Methuen, London and New York, pp. 63 88.

Low, N. (forthcoming) Beyond general systems theory — A constructivist perspective, *Urban Studies*.

Magee, B. (1973) *Popper*, Fontana, London.

Majone, G. (1980) Policies as Theories, *Omega*, vol. 8, pp. 151-162.

Mannheim, K. (1940) *Man and Society in an Age of Reconstruction*, Kegan Paul, London.

McConnell, S. (1981) *Theories for Planning*, Heinemann, London.

Meyerson, M., and Banfield, E. D. (1955) *Politics, Planning and the Public Interest*, The Free Press of Glencoe, Glencoe, Ill.

Moewes, W. (1980) *Grundfragen der Lebensraumgestaltung*, De Gruyter, Berlin/New York.

Needham, B. (1971) Planning as problem-solving, *Journal of the Royal Town Planning Institute*, vol. 57, pp. 317 319.

Needham, B., and Faludi, A. (1973) Planning and the public interest, *Journal of the Royal Town Planning Institute*, vol. 57, pp. 317-319.

Popper, K. (1961) *The Poverty of Historicism*, Routledge and Kegan Paul, London.

Popper, K. (1966, 1st ed. 1945) *The Open Society and its Enemies* (2 volumes), Routledge and Kegan Paul, London.

Popper, K. (1972) *Objective knowledge*, Oxford University Press, London.

Popper, K., and Eccles, J. (1977) *The Self and its Brain*, Springer, New York.

Rawls, J. (1971) *A Theory of Justice*, Havard University Press, Cambridge, Mass.

Reade, E. (1976) The content of 'theory' courses in planning education, in: *The Content of the Planning Theory Course*, Working Paper No. 25, Department of Town Planning, Oxford Polytechnic, Oxford.

Schilpp, P. A. (ed.) (1974) *The Philosophy of Karl Popper*, (2 volumes) The Open Court, La Salle, Ill.

Scott, A. J. and Roweis, S. T. (1977) Urban planning in theory and practice, *Environment and Planning A*, vol. 9, pp. 1097-1119.

Simon, H. A. (1976, 1st ed. 1945) *Administrative Behavior*, The Free Press, New York.

Taylor, N. (1980) *Planning theory and the philosophy of planning*, *Urban Studies*, vol. 17, pp. 159-172.

[8]

Knowledge and Action:

A Guide to Planning Theory

John Friedmann and Barclay Hudson

In a recent survey of planning theory courses taught in American universities, Henry C. Hightower distinguished "between theories of the planning process—procedural theories—and theories concerning phenomena with which planning is concerned" (1969:326). The present paper is an attempt to provide a guide to the literature of planning theory primarily in terms of Hightower's first meaning. In view of widespread skepticism about the possibilities of a general theory of planning, however, something more than a review article is intended. In the following pages, we should like to trace the contours and structure of planning theory as a distinctive field of study. This is intended as a frame of reference for students and practitioners alike. For a profound understanding of the major theories about planning should also lead to more effective practice.

The essential informtion we intend to convey is summarized in Table 1 and the bibliography. Our purpose in the text is to provide a brief commentary for this table. Although the principal works are generally known, few planners are likely to be familiar with all of the literature cited. In no sense, however, is the commentary intended to serve as a substitute for reading the books themselves. All we can hope to do is to characterize the major traditions of theoretical inquiry and point to some of the important cross-influences that have been at work.

We have resisted the temptation to extend the bibliography in several directions. First, our list is limited to key works in the field, with primary attention to books rather than journal articles. The sources selected for inclusion were generally those written by the inventors of significant concepts, or by those providing the fullest treatment of a particular theme. Second, we have omitted many earlier works which laid the foundations of social theory upon which later authors built their own ideas in planning. Finally, the paper focuses on planning theory as presently taught in American universities. We ourselves feel that graduate schools could go a great deal further in considering traditions of planning that have evolved under other ideologies, in other countries, and in other times. Here one might include both centralized and decentralized forms of socialism, pre- and post-industrial societies, and ideologically distinct movements within our own country, ranging from Shaker and Owenite communities to black separatism or Consciousness III. Many of these alternative traditions and experimental societies throw into relief the interrelations between the more conventionally separated categories of planning that this paper deals with. Because such movements tend to lie outside the mainstream of planning theory in this country, however, they are not included in our list of sources.

Before proceeding further, it will be necessary to define the subject matter of planning theory. A definition of planning will have to be devised that will be sufficiently broad to encompass the entire spectrum of published writings. A useful way to look at planning is to consider it as an activity centrally concerned with *the linkage between knowledge and organized action*. As a professional activity and as a social process, planning is therefore located precisely at the interface between knowledge and action. In one way

John Friedmann is head of the Planning Department, School of Architecture and Urban Planning, University of California, Los Angeles.

Barclay Hudson is assistant professor of urban planning, School of Architecture and Urban Planning, University of California, Los Angeles.

or another, the various theories of planning deal with this relationship, but we can distinguish at least four different intellectual traditions that grapple with this problem. One is the tradition of *philosophical synthesis*. Another approaches planning in terms of a *rationalistic* focus on decision-making in regard to specific social choices. A third stream involves a blend of empirical and normative analysis dealing with *organization development*. Finally, there is a tradition of *empiricism* concerned with studies of national and urban planning processes.

The choice of categories for these traditions was largely dictated by patterns of cross-referencing within each field. The compartmentalization is by no means watertight; nevertheless, where major works have succeeded in spanning more than one category, these seem to have been extraordinary rather than usual events, enough, at any rate, to justify the classification used in this paper.

Of all the categories, the tradition of philosophical synthesis is perhaps the least clearly defined. One of its characteristics is its interdisciplinary nature; this may account for its tendency to pose the issue of conflict between individual and societal perspectives on planning problems. More fundamentally, this tradition is distinguished by two other features: first, its concern with the larger historical context to which planning responds and, second, its normative, prescriptive concerns and its tendency to assume explicit value positions—qualities that set it off from most contemporary schools of historical study and from the mainstream of the social sciences as well. We will return to this question of combining historical with normative viewpoints at the conclusion of the paper.

THE MAJOR TRADITIONS

Table 1 is arranged to highlight the major traditions of planning theory.

Philosophical Syntheses

Here we have included all contributions which, while standing outside any of the major traditions of research, have nevertheless had (or promise to have) decisive influence on our thinking about planning. All of the authors listed have in considerable measure gone beyond the boundaries of their own discipline (sociology, economics, philosophy, political science, social psychology, and planning), reaching into whatever areas of knowledge seemed to be necessary for achieving an integrated view of planning as a social process.

The Tradition of Rationalism

This school of planning theory is predominantly concerned with how decisions can be made more rationally. Until recently, this was acknowledged to be the leading tradition, to the point where planning came to be identified almost exclusively with decisionmaking. The model of man underlying this theory is that of a utility-maximizing being, whose relations to other men are defined in purely instrumental terms.

A decision (usually about the proper allocation of resources) will be called rational when it arrives at a single "best" answer to a stated problem. Decision theory is, therefore, attempting to state the rules of logic and practice, which can lead us to an optimal solution to a problem. More recently, rationalists have pushed their thinking beyond decision theory into "policy science," a field of expert analysis where new social technologies are applied to problems of strategic decision in the central guidance of social systems.

The Tradition of Organization Development

This field of studies, now well into its second decade, is primarily focussed on ways to achieve desired changes in organizational structure and behavior. Rooted in psychology and the sociology of organizations, it has worked to elaborate a framework of analysis and action that would lead both to a closer fit between the structure of organizations and their environment and to working relations *within* organizations that maximize human potentialities and satisfactions. "Organization development," writes Warren Bennis, "is a response to change, a complex educational strategy intended to change the beliefs, attitudes, values, and structure of organizations so that they can better adapt to new technologies, markets, and challenges, and the dizzying rate of change itself" (Bennis, 1969:2). Human and organization development are thus seen as coterminous. The emphasis in planned organizational change implies a central preoccupation with innovation, the role of "change agents," and the web of interpersonal relationships of which organizations are constructed.

In contrast with the rationalist tradition of decision theory and policy science, organization development is experimental in its methods, and the development of the relevant theory is more the result of experiential learning than of logical deduction. In addition, theories of organization development are concerned with change-producing behavior. Decision theory, on the other hand, is exclusively preoccupied with the question of rational calculation. The implementation of decisions is not in itself considered a problem; it is rather assumed to follow automatically from the act of decision.

The Tradition of Empiricism

The focus here is on the functioning of large-scale political and economic systems. Far less normative than the other traditions, its emphasis has been on the measurement of system behavior as it actually exists. Decision variables are considered in the context of fairly rigid theoretical models. The notion of planned social change has little place in this tradition, which seeks a more positivistic framework for its analysis. Two mainstreams converge upon this tradition, one with its source in national planning efforts (generally in other countries), the other stemming from the study of urban politics in the United States.

1. *Studies of National Planning.*

This subject has been the province chiefly of economists, economic development specialists, and political scientists. The first empirical studies of national planning were made in the immediate postwar era (1947–1950) when the question of planning for peacetime reconstruction was openly

Table 1   *A Synoptic Guide to Major Traditions in Planning Theory*

	Philosophical Synthesis	Rationalism Systems Theory	Organization Development	Empiricism	
				Studies of National Planning	Studies of Urban Planning
1935	Karl Mannheim (planning as social reconstruction)		Chester Barnard		
	The Great Debate: F. v. Hayek and { Barbara Wootton { Karl Popper		Hawthorne Studies		
1945			Kurt Lewin		
		Decision Making		Oliver Franks	
		Herbert Simon		{ Bela Gold { Philip Selznik	
1950	Robert Dahl and Charles Lindblom (economizing and control as social processes)	Kenneth Arrow Jan Tinbergen		{ Ely Devons { Herman Somers	
1955					Martin Meyerson and Edward Banfield
			Ronald Lippitt Jeanne Watson, and Bruce Westley		
		James March and Herbert Simon			
1960		George Miller, Eugene Galanter, and Karl Pribam	W. Bennis, K. Benne, and R. Chin (eds)		{ Edward Banfield { W. H. Brown and { C. E. Gilbert
			Chris Argyris	P. J. D. Wiles { Everett Hagen { Albert Hirschman	
		Jan Tinbergen		Aaron Wildavsky	

debated, especially in Europe. Following a barren interlude of about thirteen years, a second phase of research began, this time centering on the problem of planning for economic development, with special emphasis on planning in the newly industrializing countries. Whereas in the earlier phase, theorists asserted the legitimacy of planning against critics who felt it to be a threat to the open market economy, central planning had come to be widely accepted as a necessity in Phase II of the research. The focus, therefore, shifted to a dispassionate analysis of the ways central planning worked (or did not work) in its own terms. Although the object of this phase was to deepen our understanding of developmental planning and to suggest how it might be improved, the major thrust of the research continued to be empirical.

2. *Studies of Urban Planning.*

Empirical work in urban planning, primarily in the United States, began in the mid-fifties with an analysis of public housing programs in Chicago (Meyerson and Banfield, 1955). This genre of studies came to be dominated by Edward Banfield who, together with others, helped to create the new research field of urban politics. Since planning was only one aspect of urban politics, however, relatively few empirical studies concentrated exclusively on this aspect. In general, empirical studies of urban planning used the model of rational decisionmaking as the appropriate standard against which to measure the performance of planning-in-practice. The approach was strictly behavioristic, and the tendency was to consider existing behavior (once it had been properly explained) as the "best possible" behavior. Existing behavior, because it could be "explained," was thus regarded as a "rational" adaptation to environmental circumstances. Very little effort went into questions of prescription. Politics was thought to be preemptive as a method for arriving at decisions, and the widely evident "failures" of city planning in the United States were interpreted as the result of a misplaced belief in the possibilities of rational calculation.

Table 1 *Continued*

	Philosophical Synthesis	Rationalism Systems Theory	Organization Development	Empiricism	
				Studies of National Planning	Studies of Urban Planning
1965					
		Charles Lindblom	Chris Argyris	{ Bertram Gross	Alan Altshuler
		Policy Science		{ John Friedmann	
		{ Olaf Helmer	Warren Bennis	{ Albert Waterston	
		{ R. Bauer (ed)	Paul Lawrence and	B. Akzin and Y. Dror	
	Amitai Etzioni	David Novick (ed)	Jay Lorsch	{ Bertram Gross	
	(planning as	{ R. Bauer and		{	James Wilson
	societal guidance)	{ K. Gergen (eds)	Rensis Likert	{	
		{ C. W. Churchman	{ Garth Jones	{ Albert Hirschman	Francine Rabinovitz
		Erich Jantsch (ed)	{ Edgar Schein	Stephen Cohen	Stephan Thernstrom
1970					
	The New Humanism				
	Charles Hampden-Turner (psycho-social development)			Guy Beneviste	
	{ Edgar Dunn (experi-mental evolution)	{ Harold D. Lasswell			Robert Fried
	{ Donald Schon (learning systems)	{ Yehezkel Dror		Mike Faber and	
	John Friedmann (transactive planning)	{ C. W. Churchman		Dudley Seers (eds)	

Note: authors in brackets published in the same year.

SCOPE OF THE REVIEW: LEADING CONTEMPORARY IDEAS

The rest of this article will trace each of these mainstreams of planning theory in greater detail. A final section will review some emerging trends, emphasizing what we perceive to be a dominant pattern of cross-fertilization and synthesis among the traditions which have been separated in the past by disciplinary boundaries or the overwhelming influence of particular individuals who pioneered their separate lines of inquiry in each area.

Table 1 begins with the 1930s. This was a period in history which generated special concern with planning theory and laid the professional and scholarly foundations of the planning field as taught in American universities. The history of man's endeavor to relate knowledge and action, however, goes back much farther than our own century. The scope of this article is confined to modern planning thought, but a more complete historical review of the relation between knowledge and action would go back as far as the Roman absorption of Greek and Middle Eastern culture and subsequent achievements in government, law, administration, and public works. Indeed, systematic theory of the relation between knowledge and action stems from the beginnings of urban civilization when a priesthood schooled in magical and scientific knowledge of the cosmic order and residing in monumental ceremonial centers sought to mediate between heaven and earth by extending heaven's mandate into the affairs of men (Wheatley, 1971). The scope of this article, however, is infinitely more modest. We deal here with modern theorists only, with their somewhat greater preoccupa-

tion with scientific inquiry and twentieth century notions of society in continual tension and flux. Even within this scope, however, we shall have to be exasperatingly brief, attempting no more than to provide a *Guide Michelin* to the highpoints of the intellectual landscape of contemporary planning.

THE TRADITION OF PHILOSOPHICAL SYNTHESIS

As a quick look at Table 1 will show, all but one of the major contributions to planning theory coincided with or immediately followed upon major periods of social crisis and upheaval. Karl Mannheim (1935) wrote his major book in the depths of the Great Depression and as a personally courageous, if desperate, response to the totalitarian systems of Stalinism and Fascism that had spread to much of Europe and Asia and were soon to draw the rest of the world into an agonizing and self-destructive conflict. The Great Debate (von Hayek, 1944; Wootton, 1945; Popper, 1945) commenced shortly before the war ended: the confrontation centered on the issue of freedom—whether planning enhanced freedom by clarifying real options and obstacles to social action; or whether planners, frustrated by their limited effectiveness in a free market economy, would be driven to seek increasingly coercive powers to intervene in social processes, with ever tighter constraints on individual behavior. Etzioni's major contribution (1968) was published at a time when America saw itself in the throes of a "cultural revolution" marked by a crisis of engagement in an unpopular war in Indochina and violence within the previously hallowed university community. Although the symptoms of unrest were soon to disappear, the experience of the sixties had left a deep imprint on a number of writers. Working in a time of great uncertainty and introspection, these authors (Hampden-Turner, 1970; Dunn, 1971; Schon, 1971; Friedmann, 1973) endeavored to refocus planning on a central concern with humanistic values in which existential knowledge, the life of dialogue, and self-actualizing groups would become bearers of regenerative forces in society. Only Dahl and Lindblom (1953), whose major work had appeared two decades earlier, addressed the question of planning during a period of relative quiescence.

Each of these crises—creeping totalitarianism, war and reconstruction, the collapse of a traditional normative order—posed anew and with great urgency the question of how "reason" might gain ascendancy over the insentient forces that seemed increasingly to dominate the institutions of Western society. Each crisis called forth a small number of thinkers who, trusting in the self-transcending powers of a disciplined imagination, endeavored to chart a new direction for societal guidance and planning. The metaphor which seemed most felicitous to them was that of society as a self-organizing or learning system (Von Foerster and Zopf, 1962). Accordingly, man's future would no longer be the chance result of social turbulence, nor directed by an all-powerful presidium of central technocrats. Rather it would be dispersed throughout the social system in a loosely articulated network of active learning groups.

It was Karl Mannheim who invented the idea of democratic social planning in this sense. He regarded planning as the culminating stage in an historical evolutionary process which had been preceded by the stages of chance discovery and invention. In Mannheim's view, planning appeared primarily as a way of thinking: the problem of planning therefore revolved around the possibility of comprehensive social knowledge. Mannheim attributed the contemporary crisis of bourgeois society to "perspectivist" thinking that reflected the thought patterns of groups locked into particular niches of the social order. The inherent conflict among such partial views of reality would be overcome, he believed, by applying the "relational" thinking of a small minority of uprooted intellectuals who had somehow escaped the confining visions of prevailing ideologies and were thus free to project utopian futures for society.

Mannheim distinguished between two forms of rationality: functional rationality related means to given ends, while substantial rationality dealt with the appropriate ends themselves, by inquiry into the structural relations of a social system.

Toward the end of World War II, the question of planning for peace-time reconstruction and economic stability and growth was raised in the form of immediate political options. The trauma of massive unemployment was still fresh in the mind, and the experience of the war had shown that central allocative planning was compatible with democratic freedoms. On the other hand, those who had thought most deeply about the meaning of the market economy were not only skeptical about the possibilities of replacing the allocative mechanisms of the market by central decisions, but were fearful that planning would lead—as indeed it had done in the Soviet Union—to the massive enslavement of the population. Two Austrian philosophers, Friedrich von Hayek and Karl Popper, both of whom resided in England at the time, wrote brilliantly in defense of what they called an open society. Their challenger was Barbara Wootton, an English economist, who saw in planning a way for enlarging the scope of human freedoms. The arguments were not conclusive, but had succeeded in focussing on two persisting issues in planning theory, rationality and freedom, and on the extent of their compatibility. Proponents of planning, such as Wootton and Mannheim, believed in the powers of reason to comprehend social reality and guide it towards an enhancement of the human spirit. Von Hayek and Popper, on the other hand, with far less trust in the capacities of the mind to determine the nature of the public good, feared the urge to fit human conduct to a single normative scheme.

These two opposing philosophies rested on different assumptions about man's nature. The planners understood man as essentially a social creature and society as an organic entity whose welfare could not be logically derived from an addition of individual wants; the antiplanners were atomistic in their interpretation of social meanings. In their opinion, man was essentially a self-determined creature whose social representations, in Emile Durkheim's sense, were simply the additive beliefs of individuals consulted in a public opinion poll. Eventually, these conflicting views came to rest on operational issues: how to define aggregate welfare in the context of real social choices and how to act on those choices through planning controls or other guides to social behavior.

Rational calculation and control was the dual theme of the important book by Robert Dahl and Charles Lindblom (1953). Two of America's leading social scientists, they wrote what is probably still the most complete analysis of the ways by which men arrive at choices and carry these choices into action. In comparison to their predecessors who had dealt with these themes at a highly abstract level, Dahl and Lindblom regarded rational choice and control as social processes. This permitted them to examine the several methods by which rationality is exercised in the achievement of collective purposes. This approach had the virtue of defusing the ideological conflict about planning as "the road to serfdom," and opened the way to a discussion of the unique "mix" of decision and control processes suitable to given circumstances. Being much influenced by behaviorist and economic thinking, Dahl and Lindblom revealed a strong personal preference for decisions at the margin (incrementalism) and "invisible" field controls whose effectiveness depended on their ability to constrain (and provide incentives for) individual choices.

The next major contribution was by Amitai Etzioni, an Israeli sociologist teaching during the late sixties at Columbia University. Etzioni had already earned the esteem of his colleagues for his earlier work on organization theory. His book *The Active Society* (1968) introduced him to a much wider audience and projected his voice into the forum of public discussion.

Etzioni's work is only tangentially related to planning in any of the more traditional senses. He dealt with planning as part of a broader concern with processes of societal guidance. In keeping with Herbert Simon's meaning (Simon, 1947), Etzioni defined planning as rational decisionmaking.

But more like Mannheim, he dealt with the linking of knowledge and action as components in a larger context of social system behavior, raising other central themes besides rational calculation and control. Specifically, he pointed to social alienation—or the lack of individual commitment to social purposes—as an ultimate source of social crisis. His prescription for the "sickness" of alienation was social mobilization or the formation of a group consensus around important social tasks. The greater this consensus, he argued, the less explicit, repugnant, and alienating would be the form of controls that are needed. This scheme permitted him to classify societies as follows (Etzioni, 1969):

		Controls	
		strong	weak
Consensus	high	active (example: Israel)	drifting (example: USA)
	low	over-managed (example: USSR)	passive (example: Paraguay)

Drifting and overmanaged societies he saw as being associated with relatively high levels of social alienation; only active and passive societies ranked low on this critical variable but, whereas passive societies were resigned to accept the existing state of affairs, active societies displayed both a desire and a capacity for goal attainment. Furthermore, in an active society, power needed for social control was seen to take the form of normative guides, whereas power followed a utilitarian calculus in a drifting society, became coercive in an overmanaged society, and superfluous in a passive society.

A large part of Etzioni's exposition was spent on an analysis of power and social knowledge. He defined the process of "societal guidance" in terms of the combination of downward control, or the uses of central power to overcome resistance, and upward consensus formation, or conflict resolution through an improved knowledge of societal conditions.

However breathtaking his theory as an intellectual tour de force, it nevertheless remains a curiously ambiguous statement. Despite its striking similarity to the historical experience of Israel, Etzioni's model of the active society, with its special emphasis on uses of normative power, is admittedly a utopian construct. Seeing societal guidance as a way of defining and achieving social purposes, he emphasized the importance of knowledge about the environment and about the internal states of the social system. Etzioni therefore foreshadowed the fuller discussion of a learning society which arises in the writings of subsequent authors. At the same time, however, the concept of an active society leads inescapably to the prescription of coalescing sufficient power to implement ideas. The book was addressed to the "drifting" society of America, and explored the possibilities for social mobilization and a prevalence of normative power, yet the more likely alternative, seen by Etzioni himself, was a movement in the direction of an "overmanaged" society in which a low level of social consensus would be balanced by an excessive use of coercive power. With Etzioni, a macroapproach to societal guidance seemed to have reached an impasse in dealing with contemporary social issues. Clearly, a new attack on the problem of linking knowledge with action was in order.

As if by design, a radical shift in the paradigm for planning occurred soon afterward.[1] The sixties, which through its counterculture movement, had sought to express a new humanism had also given rise to the notion of a "turbulent" environment (Emery and Trist, 1965; Emery, 1967). In the unreason of the Indochina War, the decade had revealed the absurdities of the rationalist-scientific approaches to planning. The new paradigm insisted on man's psycho-social development as a central focus of planning, and portrayed planning itself as a form of social learning. The first book of this "new wave" to appear was Charles Hampden-Turner's *Radical Man* (1970), followed by Edgar Dunn's *Economic and Social Development* (1971) and Donald A. Schon's *Beyond the Stable State* (1971). Conceived independently of the earlier studies, John Friedmann's *Retracking America: A Theory of Transactive Planning* was published two years later (1973).

All four authors rejected the bureaucratic model of organization in which traditional planning had been molded. They stressed the cognitive limits of a central intelligence and its inherent incapacity to gain a comprehensive overview of large, complex, and rapidly changing social systems. They understood planning as a form of social learning that occurred in loosely linked network structures consisting of small, temporary, nonhierarchical, and task-oriented working groups. They emphasized interpersonal transactions as the basic means of exchange between technical experts and clients. In this process, scientific and technical knowledge was seen to fuse with the personal knowledge of client actors in a process of mutual learning. They also pointed to the spoken word of dialogue as the medium through which mutual learning would occur, facilitating the transition from knowledge to action. The direct object of such planning was the innovative adaptation of social organizations to a constantly shifting environment, but its ultimate purpose was to support and enhance man's own development as a person in the course of the transforming action itself. The future was thus collapsed into the present, and the classical dichotomy of ends and means, decisions and actions, was washed out.

This new approach scarcely deserved to be called planning any longer. Societal guidance, a term borrowed from Etzioni, might be a more appropriate designation. But even "societal guidance" would not be fully adequate. In effect, the new humanists outlined the ways in which a decomposing postindustrial society might change itself into a self-organizing, negentropic learning system.

Much work remains to be done. Aside from the practical question of implementing what to many appears to be still an essentially utopian vision, future theorists will have to deal with such issues as conflict resolution, leadership roles, external system relations, imbalance in the distribution of economic and political power, the methods of policy guidance in "mixed" systems, and the ultimate question of a public philosophy suited to the needs of a learning society. The present image of the emerging system is only a partial one. But it also represents a sufficiently powerful theoretical base for further elaboration.

THE TRADITION OF RATIONALISM

For most people, including planners, planning is identified with advance decisionmaking. Planning in this view is a set of methods designed to prepare information in such a way that decisions can be made more rationally. The continuing attractiveness of this approach to planning is made evident in a recent compendium edited by Ira M. Robinson (1972). In his foreword to this volume, Britton Harris refers to it as "a well-established paradigm of the planning process" (p. 9). According to Harris, this paradigm requires the setting of goals, the formulation of alternatives, the prediction of outcomes, and the evaluation of the alternatives in relation to the goals and the outcomes.

One of the basic assumptions of the rationalist school is that decisions *precede* an action, a belief that has entered popular folklore in the exhortation: "look before you leap." This is, of course, good counsel. But suppose you don't know how to leap? The inability to leap or, more generally, the ability or inability to implement a decision is rarely taken into account in the process of decision analysis.

The theory of decisionmaking may be traced in its earliest form to Chester Barnard's work (1938) and to Herbert A. Simon who must surely be considered one of America's foremost social scientists. Simon first articulated the problem of rationality in decisions in his path-breaking study, *Administrative Behavior* (1947). He then went on to make seminal contributions to organization theory (1957) and the study of artificial intelligence (1969). But it was his clear formulation of the decision problem that laid the basis of all subsequent work in the field.

Since his original study concerned bureaucratic organizations, Simon took it for granted that decisions would be made centrally, eventually to filter down to the lower orders in the administrative hierarchy. Later on, Charles Lindblom referred to central decisionmaking of this sort as "synoptic rationality" (Lindblom, 1965).

Despite its great intellectual appeal, rational decision theory must face up to three major problems. None of these has been satisfactorily resolved within the framework of the theory.

1. The first is *the problem of knowledge.* One difficult issue that this entails is the handling of uncertainty. Since most decision analysis relates to nonrepetitive situations, the prediction of consequences and, for that matter, of external circumstances involves probability judgments that are essentially subjective (Shackle, 1961). Being subjective, they are a special mixture of hope and expectation, and no two persons are likely to have the same ingredients of judgment concerning the future. Although statisticians have succeeded in formally introducing subjective probabilities into decision models (Raiffa, 1968), this by no means eliminates this subjective and, therefore, irrational element in decision analysis.

A parallel set of difficulties lies in the information systems required to provide decisionmakers with accurate and relevant data. The problems here range from the outright falsification of data, to the loss of vital information through aggregation, the transformation of knowledge into mathematical models, and critical delays in bureaucratic responses. Some of these problems have been carefully analyzed by Oskar Morgenstern (1963) and Harold Wilensky (1967). Most of them are inherent in the structure and process of bureaucratic organizations themselves.

Finally, a serious aspect of the problem of knowledge is the inherently partial and limited validity of social models used for estimating the impact of decisions. In part this stems from the limits of man's intelligence and the consequent need for restricting the number of variables and relationships taken into account. More important, we see increasingly rapid shifts in social institutions, technological possibilities, valuation of objectives, and scientific conceptualization of key relationships. These create a "turbulent" environment for decisionmaking, denying the kind of stable framework necessary for collating relevant information, or making predictions about action consequences, or evaluating their effects. The problem is not a matter of uncertainty about the way things are, but the certainty that current knowledge and today's paradigms of social processes will mis-state the nature of conditions tomorrow. The problem is not to be solved by greater computer capacity to augment our brainpower, because the difficulty is not purely one of intelligence. Rather it is a feature of modern social dynamics that the future does not unroll incrementally but in a disjointed series of crises, breakthroughs, and transformations. Planning, in fact, has been one of the forces seeking to generate such forms of radical change. Under these conditions, however, knowledge that bears on broad social policy, unlike laboratory-based knowledge, becomes noncumulative.

2. In addition to the problem of knowledge, a second major obstacle confronting theories of rational decisionmaking has to do with what economists call a *community welfare function*, that is, a calculation of tradeoffs among a community's preferences for different objectives. Only four years after Simon's book on administrative decision processes, Kenneth J. Arrow (recipient of the Nobel Prize in economics) provided an elegant proof that, within the constraints of formal democracy (majority voting), a community welfare function could not be logically derived from premises that conform to the formalized rules of political democracy (1951). Arrow assumed, however, a form of democracy whose welfare function was expressed in terms of atomistic statements of preference by individuals. The implication of his impossibility theorem was that policy analysts would henceforth have to wait for other political processes somehow to provide them with a collective statement of objectives, either through an elite of political leaders, a process of social dialogue and development of consensus from below, or the traditional wheeling and dealing of American politics. This left the policy analyst with no independent and objective basis for valuing alternatives.

3. The third major problem relates to *coordination.* Decision theorists work on the assumption that once a decision is made, it will be carried out with a minimum of friction. Again, this belief stems from the notion that within bureaucratic organizations decisions are, in effect, commands and that commands are invariably obeyed. But empirical studies of organizational behavior have concluded that coordination not only may be difficult to achieve but may, in some cases, be altogether impossible. In his study of bureaucracy, Anthony Downs formulates three basic principles of organizational control (1967, p. 143):

> The first is the Law of Imperfect Control: *No one can fully control the behavior of a large organization.* The second is the Law of Diminishing Control: *The larger*

any organization becomes, the weaker is the control over its actions exercised by those at the top. The third is the Law of Decreasing Organization: *The larger any organization becomes, the poorer is the coordination among its actions.* These rather obvious laws are inescapable results of the fact that each person's mental capacity is limited.

Decision theory has failed to come to grips with these problems, in part because it has dealt with the problem of decisions on a purely intellectual level. The newer experimental learning approaches to planning propose a radical reorganization of the decision-action process. But these approaches have not yet penetrated the citadels of reason constructed by the normative/rational tradition.

Arrow's logical objections notwithstanding, welfare economics has continued to flourish, though no longer in the hands of mainstream economists. The mainstream retreated into an arcane positivist stance according to which values had to be given exogenously. The innovative periphery, on the other hand, developed such tools as cost-benefit analysis (Dorfman, 1965; Haveman and Margolis, 1970), PPBS (Novick, 1967), environmental economics (Mishan, 1967, Kneese, Ayres and d'Arge, 1970), and evaluative research (Caro, 1971). Still, none of these techniques could ultimately pass beyond Arrow's impossibility theorem. The weighting of values, especially of nonmonetary values, continues to be an insurmountable barrier to a "scientific politics."

The first practical application of Simon's rational decision model was Jan Tinbergen's effort to devise an econometric model for economic policy analysis (1952 and 1964). This model was so ingenious, it came not only to be used in short-range planning within the Netherlands but, under UN auspices, to inspire similar efforts throughout the world. Ultimately, it won the Nobel Prize for its author. Tinbergen was an elitist, and his model quite unabashedly assumes a top-down process of decisionmaking, including the setting of major sectoral targets. The formal logic of his model was subjected to a detailed critique by a group of like-minded economists in 1964, probably the year of its greatest popularity (Millikan, 1967). While this review was going on, however, a large number of empirical studies of the practice of economic development planning (with an emphasis on the long run) revealed gross deficiencies in the method (see the section on national planning below). The comprehensive modeling of future history (albeit restricted to economic variables) appeared to be no more successful in generating major development action in the arena of national planning than it had been in American city planning practice where comprehensiveness (or the synoptic view of decisionmaking) continued to be an essential article of every planner's faith.

Some years after Tinbergen's first published efforts, James March and Herbert Simon collaborated in a monumental study of all that was then known about organizations and organizational behavior (1959). The book dealt only in part with planning per se, but it was a significant part, much more sophisticated than Simon's original venture, and reflected a decade of work by numerous contributors to the theory of organizations and decisions. In this book, the authors backed away from pure rationalism to a more moderate position in which they advocated *satisficing* as the principle of choice. "Optimization" continued to be seen as a desirable goal in principle but unattainable in the ordinary course of events. Satisficing was the decision criterion of "bounded" rationality, according to which all one might hope to attain was a "satisfactory" decision; while not the "best," it was the best available and therefore "good enough." From this, it was only a short step to Charles Lindblom's famous description of the decision process as a "science of muddling through."

Insofar as planning was concerned, March and Simon delimited the use of planning to *nonroutine* decisionmaking. Planning was therefore inextricably involved with innovation. And the rationalists had very little to say about innovation. The discussion of planning in their book is conceptually the most advanced within the frame of rationalism, but it is curiously ambiguous and in the end trails off without resolving any of the crucial issues.

Shortly thereafter, a book was published that fell outside the main traditions of rationalism. The work of a team of psychologists, it was called *Plans and the Structure of Behavior* (Miller, Galanter, and Pribam, 1960). The importance of this work derives from the fact that its authors portrayed human behavior as essentially rational, proceeding through a series of feedback loops to the attainment of self-selected objectives. Their model of human behavior was similar to the model of rational decision and seemed to place that model on a sound empirical and theoretical foundation. Curiously, their authors made little of the natural association between feedback loops and the process of learning. Furthermore, and this is a major shortcoming of the book, the authors did not discuss *deviation-amplifying feedback* (Maruyama, 1962) and therefore had nothing to say about the processes of creativity and innovation. In any event, it stands as a landmark in the evolution of rationalist thought.

By the middle of the 1960s, Charles Lindblom reappeared with his magnum opus, *The Intelligence of Democracy* (1965). In a sense, this book draws the finish line to the theory of decision, being diametrically opposed to Herbert Simon's synoptic rationalism. (March and Simon may be regarded as the midpoint on an axis connecting Simon with Lindblom.) After a withering critique of synoptic decisionmaking, Lindblom proposes his own version of incremental decisionmaking which is aggregated into the preferred social good by a process he describes as mutual adjustment. Upon its publication in 1965, Lindblom's model was widely criticized by planners for its presumed lack of concern with structural decisions. This criticism led to an unfruitful controversy over "big" and "little" decisions, culminating in Etzioni's proposal of "mixed scanning" as a synthesis of synoptic with incremental decisionmaking (Etzioni, 1968).

Another critic of synoptic rationality was Christopher Alexander, whose *Notes on the Synthesis of Form* (1964) argued the need for rational planning explicitly to delineate the network of particular social systems affected by decisions. Though his ideas underwent modifications in later works, Alexander opened a new series of challenges to students of decisionmaking. He brought to the fore the operational significance of historical and behavioral contexts ("unselfconscious processes"), and the need to distinguish between planning for isolable social subsystems and planning for irreducibly complex networks. In the latter case, he argued, the processes of planning could not be stipulated in the abstract, but only in terms that correspond to the nature of the processes being planned for in a particular social context. Schooled in the architectural tradition of urban design and city planning, Alexander also carried planning beyond the scope of merely choosing between given options to the design of new ones.

Decision theory stagnated after 1965. Its place, however, was quickly taken by the new field of Policy Science (Dror, 1968, 1971; Lindblom, 1968; Bauer and Gergen, 1968; Jantsch, 1969; Lasswell, 1971). The latter part of the sixties witnessed a veritable implosion of ideas on how to apply the tools of rational and scientific analysis to concrete problems of public policy. A direct outgrowth of defense-supported research (and, more directly, of the War in Indochina), the new techniques spilled forth, year after year, each finding its small coterie of hopeful admirers from the President on down to directors of city planning departments. For the most part, these techniques were meant to improve the quality of central management decisions, and the logic of their structure was very much in accord with the logic of decision theory whose elaboration had gone forward during the preceding twenty years.

It is quite impossible within the scope of this paper to have a critical discussion of the several techniques of policy analysis. They include what de Jouvenel called "the art of conjecture" (de Jouvenel, 1967; Helmer, 1966; Bell, 1967); social indicators (Bauer, 1966; Gross and Springer, 1970); technology assessment (Jantsch, 1967); planning-programming-budget systems (Novick, 1967; Haveman and Margolis, 1970); systems analysis (Churchman, 1968, 1971; Quade and Boucher, 1968); and large-scale computerized simulation studies (Forrester, 1969). These defense spin-offs are exciting innovations. But, if one may ask a Simon-like question, do they suffice? Are they good enough to brush aside the serious obstacles to rational decision analysis formulated earlier in this section? Can they indeed reduce turbulent environments to order and provide a safe guide to action "beyond the stable state?" A careful analysis would probably show that they do not. Indeed, they are most likely to lead us to what Amitai Etzioni called an "overmanaged" society where, consensus being low, excessive amounts of coercive power must be used to carry out the purposes of central authorities. One result of "overmanaged" systems is an increase in social alienation. Another result is mounting social instability (nonpredictability) and error. Systems that are overmanaged tend either to fluctuate widely (to the extent they are ambitious) or to remain entrapped in repressive stagnation.

These results obviously cannot be imputed to the moral intent of the policy scientists themselves who, indeed, expect quite the contrary from their efforts. The outcome depends primarily on how the techniques will come to be used. There is little evidence from the past to suggest that they will be used wisely. Indeed, the failure rigorously to examine the epistemological foundations of policy science almost ensures that they will be wrongly used. Churchman's most recent book (1971) is the first serious attempt to remedy this situation.

Policy analysis has one great advantage: it improves with use. The agencies engaged in policy analysis are in a position to observe the results of their actions and to apply the knowledge so gained to the improvement of subsequent action. Policy analysis, therefore, becomes increasingly experience-based. This reciprocal nurturing of theory and practice approaches what the philosophical synthesizers have called social learning or evolutionary experimentation. In this way, the rich detail of concrete historical situations imposes itself upon the analysis. Whether new analytical techniques can be devised to deal with these issues remains to be seen.

In contrast to the other traditions, the emerging field of policy science has not yet a central theme or dominant personality to give it cohesion and direction. Unless a more integrated structure is evolved in the years to come, policy science may break up into relatively minor centers of intellectual gravity within the broad spectrum of planning theories.

THE TRADITION OF ORGANIZATION DEVELOPMENT

While rationalists were working to improve their models of decisionmaking, an alternative approach to planning suddenly burst on the scene in the mid-fifties which in most respects contradicted the working hypotheses of the rationalist school. Going under the label of organization development, proponents of this new field of professional practice and research understood planning not as an intellectual process of efficiently adapting means to given ends, but as primarily a method for inducing organizational change (Lippitt et al., 1958; Bennis et al., 1961). In the perspective of organization development, planning could not be meaningfully separated from implementing action, and the planner's role came accordingly to be defined as that of *change agent* (Jones, 1969; Schein, 1969). This image was congruent, as it turned out, with the experience of foreign experts in developing countries who, in rare moments of candor, admitted that the art of mapping knowledge into action involved behavior that looked very different from the assumptions of rationalist planning (Beneviste and Ilchman, 1969; Beneviste, 1972).

The operating principle of organization development is that any lasting change in process and structure must come from within the organization and involve far-reaching changes in awareness, attitudes, behavior, and values on the part of its constituents. This self-transformation may be regarded as a process of learning. Planners may be instrumental as catalysts in this process, guiding the ongoing learning in accord with its inner dynamics. To be successful in their catalytic role, they must be dealers in the human and psychological dimensions of the organization, and their mode of communication must be based on the principle of dialogue. Every attempt at organization development must be understood as an experiment from which constructive lessons may be drawn.

This new approach to planning so departs from the accepted norms of rationalism, that much of the literature of organization development remains incomprehensible to the policy scientist (Jantsch, 1971). Nor is cross-communication helped by the fact that the literature on organization development is drawn from experience with single organizations, such as private corporations. The translation of its findings to a societal scale has been extraordinarily difficult. Empirical studies of organizations have often made the bridge between institutional patterns of behavior and their larger social and cultural environments (Crozier, 1964; Blau, 1955; Beneviste, 1970), but the task of extending this to normative applications in organizational development remains to be carried out.[2]

Organization development has been most aptly characterized as a professional movement. According to Warren Bennis (1969:10–15), who more than anyone has contributed to its continued evolution,

- organization development is an *educational strategy* adopted to bring about a *planned organizational change*;
- the changes sought for are coupled directly with the *exigency* or demand the organization is trying to cope with;
- organization development relies on an educational strategy which emphasizes *experienced behavior*;
- *change agents* are for the most part, but not exclusively, external to *the client system:*
- organization development implies a *collaborative relationship* between change agent and constituents of the client system;
- change agents share a *social philosophy*, a set of values about the world in general and human organizations in particular which shape their strategies, determine their interventions, and largely govern their responses to client systems;
- change agents share a set of *normative goals* based on their philosophy, including: improvement in interpersonal competence; a shift in values so that human factors and feelings come to be considered legitimate; development of increased understanding between and within working groups in order to reduce tension; development of more effective "team management;" development of better methods of "conflict resolution;" and development of organic rather than mechanical systems.

The strong normative thrust reflected in Bennis' statement made it inevitable, perhaps, that organization development should assume a definite ideological coloring. This fact, no doubt, contributed to the rationalists' lack of comprehension of what the movement is about. For nothing could be greater anathema to a rationalist than this "messy" admixture of scientific ethos and normative enthusiasm.

Yet there is much that they and other "societal" planners could learn from the literature in organization development. The more important ideas, briefly identified below, are beginning to be integrated with the main body of planning theory, both reinforcing and complementing strands of thinking derived from other sources in the philosophical tradition (Hampden-Turner, 1970; Dunn, 1971; Schon, 1971; Goulet, 1971; Friedmann, 1973).

1. Organizations are "sociotechnical systems" in which both social organization and technical instrumentation may be viewed as complex variables in the transformation of material and informational inputs into desired outputs (Emery and Trist, 1971).

2. Organizations are composed of communication networks among individuals who themselves have basic human needs for regard, power, and opportunities for self-actualization. The achievement of interpersonal competence is therefore essential to the successful functioning of organizations (Argyris, 1962; 1965).

3. Organizational change is best regarded as a complex learning process looking to changed states of awareness and behavior on part of constituent members of organizations (Likert, 1967).

4. Critical to induced organizational change are face-to-face relations between expert and client in which "the change agent uses his own person and the relationships that he jointly builds, adapts, and terminates with the client system . . . as major tools in liberating, informing, and empowering the client to deal more aptly with itself (or himself) and its (or his) worlds" (Bennis et al., 1969:371; see also Jones, 1969; Schein, 1969).

5. Healthy organizational structures (and corresponding processes) represent an efficient adaptation to their environments. Significant aspects of such environments include the distribution of power, organizational stability, rate of environmental change, degree of openness in the system, scale and complexity, technical capacity available, and the degree of consensus about organizational ends (Lawrence and Lorsch, 1967).

6. Bureaucratic models of organization are only one form of successful organization. The contemporary environments of most organizations require adaptive structures that are significantly different and may be characterized by a high degree of internal differentiation, overlapping responsibilities, appropriate mechanisms of integration, temporary boundary arrangements, a predominance of high-capacity, horizontal channels of communication, and innovation-seeking leadership roles (Bennis, 1966; Lawrence and Lorsch, 1967; Likert, 1967; Bennis and Slater, 1968).

THE TRADITION OF EMPIRICISM

The paucity of carefully constructed empirical studies of planning comes perhaps as a surprise. The whole of wartime planning in Europe and the United States, together with the preceding antidepression planning of the New Deal, yielded only five major studies of some quality, and it was not until the 1960s that a more intensive examination of the planning process was initiated.

Several explanations of this state of affairs come to mind. As a macro-phenomenon, planning was not a natural subject for investigation by disciplines, such as empirical sociology, that tended to focus more on contemporary social "problems" on the smaller scale of organizational units. Political science had not yet developed its current behaviorist bent, while economics was taken up with formal model-building. Planning, moreover, had not yet become a salient public issue, at least in the United States, so that there was little demand for knowing more about it. City planning, though widely accepted, was tolerated as a relatively harmless activity which just possibly might do some good. National planning—after a brief flirtation with the National Resources Planning Board and its successors in the 1930s—boiled down chiefly to the Council of Economic Advisors and the grinding routines of the Bureau of the Budget (Mertins, Jr. and Gross, 1971). These were scarcely the stuff to rivet the attention of empiricists.

Yet despite their relatively small volume, the studies which did emerge produced a wealth of new insights into the character of planning practice. The results fell short of true theory, for no formal propositions were tested. Their value rather derives from the closeups they provide and their contribution to a more detailed understanding of the operational characteristics and internal dynamics of planning processes in a number of different cultural and political settings.

Rationalism had largely ignored the experience of planning practice, as indeed it had also ignored the work of organization development theories. And for good reason, for the recorded experience with planning threatened the very foundations of rationalist thinking. While rationalism argued a thin logic from first principles to derive the basis for rational choice, empiricists labored to discover how "real" planning worked or did not work—and why. And what they discovered—if nothing else—was that planning-in-practice did not at all look like planning-in-theory.

Studies of National Planning

The first few studies were carried out shortly after World War II. A clearly defined normative model of planning was practically nonexistent at that time except in socialist literature, which focused on the special case of centrally planned economies (Landauer, 1947). Americans therefore concentrated on comparing the concepts of central planning and the emerging experience of socialist countries with the classical theories of capitalism. On the whole, the authors concluded, as imperfect as the free market might be in actual operation, it still worked more efficiently in allocating resources than would a central public agency (Franks, 1947; Devons, 1950).

After this small ripple of interest in national planning had passed, the attention of social scientists turned again to other matters. For over a decade, only a single empirical study was produced, and this was in city rather than national planning (Meyerson and Banfield, 1955). The new spate of research was initiated by Peter Wiles, a British economist and Kremlinologist, who published his iconoclastic account of communist planning in 1962. Sparkling with wit and brimming with insights, Wiles' book portrayed a planning system beset by major uncertainties, lethargic response times, and grossly incomplete and inaccurate information, a system that teetered from crisis to crisis and yet managed to correlate with high economic performance. Was this a case of epiphenomenal planning where the planner only appears to be the cause? Wiles seemed to think so and cited a long list of alternate explanations for the recorded growth, including total mobilization of the population around the ends of production and an exceptionally high savings-investment rate (Wiles, Ch. 13). As for Soviet planning, it was "chiefly a system whereby each individual and organization is permanently under a quasi-legal obligation to increase output" (p. 259).

At about the time of Wiles' publication, the first harvest of studies appeared which looked at planning in the newly industrializing countries (Hagen, 1963; Hirschman, 1963). What made them especially provocative was their *comparative* format. Of particular interest is Hirschman's analysis of policymaking in the context of Latin America (op. cit.).

Here, there was no central planning modelled on Soviet experience. Nevertheless, there was a good deal of partial policy coordination for regional economic development (Brazil), rural land reform (Colombia), and financial stability (Chile). While the outcomes were not particularly impressive, Hirschman succeeded in detecting and describing what he considered to be a Latin American style of "reform-mongering" as one of the many adaptive varieties of policy planning.

Scholarly productivity continued at a fairly high level for the remainder of the decade. Bertram M. Gross edited a series of eight country studies written by a varied crew of social scientists which yielded a quite unusual array of empirical propositions about national planning. Albert Waterston worked under greater constraint than did Gross's academics (Waterston, 1965). A firm believer in the potential powers of central planning and a practitioner working with the World Bank, he identified what he thought were major planning pathologies. His book is consequently full of practical remedies. It is not clear, however, whether planning would have had a more pervasive influence on events even if all of his prescriptions had been followed from the start.

A somewhat belated entry into the field was Gross's *Action Under Planning* which reported on the proceedings of a conference on national planning which had been held three years earlier (Gross, 1967). In the same year, Albert O. Hirschman published a small classic, *Development Projects Observed*, which may well be one of the finest contributions to the development literature to date (Hirschman, 1967). Essentially a series of sophisticated case studies, the book gained cohesion through its demonstration of the "principle of the hiding hand" or what might be called the uses of ignorance in human affairs. Reliance on this principle illustrated yet again Hirschman's propensity to think of economic development as a movement proceeding via imbalances in demand or supply situations along a secular upward-bending curve of economic progress.

The decade concluded with Cohen's exemplary study of French planning (Cohen, 1969) and an analysis of educational planning in Mexico (Beneviste, 1970). The most recent contribution is a two-volume symposium on planning in the United Nations' First Development Decade which brings together what is perhaps the most sustained critical attack yet on the central planning schema promoted under Jan Tinbergen's tutelage (Faber and Seers, 1972).

This decade-long intensive intellectual preoccupation had yielded a not insignificant body of interesting concepts, models, and testable propositions about planning. It might be well quickly to allude to them. Together, they have contributed immensely to our understanding of the ways in which a technically trained intelligence can (or cannot) influence the course of historical change:

- the crisis-origins of planning (Gross, 1965, 1966; Hirshman, 1963)
- central guidance cluster (Gross, 1965)
- planning environments and styles of planning (Friedmann, 1967, 1973)
- planning as structured competition (Hirschman and Lindblom, 1962)
- political planning (Beneviste, 1970)

- planning as an extension of incremental social (po-litical-budgetary) processes (Waterston, 1965)
- reform-mongering (Hirschman, 1963)
- the principle of the hiding hand (Hirschman, 1967)
- planning as institutionalized innovation (Morse, 1969)
- the priority of current actions (Gross, 1965)
- activation of national plans (Gross, 1967)
- planners' tension (Wiles, 1962)
- manifest and latent functions of planning (Friedmann, 1965; Daland, 1967)
- cooptation (Selznick, 1949)

Studies of Urban Planning

The literature from this area of studies turned out to be much less rich in pertinent insights. As Hirschman, Gross, and Waterston had dominated the scene of national planning studies during the sixties, so Edward C. Banfield towered above other students of urban planning. His interest was less in planning than it was in politics, however, and he is generally credited with being one of the founders of the specialized field of urban politics.

His case study of public housing in Chicago, written in collaboration with Martin Meyerson, is still the most widely quoted text on the possibilities of planning in the American city (1955). Its conclusions were extremely pessimistic, however. Using Herbert Simon's model of pure rationality as a norm, Meyerson and Banfield found the realities of planning practice sadly deficient. Largely responsible for the theoretical import of this early work, Banfield succeeded in passing on his mood of profound pessimism to his students, among them James Q. Wilson and Alan A. Altshuler, both of whom also delved into the sobering realities of comprehensive physical planning (Altshuler, 1965; Wilson, 1968). This mood continued even into the third generation (Rabinovitz, 1969).

If anything, these authors proved the futility of blueprinting the future of urban America. But this result needn't surprise us; the standard of synoptic decisionmaking they used to evaluate planning practice was in any event unworkable as a realistic model for planning. This much, at least, critics like Lindblom had shown conclusively (Lindblom, 1965). It seems strange that no one should have taken Lindblom's alternate model of disjointed incrementalism as a basis for measuring the prevailing amount of rationality in urban politics. Had this been done, the conclusions of political scientists might have been more encouraging for planning practice.

Relation and Outlook

Two general conclusions may be drawn from the preceding account. First, planning cannot presently claim to be sustained by a coherent body of theoretical propositions. Second, the literature of the past twenty years is characterized by considerable coherence *within* the several research traditions which have become established. Each of these has tended to be dominated by social scientists of great brilliance and entrepreneurial acumen. Simon and Lindblom provided the necessary leadership for the evolving field of rational decision theory; Bennis and Gross set the principal directions

of empirical work in national planning, while Banfield and Wilson did much the same for urban planning. Under their influence, each group of scholars has tended to pursue an independent course. Consequently, we have yet to see substantial cross-fertilization among traditions, or the emergence of a unified planning theory.

What are the chances of such a theory and what might provide the catalyst of convergence? It would appear logical for the tradition of philosophical synthesis to evolve a framework that might integrate planning theory from the other, more specialized schools and disciplines. Yet, up to the present, the writers in this tradition have only been partially successful in this respect. The reason does not seem to be any inherent restrictions in their ability to incorporate new knowledge; a more fundamental reason appears to be that the more integrated theories of societal guidance offered by Mannheim, Etzioni, and the New Humanists have few significant applications to social practice under conditions of a free market economy. Even in the form of experimental alternatives, this country has so far failed to produce more than a very small number of major actions based on a fully synthesized theory of man and society. In short, the integration of knowledge and action which is fundamental to the idea of planning has not yet been sufficiently tested within the tradition of philosophical synthesis to make that tradition an effective vehicle for convergence among theories. We still lack a body of experience that would demonstrate the usefulness of a unified approach to guided social change and, indeed, there is not even the promise that such an approach and the theory underlying it might soon be shaped in the mold of social practice.

In contrast, both the rationalist and social organization schools of planning have independently found abundant opportunities to apply what they have preached and to develop theories from practice. Rationalism gave birth to policy science which has managed to sell its expertise to those who believed in it and could afford to pay the price. This school can probably claim to have come the closest to a unified approach to planning at the level of society. Yet rationalism has recently come under serious question as a normative guide. The revelations of the Pentagon Papers, the failures of the Development Decade in the sixties, and the uncertain control of our economy under neo-Keynesian policies have left us skeptical of models that attempt to reduce complex social problems to neat formulae. The principal failure of the rationalist school, however, is its neglect of the human side of planning. In this respect, organization development has demonstrated a far greater awareness of the reciprocity that exists between social goals and the value-permeated and power-laden nature of human relationships. Moreover, in the social laboratories of this school there seems to have emerged a greater sensitivity to the question of what is meaningful in social activities apart from what is merely possible or optimal.

This emphasis on the human seems to us the key element that might be incorporated from organization development into the philosophical tradition. To accomplish this step will demand a capacity for looking at society as a function of human potential—not as an aggregate phenomenon as depicted by social statistics, nor as a series of atomistic life patterns as implied by economic behavior, but as a *dialogue* in which planning may become more nearly synonymous with the processes that mediate between individual and social evolution.

It may be that contemporary American society—its ideology and culture, its systems of production and government—cannot generate a significant and effective demand for social theories that would allow their direct translation into practice. Some socialist societies such as China appear to have been more successful in this regard, perhaps because of the massive, ubiquitous, and urgent nature of their problems.[3] It is social crises of major dimensions that generally give scope for testing social theories in action and for generating new knowledge from practice.

One major task for the philosophical tradition of planning theory, therefore, would seem to consist in identifying the conditions in postindustrial, American society that would demand a more rigorous, ongoing, and socially permeating application of theory to practice and to demand from planners more than the value-neutral stance that social scientists and historians have clung to in the past. The significance of such a step implies a departure of planning theory from its foundations in the social sciences as we have known them. Such a move would also be able to revitalize the traditions of research on which it must continue to draw. By its historical perspective, planning theory can prevent the social sciences from growing dangerously out of touch with the problems of a society undergoing continuous transformation; by its normative perspective, it can help to generate the kinds of action that will yield new knowledge useful to the further evolution of planning theory.

NOTES

Thank you! Ed. (Emphasis added.)

1 On the role of paradigm shifts in the development of physical science, see Kuhn, 1962.

2 The literature of organization development is easily confused with that of organization theory generally. Even so, the conceptual distinction between them is of some importance. Organization theory, with its predominantly sociological and economic orientation originated with Max Weber's studies of bureaucracy, a line of thinking that has been continued by such writers as Talcott Parsons, Peter Blau, Michel Crozier, and Amitai Etzioni. Organization development, on the other hand, is primarily concerned with structural change rather than organizational behavior, and derives its focus primarily from work carried out at the Tavistock Institute of Human Relations in London, the Sloan School of Management at MIT, the Harvard Business School, and Yale University. Historically, it may be traced to the inspiring work of the German psychologist Kurt Lewin who, as Director of the Research Center for Group Dynamics at MIT, laid the basis for the later work of Ronald Lippitt, Bennis, Argyris, and other founders of OD (Lewin, 1948). An important work that may be taken to bridge the two traditions is Cyert and March's behavioral study of the firm (1963) and Chester Barnard's pioneering work (1938).

3 On the nature of these problems in China, on the role of "ideology in command", and on national preoccupation with the unity of theory and practice, see *Selected Readings from the Works of Mao Tse Tung* (Peking: Foreign Languages Press, 1971), especially the essays "On Practice" (1937), "Rectify the Party's Style of Work" (1942), and "Where Do Correct Ideas Come From?" (1963).

REFERENCES

Alexander, Christopher (1964) *Notes on the Synthesis of Form.* Cambridge, Mass.: Harvard University Press.

Altshuler, Alan A. (1965) *The City Planning Process.* Ithaca, N.Y.: Cornell University Press.

Akzin, B., and Y. Dror (1966) *Israel: High-Pressure Planning.* Syracuse: University of Syracuse Press.

Argyris, Chris (1962) *Interpersonal Competence and Organizational Effectiveness.* Homewood, Ill.: Irwin-Dorsey.

——— (1965) *Organization and Innovation.* Homewood, Ill.: Irwin Dorsey.

Arrow, Kenneth J. (1951) *Social Choice and Individual Values.* New York: John Wiley and Sons.

Banfield, Edward, C. (1961) *Political Influence.* New York: The Free Press.

Barnard, Chester I. (1938) *The Functions of the Executive.* Cambridge, Mass.: Harvard University Press.

Bauer, Raymond A., ed. (1966) *Social Indicators.* Cambridge, Mass.: The MIT Press.

———, and Kenneth J. Gergen, eds. (1968) *The Study of Policy Formation.* New York: The Free Press.

Bell, Daniel, Ed. (1967) *Toward the Year 2000: Work in Progress.* (Special issue of *Daedalus.* Journal of the American Academy of Arts and Sciences).

Beneviste, Guy (1970) *Bureaucracy and National Planning: A Sociological Case Study in Mexico.* New York: Praeger.

——— (1972) *The Politics of Expertise.* Berkeley, Cal.: The Glendessary Press.

———, and Warren F. Ilchman (1969) *Agents of Change: Professionals in Developing Countries.* New York: Praeger.

Bennis, Warren G. (1966) *Changing Organizations.* New York: McGraw-Hill.

——— (1969) *Organization Development: Its Nature, Origins, and Prospects.* Reading, Mass.: Addison-Wesley.

———, K. D. Benne, and R. Chin, eds. (1961) *The Planning of Change.* Readings in the Applied Behavioral Sciences. New York: Holt, Rinehart and Winston. A substantially revised second edition was published in 1969.

———, and P. E. Slater (1968) *The Temporary Society.* New York: Harper and Row.

Blau, Peter M. (1955) *The Dynamics of Bureaucracy,* ref. ed. Chicago: University of Chicago Press.

Brown, W. H. and C. E. Gilbert (1961) *Planning Municipal Investment.* A Case Study of Philadelphia. Philadelphia: University of Pennsylvania Press.

Caro, Francis, ed. (1971) *Readings in Evaluative Research.* New York: Russell Sage Foundation.

Churchman, Charles West (1968) *The Systems Approach.* New York: Dell.

Churchman, Charles West (1971) *The Design of Inquiring Systems: Basic Concepts of Systems and Organizations.* New York: Basic Books.

Cohen, Stephen (1969) *Modern Capitalist Planning: The French Model.* Cambridge, Mass.: Harvard University Press.

Crozier, Michel (1964) *The Bureaucratic Phenomenon.* Chicago: University of Chicago Press.

Cyert, Richard M., and James G. March (1963) *A Behavioral Theory of the Firm.* Englewood Cliffs, N.J.: Prentice Hall.

Dahl, Robert A., and Charles E. Lindblom (1953) *Politics, Economics, and Welfare.* New York: Harper and Bros.

Daland, Robert T. (1967) *Brazilian Planning.* Development Politics and Administration. Chapel Hill, N. C.: University of North Carolina Press.

de Jouvenel, Bertrand (1967 *The Art of Conjecture.* New York: Basic Books.

Devons, Ely (1950) *Planning in Practice.* Cambridge, Eng.: Cambridge University Press.

Dorfman, Robert, ed. (1965) *Measuring Benefits of Government Investments.* Washington, D. C.: The Brookings Institution.

Downs, Anthony (1967) *Inside Bureaucracy.* Boston: Little, Brown.

Dror, Yehezkel (1968) *Public Policy Reexamined.* San Francisco: Chandler.

——— (1971) *Design for Policy Sciences.* Amsterdam: Elsevier.

Dunn, Edgar S. (1971) *Economic and Social Development. A Process of Social Learning.* Baltimore: The Johns Hopkins Press.

Emery, F. E. (1967) "The Next Thirty Years: Concepts, Methods, and Anticipations," *Human Relations* 20, no. 3:199–237.

———, and E. L. Trist (1965) "The Causal Texture of Organizational Environments," *Human Relations* 18:21–32.

———, and E. L. Trist (1971) "Socio-Technical Systems," in H. Eric Frank, ed. *Organization Structuring.* London: McGraw Hill, Ch. 4. This chapter appeared originally as an article in 1965.

Etzioni, Amitai (1968) *The Active Society: A Theory of Society and Political Processes.* New York: The Free Press.

——— (1969) "Toward a Theory of Societal Guidance," in Sarajane Heidt and Amitai Etzioni, eds., *Societal Guidance: A New Approach to Social Problems.* New York: Thomas Y. Crowell.

Faber, Mike and Dudley Seers, eds. (1972) *The Crisis in Planning.* Vol. I: *The Issues;* Vol. II: *The Experience.* London: Chatto and Windus for the Sussex University Press.

Forrester, Jay W. (1969) *Urban Dynamics.* Cambridge, Mass.: The MIT Press.

Franks, Oliver (1947) *Central Planning and Control in War and Peace.* Cambridge, Mass.: Harvard University Press.

Fried, Robert (1971) *Planning the Eternal City: Roman Politics and Planning since World War II.* New Haven: Yale University Press.

Friedmann, John (1965) *Venezuela: From Doctrine to Dialogue.* Syracuse: Syracuse University Press.

——— (1967) "The Institutional Context," in Bertram M. Gross, ed., *Action Under Planning: The Guidance of Economic Development.* New York: McGraw-Hill, Ch. 2.

——— (1973) *Retracking America: A Theory of Transactive Planning.* Garden City, N.Y.: Doubleday.

Gold, Bela (1949) *Wartime Economic Planning in Agriculture.* New York: Columbia University Press.

Goulet, Denis (1971) *The Cruel Choices: A New Concept in the Theory of Development.* New York: Atheneum.

Gross, Bertram M. (1965) "National Planning: Findings and Fallacies," *Public Administration Review* 25, no. 4 (Dec.):263–273.

——— (1965) "The Managers of National Economic Change," in Roscoe C. Martin, ed., *Public Administration and Democracy: Essays in Honor of Paul H. Appleby.* Syracuse, N.Y.: Syracuse University Press.

——— (1966) "Planning as Crisis Management," A Prefatory Comment in B. Akzin and Y. Dror, *Israel: High Pressure Planning.* Syracuse, N.Y.: Syracuse University Press.

———, ed. (1967) *Action Under Planning: The Guidance of Economic Development.* New York: McGraw-Hill.

——— (1967) "Activating National Plans," in Bertram M. Gross, ed., *Action Under Planning: The Guidance of Economic Development.* New York: McGraw-Hill, Ch. 7.

———, and Michael Springer, eds. (1970) *Political Intelligence for America's Future.* Philadelphia: The American Academy of Political and Social Science.

Hagen, Everett E., ed. (1963) *Planning Economic Development.* Homewood, Ill.: Richard D. Irwin.

Hampden-Turner, Charles (1971) *Radical Man: The Process of Psycho-Social Development.* Garden City, N. Y.: Anchor Books. Originally published in 1970 by Schenkman.

Harris, Britton (1972), "Foreword" in Ira M. Robinson, ed., *Decision-Making in Urban Planning.* Beverly Hills, Cal.: Sage Publications.

Haveman, R. H., and J. Margolis, eds. (1970) *Public Expenditures and Policy Analysis.* Chicago: Markham.

Helmer, Olaf (1966) *Social Technology.* New York: Basic Books.

Hightower, Henry C. (1969) "Planning Theory in Contemporary Professional Education," *Journal of the American Institute of Planners* 35, no. 5 (Sept.):326–329.

Hirschman, Albert O. (1963) *Journeys Towards Progress: Studies of Economic Policy Making in Latin America.* New York: The Twentieth Century Fund.

——— (1967) *Development Projects Observed.* Washington, D. C.: The Brookings Institution.

———, and Charles E. Lindblom (1962) "Economic Development, Research and Development, Policy Making: Some Converging Views," *Behavioral Science* 7, no. 2 (Apr.):211–222.

Ilchman, Warren F. and Norman Thomas Uphoff (1969) *The Political Economy of Change.* Berkeley, Cal.: University of California Press.

Jantsch, Erich (1967) *Technological Forecasting in Perspective.* Paris: Organization for Economic Cooperation and Development.

———, ed. (1969) *Perspectives of Planning.* Paris: Organization for Economic Co-operation and Development.

——— (1971) Review of Warren C. Bennis et al., eds., *The Planning of Change,* 2nd ed, in *Policy Sciences* 2, no. 2 (June): 200–203.

Jones, Garth N. (1969) *Planned Organizational Change: A Study in Change Dynamics.* London: Routledge and Kegan Paul.

Kneese, A. V., R. V. Ayres, and R. C. d'Arge (1970) *Economics and the Environment: A Materials Balance Approach.* Baltimore: Johns Hopkins Press.

Kuhn, Thomas S. (1962) *The Structure of Scientific Revolutions.* Chicago: Chicago University Press.

Landauer, Carl (1947) *Theory of National Economic Planning.* Berkeley, Cal.: University of California Press.

Lasswell, Harold D. (1971) *A Preview of Policy Sciences.* Amsterdam: Elsevier.

Lawrence, Paul R., and Jay W. Lorsch (1967) *Organization and Environment: Managing Differentiation and Integration.* Boston: Graduate School of Business Administration, Harvard University.

Lewin, Kurt (1948) *Resolving Social Conflicts: Selected Papers on Group Dynamics.* New York: Harper and Bros.

Likert, Rensis (1967) *The Human Organization: Its Management and Value.* New York: McGraw-Hill.

Lindblom, Charles E. (1965) *The Intelligence of Democracy.* New York: The Free Press.

——— (1968) *The Policy-Making Process.* Englewood Cliffs, N. J.: Prentice-Hall.

Lippitt, Ronald, Jeanne Watson, and Bruce Westley (1958) *The Dynamics of Planned Change.* New York: Harcourt, Brace and World.

Mannheim, Karl (1935) *Mensch und Gesellschaft im Zeitalter des Umbaus.* Leiden: A. W. Sijthoff's Uitgeversmaatschappij N.V.; English version: (1949) *Man and Society in an Age of Reconstruction.* New York: Harcourt, Brace.

March, James Q. and Herbert A. Simon (1959) *Organizations.* New York: John Wiley and Sons.

Maruyama, Magoroh (1963) "The Second Cybernetics: Deviation-Amplifying Mutual Causal Processes," *American Scientist* 51:164–179.

Mertins, Jr., Herman, and Bertram M. Gross (1971) "Symposium on Changing Styles of Planning in Post Industrial America," *Public Administration Review* 31, no. 3 (May–June).

Meyerson, Martin, and Edward C. Banfield (1955) *Politics, Planning and the Public Interest.* The Case of Public Housing in Chicago. Glencoe, Ill.: The Free Press.

Miller, George A., Eugene Galanter, and Karl H. Pribam (1960) *Plans and the Structure of Behavior.* New York: Henry Holt.

Millikan, Max F., ed. (1967) *National Economic Planning.* National Bureau of Economic Research. New York: Columbia University Press.

Mishan, E. J. (1967) *The Costs of Economic Growth.* London: Staples Press.

Morgenstern, Oskar (1963) *On the Accuracy of Economic Observations,* 2nd ed. Princeton, N.J.: Princeton University Press.

FRIEDMANN AND HUDSON

Morse, Chandler (1969) "Becoming versus Being Modern: An Essay on Institutional Change and Economic Development," in Chandler Morse, ed., *Modernization by Design: Social Change in the Twentieth Century*. Ithaca, N.Y.: Cornell University Press, pp. 238–382.

Novick, David, ed. (1967) *Program Budgeting: Program Analysis and the Federal Budget*, 2nd ed. Cambridge, Mass.: Harvard University Press.

Popper, Karl R. (1945) *The Open Society and Its Enemies*. London: Routledge and Kegan Paul.

Quade, E. S., and W. I. Boucher, eds. (1968) *Systems Analysis and Policy Planning*. New York: American Elsevier.

Rabinovitz, Francine (1969) *City Politics and Planning*. New York: Atherton Press.

Raiffa, Howard (1968) *Decision Analysis: Introductory Lectures on Choices under Uncertainty*. Reading, Mass.: Addison-Wesley.

Robinson, Ira M., ed. (1972) *Decision-Making in Urban Planning*. Beverly Hills, Cal.: Sage Publications.

Schein, Edgar, H. (1969) *Process Consultation: Its Role in Organization Development*. Reading, Mass.: Addison-Wesley.

Schon, Donald A. (1971) *Beyond the Stable State*. New York: Random House.

Selznick, Philip (1949) *TVA and the Grass Roots*. Berkeley, Cal.: University of California Press.

Shackle, G. L. S. (1961) *Decision, Order, and Time in Human Affairs*. Cambridge, Eng.: Cambridge University Press.

Simon, Herbert A. (1947) *Administrative Behavior*. A Study of Decision-Making Processes in Administrative Organization. New York: MacMillan. 2nd edition, 1949.

——— (1957) *Models of Man: Social and Rational*. New York: John Wiley.

——— (1969) *The Sciences of the Artificial*. Cambridge, Mass.: The MIT Press.

Somers, Herman M. (1950) *Presidential Agency: OWMR: The Office of War Mobilization and Reconversion*. Cambridge, Mass.: Harvard University Press.

Thernstrom, Stephan (1969) *Poverty, Planning, and Politics in the New Boston: The Origins of ABCD*. New York: Basic Books.

Tinbergen, J. (1952) *On the Theory of Economic Policy*. Amsterdam: North Holland.

——— (1964) *Economic Policy: Principles and Design*. Amsterdam North Holland.

Von Foerster, H., and G. W. Zopf, Jr. (1962) *Principles of Self-Organization*. New York: Pergamon.

von Hayek, Friedrich A. (1944) *The Road to Serfdom*. London: George Routledge and Sons.

Waterston, Albert (1965) *Development Planning: Lessons of Experience*. Baltimore: The Johns Hopkins Press.

Wheatley, Paul (1971) *The Pivot of the Four Corners: A Preliminary Enquiry into the Origins and Character of the Ancient Chinese City*. Chicago: Aldine.

Wildavsky, Aaron (1964) *The Politics of the Budgetary Process*. Boston: Little, Brown.

Wilensky, Harold L. (1967) *Organizational Intelligence: Knowledge and Policy in Government and Industry*. New York: Basic Books.

Wiles, P. J. D. (1962) *The Political Economy of Communism*. Cambridge, Mass.: Harvard University Press.

Wilson, James Q. (1968) *City Politics and Public Policy*. New York: John Wiley and Sons.

Wootton, Barbara (1945) *Freedom Under Planning*. Chapel Hill, N.C.: The University of North Carolina Press.

[9]

RICHARD E. KLOSTERMAN

Arguments for and against planning

Planning is increasingly under attack around the world in the political arena, the popular press, and academic literature. Responding to these critiques, this article examines four major types of argument which have been made for and against planning in a modern democratic 'free market' society—economic arguments based on the advantages and deficiencies of competitive markets, pluralist arguments based on the benefits and limitations of pluralist group interactions, the traditional arguments used by the early planning profession, and recent 'neo-Marxist' arguments for and against planning. Together these perspectives suggest that planning can be defended on theoretical grounds as performing four essential social functions: promoting the collective interests of the community; considering the external effects of individual and group action; improving the information base for public and private decision-making; and protecting the interests of society's most needy members. Ultimately, however, planning can only be judged on the practical grounds of how well it performs these functions.

Formal governmental attempts to plan for and direct social change have always been controversial. However, public and academic attention to planning peaked in the 'great debate' of the 1930s and 1940s between proponents of government planning such as Karl Mannheim, Rexford Tugwell, and Barbara Wootton and defenders of 'free' markets and laissez faire such as Friedrich Hayek and Ludwig von Mises.[1] By the 1950s the debate had apparently been resolved; the grand issues of the desirability and feasibility of planning had been replaced by more concrete questions concerning particular planning techniques and alternative institutional structures for achieving society's objectives. Planning's status in modern society seemed secure; the only remaining questions appeared to be 'who shall plan, for what purposes, in what conditions, and by what devices?'[2]

Recent events in Great Britain, the United States, and other western societies indicate that planning's status is again being questioned and that the 'great debate' had never really ended. National planning efforts have been abandoned in Britain and the United States and the public agenda in both countries now focuses on deregulation, privatization, urban enterprise zones, and a host of other proposals for severely restricting government's role in economic affairs. Planning is increasingly attacked in the popular press, academic literature, and addresses to Parliament and Congress.[3] Graduate planning enrolments have declined dramatically and government retrenchment around the world has severely reduced job

6   RICHARD E. KLOSTERMAN

opportunities for professional planners at all levels.[4] At a more fundamental level, practitioners, students, and academics increasingly view planning as nothing more than a way to make a living, ignoring its potential to serve as a vocation, filling one's professional life with transcending purpose.[5]

In this environment it seems essential to return to fundamentals and examine carefully the case for and against planning in a modern industrial context. This article will critically examine four major types of argument which have been used as two-edged rhetorical swords both to criticise and defend government planning efforts and consider the implications which these arguments have for planning in the 1980s and beyond. The analysis will consider only formal governmental efforts at the local and regional level to achieve desired goals and solve novel problems in complex contexts or what in Britain is called 'town and country planning' and in America 'city and regional planning'.[6] As a result, the arguments considered below are not necessarily applicable to national economic planning or to the planning done by private individuals and organisations. Also not considered are the legal arguments for planning in particular constitutional or common law contexts or arguments such as Mannheim's[7] which have had little effect on the contemporary political debate.

Economic arguments

Contemporary arguments for abandoning planning, reducing regulation, and restricting the size of government are generally accompanied by calls for increased reliance on private entrepreneurship and the competitive forces of the market. That is, it is often argued, government regulation and planning are unnecessary and often harmful because they stifle entrepreneurial initiative, impede innovation, and impose unnecessary financial and administrative burdens on the economy.

These arguments find their historical roots in the work of Adam Smith, John Stuart Mill, and others of the classical liberal tradition.[8] Emphasising individual freedom, reliance on the 'impersonal' forces of the market, and the rule of law, these authors called for minimal state interference in society's economic affairs to protect individual liberty and promote freedom of choice and action. On pragmatic grounds they argued that competitive markets could be relied upon to coordinate the actions of individuals, provide incentives to individual action, and supply those goods and services which society wants, in the quantities which it desires, at the prices it is willing to pay.[9]

Building on these foundations, contemporary 'neo-classical' economists have demonstrated mathematically that competitive markets are capable in theory of allocating society's resources in an 'efficient' manner. That is, given an initial distribution of resources, a market-generated allocation of these resources cannot be redistributed to make some individuals better off without simultaneously making other individuals worse off.[10] However, this Pareto efficient allocation will occur only in perfectly competitive markets which satisfy the following conditions: (i) a large number of buyers and sellers trade identical goods and services; (ii) buyers and sellers possess sufficient information for rational market choice; (iii)

ARGUMENTS FOR AND AGAINST PLANNING　　7

consumer selections are unaffected by the preferences of others; (iv) individuals pursue the solitary objective of maximising profits; and (v) perfect mobility exists for production, labour, and consumption.[11]

The numerous obvious divergences between markets in the real world and economists' competitive market ideal justify a range of government actions fully consistent with private property, individual liberty, and decentralised market choice.[12] The need to increase market competition and promote informed consumer choice in a world of huge multinational firms and mass advertising helps justify restrictions on combinations in restraint of trade and prohibitions on misleading advertising. Indicative planning efforts at a national level in France and elsewhere are likewise justified as providing the information required for rational market choice. The development of municipal information systems and the preparation of long-range economic forecasts are similarly justified as promoting informed market choice with respect to locational decisions for which the relevant information is difficult to obtain, experience is limited, and mistakes can be exceptionally costly.[13]

More importantly, both classical and neo-classical economists recognise that even perfectly competitive markets require government action to correct 'market failures' involving: (i) public or collective consumption goods; (ii) externalities or spill-over effects; (iii) prisoners' dilemma conditions; and (iv) distributional issues.[14]

PUBLIC GOODS

Public goods are defined by two technical characteristics: (i) 'jointed' or 'non-rivalrous' consumption such that, once produced, they can be enjoyed simultaneously by more than one person; and (ii) 'non-excludability' or 'non-appropriability' such that it is difficult (in some cases impossible) to assign well-defined property rights or restrict consumer access.[15] Private goods such as apples, bread, and most 'normal' consumer goods exhibit neither characteristic; once produced they can be consumed by only one individual at a time. It is thus easy to restrict access to these goods and charge a price for their enjoyment. On the other hand, public goods such as open-air concerts, television broadcasts, and a healthy and pleasant environment simultaneously benefit more than one individual because one person's enjoyment does not prohibit another's enjoyment (except for any congestion effects). As a result, controlling access to these goods is either difficult, e g scramblers must be installed to restrict access to television broadcasts, or impossible, e g clean air.

Competitive markets can effectively allocate private goods which can only be enjoyed if they are purchased; as a result, the prices individuals are willing to pay for alternative goods accurately reflect their preferences for these goods. For public goods the benefit individuals receive is dependent on the total supply of the good, not on their contribution toward its production. Thus, in making voluntary market contributions to pay for, say, environmental protection, individuals are free to understate their real preferences for environmental quality in the hope that others will continue to pay for its protection—enabling them to

8   RICHARD E. KLOSTERMAN

be 'free riders', enjoying a pleasant environment at no personal expense. Of course if everyone did this, the money required to protect the environment adequately would no longer be available. Individuals may also underestimate others' willingness to contribute and 'overpay', thereby ending up with more public goods and fewer private goods than they really desire. In either case, the aggregated market preferences of individuals do not accurately reflect individual or social preferences for alternative public and private goods—the 'invisible hand' fumbles.

Similar arguments can be made for public provision of 'quasi-public' goods such as education, public health programmes, transportation facilities, and police and fire protection which simultaneously benefit particular individuals and provide shared, non-rationable benefits to society as a whole. As a result, public goods can be used to justify over 96 per cent of public purchases of goods and services and an almost open-ended range of government activities.[16]

EXTERNALITIES

Closely related to the concept of public goods are externalities or spill-over effects of production and consumption which are not taken into account in the process of voluntary market exchange.[17] The classical example is a polluting industrial plant which imposes aesthetic and health costs on neighbouring firms and individuals which are not included in its costs of production. Similar spill-over effects are revealed by land developers who can freely ignore the costs of congestion, noise, and loss of privacy which high-intensity development imposes on neighbouring landowners. Positive external economies include the increased land values associated with the construction of new transportation links and other large-scale improvements which adjoining landowners can enjoy without compensation.

As is true for public goods, the divergence between public and private costs and benefits associated with externalities causes even perfectly competitive markets to misallocate society's goods and services. Profit-maximising firms concerned only with maximising revenues and controlling costs are encourged to increase output even though the associated negative external costs vastly outweigh any increases in revenue because the external 'social' costs are not reflected in their production costs. Neighbourhood beautification projects and similar goods with positive external effects similarly tend to be under-produced because private entrepreneurs cannot appropriate the full economic benefits of their actions. In both situations the 'invisible hand' again fails to reflect accurately the needs and desires of society's members.

PRISONERS' DILEMMA CONDITIONS

Similar difficulties are revealed in circumstances in which individuals' pursuit of their own self interest does not lead to an optimal outcome for society or for the individual involved. Consider, for example, the situation faced by landlords in a declining neighbourhood who must decide whether to improve their rental property or invest their money elsewhere.[18] If a landlord improves his property and the others do not, the neighbourhood will continue to decline, making his

ARGUMENTS FOR AND AGAINST PLANNING   9

investment financially inadvisable. On the other hand, if he does not improve his property and the others improve theirs, the general improvement of the neighbourhood will allow him to raise rents without investing any money. As a result, it is in each individual's self interest to make no improvements; however, if they all refuse to do so, the neighbourhood will decline further, making things worse for everyone. An identical inevitable logic leads the competitive market to over-utilise 'common pool' resources with a limited supply and free access such as wilderness areas and a healthy environment.[19]

The fundamental problem here, as for public goods and externalities, lies in the interdependence between individual actions and the accompanying disjunction between individual benefits and costs and social benefits and costs. The only solution in all three cases is government action to deal with the public and external effects which are neglected in the pursuit of individual gain. Solutions for declining neighbourhoods include compulsory building codes, public acquisition and improvement of entire neighbourhoods, and 'enveloping'—public improvements to neighbourhood exteriors which will encourage private investments.

DISTRIBUTIONAL QUESTIONS

As was pointed out above, economists have demonstrated that, given an initial distribution of resources, perfectly competitive markets will allocate those resources in such a way that no one can benefit without someone else being harmed. However, neither the initial nor the final distribution can be assumed to be in any way 'optimal.' Both are determined largely by inherited wealth, innate talent, and blind luck and can range from states of perfect equality to extremes of tremendous wealth and abject poverty. Economic efficiency alone provides no criterion for judging one state superior in any way to another. As a result, given a societal consensus on the proper allocation of resources, e.g. that all babies should receive adequate nutrition and that the elderly should be cared for, government tax collection and income transfer programmes are justified to achieve these objectives with minimal market interference.[20]

IMPLICATIONS OF THE ECONOMIC ARGUMENTS

The preceding discussion has identified a range of government functions fully consistent with consumer sovereignty, individual freedom in production and trade, and decentralised market choice. Each of these functions justifies a major area of contemporary planning practice: first, providing the information needed for informed market choice through indicative planning, the development of urban information systems, and the preparation of long-range population, economic, and land use projections; secondly, the provision of public goods through transportation, environmental, and economic development planning; thirdly, the control of externalities and resolution of prisoner dilemma conditions through urban renewal, community development and natural resources planning and the use of traditional land regulatory devices; and lastly, health, housing, and other forms of social planning to compensate for inequities in the distribution of basic social goods and services. Specific government actions to reduce conflicts

10   RICHARD E KLOSTERMAN

between incompatible land uses, coordinate private development and public infrastructure, preserve open space and historic buildings, and examine the long-range impacts of current actions can similarly be justified as needed to correct market failures revealed in the physical development of the city.

It must be recognised, however, that while *necessary* to justify government planning in a market society, these arguments are not *sufficient* to do so. This is true, first, because those activities which are the proper responsibility of government in a market society need not be *planning* matters at all. Government decisions concerning the provision of public goods, the control of externalities, and so on can be made in a number of ways: by professional planners, by elected or appointed public officials, by the proclamations of a divine ruler, or by pure happenstance involving no deliberate decision process at all. If planning is justifed by the economic arguments for government alone, it is impossible to differentiate between government planning and government non-planning —'government' is reduced to an undifferentiated mass.

More fundamentally, the inability of existing markets to allocate society's resources adequately does not necessarily imply that government provision, regulation, or planning are necessary or even advisable. Suitably defined and administered performance standards, building codes, and development requirements may more effectively guide the land development process than traditional master planning and zoning techniques; effluent charges can often control pollution discharges more efficiently than the direct enforcement of effluent standards; and public facilities and services may be provided more equitably by leasing and voucher systems than directly by government. Thus, in these and other areas, the appropriate role for 'planning' may not be the preparation of formal end-state plans but the establishment and maintenance of an appropriate system of 'quasi-markets'.[21]

As a result, the case for planning in a market society cannot be based solely on the theoretical limitations of markets outlined above. Popular dissatisfaction with the free enterprise system is not based on an appreciation of the various theories of market failure, but on its inability to provide stable economic growth and an adequate standard of living for all of society's members. Conversely, the informed critiques of planning are not made in ignorance of the theoretical limitations of markets, but in the belief that, despite these limitations, markets are still more effective than attempts at centralised coordination by government.[22] As a result, the case for planning in a modern market society cannot be made in the abstract, but requires a careful evaluation of planning's effectiveness relative to alternative institutional mechanisms for achieving society's objectives.

Pluralist arguments

Other arguments for and against planning emerged during the 1960s and 1970s to complement the economic arguments considered above. Accepting the economic arguments for government outlined above, Lindblom, Wildavsky, and other critics of planning suggest that government actions should not be guided by long-range planning or attempts at comprehensive coordination but by increased reliance on existing political bargaining processes.[23] Underlying these arguments is a political analogue to the economists' perfectly competitive market in which competition between formal and informal groups pursuing a range of divergent goals and interests is assumed to place all important issues on the public agenda, guarantee that no group dominates the public arena, maintain political stability, and improve individuals' intellectual and deliberative skills. In this model, government has no independent role other than establishing and enforcing the rules of the game and ratifying the political adjustments worked out among the competing groups. Thus, it is assumed, political competition, like market competition, eliminates the need for independent government action, planning, and coordination.[24]

Unfortunately, the pluralist model is subject to the same fundamental limitations which face the economic model of perfect market competition. Just as real-world markets are dominated by gigantic national and multinational conglomerates, the political arena is dominated by individuals and groups who use their access to government officials and other élites to protect their status, privilege, and wealth and ensure that government acts in their interest. Particularly privileged are corporate and business leaders whose cooperation is essential for government's efforts to maintain full employment and secure stable economic growth. As a result, government officials, particularly at the local level, cannot treat business as only another special interest, but must provide incentives to stimulate desired business activity such as tax rebates and low interest-loans to attract new industry and downtown improvement projects to encourage retail and commercial activity in the central business district. Further supporting business's unique position in the group bargaining process is an unrecognised acceptance of the needs and priorities of business which pervades our political and governmental processes, media, and cultural and educational institutions.[25]

Systematically excluded from the group bargaining process are minority and low-income individuals and groups residing in decaying urban centres and rural hinterlands. Lacking the time, training, resources, leadership, information, or experience required to participate effectively in the political process, these groups have no effective voice in determining the public policies which shape their world. By thus tying individuals' political voice to underlying disparities in political power and resources, existing political processes exacerbate existing inequalities in income and wealth and fail to provide adequate information for fully informed policy-making.[26]

Group bargaining also fails adequately to provide collective goods and services which provide small benefits to a large number of individuals. In small groups, each member receives a substantial proportion of the gain from a collective good; as a result, it is clearly in their interest to ensure that the good be provided. For large groups, individual benefits are so small and organisational costs are so large that it is in no one's immediate interest to provide for the common good. The result is an 'exploitation of the great by the small' in which small groups with narrow, well-defined interests such as doctors and lawyers can organise more effectively to achieve their objectives than larger groups such as consumers who share more broadly defined interests. By turning government power over to the most interested parties and excluding the public from the policy formulation and implementation process, pluralist bargaining systematically neglects the political spill-over effects of government actions and policies on unrepresented groups and individuals.[27]

The limitations of pluralist bargaining, like the limitations of market competition, provide the theoretical justification for a wide range of planning functions. Accepting the critiques of comprehensive planning by Lindblom and others, some authors propose that planning be limited to the 'adjunctive' functions of providing information, analysing alternative public policies, and identifying bases for improved group interaction. The objective here, as for indicative planning, is improving existing decentralised decision processes by providing the information needed for more informed decision-making.[28]

The pluralist model is incorporated directly in the advocacy planning approach which rejects the preparation of value-neutral 'unitary' plans representing the overall community interest for the explicit advocacy of 'plural plans' representing all of the interests involved in the physical development of the city.[29] Recognising the inequities of existing political processes, advocate planners have acted primarily as advocates for society's poor and minority members. Particularly noteworthy here are the efforts of the Cleveland Planning Commission to promote 'a wider range of choices for those Cleveland residents who have few, if any, choices'.[30]

Experience has demonstrated, however, that advocacy planning shares many of the limitations of the pluralist model on which it is based: (i) urban neighbourhoods are no more homogeneous and the neighbourhood interest no more easy to identify than is true at the community level; (ii) group leaders are not representative of the group's membership; (iii) it is easier to represent narrowly-defined interests and preserve the status quo than to advocate diffuse and widely-shared interests or propose new alternatives; and (iv) public officials still lack the information required for adequate decision-making.[31]

As a result, there remains a fundamental need for public sector planners who can represent the shared interests of the community, coordinate the actions of individuals and groups, and consider the long range effects of current actions. This does not imply that the shared interests of the community are superior to the private interests of individuals and groups or that the external and long-term effects of action are more important than their direct and immediate impacts. It assumes only that these considerations are particularly important *politically* because only government can ensure that they will be considered at all.[32] It is on these foundations that the traditional arguments for town and country planning have been made.

Traditional arguments

The planning profession originated at the turn of the century with the widespread dissatisfaction with the results of existing market and political processes reflected in the physical squalour and political corruption of the emerging industrial city.

ARGUMENTS FOR AND AGAINST PLANNING   13

The profession's organisational roots in architecture and landscape architecture were reflected in early views of planning as 'do|ing| for the city what ... architecture does for the home'—improving the built environment to raise amenity levels, increase efficiency in the performance of necessary functions, and promote health, safety, and convenience. The profession's political roots in progressive reform were reflected in arguments for planning as an independent 'fourth power' of government promoting the general or public interest over the narrow conflicting interests of individuals and groups. Others viewed planning as a mechanism for coordinating the impacts of public and private land uses on adjoining property owners and considering the future consequences of present actions in isolation from day-to-day operating responsibilities. Underlying all of these arguments was the belief that the conscious application of professional expertise, instrumental rationality, and scientific methods could more effectively promote economic growth and political stability than the unplanned forces of market and political competition.[33]

Implicit in these traditional arguments for planning are many of the more formal justifications examined above. The arguments for planning as an independent function of government promoting the collective public interest obviously parallel the economic and pluralist arguments for government action to provide public or collective consumption goods. The calls for planning as comprehensive coordination similarly recognise the need for dealing with the external effects of individual and group action. And the arguments for planning which consider the long-range effects of current actions likewise acknowledge the need for more informed public policy-making. Noteworthy by its absence is any concern with the distributional effects of government and private actions which were largely ignored in planners' attempts to promote a collective public interest.[34]

By mid-century social scientists who had joined the ranks of academic planners began severely to question each of these arguments for public sector planning: planners' concern with the physical city was viewed as overly restrictive; their perceptions of the urban development process seen as politically naive; their technical solutions found to reflect their protestant middle-class views of city life; their attempts to promote a collective public interest revealed to serve primarily the needs of civic and business élites; and democratic comprehensive coordination of public and private development proven to be organisationally and politically impossible.[35]

Accompanying these critiques were new conceptions of planning as a value-neutral, rational process of problem identification, goal definition, analysis, implementation, and evaluation. In recent years the rational planning model has come under severe attack as well for failing to recognise the fundamental constraints on private and organisational decision-making, the inherently political and ethical nature of planning practice, and the organisational, social and psychological realities of planning practice. As a result, while the social need for providing collective goods, dealing with externalities, and so on remains, the planning profession currently lacks a widely accepted procedural model for defining planning problems or justifying planning solutions.[36]

Marxist arguments

The recent emergence of Marxist theories of urban development has added a new dimension to the debate about the desirability and feasibility of planning.[37] From the Marxist perspective, the role of planning in contemporary society can only be understood by recognising the structure of modern capitalism as it relates to the physical environment. That is, it is argued, the fundamental social and economic institutions of capitalist society systematically promote the interests of those who control society's productive capital over those of the remainder of society. The formal organisation of the state is likewise assumed to serve the long-term interests of capital by creating and maintaining conditions conducive to the efficient accumulation of capital in the private sector, subordinating the conflicting short-run interests of the factions of capital to the long-run interests of the capitalist class, and containing civil strife which threaten the capitalist order. These actions are legitimised by a prevailing democratic ideology which portrays the state as a neutral instrument serving the interests of society as a whole.

Marxists argue that fundamental social improvements can result only from the revolutionary activity of labour and the replacement of existing social institutions benefiting capital by new ones which serve the interests of society at large. Essential reforms include public ownership of the means of production and centralised planning which would replace existing market and political decision processes by the comprehensive coordination of investment decisions and democratic procedures for formulating social priorities and restricting individual actions which conflict with the long-term interests of society.[38]

Applying this perspective to urban planning, Marxist scholars have been highly critical of traditional planning practice and planning theory. The arguments for and against planning examined above are dismissed as mere ideological rationalisations which fail to recognise the material conditions and historical and political forces which allowed planning to emerge and define its role in society. Accepting the limitations of market and political competition outlined above, Marxists interpret planners' actions in each sphere as primarily serving the interests of capital at the expense of the rest of society. Planners' attempts to provide collective goods and control externalities are assumed to serve the needs of capital by helping manage the inevitable contradictions of capitalism revealed in the physical and social development of the city. Planners' attempts to employ scientific techniques and professional expertise are seen as helping legitimise state action in the interest of capital by casting it in terms of the public interest, neutral professionalism, and scientific rationality. And planners' attempts to advance the interests of deprived groups are dismissed as merely coopting these groups, forestalling the structural reforms which are ultimately required for real improvement to their positions in society.[39]

While extremely valuable in helping reveal the underlying nature of contemporary planning, the Marxist perspective has obvious limitations as a guide to planning practice.[40] A strict Marxist analysis which sees all social relations and all government actions as serving the interests of capital identifies no mechanism for reform other than a radical transformation of society which is highly unlikely in

ARGUMENTS FOR AND AGAINST PLANNING　　　15

the near future: If needed reforms can result only from the revolutionary action of labour and all attempts to help the needy merely delay necessary structural changes, there is no significant role for reform-minded planners who occupy an ambiguous class position between labour and capital. And rejection of planners' attempts to apply professional expertise and scientific methods to public policy-making as merely legitimising and maintaining existing social and economic relations deprives professional planners of their main political resource for dealing with other political actors—their claims to professional expertise.

As a result, as was true for the arguments for and against planning examined earlier, the Marxist arguments cannot be evaluated in the abstract but must be examined critically in the light of present economic and political realities. Thus while it may be desirable in the abstract to replace existing market and political decision processes, this is highly unlikely in most Western democracies. The lack of a revolutionary role for planners in traditional Marxist analysis does not mean that they cannot work effectively for short-term reforms with other progressive professionals and community-based organisations. And while contemporary planning may indeed serve the interests of capital, it need not serve these interests alone and is clearly preferable to exclusive reliance on the fundamentally flawed processes of market and political competition.

Conclusions and implications

The preceding discussion has examined a variety of arguments for and against planning in a modern industrial context. Underlying this apparent diversity is an implicit consensus about the need for public sector planning to perform four vital social functions—promoting the common or collective interests of the community, considering the external effects of individual and group action, improving the information base for public and private decision-making, and considering the distributional effects of public and private action.

The first need is reflected in the economic arguments for government action to resolve prisoners' dilemma conditions and provide public or collective consumption goods such as a healthy and pleasant environment which cannot be provided adequately by even perfectly competitive markets. The second results from the inability of markets to deal with social costs and benefits of production and consumption which are not reflected in market prices or revenues. The third is reflected in the public and private need for improved information on the long-term effects of locational decisions necessary for making adequately informed market decisions. And the fourth results from the fact that market competition alone is incapable in principle of resolving distributional questions in a socially acceptable manner.

From the pluralist perspective, planning is required to represent broadly defined interests which are neglected in the competition between organised groups representing more narrow interests. And it is required to represent the external effects of political decisions on groups and individuals who are not directly involved in the political bargaining process. Improved information on the short- and long-term consequences of alternative public policies and actions is required to facilitate the group bargaining process. And planners are required to serve as advocates for society's most needy members who are systematically excluded from the group bargaining process.

The traditional arguments for planning reflect the need for representing the collective interests of the community in the cails for planning as an independent function of government charged with promoting the public interest. The need for considering the external effects of individual action is reflected in the conceptions of planning as comprehensive coordination. From this perspective, planning is required to provide information on the physical development of the city and the long-range implications of current actions. Distributional questions were regretfully largely ignored in traditional planning's efforts to promote an aggregate public interest.

While largely critical of contemporary planning practice, the Marxist perspective recognises each of the arguments for planning identified by the other perspectives. The need for representing the collective interests of the community is reflected in the Marxist prescriptions for replacing existing decentralised markets by centralised planning in the interests of society as a whole. The need for considering externalities is reflected in calls for the comprehensive coordination of investment decisions. From the Marxist perspective, traditional forms of planning information primarily serve the interests of capital; thus to promote fundamental social change planners are called upon to inform the public of the underlying realities of capitalist society. And the need to correct the structural imbalances in power and wealth which shape contemporary society underlies the Marxist call for the radical reformation of society.

While all four perspectives propose that planning is required *in theory* to fulfil these fundamental social requirements, they each recognise in their own way that these theoretical arguments for planning are insufficient. Contemporary economists argue that market competition, properly structured and augmented, can be more efficient and equitable than traditional forms of public-sector planning and regulation. Critics such as Lindblom have revealed planners' traditional models of centralised coordination to be impossible in a decentralised democratic society. And the social critics of the 1960s and 1970s and Marxist critics of today have demonstrated convincingly that traditional planning practice, while couched in terms of neutral technical competence and the public interest, has primarily served the interests of society's most powerful and wealthy members.

An objective evaluation of sixty years' experience with town and country planning in Great Britain and the United States must recognise the tremendous gap between planning's potential and its performance. While there have been several remarkable successes, much of contemporary practice is still limited to the preparation of 'boiler plate' plans, the avoidance of political controversy, and the routine administration of overly rigid and conservative regulations.[41] It is thus an open question whether planning, as currently practised the world over, deserves high levels of public support or whether other professional groups and institutional arrangements can better perform the vital social functions identified above. As a result, the arguments for planning outlined above cannot be taken as a defence of the status quo in planning, but must serve as a challenge to the

ARGUMENTS FOR AND AGAINST PLANNING   17

profession to learn from its mistakes and build on new and expanded conceptions of the public interest, information, and political action to realise its ultimate potential.[42]

NOTES AND REFERENCES

1 See, for example, Mannheim, Karl, *Man and Society in an Age of Reconstruction: Studies in Modern Social Structure*, New York, Harcourt, Brace, and World, 1944, pp. 41–75; Tugwell, Rexford G., 'Implementing the General Interest', *Public Administration Review*, 1 (1) Autumn 1940, pp. 32–49; Wootton, Barbara, *Freedom Under Planning*, Chapel Hill, University of North Carolina Press, 1945; Hayek, Friedrich A., *The Road to Serfdom*, Chicago, University of Chicago Press, 1944; and von Mises, Ludwig, *Planning for Freedom and Other Essays*, South Holland, Illinois, Libertarian Press, 1952.

2 Examples here include Schonfield, Andrew, *Modern Capitalism*, New York, Oxford University Press, 1965; and Dahl, Robert A. and Lindblom, Charles E., *Politics, Economics, and Welfare*, New York, Harper and Row, 1953. The quotation is from Dahl and Lindblom, p. 5.

3 For recent critiques of planning see Friedman, Milton and Friedman, Rose, *Free to Choose: A Personal Statement*, New York, Harcourt, Brace and Jovanovich, 1979; Simon, William E., *A Time for Truth*, New York, Reader's Digest Press, 1978; and Wildavsky, Aaron, 'If Planning is Everything, Maybe It's Nothing,' *Policy Sciences*, 4 (3) June 1973, pp. 277–295.

4 The dramatically declining enrolments in American planning schools are documented and analysed by Krueckeberg, Donald A., 'Planning and the New Depression in the Social Sciences', *Journal of Planning Education and Research*, 3 (2) Winter 1984, pp. 78–86.

5 Friedmann, John, 'Planning as a Vocation', *Plan (Canada)*, 6 (2) April 1966, pp. 99–124 and 7 (3) July 1966, pp. 8–26.

6 A similar definition of planning is proposed by Alexander, Ernest R., 'If Planning Isn't Everything, Maybe It's Something', *Town Planning Review*, 52 (2) April 1981, pp. 131–142.

7 Mannheim, op. cit.

8 These writers are 'classical' liberals in that their views of government and liberty are fundamentally different from those associated with contemporary liberalism. Classical liberals define liberty in the negative sense in which freedom is determined by the extent to which individuals' actions are *externally* constrained by the actions of others; the wider the sphere of non-interference, the greater an individual's liberty. Thus to increase the (negative) liberty of individuals by decreasing the external interference of the state, classical liberals call for a sharply reduced role for government in the domestic and foreign economy. 'Contemporary' liberals, on the other hand, view liberty largely in the positive sense in which individuals are free when no *internal* constraints such as a lack of knowledge, resources, or opportunities restrain their actions. From this perspective, increasing the (positive) liberty of individuals, particularly the most deprived, requires deliberate government action to promote social welfare and reduce the internal constraints on individual action, even though this may restrain the actions (and negative liberty) of some individuals. Compare Friedman, Milton, *Capitalism and Freedom*, Chicago, University of Chicago Press, 1962, pp. 5–6; and Finer, Herman, *Road to Reaction*, Boston, Little Brown and Co., 1945, pp. 221–228. Contemporary examples of the classical liberal argument include Hayek, op. cit., Friedman and Friedman, op. cit., Friedman, op. cit. and Sorensen, Anthony D. and Day, Richard A., 'Libertarian Planning', *Town Planning Review*, 52 (4) October 1981, pp. 390–402.

9 Heilbroner, Robert L., *The Worldly Philosophers*, New York, Simon and Schuster, 1969 (3rd edn.), pp. 48–61; Friedman and Friedman, op. cit., pp. 9–27.

10 See, for example, Bator, Francis M., 'The Simple Analytics of Welfare Maximization', *American Economic Review*, 47 (1) March 1957, pp. 22–59.

11 Seventeen more restrictive assumptions including perfectly divisible capital and consumer goods and an absence of risk and uncertainty are identified by De. V. Graaff, J., *Theoretical Welfare Economics*, London, Cambridge University Press, 1957.

12 For analyses of the many empirical limitations of real markets see Lindblom, Charles E., *Politics and Markets: The World's Politics-Economic Systems*, New York, Basic Books, 1977, pp. 76–89 and 144–157; and Heilbroner, Robert L. and

18 RICHARD E. KLOSTERMAN

Thurow, Lester C., *The Economic Problem*, Englewood Cliffs, Prentice Hall, 1978 (5th edn.), pp. 201–219.

13 Cohen, Stephen, *Modern Capitalist Planning: The French Model*, Cambridge, Harvard University Press, 1969; Foster, Christopher, 'Planning and the Market', in Cowan, Peter (ed.), *The Future of Planning: A Study Sponsored by the Centre for Environmental Studies*, London, Heinemann, 1973, pp. 135–140; Meyerson, Martin, 'Building the Middle-range Bridge for Comprehensive Planning', *Journal of the American Institute of Planners*, 22 (1) 1956, pp. 58–64; and Skjei, Stephen S., 'Urban Problems and the Theoretical Justification of Urban Planning', *Urban Affairs Quarterly*, 11 (3) March 1976, pp. 323–344.

14 Thus, for example, Adam Smith recognised that government must be responsible for: (i) 'protecting the society from the violence and invasion of other independent societies'; (ii) 'establishing an exact administration of justice'; and (iii) 'erecting and maintaining those public institutions and those public works, which . . . are . . . of such a nature that the profit could never repay the expense of an individual or small number of individuals', Smith, Adam, *An Enquiry into the Nature and Causes of the Wealth of Nations* (edited by Edwin Cannon), New York, Modern Library, 1937, pp. 653, 669, and 681; his third category of justified state functions is discussed in pages 681–740. Other government functions recommended by the classical economists include: the regulation of public utilities, the establishment of social insurance systems, the enactment of protective labour legislation, and compensatory fiscal and monetary policy. See Robbins, Lionel, *The Theory of Economic Policy in English Classical Political Economy*, London, Macmillan, 1952, esp. pp. 55–61.

15 The literature on public goods is extensive. For excellent reviews see Burkhead, Jesse and Miner, Jerry, *Public Expenditure*, Chicago, Aldine, 1971; and Head, John G., *Public Goods and Public Welfare*, Durham, North Carolina, Duke University Press, 1974, pp. 68–92 and 164–183. In the planning literature see Moore, Terry, 'Why Allow Planners to do What They Do? A Justification From Economic Theory', *Journal of the American Institute of Planners*, 44 (4) October 1978, pp. 387–398. The discussion below generally follows that in Bator, Francis M., *The Question of Government Spending: Public Needs and Private Wants*, New York, Collier Books, 1960. pp. 80–102.

16 Bator, op. cit., p. 104; Friedman and Friedman, op. cit., pp. 27–37. Similar arguments can be used to justify government provision of highways, dams, and other 'decreasing cost' goods with large initial costs and decreasing marginal costs; see Bator, op. cit., pp. 93–95.

17 The relevant literature here is extensive as well. For excellent reviews see Mishan, E. J., 'The Postwar Literature on Externalities: An Interpretive Review', *Journal of Economic Literature*, 9 (1) March 1971, pp. 1–28, and Head, op. cit., pp. 184–213. In the planning literature see Lee, Douglas B. Jr., 'Land Use Planning as a Response to Market Failure' in de Neufville, Judith I., (ed.), *The Land Use Planning Debate in the United States*, New York, Pleneum Press, 1981, pp. 153–154.

18 This example is adapted from Davis, Otto A., and Whinston, Andrew B., 'The Economics of Urban Renewal', *Law and Contemporary Problems*, 26 (2) Winter 1961, pp. 106–117.

19 See the classic article by Garret Hardin, 'The Tragedy of the Commons', *Science*, 162, 13 December 1968, pp. 242–248. For more general discussions see Luce, Duncan and Raiffa, Howard, *Games and Decision: Introduction and Critical Survey*, New York, John Wiley, 1957, pp. 88–154. In the planning literature see Moore, op. cit.

20 Bator, op. cit., pp 87–89; Musgrave, Richard S., *The Theory of Public Finance: A Study in Public Economy*, New York, McGraw Hill, pp. 17–22. These points do not, of course, exhaust the economic arguments for and against planning. Thus while Friedman, op. cit., pp. 7–21, and Hayek, op. cit., pp. 43–118, defend unrestricted markets as necessary to protect individual liberty, Barbara Wootton, op. cit., argues that government planning is fully compatible with the whole range of cultural, civil, political, and economic freedoms. For other economic arguments for planning see Webber, Melvin, 'Planning in an Environment of Change, Part Two: Permissive Planning', *Town Planning Review*, 39 (4) January 1969, pp. 282–284; Oxley, op. cit.; and Lee, op. cit. More fundamental 'Marxist' critiques of reliance on competitive markets are considered below.

21 See Webber, op. cit., pp. 284–295; Lee, op. cit., pp. 158–164; Friedman, op. cit., pp. 84–107; Moore, op. cit., pp. 393–396; and Foster, op. cit., pp. 153–165.

22 See, for example, Becker, Gary S., 'Competition and Democracy', *Journal of Law and Economics*, 1, October 1958, pp. 105–109, and Wolf, Charles Jr., 'A Theory of Nonmarket Failure: Framework for Implementation Analysis', *Journal of Law and Economics*, 22 (1) April 1979, pp. 107–140.

23 See, for example, Lindblom, Charles E., 'The Science of Muddling Through', *Public Admin-*

ARGUMENTS FOR AND AGAINST PLANNING   19

istration Review, 19 (1) January 1959, pp. 79–88 and Wildavsky, op. cit.

24 Conolly, William E. (ed.), *The Bias of Pluralism*, New York, Atherton, 1969, pp. 3–13.

25 Lindblom, op. cit., pp. 170–233; Elkin, Stephen L., 'Market and Politics in Liberal Democracy', *Ethics*, 92 (4) July 1982, pp. 720–732; Miliband, Ralph, *The State in Capitalist Society*, New York, Basic Books, 1969.

26 Gamson, William A., 'Stable Underrepresentation in American Society', *American Behavioral Scientist*, 12 (1) November/December 1968, pp. 15–21; Skjei, Stephen S., 'Urban Systems Advocacy', *Journal of the American Institute of Planners*, 38 (1) January 1972, pp. 11–24; also see Dye, Thomas R. and Zeigler, L. Harmon, *The Irony of Democracy: An Uncommon Introduction to American Politics*, North Scituate, Mass., Duxbury Press, 1975 (3rd edn.), pp. 225–284.

27 Olson, Mancur, *The Logic of Collective Action: Public Goods and the Theory of Groups*, Cambridge, Harvard University Press, 1965; Lowi, Theodore J., 'The Public Philosophy: Interest-group Liberalism', *American Political Science Review*, 61 (1) March 1967, pp. 5–24. For an extensive discussion of other forms of 'non-market failure' see Wolf, op. cit.

28 See, for example, Rondinelli, Dennis A., 'Adjunctive Planning and Urban Policy Development', *Urban Affairs Quarterly*, 6 (1) September 1971, pp. 13–39; and Skjei, Stephen S., 'Urban Problems and the Theoretical Justification of Planning', *Urban Affairs Quarterly*, 11 (3) March 1976, pp. 323–344.

29 Davidoff, Paul, 'Advocacy and Pluralism in Planning', *Journal of the American Institute of Planners*, 31 (6) November 1965, pp. 331–338.

30 Krumholz, Norman, Cogger, Janice and Linner, John, 'The Cleveland Policy Planning Report', *Journal of the American Institute of Planners*, 41 (3) September 1975, pp. 298–304; Krumholz, Norman, 'A Retrospective View of Equity Planning: Cleveland, 1969–1979', *Journal of the American Planning Association*, 48 (2) Spring 1982, pp. 163–174.

31 Peattie, Lisa R., 'Reflections on Advocacy Planning', *Journal of the American Institute of Planners*, 34 (2) March 1968, pp. 80–88; Skjei, Stephen S., 'Urban Systems Advocacy', *Journal of the American Institute of Planners*, 38 (1) January 1972, pp. 11–24; Mazziotti, Donald F., 'The Underlying Assumptions of Advocacy Planning: Pluralism and Reform', *Journal of the American Institute of Planners*, 40 (1) January 1974, pp. 38, 40–47.

32 Klosterman, Richard E., 'A Public Interest Criterion', *Journal of the American Planning Association*, 46 (3) July 1980, p. 330; Barry, Brian, *Political Argument*, New York, Humanities Press, 1965, pp. 234–235.

33 For examples of each argument see: (i) Robinson, Charles Mulford, *City Planning*, New York, G. P. Putnams, 1916, pp. 291–303 (the quotation is from p. 291); (ii) Howard, John T., 'In Defense of Planning Commissions', *Journal of the American Institute of Planners*, 17 (1) Spring 1951, pp. 89–93, and Tugwell, op. cit.; and (iii) Bettman, Alfred, *City and Regional Planning Papers* (edited by Arthur C. Comey), Cambridge, Mass., Harvard University Press, pp. 5–30, and Dunham, Allison, 'A Legal and Economic Basis for City Planning', *Columbia Law Review*, 58, 1958, pp. 650–671.

34 The earliest example of this concern in the planning literature known to the author is Webber, Melvin M., 'Comprehensive Planning and Social Responsibility: Toward an AIP Consensus on the Profession's Role and Purposes', *Journal of the American Institute of Planners*, 29 (4) November 1963, pp. 232–241.

35 For examples of these now-familiar critiques see Gans, Herbert J., 'City Planning in America: A Sociological Analysis' in Gans, Herbert J., *People and Plans: Essays on Urban Problems and Solutions*, New York, Basic Books, 1963; Altshuler, Alan A., 'The Goals of Comprehensive Planning', *Journal of the American Institute of Planners*, 31 (5) August 1965, pp. 186–195; Bolan, Richard S., 'Emerging Views of Planning', *Journal of the American Institute of Planners*, 33 (4) July 1967, pp. 233–246; and Kravitz, Alan S., 'Mandaranism: Planning as Handmaiden to Conservative Politics' in Beyle, Thad L., and Lathrop George T. (eds.), *Planning and Politics: Uneasy Partnership*, New York, Odyssey Press, 1970.

36 Critiques of the 'rational' planning model have dominated the planning theory literature for the last decade. For reviews of this literature and their implications for contemporary planning practice see DiMento, Joseph F., *The Consistency Doctrine and the Limits of Planning*, Cambridge, Mass., Oelgeschlager, Gunn, and Hain, 1980, pp. 44–117; and Alexander, Ernest R., 'After Rationality, What? A Review of Responses to Paradigm Breakdown', *Journal of the American Planning Association*, 50 (1) Winter 1984, pp. 62–69.

37 Examples here include Castells, Manuel, *The Urban Question: A Marxist Approach*, Cambridge, Mass., The MIT Press, 1977; Harvey, David, *Social Justice and the City*, Baltimore, Johns Hopkins University Press, 1973, pp. 195–238; Paris, Chris (ed.), *Critical Readings in Planning Theory*, Oxford,

20 RICHARD E. KLOSTERMAN

Pergamon, 1982; and the articles cited in footnote 39 below.

38 Harrington, Michael, *Socialism*, New York, Saturday Review Press, 1972, pp. 270–307; Baran, Paul A., *The Longer View: Essays Toward a Critique of Political Economy*, New York, Monthly Review Press, 1969, pp. 144–149; Huberman, Leo and Sweezy, Paul M., *Introduction to Socialism*, New York, Monthly Review Press, 1968, pp. 60–65.

39 See, for example, Fainstein, Norman I. and Fainstein, Susan S., 'New Debates in Urban Planning: The Impact of Marxist Theory Within the United States', *International Journal of Urban and Regional Research*, 3 (3) September 1979, pp. 381–403; Beauregard, Robert A., 'Planning in an Advanced Capitalist State' in Burchell, Robert W. and Sternlieb, George (eds.), *Planning Theory in the 1980's: A Search for New Directions*, New Brunswick, NJ, Center for Urban Policy Research, 1978; Harvey, David, 'On Planning the Ideology of Planning' in ibid.; Boyer, M. Christine, *Dreaming the Rational City: The Myth of City Planning*, Cambridge, Mass., The MIT Press, 1983.

40 The discussion here draws heavily on that in Fainstein and Fainstein, op. cit.

41 Also see Branch, Melville C., 'Delusions and Defusions of City Planning in the United States', *Management Science*, 16 (12) August 1970, pp. 714–732, and Branch, Melville C., 'Sins of City Planners', *Public Administration Review*, 42 (1) January/February 1982, pp. 1–5.

42 See Alexander, op. cit., pp. 138–140; Klosterman, op. cit.; Forester, John, 'Critical Theory and Planning Practice', *Journal of the American Planning Association*, 46 (3) July 1980, pp. 275–286; Clavel, Pierre, Forester, John and Goldsmith, William W. (eds.), *Urban and Regional Planning in an Age of Austerity*, New York, Pergamon, 1980; and Dyckman, John W., 'Reflections on Planning Practice in an Age of Reaction', *Journal of Planning Education and Research*, 3 (1) Summer 1983, pp. 5–12.

ACKNOWLEDGEMENTS

The author gratefully acknowledges the valuable comments received from Robert A. Beauregard of Rutgers University, Jay M. Stein of the Georgia Institute of Technology, and the anonymous reviewers of this journal.

Part III
Modelling Approaches and Evaluation

[10]

Urban Modelling and Planning: Reflections, Retrodictions and Prescriptions

Michael Batty

There are no such things as applied sciences, only applications of science.

Louis Pasteur

Introduction

This chapter reflects upon the development of urban models for planning purposes which were first applied in the United States in the late 1950s. The notion that such activity constitutes a 'science' is questioned, for it is argued that the field entirely owes its conception and existence to the demands of public policy. The rise and decline of modelling in practice is traced, the types of models identified and some important achievements are noted. As the demands of policy changed and the rationale for models disappeared, the field continued, institutionalized in academia and shielded from the harsher worlds of practice. The reasons for this changing context are briefly sketched and the discussion then turns to a possible re-emergence of the field as this time those remaining in it respond to the new landscape of practice. This emergent context is quite different from that of a generation ago, and it is still unclear as to the applicability of models in this changed environment. Finally some prescriptions for the field are noted and the value of modelling as a mode of thinking in the computer age is emphasized.

Urban models first emerged in the late 1950s in the United States. They were preceded by the development of transportation models which developed in response to the growing need to cater for the automobile. The driving force for these developments was practice. There was no science as such on which to build, and the field was constructed from such bits and pieces of theory which the model-builders and planners could easily lay their hands on. The intellectual landscape to which these techniques related was a peculiar mix of economics and engineering,

147

Michael Batty

and models were 'invented' in a practical, policy-based context. If there is ever an area which contradicts Pasteur's view that science exists independently of its applications, it is urban modelling, for the field emerged in response to applications, and it remains an open question as to whether or not it would still have developed without the driving force of urban policy.

This intimate connection with practice means that the field will never be to able to escape the volatility of its social context. Urban planning and policy-making have changed dramatically over the past twenty-five years and the development and popularity of modelling is closely reflected in such changes. As the post-war boom turned to recession, and as the emphasis in western industrialized societies turned from strategic planning to short-term tactical management, as urban society began its transition from industrial to post-industrial, and as the economy began to radically restructure itself into one based on information, urban models moved from the centre stage of strategic urban planning to the edge, to disappear finally in the form they were originally cast a generation or more ago. The intellectual and practice-based landscape is still littered with their remains and much of the landscape has been moulded by their development, but the cutting edge which these techniques once represented in planning practice and theory is long gone. The purpose of this essay is to reflect on these developments and to explain why. But this is not simply a retrospective affair. The discussion will also be prescriptive and critical, and will attempt to assess the continuing role for such activity, particularly in the context of the emergent computer age. There is a new driving force to modelling which once again represents a way of thinking about and 'doing' planning. This we will attempt to assess.

It is not easy to provide balanced reflections on a field which one has been close to for so long. Indeed, good critiques are usually produced by those who stand at arm's length from the field, those whose views are fresher and keener, and who are less committed in the first instance. There is much to Max Planck's oft-quoted dictum that a scientific theory only finally dies when those who have cut their teeth on it disappear from the scene too. There have been dramatic changes in many areas of social policy-making and intellectual life over this period in which we are reflecting on the development of urban modelling. To introduce this drama, it is worth providing a personal example to illustrate the sorts of changes which have occurred, so that these might be put in perspective. Some three months before the Oxford conference, I began to teach a course which I had not studied in any detail since my student days; this was urban design, the interface between planning and architecture. Of course, I was well aware of the reactions against large-scale public architecture, especially in the form of housing which marked a transition from the boom years of the 1960s to the massive disengagement from public sector involvement in such areas in the 1980s. But what I was not prepared for was the almost total switch in architectural style, fashion, method – theory in fact, which has occurred over the past twenty years.

Urban Modelling and Planning

To those like myself who had been reared, indoctrinated even, on the tenets of modern architecture embodied in Louis Sullivan's hallowed phrase 'form follows function', who could not accept any form of ornamentation on buildings because such detail conflicted with the aesthetics of the day, the transition which has occurred in practice is a shock. In post-modern architecture, anything goes and form very definitely does *not* follow function. Architecture of the 1980s is a total reaction to the concrete towers of the 1960s and the emerging 'style' is pluralist to the point where style no longer has any meaning. Skyscapers are now being built in New York which are festooned with Gothic and Georgian ornament, and there has been a neo-classical revival at all levels from the most domestic to the most public of architecture. If you stand away from a field and only follow it in 'lay' terms for a generation, when you return it is bound to contain surprises, but the sort of thing now going on within architecture would have been unthinkable in the heyday of modernism. Cosgrove uses similar examples in his chapter in explaining the logic of the humanist approach in contrast to the quantitative as the appropriate basis for theoretical geography.

Architecture, as Denys Lasdun has remarked 'is a social art' (quoted in Knevitt, 1985) and its driving force is very definitely public acceptability. The social milieu in which it exists is so strong that no individual ingenuity and flair can counter the structural trends at work. A remarkable demonstration of the power of this driving force is involved in the proposal, now rejected, for the construction of a Mies van der Rohe building in London's Mansion House Square. The building originally designed by one of the world's great modernists before his death in the late 1960s, was then approved, but it took nearly twenty years to assemble the site. By the time this had happened, the ground rules had so changed that even one of the world's great architects could no longer fight the turning tide. At a more modest level, one could construct examples involving the application of urban models and planning techniques in the 1980s which would simply be regarded by planning practice as curios from the past. They would no longer be understood.

I tell this story because it illustrates the sort of dramatic change in the social context of ideas which we are reflecting upon here – where the intellectual terrain exists in response to an applied context, where the science exists because of applications, not despite them. It is easy to forget that the field in question – urban modelling – was developed in response to the burning policy questions of the day in the North America and Britain of the 1950s and 1960s. The field, like so many areas in the social sciences, has since been institutionalized and professionalized, and this can blind one to thinking that it exists separately from its context. To a degree, elements of the field have been adopted by academic geography and in the past ten or fifteen years a synergy has developed between geography and modelling. Modelling is now very much a theme which builds on geography's quantitative revolution, which in turn has been central to that discipline's development. But after I have developed my

Michael Batty

own assessment of the field, I will also argue that modelling can never be a central construct of geographical theory although it does represent a way of thinking and 'doing' geography (in Johnston's (1986b) phrase) which is important and has lasting value. The particular models of the 1960s and the articulations of the urban system which they embody are no longer widely accepted. The social context has changed, and it is unforgiving in its rejection of all that has gone before. Indeed, Pasteur's quote which introduces this chapter is very much cast in doubt when one examines this field, and perhaps it sows this doubt throughout geography itself, indeed possibly throughout the social sciences.

The intellectual landscape which we will survey is a very different one from that which dominated the 1960s. Many remnants of those days remain and remain useful, but their *coherence* has gone. As I was involved, like many speaking at the conference, in moulding a bit of the landscape, I would like to be able to explain how it has changed, of course because of the need to develop applicable knowledge for urban planning, but also because I cannot accept that my responses then or now to this area are in any sense 'wrong' or inappropriate. And more important-antly, such reflection is necessary so that we can adapt such experiences and the formal intellectual apparatus which has been constructed, to the continually changing context.

First we will sketch the context and identify how this acts as a driving force to the field. A variety of approaches to urban modelling have emerged over the past twenty-five years, and from the vantage point of the 1980s it is easy to identify different schools of thought based on social physics, micro-economics, structural dynamics, and so on. Here we will note the achievements too which have been particularly impressive with respect to synthesis and the convergence of ideas. One of the most interesting features of the field has been its institutionalization, and because the conference is a reflection on models in geography, a little time will be spent in tracing the interaction between this field and mainstream human and theoretical geography. We will then examine how the context to urban modelling has changed, noting the emergence of practical problems and ideological challenges. But most of all, these changes have been spurred by the transition from industrial to post-industrial, by the rise of information technology and for modelling, we will argue, these trends represent a mixed blessing. The cult of informa-tion, as Roszak (1986) calls it, involves an obsession with data, and ideological change has led to the development of the private sector as the main means of transition to the information society. Computers have always been essential to modelling but what is currently emerging by no means marks a resurrection of this field in the form it was predicated a generation ago.

Articulating Applicable Models

In the 1950s when all this began, social science was in awe of the physical sciences. There seemed nothing more appropriate than 'big science'. To mimic big science was the implicit goal of many a social scientist and there were countless public statements of this quest which implied that a science of society was quite literally around the corner. What gave rise to this optimism was the optimism of society at that time. Dramatic advances in theoretical science which had demonstrated their power in nuclear physics were just sinking in, in society-at-large; the war had ended in a moral victory for the Allies; in trade cycle terms, the fourth Kondratieff marking the recession of the 1930s was over and fifth long wave spawned by the invention of the computer had begun. General systems theory, cybernetics, operations research, all heralded the prospect of new frameworks for synthesizing the ad hoc knowledge which dominated the social sciences. Economics in particular, following the remarkable example of Keynes in the 1930s, looked more and more like a science in its structure and application. Moreover, much of the intellectual apparatus being assembled looked as though it might work in everyday life.

In land-use and transportation planning, the real quest was to contain growth and to accommodate the automobile. New infrastructure was urgently required and the link between land-use and transportation was becoming more clearly articulated. The context was right in that demands by urban policy-makers for new transportation infrastructure set in train the development of methods for dealing with the emergent complexity of spatial interaction. And if the context was right, the computer made it possible. For the first time, the sort of extensive complexity characterizing cities (as well as other such systems in both the physical and social sciences) could be managed, manipulated and explored using computer models. In short, the computer presented a working environment or medium akin to the physical scientist's laboratory. Such analogies were not lost on those involved; indeed they were positively exploited (Dyckman, 1963). Transportation planning studies were started for several U.S. cities in the mid-1950s (Voorhees, 1955) and by the late 1950s the first land-use models were under construction. A wave of such models appeared in the early 1960s and the speed at which they came to dominate the planning scene is illustrated by the special issue of the *Journal of the American Institute of Planners* devoted to land-use modelling published in May 1965 (Harris, 1965).

The types of models then developed now appear to represent a rather narrow conception of the urban system: essentially distinct land uses, articulated in measurable economic and demographic activities formed the subject matter of these models which were designed to locate such activities in spatial units represented by zones at the level of census tracts. Interaction between such activities in the form of transportation and inter-industry linkages were central to the workings of the models.

Michael Batty

Spatial interaction and trip-making were embodied in gravitational analogues while model structures were conceived along simple econometric lines, with some emphasis on algorithmic computer-orientated solution methods. The emphasis was more technique-based than substantive, but the models were informal and rather pragmatic in that they avoided mainstream statistical theory.

There was a key distinction between comprehensive models – models dealing with two or more sectors/activities of the urban system and their consequent interactions – and partial or single-activity models. Lowry's (1964) Pittsburgh model represented the former, while Lakshmanan and Hansen's (1965) retail model for Baltimore, the latter. These models were largely one-off, static descriptions of the urban system, calibrated or massaged to fit some base date at which data were available, and then deemed suitable for making forecasts. There was only limited emphasis on optimization modelling despite (or perhaps because of) the fact that the planning system in which such models were embedded was designed to find best or optimal solutions. Schlager's (1965) land-use plan design model was conceived in the operations research tradition as a linear programming model, but there was really only one optimization model which signalled anything like the sophistication of urban and regional theory which would come to characterize such efforts over the next two decades. This was the housing market model designed by Herbert and Stevens (1960) for the Penn–Jersey Transportation Study which reflected a unique synthesis of urban economic theory with transportation through the mechanisms of the land market modelled at the individual level in terms of utility maximization.

This lack of focus on optimization is intriguing. It was almost as if the strategic planning systems themselves were regarded as being superior to any formal method of optimization, and it was perhaps implicit recognition of the fact that planning, in the last analysis, was a satisficing rather than optimizing process. This reflected the consensus type of society in which this style of planning was embedded, and it also reflected the positivist flavour of the behavioural–social sciences in North America (Simon, 1977). Yet the models which were developed in no way represented a science in the making. Everything was in response to the policy context and the whole show was driven by publicly articulated needs. Indeed, as far back as the French Physiocrats in the 18th century and certainly back to Ravenstein (1885) and Reilly (1929), methods of social physics which were so important to the emergence of this field were driven by the demands of the market and/or urban–economic policy. Even the maverick attempt in the late 1960s by Forrester (1969) to apply his technique of systems dynamics to urban problems was grounded in a public-policy context.

It could be argued, perhaps, that all science is driven this way, and there is clearly a school of thought within the history of science which suggests that the structure of science is dependent on its social context. But in the traditional sciences the knowledge base does stand apart from its applications, as Pasteur implies, if only because the base seems more stable, less controversial and hence easier to institutionalize. The point really is that the emergent field of urban modelling in the 1960s was fundamentally dependent on applications and practice for its very existence. Its development was pragmatically conceived, hence highly responsive to its environment. At the time, another revolution was proceeding within geography – the quantitative revolution – but this was proceeding in a parallel world, initially with very little contact with transportation and land-use modelling. Quantitative geography was building a spatial science, slowly adapting location theory on the one hand, and formalizing spatial statistics on the other, and this was taking place worlds away in academia. In urban modelling the *modus operandi* was very different in that models were built and researched mainly in practice and were not characterized by any of the elegance associated with spatial statistics and location theory. Indeed, Wilson (1984), in writing about his own involvement with the quantitative revolution in geography, considers his work to have been well outside the mainstream, in planning rather than geography in this period.

In the late 1960s, after the first wave of ideas had been absorbed in the U.S., these techniques began to diffuse globally, first to the U.K. and then to other western industrialized societies, and eventually to the developing world (Mohan, 1979). In the U.K., a planning system had emerged which embodied a hierarchy of planning instruments, from regional policy to structure plans down to local and district plans. The emphasis on strategic thinking, on growth and on positive intervention in the land market provided a well-fitting context for the development of models. Looking back even the language being spoken at the time appeared model-based, sometimes by persons such as those preparing the Planning Advisory Group Report which led to the new strategic planning system, persons who have never heard of gravity models and location theory.

In the late 1960s, as urban modelling swept through the U.K., the models built were a little more sophisticated than their earlier U.S. counterparts. Some early difficulties had been resolved and there was not the wealth of applications or the variety that had characterized the U.S. experience. Consultants were much less involved in their development because the U.K. environment was much less supportive of such possibilities than that in North America, and thus the U.K. scene was dominated by research centres such as the Centre for Environmental Studies (CES) in London, the Urban Systems Research Unit in Reading, and the Centre for Land Use and Built Form Studies in Cambridge. By the mid-1970s the CES work had diffused to Leeds and a Planning Research Applications Group had been started by the CES. The object of many of these groups was to both research the emerging 'science' of urban modelling and to 'apply' such science, often in the form of advice to strategic planning authorities. Yet despite this arms'-length distancing from practice, the first models were spurred by the practical context: the Lakshmanan and Hansen shopping model was first applied by

Michael Batty

McLoughlin et al. (1966) to evaluate the impact of a proposed out-of-town shopping centre in northwest England, while Cripps and Foot (1968) developed a more comprehensive 'Lowry-style' model for statutory planning in the county of Bedfordshire.

The 1970s saw the beginnings of the institutionalization of this area. A critical mass of researchers had been assembled and their interests lay in improving and researching the same models further. But the real irony was that modelling had been developed to the point of take-off at the very end of the post-war boom. As boom turned to recession, optimism turned to pessimism, idealism to disillusion. The story is well known, but to anticipate the reaction that set in, in the early 1970s, the policy context changed so dramatically that urban models could no longer inform policy-makers about the most important questions they had begun to ask. This growing practical disillusion, which was accompanied by a new cutting edge in the form of a resurrection of political economy in the social sciences, combined to change the context entirely. But alongside this there was technical and organizational disillusion in that some models were oversold, their data demands were too great, they were technically inconsistent, they produced poor or incoherent forecasts, and so on. There was a catalogue of practical disasters which were largely due to learning on-the-job, so to speak (Brewer, 1973). None of this helped improve either the image or the applicability of these techniques. Yet there was a good deal of important work with models started in the 1970s and some impressive achievements have resulted. To set these in context before the retreat from modelling is charted, we must take one step back and examine what exactly these urban models attempted to do so that we can appreciate their limitations.

Model-based Conceptions of the City System

Urban models are based on a conception of the urban system which is articulated in terms of urban activities. As demographic and economic mechanisms essentially underpin such model workings, the models are constructed to embody rudimentary economic processes reflecting the spatial demand and supply of labour and produced goods. The link in these models to the observable superficiality of the system – the physical configuration of buildings and land uses – is tentative, although a one–one correspondence, which is assumed to be unproblematic, exists between land uses and activities. In this sense then, although the models are essentially economic in focus, their treatment of the local economy is simplistic and they are often referred to by urban economists as 'physical' models (Anas, 1986).

Location in such models is essentially regarded as a way of accounting for spatial interaction either in terms of trip-making expressed as travel demands or in terms of inter-industry flows as reflected in the workings of the macro-economy. Essentially the models of the 1960s and early

1970s represent a fusion, albeit sophisticated, of gravitational concepts underpinning spatial interaction with macro-economic theory as reflected in input–output and economic base analysis. Demographic processes have occasionally been integrated into these frameworks but the labour market is normally represented in a somewhat naive fashion in such models. In structure, such models are largely based on linear mathematics at the level of coupling activities and are usually static in conception, embodying no possibilities for qualitative change. For example, models in the Lowry (1964) tradition which dominate the field, are essentially mechanical artifacts reflecting social physics based on Newton and classical economics based on Keynes.

Right from the inception of the field there has been a vibrant debate about the degree of comprehensiveness of such model structures. In practice there was some early pressure for partial models, particularly in retailing, but the main forces have been towards comprehensiveness and integration. The nature of the planning system into which such models were embedded, the quest to integrate land use with transportation, the desire by model-builders to follow the general systems dictum that 'the whole is greater than the sum of the parts', as well as the 'biggest is best' syndrome, all forced the pace towards large-scale modelling (Lee, 1973). Although at the time I argued that the experience was not dominated by large-scale thinking (Batty, 1975), in hindsight that style of thinking, emanating from the 1960s, was quite different from the partial, even parochial, certainly more self-interested thinking which characterizes public policy in the mid- to late-1980s.

After the first wave of models in the U.S. and almost as soon as modelling began in the U.K., many reviews appeared which were concerned with how the field should develop. Remarkably, again in hindsight, such reviews seldom addressed new models for new policy questions, for the policy context was regarded as stable: the agenda was essentially a research agenda dominated by discussion of the need for greater comprehensiveness, the need for dynamics, the need for better mathematics and statistics, and the continuing plea for better integration with economic theory. Since then, some progress has been made on all these fronts, some of it rather impressive in technical terms and some of it having lasting importance with respect to the art of modelling. But among model-builders, the emphasis has been on the models themselves, never on the context of application. It is an open question, however, whether model-builders could have influenced the degree to which these tools were applied had they concentrated their fire on policy rather than technical questions.

The easiest nuts to crack in urban modelling have been the most obvious, namely those involving statistical estimation. In some respects, advances in these areas have simply been a matter of learning the appropriate mathematics and statistics and applying it. But from this has also emerged the most dramatic accomplishment, and that relates to a theoretical synthesis of model estimation, specification and application

Michael Batty

around the underlying idea of optimization. Extremal methods initially to generate consistent models were introduced into spatial interaction and transportation modelling in the mid-1960s by Wilson (1967) amongst others. His entropy-maximizing methods were quickly seen as possible structures for statistical estimation through reconciling entropy with likelihood. Maximizing entropy or likelihood enables best estimation of such models, such estimation being conceived as an optimization process. The methodological link from entropy to likelihood to statistical optimization was quickly worked out, and then came the breakthrough. Calibration was none other than a kind of substantive optimization, and once the mathematical machinery was in place, could be used to optimize the model in other ways, in ways for example that planners and policy-makers might wish.

There is another link through to economic optimization which we will come to in a moment but the work of Murchland, Wilson, Evans, Coelho and Williams represents a peculiarly British contribution of great theoretical importance to this area (see the book by Wilson, Coelho, Macgill and Williams, 1981). In a sense, though, it came too late to save the field. The link between modelling, planning and optimization had finally been worked out. In fact it was up to others, particularly Brotchie, Dickey and Sharpe (1980), to apply such models with impressive results but in a different time and place. There remain even more extensions to be worked through. The link between model structure and optimization is a rich seam which enables models not only to be optimized but to be inverted and solved in diverse ways (Batty, 1986), and there remains a field day in such research for the technically minded. It is an irony of history that such good models finally exist which could well have produced excellent advice in their day had they been available. But that day has passed.

Research into making static models dynamic proceeded on two fronts. Adding time onto static structures, producing pseudo-dynamic models, has met with limited success for such developments represent no more than simply indexing the cross-section with respect to time. There has also been some cross-fertilization with the types of space–time models emerging from quantitative geography (Bennett, 1981), but the real drama in model development has been much more research-orientated. Embedding static model structures into quite well-worked-out dynamic frameworks which involved qualitative or structural changes in the urban system has been a major force. Simple non-linear equation systems which are coupled with one another can give rise to quite sharp discontinuities or bifurcations in the development trajectory of the system if model parameters change continuously across certain thresholds. The idea of a catastrophe and catastrophe theory provides a useful image of the types of effect such model systems can capture. Wilson (1981a) shows how such models can be used to generate discontinuities in locational development, accounting for the growth of new shopping centres, for example. Allen (1983) develops similar frameworks to show how new cities can form and even get started in the first place.

All this work is very much in the tradition of building an urban science through modelling, and although it has some important conceptual implications for urban policy-making, these types of models are not applicable in the same way as those sketched earlier. And may be it is no accident either that such approaches have become popular in the age of discontinuity, as technological change is forcing such discontinuities onto what were comparatively stable industrial cultures. Indeed, there are some who have drawn their inspiration for describing social change from these sources (see Prigogine and Stengers, 1984).

There are other achievements which must be charted, and the most important one remaining involves further extension of the optimization paradigm. The original Penn–Jersey model due to Herbert and Stevens (1960) involved optimization by maximizing utility in a spatial context. The entropy–likelihood–optimization paradigm was easily extended to embrace utility in the early 1970s and then there emerged a remarkable convergence of these styles of macro-urban modelling with micro. In the late 1960s a theory of utility maximization involving a random element of choice was introduced by McFadden, and then began the development of a new style of travel demand modelling referred to as discrete choice analysis. The optimization paradigm was formally extended to embrace random utility theory (Williams, 1977) and the link between micro- and macro-modelling, so long a source of difficulty and contention began to fall into place. Most of these developments occurred in the U.S. where there have been many practical applications in transportation planning, and which remains a fairly vibrant model-based area of public policy-making (Ben Akiva and Lerman, 1985). In this area too there have been contributions by geographers, particularly in the area of discrete or categorical modelling which also emerge from developments in mainstream applied statistics (Wrigley, 1985).

Some of these developments have resulted in quite sophisticated applications, but usually from the standpoint of applied research rather than policy-making. Anas (1982) has provided a synthetic model linking traditional spatial interaction, discrete choice theory and urban economic processes which use state-of-the-art estimation and optimization methods. Putman (1983) has developed a variety of integrated urban models building on the tradition of comprehensive modelling and also developing these in an applied context. There has been much work at the coal face on zoning, calibration, model structure and data description. But there have been very few attempts to extend the battery of methods and techniques now available to other sectors of the urban system or to other substantive questions. Policy questions have been rarely researched at other than the speculative level and, in hindsight, it is hard not to brand this field as the province of technicians. Much of the achievement has been thoughtful and careful but there has not been a distinct group of researchers ever tackling new substantive issues and new policy questions from a modelling perspective. This will be all too apparent when we

Michael Batty

discuss the retreat from modelling but before then, we will turn to the institutionalization of this field.

The Institutionalization of Modelling

The argument of this chapter is that modelling can never represent a science because its intellectual rationale is entirely determined by a volatile social context. It is driven by urban policy and, as policy is an inherently unstable affair, the structure of knowledge demanded will also reflect this volatility. Of course various bits and pieces of the field will have lasting importance, but the map of its intellectual terrain is continually changing, just as the image of architecture is dictated ultimately by public acceptability. Yet modelling has acquired a life of its own for social reasons. It has become institutionalized, in the U.K. within geography to some extent, and it has become partly professionalized. In this section we will attempt to explain this phenomenon.

The disciplines from which model-builders drew their inspiration in the early 1960s represented an eclectic set of subjects broadly spanning the range from economics through to engineering. These subjects were in themselves developed in an ad hoc manner comprising an amalgam of inconsistent theories and techniques, and the resulting models reflected this to an even greater degree. But in the 1950s and 1960s there was some real hope that emergent frameworks involving ideas in systems theory and cybernetics, new forms of applied mathematics in operations research, and the new medium of empirical testing – the computer – would all come together to produce a 'science of society'. Although the structure of these fields then, as now, looked as though they could never by systematized, the hope of such restructuring was uppermost in academic minds.

In the groves of academia itself, new subject areas such as planning and other social sciences spawned through a variety of social and intellectual spin-offs from more established areas were particularly attracted to these emerging ideas. These areas were extremely fragile in terms of their knowledge base, and systems theory and the like seemed to provide the path to intellectual salvation. There was also a growing core of researchers trained in little else, or at least having been exposed to little else, who required some stability to reinforce their interests. The field attracted bright and active minds, its advocates learnt fast and there were some impressive advances at the technical level such as those referred to above. The post-war boom which had created a massive expansion of the university system in all western industrialized societies was still working itself out in academia through increasing demands for journals, textbooks, research grants and such like which all fuelled the drive to institutionalization.

Yet again in hindsight, the institutionalization was half-baked, as indeed it was for many other areas of the social sciences. In general the field was not attractive enough to persuade enough research students to fly under its banner, although, this said, many other areas in the social sciences faced and continue to face the same prospect. But more importantly, the volatile practical context to such work also detracted from the vibrant growth which occurred on its inception in the 1960s. The field has continued in its original fashion in the more pragmatic environment of North America but in some continental European countries, for example France, it has never developed. Only in Britain does it appear to have attempted an institutionalization in areas such as geography and planning.

Nevertheless, examining the scale of work in this field, what has been produced is impressive. The Oxford conference itself indicates the seriousness with which the broader context of modelling and quantification is treated. In the narrow context of urban and regional modelling, at least ten textbooks have been produced between 1972 and 1982, three of these being of the more advanced type. Around ten technical monographs akin to textbooks have been written and there are many books which include important sections on the field. There are at least twenty books reflecting conference proceedings and there are thousands of articles. Indeed in the analysis of citations by Wrigley and Matthews (1986), two of the top five most cited books and papers in geography are associated with this field. But during the last five years, momentum in the field has decreased. The last textbook was written in 1982 (Foot, 1982) and although there are conference proceedings still being produced, my impressions are that the rate of production of modelling work, in the tradition sketched here at least, is slackening. There are, however, new directions which we will pick up later.

Developments in quantitative geography ran parallel to urban modelling, as indicated earlier. Quantitative geography was dominated by a concern for spatial statistics which initially was focused on developing appropriate statistical assumptions incorporating space. This was a very different tradition, not exposed to public policy issues at all but concentrating on issues such as spatial autocorrelation, point patterns, diffusion theory and latterly space–time modelling. In fact, quantitative geography has been largely statistical in emphasis and even substantive theories of location in the classical tradition have been more the prerogative of urban and regional economists than geographers. Nevertheless, as urban modelling became institutionalized within the confines of geography, cross-fertilization of ideas did begin, particularly in more recent developments involving discrete choice theory, urban dynamics and estimation theory for models.

The overlap between geography and this style of modelling is of interest. A measure of how these parallel worlds interact and intersect can be produced by examining the participants at a series of key conferences on urban modelling over the last twenty years. In fact, urban modelling is characterized by a string of conferences dating back to the early 1960s, starting with Philadelphia in 1964, Dartmouth 1967, Liver-

Michael Batty

Table 10.1   An analysis of modellers by professional training and work affiliation

Conference	Arch.	Geog.	Plan.	Econ.	Eng.	Math.	Sci.	Arts/ Other
Dartmouth	8	7	5	15	40	7	11	7
1967	(0)	(0)	(16)	(5)	(12)	(0)	(3)	(63)
Cambridge	25	8	6	11	19	11	11	8
1974	(14)	(8)	(25)	(8)	(14)	(3)	(6)	(22)
Oxford	14	13	10	13	13	3	20	10
1980	(3)	(7)	(40)	(17)	(13)	(0)	(7)	(13)
Waterloo	9	11	6	17	35	11	11	0
1983	(2)	(11)	(26)	(9)	(28)	(0)	(9)	(15)
Total	13	9	6	14	32	8	12	5
(four events)	(4)	(6)	(24)	(9)	(17)	(1)	(6)	(34)

The first line associated with each conference gives the percentage of modellers in terms of disciplinary degree. The second line (figures in parentheses) gives the percentage by work affiliation. In the case of 'Other', this refers to practice.

pool 1970, Cambridge in 1972 and 1974, Oxford in 1980 and Waterloo in 1983. There have been more specialist conferences on urban dynamics, on spatial interaction and other topic areas but those listed represent events which attempted to provide state-of-the-art evaluations of the field. In fact, we will not examine the Philadelphia conference in 1964, nor the Liverpool 1970 and Cambridge 1972 conferences because these represented rather smaller, more exclusive events, and were less typical than the remaining four state-of-the-art meetings.

In table 10.1 we show the percentage of participants (persons giving papers and/or discussants) with respect to their main disciplinary training and (in parentheses) with respect to their then present work affiliation. There are some striking points: first the relatively high proportions of engineers by training and present affiliation; second the high proportion of persons now affiliated to academic planning institutions; third the decreasing proportion of others (bureaucrats, practitioners, consultants) represented at each of the successive meetings; and finally the low porportion of geographers by training and present affiliation contributing to the subject area. In fact this is also borne out by an analysis of publications of the ten texts. Only one is written by a person trained as a geographer, whereas three were written by persons now working in geography departments, none of whom was trained as a geographer. This may sound as if the field wishes to distance itself from geography, but this is not so. The analysis simply makes the point that the area is professionally eclectic. Although it may be institutionalizing itself in part in geography, it remains diverse, rooted to practical applications and indeed dependent upon practical needs for its very survival.

It is worth posing two hypothetical questions to conclude this section which represent retrodictions – predictions of what might have happened to this field if the social context and needs of urban policy-makers had been different. Firstly, would the field have emerged anyway as geographers and economists continued in their quest to build a spatial science? The answer is probably no. The eclecticism of the field is its great strength, but equally its vulnerability in that the field has been awash with ideas but the area has not attracted a very large or stable core following. Interestingly, urban economics has always stood aloof from urban modelling and consequently it is much less applicable but stronger. If there was a driving force intellectually in urban modelling, it was transportation which initially spawned or provided the seed beds for spatial interaction and discrete choice modelling.

The second question is more speculative and relates to the extent to which this field has provided any basic material for the science of geography. In fact, the strength of the field is not in its theorizing about cities – in this it is eclectic and draws on anything at hand – but in providing new ways of thinking about cities, and new ways of 'doing' planning. The computer age has provided a powerful medium for enabling us to articulate new insights into all kinds of material and social phenomena, and the method of creating such insights is in general a form of modelling. Exploring ideas on computers does represent a new kind of investigation, different from formal mathematical and scientific traditions. In one sense as in adopting any theoretical position, it takes an act of faith to accept the approach, but geography is in a unique position among many social sciences as having a sufficiently strong basis of modelling to inform the area without it dominating the intellectual superstructure.

Criticisms: the Retreat from Rationality

Before we digressed to talk about the institutionalization of modelling, we had painted a picture of the emergence of urban modelling as a response to growth created in the boom years of the 1950s and 1960s. But along with models emerged a strong planning system at least in Britain which represented a vehicle on which models were carried and applied. This highly structured approach to planning was itself a process of optimization rather than management, of problem-solving predicated on the rational decision model which has emerged in many fields of inquiry since the late 1930s. The rational decision model portrayed the planning process as one in which goals were set, problems defined, solutions generated by searching across a sample of alternatives characterizing the solution space, with the best plans chosen, then implemented after solutions had been rigorously evaluated against the prior set of goals. The process was cyclic, solutions were generated iteratively and revised continually, and the optimization paradigm was frequently invoked (Harris, 1967).

Urban models represented the *modus operandi* of a strategic planning system based on this rational process. What emerged was a model-based

Michael Batty

planning but not strictly speaking planning models. Planning was regarding as being almost too complex to be formally structured as a process of optimization and, as such, models came to be applied predictively within planning rather than planning being specified as the control function within sets of urban models (Batty, 1985). This is why optimization models never really caught on: such formality lay beyond the bounds of a highly complex, uncertain system, and in any case, the ultimate power of advice and solution lay in the professional credibility of planners and policy-makers themselves.

This style of planning characterized the application of land-use–transportation models in the U.S. in the 1960s (Boyce, Day and McDonald, 1970) and the early wave of structure plans in the 1970s in the U.K. Indeed, a Department of Environment (DoE) publication, *Using Models in Structure Planning*, produced in 1973, provided some guarded support for the use of models in planning. But it had taken twenty years for this context to be established, and by the time it all came on stream the world had begun to change. Boom turned to recession, the western economies began to overheat as the fifth Kondratieff entered the mature phase of its product cycle, deindustrialization emerged as a phenomenon, and the questions that planners came to be concerned with were no longer those which models could inform them about.

Growth turned to decline, but urban models were equally good at subtracting activity as adding it, and thus it was not the shift from positive to negative that provided the problem. It was the shift from *planning* growth to *managing* decline that was at issue. This marked not only a disillusion with modelling but with planning itself. Indeed, strategic planning, particularly in the U.K., and with it the vehicle which carried the models and the organization in which they were embedded, has disappeared. Questions in planning were no longer seen in terms of allocation or distribution across space but of competing for economic growth, of alleviating the worst effects of decline, of conserving what was under threat and of opening up the market to whatever economic activity showed any signs of life. Consequently the grand strategies of containment which dominated British planning for a century disappeared almost overnight.

Changes in the questions asked, abandoning strategic long-term planning for short-term expediencies, the growth of new paradigms seeking to answer 'bigger' questions than the modelling fraternity had ever considered were there for the asking, combined with practical disillusion through difficulties of learning how to do intelligent modelling in practice all conspired to quell the original enthusiasm for these new techniques. Models were also expensive and were mystical in their operation. In the reaction there was always an element of 'Ludditism'. The last large-scale urban models applied in British planning practice were the models developed by PRAG (Planning Research Appliations Group) in the Teesside area in the 1976–7. Some retail modelling continued but Development Control Policy Note 13 issued in 1977 by the DoE advised local authorities even to abandon these, for them only to be picked up by the retailing chains in the mid-1980s intent on increasing their market share. We will return to this point later, for any resurgence there has been of late for modelling relates to this type of private sector response.

By 1980, structure planning and regional policy were being dismantled to be replaced by ad hoc agreements and responses. New types of local area-based government agency had come to dominate the planning scene, cutting across the notion of comprehensive planning. The final demise of the metropolitan counties in 1986 represented the end of a long saga of attacks on the notion of comprehensive planning, and now it appears that this response is part of a wider change in attitudes and policies towards the welfare state itself. This is an interesting and complex argument which also marks the transition from industrial to post-industrial society but in all of this, which we cannot explore further here, models were long gone.

The good work accomplished in modelling during the 1970s, in particular the development of the optimization paradigm, has never come to be applied in practice. The questions had changed so radically by the time such work emerged that this work could be regarded as little else than advances in the science rather than application of modelling. A couple of examples will serve to impress the point. In the mid-1970s Sayer (1976) criticized one of the assumptions of the economic base model as being unidirectional in causation, of not embodying any feedback between basic and non-basic components of employment, the division into which was arbitrary. In fact, by the early 1980s, work had been done which resolved these criticisms in that model structures were available which incorporated every possible feedback loop (Batty, 1983). The division between basic and non-basic was inevitably arbitrary to some extent, but models did emerge in which this arbitrariness could be dealt with. However, Sayer's criticism now looks somewhat mild in comparison with the wholesale disappearance of the traditional basic sector from many areas. In the transition to a post-industrial, deindustrial urban society, the basic–non-basic split itself has changed, and the transition has been so swift that the components of what is now 'basic' to the economy are not at all clear.

The second example also relates to this transition to a different style of economy. Traditionally, questions of competition are handled in urban models by mechanisms involving substitution. For example in modal split, a new transport mode directly competes for its patronage with other modes. However, new forms of communications involving information transfer are now emerging which are increasing interaction, and rather than competing with existing modes as originally anticipated, these are increasing the capacity of every mode. Such additions and complementations are extremely difficult to model because they constitute qualitative changes of a novel and surprising kind. Indeed, there are many such examples which betray a subtlety to urban systems that most current theories, and certainly urban models, are not able to handle.

Environment, Land Use and Urban Policy

Michael Batty

The kind of milieu of planning which has emerged is essentially pragmatic, reflecting a collapse of the consensus of the past fifty years and an abandonment of comprehensive thinking. Ideological change reflecting an increasing self-interest and technological change have changed the questions being asked so radically that most theories culled in the years prior to the current transition now seem irrelevant. Indeed, the speed at which new theories have been developed during the past twenty years marks this degree of change. The driving force for modelling the urban system in traditional spatial terms has gone, but in its place there is a new context. The new landscape is one of a weak public sector and increasingly dominant self-interest. The situation is one where, if models are demanded at all, it is to enhance self-interest, not to embody any of the goals for which they were originally designed. The questions being asked about spatial differentials are just as interesting as they ever were but the interest in using models to address them is quite different from those of a generation ago. The new rationale for modelling, if it can be seen as such, is one of narrow, sectoral interest, involving the bits and pieces of models that would appear to enable as much profit to be extracted as quickly as possible in spatial terms. In fact, the landscape is somewhat indifferent to modelling, as we will show. Nevertheless this is an applied context which is still fuelling a little research.

The Cult of Information

The social context in which we now find ourselves is dominated by self-interest. The notion of a collective or public interest and of planners working for it or towards it has more or less disappeared, and thus local agencies and governments have become caught up in this increase in the competitive edge. Thus ideological change conspires with technological change to make the theories and models, which had taken half a century to develop to the form in which they might be applicable, barely relevant. Not only have the questions changed but so have the answers. The configuration of activities in the post-industrial city is a very different affair from that it has replaced, and even the causal processes appear different. As noted above, the very classification of activities is now in doubt for, with the rise of the information sector, the growth of multi-national corporatism, and the decline of manufacturing base, location theory must be rewritten if it is to be useful in planning the future city.

Space is still important and thus spatial models are still in principle useful vehicles for exploring planning policies. But telecommunications, if not replacing traditional transport infrastructure and modes, is elaborating spatial structure to a new level of complexity. Information networks, data bases and new methods of automation are changing the structure of parts of the city beyond recognition. The model-based conceptions referred to in an earlier section are no longer very appropriate, for not only have new activities based on information emerged but also new infrastructures based on telecommunications, and new methods of communication and causality have appeared. Information not energy has become the new source of power, and the computer represents its driving force.

There is a quiet irony in all of this. An information age centred on computer-based systems would seem to imply that an age of computer modelling was about to emerge. In fact quite the opposite has occurred. Although the computer spawned the urban model in the late 1950s, the power of computation to change the context in turn changed the very rationale that led to modelling. In the very early days in the 1960s some models failed because of limits on computer memory available. But such constraints quickly disappeared and, in the review of modelling already discussed in this chapter, the role of the computer other than that of a facilitator of models has rarely been mentioned. Nevertheless the massive diffusion of computers throughout society has the potential to make models more transparent and to enable communication of their operation and results through new modes of computation such as expert system and computer graphics. These are all prospects which are immediately realizable but, apart from occasional examples, there is little sign of the computer revolution having affected modelling in these or any other ways.

In fact it is a concern for information rather than modelling which marks the information age. In a recent survey of British local planning authorities, Bardon, Elliott and Stothers (1984) report that of 335 planning authorities found to be using computers (66 per cent of all authorities), nearly one half (49 per cent) were using computers to process development control data; 32 per cent were using computers to process census data while 14 per cent were involved with digital mapping in some form. In contrast only 3 per cent were using retail models and the most popular (and standard) forecasting technique used was population projection, with 12 per cent using such methods. These are striking figures which indicate that models are barely used at all in British planning at present. In contrast, there is substantial interest in information systems. However, one must ask the question as to how such information is processed once it has been stored, and it is here of course that models are most appropriate.

This cult of information is increasingly problematic (Roszak, 1986). Information is power, and many private agencies and firms have emerged who work in the market for information. Information systems have become big business and consultants specializing in mapping and analysis of information have grown rapidly in the past decade. It is easy to overestimate the size of this market and the number of firms involved. In Britain, perhaps there are a dozen like CACI, Pinpoint, MVA Systematica and so on who specialize in information analysis with a spatial basis, and there may be many more who are involved in occasional research work for other parts of the private and sometimes public sector. Some of these companies are involved in using models, but the models which have

Michael Batty

been picked up are only ever partial in scope, usually involving retailing or other forms of market share. Such models appear to be those of the first generation and are rarely those which represent the state-of-the-art. These companies are able to exploit the intellectual terrain and choose models which enable them to predict market share on a spatial basis. But the evidence on the scale of their use is ambiguous and the advantages to advancing the state-of-the-art unclear.

This is particularly true in the area of retail modelling where some retail companies have large research staffs using models. Yet there is some uncertainty as to whether the models can produce good predictions. They are based essentially on the Lakshmanan and Hansen shopping model which was first specified by Huff (1963) some twenty-five years ago. At least the researches over the intervening years have showed how such models can be improved in practice, but little of the insights into zoning, specification, estimation and optimization, which are all available possibilities now, have been incorporated. Clarke and Wilson (1987) see some hope for a resurgence of modelling in these developments but I remain sceptical. The practice which has emerged is even more unforgiving than that of earlier generations.

Data, Data Everywhere and Not a Thought to Think

The diffusion of computer technology and the rise of data banks which contain facts and information about individuals across whole arrays of issues is one of the more sinister features of the emerging information society. There is a sense in which computers attract data in that the availability of information systems leads to their rather unselective use. In the past, before the advent of universal computer technology, information was filtered by those whose job it was to store and process it, but the cult of information presumes that all information is good. Data banks are being filled daily with all sorts of information which a generation ago would have been discarded as worthless. This proliferation of data, and the many banks which now exist, are available only to those who have the power to buy it, or control it; and although there are clearly better data sets available than there were a generation ago to aid our understanding of cities, for example, access to these data is restricted. There is something rather strange about a situation where data can be collected about ourselves 'freely' but then only made available to us at a cost. The commodification of information is an issue that is becoming central to the information society, and threatens to become one of the most problematic features of the economic future (Goddard and Openshaw, 1987).

It might appear that one of the original problems of applying modelling in practice has disappeared in the intervening years. Models had always run into data problems, and lack of data, or at least the right kind of data, clearly did influence the development of the field. But lack of data has never really been a central issue, and in any case it is an open question as to whether any of the appropriate data is available now. Some spatial interaction data on retail behaviour is clearly now collected as a matter of routine by the large retailing companies, and for those building shopping models this is clearly very useful. Some panel data collected by market research companies would also be useful in some model-building but, in general, the increase in data available has also to be seen in the context of government reducing its organized collection and aggregation of data at many levels. It will clearly be necessary to explore these new sources of data, as Rhind suggests in his chapter, but they are unlikely to provide a new momentum for urban modelling.

Thus data availability has never been the key issue in modelling. As Shubik (1979) says: 'Ours is a data-rich and information-poor society'. The real critique of models relates to more substantive issues, to the questions which models are able to respond to, not to the data which are available. Indeed, there may be many questions for which data are not available, but this has rarely been the case in model development. Urban models were originally constructed around conceptions of the urban system which were readily measurable and quantifiable. The data were never perfect and there were gaps, but there was always enough to get going. At present, however, there are many issues pertaining to urban spatial structure which do require better data if they are to be understood, but the data being collected by the private sector in its penchant for continual data-gathering are unlikely to be very useful in this quest. Once again there is the obvious point that useful information can be collected only if some idea of what it is likely to be used for has been established. This sounds trite, but the cult of information seems to provide a context in which it is often forgotten. The issue is as much one of better theory as it always has been than of better data, as Harvey and Scott and Macmillan also argue in their chapters.

In fact, one of the criticisms of modelling is that models produce too much data and that their outputs are difficult to assess. This is clearly the case. Anyone who has ever operated a spatial interaction model will know that some way of summarizing – usually through statistical measures, averages and so on – is required if the predictions of such a model are to be evaluated. One of the problems is actually producing reasonable statistics which indicate how well such models do perform. Over the years there has been quite some debate about model performance and invariably good statistical performance (high R^2 values, for example) has not been borne out when the data predictions are examined in more comprehensive ways, by mapping for example. What the computer revolution has enabled is much better ways of summarizing data using text and graphics, and there is some work which indicates that the results of modelling can now be better communicated to model-builders as well as model-users using new forms of display technology and the like. We will return to these points in our conclusions. One thing, however, is clear, and that is that modelling is antipathetic to data for data's sake, but that

Michael Batty

the growth in computer technology has indeed become coincident with
the cult of information.

The present obsession with data is thus quite inconsistent with good
modelling. As Wildavsky (1973) once rather humorously remarked: 'if
the data are thicker than your thumb ... they are not likely to be
comprehensible to anyone'. Shubik's (1969) observation that 'Most
simulations have a value inversely related to the fourth power of the
quantity of computer output' further impresses the need to impose great
structure on data in order to ensure highly intelligible modelling in the
computer age.

Conclusions: the Future is Not Like it Was

A generation ago, chapters like this were concluded with a long agenda
about how we should improve urban modelling. I will not attempt
anything so presumptuous here, but I will reinforce the value which
modelling has as one form of communication and understanding which is
now reasonably well established in the social sciences. My own work is
now very much in the area of communicating model-based ideas, and
data in intelligible forms using computer graphics, and the kind of styles
one is now able to bring to modelling have opened up dramatic new
prospects for communicating and handling complex issues. A generation
ago, when you wished to communicate modelling ideas, you would sit
down with a stack of printout and hopefully convince your audience that
this was where it was all at. Today, computer graphics is a much more
effective medium, and in spatial problems it is essential. Models have got
to 'look' right to be acceptable, as well as 'compute' right. I will only note
this in passing, but a new physicalism is emerging in the sciences based on
the power of computers to enable visualization of ideas which have
always remained complex, abstract and inaccessible to most people.
Interestingly, similar trends appear at work in other branches of geography, for example in the climate models presented here by Henderson-
Sellers.

There are of course technical and theoretical areas where models can
continue to be improved a little. Enabling qualitative change to be
handled, and devising new models but in the same tradition to simulate
relationships between new categorical descriptions of the urban system,
are worthy tasks. But these are likely to remain in the confines of
academia. In practice there are situations emerging where models provide
eminently sensible ways of communicating ideas. Modelling as a kind of
bargaining process (Dutton and Kraemer, 1985) is a prospect which
holds promise, counter-modelling in Greenberger, Crenson and Crissey's
(1976) phrase still characterizes econometric modelling where models
compete with respect to forecasts, and modelling as a way of summarizing and making data intelligible is an area which could dominate the
applied scene. There are opportunities in district health authorities, in

Urban Modelling and Planning

retailing, in utility management and so on, for modest applications (see Openshaw's chapter). But the drive from practice, from policy-making for new sorts of models is no longer there and shows little prospect of returning. The field can never be like it was again, and it is now being fashioned in a manner much more akin to the way operations research has developed. Operations research has never warranted an agenda for future research and applications, and one is not warranted for modelling here. Modelling has now been absorbed into the intellectual culture surrounding geography and planning. Its future prospects are unlikely to be determined by dramatic conversions to its ideology but more by its pragmatic value to researchers and policy-makers, sentiments which are echoed in many of the contributions to this book.

References

Allen, P. 1983: Planning and decision-making in human systems: modelling self-organisation. In M. Batty and B. Hutchinson (eds), *Systems Analysis in Urban Policy-Making and Planning*, Plenum Press, 491–524.

Anas, A. 1982: *Residential Location Markets and Urban Transportation*, Academic Press.

—— 1986: From physical to economic urban models: the Lowry framework revisited. In B. Hutchinson and M. Batty (eds), *Advances in Urban Systems Modelling*, North-Holland, 163–72.

Bardon, K., Elliott, C. and Stothers, N. 1984: *Computer Applications in Local Authority Planning Departments: A Review*, Birmingham, U.K.: Birmingham Polytechnic.

Batty, M. 1975: In defence of urban modelling. *The Planner*, 61, 184–7.

—— 1983: Linear urban models. *Papers of the Regional Science Association*, 53, 5–25.

—— 1985: Formal reasoning in urban planning. In M. Breheny and A. Hooper (eds), *Rationality in Planning*, Pion, 98–119.

—— 1986: Technical issues in urban model development: a review of linear and nonlinear model structures. In B. Hutchinson and M. Batty (eds), *Advances in Urban Systems Modelling*, North-Holland, 133–62.

Ben Akiva, M. and Lerman, S. 1985: *Discrete Choice Analysis: Theory and Application to Travel Demand*, MIT Press.

Bennett, R. J. 1981: Spatial and temporal analysis: spatial time series. In N. Wrigley and R. J. Bennett (eds), *Quantitative Geography*. Routledge & Kegan Paul, 97–103.

Boyce, D., Day, N. and McDonald, C. 1970: *Metropolitan Plan-Making*, Philadelphia, Pennsylvania: The Regional Science Research Institute.

Brewer, G. D. 1973: *Politicians, Bureaucrats and the Consultant: a critique of urban problem solving*, Basic Books.

Brotchie, J. F., Dickey, J. W. and Sharpe, R. 1980: *TOPAZ – General Planning Technique and its Applications at the Regional, Urban and Facility Planning Levels*, Springer-Verlag.

Clarke, M. and Wilson, A. G. 1987: Towards an applicable human geography: some developments and observations, *Environment and Planning A*, 19(11), 1525–41.

Cripps, E. and Foot, D. 1968: Evaluating alternative strategies, *Official Architecture and Planning*, 31, 928–38.

Dutton, W. H. and Kraemer, K. L. 1985: *Modelling as Negotiating*, Ablex.

Dyckmanm, J. W. 1963: The scientific world of the city planners. *American Behavioral Scientist*, 6, 46–50.

Foot, D. 1982: *Operational Urban Models*, Methuen.

Forrester, J. W. 1969: *Urban Dynamics*, MIT Press.

Goddard, J. and Openshaw, S. 1987: The use and availability of computerised data and the commodification of information. *Environment and Planning A*.

Greenberger, M., Crenson, M. A. and Crissey, B. L. 1976: *Models in the Policy Process: public decision-making in the computer era*. Russell Sage Foundation.

Harris, B. 1965: New tools for planning. *Journal of the American Institute of Planners*, 31, 90–5.

—— 1967: The city of the future: the problems of optimal design. *Papers of the Regional Science Association*, 19, 185–95.

Herbert, J. D. and Stevens, B. H. 1960: A model for the distribution of residential activity in urban areas. *Journal of Regional Science*, 2, 21–36.

Huff, D. L. 1963: A probabilistic analysis of shopping center trade areas. *Land Economics*, 39, 81–90.

Johnston, R. J. 1986b: *On Human Geography*, Basil Blackwell.

Knevitt, C. 1985: *Space on Earth: Architecture, People and Buildings*, Thames/Methuen.

Lakshmanan, T. R. and Hansen, W. G. 1965: A retail market potential model. *Journal of the American Institute of Planners*, 31, 134–43.

Lee, D. B. 1973: Requiem for large-scale models. *Journal of the American Institute of Planners*, 39, 163–78.

Lowry, I. S. 1964: *A Model of Metropolis*, The Rand Corporation.

Mohan, R. 1979: *Urban Economic and Planning Models*, Baltimore, Maryland: Johns Hopkins University Press.

Prigogine, I. and Stengers, I. 1984: *Order Out of Chaos*, Bantam Books.

Putman, S. H. 1983: *Integrated Urban Models*, Pion.

Ravenstein, E. G. 1885: The laws of migration. *Journal of the Royal Statistical Society*, 48, 167–235.

Reilly, W. J. 1929: Methods for the study of retail relationships. *Bulletin No. 2944*, Houston, Texas: University of Texas.

Roszak, T. 1986: *The Cult of Information*, Lutterworths.

Sayer, A. 1976: A critique of urban modelling. *Progress in Planning*, 6, 187–254.

Schlager, K. J. 1965: A land use plan design model. *Journal of the American Institute of Planners*, 31, 103–11.

Shubik, M. 1969: Processing the future. *Science*, 166, 1257–8.

—— 1979: Computers and modelling. In M. L. Dertouzos and J. Moses (eds), *The Computer Age: a twenty year view*, MIT Press, 285–305.

Simon, H. A. 1977: *Models of Discovery*, Reidel.

Voorhees, A. M. 1955: A general theory of traffic movement. *Proceedings of the Institute of Traffic Engineering*, 1, 46–56.

Wildavsky, A. 1973: Consumer report. *Science*, 182, 1335–8.

Williams, H. C. W. L. 1977: On the formation of travel demand models and economic evaluation measures of user benefit. *Environment Planning A*, 9, 285–344.

Wilson, A. G. 1967: A statistical theory of spatial distribution models. *Transportation Research*, 1, 253–69.

—— 1981a: *Catastrophe Theory and Bifurcation: applications to urban and regional systems*, Croom Helm.

—— 1984: One man's quantitative geography: frameworks, evaluations, uses and prospects. In M. Billinge, D. Gregory and R. Martin (eds), *Recollections of a Revolution*, Macmillan, 200–26.

——, Coelho, J. D., Macgill, S. M. and Williams, H. C. W. L. 1981: *Optimization in Locational and Transport Analysis*, Wiley.

Wrigley, N. 1985: *Categorical Data Analysis for Geographers and Environmental Scientists*, Longmans.

—— and Matthews, S. 1986: Citation classics and citation levels in geography. *Area*, 18, 185–94.

Project Appraisal, volume 7, number 3, September 1992, pages 126-136, Beech Tree Publishing, 10 Watford Close, Guildford, Surrey GU1 2EP, England.

Strategic environmental assessment: an overview

N Lee and F Walsh

Current SEA provision and proposed developments in different parts of the world are reviewed, highlighting a 15 year time lag between the development of SEA and EIA. The reasons for the recent growth of interest in SEA are examined, focusing on the limitations of project-level EIA and new assessment requirements arising from policy commitments to sustainable development. The similarities and differences between SEA and EIA are considered, in order to identify the distinctive features of SEA, by reference to tiering, the range and types of actions assessed, the processes and procedures followed and the assessment methods applied. Conclusions are drawn and a number of proposals are made to strengthen SEA practice in the future.

Keywords: strategic environmental assessment; environmental impact assessment; tiering; policies, plans and programmes; sustainable development

Norman Lee and Fiona Walsh are, respectively, Co-Director and Research Assistant at the Environmental Impact Assessment Centre, University of Manchester, Manchester M13 9PL, UK.

STRATEGIC ENVIRONMENTAL assessment (SEA) is the term used to describe the environmental assessment process for policies, plans and programmes[1] which are approved earlier than the authorisation of individual projects.

The purpose of this opening article is to review the development and future potential of SEA as an instrument in the policy-making and planning process. It covers provisions for SEA in different areas of the world, the reasons for its development, the types of actions to which it may be applied, the main components of the process, its similarities with and differences to EIA, and SEA methods. It concludes with a summary of findings and recommendations.

The other contributions to this special issue are of two kinds:

- Those reviewing SEA experience and developments in certain countries where some provisions for SEA and/or experience in its use currently exist. These relate to the USA (Webb and Sigal), Australia and New Zealand (Wood) and the Netherlands (Verheem).
- Those exploring SEA application for a particular category of action in the United Kingdom. These are for land-use planning (Pinfield), the water environment (Gardiner) and the transport sector (Sheate).

SEA is a relatively new concept and, so far, it has received limited treatment in professional and academic journals. It is hoped that this special issue will stimulate further investigations and a sharing

> **The European Commission has signalled its intention, in its latest Environment Programme, to propose a new Directive for the application of environmental assessment to certain policies, plans and programmes in Member States**

of experience in what is a developing area of activity.

Current SEA provision

In reviewing current SEA provision it is possible to distinguish between:

- those countries and organisations that have established formalised and mandatory provisions for SEA which contain most of its constituent features;
- those that have incorporated some elements of a more limited form of environmental evaluation (EE) into their planning procedures;
- those that envisage introducing SEA or EE into their procedures or to strengthen their existing arrangements.

The number of examples in the first category is still quite small, numbers in the second category are greater, whilst those in the third category may be greatest of all. In this respect the current SEA situation is not dissimilar to that of EIA in the mid-1970s. Hence, practical experience in the use of SEA is still fairly limited outside some countries and particular sectors; less formalised and more restricted EE experience is somewhat greater.

Within the European Community, France, Germany and the Netherlands already make some provision for the environmental assessment of certain policies, plans and programmes (PPPs) within the framework of their existing project-level EIA legislation. However, the scope of their coverage is fairly limited — mainly, certain land-use plans in France and Germany and policy-plans in the Netherlands (see Verheem in this issue).

New proposals to incorporate environmental considerations into policy-level assessments are now being considered in the Netherlands (see Verheem). Italy has prepared draft legislation which provides not only for the application of environmental assessment to a wider range of projects than at present, but also for the assessment of certain types of plans and programmes, though not of policies (Matarrese, 1991). In Germany, a guideline has existed since 1975 making provision for the

environmental assessment of federal programmes, plans and policies but, to date, it has only been applied in a limited number of cases (Kleinschmidt, 1991).

A number of other Member States use some elements of environmental evaluation in PPP preparation (especially in preparing land-use plans) and envisage their greater use in the future. Two recent developments in the UK are the publication of a guide, for use in government departments, on *Policy Appraisal and the Environment* (DOE, 1991), and official acceptance of the need for earlier use of environmental assessment in the planning of new roads (DOT, 1992).

Additionally, it is worth noting that the list of Annex II projects in Directive 85/337/EEC (Commission of the European Communities, 1985), to which environmental assessment should be applied, includes 'industrial estate projects', 'urban development projects' and 'holiday villages' which may contain multiple developments whose environmental assessment could take on some of the characteristics of a plan or programme SEA.

The EC now requires the provision of environmental information in support of Member State regional development plans and programmes which seek financial assistance from the Community's Structural Funds. The implementation of these provisions is still in its infancy but it should eventually lead to the integration of a form of SEA into certain plan- and programme- making processes (Directorate-General for Environment, 1990).

Finally, the European Commission has signalled its intention, in its latest Environment Programme, to propose a new Directive for the application of environmental assessment to certain policies, plans and programmes in Member States (Commission of the European Communities, 1992).

The Convention on EIA in a Transboundary Context, which was agreed at the Economic Commission for Europe (ECE) meeting in Espoo in 1991, is primarily concerned with the assessment of transborder impacts from projects, but it also encourages "to the extent appropriate" the environmental assessment of transborder impacts from PPPs (United Nations Economic Commission for Europe, 1991). Additionally, an ECE Task Force has been reviewing environmental assessment practice and potential at the PPP level and its findings will be published shortly (United Nations Economic Commission for Europe, 1992).

A number of other European countries currently outside the European Communities are exploring the potential for applying environmental assessment at a more strategic level. These include the member countries of the Nordic Council (Lind, 1991) and some East European countries.

In the USA, under the provisions of the National Environmental Policy Act (NEPA) (1969), there has been provision for 'program-

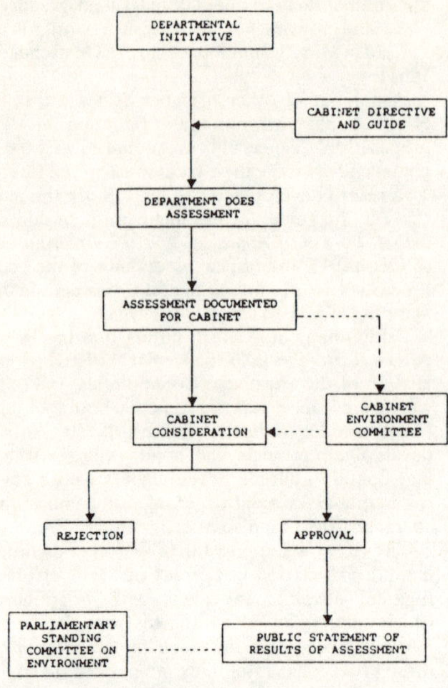

Figure 1. Assessment of proposals needing Cabinet decision

Source: Federal Environmental Assessment Review Office
(1991), *Flowchart for Policy and Program Assessments* (Federal Enviromental Assessment Review
office, Hull, Quebec, Canada).

matic' EIAs for many years, although this has not
been used to anything like the same extent as for
project EIAs (see Webb and Sigal in this issue). At
the State level, California possesses a more fully-
developed, tiered, EIA system (Bass, 1990).

In New Zealand, the provisions of the Resource
Management Act (1991) place an obligation on
decision-makers to anticipate and assess the impacts of their policies, and on consent applicants to
assess the impacts of their proposals. These impact
assessments are to be integrated respectively into
plan-making and into the consent process (Wells,
1991).

In Australia, some legal provisions relating to
SEA, though of a discretionary nature, have
existed for many years but, to date, have been used
relatively infrequently. However, interest in their
greater use has grown recently. A review by Wood
of such provisions in New Zealand and Australia
appears later in this issue.

In Canada, in January 1990, the Federal Environmental Minister tabled a Bill for an Environmental Assessment Act and a commitment by the
Federal Cabinet to assess the environmental impacts of all of its policy decisions. The Bill was

subsequently amended and has recently been approved. Whilst it relates only to project level assessments it does contain requirements relating to
the coverage of alternatives, cumulative effects
and resource sustainability (Couch, 1991).

The Cabinet procedures to be followed in assessing the environmental impacts of its decisions
have been established (see Figure 1). As a consequence, between June 1990 and June 1992, nearly
90 Policy Memoranda to Cabinet were assessed for
environmental impacts. Guidance for government
officials on how to assess policy impacts is being
prepared and further research in this area is also
supported (LeBlanc, 1991).

Independently of this Bill, there have been a
number of workshops and studies, involving researchers from Canada and other countries, relating particularly to cumulative impact assessment
and sustainability assessment (see, for example,
Canadian Environmental Assessment Research
Council, 1986; Cocklin, Parker and Hay, 1992).

Many multi-national and bi-national aid agencies and banks now require EIA before providing
financial assistance for projects. However, some of
these are now also showing interest in, and a
measure of commitment to, the extension of environmental assessment to more strategic levels of
planning and decision- making. This is reflected in
a number of published policy and guidance statements (see Box 1 for examples). However, as often
elsewhere, actual practice in the use of SEA is to
date fairly limited.

Growth of interest

The recent growth of interest in the use of environmental assessment at earlier stages of the planning
process stems from two sources:

- greater awareness of the limitations of environmental assessments confined to the relatively
  late stage of individual project authorisation;
- increasing support for measures to promote sustainable development which require the integration of environmental considerations into
  development planning.

Each of these is briefly reviewed below.

**Evaluations of the use of EIA are
positive in terms of improvements to
the planning and design of projects,
in the quality of decision-making and
of cost-effectiveness: some
deficiencies have also been identified**

Box 1. Policies and guidance relating to environmental assessment and development aid

The World Bank

"EA procedures may be applied to development activities other than specific projects. EA can be adapted to regional or sectoral scales and used to assess impacts of sector-wide programs, multiple projects, or development policies and plans. A regional or sectoral EA can reduce the time and effort required for project-specific EAs in the same region or sector by identifying issues, initiating baseline data collection, and assembling existing data in advance, or, in certain cases, by eliminating the need for project-specific EA altogether."

(World Bank, 1991a, chapter 1, para 39)

"... regional EAs are generally more efficient than a series of project-specific EAs. They may identify issues that the latter might overlook (e.g., inter-action among effluents or competition for natural resources). Regional EAs compare alternative development scenarios and recommend environmentally sustainable development and land use patterns and policies."

(World Bank, 1991b, para 5)

"Sectoral EAs ... are particularly suitable for reviewing (a) sector investment alternatives; (b) the effect of sector policy changes; (c) institutional capacities and requirements for environmental review, implementation, and monitoring at the sectoral level; and (d) the cumulative impacts of many relatively small, similar investments that do not merit individual project- specific EAs."

(World Bank, 1991b, para 6)

Asian Development Bank

The Asian Development Bank advocates a system whereby:

"... a full-scale economic-cum-environmental plan is derived which integrates environmental needs into economic development planning. The limited regional environmental development plan, which is done without tie-in with economic planning, nevertheless involves demonstration of the economic affordability of the plan's recommendations."

(Asian Development Bank, 1988, Section 1.1)

OECD

"... the environmental assessment process needs to be integrated at an early stage of project and programme planning; co-ordinated with the host country government; reflected in the implementation of the activity and followed up by monitoring and post-audit evaluation."

(OECD, 1986, page 77)

"Ministers welcomed recent efforts by OECD countries to expand support for environmental assistance to developing countries. They stressed that all programmes and projects of bilateral and multilateral development organisations should be consistent with sustainable development goals, and that systematic application of environmental impact assessment instruments is essential."

(OECD, 1991)

Limitations of project-level EIA

EIA is now widely practised, at the project level, in a large number of developed and developing countries and international aid organisations. The evaluations of its use, particularly after the initial 'settling-in' phase, are positive, in terms of improvements to the planning and design of projects, in the quality of decision-making, and of cost-effectiveness. However, some deficiencies have been identified. Certain of these can be remedied within the framework of project-level EIA itself, others may only be achieved by extending environmental assessment to earlier stages of the planning process. It is the latter which are of concern here.

Assessing impacts from ancillary developments. Difficulties can arise in evaluating the environmental impacts which may result from the indirect and induced activities stemming from a major development. For example, the Channel Tunnel project is expected to require major improvements to the UK rail system, development of major freight transhipment facilities, and so on. These may be of a sufficient scale to induce significant new development in their vicinity. The environmental impacts of these indirect and induced developments may exceed those of the Channel Tunnel project itself.

However, it is questionable how far, under present arrangements, these additional impacts could have been included within the EIA of the initial project. A number of the ancillary developments may be subject to separate, project-level, EIAs subsequent to the approval of the Channel Link project. Nevertheless, sequential, as distinct from simultaneous, assessments tend to reduce the number of alternatives (including the zero option) that can be effectively considered and hamper the evaluation of the cumulative impacts associated with the development as a whole.

Foreclosure of alternatives. Typically, by the project assessment stage, a number of options, which have potentially different environmental consequences from the chosen one, have been eliminated by decisions taken at earlier stages in the planning process, at which no satisfactory environmental assessment may have taken place. For example:

- The planning and design of a motorway section may be constrained by an earlier decision to build the motorway, part of which may already have been constructed. In turn, the decision to build the motorway may be constrained by an earlier decision to construct a motorway network as the preferred means of meeting national transport needs.
- A proposal to build a particular nuclear power station may result from earlier energy policy and planning decisions relating to energy requirements and the most appropriate means of meeting these.

Options of not constructing the road scheme or power station, of greatly altering their scale or location, or changing the technology cannot be examined from an environmental viewpoint unless the earlier policy and planning decisions themselves can be re-examined. To do so on a project-by-project basis would be unnecessarily inefficient and contentious. Almost certainly, it is preferable to introduce some form of environmental assessment into the earlier stages of the planning process.

Cumulative impacts. The need to assess cumulative impacts (that is, the combined environmental impacts of a number of activities) is not confined to the case where a large project stimulates other related developments, as discussed earlier. It also arises where proposals are made:

- to promote or regulate multiple developments within a prescribed geographical area (as in a development plan or land-use plan); or
- to expand or modify activities within a particular sector (for instance, through policies, plans or programmes relating to energy, transport, forestry or tourism activities).

The difficulties in relying exclusively on project-level environmental assessments in these cases are:

- the base line against which the individual project's impact is assessed can easily ignore or incorrectly estimate the changes to environmental conditions that will result from the other developments;
- because environmental damage functions are typically non-linear, and impacts from different activities may have synergistic or partially neutralising effects, the aggregate environmental impacts from multiple activities cannot be obtained by a simple summation of individual project-level assessment data.

Project-level EIAs should be sensitive to the phenomenon of cumulative impacts but they are unlikely to be satisfactorily handled in the absence of earlier sectoral and/or area-wide environmental assessments.

Other deficiencies. There are two categories of actions which tend to fall outside project-level EIA procedures but which can be collectively important from an environmental viewpoint:

- small projects which are not individually expected to cause significant impacts but collectively may do so (such as multiple housing or tourist developments within the same area);
- non-project actions which may have significant environmental consequences that cannot be satisfactorily regulated through the approval of capital schemes (for instance, changes in farming and forest management practices which en-

courage increased use of fertilisers and pesticides, livestock intensification and removal of hedgerows).

These types of actions may be more effectively handled at a policy, plan or programme level of assessment.

Earlier environmental assessments should help to overcome some of the deficiencies in project-level EIA, but they may also reduce the EIA workload at the project-level in the following ways:

- policy, plan and programme assessment issues should no longer intrude into each project-level assessment;
- more effective screening of projects is possible: some activities which have been satisfactorily assessed at earlier stages in the planning process may not require project-level assessment;
- more effective scoping of the coverage of project-level environmental assessments is possible using the information obtained and analysis undertaken at earlier stages of assessment.

Requirements for sustainable development

'Sustainable development' has been defined in a variety of ways but, in all cases, it implies the adoption of a collection of economic, social and environmental goals which are consistent with each other and mutually attainable. This entails the integration of economic, social and environmental considerations when planning or guiding future development. Thus:

"There is ... no contradiction in arguing both for economic growth and for environmental good sense, the challenge is to integrate the two ... The Government needs to ensure that its policies fit together in every sector; that we are not undoing in one area what we are trying to do in another; and that policies are based on a harmonious set of principles rather than a clutter of expedients." (UK Government, 1990, pages 8-9)

"Given the goal of achieving sustainable development it seems only logical, if not essential, to apply an assessment of the environmental implications of all relevant policies, plans and programmes. The integration of environmental assessment within the macro-planning process would not only enhance the protection of the environment and encourage optimisation of resource management but would also help to reduce those disparities in the international and inter-regional competition for new development projects which at present arise from disparities in assessment practices in the

> **Sustainable development requires the setting of environmental quality goals; institution strengthening; greater use of economic instruments; and the strengthening of procedures and assessment methods**

Member States." (Commission of the European Communities, 1992, para 7.3).

The most effective means of promoting sustainable development are still being debated but four types of measure are commonly identified:

- Setting environmental quality goals and/or emission targets to achieve these goals.
- Institution strengthening to promote the combined attainment of environmental quality and economic development goals.
- Greater use of economic instruments to guide economies on to more sustainable development pathways.
- Strengthening of procedures and assessment methods for the integration of environmental considerations, alongside economic and social considerations, in formulating and evaluating

new policies, plans, programmes and projects at all levels of decision-making.

The fourth of these measures, which entails the combined use of SEA and EIA procedures and methods, is of concern here. However, in a well-functioning system, all four are needed.

SEA and EIA: a comparison

Tiering

SEA and EIA share the same objectives, and should closely relate to each other within the same policy and planning process. They are intended to be complementary to each other. This can be illustrated through the concept of 'tiering'. The essential features of a tiered system of planning and environmental assessment are illustrated, in simplified form, in Figure 2. Thus:

- more strategic types of environmental assessment (SEAs) are to be carried out at policy, plan and/or programme level prior to more detailed environmental impact assessments (EIAs) at the individual project level;
- environmental impacts should be assessed at the relevant level of detail and be taken into account at those stages (policy, plan, programme or project authorisation) in the planning process

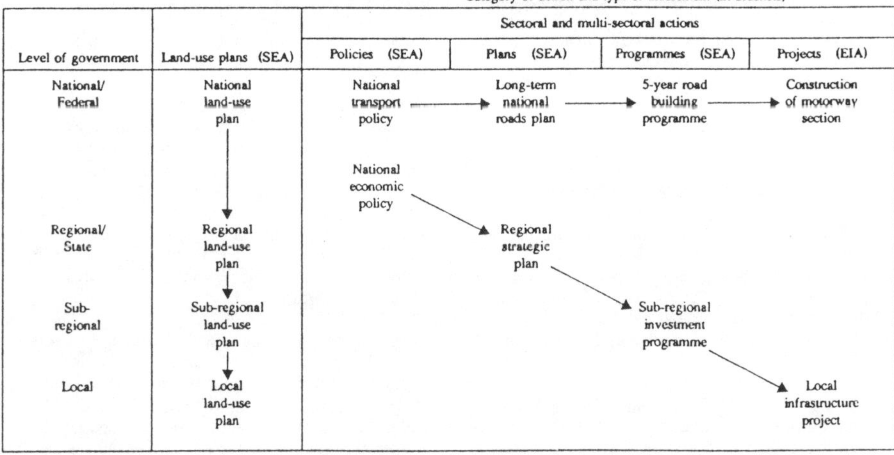

Level of government	Land-use plans (SEA)	Sectoral and multi-sectoral actions			
		Policies (SEA)	Plans (SEA)	Programmes (SEA)	Projects (EIA)
National/ Federal	National land-use plan	National transport policy →	Long-term national roads plan →	5-year road building programme →	Construction of motorway section
		National economic policy			
Regional/ State	Regional land-use plan		Regional strategic plan		
Sub-regional	Sub-regional land-use plan			Sub-regional investment programme	
Local	Local land-use plan				Local infrastructure project

N.B. This is a simplified representation of what, in reality, could be a more complex set of relationships. In general, those actions at the highest tier level (e.g. national policies) are likely to require the broadest and least detailed form of strategic environmental assessment.

Figure 2. Sequence of actions and assessments within a tiered planning and assessment system

Source: Based on N Lee and C Wood (1978), "EIA — a European perspective", *Built Environment*, 4(2), pages 101-110.

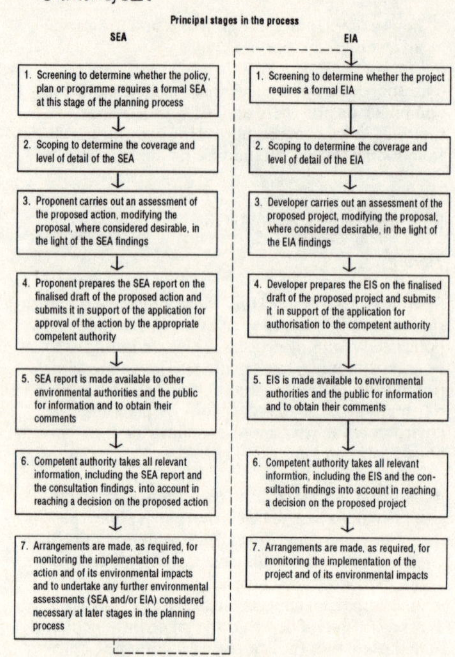

Figure 3. SEA and EIA: a comparison

which are most appropriate for their consideration in decision-making;

- assessments carried out at different stages in the planning process should be consistent with each other and should avoid unnecessary duplication.

Actions to be submitted to SEA

In principle, the actions submitted to SEA are those whose subsequent implementation is likely to give rise to significant environmental impacts *to the extent that these cannot be more satisfactorily assessed and/or mitigated at other (earlier or later) stages in the planning process*. This qualification is important and should greatly reduce both the number and scope of SEAs that need to be carried out at any given stage of the planning process. It implies:

- listing the categories of policies, plans and programmes which, in relation to alternatives, cumulative and/or non-project impacts, are likely to need assessment at some stage of the planning process before project-level authorisation; and
- establishing a screening mechanism for determining, within each of these categories, the most appropriate stage/s at which SEAs should take place.

Some form of SEA may be justified, on this basis, within the following sectors:

- primary sector: for example, agriculture, forestry, extractive industry, water supply and treatment;
- secondary sector: for example, energy production, chemicals, metals production and processing, construction;
- tertiary sector: for example, tourism, transport.

These sectors contain most of the types of projects that are covered by EIA regulations. However, the frequency distribution of SEAs by sector may not closely mirror the frequency distribution of EIAs.

Additionally, some form of SEA may be justified for certain multi-sectoral policies, plans and programmes, such as: land-use and regional development plans which promote or regulate different sectoral activities within a specified geographical area; fiscal policies which influence patterns of development and their environmental side-effects; and R&D policies, plans and programmes which influence the direction of technological change and its environmental consequences.

Similarities between processes

Since SEA and EIA processes are based on common principles, their components are also similar, even though their detailed form may differ. This is illustrated in Figure 3 and is briefly explained below in relation to the environmental inputs to the planning process — other inputs (economic, social, technical, and so on) are not considered, other than very briefly, at this point.

Stage 1. The first stage, in both SEA and EIA processes, is to establish whether an environmental assessment is likely to be required. The initiative should be taken early by the proponent of the action — he/she should be able to consult lists of actions contained in regulations or guidelines and/or use screening procedures to assist in this. There should be a competent authority or appeals authority to make final decisions in cases of doubt or dispute.

Stage 2. The next stage, in both cases, involves determining the scope (coverage) of the assessment. The initiative should normally be taken by the proponent of the action but scoping should be undertaken in consultation with the competent and environmental authorities and, except where there are real difficulties over confidential matters, with the public. Consideration should be given to the tier in the process at which the assessment is to be carried out since this will influence the types of alternatives and impacts to be investigated, the level of detail of the assessment and the methods to be used.

Stage 3. The third stage involves the proponent, assisted where necessary by consultants and others with environmental expertise, carrying out the environmental assessment of the proposed action. In the case of both SEA and EIA this assessment may pass through a number of iterations as new environmental information (and other information from parallel technical and socio-economic studies) is transmitted back into the planning process to help in improving the design and content of the action.

Stage 4. Once this is completed and the proposed action is finalised, the proponent prepares the SEA report (or EIS, in the case of a project). This should contain a summary of the proposed action, a description of the environment that may be affected by its implementation, a prediction of the likely significant environmental impacts that may result (having regard to environmental objectives, targets, standards, and so on which have been established) and a statement of any mitigatory measures including monitoring arrangements that are proposed. This is submitted, together with any other relevant information, to the competent authority when seeking approval for the action.

Stage 5. When the SEA report (or EIS, in the case of projects) is submitted to the competent authority it should also be made available to other environmental authorities and the general public for information and comment. In certain situations there may also be provision for the SEA/EIA report to be reviewed by an independent authority (for instance, a special environmental commission). This may be of particular importance where the proponent and the competent authority belong to the same organisation.

The forms in which the public are consulted may differ between SEA and EIA procedures, with greater emphasis being placed on consultations with public interest groups in the former case. The nature of the information provided and the issues discussed in the SEA report are likely to be of a more strategic nature and the numbers of people potentially involved in any consultative exercise in the former case is considerably greater. In both cases, the results of the consultations should be recorded in a form suitable for them to be taken

> **Despite the similarities between SEA and EIA processes, there are some differences, largely stemming from SEA being applied at an earlier stage in the planning process than EIA, which are of practical significance**

into account when a decision is being made on the proposed action.

Stages 6 and 7. The competent authority should take all of the relevant documentation, including the SEA report (or EIS, in the case of projects) and the findings of the consultations, into account in reaching a decision on the proposed action. The decision may involve changes to the proposed action, setting monitoring requirements and/or requirements for some additional environmental assessment to be undertaken at subsequent stages of the planning process.

Procedural differences between SEA and EIA

Despite the similarities between SEA and EIA processes, there are some differences between them, largely stemming from SEA being applied at an earlier stage in the planning process than EIA, which are of practical significance. In particular, five procedural issues relating to the SEA process merit attention.

Confidentiality The draft contents of certain policies (such as details of central government budget proposals), plans and programmes, may be considered too sensitive to release for public consultation prior to their approval. As in the case of EIA, this may be handled by exemptions from certain consultation arrangements in those cases where confidentiality justifies this. It is too early to judge whether such exemptions are likely to be relatively more extensive in SEA than in EIA.

Constitutional issue Certain actions (such as high-level policy decisions) are approved by national cabinets acting under conditions of collective ministerial responsibility. If these were subject to SEA law, the cabinet decisions relating to them may be subject to legal challenge in the courts. In Canada, this has been addressed by incorporating an environmental assessment procedure within federal cabinet decision-making procedures (Figure 1).

Procedural deficiencies SEA, to be effective, should be integrated into existing procedures at key decision-making points for policies, plans and programmes. These procedures should have the potential to meet SEA requirements relating to the provision of documentation by the proponent, for consultations based on this and the use of this combined information in decision-making by the competent authority.

The extent of existing provisions of this kind, within the earlier phases of planning processes in many countries, is variable. However, within a tiered system of environmental assessment, there is considerable flexibility in selecting the stages in the planning process at which to carry out assessments; the existence of suitable planning procedures into which these may be integrated is one of the factors in making that selection. Nevertheless, in certain cases, some institutional and procedural strengthening may still be desirable.

Proponent-competent authority relationship In certain cases, the proponent belongs to the same organisation as the competent authority. In the case of policies, plans and programmes, this is likely to occur frequently. One means of safe-guarding the objectivity and quality of the EIA process, in this type of situation, at the project level is to submit the EIS to review by an independent environmental authority or commission. A similar kind of solution may be needed to safeguard the SEA process.

Curtailment of competencies SEA may be resisted by some government departments as an intrusion into their area of competence. In fact, SEA (like EIA) is not intended to change the decision-making responsibilities of competent authorities. However, there is little doubt that the introduction of SEA, particularly at the national policy-making level, is a sensitive issue. It provides a real challenge to governments and, more particularly, Departments with developmental responsibilities, to give greater meaning and credibility to their role in promoting sustainable development.

Methodological differences

There are also similarities to, and differences between, the assessment tasks and methods used for SEA and EIA. The broad assessment tasks are fundamentally the same (see Figure 3) but there are some significant differences in detail, for the reasons given below.

First, the *scale* of an SEA tends to be considerably greater than that of an EIA because:

- the proposed action contains a number of different activities rather than a single project;
- the range of alternatives that may be considered is greater (for instance, including alternative locations, technologies, and land-use patterns);
- the area over which the assessment is conducted is larger because impacts are likely to be more geographically diffuse;
- the range of environmental impacts to be assessed may be greater (for instance certain resource use impacts — water, fuel use, and so on — may be significant at the strategic planning level but not at the project assessment level).

Second, the *time interval* between planning and approving an action and the implementation of the specific activities which give rise to environmental impacts is much longer in SEA than in EIA. As a consequence, the content of the proposed

action is known in less detail; it is more likely to change at later stages in the planning process; and the impact predictions are subject to greater uncertainty.

These scale and time differences increase the potential complexity of SEA relative to EIA. However, two other differences may operate in the opposite direction:

- the degree of *detail* and the level of *accuracy* of information needed for policy, plan and programme decision-making is generally less than that needed for project evaluation and decision-making. It will often be much less at the highest tiers in the planning process;
- the *time available* for gathering and analysing information for an SEA is, with the important exception of some policy decisions, greater than for EIA.

Wood and Djeddour (1992) identify a range of different assessment methods that may be used to undertake each of the tasks in the SEA process. These are broadly of two kinds:

- those already in use in project-level EIA but which can be adapted for use at more strategic levels of assessment. These include many of the methods used to identify impacts (checklists, matrices, network analyses), for describing baseline conditions, for predicting pollution impacts from multiple sources, and so on.
- those already used in policy analysis and planning studies which can be adapted for use in SEA. These include various forms of scenario and simulation analysis, regional forecasting and input-output techniques, site selection and land suitability analysis, geographic information systems (GIS), systems modelling (for instance, for traffic networks, energy systems, water resources systems), policy and programme evaluation techniques (such as multi-criteria analysis, goals achievement analysis, planning balance sheet approaches, cost-benefit analysis, constrained cost minimisation analysis, sensitivity analysis and other techniques for handling uncertainty).

Among the SEA tasks to be undertaken, the following are likely to be the most challenging (see items 2 and 3 in Figure 3):

- Describing the action, and its alternatives, in a way which enables the principal environmental impacts to be identified and subsequently assessed at the appropriate level of detail.
- Identifying the types of areas likely to be affected by the action and to describe, at the appropriate level of detail, their baseline environmental conditions.
- Predicting, on the basis of the above informa-

tion, the likely size and significance of the impacts at the appropriate level of detail.

- Integrating the SEA findings into the overall evaluation of the policy, plan or programme.
- Ensuring that uncertainty is satisfactorily handled at each stage in the assessment process.

The kinds of assessment methods needed to perform these tasks exist but, in a number of cases, some further work may be needed to adapt them for SEA use. Additionally, guidance and training in their use may be needed for practitioners with insufficient relevant experience.

Conclusions and recommendations

Formal provisions for environmental impact assessment (EIA), as an integral element of project approval and decision-making, now exist in many countries and are included in the procedures of many overseas development agencies. The quality of EIA practice is variable but it is improving as experience grows and as guidance and training is strengthened.

Formal provisions for strategic environmental assessment (SEA), as an integral element of appraisal and decision-making for policies, plans and programmes, are much less developed. However, SEA is already used, in both sector and land-use planning, in some countries. Also, less formalised and comprehensive environmental evaluation procedures are used in a greater number of countries. In this sense, the current status of SEA in many countries is not unlike that of EIA in the mid-1970s.

However, the situation is changing. A number of countries and aid agencies are in the process of adopting, extending or strengthening procedures for incorporating some form of environmental assessment into the earlier stages of the planning process. Others are carrying out studies into the desirability of doing so. This has been stimulated by two developments:

- a growing recognition that some important aspects of environmental assessment cannot be satisfactorily undertaken at the project evaluation stage and must, therefore, be carried out

---

Formal provisions for EIA as an integral element of project approval now exist in many countries and are included in the procedures of many development agencies: provisions for SEA are much less developed

---

at earlier stages in the planning process;
- an increasing appreciation that the implementation of sustainable development strategies will require the use of environmental assessment procedures and methods in the formulation of policies, plans and programmes for the principal sectors of national economies.

With the developing interest in a more strategic approach to environmental assessment, there needs to be a better understanding of the principal elements of the SEA process itself. In particular, to avoid confusion and misunderstanding, it is necessary to clarify its relationship to EIA. SEA and EIA share the same objectives, belong to the same 'tiered' system of assessment (see Figure 2) and contain similar assessment stages and tasks (see Figure 3). However, because they operate at different points in the planning process, and at different levels of generality, there are likely to be some procedural and methodological differences between them.

At the procedural level, some adaptations to the EIA 'model' are likely to be needed for SEA application including: modifications to procedures where cabinet decision-making is involved and/or to consultation procedures where real issues of confidentiality apply; modifications to the form of public consultations, placing greater reliance on consultations with community and group representatives; and the strengthening of screening and scoping procedures to avoid excessive and duplicatory use of SEA at different stages in the planning process.

Similarly, at the methodological level, some modification to the methods used at the project level of assessment may be necessary. The SEA methods used will be mainly drawn from two sources: adaptations to certain methods currently being used successfully in project EIAs; and adaptations to assessment methods currently being used in policy analyses and planning studies outside the environmental sector.

The use of both of these sources is already evident in existing SEA practice and further adaptations of methods drawn from them are to be expected. However, because of its more recent development, both knowledge of these SEA methods and experience in their use is fairly restricted at present, outside a relatively small number of countries and sectors.

In view of these conclusions, there are a number of initiatives that could be taken to encourage more effective use of SEA in the future:

Increase the general understanding of SEA, especially among community representatives, administrators and technical staff involved in the earlier stages of policy-making and planning. Particular attention is needed to the following topics: the types of actions to which SEA may be usefully applied and how it would operate in practice; its relationship to existing policy and planning arrangements; its relationship to existing EIA and sustainable development policies; and the main benefits and costs of using it.

Clarify any procedural issues which are potential sources of confusion or concern, including: at which decision point/s in a given planning process should SEA be inserted; how should SEA be applied to high-level policy decisions and where confidentiality, prior to decision-making, is considered important; what screening and scoping procedures are required; what are the content requirements of an SEA report; what forms of consultation would be most appropriate; how are the SEA findings to be integrated with other policy and planning considerations in decision-making; what forms of monitoring are most appropriate?

Clarify any methodological uncertainties and strengthen the practical application of appropriate SEA methods. This may be promoted by: assembling an inventory of appropriate SEA methods, classified according to assessment task and cross-referenced to the practical situations in which they have already been used; carrying out further developmental work, where needed, to adapt other methods for SEA use; undertaking pilot studies or 'trial runs'; assembling collections of SEA case studies which exemplify how environmental assessments of particular policies, plans and programmes have been carried out and the methods that have been used for this purpose; preparing guidance (procedural and methodological) on 'how to do' SEA and providing training in its use.

Review existing environmental data sources to assess their potential in terms of content, access, and so on for use in SEA and to prioritise measures for correcting any deficiencies.

If measures of this kind are carried out, the next phase of SEA development could proceed on a better-prepared and more fully-informed basis.

Note

1. The terms 'policy', 'plan' and 'programme' are each often used differently, and sometimes interchangeably. In the context of SEA it is generally not helpful to draw sharp distinctions between them but to regard each as actions to be approved at different stages in the planning process prior to the project approval stage.

References

Asian Development Bank (1988), *Guidelines for Integrated Regional Economic-cum-Environmental Development Planning — a Review of Regional Environmental Development Planning Studies in Asia (Volume I)* (Environment Unit, Asian Development Bank, Manila, The Philippines).

R Bass (1990), "California's experience with environmental impact reports", *Project Appraisal*, 5(4), pages 220-224.

Canadian Environmental Assessment Research Council (1986), *Proceedings of the Workshop on Cumulative Environmental Effects: a Binational Perspective* (Federal Environmental Assessment Review Office, Hull, Quebec, Canada).

C Cocklin, S Parker and J Hay (1992), "Notes on cumulative environmental change", *Journal of Environmental Management*, 35, pages 31-67.

Commission of the European Communities (1985), "Council directive of 27 June 1985 on the assessment of the effects of certain public and private projects on the environment",*Official Journal of the European Communities*, L175, pages 40-48.

Commission of the European Communities (1992), *Towards Sustainability — a European Community Programme of Policy and Action in Relation to the Environment and Sustainable Development*, COM(92) 23 final - vol II (Commission of the European Communities, Brussels, Belgium).

W Couch (1991), "Recent EIA developments in Canada", *EIA Newsletter*, 6, pages 17-18.

Department of the Environment (1991), *Policy Appraisal and the Environment* (HMSO, London, UK).

Department of Transport (1992), *Assessing the Environmental Impact of Road Schemes — Response by Department of Transport to the Report by the Standing Committee on Trunk Road Assessment (SACTRA)* (HMSO, London, UK).

Directorate-General for Environment, Commission of the European Communities (1990), *Vade Mecum for use in Providing Environmental Information relating to Plans, Programmes and Projects financed through the Structural Funds* (DGXI, Commission of the European Communities, Brussels, Belgium).

V Kleinschmidt (1991), "Strategic environmental assessment of technological research proposals", *EIA Newsletter*, 6, page 4.

P LeBlanc (1991), "Canadian Environmental Assessment Research Council activities", *EIA Newsletter*, 6, pages 21-22.

T Lind (1991), "Nordic co-operation on environmental impact assessment", *EIA Newsletter*, 6, pages 15-16.

G Matarrese (1991), "EIA in Italy", *EIA Newsletter*, 6, page 10.

Organisation for Economic Co-operation and Development (1986), *Environmental Assessment and Development Assistance*, OECD Environmental Monograph no 4 (OECD, Paris, France).

Organisation for Economic Co-operation and Development (1991), *Communique — an Environmental Strategy in the 1990s*, SG/Press(91)9 (OECD, Paris, France).

United Kingdom Government (1990), *This Common Inheritance — Britain's Environmental Strategy*, Cm 1200 (HMSO, London, UK).

United Nations Economic Commission for Europe (1991), *Convention on Environmental Impact Assessment in a Transboundary Context* (United Nations, Geneva, Switzerland).

United Nations Economic Commission for Europe (1992), *Application of Environmental Impact Assessment Principles to Policies, Plans and Programmes (ECE/ENVWA/27)*, Environmental Series no 5 (United Nations, Geneva, Switzerland, forthcoming).

C Wells (1991), "Impact assessment in New Zealand: the Resource Management Act", *EIA Newsletter*, 6, pages 19- 20.

C Wood and M Djeddour (1992), "Strategic environmental assessment: EA of policies, plans and programmes", *Impact Assessment Bulletin*, 10(1), pages 3-22.

World Bank (1991a), *Environmental Assessment Sourcebook Volume I — Policies, Procedures, and Cross-Sectoral Issues*, World Bank Technical Paper 139 (The World Bank, Washington, DC, USA).

World Bank (1991b), *Operational Directive 4.01: Environmental Assessment* (The World Bank, Washington, DC, USA).

[12]

Regional Studies. Vol. 4, pp. 151–165. Pergamon Press 1970. Printed in Great Britain

SfB Aa4

UDC 338.984:
711

Evaluation Methodology of Urban and Regional Plans: A Review

NATHANIEL LICHFIELD

School of Environmental Studies, University College London

(Received 28 April 1970)

LICHFIELD N. (1970) Evaluation methodology of urban and regional plans: A Review, *Reg. Studies* **4,** 151–165. Of recent years there has been advancement in the urban and regional planning process in terms of the conscious searching out of alternative policies, projects and plans with a view to selection amongst them of the preferred solution. The search may be confined to the design process of the professional planners culminating in one preferred solution to the political decision makers; or it may lead to the presentation of alternatives to the decision makers, with or without a recommendation as to choice. In both cases there is need for formal testing of the alternatives with a view to indicating the preferred choice. There has also been advancement in such testing methodologies. But a distinction is here made between tests in general and the particular test of a plan or project as a whole with a view to choice of that which is best in terms of community welfare. Such a test is here called Plan Evaluation.

After describing the generalities of tests the article makes a comparative review of some twenty plan evaluation methodologies which have been used in practice or advocated in the literature. It does so by reference to ten criteria to which comprehensive evaluation methodologies should conform if they are to suit the purpose, concerning itself with the potential of the methodology rather than the actual example of its use. It concludes in favour of the Planning Balance Sheet, that is cost–benefit analysis as applied to urban and regional planning, as having the greater potential.

Planning   Decision making in planning   Testing of plans   Evaluation of plans   Planning balance sheet   Cost–benefit analysis   Project appraisal   Linear programming   Goal achievement

THE PURPOSE of this article is to make a review of methods currently used or proposed for evaluation of both or either urban and regional plans. The aim of the review is to describe comparatively the broad range of methods available rather than offer a critique of their efficiency and value.

Evaluation here is the means of aiding the selection by the decision makers (those commissioning the plan) as to which of alternative plans they will adopt as the "best" for the community for whom they are planning; or aiding the planners themselves during the planning process in the similar need for selection, that is the rejection of alternatives that they do not intend to offer to the decision makers for adoption. *Evaluation* in this sense is one form of what is called the *testing* of plans or parts of plans, also with a view to selection as among alternatives.

Thus testing and evaluation are linked in practice, and in the minds of planners. Accordingly the article starts with a review of what is normally meant by testing so that the contrast between testing and evaluation, and their respective places in the planning process, can be the more readily seen. But it is not the intention here that the linkage between the two be specifically brought out and for the contribution that testing in general could make to evaluation.

REVIEW OF PLAN TESTS

The simplest way of visualizing what is here meant by the testing (in the broad sense) of a plan or project is to imagine that somebody is intent on making a critical examination of it: for example, the planners themselves, the commissioning body, a Ministry examining the plan of a local planning authority, an Inspector or Commission at a public hearing, other planners or a writer reviewing the plan for a journal. The review could take many forms. One simple form could be the listing of a series of critical questions (criteria) with a view to finding the answers which indicate whether the plan is satisfactory or not, on the criteria posed. Such questions might be: does the plan conform to acceptable planning standards (of open space, density, width of green belt) or planning principles (distribution of neighbourhood centres or segregation of pedestrians and vehicles) or has it been designed with acceptable technical skill (in highway or town centre lay-out)? Will the plan solution in fact cater for the current and future problems in the area under study? Will there be the economic resources and demand for the development envisaged? Are the relevant development agencies likely to be able to afford a particular project (LICHFIELD, 1964)?

While such tests will enable answers to be formulated to the questions on a particular plan they will also enable comparisons to be made between alternative plans for the same area, with a view to deciding which is the "best", and also possibly to permit of the generation of a plan which is "better" than those which have been put forward. In this context the "best" and "better" are chosen according to the pre-selected criterion, which can limit the degree of optimality of the final choice.

It is possible to carry out such tests when any particular plan or alternatives have been formulated by the planners for review in this way. However it is implicit in the planning process itself that the tests are carried out at appropriate stages during the plan preparation, so that plans which do not meet the tests are not proceeded with or, more generally, particular elements of the plan are accordingly re-designed. This will clearly apply to the selection of land for new development which will not fail on tests of physical suitability, or location in relation to other development, or inadequacy of public utilities without new major construction. It is by the application of such tests throughout the planning process that one or more solutions eventually evolve which are both feasible and also as optimal as the particular planning process allows.

Tests of this kind have always been germane to the planning process, even though certain plans of the past raise doubts as to whether such questions were seriously asked and answered. But although the testing process is an old one it is today being introduced at a more sophisticated level. The reasons are that a conscious search for alternatives plays a much greater part in the planning process today than before, as does the conscious presentation of alternatives to the decision makers for selection, such very presentation requiring a statement of the tests which have been introduced and the reasons why they have led to the alternative which is put forward for recommendation. But there is another reason, namely that the introduction of urban and regional models of various kinds enables more alternatives to be formulated and the alternatives to be tested by the use of computers, which both facilitates the introduction of the tests and also provides facilities for using them. These facilities have themselves enriched the planning process in making it possible to proceed to a particular solution on a "cyclical" rather than "linear" approach. In the latter there would be an attempt to generate the particular solution, in the somewhat step-by-step approach of the 1947 Act development plans which in brief envisaged the survey followed by the analysis followed by the plan and programme. An example of the former is seen in a recent sub-regional study (NOTTS-DERBY, 1969) where the plan finally put forward was evolved through four separate stages which moved from a broad review of a large number of possible strategies which were not precisely quantified to a small number of strategies which were very precisely delineated. The plan making process thus comprised four main cycles in each of which the sequence—formulation of concepts; translation into numerical and spatial form; testing; evaluation and conclusion—was followed. The conclusions from one cycle led directly to the plan formulation stage of the next cycle, and in this way the various alternatives considered at the beginning of Stage I were progressively reduced until the preferred strategy was put forward for testing in Stage IV. During these stages varying kinds of tests were carried out which led to the rejection of alternatives, tests such as the delimitation of areas having potential for development, the establishment of locations by modelling, a sieve map for eliminating areas unsuitable for development, testing of retailing locations by modelling.

This brief review of testing shows that the tests can be of varied kinds and used in varied ways. Further consideration of them is outside the scope of this article except in so far as some such tests are also used, as it will be seen, for the kind of evaluation which is of concern here.

But before leaving tests in the broad sense it is useful to attempt some categorization of them so that their link with the evaluation tests can be seen. A tentative categorization could be as follows:

1. *Internal consistency*

Do the varying quantitative elements in the plan (e.g. population, employment needs, employment opportunities, motor-car ownership, traffic flows, etc.) relate to each other in the statistical sense? This question can be applied to the total system dealt with by the plan or to part of the system, an example of the latter being the consistency between the traffic which will be generated by the land uses and the capacity of the traffic system to take such traffic, both in movement and when the vehicle is stationary.

2. *Locational suitability*

To what degree are the locations of the varying activities and functions appropriate in the sense that they are suitable to the activity (e.g. industrial location) and suitable to the people who will use them (e.g. residential location)?

3. *Conformity to standards and principles*

Are the elements in the plan appropriate from the viewpoint of standards and principles which are accepted in plans of the kind under consideration, such as acceptability being related to levels of performance?

4. *Problem solving*

Will the planning solution solve the problems of the area, both current and future, which have emerged from an analysis of the studies and forecasts in the planning process?

5. *Feasibility*

Are the planning proposals feasible, i.e. practicable, in regard to the various constraints which apply? These are several in character. Under economic feasibility will arise the question as to whether there will be the demand for the new accommodation of various kinds to be provided and also whether there will be available at acceptable prices the various factors necessary for the supply of the accommodation. Under financial feasibility comes a question of whether all the particular agencies who will be concerned with implementing the plan will find the relationship between revenues to be earned and cost to be incurred sufficient to attract their enterprise. Clearly differing rules will apply as between the private and public sectors; for the public sector there is question of whether the cost to be incurred can be matched by the revenues which will need to be raised, after allowing for grants, subsidies, etc. There then arises the question of administrative or organizational feasibility, for example whether the necessary statutory powers are available or the administrative organization to implement the plan. A final instance could be political feasibility; whether the proposals are acceptable to the people who will be affected, to their elected representatives and to the higher level or lower level political decision making bodies concerned.

6. *Design*

Having regard to all the preceding tests is the level of design, i.e. the level of creativity which has been introduced into the problem by the planners, of a good order, from the acceptable to the commendable?

7. *Flexibility and open-endedness*

Since the future is uncertain there must be provision in the plans for changing course if reviews after a few years show this to be necessary. Therefore some test needs to be made whether the planning proposals themselves are capable of such adjustment, in the light of what are shown by forecasts to be the main uncertainties.

From this categorization it is seen that these tests have as their general aim the production of plans which are technically competent and acceptable, and also generally practicable and feasible.

REVIEW AND CATEGORISATION OF PLAN EVALUATION METHODOLOGY

As just indicated, plan evaluation is a distinctive kind of plan testing. Its distinction lies in the fact that it is properly applied when the other tests have been met and also, as in all tests, in the questions which plan evaluation aims to answer. Put more simply (LICHFIELD, 1969), a town is a complex organism catering for the operational demands of all its inhabitants and users. Any proposals for its alteration or development will have advantages and disadvantages for every individual within it. A plan is intended to provide for all these operational demands, both current and prospective. While it is impossible to plan for optimum conditions for every current or future inhabitant or user, the plan proposals should aim to provide the best solution for as many requirements as possible, or the greatest aggregate net benefit for all concerned. Accordingly, any method of evaluation of alternative plans must be able to demonstrate how the operational demands of all the individuals concerned have been catered for (the benefits), and what consequential costs would fall on them.

It is in order to attempt an answer to these questions that the Planning Balance Sheet methodology has been devised and applied in a series of case studies (starting with LICHFIELD, 1960). But other methods have been used, some attempting to answer different questions (e.g. STONE, 1963), some attempting the same question but using different methodologies (e.g. BEN-SHAHAR, *et al.*, 1969).

An earlier review of plan evaluation methodologies critically examined six, drawing attention to their limitations for the purpose in hand, and concluded "that in my view these widely ranging methodologies of plan evaluation fall short of the full needs of planning decision makers for evaluating plans in terms of what the community is asked to give up and what it would achieve" (LICHFIELD, 1968). In this article a more comprehensive review is made of the methodologies previously discussed and of others, but in a more systematic way. This is attempted by listing ten criteria which in my view a plan evaluation methodology should satisfy to discharge its full function, and by showing how the various methodologies, including the Planning Balance Sheet, fall short on these criteria.

The ten criteria are shown in Table 1. In brief the evaluation methodology should:

1. Have regard to the stated or implied objective (ends, values) of the decision makers (which may or may not be the objectives of those for whom they are planning).
2. Cover all systems of urban and regional facilities which are encompassed in the plan.
3. Cover all sectors of the community which are affected, that is which should be included within the decision maker's concern.
4. Sub-divide the sectors into producers/operators of the plan output and its consumers so that all the "transactions" implicit in the plan are considered.
5. Take account of all costs to all sectors, including externalities.
6. Take account of all benefits to sectors, including externalities.
7. Measure all the costs and benefits in money terms.
8. Facilitate the adoption of a satisfactory criterion for choice.
9. Show the incidence of the costs and benefits on all sectors of the community.
10. Be useable as an optimizing tool with a view to ensuring the best solution.

Each of the columns in Table 1 are sub-divided to show whether the methodology under review caters for the criterion in a partial (*P*) or full (*F*) sense. A × in the Table shows whether the treatment in this instance is partial or full but no attempt is made to distinguish between degrees of achievement (in which considerable variations exist). And a blank in the Table shows that the item is not considered at all, even by implication.

Coming now to the evaluation methodologies themselves it will be seen from the Table that eight distinct groups are attempted, these merely being convenient ways of dealing with groups of cognate methods which have originated from different sources. The groups start with the Planning Balance Sheet analysis, being the most comprehensive, with an indication of whether it partially or fully meets the ten criteria. From the Table it will be seen that it fulfils them fully on seven of the ten counts but only partially on three. This arises because it is recognized that all items cannot be measured in money terms with current measurement methodology (7) and applies itself to the questions of evaluation where some and perhaps many of the items of necessity are measured only in physical units, or are crudely ranked in order or are quite non-measurable. For this reason the full range of criteria of choice may not necessarily be available (8). And finally while the Planning Balance Sheet attempts to find the best solution among alternatives, and in this sense optimizes as far as possible, it is not inherently an optimizing analysis, as for example is linear programming (10).

This statement in relation to each of the criteria is then compared in the remainder of the Table with the other methodologies which are grouped under headings 2–8:

2. Checklist of Criteria
3. Investment Appraisal Financial
4. Investment Appraisal Economic
5. Goal Achievement
6. Cost Minimization
7. Cost Effectiveness
8. Cost–Benefit Analysis

We now proceed to each of these in turn, with sub-variants in each group, making 24 methods in all. Against each method is an indication of whether it has been used in practice on an actual problem or whether it is simply proposed in the literature. In the latter case some inference has necessarily been drawn as to the potential for the purpose of Table 1.

This wide ranging review probably means that in the space available some accuracy in description has been lost and some injustice done. But it is hoped that these are small.

1. *Planning Balance Sheet*

The reasoning behind the Planning Balance Sheet methodology for the purpose of plan

Table 1. Comparison of plan evaluation methodology by criteria*

Group No.	Description	Source			1		2		3		4		5		6		7		8		9		10	
			Theory practice		Objectives		Systems		Sectors		Producers Consumers		Costs		Benefits		Measured		Criterion		Inci-dence		Optim-izing	
			T	P	P	F	P	F	P	F	P	F	P	F	P	F	P	F	P	F	P	F	P	F
1	*Planning Balance Sheet*	Lichfield (1960)		×		×		×		×		×		×		×	×		×			×	×	
2	*Checklist of criteria*																								
2.1	Advantages and disadvantages	Kitching (1963)		×	×				×	×			×						×				×	
2.2	Checklist of criteria	Kitching (1969)		×	×				×	×			×		×		×		×				×	
2.3	Checklist and costing	Llewelyn-Davies et al. (1970)		×	×				×	×			×		×		×		×				×	
3	*Investment appraisal—Financial*																								
3.1	Public development agencies	Lichfield and Wendt (1969), Wendt (1967)		×	×		×		×		×		×		×		×		×		×		×	
3.2	Public operating agencies	Mace (1961)		×	×		×		×		×		×		×		×		×		×		×	
3.3	All agencies—development and operating						×		×		×		×		×		×		×		×		×	
4	*Investment appraisal—Economic*																								
4.1	Highways			×	×		×		×		×		×		×		×		×		×			×
4.2	Municipal enterprise	I.M.T.A. (1969)		×	×		×		×		×		×		×		×		×		×		×	
4.3	Recreation	McCarthy and Dower (1967)		×			×		×		×		×		×		×		×		×			
5	*Goal achievement*																								
5.1	Bending on	Shankland Cox (1966)		×	×				×	×					×				×				×	
5.2	Policy evaluation matrix	Kreditor (1967)		×	×				×	×					×				×					
5.3	Goals achievement matrix	Hill (1967)	×				×		×				×		×		×		×		×			×
5.4	Objective fulfilment analysis	Schlager (1968)	×				×		×				×		×		×		×					
6	*Cost minimization*																								
6.1	Costs in use	Stone (1967)		×	×				×		×						×		×		×		×	
6.2	Threshold theory	Kozlowski and Hughes (1967)		×	×		×		×		×		×				×		×		×		×	
7	*Cost effectiveness*																								
7.1	Planning, programming and budgeting			×	×				×		×				×		×		×		×		×	
8	*Cost–benefit analysis*																								
8.1	Warsaw optimization planning	Planning Research Unit (1970)	×		×		×		×				×		×		×		×		×		×	
8.2	Linear programming	Ben-Shahar (1969)		×	×		×		×				×		×		×		×					×
8.3	Maximize land values	Lean and Goodall (1966)	×	×			×		×				×		×		×		×					
8.4	Cost–benefit analysis:																								
8.4.1	Rothenberg (1967)			×	×		×		×				×		×		×		×				×	
8.4.2	Mao (1966)			×	×		×		×				×		×		×		×				×	
8.4.3	Commission on T.L.A. (1970)			×				×		×				×		×		×		×	×			×

* By "plan" here is meant either a project or a complete plan.

evaluation has been described elsewhere (LICH-
FIELD, 1960 and LICHFIELD, 1964), and also the
application to case studies, demonstrating its
potential (LICHFIELD and CHAPMAN, 1968) and
also the research needs for its greater maturity
(LICHFIELD, 1964). Thus it is thought necessary
for this review only to restate the approach in
simple terms. "To evaluate alternatives from the
point of view of every individual concerned
would be a virtual impossibility. Therefore, the
planning balance sheet groups the community
into various homogeneous sectors distinguished
by the kind of operations they wish to perform.
It then evaluates and compares the alternatives
from the point of view of the advantages (benefits) and disadvantages (costs) accruing to every
sector from each alternative, to see which would
provide the maximum net advantage (benefit).
Since the analysis is being made in respect of
urban and regional plans, it must include all
features of relevance in such plans. It follows
that as well as those benefits and costs which are
measurable in money terms, there are others
that are only measurable in some other unit
(time, physical) and others that are non-measurable. Thus, the balance sheet cannot, and does not,
aim to provide a conclusion in terms of rate of
return or net profit measured by money values
as is the case in some typical cost–benefit studies.
Its value lies in exposing the implications of each
set of proposals to the whole community and to
the various groups within that community, and
also in indicating how the alternatives might be
improved or amalgamated to produce a better
result. The purpose of the approach is the selection of a plan which, on the information available, is likely to best serve the total interests of
the community" (LICHFIELD, 1969).

2. Checklist of criteria

The second group deals with methodologies
developed amongst physical planners.

2.1. Enumeration of advantages and disadvantages.
KITCHING (1963) demonstrates this method in
relation to alternative possible plans for Greater
London. He takes as a starting point the expected
population increase of two to four million in
South-East England between 1963 and 1981 and
suggests five possible basic patterns which could
be followed for its accommodation. These are
briefly: unrestricted growth of London, following present pattern of development plans,
concentration of growth into one new city,
six to twelve new cities or linear towns stretching
radially from London. From the "balance sheet"
of advantages and disadvantages Kitching draws
conclusions on each and then puts forward a

composite pattern which in his view would be
the most satisfactory. In relation to the criteria of
Table 1, it will be seen that the aim is to consider
all the systems concerned in the plan but there is
only implied reference to objectives, sectors of the
community, costs and benefits. The criterion is
limited (the greatest net advantage). The method
is only partially optimizing, in the trial and error
sense. There is no attempt to distinguish between
the producers/consumers, nor is the incidence of
the advantages and disadvantages brought out.
Nor is there any attempt at measurement, so that
the comparison is entirely subjective to the
analyst.

2.2. Checklist of criteria. KITCHING (1969) has also
demonstrated this approach in relation to the
regional planning considerations affecting the
four sites selected by the Roskill Commission
for the Third London Airport. He first enum-
erates seven characteristics which one would
ideally seek in siting a major international airport
in the South-East Region: communications, airport noise, growth potential of population and
industry, labour costs, amenity and agriculture
and services. He then examines each of the four
possible sites in relation to each of these criteria,
using such data as are available and forms a
judgement as to the order of choice in relation to
each. These are set out in a summary table with
the sites ranked 1–4 for each, 1 being the best and
4 the worst. From this table of crude, that is
unweighted, ranking he draws conclusions. In
relation to the criteria in Table 1, the method is
much the same as that of "advantages and disadvantages", except that there is a certain
degree of measurement introduced, by ordinal
ranking. As to optimizing, there has been no
attempt to find a better site than the best of the
four, since this was not the point at issue, but
inherently the method could be used for this
purpose.

A combination of the methods in 2.1 and 2.2
appears in a study analysing four alternatives for
the designated area of a new town in Lancashire
(MATHEW *et al.*, 1967). After studying the theoretical basis of urban form the study established
a list of nine criteria as a sieve through which the
various options for development were assessed.
Ten possible options were thus reduced to three
which were then developed in greater detail and
reassessed against the nine criteria by listing each
one's advantages and disadvantages from which
the preferred option, modified slightly, emerged.

2.3. Checklist of criteria and costing. An improvement on the methods in 2.1 and 2.2 was developed
by Consultants appointed by the Roskill Commission to find suitable locations for the associated urban development of each of the four

alternative airport sites, following a comparison of alternatives (LLEWELYN-DAVIES *et al.*, 1970). The process of comparison and selection was agreed with the Commission and was basically the same for all four sites. The approach was as follows.

Firstly, certain elements in the development were costed (construction of site development, engineering, transportation, provision of major services and shopping centres, land acquisition, losses in agricultural output, user transportation costs) and then there were listed a large number of criteria on which schemes were not costed. These criteria were applied to the alternative strategies in two stages. At the first stage the strategies (including those which had been costed) were roughly ranked on a five-point scale in respect of each criterion without costing. Pairs of strategies were then compared and when one dominated (that is had an inferior ranking for at least one criterion and no lower rankings) it was rejected, so reducing the number of alternatives. At the second stage the costed items were introduced, the alternative with the lowest total cost being provisionally selected. The uncosted criteria were then examined to establish whether there were any factors that might outweigh the least cost. This was the final judgement leading to a selection of the preferred strategy.

From the criteria in Table 1 it is seen that although the amount of scrutiny and costing is greater than in the two previous methods, and is thus more likely to lead to a better selection, inherently the method is a more sophisticated attempt at the checklist of criteria of 2.2. But it does introduce the important feature of offsetting measured money costs against features which cannot be costed as a basis for judgement.

3. *Investment appraisal—Financial*

The next group of evaluation methods stems from the quite different source of those concerned with the financial appraisal of investment, that is financial costs and returns which will flow to the particular decision maker who is considering alternative investment possibilities. The source here comes jointly from economics, accountancy and real estate valuation (LICHFIELD, 1956; LICHFIELD, 1967). The feature of the method is that only the financial costs and returns directly of interest to the investing or decision making body are of interest, and not the inevitable external repercussions affecting others.

3.1. *Public development agencies.* Although not intended as an evaluation exercise, LICHFIELD and WENDT (1969) demonstrated in their analysis of the financial experience and expectations of six English new towns the manner in which the analysis could be used for evaluation. After introducing the cost elements for the new towns as a whole, including all agencies, they concentrated on the experience of the New Town Development Corporation, both as regards the financial costs which fell upon them and the financial returns they would obtain. Writing in 1962, they reviewed the experience to 1961 and then made forecasts on a comparable basis to the expected dates on the completion of the towns. On the costs side came all investment and on the revenue side came all rents, after deducting real estate operating expenditures.

The interest in this particular study was the costs and returns at the dates mentioned, which were of relevance. But investment appraisal as such would necessarily include discounting of the expected streams of costs and returns to the date of decision. WENDT (1967) has applied such a model to private enterprise real estate development in the United States.

In Table 1 the method is related to the criteria irrespective of whether discounting is or is not applied. From the Table it will be seen that only part of the objectives, systems and sectors are examined, and only part of the costs and benefits and therefore incidence. There is a clear distinction between producers and consumers, all relevant costs and returns are measured, thus providing full opportunity for the use of the relevant criteria, but the range of costs and benefits and of criteria are still partial in the planning sense. The model is an optimizing one, as adapted for computer use (WENDT, 1967), but again is only partial for planning purposes.

3.2. *Public operating agencies.* Coming from quite a different source are the appraisals of costs and returns to public operating agencies, notably local authorities concerned with developments affecting their municipality. These are known in this country in the everyday exercises of municipal treasurers for their short-term or long-term budgets. An early example for planning was found in the Development Plan for Middlesbrough (County Borough of Middlesbrough, 1951). But the methodology is much more developed in the United States under the general heading of cost revenue analysis. MACE (1961) gives a full review of their relevant studies in the U.S.A. Here again the emphasis is mainly on the particular public sector of the local authority, and of main interest is their financial investment and operating costs on the one hand and their revenues from the tax base so created on the other. From this it follows that the suitability of the analysis of planning methodology is similar to that in 3.1, the difference between the two being the concern with investment in the first and with development and operation in the second.

3.3. *All agencies—development and operating.* With the growing number of new towns and large-scale urban renewal plans of recent years there has also been growing the tendency for full-scale financial appraisal of the alternatives. Many examples exist of cost estimates of construction (e.g. WELLS, 1963 and BUCHANAN, 1967). Some also have attempted the total stream of costs and revenues from development falling on all agencies (LICHFIELD, 1967, 1968). Lichfield and Associates (1969) have also presented an analysis for the financial implications of alternative urban renewal projects having regard to all sectors of the community who would be affected as producers and consumers.

However there still remains to be attempted the comprehensive financial analysis which will have regard not only to all agencies but to both initial and continuing costs and returns. If this were done it would meet the criteria of Table 1 in the manner shown. Firstly it would cover all systems and sectors (in contrast to methods 3.1 and 3.2) but in all other respects would be the same as those two methods. Secondly to some degree it would take account of externalities, in the sense that concurrent estimates for all agencies would avoid having regard to costs or returns without compensating adjustments on other sectors. But the coverage would still not be full in the planning sense; since the costs and returns would relate only to the financial flows there would not be considered those costs and benefits to which money does not pass (for example, time spent in travel, effect of noise, injury to landscape views).

4. Investment appraisal—Economic

The next group comes from the distinct source of economists applying cost–benefit analysis techniques to particular public sector investments following the initiation of such attempts by engineers. While the theory goes back further (KRUTILLA and ECKSTEIN, 1958) modern attempts started with application in the United States to water resource and highway projects and since then the application has ramified throughout the whole of the public sector, with economists attempting to find some economic rationale for public sector investment projects, such as health, education and defence. PREST and TURVEY (1966) give a wide-ranging review of both the literature and the application. If a common feature is to be sought on the application it is in the isolation of the particular system under examination from the remainder of systems, the measurement of costs and benefits relating to that system with regard only to

externalities affecting that system. Accordingly it is necessary to consider only one form or facility as an example, and highways are chosen since they are of great relevance in planning and highway cost–benefit analysis has advanced considerably.

4.1. *Highway.* Highway cost–benefit analysis methodology has been greatly advanced since the pioneering work in the United States. More recent examples of the analysis in this country are in the London Transportation Study (GREATER LONDON COUNCIL, 1969) and in THOMPSON (1969). From what has been said above it is apparent that since only part of the urban system is being analysed there is only partial reference in the planning sense to most of the criteria referred to in Table 1. An implicit distinction is made between producers and consumers. But there is considerable advancement in relation to optimizing. With the great development in urban transportation models and the use of computers it is possible for the analysis of costs and benefits to be used to optimize the system, as a whole taking account of marginal changes on the whole network.

4.2. *Municipal project.* A recent most interesting development has come from the marriage of those concerned with municipal finances who have previously worked under group 3.2 above but have seen the need to widen their analysis in the direction of cost–benefit. The result has been the generation of a series of wide-ranging case studies covering many aspects of municipal work, from alternative means of expanding a town to the question of whether refuse containers at houses should be in dustbins or paper sacks (I.M.T.A., 1969). The approach has extended towards the planning balance sheet analysis but otherwise the studies have contributed little towards the development of the technique in relation to municipal projects and are accordingly so shown in Table 1, except for optimizing since the analysis is not always applicable to computers.

4.3. *Recreation.* Although coming within the same area of endeavour as item 4.2 special mention should be made of a pioneer attempt in recreation planning since it was initiated from another source, by physical planners (McCARTHY and DOWER, 1967). This essay is notable for its placing of the technique within a comprehensible decision making process and also for the attempt to measure the capacity of natural resources for use by holiday makers, tourists, visitors, etc. From this capacity is generated the benefits which the use of the facility will generate. These are then compared with the cost of providing the facilities. This leads to a planning budgeting process, which measures the investment required in financial terms. However while the approach could be applied more extensively it is nonetheless only partial in terms of Table 1 and is shown in a manner similar to municipal project appraisals in item 4.2.

5. *Goal achievement*

The next group of evaluation tests have derived from varying sources but have in common a simple approach: to what extent will the plan as designed meet objectives which have been set in advance. In general it is these objectives which are the benefits to be derived and it is the likely success or failure in doing (as opposed to the costs involved) on which the plans are compared. But in each case the approach is somewhat different, thus needing separate treatment.

5.1. *Bending on.* This popular term is applied to a process used in Britain which in essence attempts to find the ideal urban or regional form and then tests alternative plans as to whether or not they approximate to the form. An example in relation to the expansion of Ipswich will illustrate (SHANKLAND, COX and ASSOCIATES, 1966) although others exist (BUCHANAN, 1967). This formulated some social and economic objectives in general terms and then tested them (by simple ranking) against alternative diagrammatic ideal urban forms for the expansion of the town. The ranking led to a preferred alternative which was then developed in detail as the solution, by bending on to the site in question, having regard to the opportunities and constraints on the ground.

There is therefore only a tenuous link between objectives and the ideal urban form and there is no certainty that the bent-on variation from the ideal is better or worse in a particular situation than a bent-on version of another diagrammatic form that has been rejected. Furthermore there is no attention to the costs of achieving the benefits that are so derived. The outcome is shown in Table 1 according to the criteria. While the attempt is made to consider all systems there is no attempt to cover all sectors in the analysis. Producers and consumers are not distinguished and nor are the costs falling on them. There is partial attention to benefits in terms of objectives but these are not measured, so that only a partial criterion is available with little reference to incidence. To some degree the attempt is an optimizing one in the sense that it is the ideal form which is sought by design before the process is started.

5.2. *Policy evaluation matrix.* KREDITOR (1967) compares more directly the objectives for the actual plan proposals. He sets up a matrix whereby alternative plan proposals are ranked against a series of objectives to show whether each is affected directly, marginally, negatively or not at all, by each hypothesis. The result is a visual ranking in these terms from which the preferred solution is selected for study. This approach is useful in linking objective and end product but is not comprehensive as to objectives, would not for example show the distinction between cost (input) and benefit (output) nor indicate the marginal differences in such costs and benefits which are necessary to show the best scheme. And there is no attention to incidence. From this it follows that much the same position is recorded on Table 1 as item 5.1, although there is less conscious search for the optimal.

5.3. *Goals achievement matrix.* HILL (1967, 1968) has developed the goal achievement approach, under the title of goals achievement matrix, to a more sophisticated level. Essentially it is the same approach as in item 5.2, but there is considerable improvement in that the whole issue of objectives is more carefully considered, the analysis is by sectors and objections are pre-weighted in the analysis so that the decision makers are faced with results in terms of prior weighted preferences as to these matters. These differences are reflected in Table 1. This method in its potential is the nearest in comprehensiveness to the Planning Balance Sheet, but by comparison with that method is less developed in terms of costs and benefits and measurement.

A characteristic of this method is that both costs and benefits are always defined in terms of goal achievement. Thus benefits represent progress towards desired objectives while costs represent retrogression from desired objectives. Each objective thus has its characteristic set of costs and benefits measured in the same terms as the objectives. The preferred outcome is determined on the basis of a goals-achievement account, by weighted indices of goals-achievement or by means of goals-achievement transformation function. The goals-achievements account is similar in form to the outcome of the planning balance sheet. Weighted indices of goal achievement can lead to single unequivocal outcomes but are greatly dependent on the validity of the weighting and the measurement scales employed. Goals-achievement transformation functions are theoretically promising but would be very difficult to apply in practice. The approach lends itself to incorporation in programming techniques. One such approach (HILL and SHECHTER, 1970) employing weighted indices of goals achievement in a zero-one Boolean programming model is applied to the planning of outdoor recreation facilities. Objectives considered include national and regional economic benefits, equity, choice, participation and nature preservation.

5.4. Objective fulfilment analysis. An extension of the approach by Hill is given by SCHLAGER (1968). The extension relates in even greater differentiation between the fulfilment of the objective. "In each case, the objectives already defined were grouped into three major categories. These categories of objectives were ranked in order of their increasing importance. Then the three alternative plans were ranked on each category of objective in order of their increasing ability to meet each category . . . These weighted scores were summed for each alternative achieving an overall score for each plan. Finally, this score was weighted by a 'probability of implementation' subjectively reflecting the difficulty of implementing the plan. The alternative with the highest weighted score was considered to be the preferred alternative." From this description it will be seen why the method is described as "rank-based expected value". Features of the system are shown in Table 1. It corresponds with item 5.3 except that there would appear to be less emphasis on sector and incidence. But the criterion elements is strengthened through the introduction of the ranking for probability of implementation.

6. Cost minimization

The next group relates to attempts from a differing source to evaluate alternatives in terms of the input costs, the criterion being one of cost minimization.

6.1. Costs in use. STONE (1963, 1968) has developed methods for estimating private and public capital and operating costs in town development for "comparing alternative means broadly to the same ends, any differences in the end product being regarded as imponderables to be assessed against the costs differences". For such costs he has used the phrase "costs in use" which relate to average per capita costs of the whole plan or its phases. Stone has applied the technique to theoretical urban forms of different sizes. The method has direct links with the group of methods under 3 above, financial investment appraisal, except that a feature of the analysis is to distinguish also between resource and financial costs. The conclusions for plan evaluation are drawn in Table 1. In terms of systems and sectors the attempt is to be comprehensive, but the formulation of objectives is very limited, being related only to cost; as to costs little regard is paid to externalities and benefits are ignored. Within the limitations described the

measurement is full in money terms but the criterion and incidence are also limited. As with other methods it can be used on a trial and error basis for optimization.

6.2. Threshold theory. The theory and application which is becoming widely known under the title "threshold" has quite different origins, stemming in the main from physical planning and also from Poland (MALISZ, 1966; KOZLOWSKI, 1968; KOZLOWSKI and HUGHES, 1967; HUGHES and KOZLOWSKI, 1968). In essence it is the application to plan design of simple rules in economics, namely that investment gives rise to both fixed or overhead costs and also variable or operating costs. Whereas the costs per unit of supply must decline in relation to overhead costs, it can follow different curves in relation to operating costs. The aim is to find that degree of investment in which the combination of overhead and operating costs are at a minimum. The search for these points recognizes that the threshold (the points of minimum cost of investment) can be divided threefold into physical constraints (topographic and land resource costs), quantitative constraints (limiting capacities of existing public utilities), and structural constraints (limitations of existing urban development). While the method can be used for cost minimization in certain systems and sectors it is essentially an optimizing and design tool for searching out those thresholds which will produce cost minima.

The features are shown in Table 1. As indicated the objectives are limited and the coverage is only for part of the system and accordingly only some of the sectors. There is regard only to the costs of production and normally no regard to benefits. Within these limitations, the measurement, criterion and incidence are partial and while the method aims at optimizing as regards minimal cost, since there is regard only to cost minimization it cannot be called an optimizing method in the full sense.

7. Cost effectiveness

Whereas in cost minimization it is the end product which is assumed to be constant so that the aim is the minimization of cost, in cost effectiveness the reverse is applied. Here it is the cost which is assumed to be constant and it is the effectiveness of using such cost (in different situations) which is compared. The origins of this approach are in systems analysis which was initially applied to problems of defence in the United States (HITCH and McKEAN, 1960) and since 1965 has been attempted for civilian departments in the United States and more recently in this country (NOVICK, 1967).

7.1. Planning, programming and budgeting. It is

under this title that the application has been developed to civilian expenditures. Essentially the need is to be able to measure the outputs from particular expenditures. However, since by definition the outputs are rarely transacted in the market, the problem becomes one of measurement of public goods and intangibles. The search for such measurement has been pursued not only in typical cost–benefit studies but also as social as opposed to economic indicators (BAUER, 1966). Inherently therefore the approach is usable for urban and regional plans but to date there has been no formal application. However from the theory and literature it is possible to visualize the nature of the application to plan evaluation and this is suggested in Table 1. In essence we have a similar scoring as for costs in use, the method simply being the reverse side of the coin, where benefits are explored rather than costs. But P.P.B. is very strong on the formulation of objectives, which are an essential feature of measurement of output; and by the same token weak on measurement itself because of the difficulties mentioned above. However there is no reason why costs should also not be introduced, where these are variables. In the Planning Balance Sheet literature this becomes known as cost utility analysis and as such is indistinguishable from cost–benefit analysis, to which we now turn.

8. Cost–benefit analysis

Not all the evaluation methods included under this head can be called cost–benefit analysis, for this has somewhat a rigorous economic connotation. However there are other methods which recognize both the cost and benefit side of the evaluation problem, and for that reason are mentioned here, and first:

8.1. *Warsaw optimization planning.* Under this head are described the developments of threshold theory in Poland, where the attempt is not simply to minimize investment costs but also concurrently to maximize the effects which are outputs from the investment. Although already applied by Polish planners on a limited scale, to residential functions only, in the plans for Warsaw and Skopje, the method is still in the research stage in this country. As with the threshold analysis it is a practical planning tool for searching out solutions, hopefully optimal ones, and thus lends itself to evaluation in the same terms. Briefly, it is visualized that the first phase of the process is to search out the costs of developing the land in question, the second is to search out the best way of using the land and in the third phase to combine the two sets of findings by means of a computer programme.

Just how the method would work over a comprehensive plan has been suggested (PLANNING RESEARCH UNIT, 1970). For the purpose of Table 1 all that would appear to be claimed is for a partial treatment of systems and sectors, and also costs, benefits, criteria and incidence. But if the research were successful it might well be that the method would be an optimizing tool, in at least a partial sense.

8.2. *Linear programming.* Linear programming is an operational research technique permitting the optimization of an objective function which is subject to a number of well-defined linear inequality constraints (DUCKWORTH, 1965). As such the technique has had wide application (DORFMAN *et al.*, 1958) and since the early 1960s has been applied in land-use allocation models (HARRIS, 1965). More recently it has been developed in Israel as a means of finding optimal solutions to planning problems, the aim being to use it for most types of plans (BEN-SHAHAR *et al.*, 1969). The authors recognize that "the purpose of the town planners is to make a feasible plan which conforms with the existing constraints and maximises the value of an accepted social welfare function as well". They recognize that the list of constraints is very long, that some can be translated into money values and others not. The items which can be translated into money values are expressed in the objective function and those which cannot are expressed as constraints. These are expressed in linear programming form, so that the computer searches out all possible alternatives and determines "simultaneously the quantity of every component of the efficient programme, that is the programme in which the present value of the welfare function is maximised", subject of course to the constraints. The method can also produce useful by-products, such as the shadow price of the constraints (which might have been subjectively determined) and also the marginal output on the land.

The strength of this approach is clearly its ability to search out the preferred of a large range of alternatives, to optimize simultaneously and to generate shadow prices for marginal elements of constraints. As such it is the most powerful of the optimizing models. However the limitations must rest with the limitations of linear programming as such, namely that the objective function is most difficult of specification, the relationships of the function and constraints are not simply linear and the definition of the constraints cannot always be simply made in mathematical form. Thus it has been argued that linear programming "can be useful if used for exploration to suggest possibilities;

but also it ignores so much, and simplifies so much, that it should probably never be used in any more exalted way" (Parry-Lewis, 1970). Thus the technique can only solve problems for which it is suited. This the authors recognize, and suggest that such problems will be solvable with the use of non-linear techniques, such as quadratic programming, whereby certain non-linear aspects such as economies of scale and differential weights in the concentration of urban centres can be dealt with (Ben-Shahar et al., 1969).

On the basis that linear programming can only do what the programme permits it to do, then its contribution to plan evaluation is shown in Table 1. Clearly it is a method of partial analysis throughout, because it does not throw up the differences between producers and consumers nor does it show incidence. However it is very strong as an optimizing tool.

8.3. *Maximize land values.* The difficulties in the linear programming model of finding the correct objective function are treated very lightly in the suggestion that such a single index of social welfare can be found in aggregate land values. Lean and Goodall (1966) state: "if it is calculated that town planning will lead to higher land values than would exist without it, then it is desirable from an economic point of view. The town plan that would lead to the highest aggregate land values is the best economically." The simple basis for the approach is derived from rent theory, that the greater the aggregate land values (capital returns minus capital costs of construction) the greater overall benefit to the community to be derived from the plan.

This would be an attractively simple index. But there are difficulties. Lean admits that the theoretical difficulty of placing money values on non-revenue-producing public sector development, a large part of any town, is insuperable. Furthermore, in practice, valuation of the revenue-producing investment can only reflect from empirical data the imperfections of market values as the index of the social values which are of interest in plan evaluation; and they cannot make forecasts which are of sufficient sensitivity to reflect significant differences in quality of the alternative plans as a basis for comparison with planning objectives (Lichfield, 1968). Evans (1969) has criticized the maximum land value formulation with the conclusion that "it is incorrect theoretically and inapplicable practically". However if it were to be applicable on the lines visualized by Lean and Goodall then it would attract the features shown in Table 1. On the whole it could only contribute a partial analysis for objectives, systems and sectors, would be silent as to producers and consumers, would not give costs and benefits but only their difference, which is of limited use as a criterion and would not give incidence.

8.4. *Cost–benefit analysis.* As indicated earlier under Section 4 above, cost–benefit analysis has a long history of application to public investment and policy projects. But it is only recently that it has been used for urban and regional planning. In the main this use has been the extension by economists of the analysis into the field. This approach is in contrast to that of the writer who has visualized the problem as a planner and attempted to adapt the technique of analysis to the purpose, thus leading to the Planning Balance Sheet which has been described above.

8.4.1. *Rothenberg.* Rothenberg (1967) has applied the analysis to the problem of urban renewal and has attempted to use it in particular cases. In the cases the costs are the resource costs of implementing the renewal project (that is excluding land acquisition) and the benefits are measured by increased site values. The difference is compared with the spillover effect in terms of increased values in neighbouring real estate and decreased social costs associated with slums.

This brief formulation shows that the analysis uses as the main source of benefits the increase in real estate site values and is therefore open to the same kind of criticism as was given in relation to land values in 8.3 above and also to objections as to use of meaning of real estate data in urban renewal situations. And any objections to using the index for a new town (as proposed by Lean and Goodall) must be increased when it is proposed to apply it in the complex situation of urban renewal, for then the interdependency with established real estate values offers complexity. Accordingly Table 1 shows the method has the same features as Section 8.3. It is only of limited application.

8.4.2. *Mao.* Mao (1966) also tackles urban renewal projects in the United States with an approach quite similar to that of Rothenberg. However he extends the analysis by attempting to measure the decreased social costs associated with the elimination of slums in terms of municipal savings and such matters as fire, health and police protection. A difference in the financial costs is struck which is then compared with the intangible costs and benefits that would be involved. This presents the essential decision framework for the decision maker. Thus the approach is more helpful than that of Rothenberg, by making more specific the social benefits from removing slums and also throwing into the balance the intangibles which have not been measured. However the analysis as a whole is still partial in terms of Table 1.

8.4.3. *Roskill commission research team.* From the urban renewal analyses just mentioned to the cost–benefit analysis for the Third London Airport produced by the Roskill Commission Research Team (Commission on the Third London Airport, 1970) is a very big step, for the team has produced the most thorough-going cost–benefit analysis in urban and regional planning so far. Taking as the starting point four sites which have already been located for the airport by the Commission, the analysis explores exhaustively all the consequential costs and benefits that will flow and measures them, and concludes with a summary of best estimates of total costs and benefits. This summary is then adjusted by means of sensitivity analysis of certain of the variables. Since the cost–benefit analysis is so comprehensive, the question arises as to whether it is or is not the same as the Planning Balance Sheet appraisal, which applies cost–benefit analysis to urban and regional planning problems. The answer to this question can be given simply because a Planning Balance Sheet analysis of the identical four sites was also made for submission as evidence to the Commission at Stage III of the Inquiry (LICHFIELD and ASSO-CIATES, 1969), thus enabling a close comparison to be made. The differences in methodology can be seen from Table 1. The Planning Balance Sheet is more specific on objectives. Both cover the total system and all the sectors and both attempt the measurement of all the costs and benefits, but the Research Team has measured all the items whereas the Planning Balance Sheet analysis, for want of time and resources, had to leave many as unmeasured. Accordingly the criterion for the cost–benefit analysis can be more easily formulated and used, and accordingly the analysis can be better used as an optimizing tool than can the Planning Balance Sheet. Further differences lie in the fact that the Research Team have not generated their results in terms of producers and consumers, there is no particular logic or order in the manner of treatment of the elements, and they have also not had full re-gard to the incidence of the costs and benefits.

These differences are ones of degree only. In a Planning Balance Sheet analysis there is every endeavour to measure what can be measured; but there is also the recognition that the time resources for such full measurement are not normally available so that recourse must be had to the treatment of measurables and intangibles in the same analysis. Equally well the Research Team could have, had they wished, made their approach to the analysis more operational by grouping the elements in more orderly form in relation to producers and consumers, and brought out the incidence more carefully.

In brief, where a cost–benefit analysis is carried out in a comprehensive manner, that is comprehensive in relation to the systems and sectors which are of interest in urban and regional planning, such analysis becomes in effect a Planning Balance Sheet. Put alternatively, although it must be recognized that the failure to measure costs and benefits leads to difficulty in interpretation of the results, a Planning Balance Sheet applies cost–benefit analysis as far as it can be taken in the absence of full measurement.

CONCLUSION

Thus we have completed the circle in this review of planning evaluation methodologies. As Table 1 shows, of all the methods that have been put forward, whether tried in practice or not, only the Planning Balance Sheet, or cost-benefit analysis, as used by the Roskill Commission Research Team, gives a sufficiently comprehensive treatment to justify the description of comprehensiveness in plan evaluation; and even these fall short on the ten criteria shown in Table 1.

This should not lead to discouragement in the U.K. of other plan evaluation methodologies, where the conclusions can be reached simply and quickly. Some conscious evaluation is better than the failure to generate and consciously compare alternatives. And the best here can be the enemy of the good.

But if it is the best plan which is sought then only the more comprehensive analysis can be relied upon to aid in its selection.

Acknowledgements—I must thank my colleagues in Nathaniel Lichfield and Associates for their comments on the draft. One of them said: "I think it inevitable that in reviewing so many methods the review cannot do justice to either reviewer or the reviewed or to those not reviewed". I hope he is wrong.

REFERENCES

BAUER R. A. ed. (1966) *Social Indicators*, M.I.T. Press.
BEN-SHAHAR H., MAZOR A. and PINES D. (1969) Town planning and welfare maximization: A methodological approach, *Reg. Studies* **3**, 105–113.
BUCHANAN C. and PARTNERS (1966) *South Hampshire Study*.
BUCHANAN C. and PARTNERS (1967) *Ashford Study*, H.M.S.O. London.
Commission on the Third London Airport (1970) *Papers and Proceedings*, Vol. VII, Parts 1 and 2, H.M.S.O., London.
County Borough of Middlesbrough, *Middlesbrough Development Plan* (1951), Report of the Survey, p. 85.
DORFMAN R., SAMULSON P. and SOLOW P. (1958) *Linear Programming and Economic Analysis*, McGraw-Hill, New York.
DUCKWORTH E. (1965) *A Guide to Operation Research*, Methuen, London.
EVANS A. (1969) Two Economic Rules for Town Planning: A Critical Note, *Urban Studies* **6**, 229.
Greater London Council (1969) *Movement in London*, The G.L.C., London.
HARRIS B. (1965) Models in urban planning, *J. Am. Inst. Plann.* **31**, 2.
HILL M. (1967) A Method for Evaluating Alternative Plans, The Goals–Achievement Matrix Applied to Transportation Plans (unpublished, Ph.D. Thesis).
HILL M. (1968) A goals–achievement matrix in evaluation alternative plans, *J. Am. Inst. Plann.* **34**, 2.
HILL M. and SHECHTER M. (1970) *Optimal Goal Achievement in the Development of Outdoor Recreation Facilities*, Studies in Regional Science.
HITCH C. N. and McKEAN R. N. (1960) *Economics of Defence in a Nuclear Age*, Oxford University Press.
HUGHES J. T. and KOZLOWSKI J. (1968) Threshold analysis—An economic tool for town and regional planning, *Urban Studies* **5**, 132–143.
I.M.T.A. (1969) *Cost–Benefit Analysis*, I.M.T.A., London.
KITCHING L. C. (1963) Conurbation into city region: how should London grow? *J. Tn Plann. Inst. Lond.* **49**, 316.
KITCHING L. C. (1969) Regional planning considerations, in Cambridgeshire et al, *Commission on the Third London Airport, Evidence Submitted at Stage III*, Chapter 2.
KOZLOWSKI J. (1968) Threshold theory and the sub-regional plan, *Tn Plann. Rev.* **39**, 99–116.
KOZLOWSKI J. and HUGHES J. T. (1967) Urban threshold theory and analysis, *J. Tn Plann. Inst.* **53**.
KREDITOR A. (1967) The provisional plan, *Industrial Development and the Development Plan*, Chapter 8, An Foras Forbartha, Dublin.
KRUTILLA J. V. and ECKSTEIN O. (1958) *Multiple Purpose River Development*, Johns Hopkins, Baltimore.
LEAN W. and GOODALL B. (1966) *Aspects of Land Economics*, Estates Gazette, London.
LICHFIELD N. (1956) *Economics of Planned Development*, Chapters 10 and 11, Estates Gazette, London.
LICHFIELD N. (1960) Cost–benefit analysis in city planning, *J. Am. Inst. Plann.* **26**, 273–279.
LICHFIELD N. (1964) Cost–benefit analysis in plan evaluation, *Tn. Plann. Rev.* **35**, 160–169.
LICHFIELD N. (1967) The evaluation of capital investment projects in town centre redevelopment, *Public Admin.* **45**, 132–134.
LICHFIELD N. (1968) Economics in town planning: A basis for decision making, *Tn Plann. Rev.* **39**, 13–15.
LICHFIELD N. (1969) Cost–benefit analysis in urban expansion: A case study, Peterborough, *Reg. Studies* **3**, 123–155.
LICHFIELD N. and WENDT P. F. (1969) Six English new towns: A financial appraisal, *Tn Plann. Rev.* **40**, 284–314.
LICHFIELD N. and CHAPMAN H. (1968) Road proposals for a shopping centre, *J. Trans. Econ. Policy.* II, **3**, 280–320.
LICHFIELD N. and ASSOCIATES (1967) Cramlington New Town, Report No. 13, Information Required for Financial Appraisal of Master Plan (unpublished).
LICHFIELD N. and ASSOCIATES with HANCOCK/HAWKES, DAVIS, BELFIELD and EVEREST, PARSONS BROWN and PARTNERS (1968) Greater Peterborough Draft Basic Plan, Financial Appraisal (unpublished).
LICHFIELD N. and ASSOCIATES, Appendix V in Civic Trust for the North West (1969) *Environmental Recovery, Skelmersdale*, Civic Trust for the North West, Manchester.
LICHFIELD N. and ASSOCIATES (1969) Chapter 14 in Cambridgeshire and the Isle of Ely, Essex and Hertfordshire County Councils, *Commission on the Third London Airport, Evidence Submitted at Stage III*.
LLEWELYN-DAVIES, WEEKS, FORESTIER-WALKER and BOR and SHANKLAND, COX and ASSOCIATES (1970) *Airport City: Urbanisation Studies for the Third London Airport*, London: H.M.S.O.
MACE R. (1961) *Municipal Cost-Revenue Research in the United States*, The Institute of Government, The University of North Carolina.
MAO J. C. T. (1966) Efficiency in public urban renewal expenditures through benefit–cost analysis, *J. Am. Inst. Plann.* **32**, 95–107.

Evaluation Methodology of Urban and Regional Plans: A Review   165

MALISZ B. (1966) Urban planning theory methods and results, in *City and Regional Planning in Poland*, (Edited by FISHER J. C.) Cornell University Press, Ithaca, N.Y.

McCARTHY P. E. and DOWER M. (1967) Planning for conservation and development: an exercise in the process of decision making, *J. Tn Plann. Inst.* **53**, 99–105.

MATHEW R., JOHNSON MARSHALL P. and PARTNERS (1967) *Central Lancashire, Study for a City*, H.M.S.O., London.

NOTTS-DERBY SUB-REGIONAL PLANNING UNIT (1969) *Notts-Derby Sub-Regional Plan*, Notts-Derby Sub-Regional Planning Unit, Nottingham.

NOVICK D. (Ed.) (1967) *Program Budgeting: Program Analysis and the Federal Budget*, Harvard University Press, Cambridge, Mass.

PARRY-LEWIS J. (1970) The Invasion of Planning, *J. Tn Plann. Inst.* **56**, 101.

PLANNING RESEARCH UNIT and INSTITUTE OF TOWN PLANNING AND ARCHITECTURE (1970) *Threshold Analysis Optimisation*, Planning Research Unit, Edinburgh.

PREST A. R. and TURVEY R. (1966) Cost-benefit analysis: A survey, *Econ. J.* **75**, 155–207.

ROTHENBERG J. (1967) *Economic Evaluation of Urban Renewal*, The Brookings Institution, Washington D.C.

SCHLAGER K. (1968) The Rank Based Expected Value Method of Plan Evaluation, *Highway Research Record, No. 238*, Highway Research Board, Washington D.C. The description is quoted from Boyce E. and Day, N.D. (1969) *Metropolitan Plan Evaluation Methodology*, pp. 45–47, Institute for Environmental Studies, University of Pennsylvania.

SHANKLAND, COX and ASSOCIATES (1966) *Expansion of Ipswich—Designation Proposals*, Chapters 1–5, H.M.S.O., London.

STONE P. A. (1963) *Housing, Town Development, Land and Costs*, Estates Gazette, London.

STONE P. A. (1968) Town Structure, Size and Costs (unpublished).

THOMPSON J. M. (1969) *Motorways in London*, Gerald Duckworth, London.

WELLS H. (1963) Peterborough Expansion Study.

WENDT P. F. (1967) Large scale community development, *J. Finance* **22**, 220–239.

[13]

JOURNAL OF REGIONAL SCIENCE, VOL. 25, NO. 4, 1985

MODELS OF LAND-USE, HOUSING, AND RENT: AN EVALUATION

Richard F. Muth*

1. INTRODUCTION

It is indeed fitting that this special anniversary issue of the *Journal of Regional Science* should contain an article on models of urban land use. For, like the *Journal* itself, such models are about a quarter of a century old. Moreover, such models form the core of a new field both of economics and of regional science, which is itself of about the same age.

It is ironic that models of urban land-use should have much in common with, indeed some would say derive from, the von Thünen analysis of agricultural production. I find it especially ironic in view of the fact that this analysis no longer is very useful in explaining the location of agricultural production. While some of us are old enough to remember areas of truck-farming surrounding major U.S. cities, with the development of refigerator cars and fast freight, different kinds of crop areas would seem to be determined primarily by climate and soil conditions rather than location vis-à-vis major population centers. In a somewhat similar fashion, some early urban models stressed the annular nature of different types of urban land-use. Such, in my judgment, is not very fruitful. For, apart from the Central Business District (CBD), which is almost exclusively nonresidential, and the remainder of the city, which is principally although not exclusively residential, most features of cities would seem to be noncentral. Despite some attempts to model the structure of the CBD itself, most urban models have taken the latter as given and focused upon the residential annulus.

In the following pages I will first outline the standard monocentric model of urban residential land-use. I will then discuss the effect of modifying most of the assumptions typically made in the standard model. Finally, I will discuss a variety of noncentral aspects of cities that may be treated under the rubric "clustering."

In so doing I will make no attempt to survey the literature. This has been ably done in articles for the forthcoming *Encyclopedia of Economics* by Fujita (1984) and Kanemoto (1984). Rather, I shall attempt primarily to appraise the usefulness of the analysis for understanding and predicting urban form and structure and, especially, to indicate those urban features for which our current models provide little explanation. Nor will I attempt to impose on the reader yet another seemingly endless progression of arcane mathematics. There currently exists a surfeit of books and articles which do so. Having tried to teach the subject to undergraduates

---

*Fuller E. Callaway Professor and Chairman, Department of Economics, Emory University.

593

for almost 15 years now, I have become increasingly convinced that most of the subject can be discussed rigorously—although perhaps it could not have been discovered—in old-fashioned verbal form. Those wishing a mathematical treatment should refer to Wheaton (1974), which is one of the best such treatments.

2. THE STANDARD MONOCENTRIC MODEL

In most statements of it, some very restrictive assumptions are made in the standard monocentric model regarding employment, transportation, land, and households. Urban models are often criticized for the restrictiveness of these assumptions. As I hope will become clear in the following section, however, such assumptions are sufficient rather than necessary conditions for the conclusions reached. Together they form what is best regarded as a kind of canonical form, from which more complicated situations can be derived through transformation or elaboration.

First, all employment is assumed to take place at a single point in space. This point is typically called the CBD, after what in most cities still contains by far the highest level of employment per unit of land. Workers are assumed to commute to jobs in the CBD from residences surrounding it. The cost of their commuting is assumed to be the same in all directions and to be exogenously fixed. These costs are usually presumed to include the opportunity costs of the commuter's time as well as direct money outlays, although the allocation of time itself is usually not explicitly included in the analysis.

Even the earliest presentations of the monocentric urban model differed considerably in their treatment of the nature of land. Most analyses, of course, assume that useable land surrounds the CBD in all directions, although it is but a trivial modification to substitute a pie slice for two *pi* radians. All statements of the model with which I am familiar assume that all land surrounding the CBD is the same. While less unrealistic for housing and other urban land-uses than for agriculture, differences in subsoil conditions and slope may have an important effect upon the cost of construction upon different lots. It is principally in what is assumed about construction that most urban models differ, however.

Even today, many analyses neglect construction altogether. In the case of housing, land itself along with all other commodities is taken as an argument of household utility functions. The principal justification for doing so is that housing capital is very durable, and models involving durable capital stocks tend to be quite intractable analytically. Although I have never been one to insist upon descriptive realism, it has always seemed to me that neglecting housing production altogether was a case of surrendering too easily. Treating land as an input into housing production along with nondurable capital is but little different from similar treatment in other areas of economics. Moreover, I am convinced that so treating land is insightful, in that doing so leads to empirical implications which seem to be borne out by real-world behavior. I will, of course, discuss durability and what little we know of its implications in the following section.

Regarding households, it is most commonly assumed that they are identical. This means not only do households have the same utility functions, but also that they have the same incomes. The latter is, of course, quite unrealistic descriptively, and many have argued that income differences among households are of considerable substantive importance for the nature of cities. Unlike the durability of housing capital, it is not difficult analytically to incorporate income differences among households into the analysis. Doing so in models that retain the other standard assumptions described above, however, greatly overpredicts the extent to which average household income increases with distance. I will elaborate upon this last point in the following section.

Under the assumptions described above, it follows immediately that the rental value per unit of housing service must decline with distance from the CBD. For, if it did not, otherwise identical households located a greater distance from the CBD would not be able to achieve as high a utility level as those located closer. Those more distant would thus bid up the rentals of dwellings closer to the CBD, while the rentals of those more distant from it would fall. To a first approximation, the condition for utility to be constant with a slight move in any direction is that real income be constant. The latter requires that the change in the expenditure necessary to rent a given dwelling just offset the change in commuting cost incurred, or that the percentage change in the rental of a given dwelling be numerically equal, but opposite in sign, to the ratio of the change in commuting costs to housing expenditures. Simple calculations suggest that this ratio is currently of the order of 2 percent per mile [see Muth (1984, pp. 94–100)]. It is difficult to isolate the variation in dwelling rentals or prices with location from other factors, especially the characteristics relating to the size of dwellings themselves. Some studies, however, have found the expected negative, although small, relationship with distance from the CBD [see Ball (1973)].

The decline in housing prices with distance implies that land rentals must likewise fall. For, if they did not and other factor prices were the same everywhere, producers of housing services located farther away from the CBD would earn lower net incomes. Hence, they would bid up the rentals of closer sites. Moreoever, unlike housing prices themselves, land rentals and values are likely to show substantial variation with location. Since, as data on new homes financed by FHA-insured mortgages suggest to me, raw land costs are only about one-tenth of the total costs of these houses, land rentals would have to vary 10 times as much as housing prices to keep the profits of producers unchanged with location. Data analyzed by Wieand and Muth (1972) suggest, indeed, that land values decline by the expected 20 percent per mile from downtown St. Louis.[1] Since relatively few sales of undeveloped land occur in built-up areas of U.S. cities, however, it is difficult to test this implication of urban models using market data.

Decreases in house prices with distance also imply that otherwise identical households will consume greater amounts of housing services per unit of time at greater distances from the CBD. With real price elasticities of housing demand of about unity or somewhat smaller numerically, however, variations in consumption per household would be small. Variations in expenditure per household, which

---

[1]Most empirical studies use the CBD as identified by the Census of Retail Trade as the city center.

596　　JOURNAL OF REGIONAL SCIENCE, VOL. 25, NO. 4, 1985

rentals or house prices measure, would be smaller still. Empirically, one would expect income differences to be the principal source of differences in housing consumption with location in cities.

Variations in the output of housing per unit of land with location are quite another matter, however. The latter depend upon variation in land rentals, which theory predicts would be greater than the variation in house prices. Given elasticities of substitution of land for structures in the production of housing services of the order of unity, the output of housing services per unit of land would vary by almost the same relative amount with location as land rentals. I know of no studies other than my own [Muth (1969)] that have examined output per unit of land empirically. That study showed variations consistent in magnitude with predictions of the theory. That residential land is more intensively used closer to downtown parts of cities is obvious, however, from casual observation.

Most readily apparent on the basis of casual observation, however, is the variation in population density with location. Moreover, a considerable amount of empirical evidence on population densities is available. Population density, which is persons per unit of land, is simply the output of housing per unit of land divided by the consumption of housing services per capita. Although the increase in the latter with distance is small, the former declines by an amount almost 10 times the decline of the price of housing services with distance. Consequently, population densitities would do likewise. Beginning with Clark's (1951) classical investigation, every study of which I am aware has found the expected decline with distance from the city center. Most recently, a study by Kau and Lee (1977) found, for 30 of the 50 cities studied, a relative decline of from 10 to 20 percent per mile, which is the approximate magnitude that the model predicts.

The standard monocentric model also has important implications for changes over time. Most obvious is the predicted effect of population growth. The latter would lead to a bidding up of housing prices and hence an increase in residential land rents throughout the city. The increase at the urban-rural boundary would make conversion of nonurban to urban land profitable, and the land area of the city would grow. There is nothing in the standard model which would lead one to expect that the density gradient—the relative rate of decline of population densities with distance from the CBD—would decline with population growth. Indeed, one is tempted to argue that marginal commuting costs would rise with population growth as more workers travel to and from the city center. Empirically, however, the evidence for such a decline is quite strong. Although several ad hoc explanations have been offered for such a decline, in my judgment the reasons are not really understood.

It also seems obvious to anyone who has lived through the post-war period that improvements in transportation would lead to urban decentralization, a greater relative growth in population in the outer parts of urban areas. In the monocentric model, the decline in transport costs leads to a decline in the rate of price decline with distance. If prices were fixed at the old urban-rural boundary, prices would fall throughout the city and an excess demand for housing would result. Hence, prices must rise at the boundary. Consequently, prices rise relatively more in the outer parts of the cities, as do the output of housing and population per unit of land.[2] Studies by Winsborough (1960) of Chicago and Mills (1970) for a variety of U.S. cities both suggest that population density gradients have declined more or less persistently over time. The greatest declines, however, appear to have occurred during the 1880's, 1920's, and following 1948. These coincide with the development of the electric street railway, the automobile, and the urban expressway.

Apart from population growth, one of the reasons suggested by the monocentric model for declining density gradients is the growth of average income. An increase in income resulting from a growth in earnings would increase both the time cost of travel and expenditures on housing. Time costs, however, are only about one-half of the marginal cost of commuting [Muth (1984)], so with any believable estimate of the income elasticity of housing demand the price gradient would tend to fall as income increases. The increase in income by itself would result in an excess demand for housing so that housing prices would tend to rise throughout the city. Consequently, I would expect the city to grow, and to grow relatively more rapidly in its outer parts as income does. Calculations I have made [Muth (1975)] embodying these effects as well as those of population growth and increased travel speed imply that the density gradient would have declined about by one-half between 1950 and 1970. Such a decline agrees remarkably well with subsequently published estimates for 1970 by Kau and Lee (1977). Yet, statistical comparisons by me [Muth (1969)] and others do not provide much confirmation.

3. VARIATIONS ON THE MONOCENTRIC MODEL

The empirical evidence cited in the preceding section suggests that the implications of the standard monocentric model agree relatively well with empirical evidence. Like those of any model, its predictions could be improved, of course. Elaboration of the standard model, to say nothing of criticisms of it, would seem to be motivated more by a desire for descriptive realism than by an effort to improve its predictions of real-world behavior. Some elaborations, of course, have been intended to extend the range of phenomena which the model might explain. Unfortunately, however, many of these seek to incorporate in the basic model aspects of the world which have little to do with spatial structure and which might best be studied by themselves.

One of the standard assumptions most often criticized is that regarding employment. The 1970 population census, the first to present data on place of employment, suggested that only 7.5 percent of total employment in SMSA's was located in the CBD. Casual observation, however, suggests that people commute to CBD jobs in significant numbers throughout the whole of the metropolitan area. There is no reason to believe that CBD workers are heavily concentrated in the residential areas immediately surrounding it. If CBD workers are to be compen-

---

[2]Prices, however, and thus population densities, must fall close to the center. If prices were to be unchanged or rise at the center, they would be higher everywhere throughout the city. The quantity of housing services supplied would thus increase. But, apart from a possible income effect, which, in any event, is small, there is nothing in the fall of commuting costs to increase the quantity of housing services demanded.

sated for longer commutes, then housing prices must fall in exactly the same fashion, given the marginal costs of commuting, as they would if everyone worked in the CBD. With given transportation facilities, a decline in the number of CBD commuters, of course, by reducing congestion would tend to reduce the rate of decline in housing prices and increase decentralization. What remains to be explained, however, is the impact of non-CBD employment.

To a great extent, non-CBD employment might be characterized as local. By the latter I mean occurring in such small concentrations that everyone so employed could live adjacent to his/her workplace and incur no commuting costs. Housing prices would still have to decline with distance from the CBD, of course, to compensate CBD commuters. Constant money wages for local workers in all locations, together with housing prices which declined with distance, would mean that otherwise identical local workers would be better off the more distant their residential/employment location from the CBD. To maintain equilibrium, money wages would thus have to decline with distance from the CBD. Since the prices of nonhousing commodities are presumably the same everywhere, however, the relative decline in money wages would be but a fraction of that in housing prices, which is itself small.

The effects of non-CBD concentrations of employment are no more difficult to analyze. First, persons working in different centers would tend to live in disjoint residential areas so long as they are concerned only with the cost of commuting and housing prices. The boundary separating the residential areas of workers in different centers would be defined by the condition that the utility level attained by otherwise identical households would be independent of place of work. Within each residential area, housing prices, thus the intensity of residential land use and population densities, would all decline with distance from the center. Such an analysis might well be applicable to so-called twin cities such as Minneapolis/St. Paul. It is an open question empirically, however, whether non-CBD concentrations of employment are important enough in the typical U.S. city to produce noticeable effects.

One other modification of the standard model related to employment has to do with the spatial patterns of nonresidential concentrations of land-use. The CBD itself has been modeled as an inner annulus governed by accessibility to a center, perhaps rail terminals. The folklore of location theory, however, attributes such concentrations to the need for face-to-face contact. The CBD might thus better be analyzed using methods similar to Beckmann's (1976) model of household interaction, which produces a density pattern similar to that of the monocentric model. Outside the CBD, concentrations of employment, especially of processing firms, might be explainable by accessibility to transportation routes such as rail lines. That such concentrations occur was obvious in the days when people rode passenger railroads. Moses and Williamson (1967) have demonstrated the importance of such factors for Chicago. This is but one instance in which the importance of centrality breaks down, as will be elaborated upon in the following section.

Unlike the assumption made by standard monocentric models, transport costs may both vary with direction from the CBD and be determined endogenously by the volume of travel at any point. The former is relatively easy to handle analytically. Variations with direction in effect produce a deformation of Euclidean space, stretching it in the direction where transportation is less costly. Even sharply discontinuous variation in commuting costs such as might result from the building of a freeway or rail system may still produce a one-to-one continuous mapping of a circular city onto the actual one, as the example in Mohring (1961) shows. In space so deformed, the contours of constant commuting cost, which define generalized distance or accessibility, might be highly irregular in shape. Along them, however, housing prices and thus residential land rentals and the intensity of residential land use would all be constant. In other respects, however, the analysis is essentially the same as in the standard case.

Endogenous determination of transport costs is much more difficult to handle analytically. In the study of transportation itself, these costs are typically made to depend upon the volume of travel on a given mode in some given corridor. After some point, which might be called capacity, costs per traveler rise because of congestion. The problem has been well understood at least since the work of Strotz (1964). In the context of an explicit spatial model, the marginal cost of transport at any point is made to depend upon total travel past, hence total population living beyond, that point. While it is easy enough to state the conditions which must hold in such cases, it is quite difficult to find explicit analytic solutions in two-dimensional space. Hence, one saw a spate of articles on long, narrow cities for a time. It is relatively easy to solve two-dimensional models numerically by computer, however.

Substantively, the issue of greatest interest, when congestion phenomena in commuter transportation are introduced into urban models, is the effect of the pricing of commuting on urban structure. It is well known in the transportation literature that, when congestion phenomena exist and its use is unregulated, the transport mode will be overused in the sense that the marginal social cost exceeds marginal private benefit. In an explicit spatial setting it is widely appreciated intuitively that a city will occupy a larger land area and be less densely populated than it would otherwise if commuter transport is unregulated. My own calculations [Muth (1975)], however, suggest that for conditions as they existed in 1950, the principal source of inefficiency was in allocating too high a fraction of land to transportation. Given this allocation of land, the speed of commuter travel slowed noticeably only at distances very close to the center. These same calculations suggest that with land allocated to transportation in such a way that its implicit rental value equals that of residential land and with marginal cost pricing of commuting, the land area occupied by the typical 1950 city would have been about 40 percent smaller than it was in fact.

As was pointed out in the preceding section, standard models assume that land is an argument either of the utility functions of households or, along with nondurable capital, of the production function for housing services. Neither treatment seems very realistic on purely descriptive grounds. A more defensible objection to the standard treatment, it seems to me, is that the standard models do not enable one to treat what are essentially short-run questions such as the effects of an urban redevelopment project. Of course, it is not at all obvious that such questions are inherently spatial in nature and cannot be analyzed by traditional methods which neglect questions of spatial structure. Nonetheless, considerable effort has been exerted in the past decade or so in the development of models of urban spatial structure with durable capital inputs.

If the focus of this paper were on models instead of real-world behavior and the conformity of models to it, this portion on durability would be considerably longer than it is. For an almost bewildering variety of different papers have been written on the question and a considerable amount of professional expertise has been expended on them. Yet, I believe it fair to say that these papers, including my own, have added little to our ability to predict real-world phenomena. Models involving durable capital have proved to be analytically intractable in all but the simplest cases. Partly for this reason, in most papers the formulation has been exceedingly general, so that only the most general kinds of conclusions have been derivable. Moreover, among these are: (1) under appropriate conditions population densities may increase with greater commuting distances and (2) urban development might proceed toward the center of the city over time rather than away from it. No doubt, there are those to whom this greater richness of conceptually possible outcomes would have a certain appeal. Since such phenomena have never, to my knowledge, been observed, however, it is by no means clear that our understanding of the real world has been at all advanced by models consistent with them.

Most analyses to date have assumed that residential capital is totally durable. By this is meant that, while it may be abandoned, it cannot be replaced. One of the few to suppose otherwise is a recent paper by Wheaton (1982).[3] On the basis of numerical solutions calculated, Wheaton concludes that replaceable capital models predict results much more in accord with those of earlier models with nondurable capital than do models with durable capital and no replacement. Although I view Wheaton's efforts as encouraging, it is yet to be demonstrated that durable although replaceable capital models predict the actual structure of real-world cities better than nondurable capital ones.

The treatment of income differences among households is considerably easier analytically than that of durable nonland capital inputs. The conclusions are no more satisfactory empirically, however, if the other assumptions of the standard monocentric model are retained. Like the effects of an increase in income in the standard model, the locational effects of income differences depend upon their relative effects upon marginal commuting costs and housing expenditures. As was suggested earlier, on empirical grounds one would expect the latter effect to be the relatively larger. Consequently, provided that the second-order conditions for locational equilibrium hold, higher income households would tend to live farther from the city center. [See Muth (1969) for details.]

The difficulty with this seemingly sensible result is that it greatly overpredicts the tendency for average income to increase with distance from the CBD. The average incomes of suburbanites are indeed higher than those of central city residents, but the differences are not nearly as great as commonly believed. As reported by the 1980 housing census, in 1979 the average household income in

---

[3]Wheaton's paper cited above contains references to most of the major papers on urban spatial models with durable capital stocks.

SMSA's was about $21,300, while it was $18,600 in central cities. The difference was almost wholly due to the higher proportion of renters in central cities. On the hypothesis that average income increases monotonically with distance from the center, the central cities would have contained the lowest 42.2 percent of households by income—those whose incomes were $15,008 or less. The average income for this group in SMSA's was only about $7,800, considerably smaller than the actual central city average.

One way to explain the discrepancy is to note that only about 7 percent of all SMSA workers were employed in the CBD in 1980. If all other workers were locally employed, their wage incomes would decline by an amount just sufficient to compensate for the decline in housing prices with distance and leave them at the same level of utility as otherwise comparable workers employed in the CBD. Since this amount is small, for simplicity assume that non-CBD employed central city workers are 93 percent of the total and that their incomes equal the SMSA average. If, then, the average incomes of the 7 percent of central city households with CBD workers equal $7,800, the average income of all central city households would have been about $20,350. Although somewhat higher than the actual value, it is much closer than that predicted on the assumption that all workers are employed in the CBD.

Indeed, a little casual observation suggests that the matter of the determinants of location by income is still more complicated. Everyone is familiar with the existence of central city, high-income neighborhoods such as Georgetown in Washington, D.C., the Gold Coast in Chicago, and Pacific Heights in San Francisco. These are but one example of the phenomenon of clustering. While this is, in my judgment, as important as centrality in explaining urban structure and form, it has received far less attention in the literature. That which it has received has been largely in connection with the emotionally charged matter of racial segregation in U.S. cities. The following section explores the question of clustering more fully.

4. CLUSTERING OF LIKE LAND-USES

In addition to segregation by race and by income, there are many examples of clustering of like land-uses in U.S. cities. One of the most famous is the garment district of New York City, where firms engaged in various stages of the production of women's clothing are located in close proximity to each other. Many large U.S. cities have entertainment districts. Most have stretches of major streets along which auto dealers are arranged one after another. To take but one other nonresidential example, prior to the automobile and the suburban shopping center, non-CBD commerical areas grew up in large cities, especially at the intersections of major streets such as 63rd and Halstead on Chicago's south side. Moreover, residential segregation is hardly unique to the U.S. As we became aware from television news broadcasts covering events in Northern Ireland, Catholics and Protestants tend to live in disjoint residential areas in Belfast and other cities of Northern Ireland. Similarily, Christians and Muslims occupy separate areas of Beirut.

Cases of such spatial clustering are all consistent with Bailey's (1959) analysis.

Suppose there are two types of land users, I and II. Further, suppose that type I users prefer segregation in that they will offer a premium for land or for real estate located in the vicinity of other type I users. Type II users may prefer integration in that they, too, will offer a premium for land or real estate in the vicinity of type I users. Alternatively, type II users may prefer segregation and will offer a premium for sites in the vicinity of other type II users.

Consider now an initial, random scattering of type I and II users over the urban landscape. Such a scattering would not, of course, produce perfect uniformity but rather clusters of type I and II users. These clusters would, in general, be unstable over time, however. Provided that type I users would offer more of a premium to inhabit sites in the vicinity of other type I users than type II users, it would be mutually profitable for type I users to buy out any type II users in predominantly type I areas, and vice versa. Even if transactions costs were high enough to prevent this, as type II users moved from structures in predominantly type I areas for other reasons, their places would tend to be taken by type I users. Thus over time, the initial clusters would evolve into wholly segregated land-use areas.

For segregation to develop it is by no means necessary for type II users to prefer segregation, that is, offer a premium to occupy sites in the vicinity of other type II users. Rather, it is only necessary that type I users offer more of a premium for segregation than type II users would for integration. Those few empirical studies that have inquired into the matter, indeed, find that whites occupying areas contiguous to blacks pay lesser amounts for housing. Blacks contiguous to whites, however, would appear to pay more for housing than those blacks surrounded by other blacks. Although I know of no studies of the questions, one presumes that both in Beirut and in Belfast members of each of the two principal religious groups would offer a premium for sites in the vicinity of others of the same group.

Firms in the women's garment industry are typically highly specialized by function, and partly finished goods are often transported from one firm to another. Under these conditions, one supposes that firms would pay a premium for sites in the vicinity of other garment firms, although other land users might be indifferent to location vis-à-vis a garment firm. The situation is probably similar in the automobile dealer case, where persons shopping for a car are more likely to visit a particular lot if located close to other car lots. The shopping center case too is similar. Not only would stores selling, say, women's clothing attract customers because of other such stores in the center, but shoppers may well prefer to purchase more than one kind of item on a single trip. Shopping center formation is also encouraged by the prospect of more efficient usage of certain facilities such as parking. In the entertainment district case, however, residential users, at least, would doubtless find the noise at night objectionable and thus offer less for sites adjacent to an entertainment district.

Along boundaries separating areas of unlike land-use, rentals of sites or sites plus structures may differ from those of otherwise identical parcels remote from the boundary. Differentials such as these arise because of proximity to the other group and are often called boundary externalities. Assuming type I users prefer segregation from type II's, the rentals of land plus structures will be lower along the boundary in the type I area than in its interior. Rentals in the type II area along the boundary may be either higher or lower than in the interior, depending upon whether type II users prefer integration or segregation. As was noted earlier, such differentials have indeed been observed in a few studies of the effect of race on housing prices in the U.S. Somewhat surprising, however, is the fact that the few available studies fail to reveal significant boundary effects on the values of single-family properties generally [see Avrin (1974)].

From the examples discussed above, it would seem that the phenomenon of clustering is both pervasive and readily explicable on the basis of market transactions. Less readily explainable, however, is the matter of the shapes and spatial locations of clusters of like land uses. One is tempted to suppose that, to minimize externalities that occur along boundaries separating areas of unlike land uses, clusters would be so shaped as to minimize the length of their perimeters. Such an hypothesis must confront two difficulties, however. First, I know of no market process involving individual transactions, as in their formation, through which perimeters of these clusters might be minimized. One might have to suppose that certain very large institutions such as insurance companies would buy up substantial parts of a city and relocate site users so as to minimize perimeters. Alternatively, governments might do so under urban renewal type programs. Secondly, depending upon their size, such clusters might be either annular, surrounding the center, or, if sufficiently large, wedge shaped. These shapes would seem to have a certain empirical relevance. Loury (1978), however, has shown that perimeter-minimizing areas are lens-shaped, determined by the intersection of the urban-rural boundary and another circle.

Virtually unnoticed by the literature, but almost as important empirically as centrality, is the phenomenon called sectoring. Not quite 50 years ago, Hoyt (1939) argued, partly on the basis of some very convincing diagrams, that higher-income residential areas in U.S. cities tend to proceed out from the center along certain radials. Unlike central tendencies, which are very similar everywhere, the directions of these radials differ considerably from city to city, however. Although I am not aware of any study of it as comprehensive as Hoyt's, much the same might be said of black residential areas in many U.S. cities.

One possible explanation for the development of sectors is the historical growth process. When initially established, a settlement consisting of two income groups would segregate along the lines suggested above if members of the higher income group prefer segregation more than the lower income group members prefer integration. If it is cheaper to build on the periphery of the existing higher income area than to convert existing lower income structures into higher income ones along the boundary of the existing higher income area, the latter would extend outward along a given radial from the center as the size of the place grows over time.

The situation is somewhat similar when the residential area of a lower income or minority group expands into an already developed residential area as the group grows in size. Boundary price differences or the availability of information about the housing market would both suggest that the area inhabited by the group would grow along its borders. The specific direction taken by the expansion, however, might well depend upon that in which the available housing stock is most suitable for occupancy by the expanding group. In this context, suitable, of course, means that for which the relative rental offers of the expanding group are highest relative to those of the existing residents. Brueckner (1977) found, indeed, that indicators of the size of existing dwellings such as average rent and age variables are important determinants of residential succession.

One of the oldest ideas in the fields of real estate and urban economics is that of filtering. Filtering, as I would interpret it, means the progressive relative decline of the incomes of a structure's inhabitants as the structure ages. Classic discussions of the notion of filtering suggest that new dwellings are built primarily for the highest income groups.[4] Existing dwellings are passed down to relatively lower groups on the income scale as they age rather like clothing from older to younger brothers or sisters.

I find several difficulties with the filtering hypothesis, however. First, casual observation suggests many examples of neighborhoods or whole suburbs that have maintained their relative income levels for protracted periods of time. On the other hand, many of the changes in the character of neighborhoods that have occurred in U.S. cities have been sudden ones, as a lower income or minority group expands out of its previous residential area. Moreover, housing census data suggest to me that there is surprisingly little variation of income with age of structure. Income in 1979, for example, averaged about $25,000 for households in structures built from 1975 through March, 1980, and almost $18,000 for those living in structures built prior to 1940. However, if the highest income households lived in the newest housing and vice versa, average household income would have been roughly $58,400 in structures built since 1974 as compared with only $4,700 in pre-1940 structures. On the whole, it would seem that we have very little understanding of the process by which people of different income levels are distributed over space and the existing housing stock.

5. CONCLUDING OBSERVATIONS

After reading over the preceding, I found no major changes I thought were needed. I felt something was lacking, however, rather like a sauce that wanted a little more oregano. After considerable thought, it occurred to me that some comments on the direction future work might best take were in order. Since I am soon to enter upon my seventh decade, I would imagine that I am accorded the privilege of speaking out on such questions, although it would be presumptuous to expect anyone to take my words seriously.

---

[4]More recent treatments of filtering, of course, have relaxed this assumption. All that I am aware of, however, maintain the assumption of a nonzero size or quality level below which new dwellings are not built. The lowest income groups are presumed to live only in hand-me-down housing. In my judgment, although the average rental value of newly built dwellings, however defined, is higher than that of existing ones, distributions of dwellings by rental value reveal no evidence of a rental level below which no new units are built.

One's agenda for the future would depend critically upon whether one's goal is mathematical interest or empirical relevance. For those to whom it is not obvious which I prefer, let me simply say that I fully agree with McCracken (1984, ρ. 328). He commented to the effect that we use mathematical tools not so much to understand economic phenomena as we use economic phenomena as an excuse to play with mathematical tools. I am admittedly old fashioned enough to think calculus more useful than topology. Yet I know enough mathematics to realize that which is used by the most facile of economists and regional scientists is at most fourth-year undergraduate or first-year graduate level mathematics. Pure mathematics is far more interesting mathematically than economic or spatial phenomena. Therefore, if we are to be more than second-rate mathematicians, it is the real world that should receive our primary attention.

In studying the real world, economics and regional science are far behind other fields in adapting to the use of the computer. Admittedly, our graduate students run countless regressions on the computer and write their dissertations on it. Yet we have been most laggard in adapting our way of thought to the possibilities it presents. It is still all too common to set up problems so that by employing the most currently fashionable mathematics they are analytically tractable. Yet a far wider class of problems is susceptible to numerical solution by computer than by traditional analytic methods. Moreover, when looking over numerical output one is forced to think in terms not only of direction of change but of quantitative significance. The computer, it seems to me, offers as much potential for progress in understanding economic and spatial phenomena as did the new methods of statistical inference when this *Journal* was born.

What might be done to encourage better work? One suggestion is a micro computer in every faculty office. The \$100 or so per month per office which such would cost could easily be saved from the secretarial budget through using its word processing capabilities alone. More important, it is up to us as senior faculty and department chairs to throw away our rulers. Rather than measuring the length of a candidate's *Curriculum Vitae*, I would make the revolutionary recommendation that we actually read the items on it. Regardless of what the Supreme Court says regarding "one man, one vote," we should realize that not all articles in refereed journals are the same. Journal editors and referees, too, should realize that papers which show some sign of originality and the ability to focus upon the critical aspects of a new and substantively interesting problem are far more valuable than yet another proof of the existence of a competitive equilibrium. If professional recognition were to be had for truly good work, as an economist I am confident that more such work would be forthcoming.

REFERENCES

Avrin, Marcy Elkind. "Some Economic Effects of Residential Zoning in San Francisco," unpublished Ph.D. dissertation, Stanford University, 1974.

Bailey, Martin J. "Note on the Economics of Residential Zoning and Urban Renewal," *Land Economics*, 35 (1959), 288–292.

Ball, Michael J. "Recent Empirical Work on the Determinants of Relative House Prices," *Urban Studies*, 10 (1973), 213–231.

Beckmann, Martin J. "Spatial Equilibrium in the Dispersed City," in George Papageorgiou (ed.), *Mathematical Land Use Theory.* Lexington, MA: D.C. Heath and Company, 1976, pp. 117–125.

Brueckner, Jan. "The Determinants of Residential Succession," *Journal of Urban Economics,* 4 (1977), 45–59.

Clark, Colin. "Urban Population Densities," *Journal of the Royal Statistical Society, A,* 114 (1951), 490–496.

Fujita, Masahisa. "Urban Land Use Theory," unpublished manuscript, 1984.

Hoyt, Homer. *The Structure and Growth of Residential Neighborhoods in American Cities.* Washington, D.C.: Government Printing Office, 1939.

Kanemoto, Yoshitsugu. "Externalities in Space," unpublished manuscript, 1984.

Kau, James B. and Cheng F. Lee. "A Random Coefficient Model to Estimate a Stochastic Density Gradient," *Regional Science and Urban Economics,* 7 (1977), 169–177.

Loury, Glenn C. "The Minimum Border Length Hypothesis Does Not Explain the Shape of Black Ghettos," *Journal of Urban Economics,* 5 (1978), 147–153.

McCracken, Paul W. "Has Macro-Theory Failed Economic Policy?," *Southern Economic Journal,* 51 (1984), 319–329.

Mills, Edwin. "Urban Density Functions," *Urban Studies,* 7 (1970), 5–20.

Mohring, Herbert. "Land Values and the Measurement of Highway Benefits," *Journal of Political Economy,* 49 (1961), 236–249.

Moses, Leon and Harold F. Williamson, Jr. "The Location of Economic Activity in Cities," *American Economic Review,* 57 (1967), 211–222.

Muth, Richard F. *Cities and Housing.* Chicago: University of Chicago Press, 1969.

———. "Numerical Solution of Urban Residential Land-Use Models," *Journal of Urban Economics,* 2 (1975), 307–332.

———. "Energy Prices and Urban Decentralization," in Anthony Downs and Katherine L. Bradbury (eds.), *Energy Costs and Urban Development.* Washington, D.C.: The Brookings Institution, 1984, pp. 85–104.

Strotz, Robert H. "Urban Transportation Parables," in Julius Margolis (ed.), *The Public Economy of Urban Communities.* Washington, D.C.: Resources for the Future, 1964, pp. 127–169.

Wheaton, William. "A Comparative Static Analysis of Urban Spatial Structure," *Journal of Economic Theory,* 9 (1974), 223–237.

———. "Urban Spatial Development with Durable but Replaceable Capital," *Journal of Urban Economics,* 12 (1982), 53–67.

Wieand, Kenneth and Richard F. Muth. "A Note on the Variation of Land Values in St. Louis," *Journal of Regional Science,* 12 (1972), 469–473.

Winsborough, Halliman H. "A Comparative Study of Urban Residential Densities," unpublished Ph.D. dissertation, University of Chicago, 1960.

[14]

A Critique of Urban Modelling

From Regional Science to Urban and Regional Political Economy

R. ANDREW SAYER

School of Social Sciences,
University of Sussex, Falmer, Brighton BN1 9QN, Sussex

Contents

Acknowledgements

This book is based upon part of my D.Phil thesis, 'Dynamic Spatial Models of Urban and Regional Systems'. It may seem superfluous to acknowledge intellectual debts to other writers, for the bibliography serves as a list of these debts, but it is worth noting that significantly, I owe most to writers outside urban modelling — particularly David Harvey, Leslie Curry, Joan Robinson and Maurice Dobb. Urban modellers please take note.

I am also indebted to my research supervisors, Tony Fielding of the School of Social Sciences, University of Sussex, and Ray Curnow of the Science Policy Research Unit at Sussex for their unfailing interest and help in my work and not least for their progressive attitude towards D.Phil's!

I would like to thank Doreen Mitten for doing most of the typing, and my friends, family and former teachers for wittingly or unwittingly providing invaluable moral support. Finally, this book is dedicated to Hazel with love, respect and thanks.   [*189*]

CHAPTER 1

Introduction

This book is a reaction against the conventional wisdom in urban modelling and regional
science. The first two decades in the development of the overlapping interdisciplinary subjects
of regional science, spatial analysis and urban modelling have not, until recently, been disturbed
by any fundamental challenges to their methodology and content. To borrow Kuhn's
terminology, there has truly been a period of 'normal science' in which researchers have
accepted certain basic premises without question (Kuhn, 1970, 2nd edn.). Those disputes which
have arisen, have been limited to technical or secondary issues which do not bring these basic
premises into question. For example, urban modellers have had their disputes over the question
of the appropriate *size* of urban models (Lee, 1973), and over the way in which they should be
used in planning (Batty, 1975), but the logically prior question of whether urban models have
any validity at all, has not been raised.

If science progresses by means of conjecture and refutation rather than as a gradual process
of accretion of knowledge, then this lack of fundamental criticism in the regional science
literature must be a source of concern. In trying to provide such a critique we have to explore
the bases of the consensus in regional science. Despite the diverse disciplinary origins of regional
scientists, most of the models and techniques imported into the subject from outside are
compatible, and where there are exceptions of contradictory models, they are not brought into
conflict, but kept separate. Models have been developed chiefly as techniques, as *computational
devices*, rather than as embodiments of theories about the space economy. Whereas clashes
between theories are difficult to hide, it is not so easy to find contradictions between models
which are little more than convenient computational devices. We intend to attack regional
science both for its lack of theory and for the poverty of such theory that it does contain.

One of the most important bases of consensus concerns the use of theory and models
derived from neoclassical economics. Judging by the economic content of the literature in
regional science, one would scarcely imagine that the very foundations of the 'mother subject'
of neoclassical economics were disintegrating under mounting criticism from the British
Cambridge School of economists and their supporters.[1] Despite this, the derived neoclassical
models continue to be used without question.

Geographers involved in urban modelling and regional science have also failed to break with
this consensus, indeed they have reinforced it. It will be argued in the following chapters that
many spatial models, including those with no explicit economic content, use the same
methodology as neoclassical economics. As a result, they share structurally identical errors. This
shared methodology is perhaps clearest in the case of entropy-maximizing or gravity models and
neoclassical utility theory (Apps, 1971; Wilson, 1970; Hansen, 1972; Batty, 1973). However,
regional scientists have interpreted this compatibility as a new form of confirmation of the
validity of both sets of models. We shall argue that this compatibility merely confirms their
mutual inadequacy.

This shared methodology has many elements, but the most important one is functionalism.
As the name implies, functionalism analyzes social phenomena in terms of how they function,
and how they support the system of which they are a part. Temporal and cause-and-effect
modes of explanation (see Harvey, 1969, part VI) are largely excluded so that even urban
development is described, not in terms of a historical sequence, but as an extrapolation of
present patterns of functioning. For example, Lowry models do not refer to the real world
development processes of land acquisition, financing and development, but merely extrapolate
the superficial evidence of urban 'functioning', in terms of certain types of spatial interaction,

into the future. Functionalism has been widely discredited in more methodologically aware social sciences such as sociology and social anthropology, and it can be shown that this critique is also applicable to regional science.

Having demonstrated that the errors and inadequacies of this paradigm cannot be removed without rejecting the paradigm itself, it will be argued that there should be a shift towards the development of theories of the political economy of cities and regions. Some former regional scientists have already made this shift, e.g. Harvey (1973), Massey (1974), Edel (1975), but, perhaps understandably, they have been preoccupied with pursuing their new interests rather than spending or wasting their time on detailed, retrospective critiques of the old paradigm. However, without this kind of critique, the adoption of the new paradigm may appear to be dependent on some mystical conversion experience. Worse still, the new political economy school may be dismissed as an eccentric alternative to conventional regional science which we may either take or leave. More cynically, in view of the ignorance and suspicion of its Marxian content, one suspects that many regional scientists would indeed be happy to dismiss it as outlet for 'radicals' which cannot challenge 'objective', 'neutral', regional science. Hopefully, this book will combat such views, and show that conventional regional science must be overthrown, and that the adoption of a political economy approach which is predicated upon its destruction, is not optional but imperative.

Communication between members of different paradigms is always difficult, for by definition, their conceptual apparatus differ so greatly that they may interpret the same phenomena in entirely opposed ways; they will attach different levels of significance to these phenomena and each side will use jargon which is mystifying to the other. Nevertheless, if we are to avoid lapsing into an indifferent relativist view of the two paradigms, the attempt to communicate must be made. Consequently, our tactics will be to begin the critique very much upon the home ground of conventional regional science. Pride of place will be given to attacks on the validity of the reasoning used, rather than the ideological content of regional science. Certainly, there are very important connections between questions of logic and ideological content, and we shall attempt to point these out, but positivist regional scientists who are unaware of the impossibility of value-free social science may simply rule an ideological critique out of court. However, they can hardly turn away from a challenge to the validity of their reasoning.

The book is chiefly aimed at urban modellers, and it therefore starts by looking at some so-called technical problems of popular models such as Lowry-type models and gravity/entropy-maximizing models. Amongst the most important of these problems are those that have surfaced through the long-standing search for *dynamic spatial* models in regional science.

As a result of this analysis, structurally identical errors and ambiguities in the logic of these models are revealed. Mathematical modellers may be surprised that we find no fault with their mathematics, and yet claim that their models are incorrect. The point is that urban models are supposed to make statements about the real world, and hence their interpretation and meaning must be evaluated: mathematical consistency is only a minimal requirement.

Implicit in our critique is the view that the all-absorbing preoccupation with mathematical form which typifies so much of regional science is symptomatic of an inadequate and highly inhibiting conception of the nature of 'science'. The dominant positivist conception of science is *not* the only scientific epistemology. The view that the social sciences can be made truly 'scientific' or 'hard' by mimicking physics or by mere application of rigorous mathematical techniques is popular but misconceived, for it fails to specify any particular ontology (theory of what exists). The question is, to what do we apply such techniques? The danger of this inhibiting epistemology is that it sweeps all the problems of developing theories of society under the carpet; the fundamental questions of what aspect of social reality we should examine and how we should go about the process of *abstraction* are considered unproblematic. The lack of theoretical content in the mathematical models would seem to imply either an ignorance of social theory or dismissal of the latter as 'unscientific'. Even though mathematical modellers may give the impression that 'science' is just a matter of 'defining variables' and performing rigorous mathematical operations upon them,[2] their choice of substantive content is by no means neutral. As Wright Mills (1959, Chapter 3) observed, their explanations are characteristically ahistorical, biased towards psychologism (attributing behaviour to innate, autonomous desires, needs, demands) and conversely biased against explanation in terms of social structure.

However, while it seems wise to give the reader advance warning of the main thrust of the critique, in order to keep to our strategy of starting on the ground of conventional regional science before showing that a shift away from it is necessary, the above methodological arguments will only be developed fully *after* the discussion on more familiar territory of the problems and inadequacies of particular models.

Planners and researchers interested in planning issues may have little time for methodological critiques such as this, and may complain that it is not sufficiently relevant to planning. Firstly, although it may seem more 'practical' and 'relevant' to work on the application and refinement of models in planning, the validity of this work depends upon the validity of these models. If it is not worth building Lowry models, it is not worth building them well. Secondly, the implication that regional science or urban studies should be primarily a 'support-science' for planning is rejected, for such a view does no justice to either planning or urban studies. On the one hand, those who are interested in planning may develop a misleading picture of planning by failing to recognize its relative impotence *vis-à-vis* more powerful forces of production and investment in the built environment in urban and regional development, and on the other hand urban studies or regional science may remain in an emasculated state, and fail to understand this development through a neglect of these forces.

To those who have already developed an interest in the political economy of cities and regions, much of this critique may seem redundant or at least pitched too much on conventional regional science's own terms. A more abstract critique of positivist, idealist social science, using regional science as an example, might have been preferred. Several good texts in this vein have appeared recently and although their arguments are not directed against regional science they are highly recommended (e.g. Blackburn 1972; Giddens, 1974; Hollis and Nell, 1975; Keat and Urry, 1975.) However, their discussions are perhaps pitched at too high a level of generality to provide a convincing demonstration that the specific problems of particular models are *symptomatic* of the fallibility of this approach to social science. These texts also fail to provide discussions of the problems involved with regional science's distinctive concern with *space*. These are the gaps in the literature which this book intends to fill.

As regards the prescriptions arising from the critique, limitations of space exclude more than the presentation of the barest outlines of the alternative political economy approach. The best way of understanding the distinctive features of this approach is undoubtedly to look at some examples. Harvey's *Social Justice and the City* (1973) is perhaps the best known, and its persuasiveness owes much to its *sequential development* of ideas and shifts of position, starting off from a liberal standpoint and evolving towards the beginnings of a Marxist approach. The influence of its form on this book should be obvious. Harvey's more recent work on the political economy of housing, urbanization and capital accumulation represent maturer applications of this approach. Less well-known, but equally impressive and readable is Murray's analysis of the political economy of uneven development (1972). At a more advanced and unfortunately, in some cases somewhat less readable, level there is the work of Frank on dependency theory and underdevelopment (1967), and the French Marxist studies of urbanization and urbanism, e.g. Castells, 1972; Pickvance, 1976.[3] From a reading of this type of material the distinctive characteristics of the political economy approach should rapidly become apparent; the rejection of the search for eternal, immutable, social laws, the rejection of the possibility of separate studies of economics, sociology, politics and history, the use of a materialist concept of history, and so on. But perhaps the most compelling of the first impressions one has of political economy are of its comprehensiveness, its power of demystification and its firm grounding in human practice. These three characteristics clearly overlap. Its comprehensiveness makes the synthesizing claims of systems analysis look foolish; whereas the systems approach often treats, say, housing, as something merely dependent on 'preferences' and employment location, the political economy approach situates it in an economic, social, political and historical context, dealing with its financing, its production, its consumption, its implications for economy and society as a whole, its ideological import, plus the connections between these aspects. On the basis of general knowledge we know that all these aspects of housing are interlinked: on the basis of liberal social science, we are led to believe it has to be dismembered and the parts distributed among 'experts' in social administration, sociology, economics and geography for discipline-based or technique-based interpretation, so that we may understand it. Conventional urban studies and regional science also mystify social phenomena by failing to base their abstractions on human practice. Harvey (1974) gives a simple example; in neo-classical economics, rent is a payment to a scarce factor of production, in political economy, it is a payment to a person who happens to own property. The first form of abstraction obscures the relation between the social and the economic, the latter illuminates it, and which corresponds more with our experience?

Having hinted at the 'promise' of urban and regional political economy, let us now explore the inadequacies of conventional regional science and urban modelling in detail and try to defend our claim that adoption of the political economy approach is obligatory rather than optional.

NOTES: CHAPTER 1

1. Also variously known as post or left-Keynesians, neo-Marxists, or neo-Ricardians, they include Joan Robinson, Dobb, Sraffa, Kaldor, Eatwell, Kregel, Pasinetti, Harcourt, Nell, Kalecki, Kornai (see Chapter 5 and Appendix 1).
2. See Wilson, 1974, especially sections 11.7 and 11.8 for some beautiful examples.
3. In parallel to this reading, it is advisable to consult introductory texts on general political economic theory, e.g. Kay, 1975; Robinson and Eatwell, 1973; Barratt-Brown, 1970; Mandel, 1968.

CHAPTER 2

The Economic Base Model

2.1. UNDERMINING THE LOWRY MODEL'S ECONOMIC BASE MECHANISM

We open our critique with a discussion of the problems of a very simple, long established model – the economic base model, as it is used within the Lowry model.

From one point of view, looking at the long history of criticisms of the economic base model,[1] one might be excused for expecting that it should surely have died the 'death of a thousand refutations' by now. Nevertheless, it persists, and in a very crude form within the Lowry model, and by virtue of this, it could be claimed to have widespread support. In British regional sciences, Lowry models have aroused unparalleled interest, reflected in a formidable body of research literature devoted to refinements and applications of the original Lowry model.[2] Batty (1971) has described it as the first general model of an urban system, and later (1975), as a 'fundamental paradigm (sic) of urban structure' and 'a grand and elegant conception, ... (which) stands head and shoulders above any other of its competitors'.

We shall argue that this judgement could scarcely be more grossly mistaken, that its two main components – the economic base mechanism and gravity/entropy-maximizing models (see Chapter 3) – share serious, structurally identical errors, which have failed to be identified by this vast body of research literature. The very fact that almost all of this literature makes no reference to these errors, means that we need cite only a few, original works, for the same criticisms apply throughout the field.

Firstly, let us set out the context in which the economic base model is used here. The Lowry model uses an economic base model to generate estimates of population and service employment associated with a given amount of basic employment in an urban area or subregion. Basic employment refers to industries which are not dependent on the local market of the area in which they are located, whereas the non-basic or service industries depend on the local population and other local industry for their markets. Changes in basic employment are therefore treated as being independent of changes in the area in which they are located. In order to derive the estimates of services employment and population, the model also makes use of certain empirical regularities in the relationships between population and employment – the activity rate and the population-serving ratio. Given an exogenous estimate of basic employment, we can multiply this by the inverse activity rate (the ratio of population to jobs) to derive the population associated with that basic employment. Similarly, the number of non-basic jobs required to serve this population is derived by multiplying the latter by the population-serving ratio. This gives us a new total of jobs (basic plus non-basic) which can in turn be used to generate more population (see Fig. 2.1).

By iterating this sequence of calculations, the totals for population and service employment converge towards an equilibrium level which is ultimately dependent on basic employment.

(A quick method of finding this equilibrium state which does not require an iterative solution uses the following formulae:

$$P = a \; \frac{E^B}{1-(a\beta)} \qquad\qquad (2.1.)$$

and for equilibrium service employment,

$$S = a\beta \, \frac{E^B}{1-(a\beta)} \qquad\qquad (2.2.)$$

where P is population; S is service employment; E^B is basic employment; a is the inverse activity rate; and β the population-serving ratio).

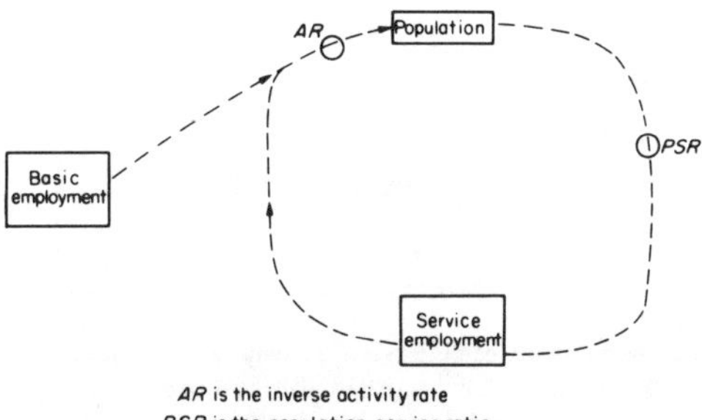

FIG. 2.1. The economic base mechanism in the Lowry model.

Now it should be noted that urban modellers have claimed that such models exemplify the well-known dictum that 'in the city, everything affects everything else' — indeed this ability to handle complex interactions has formed a major part of the rhetoric of the 'systems approach'. This claim surely implies that the causal structure of urban models should contain *two-way* causation between the major elements of the system. In the Lowry model, the only example of two-way causation is in the relationship between population and service jobs, where the former creates a demand for the latter, which, in turn creates a demand for population. In the absence of any basic jobs, the population and service job levels should decline to zero, provided that $a \times \beta < 1$. Therefore, all change in these levels is ultimately attributable to the level of basic jobs and its rate of change. It follows that there is a *one-way causation* from basic jobs to population in the model and basic jobs are totally independent of population constraints. This means that the Lowry model is a demand model where demand for employees in basic industry creates its own supply of people perfectly and instantly and these, in turn, create their own supply of services in similar fashion.

Clearly, in this model, everything does *not* affect everything else, and one can only infer that ultimately, the entire urban system, as represented in these models, is driven by 'insatiable consumer demand' for the products of basic industry (Harvey, 1973, 238). Subsystems or elements of the model have no independence of operation, but function together in machine-like harmony, where troublesome realities such as unemployment, labour shortages and other disequilibria, simply cannot exist.

This much has already been recognized in critiques of the economic base model, which have argued that it is a *demand-oriented* model (Pfouts, 1960; Thompson, 1965). This criticism has tended to be fended off by users of the model, by means of the familiar argument that the omission of the supply-side is merely a *simplifying assumption*. After all, simplifying assumptions are supposed to be essential to the hallowed hypothetico-deductive method of regional science, and there is always the comforting belief that, having used this simplification to gain an understanding of the fundamentals of the problem, it can later be replaced by more realistic assumptions. However, it will be shown that there is more than just a simplifying assumption here — there is a serious but very simple logical error.

Users of the model might be tempted to defend this causal structure by appealing to the empirical observation that real world activity rates and population—serving ratios tend to be stable, so that when we fit a Lowry model to the existing situation in a region, we are modelling an equilibrium between demand and supply forces, and hence argue that population can be forecasted simply by multiplying projected jobs by the inverse activity rate. In diagrammatic form, the 'real world' relationships:

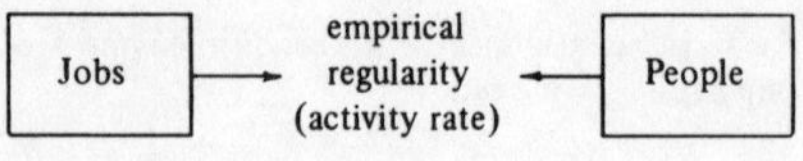

can be interpreted as:

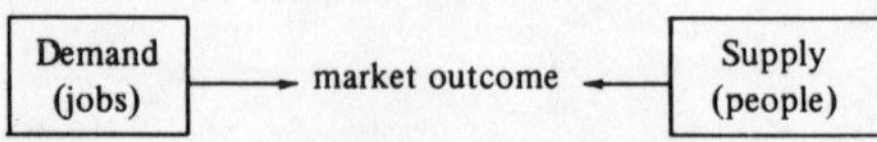

so that we can use them to forecast population by the model

$$\text{Demand} \quad \times \quad \underset{\text{(inverse activity rate)}}{\text{market outcome}} \quad = \quad \text{Population}$$

However, the observed stability of the (inverse) activity rate provides no justification for this procedure whatsoever: if it did, then it would be equally justifiable to multiply projected population by the activity rate to derive a forecast of jobs! —

$$\text{Population} \quad \times \quad \text{activity rate} \quad = \quad \text{Jobs}$$

To detect the logical error, we must first eliminate the considerable ambiguity of meaning of the variables labelled as 'jobs' or 'employment'. Moreover, it is essential to distinguish between *ex ante* quantities (referring to market expectations and intentions) and *ex post* quantities (referring to actual, realized quantities). When this distinction is made, it can readily be seen that the relative forces of 'demand' and 'supply' can change without disturbing the empirical regularity of the activity rate. For example, there may be, at the present time in a certain place, 250 people for every 100 workers, thus giving an activity rate of 40%. However, this does not necessarily mean that if we create another 100 jobs we will get another 250 people. The new jobs will represent an *ex ante* demand for labour — job vacancies which may or may not be taken up, depending on the supply of labour. If only fifty of the new jobs are filled because no more workers exist in the region or can migrate in from outside, we are likely to get a total increase in population of 125 (ignoring multiplier effects). The inverse activity rate of 2.5 people per worker will therefore be maintained as an *ex post relation*, irrespective of whether the demand for labour can succeed in creating its own supply or not. Lowry models do not model the two-way interaction of urban subsystems, but merely take the particular *ex post* market outcome that obtains in the base year, and extrapolate it in a way which 'freezes' that particular demand—supply balance.[3]

Undoubtedly, the illusion of the economic base mechanism's validity is produced by its static nature which excludes the possibility of distinguishing between *ex ante* and *ex post* quantities, and which camouflages the definitional ambiguity of variables such as basic 'jobs' or basic 'employment'. The static framework produces a 'sleight-of-hand' whereby an input of new jobs into a region is surreptitiously redefined 'employment' thus letting in the hidden assumption that all these jobs can be filled. 'Jobs' therefore, tautologically become 'employment' which similarly becomes 'labour' and hence 'population'.[4] The definitional identity of the *ex post* quantities demanded and supplied can easily give an impression of some genuine lasting equilibrium, which completely conceals unsatisfied demand and unemployed supplies. In a consistent model we need to satisfy the definitional *ex post* equalities *and* the unrealized *ex ante* quantities. It is a pity that those who have advocated the use of accounting frameworks in modelling have frequently failed to account for *ex ante* disequilibria, and have included only *ex post* 'definitional—equilibrium quantities'.

Some regional scientists might still object that they are well aware that they are assuming that demand for labour creates its own supply and as long as it is acknowledged, that is all that matters. We would answer that one may indeed treat the whole matter as one of choice of assumptions, so long as it is realized that this selfconscious choice does not *remove* the logical error, but merely conceals it.

2.2. IDENTIFICATION ERRORS

The economic base model contains a typical example of an *Identification Error* — it places a false interpretation upon an empirical regularity. *Identification Problems* are very common in economics where it is often found that the value of a single variable is determined by the interplay of several others. For example, if we plot the sales and price of a certain commodity over time on a demand—supply diagram, as in Fig. 2.2., the interpretation of the changes in

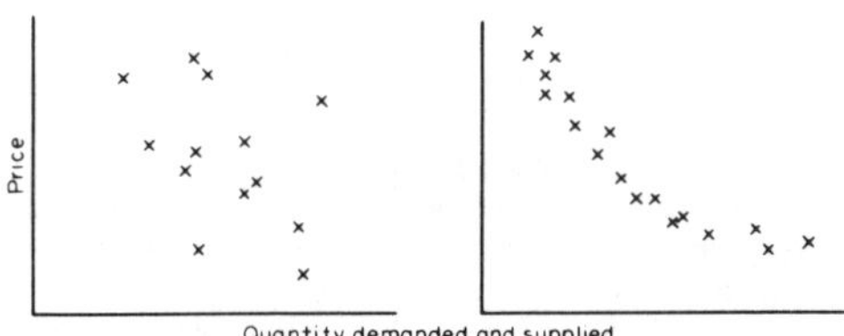

FIG. 2.2. The identification problem (after Hollis and Nell, 1975, p. 82).

price and quantity demanded and supplied is ambiguous. This is not only the case in the left-hand diagram where there is no apparent order whatsoever; for even where the points fall in an orderly manner as indicated in the right-hand diagram, we cannot decide, *on this basis alone,* that this is a downward sloping demand curve. The pattern might equally be interpreted as the outcome of a situation of rapidly increasing economics of scale, or a mixture of several elements. Additional evidence is required in order to avoid an identification error. In the case of the economic base mechanism in the Lowry model, additional information about the supply of labour and population is required.

2.3. SOME IMPLICATIONS OF THE IDENTIFICATION ERROR IN THE ECONOMIC BASE MODEL

It will be shown later on that identification errors are quite common in regional science, but for now it is useful to dwell upon some of the implications of their occurrence in the economic base model.

2.3.1. Lowry Models and Population Forecasting

Firstly, this example points out an important contradiction in regional science involved in the widespread acceptance of population forecasts generated by Lowry models. On one level, the point that additional information about the supply of population is required is hardly contentious, for the idea that jobs 'create' population instantaneously and without any constraints obviously offends against our intuition. Also, if asked to produce a population forecast for a region, most regional scientists would surely use the most well-researched population-forecasting models — perhaps a cohort-survival model of the type developed by Rogers (1971); they would be unlikely to use anything as crude as an economic base model. However, in another context, one suspects that they might *accept or condone the use of a* Lowry model in planning, even though the model's chief output is a forecast of population, together with its spatial distribution within the region.

It might be objected that this is not the case and that the Lowry model is purely a *spatial* model; for example, Lee writes:

All of the models to be discussed are models for predicting the location of activities within urban regions or the interactions between activities once the level of activities has been determined. The range of models which are available for forecasting the *levels* of urban activities are not dealt with. (C. Lee, 1973, x).

Such an assertion is wholly unfounded because the Lowry model (which Lee later discusses), *does* forecast levels of activities and because a spatial distribution can have no meaning unless the quantities involved are defined: there can be no spatial form without content (cf. Sack, 1974). Therefore the aims of a regional population-forecasting model and a Lowry model have a common element, but the former is considerably more suitable for this common purpose.

2.3.2. Lowry Models: Statics, Dynamics and the Supply of Population.

One of the best known criticisms of the Lowry model, first raised by Lowry himself, is that it is static: it is a model of *'instant metropolis'*. We have argued above, that the static format of the economic base model tends to conceal its identification error, and so it would be of interest to consider the effect of making the model *dynamic*.

However, there are several very different ways of doing this. The simplest method is to allow basic jobs to vary over time, and make population change proportionately over time too. Since this method preserves the one-way causation from jobs to population and hence the identification error too, we shall label it a 'trivial dynamic model'. A Lowry model made dynamic in this manner could accordingly be labelled a 'dynamic instant metropolis model', since population is still created instantaneously as jobs change. Batty's 'dynamic' model of the Reading area could be included in this category, for it uses equations of the type:

$$P^{t+1} = A_i \sum_j E_j^{t+1} \exp(-\beta c_{ij}), \tag{2.3.}$$

which retain assumptions of static equilibrium despite the time superscripts and the fact that E_j may be obtained from a separate equation that involves an explicit time description (Cordey-Hayes, 1972, p.19). In such models the functional relationship between variables remains constant and static: dependent variables change instantaneously as a linear function of some exogenously determined rate of change in an independent variable.

It would be a slight improvement to insert time lags of predetermined length so that population is not 'created' instantaneously in response to changes in basic jobs, but with a delay. Nevertheless, the functional relationship between stimulus and response is still fixed, and population is still ultimately determined by basic jobs, however long the delay, and so this type of dynamic model can be labelled a *'semi-trivial* dynamic model' (see Fig. 2.3. and Sayer (1974), for an example of a semi-trivial dynamic Lowry model).

In order to construct a non-trivial dynamic model, two-way causation or interaction has to be represented, where it exists, explicitly. In the case of the economic base model, this means that the *ex post* quantities of labour demanded and supplied must not be misrepresented as reflecting a one-way dependence of population on basic jobs, but must be derived as the *outcome* of two-way interaction of population and job supply. The unhelpfully crude dichotomy of independent variable/dependent variable must be rejected, so that, e.g. the two sides of the labour market each have some degree of independence as well as mutual dependence. Although immigration into a region may be strongly influenced by job vacancies, birth and death rates are almost completely independent of them.

Mathematicians might be tempted to describe this kind of population change as a *non-linear function* of economic change, but such a conceptualization misses the whole point for it reintroduces, by implication, the notion of one-way dependence and with it the identification error.

Thus, while it is clear that static equilibrium models conceal identification errors particularly successfully, trivial and semi-trivial dynamic models do so too because they retain implicit static equilibrium assumptions within an outwardly dynamic form. The type of thinking which treats the task of making dynamic models purely as a *mathematical* problem, as one of adding a

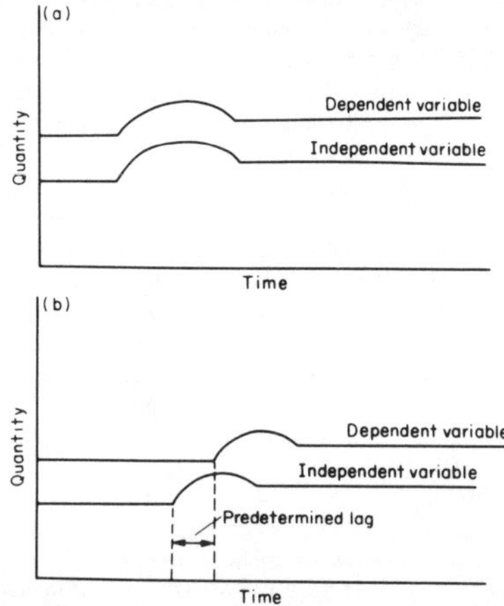

FIG. 2.3. (a): Stimulus and response in 'trivial' dynamic models.
(b): Stimulus and response in 'semi-trivial' dynamic models.

judicious sprinkling of time subscripts here and there to an existing static model, invites this kind of mis-specification.[5] To build a non-trivial dynamic model, the real world processes must be looked at anew, and the meanings of the variables (especially in terms of the *ex ante/ex post* distinction) must be checked; the problem of mathematical form becomes entirely *subsidiary* to the problem of finding an appropriate conceptualization of the system.

We may wish to make the economic base model a non-trivial dynamic model, but this is impossible as long as it remains a purely demand-oriented model, for the supply of population is essential to the dynamics. If we do not know the extent to which migration responds to changes in jobs, we cannot specify the dynamics. If we use a static model, we are forced to opt for one-way causation where the situation is either supply determined or demand determined. It becomes clear that the dynamics of a (labour) market can be determined only when the semi-independent behaviour of the supply-side (population) is modelled; and conversely the contribution of the supply-side to overall behaviour can only be determined within a dynamic framework. If we instead opt for the unidirectional causation of a semi-trivial dynamic model, we immediately create the artificial problem of having to determine lags and responses *a priori*, whereas a non-trivial dynamic model can do this for us. And if, of course, we opt for trivial dynamic.or static formats we have to live with the absurd assumption that demand for labour creates its own supply of population.

2.3.3. Lowry Models Versus Population Forecasting Models

This discussion of an example of a particularly important identification error in regional science, raises some further implications which reveal some surprising contradictions between some familiar, well-worn, models. Let us examine the contradictions between the economic base model, cohort-survival population models and migration models. Now it is well-known that at urban and regional scales the most volatile element of population dynamics is migration, and yet most population-forecasting models use *fixed*, (age-/sex-specific) migration coefficients. Admittedly, in an age-disaggregated model, the age-structure of the population may change and with it the sizes of the migration flows, but the actual coefficients used to generate the flows from the 'stocks' of population are constant. This assumption therefore contradicts our empirical knowledge. Just as, in the economic base model, population dynamics present no problem for employment generation, so, in these population-forecasting models, the varying influences of changes in employment on migration are ignored.

Coexisting with this body of theoretical and empirical knowledge, but apparently occupying a separate pigeonhole in the minds of most regional scientists, are migration models, which purport to explain this crucial element of population dynamics. Furthermore, most migration models, whether descriptive or predictive, relate migration flows to economic conditions in greater or lesser degree. On the one hand, these contradictions arise from the treatment of migration models, population-forecasting models and Lowry models as separate, unrelated bodies of knowledge in the modeller's 'tool-kit' (see section 6.3).[6] However, in a different sense, we could argue that these conceptual contradictions have some grounding in reality, for is it not the case that the activity rates and migration flows are the outcome of the interaction, conflict, or mutual adjustment, between the dynamics of the semi-autonomous economic and demographic subsystems? Non-trivial dynamic models can internalize this conflict between different subsystems, although usually at the expense of using simulation rather than analytical solutions. Static, trivial or semi-trivial models can only assume this conflict away and replace it with one-way causation, as does the economic base mechanism.

NOTES: CHAPTER 2

1. See especially, the book of readings by Pfouts (1960).

2. Lowry, 1964; Wilson, 1970; Batty, 1969, 1970a, 1970b, 1971, 1972; Cripps and Foot, 1969; Echenique, *et al.*, 1969; Goldner, 1971; Turner, 1971, – plus journals such as *Environment and Planning A*, and *Regional Studies*.

3. Cf. Kirwan and Martin (1970).

4. The reader should note that this curious combination of rigour in mathematical formulation and sloppiness and ambiguity in definition of variables will be encountered in many other models.

5. Cf. Finkelstein and Thimm, (1973, p. 325) 'Much – but not all – of current dynamic analysis is still a methodological continuation of partial equilibrium analysis. Starting with a static model, a few variables are made dynamic, whereas for the others, the *ceteris paribus* assumption still prevails. The results are neat, precise models which have little operational usefulness. Worse, this methodology has cut off the economist from the biologist and engineer who also deal with complex dynamic systems. Conceptually, the specific explicit awareness of dependency, feedback, and delay as the prime characteristics of dynamic systems that has been developed by the systems engineer, ecologist, and biologist has until recently been lacking in economics . . . . ' Also, Kregel (1973, p. 32) 'Even neo-classical dynamic analysis is essentially static, for the static equilibrium position is preserved despite differentiation of the variables with respect to time.'

6. See Sayer (1974) for an example of a dynamic Lowry model which is coupled to migration and population-forecasting models.

CHAPTER 3

The Critique of Gravity/Entropy-Maximizing Models

3.1. AIMS OF THE CRITIQUE

Having examined a very simple example of an identification error in the economic base model, we can now turn to a more complex and subtle type which occurs in the other major submodels — in the gravity or entropy-maximizing models. Here, it will be shown that mis-specification or identification errors occur not only in the calculation of *quantities* but also in the calculation of their *spatial distribution*. In this case the basic errors underlie several fairly familiar 'technical puzzles' of gravity/entropy-maximizing models; the demand-oriented nature of gravity-models, the arbitrary separation of trip-generation and distribution, the problem of spatial autocorrelation, and other less well-known puzzles such as the use of an untenable concept of absolute space and the ambiguous definition of variables. We will attempt to show that these 'symptoms' are all related, and stem from a fundamental error in the conceptualization of spatial interaction and location. The tendency has been to treat these symptoms as being capable of solution within the existing conceptual framework — perhaps by the addition of a few more terms to the existing equations, but we shall show that their solution is dependent on the *dissolution* of gravity/entropy-maximizing models.

Before attempting this critique, we must prepare the ground by providing a brief description of gravity/entropy-maximizing models for the benefit of readers who may be unfamiliar with them, and then clarify certain issues about the method of criticizing such models.

3.2. GRAVITY/ENTROPY-MAXIMIZING MODELS: A BRIEF DESCRIPTION

Gravity models have had an exceptionally long history of use in the study of the space economy, dating back to Carey (1858) and Ravenstein (1885). In recent years their development has been greatly accelerated and some measure of theoretical consistency achieved through efforts made in regional science and transportation studies. This is not the place to review this development in depth and the reader wishing to pursue this is referred to the reviews by Carrothers (1956), Isard (1960), Olsson (1965) and Styles (1968). Instead, we will outline the most recent stage in their development — their derivation from first principles by Wilson (e.g. Wilson, 1970).

Wilson's work has apparently strengthened the theoretical basis of gravity models considerably by showing that they can be derived from principles of statistical mechanics and information theory. This approach has enabled other models to be developed which can handle more complex situations (e.g. disaggregated populations) and has rendered the heavily criticized Newtonian analogy redundant. Therefore, the term 'gravity model', although still in usage in regional science has become a misnomer and is sometimes replaced by 'spatial interaction model'. The former term will be retained here because of its continued popularity and because the latter term is misleading as there are a large number of spatial interaction models which do not belong to the entropy-maximizing type, e.g. diffusion models.

Using the procedure of entropy-maximization Wilson derived several types of models, each one appropriate to a different context and termed by Wilson 'a family of spatial interaction models' (Wilson, 1971). For a spatial system of zones we may have certain forms of information about spatial interaction within the system. For example, there may be independent estimates of the origins (O_i) and destinations (D_j) which can be used as constraints.

$$\sum_j T_{ij} = O_i \tag{3.1.}$$

$$\sum_i T_{ij} = D_j \tag{3.2.}$$

A third constraint is also required to define the total expenditure on travel

$$\sum_i \sum_j T_{ij} c_{ij} = C \tag{3.3.}$$

where T_{ij} are trips from zone i to j; O_i are trip origins in i, and D_j are trip destinations in j; c_{ij} is travel cost between i and j; C is total expenditure on travel.

Given this limited amount of information, for even a small population, there are millions of different ways each individual in each origin zone could be assigned to individual destinations in each destination zone. These assignments are known as 'micro-states'. Several different micro-states could give rise to the same 'macro-state' — which tells us simply how many individuals travel between each origin-destination pair. The entropy-maximizing procedure (which is also a probability-maximizing procedure) assumes that the most probable macro-state is that which maximizes the number of different ways of occurring (micro-states), subject to the above constraint equations (3.1; 3.2; 3.3.), and estimates this macro-state. (The reader is referred to Wilson, 1970, for mathematical proofs.)

The three most widely used members of the 'family of spatial interaction or gravity models' are

(1)   the production-attraction constrained model;
(2)   the production-constrained model;
(3)   the attraction-constrained model.

(1) is sometimes termed the 'doubly-constrained' model and (2) and (3), 'singly-constrained' models.

(1) *The Production-Attraction-Constrained Gravity Model.* All three constraints are operative. Given independent estimates of the O_i's and D_j's, the objective is to generate the trip distribution.

$$T_{ij} = A_i B_j O_i D_j \exp(^{-\beta c_{ij}}) \tag{3.4.}$$

where,

$$A_i = [\sum_j B_j D_j \exp(^{-\beta c_{ij}})]^{-1} \tag{3.5.}$$

iterate

$$B_j = [\sum_i A_i O_i \exp(^{-\beta c_{ij}})]^{-1} \tag{3.6.}$$

A_i and B_j are 'balancing factors' (see Wilson, 1970), and β is a parameter.

(2) *The Production-Constrained Gravity Model.* If the constraint on destinations is dropped (eq 3.2), the model becomes 'production-constrained'. Given an independent estimate of the O_i (trip producers) plus the c_{ij} matrix and an index X_j representing the intrinsic attractiveness of zone j, the most probable distribution of trips *and* of trip destinations can be estimated. Therefore, this can be considered a *location* model.

$$T_{ij} = A_i O_i X_j \exp(^{-\beta c_{ij}}) \tag{3.7.}$$

where,

$$A_i = [\sum_j X_j \exp(^{-\beta c_{ij}})]^{-1} \tag{3.8.}$$

This can also be written,

$$T_{ij} = \frac{O_i X_j \exp(-\beta c_{ij})}{\sum_j X_j \exp(-\beta c_{ij})} \qquad (3.9.)$$

By summing the T_{ij} over i, estimates of trip destinations D_j can be obtained. The total number of trips leaving each zone is completely determined in this model, and the X_j can only influence, but not fully determine the destinations. The X_j are sometimes termed 'competition factors' as they can be interpreted as representing the competing attractions of different zones for trips.

(3) *The Attraction-Constrained Gravity Model.* This is simply the mirror opposite of the production-constrained model. Trip destinations are given, and the object is to forecast trip origins.

$$T_{ij} = \frac{D_j W_i \exp(-\beta c_{ij})}{\sum_i W_i \exp(-\beta c_{ij})} \qquad (3.10.)$$

W_i is the intrinsic attractiveness of zone i for location of trip origins. The location of origins is found by summing the T_{ij} over j.

From the point of view of the entropy-maximizing derivation of these models, the singly-constrained models (2) and (3) differ from the doubly-constrained model (1) only by the dropping of one constraint, which means that we have less information restricting the range of possible outcomes. However, the reader should note, in anticipation of criticisms to follow, that the singly-constrained models' causal structures are markedly different from that of the doubly-constrained model. In the latter, the use of independent estimates of both trip ends and the associated constraints implies that they are independent of the trip distribution, which, conversely, is contingent upon these determining relations, whereas in the singly-constrained models, the location of the trip destinations is largely dependent on the trip distribution.

3.3. METHODS OF CRITICIZING MATHEMATICAL MODELS

There are almost certainly large differences of opinion amongst regional scientists regarding the nature of legitimate forms of criticism of mathematical models. As the types of criticism adopted here are somewhat unorthodox, some justification is required.

Firstly, it is argued that the types of criticism should be chosen according to the *manner* in which models have been presented, and the significance which has been conferred upon them by their advocates. The implicit criteria of validity which seem to be dominant in the literature on entropy-maximizing models do not extend much beyond the minimal requirement of mathematical consistency. Nevertheless, this extraordinarily voluminous literature often (perhaps unwittingly) gives the impression that the entropy-maximizing procedure provides a near-foolproof method of constructing models.[1] The analyst (or 'entropy-maximizer') should formulate all the information available about a system of interest in terms of constraints on its behaviour, and then find the most probable macro-state of the system (e.g. trip distribution) subject to these constraints. It has been contended that this technique forces the analyst to specify the model unambiguously and consistently, for, provided that the constraints contain all known information, the model will be the most impartial one with respect to that information. However, mathematical consistency is no guarantee of theoretical consistency, for the latter also depends on the assumptions and the type of 'abstraction' used, and, in this context, the way in which constraints are specified. By 'type or mode of abstraction' we refer to the crucial issue of choice of variables, the definition of the system of interest, the choices made regarding exclusion of certain phenomena which are considered to be irrelevant, and above all, the interpretation and definition of the included phenomena.

Therefore, in the following critique, there is no argument whatsoever about mathematical consistency, and instead we concentrate on the meaning of the assumptions of gravity models. The mathematicians may protest that if there is no challenge to their mathematics there is no real challenge to the validity of their models, for the criticisms will be no more than subjective interpretations. However, that is exactly the status of the assumptions used in any model, and the employment of a mathematical technique cannot possibly make them objective. We are not criticizing a piece of algebra, we are criticizing a model which purports to describe, and in some cases predict, the state of a part of the world.[2]

Critical interpretation of mathematical models is regarded as essential for four main reasons.

(1) As Feyerabend (1975, p. 76) argues, to eliminate interpretations is to eliminate the ability to think and to perceive. To try to understand a model without these interpretations would leave us completely disoriented, we could not even start the business of science.

(2) It is generally the hidden assumptions, the hidden ambiguities in the definition of variables which are the most stubborn and insidious, as the example of the economic base mechanism showed.

(3) It must always be remembered that

In life . . . . we use mathematical propositions *only* in order to infer from propositions which do not belong to mathematics to others which equally do not belong to mathematics. (Wittgenstein, quoted in Dobb, 1973).

The use of mathematical models involves three difficult stages of translation between ordinary verbal language and mathematical language.

(a) We have to find appropriate ways of translating our selected data (as defined by some theory) into algebra when we construct a model, e.g. we may define a certain kind of spatial interaction as 'T'. This translation process is by no means as straightforward as it might at first appear.

(b) There is the problem of checking whether the mathematical operations performed on the variables, adequately correspond to real world processes, e.g. if trips are *simultaneously* allocated across all destinations and origins in the model, does it matter if the real world allocation process is sequential?

(c) There are difficulties in translating the output of the model back into interpretable statements about the real world, e.g. how do we attach meaning to a forecast which is undated?

(4) The third justification for critical interpretation is simply, that in terms of scientific progress, falsification may be a more constructive activity than the more normal activities of replication and refinement of existing models. Accordingly, methodologies which take a complacent attitude towards assumptions and interpretation (e.g. 'instrumentalism' which allows any assumption, and only requires that the model 'fits' reality) are rejected as an invitation to bad science. Therefore, not only the models themselves but also the methodological premises of the model-builders are under attack.

3.4. TOWARDS THE REFUTATION OF GRAVITY/ENTROPY-MAXIMIZING MODELS

The criticisms are presented in the form of a list, although the reader will note interconnections and overlap among the separate points. Some of the points may already be familiar, while others may seem curious and obscure from the point of view of the existing paradigm (e.g. concerning the assumption of absolute space), but from the point of view of our alternative paradigm, they are central, and their relevance should become clearer when the reinforcements of the evidence in later chapters is encountered.

3.4.1. *Fixed Expenditure on Travel and Separation of Trip Generation and Distribution*

Both doubly- and singly-constrained gravity models assume a fixed amount of expenditure on travel and therefore an inelastic demand for travel. Consequently, they give no indication of the effects of changes in travel costs on the overall amount of travel in the system. This is one of the reasons why a gravity model which is calibrated to a base-year and then used for prediction merely extrapolates the *status quo* — both in process terms (travel costs) and spatial terms (see below 3.4.7.).

This leads us to one of the most long-standing problems of gravity models, and one which the entropy-maximizing derivation has done nothing to mitigate — namely, the artificial separation of trip generation and trip distribution, which accounts for the fixed travel cost assumption. Since the travel cost for the system is fixed, the model implicitly assumes that the efficiency of the spatial organization of the city or region makes absolutely no difference to the overall level of activity. Needless to say, if this were really true, there would be little point in regional analysis! The use of the models which make this assumption in planning must surely be one of the outstanding contradictions of regional science. For example, in the Lowry model, changes in spatial organization can only make a difference to the overall activity levels of the region if there is a transfer of activities to any external zone(s) which may be defined.

Singly-constrained location models have the unfortunate characteristic of predicting changes in trip-end distributions which would imply the violation of the *ceteris paribus* assumption (of fixed travel cost) upon which they are based. In a properly constituted location model there should be feedback from changes in location patterns and travel costs to changes in the *amount* of traffic generated and the *amount* of further activities located.

3.4.2. The Mode of Abstraction Used in Gravity Models

The last point may be enlarged and looked at from the viewpoint of the 'mode of abstraction' used in gravity models. All models, by definition, abstract from reality. The modelling problems is to choose the most enlightening form of abstraction. It is considered that the form of abstraction on which gravity models are based is unhelpful. By arbitrarily separating trip generation and trip distribution, gravity models fail to specify the essential links between the two. They abstract from the social and economic relations which determine the supply and demand for travel. As many writers have observed (Caruso and Palm, 1973; Curry, 1972; Hansen, 1972; Paelinck, 1973; Sack, 1973), gravity models use a *posterior form of analysis*. The origin and destination constraints from which the models are derived are market *outputs*, and *not* market *determinants* (Kirwan and Martin, 1971). As such, these *ex post* constraints are nothing more than tautologies or arithmetical truisms which may make for mathematical consistency, but which hide the *ex ante* determinants of behaviour. The number of trips originating in zone *i* equals the number of trip origins in zone *i*. Therefore, gravity models use a concept of revealed preference, which renders them incapable of revealing those potential or unrealized demands for travel which do not appear in the trip data to which they are fitted.

> Most of the models base generation . . . . on regression analysis; such statistical formulae reflect the actual traveller's behaviour without setting out the multiple constraints from which they are derived; economical, psychological, cultural and social. (Le Boulanger, 1971, p. 116).

One might expect that singly-constrained location models would supply the determinants of travel for a doubly-constrained traffic model, but this is not so because location gravity models are also posterior forms of analysis based on the same type of tautological *ex post* constraints. In order to explain the determinants of trip behaviour, we must choose a type of abstraction which refers, e.g. to the buyer's motivation and circumstances in choosing a house and car (Le Boulanger, 1971, p. 115).

The entropy-maximizing procedure is supposed to allow us to include all relevant information in constraint form, but behavioural constraints cannot usefully be specified in the *ex post* form that gravity models demand. Moreover, important spatial constraints are omitted, relating to the effect of use of a bounded area, of spatial autocorrelation in origins and destinations, and of use of points as surrogates for areas in the definition of zones:

> . . . it is difficult to believe that distance could be the only relevant spatial measure of flows and therefore information must be being thrown away i.e. spatial constraints should be added. (Curry, 1972, p. 135).

Because so many constraints are omitted, and because those that are included are in *ex post* form, gravity models falsely represent the journey-to-work as an area of behaviour in which there is great freedom of choice. The doubly-constrained model can be interpreted as assuming that all workers have access to all jobs so that when the distribution of jobs changes, they can all adjust their trip-making behaviour and choice instantaneously and in a way consistent with the parameters of the model. Workers do of course, in most cases choose their workplace and home but this does not mean they have complete freedom of choice.[3]

Once workers have got their jobs and homes, their journey-to-work trips should be treated as fixed and compulsory. Journey-to-work trips are *contingent*[4] upon location – the costs of travel may intervene at the stage of choice of location along with a large number of other constraints, but once the job and home locations are fixed, the trip-making behaviour is also fixed and therefore, in an important sense, a distance 'factor' is *redundant* in a behavioural explanation of *ex post* journey-to-work patterns.

Gravity models ignore the contingent nature of travel, by abstracting trip distribution from its determining social, economic and spatial relations, and by giving it a separate existence as if it represented the essence of reality instead of one contingent facet of reality.[5] This also emphasizes the reversal of causality encountered when switching from a traffic model to a location model; the contingent relations of the former become the determining relations of the latter.

As Le Boulanger (1971) advocates, when looking at the socio-economic determinants, we should distinguish between compulsory and optional trip-making behaviour. The former's explanation may include travel costs and time costs at the stage of choice of location of trip ends, while the latter may include it in the stage of trip distribution as well. However, for many travel purposes, including shopping, travel is optional only over a very short period, and over a longer period – say several months – it could be regarded as compulsory and inelastic with respect to travel costs.[6]

3.4.3. Dynamic and Static Interpretations of Gravity Models

Further implications of the contingent nature of journey-to-work trips for spatial interaction modelling become apparent when we compare static and dynamic interpretations of gravity models. For example, in a doubly-constrained journey-to-work model, there is an implicit assumption of instantaneous equilibrium such that *all* that is required to explain a trip distribution at time t is the distribution of homes and jobs at the time t. A clear understanding of the error of this assumption in the journey-to-work context is essential for providing a basis for an alternative model. Jobs and homes are taken up over a period of time, and since journey-to-work trips are compulsory, regular, and tied to these origins and destinations for considerable periods of time, the actual trip distribution at time t in fact represents many *past* location decisions. While the assumption that the number of work-trip origins in a residential zone is equal to the number of trips made from that zone cannot fail to be true, it is hard to see why, in a purely static context, workers should conveniently distribute themselves in such a way as to ensure that each job destination zone receives exactly the same number of trip-ends as it has jobs. Static, *ex post* models have to produce this result without specifying the dynamic process by which it came into being. This accounts for the necessity of using the clumsy device of iterating the A_i and B_j terms in a doubly-constrained model in order to satisfy the constraints. In Curry's words, this procedure

> . . . is intended to take account of all the problems of the relative spatial distribution of jobs and homes. Thus all the difficult and interesting questions raised by the geography of the area are loaded on to a suspect calibration procedure'. (Curry, 1972, p. 135).

The trip distribution is time-dependent and *not* time-independent as is usually assumed. As Piaget says in a more general context:

> . . . final states illuminate the process from which they result as much as that process is necessary to the development of those states. (Piaget, 1973, p. 56).

Therefore, in order to explain a trip distribution we have to explain how the job and residential locations of the people making those trips came into being in the time periods previous to t, and in so doing we begin to specify the social relations governing trip distribution.

3.4.4. The Implicit Assumption of Absolute Space

The distance terms $(\exp(-\beta c_{ij}))$ in the models can be interpreted as representing an implicit assumption of absolute space. They imply that trip frequency declines in an absolute (empty) space as a function of distance, and independently of objects located in space. Some users of gravity models would probably deny that they are assuming space to be absolute, and would argue that they are taking the distance-decay of trips as nothing more than an empirical regularity. This argument seems quite acceptable as long as it is restricted to the *a posteriori* analysis of *ex post* spatial interactions. However, as soon as we represent the distance-decay effect as a distance term in a gravity model which can be used in an *a priori* manner to generate the locational pattern of trip-ends, as is the case in singly-constrained models, then absolute space connotations become harder to resist for it appears that trip lengths have some independent, determining role and meaning.

Such is the weight of philosophical evidence against the possibility of absolute space, that its (witting or unwitting) use in spatial interaction modelling should be suspected. Firstly, there can be no such thing as empty space 'for what is empty is nothing, and what is nothing cannot be' (Blaut, 1961). Furthermore, the distance term cannot be held to represent the 'friction of distance' as this is non-existent — there can only be coefficients of friction for particular *substances*, and they are only capable of empirical observation (Sack, 1973).

The only sound concept of space is that of 'relative' or 'relational' space,[7] which is actually *defined* by the interactions and physical elements themselves. This concept recognizes that there can be no content without form, and no form without content and that distance must ideally be measured in terms of process activity (Harvey, 1969, p. 210). Whereas, as Sack (1973) shows, the concept of absolute space does not even qualify as a meaningful concept because it fails to specify relevant substance referents (since it refers to emptiness and nothingness), the concept of relative space allows us to make testable hypotheses about the space economy because it is defined by the substance terms capable of empirical observation.

Isard (1972), gives a more concrete example of the necessity of using a concept of relative space:

> In regional science we well know that the significance (employment- and income-generating capability) of an industry mass (say an integrated iron and steel works) is affected by the geometry of the space-time as reflected at the point at which it is located, and in turn affects the geometry of social, economic and political space-time. This is in keeping with that traditional agglomeration thinking of economics and regional science which we have never been able to incorporate in a satisfactory theory.

and, more formally:

> ... the properties of any mass present at any given point of space-time are affected by the geometry of that space-time and simultaneously affect that geometry. (Isard, 1972, p. 150).

Thus, what at first might seem to be a minor philosophical debating point, has in fact great relevance for the understanding of the space-economy.[8]

3.4.5. *The Implicit Concept of Relative Space*

Gravity models can also be interpreted as containing a partial concept of relative space which is implicit in the accounting constraints on origins and destinations (3.1.) and (3.2.). These 'tie' all trips to origins and destinations, so that in the doubly-constrained model there are no trips ending or beginning without any identified destinations or origins. Thus the spatial interaction is in one sense modelled in terms *relative to*, and contingent upon, the map pattern of origins and destinations. This interaction, however, is modified by the subsidiary concept of absolute space, so that within the 'relative space constraints', interaction is also influenced by the so-called 'friction of distance', or travel cost. Nevertheless, for any given set of origins and destinations, one can meet the constraints exactly using very different distance (β) parameters (Curry, 1972, p. 132).

The important point is that the absolute and relative space concepts are quite incompatible and their incompatibility is probably an underlying reason for many of the problems of gravity models, which still remain in the form of the necessity of using an iterative solution for the A_i and B_j terms.

The accounting constraints (3.1.) and (3.2.) in the doubly-constrained model are *inputs* which have to be satisfied, but the value of the overall travel cost constraint C is an *output* of the model which is determined from the calibration process: it is fitted, not predetermined. This fact in itself suggests that it is a hopeless task to try to treat the effect of distance or travel cost on interaction as separable from the effect of map pattern constraints. If the distance decay term in the model is a negative exponential, there is no guarantee that the predicted trip distribution will be negative exponential because of the interference of the map pattern constraints (Curry, 1972, p. 136). For example, one could imagine the case of a spatial system in which the majority of workers lived in a large town but worked mostly in a small, compact industrial centre at some distance from the town. In such a case, journey-to-work trip frequency would *increase* with distance up to a point.

Coincidence of the relative space (interaction patterns 'purely' due to the map pattern of origins and destinations) and absolute space (interaction patterns 'purely' due to the 'friction of distance') could only occur in an unbounded, isotropic region having a regular distribution of an undifferentiated set of origins and destinations (Curry, 1972, p. 132).

3.4.6. The Interference of Spatial Autocorrelation

Regardless of whether physical distance or travel cost is a constraint on interaction, as long as there is spatial autocorrelation in the origins and destinations, the calibration process will produce a value for the parameter in the distance-cost term (Curry, p. 132). It would only be in the unlikely event of zero autocorrelation that the β parameter could be read directly as an unambiguous index of the difficulty of travel between origins and destinations. Therefore, because of map pattern interference and the lack of a substantive meaning for the β parameter, any calibration for a real world region is specific to the particular relative distribution of origins and destinations (Curry, 1972, p. 132). In dealing with the highly autocorrelated spatial systems characteristic of urban and intra-urban situations, it is clear that there will be considerable confounding of the effects of distance friction (if there could be such a thing) and map pattern, although, as Cliff *et al*. (1974) show, at the inter-urban scale, the problem is likely to be much less serious.

However, in the case of *urban development* models, the problem has another aspect, in that the relative contributions of the map pattern effect and the 'gravity' effect in determining the spatial interaction, are almost certain to change during any phase of urban physical expansion. For example, Fig. 3.1 represents an urban area in which most jobs, J, are concentrated in the

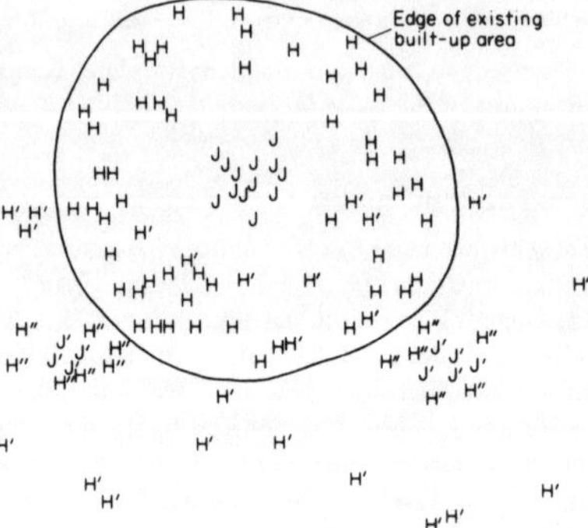

FIG. 3.1. Changes in average trip length during urban
expansion.

centre and most workers' homes H lie towards the periphery of the urban area, giving rise to long journey-to-work trips. If new jobs are created J' outside the urban area, a gravity model fitted to the original situation would tend to locate new workers' home H' at similar long distances from these jobs, although this tendency may be modified slightly by the influence of intrinsic attractiveness terminal descriptors in the model. However, given the free-standing position of J', H' would be a more probable location for, as would not be the case within the built-up area, there would be few physical constraints to separate them.[9] In these circumstances it would seem likely that the contribution of the map pattern effect would weaken relative to the 'gravity' effect, and so the original value of the β parameter would cease to apply to the new situation, if the model were recalibrated.

3.4.7. Preliminary Conclusions from the Critique

Summarizing this critique, we can say that gravity models fail to capture the complex but essential dialectic of location and interaction, because they ignore too many of the essential qualities of the universals of space, time and process. The concepts of location and spatial interaction have obvious temporal connotations, and the use of static models may deny us the possibility of capturing their interrelation. At any one time spatial interaction is determined by, and operates within, the constraints of the relative locations of people, organizations and places. Decisions regarding location of a new activity are made not only with respect to existing patterns of location and spatial interaction, but also with respect to future patterns of interaction which will result from the location of this activity.[10] To collapse this complex interrelationship into a single point in time is to obfuscate both location and spatial interaction.

The reader may have already noticed some parallels with the critique of the Lowry model's economic base submodel. The arguments under 3.4.6 can be interpreted as an identification error caused by the extrapolation of *ex post* spatial relations to new locational patterns, similar to the invalid extrapolation of *ex post* demand and supply relations in the labour market. Also, the singly-constrained gravity models are *demand-oriented* models – demands for trip-ends creates its own supply perfectly and instantly. There will be many more such parallels in the subsequent chapters, and their synthesis will be left till Chapter 6.

As was noted before, although the criticisms of gravity models have been presented as a list of separate points, they overlap considerably; indeed it is a crucial part of the argument that is being developed, that the points are interconnected, for if they are, then we can no longer regard each one as an isolated technical problem capable of eventual solution within the existing conceptual framework. For example, as will be shown later, the spatial autocorrelation 'problem' is partly created by an incorrect representation of *temporal* sequences, and economic *processes*, so that we cannot expect to resolve the 'technical problems' without changing the whole 'mode of abstraction' that we use in urban modelling.

However, before this integration of these criticisms can be achieved in such a way as to show that there are *necessary* connections between them, we must examine some related models for similar faults in order to demonstrate their universality. These related models are the intervening-opportunities model (Section 3.5), Curry's model (Section 3.6), models based on utility theory (Section 3.7) and disaggregated residential location models (Section 3.8).

3.5. THE INTERVENING-OPPORTUNITIES MODEL

The intervening-opportunities model, originally developed by Stouffler (1940), is similar to the gravity model, though less widely used. The chief difference is that it uses an ordinal measure of distance. For each zone, destination opportunities are ranked in terms of distance away from the zone, and interaction is inversely proportional to the cumulated points (substitutable places) encountered along a sequence (Sack, 1973, p. 22; Wilson, 1970, p. 151; Curry, 1972, p. 133). As Sack shows, although there is no explicit 'friction-of-distance' term in the model, it nevertheless retains an implicit assumption of absolute space, for it fails to specify why such a ranking of opportunities should be relevant in *process* terms. We find that the same points listed above for gravity models, apply in slightly modified form to the intervening-opportunities model, with the most clear problems again arising out of the collapsing of the sequential relations between location and spatial interaction, which account for the evolution of the present trip distribution, into a single point in time.

3.6. CURRY'S MODEL

Curry's paper 'A spatial analysis of gravity flows' (1972), is perhaps the most profound challenge to gravity models in the literature. Curry shows how gravity models confuse spatial effects created by 'distance' (the so-called 'gravity effect') with those created by spatial autocorrelation of origins and destinations (the 'map pattern effect'). By formally separating out these effects in his alternative model, Curry is able to restore linearity and obviate the necessity for an iterative solution to the map pattern constraints (i.e. iterating the A_i and B_j in eqs. (3.5. and 3.6.)). Curry's model combines the location of trip-ends through time with trip distribution in such a way that not only does origin and destination location determine travel patterns, but existing travel patterns also influence future trip-end location. It therefore attempts to specify the sequential relations between location and spatial interaction which we found were absent in the gravity models. It distinguishes clearly between spatial interaction according to *preference* (willingness and ability to travel) and spatial interaction according to *need* (the actual existing map pattern of origins and destinations), where the gravity model only confounds the two. Curry made an important theoretical advance in proposing a dynamic model of the *evolution* of patterns of spatial interaction, but, as we shall see in Chapter 4, while the introduction of time enabled the importance of 'gravity' to be reduced, he was unable to banish the absolute space 'concept' completely, owing to a mis-specification of *process*. Curry's concept of 'gravity' is used to account for the residual element of travel which would still occur even in the event of zero autocorrelation of origins and destinations. Thus while Curry usefully limits its domain, he still *retains* an implicit assumption of absolute space in his model, where trip-lengths are determined by physical distance.

However, Curry's abstruse critique and alternative model has some curiously paradoxical, but very important aspects. In one sense, Curry heightened awareness of the conflict of relative and absolute space in the gravity model, insofar as trips, as a function of physical distance (absolute space) have to be tied to (and are therefore relative to), the map pattern (relative space). And yet, from the point of view of the map pattern of origins and destinations itself, we must note that this is *described* in terms of spatial autocorrelation which uses physical distance as its measure — that is, it is described in absolute space terms. Therefore, the paradox is that Curry only managed to demonstrate the shortcomings of one type of absolute space 'concept' — the 'gravity effect', by using another absolute space 'concept' — spatial autocorrelation, but which nevertheless, when interpreted in the context of the gravity model, has important relative space implications. Thus, while Curry succeeded in revealing some of the technical problems and internal contradictions of gravity models, he did so on the same ground of absolute space. Gravity models and Curry's models are both 'spatial separatist'[11] models (although Curry's model is by far the more sophisticated in that it uses a wider range of 'spatial concepts', e.g. spatial moving averages) and as such, they abstract almost completely from the very socio-economic processes which create the spatial distributions that they describe.

In our alternative approach described in Chapter 4 we show that what Curry calls the 'gravity effect' can be explained entirely in substance terms by examining the social relations and temporal evolution of the spatial interaction explicitly. Curry, does however, hint rather enigmatically that '(p)erhaps gravity as such does not deserve such an extensive discussion . . . . ' (1972, p. 146).

Before going on to propose our alternative approach, models based on utility theory and disaggregated models will be examined in similar fashion, for in some cases, these have been developed in order to replace the abstractions of the social physics approach by more behavioural, process-oriented models, but nevertheless, they can be shown to share the same types of error.

3.7. UTILITY THEORY AND GRAVITY MODELS

Most models of urban and regional systems produced to date have been aggregate, descriptive models of 'macro-states'. Recently, regional scientists have begun to explore the possibilities of disaggregating these models and relating them to theories of micro-economic

behaviour. Interest has focused mainly upon utility theory and the development of a
utility-maximizing derivation of aggregate urban models in the hope of giving the latter a
sounder behavioural basis.

Although utility is becoming very fashionable in regional science, its users almost invariably
neglect to explain what utility is — its relevance is taken for granted. Utility functions are
simply defined algebraically — U is utility, and utility is U and that is all there is to the matter.
If we look at definitions of utility given in standard economics textbooks, it becomes more
obvious why urban model-builders are reticent about explaining its meaning. For example,
Lancaster (1969), writes:

> The 'something' that goods produce or give rise to is usually called utility. A given collection of goods is
> associated with a certain level of utility. 'Utility' is something such that more of it is always desirable, so a
> collection with *higher* utility is *preferred*, collections with the *same* utility are indifferent . . . . For a
> utility function, we can measure inputs but *we cannot measure output* which is a subjective 'something'
> felt only by the particular consumer. Thus a utility function is not only *subjective* (the relationship will
> differ from consumer to consumer), but it is not observable.[12] (Lancaster, 1969, p. 196).

and Cole (1973) is no more illuminating:

> We shall resolutely refuse to define utility as 'happiness' 'pleasure', 'satisfaction', or, most certainly as
> 'usefulness'. Utility is simply an index that increases whenever his (the consumer's) sense of well-being has
> increased as a result of making some thing, or collection of things, his own. (Cole, 1973, p. 35).

It is hard to believe that this is the stuff of which economic 'science' is made, but that is the
case. Fortunately, Joan Robinson offers us some good sense and banishes utility to the realms
of economic theology:

> *Utility* is a metaphysical concept of impregnable circularity; *utility* is the quality in commodities that
> makes individuals want to buy them and the fact that individuals want to buy commodities shows that
> they have *utility*. (Robinson, 1962, p. 48).

Not surprisingly, such a flimsy concept has no empirical status and the statement that
consumers maximize their utility is one of the many unverifiable propositions of equilibrium
economics (Kaldor, 1972, p. 1238). When set out in a diagram or equation, utility purports to
be a quantity, and yet it is not measurable against any independent scale. It is unhelpful to
know that an individual consumes good, x, up to the point where its marginal utility is equal to
its price, because price is the measure of marginal utility. Furthermore, none of the modern
refinements of this empty, tautologous concept has done anything to give it any substance
(Robinson, 1962, p. 50), and this applies to Strotz's 'utility trees', and Evans' valuations of the
utility of time, and Lancaster's attempt to replace goods by 'characteristics' as the object of
preference or utility.

Preferences are assumed to be expressed adequately in market outcomes: this is Samuelson's
popular concept of 'revealed preference', which, as Harvey (1973, p. 157), Robinson and
Eatwell (1973, p. 202), and Kornai (1971, p. 147) and many others have noted, is distinctly
unrevealing because it merely says that people behave as they behave. As Dobb (1937) shows,
this concept implies that economic desires are equal to satisfactions and, in temporal terms,
that *ex ante* demand is fully realized in *ex post* demand.

Kornai (1971, p. 147), finds preference theory and utility theory simply unnecessary.
Kornai expects a preference model to have the structure:

$$\text{Explanatory Factors} \rightarrow \text{Preference Ordering} \rightarrow \text{Decisions}$$

The intermediate state of examining preference ordering is redundent: but even if we allow
preference ordering to be retained, preference theory and utility theory invert and confuse the
whole problem, because they derive preferences from *ex post* decisions, and not vice versa.
Usually the set of 'explanatory factors' used to rationalize the revealed preferences is
incomplete and heavily biased towards demand-side factors, so that the consumer is
misrepresented as 'sovereign' and supply takes on a completely passive role. As long as supply is
not infinitely elastic, the translation of 'desires' into 'satisfactions' is not likely to be linear and
straightforward (Dobb, 1937, p. 63). The relationship between demand-side explanatory factors
and market outcomes is continually changed by the market conditions which they meet, in the
shape of prices, supply, and market information. When we take these factors into account it is

easily seen that we have little reason for assuming that preference scales are the creators rather than the creatures of market price (Dobb, 1937, pp. 71–72). This, of course, is another example of an identification error (see above, Section 2.2).

The practice of using procedures of statistical inference to 'estimate' the explanatory factors is not an adequate substitute for empirical research and a properly constituted theory of market behaviour. Without such a basis, the demand schedules of individuals cannot be conceived to rest upon anything ultimate or fundamental, and therefore they cannot provide a basis for prediction.

Clarkson (1963), finds that utility theory and the theory of demand cannot belong to empirical science because they fail to conform to accepted positivist models of scientific explanation:

> Unless preference orderings can be established prior to and independently of the collection of data, it is meaningless to examine the data with the hope of both establishing the preference orderings and of using these orderings for an empirical test of the 'ideal' laws. (i.e. of utility maximization). (Clarkson, 1973, p. 77).

(However, it must be noted that some exercises in utility theory have used independent attitude or preference surveys to establish people's *ex ante* evaluations of goods, and accordingly these are exempted from these criticisms as they break the revealed preference circularity and hence are testable.)

The deficiencies of gravity models and utility theory are strikingly similar. When used for prediction, both extrapolate the *status quo*, with no means of showing how the relationships might change. In the same way that the problem of trip distribution is cut off from its determining spatial, and socio-economic relations in gravity models as Curry and Le Boulanger emphasized, in utility theory, *ex post* economic behaviour is examined in abstraction from its determinants of human needs and supply conditions.

These shared characteristics of gravity models and utility theory can be illustrated very clearly by an example similar to that used in Fig. 3.1 to demonstrate how map pattern and 'gravity effects' change during urban expansion.

Imagine a gravity model of retail location in a town which is fitted to an existing distribution of shops and homes. A number of people may be found to be living on top of, or at least very close to, shops. Considering the situation in isolation, it might be inferred that these people have chosen to live there in order to be close to the shops. This inference might be reinforced if we then used a gravity location model to forecast the relative spatial distributions of some given increments of population and shops for it would be calibrated to the existing situation, and therefore would stipulate that the new people would again locate at high density close to the shops. Of course, the inference is unwarranted because the proximity of the homes and shops may be quite coincidental and fortuitous or may be a result of quite different locational influences.

A utility maximizing model of the same situation would fall into exactly the same category of trap, only more heavily because of its explicit assumption that the locational pattern revealed the locational preferences of the individuals. Therefore, we can consider the influence of *'map pattern constraints'* on the journey-to-work trip distribution (after Curry), to be directly equivalent to the influence of the *'explanatory factors'* on revealed preferences for shopping trips (after Dobb and Kornai). Indeed, we can say that the map pattern is the *spatial expression* of the determining socio-economic relations of the revealed preferences for trips. Both gravity and utility-maximizing models abstract the *contingent* spatial and exchange relations from the very contexts and *determining relations* which give rise to them, and treat them in an isolation which excludes the possibility of proper explanation. As a result both models can only be descriptive rather than explanatory and while they may be fitted with reasonable success, they do not offer worthwhile testable explanatory hypotheses.

Moreover, this shows that although such models might refer to travel *costs* and not *distance*, and hence seem to escape the absolute space implications described above, their faults, though superficially 'economic' rather than 'spatial' are structurally identical.[13]

There is, of course, nothing wrong with examining *ex post* market relations, provided it is realized that the insights gained from such studies are very limited. However, such studies do not gain anything through being related to the rationalizations of utility theory: they can stand up on their own (Kornai, 1971, p. 258; Lancaster, 1969, p. 197). This is equally true in the context of urban modelling. The second of the following pairs of equations adds nothing to the information supplied by the first:

$$P_{ij} = \frac{T_{ij}}{\sum_i \sum_j T_{ij}} \qquad (3.11.)$$

$$P_{ij} = \frac{U_{ij}}{\sum_i \sum_j U_{ij}} \qquad (3.12.)$$

where P_{ij} is the probability of trips from i to j, and U_{ij} is the utility of trips from i to j as revealed *ex post*. Some model-builders do acknowledge this (e.g. see Wilson, 1970a, p. 105; and Apps, 1971, 5n), but the latter justifies the retention of utility theory on the grounds that it 'provides a connecting base to classical [14] economic theory'. As we have seen, this base is a tautology. Regional scientists are correct in thinking that utility theory and gravity models are compatible: exactly, *they share the same defective mode of abstraction.*

3.8. DISAGGREGATED RESIDENTIAL LOCATION MODELS

It is worthwhile to extend the critique to the disaggregated location models developed by Wilson (1970). These models are of interest because it is considered that they compound the same type of deficiencies noted above, and reveal them much more clearly because of their more explicit behavioural interpretation and their more stringent calibration requirements.

Disaggregated models were first developed by Wilson (1970, p. 77), using the entropy-maximizing procedure. The population is split into different income groups, different wage levels by location, different types of house, and different prices of houses by location. Assuming each household has only one worker, the following variables are defined.[15]

T_{ij}^{kw} — workers of wage w in zone j living in zone i in type k houses.

H_i^k — houses in zone i of type k.

E_j^w jobs in zone j offering wage w.

T_{ij}^{kw} must satisfy the following constraints:

$$\sum_j \sum_w T_{ij}^{kw} = H_i^k \qquad (3.13.)$$

$$\sum_i \sum_k T_{ij}^{kw} = E_j^w \qquad (3.14.)$$

$$\sum_i \sum_j \sum_k T_{ij}^{kw} c_{ij} = C^w \qquad (3.15.)$$

Although constraints (3.13.) and (3.14.) are used to derive the model, they refer to *ex post* market outputs and the value of C^w in (3.15.) is an output of the calibration process. In this respect they do not differ from elementary aggregate gravity models.

Other constraints are also introduced to make sure that workers will, within limits, live in houses they can afford. Let:

p_i^k be the price of type k house in zone i;

q^w be the average percentage of income (after transport costs have been deducted) which a member of income group w spends on housing; and

c_{ij} be that component of the usual *generalized* journey-to-work cost c_{ij}, which is the actual money paid.

Again these are empirically derived market outputs.

In order to show the *spread* of actual expenditure around the mean and to relate this to the house price variable, $p_i^{\,k}$, the following constraint is introduced.

$$\sum_i \sum_j \sum_k T_{ij}^{kw}\,[p_i^{\,k} - q^w(w - c'_{ij})]^2 = \sigma^{w\,2} \qquad (3.16.)$$

where $\sigma^{w\,2}$ is the variance of the normal distribution for income group w.[16]

The model which Wilson derives from these constraints is:

$$T_{ij}^{kw} = A_i^{\,k} B_j^{\,w} H_i^{\,k} E_j^{\,w}\,\exp(-\beta^w c_{ij})\,\exp\{-\mu^w\,[p_i^{\,k} - q^w(w - c'_{ij})]^2\} \qquad (3.17.)$$

where,

$$A_i^{\,k} = (\sum_j \sum_w B_j^{\,w} E_j^{\,w}\,\exp(-\beta^w c_{ij})\,\exp\{-\mu^w\,[p_i^{\,k} - q^w(w - c'_{ij})]^2\})^{-1} \qquad (3.18.)$$

and

$$B_j^{\,w} = (\sum_i \sum_k A_i^{\,k} H_i^{\,k}\,\exp(-\beta^w c_{ij})\,\exp\{-\mu^w\,[p_i^{\,k} - q^w(w - c'_{ij})]^2\})^{-1} \qquad (3.19.)$$

The $A_i^{\,k}$ and $B_j^{\,w}$ terms are iterated as in the aggregate, gravity model in order to satisfy constraints (3.13.) and (3.14.), which are the disaggregated versions of map pattern constraints. Therefore, the $A_i^{\,k}$ and $B_j^{\,w}$ terms ensure that the spatial constraints and the constraints on the *ex post* demand and supply relations in the housing market are satisfied. Just as, in a gravity model, the origin destination constraints can be satisfied no matter what the value of the β (distance) parameter is,[17] in the disaggregated model, we also find that the *ex post* demand and supply conditions can be satisfied no matter what the value of the μ parameter is.

Senior and Wilson (1972) have fitted a version of this model to Leeds County Borough with reasonable success and Cripps and Cater (1972) have fitted a singly-constrained version to the Reading subregion. The latter application highlights the problems of these models particularly well. Constraint (3.13.) was dropped so that the model could be used for predicting the number of type k houses demanded at i as an outcome of the allocation of workers of wage w from the zones j. It is implicitly assumed that demand for houses creates its own supply. They use the following model.[18]

$$T_{ij}^{kw} = B_j^{\,w} E_j^{\,w} H_i^{\,k}\,\exp(-\beta^w c_{ij})\,\exp\{-\mu^w\,[p_i^{\,k} - q^w(w - c'_{ij})]^2\} \qquad (3.20.)$$

where,

$$B_j^{\,w} = (\sum_i \sum_k H_i^{\,k}\,\exp(-\beta^w c_{ij})\,\exp\{-\mu^w\,[p_i^{\,k} - q^w(w - c'_{ij})]^2\})^{-1} \qquad (3.21.)$$

The model specifies that workers in type w jobs in job locations j will be allocated to type k housing in residential zones i:

(a) in direct proportion to the number of type k houses in i;
(b) inversely in proportion to the cost of travelling from i to j; and
(c) as a function of the degree to which the average available expenditure on housing of type w households varies from the price of k type houses in each residential zone i, after transport costs have been accounted for (Cripps and Cater, 1973, p. 129).

During the calibration of this model, it was found that some of the values of the μ parameter were negative. This contradicts the hypothesis suggested by eqn (3.16.); the negative values imply that the *greater* the difference between the price of a new type k house in a residential zone i and the available expenditure of a w type household, the more attractive is the k type house and residential zone i to this household type.

One can attribute this to data problems and/or mis-specification of the model. It is interesting to note that both Senior and Wilson and Cripps and Cater come out solidly on the side of data problems as the reason, although Cripps and Cater do concede that a normal distribution may be inappropriate for describing the distribution of prices around the values of average expenditure on housing. They note the severe data collection problems of such models and the difficulties of choosing classification schemes and using averages. All this is accepted.

Senior and Wilson (1972) offer the following explanation of the negative μ value. Figure 3.2 shows a severe mismatch between housing demand and housing supply.

> In trying to correct for this inconsistency the value of μ has become nonsensical. To be more explicit, what happens is that the mean housing expenditure for certain income groups (w) tends to be matched in price by only a few houses . . . In this hypothetical case the mean housing expenditure of income group 1 is matched by the prices of numerous housing opportunities so μ^1 would be positive. For income groups 2 and 3 the mean housing expenditure coincides with a 'depression' in the surface of housing opportunities by price. Hence to obtain a fit, μ^2 and μ^3 must 'push' residential locators in such groups away from their mean housing expenditure. So instead of obtaining the normal distribution of housing expenditure hypothesised in the housing budget mechanism . . . , negative values of μ^2 and μ^3 imply an inverted normal distribution, hence matching housing expenditure to the peculiarities of the surface of housing opportunities by price. (Senior and Wilson, 1972, p. 17).

The problem is perhaps not surprising when we consider that variations in the distribution of housing expenditures are a *market output*, contingent upon the demand and supply relations, and yet in the model, the curve chosen to represent this distribution is chosen *a priori*, and separately from the determination of the demand and supply constraints.

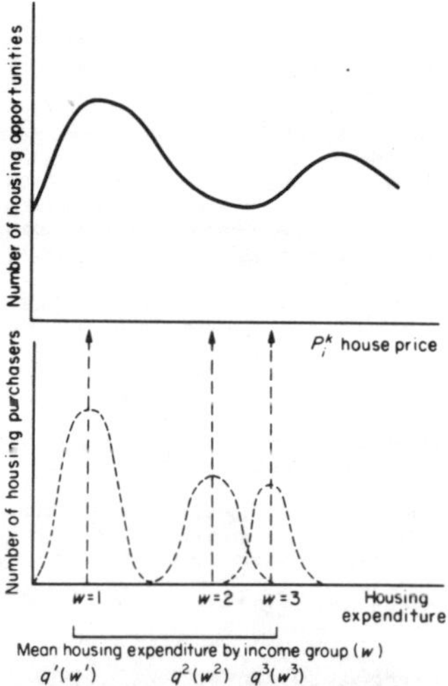

FIG. 3.2. One possible type of imbalance
between housing costs and housing expenditures
(from Senior and Wilson, 1972, p. 19).

In a doubly-constrained model where *ex post* supply and demand constraints are specified, this approach may be satisfactory, although the corollaries of such a model are very limited. In the singly-constrained model used by Cripps and Cater the constraints on housing supply are removed, and so we would expect the model to give a different result from those of a doubly-constrained model used in the same situation. Therefore, one of the reasons for the negative μ values found by Cripps and Cater may simply be that they were trying to fit a demand-oriented model without housing supply constraints into a real world situation where supply-side constraints are binding.

Senior and Wilson's policy of using 'data consistency factors' to bring *total* housing expenditure and *total* housing costs into equality is highly questionable, especially where they are used for each income group. A less flattering term might be 'fudge-factors'. A more worthwhile approach would be to trace and remedy the logical shortcomings of the model's causal structure.

At first sight, these problems may seem to be purely 'technical' and unrelated to the foregoing arguments of this chapter. However, when these problems are looked at in the context of the whole 'mode of abstraction' used in these models, it becomes clear that they are, like the spatial autocorrelation and revealed preference problems, merely symptoms of more fundamental errors. Despite the fact that disaggregated residential location models attempt to relate spatial interaction and market behaviour to clearly defined socio-economic categories of people, jobs and houses, they still represent *posterior forms of analysis*, and in their predictive role (e.g. the Cripps and Cater model) they compound several identification errors by falsely assuming that the contingent spatial interaction patterns and exchange relations (i.e. market outputs) to which they are fitted can be used to predict their determining relations (i.e. the amount and spatial distribution of the socio-economic categories). Again, they share the same defects as their undisaggregated antecedents.

NOTES: CHAPTER 3

1. Cf. especially Wilson (1974).

2. Cf. Dobb, 1973, chapter 1, for a fuller development of this argument.

3. Dobb makes a similar point in his criticism of neoclassical theories of demand which ignore the socio-economic constraints on consumer choices. 'The mere absence of any such qualification means that the statement that individuals *choose*, as soon as it is made concrete in the form that individuals choose *in a particular* way' (in our case, a particular journey-to-work pattern) 'becomes the false statement that individuals choose freely . . . ' (Dobb, 1937, p. 75).

4. 'Contingent' is used in preference to 'dependent' to avoid the misleading connotations of the 'dependent' and 'independent' variable dichotomy, with its implicit assumption of simple one-way causation from independent to dependent variable. By 'contingent variable' is meant one which is largely, but not entirely, dependent on another and has limited autonomous elements: by 'determining relation' or 'variable' is meant one which is largely, but not entirely, responsible for controlling another. Thus we replace the rigid dichotomy with a more flexible continuum allowing for two-way causation, but with control dominant in one of the directions.

5. This argument also owes much to Dobb's causal analysis of modes of explanation in static neoclassical economies in which he shows how abstraction of contingent exchange relations from their determining social relations is made in order to treat the former as the essence of the economic situation, thereby concealing social implications and denying the possibility of relating the models to the real world (Dobb, 1937, p. 43).

6. Wilson (1973) outlines a complex transport model which recognizes these different elasticities of demand.

7. The terms 'relative' and 'relational' space have sometimes been used interchangeably and sometimes as distinct concepts e.g. Harvey (1973). Also, note that by 'absolute space' we do not refer to Harvey's *socially-defined* absolute space.

8. For a thorough discussion of the dangers and limitations of 'spatial separatist' approaches (of which gravity models are an example) for understanding the space economy, see Sack (1974).

9. Baxter and Williams (1973) put forward a similar example and argument, although without referring to spatial autocorrelation explicitly.

10. See above, Section 3.4.4. Isard quotations and Sections 5.3. to 5.5.

11. Sack, 1974.

12. Lancaster's emphasis.

13. This connection is analyzed more fully in Chapter 6.

14. Or more correctly, *neo*classical economic theory.

15. This description is based on Wilson's own account (1970, p. 77).

16. Distribution other than the normal could be used.

17. See above, Section 3.4.5.

18. The notation of the Cripps and Cater model has been altered to correspond to that of Senior and Wilson.

CHAPTER 4

Towards an Alternative Approach

4.1. THE RELATIVE SPACE MODEL AS A CRITICAL DEVICE

An alternative approach to modelling urban spatial change can now be outlined, using a 'relative space model' as an example. This model is intended to provide an antithesis to the models discussed in Chapter 3. The relative space model is not presented as an alternative, fully completed and formalized simulation model *in its own right*. It is intended to serve as a critical device: to demonstrate an alternative 'mode of abstraction' which solves or dissolves the problems of conventional models. In order to fulfil this function, the subject of this model has to be close enough to that of conventional models to permit overlap and critical comparison, but it cannot be identical, for we are arguing that existing models not only use the wrong methods, but answer the wrong questions.[1]

Once the relative space model has served its purpose as a critical device and an introduction to our alternative approach, it can be dropped and replaced by the development of theory in urban political economy which is more appropriate to this approach. Therefore, the relative space model also attempts to bridge a gap between two very different approaches or methods between the conventional functionalist systems approach and our alternative structuralist approach, and between two different objects of study — between the study of urban spatial systems and urban political economy. Figure 4.1. represents these relationships diagrammatically.

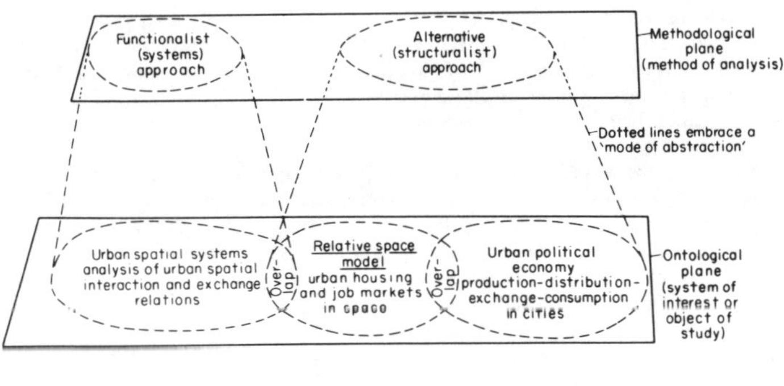

FIG. 4.1. The relative space model: where it stands.

The particular combination of a methodology and an appropriate ontology are broadly equivalent to the concept of a 'mode of abstraction'. It may be that the urban political economy mode and the urban systems analysis mode may be incommensurable. Therefore without some intermediate model the urban political-economy mode may simply appear as an optional alternative which we can take or leave as the mood takes us. The relative space model is intended to show that this is not the case, but that the urban systems analysis mode is misconceived, and that the alternative mode can be constructed out of its demolition, in which case, adoption of the urban political economy becomes *necessary*, instead of optional.

4.2. THE RELATIVE SPACE MODEL

In the relative space model, we recognize explicitly both that urban space is relative and socially defined and that decisions are made on the basis of an irrecoverable past and an uncertain future. Therefore, throughout, we insist on the distinction between *ex ante* economic expectations and intentions and *ex post* or realized activities.

We retain a set of zones or coordinates comprising the real or hypothetical urban area we wish to model. The use of a set of zones as in existing models, need not clash with the use of a concept of relative space in modelling processes because a Euclidean spatial reference system is necessary to permit public identification of these processes (Sack, 1973, p. 26), and is preferable to the obscure and highly abstruse non-Euclidean geometries.

The output of the model would be urban residential location and development, at a level of resolution approximately the same as that of the disaggregated residential location models described in Section 3.8. However, the causal structure of the model has a more micro-level flavour. In contrast to existing models which centre around trip distributions (and, in disaggregated versions, around *ex post* price relations also), and which do not relate to processes in the housing and job markets explictly, the 'Relative Space Model' emphasizes these latter processes, and relegates trip distributions and *ex post* prices to the role of model outputs.

The crucial processes modelled are the allocation of workers to jobs and of households to housing units. Imagine, for example, that at a certain time, a new job vacancy is created in zone j offering wage w. There is a small pool of workers able to take up this vacancy. Some of these workers will already be resident in the region and will have voluntarily or involuntarily become unemployed. If these workers can afford to travel to this job (i.e. if their journey-to-work costs will not exceed their potential income minus housing and other costs), they will compete for the vacancy.

The set of unemployed workers may include potential inmigrant workers. Potential inmigrants may enter the region if, in competition with others, they can find housing for sale of adequate size whose cost (including transport cost for travelling to their prospective job) is within their budget, and if they can find employment. If any of these conditions are not satisfied, potential inmigrants will not be able to enter the region. (However, decision rules could also be devised for unemployed inmigrants to take up homes, which could then be used as a local base for job search.) Similarly, the unsuccessful 'applicants' already resident in the region will remain unemployed. If one of the workers does get the job (and house), the model records that either a new worker (in the case of an immigrant) has taken up a house of type k in zone i, and a job offering income w in zone j, or that a worker resident in a type k house in zone i has taken up a job, wage w, in zone j. Whichever is the case, while the worker has this job and this house, his or her journey-to-work trips are assumed to be absolutely regular and fixed. This means that trip distribution is no longer a problem in itself, it is merely a model output which is contingent upon the operation of the housing and job markets when defined spatially and dynamically. The recording of the journey-to-work trip distribution is simply a bookkeeping operation and an 'entry' is not revised until the worker changes job and/or house again. Therefore, we follow Le Boulanger (1971) in emphasizing that choices of trip-ends and their characteristics are the determining relations of trip distribution, so that a journey-to-work trip is simply dependent on the worker's attachment to a particular job and to a particular house. Transport costs are merely one of the limiting factors influencing the choice of house and/or job. Once that choice has been made, transport costs no longer play any role whatsoever in the determination of the journey-to-work trip distribution, because the trips are compulsory.

The model recognizes that workers and their dependants move house infrequently, and assumes that their decision 'when-to-move' is chiefly an internal one relating to age and income, and so their *ex ante* moving desires have a large degree of independence of external, supply conditions.

It also recognizes the considerable constraints on their area of choice when they do want to move. Similarly, their choice of job is often very limited, although the decision, when to change job may be influenced by external factors such as recent and current rates of unemployment.

The important point is that the processes by which the model should represent spatial development are very similar to those operating in the real world. We do *not* have to assume that at any time each worker may choose any job or home — there is no 'instant metropolis' whether dynamic or static. Instead the worker's 'choice' of trip is no more than the (incidental) spatial expression of his experience in the job and housing markets. We can abandon the unhelpful conceptualization of the trip distribution and the workplace-residence connections it reflects as an equilibrating system. Instead, we take the view, recalling Piaget again, that

> ... final states illuminate the process from which they result as much as that process is necessary to the development of those states. (Piaget, 1973, p. 56).

Hence, in our context, the present pattern of work trips of an urban area can illuminate the historical processes of residential and job location as much as those processes are necessary to the development of the present state. Accordingly, if a worker has been making a certain work-trip for 6 years, we know that we shall find the explanation of his present trip-making behaviour in the conditions which led him to take up his house and/or job 6 years ago, and to maintain them over the intervening period. These conditions include the worker's income, his skills, his age, the demand for his skills, his housing requirements, the availability of suitable jobs and houses and their relative location, and the competition for those opportunities — all as they existed 6 years ago and since that time.

We can now look back and see the defects of gravity models and Curry's alternative model more clearly. In the relative space model, work-trips are modelled entirely as functions of the map pattern of jobs and houses, but we do not abstract excessively from the non-spatial attributes of these origins and destinations as Curry tends to do. Using this approach, we can easily explain in behavioural terms what Curry called the 'pure gravity effect' — i.e. that element of travel which is 'relative to distance alone in unconstrained situations', or, in our context, the trip distribution which would occur given zero spatial autocorrelation of jobs and homes (Curry, 1972, p. 132). Firstly, when we differentiate homes and jobs by type, we recognize that, even if each worker lived above a workplace, work trips would still be necessary because only a small sub-set of all jobs are suitable for each worker, and so it does not follow that all workers would find jobs on their doorsteps. Secondly, when we note the permanence of jobs and homes and the limited number of vacancies available at any one time, it becomes clear that work-trips would probably persist even if each worker did live above a job fitted to his skills because it might not be possible for workers to wait for job (house) vacancies immediately adjacent to their present home (job). Thus, the limited supply of vacancies at any one *time*, coupled with the physical exclusivity of housing and workplaces in space, and the differentiation of the *types* of workers and jobs, can account for a wide distribution of journey-to-work distances.

Thirdly, as has usually been recognized, differences in income, in car ownership rates, and in the supply of transport facilities, also give rise to a range of work-trip lengths, although, since the trips are compulsory, these factors may only be considered relevant at the stage of job and home selection. Therefore, if we are willing to look at the historical development of the city as a space-packing problem (as Harvey, 1973 and Hägerstrand, 1973, recommend), and furthermore to model location processes realistically with respect to time, we can dispense with the metaphysical 'gravity effect' altogether. A consequence of this approach is that in the relative space model, disaggregation of population and job is not merely an attractive 'optional extra' to be pursued in further research, but a logical necessity stemming from the use of a concept of relative space in which we have to differentiate between population subgroups and job-categories in order to explain their location and spatial behaviour.

It can now be seen that when we calibrate the distance-decay function of a gravity model, we are blindly approximating the effects of all these factors and processes. One might, of course, take the view that the relatively simple task of fitting a gravity model is preferable to the onerous task of disaggregating the variables and modelling these processes over time, but if so, we should at least realize what we are doing and thus be able to understand why gravity models are so unrobust.

In the relative space model, the purely technical modelling problems of gravity models (e.g. calibration of distance-decay parameters) are replaced by problems of understanding and modelling the operation of the job and housing markets within a city. While the housing market has been the subject of considerable research, the study of the job market has curiously been largely neglected in urban studies. We would argue that production and the job market are too important in urban dynamics to be excluded, indeed we can hardly expect to understand spatial interaction in abstraction from them. In fact, the dynamics of these two markets are very similar, although the job market is perhaps simpler to model, and therefore we begin a more detailed account of the relative space model with an outline of a possible job-market submodel.

4.3. MODELLING THE JOB MARKET[2]

Since the principal objective of this particular relative space model would be to explain the development of housing and its occupance in a city, the representation of the job market plays only a supporting role. Total employment required by industry might be considered as an exogenous input into the model, but this would be modified endogenously by the movement of workers and by population dynamics generally, affecting the levels of filled jobs. We focus on the two most important stocks in the labour market — the stocks of unemployed workers and job vacancies, and the interactions between them. Those switching jobs without a break are assumed to be temporarily unemployed.

The prices at which workers try to sell their labour can best be assumed to be equivalent to the wages actually paid to workers of similar skills for similar work in the recent past. Firms are assumed to attempt to minimize the gap between actual and required labour force size. They may raise wages by a few per cent if they have to wait a long time to fill vacancies, but it is assumed that they cannot lower wages. However, the worker's minimum acceptance wage may fall with duration of unemployment as outlined below (see Fig. 4.3.). Unemployment and vacancies can exist simultaneously because job-seeking is a complex, time-consuming process arising from the nonstandardization of jobs and workers and lack of perfect knowledge (Holt and David, 1966).

Figure 4.2 describes the structure of the model. The hiring of an unemployed worker reduces by one the stocks of both unemployed workers and vacancies. 'Quits' are highest when the stock of unemployed is lowest, and they have the effect of increasing unemployed and vacancies stocks. Layoffs increase unemployment only. Unemployed workers and job vacancies flow into the market and accumulate until the acceptance levels drift down far enough to meet the wage-levels offered by the employers, which are moving slowly upward, when the market operates by randomly pairing off unemployed workers and vacancies. In the Holt–David model, the probability per period of time P_u that an unemployed worker would find an acceptable job vancancy is in direct proportion to the total number of vacancies available:

$$P_u = kV \qquad (4.1.)$$

where k is a constant,

and similarly, the probability per period of time P_v, that a vacancy will be filled is in direct proportion to the total number of unemployed:

$$P_v = kU \qquad (4.2.)$$

Where V is vacancies, and U, unemployed.

Thus, where the vacancy level is fairly stable and other factors affecting this probability are unimportant, we would expect to observe an exponential distribution for duration of unemployment. k will be small where the skill-level of the unemployed differs widely from that required by industry.

Gross flows in and out of U and V may be high, but net changes in either will usually be

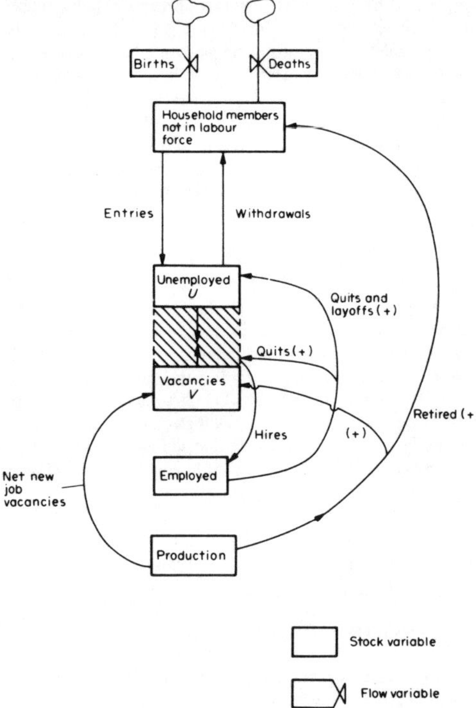

FIG. 4.2. Chief stocks and flows in the job market (based on Holt and David, 1966).

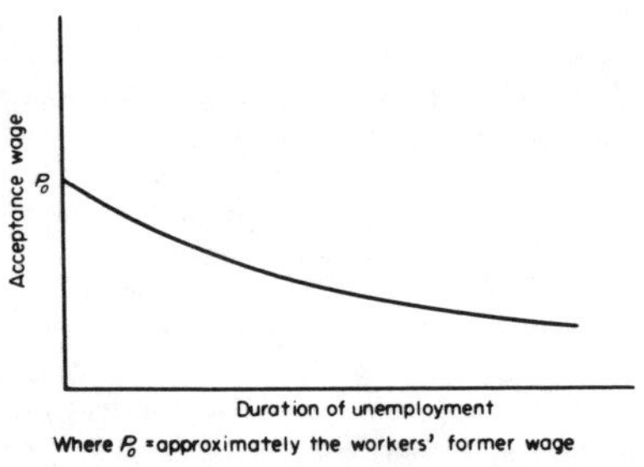

FIG. 4.3. Workers' acceptance wages.

relatively small. However, we have to model gross flows because only by doing so can we recognize the constraints on job selection of housing location and vice versa. As Holt and David recommend, a stochastic model would probably be most suitable for modelling the actual pairing of unemployed workers with job vacancies. In each time period workers with acceptance wages equal to or less than vacancy wages offered would be determined first and then, from these, worker and vacancy pairs would be selected and the process continued until either all unemployed workers and/or vacancies had been used up or until the number of unemployed given jobs equals kV, or the number of vacancies filled in the time period equals kU. Spatial constraints on these job market processes are discussed below in Section 4.8.

4.4. HOUSING

As this is primarily a residential location model, the housing market is modelled in more detail than the job market. Whereas it was suggested that employment required might be treated as largely exogenous in the job market submodel, newly constructed housing and hence the supply of housing are endogenously determined. Although newly constructed houses[3] form a tiny proportion of the housing stock at any one time, we must not fall into the trap characteristic of static models, where the total stock is assumed to be determined by *present* functional interrelationships — we must remember that all houses were once newly constructed and that therefore, the explanation of the location of houses which are 10 years old lies in the state of the urban system at that time.

Having noted these basic truisms, we now have before us the difficult task of suggesting a method for modelling the way in which workers of a certain age, income and job location and their dependants take up houses of a certain price, size and location.

4.5. THE SUPPLY OF HOUSING[4]

At any one time, only a small proportion of the total stock of housing is actually available for purchase. The available supply consists of:

(a) vacant newly-completed houses and 'second-hand' houses offered for sale; and
(b) presently-occupied units being offered for sale.

The latter could be described as *ex ante* vacancies for the seller often does not actually vacate his house until he has found a new house for himself, and a buyer for his present house. Vacant second-hand houses usually come into being through household deaths or are the property of owners with more than one home.

Given these characteristics plus the fact that urban growth in developed countries is usually very slow, the number of *ex ante* buyers is approximately equal to the number of *ex ante* sellers, indeed many of the movers are in both categories. Therefore, in a limited sense, the supply and demand for houses create each other. However, because the stocks of people and houses are differentiated by characteristics and location, it does not follow that there is a harmonious equilibrium where supply satisfies demand. As the income and demographic structure of the population changes, and as accessibilities of different residential areas to work-places change, pressures will be set up in certain sections of the market. Also, we must remember that the housing market has strong monopoly characteristics owing to the highly inelastic long run demand for housing and the spatial (physical) exclusivity and temporal longevity of housing which allow the owner to have a monopoly of his house's particular *relational qualities* (its proximity to urban facilities — shops, commercial activities, entertainment centres etc.), as well as the house itself (Harvey, 1973, p. 186).

In order to model these characteristics faithfully, we must reject the all too familiar neoclassical approaches of finding 'optimum' or 'equilibrium' prices for the market system, which abstract totally from the realities described above. Instead, we use a modified version of a price-setting model suggested by Bliss (1972) for the housing market.

At time t, potential sellers of type k houses in zone i set their *ex ante* prices at levels approximately consistent with *ex post* prices recently reached for similar housing in similar areas. If recent rates of buying of similar houses have been high, the new potential sellers may raise their own prices by a few per cent in the belief that buyers can be induced to pay more. In the next time period $t + 1$, potential sellers will in turn set their *ex ante* prices by reference to these new prices, and if the market is still healthy, may raise these by a further few per cent. Time lags for the perception of the state of the market will of course be evident in this process.

This process sets off interesting repercussions. If buying rates are high, selling rates will of course be high also, but the increase in prices as a result of increased mobility will also sooner or later reduce that rate of mobility, and the stock of people waiting to move will also become depleted. As the market slows down and *ex ante* sellers find that they have to wait long periods in order to find buyers, they may lower their prices by a few per cent. Meanwhile, subsequent *ex ante* sellers will set their prices with reference to these new lowered prices.

As there are limitations on numbers of people wishing to move (in the model we would use a pool of potential movers), the price mechanism shown in Fig. 4.4 is likely to be fairly stable, although price elasticity may be significantly higher for upward price movements than for downward movements. Long-term increases in prices may result from increased incomes or increased availability of mortgages which will push up the rate of buying.

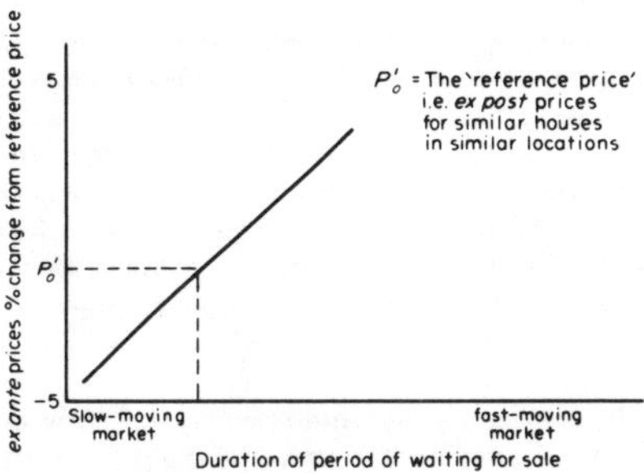

FIG. 4.4. Mechanism for setting *ex ante* house prices.

In any case, as Smith (1970, p. 140) argues, house prices are not necessarily a very important variable of interest; actual quantities demanded and supplied *ex post*, excess demand and supply, and actual pairings of houses and households according to their respective characteristics are probably of more interest.

4.6. NEW CONSTRUCTION

Before discussing these important features, we must briefly describe the process by which the housing stock originates – new construction. This may prove to be the most difficult process to model of all, and it is also one of the most important. Maisel (1963), suggests that the number of new starts made is a function of the number of vacancies available, and the rate of take-up of vacancies. However, the location of these new starts and the type of houses constructed are more difficult to model. The former is strongly influenced by land values, which express perceptions of the present and expected future relational qualities of vacant land, and by planning constraints, and the latter is probably a function of recent and expected demand for specific types of houses. Clearly, there are many difficulties here because of lack of understanding of the processes involved and the significance of institutional influences and the speculative behaviour of very small numbers of decision-makers. The very fact, that at any one time we are dealing with the behaviour of a very small group of decision-makers, not so much responding to a current state-of-affairs, but trying to manufacture a future which is favourable to them, means that we will have very great difficulty in making robust generalizations.

On the other hand, this kind of mental model is useful in that it helps us to look at other residential location models in a more critical light. Firstly, the disaggregated residential location models described above (Chapter 3.8.) do not even distinguish between new construction and existing houses. Secondly, when we appreciate the degree of independence of the new construction process from subsequent functional relations between houses, people and jobs, it becomes obvious that models which represent the supply of housing as being determined by the demands of present-day functional relations between homes and jobs (e.g. Cripps and Cater's singly-constrained disaggregated model) are teleological and grossly misleading.

Ironically, the very processes by which houses come into being have been virtually ignored by urban modellers, or else have been misleadingly misrepresented as a simple dependent variable of 'housing demand'. Until very recently there has been a conspicuous lack of research on the political economy of housing[5] — that is on the control mechanisms *behind* the housing market, in particular, on the social regulation of scarcity required to prevent prices and rents falling. However, this is at least implicit in Maisel's model, which could provide a possible starting point for development of a spatial model.

4.7. THE HOUSING MARKET

The major problem in modelling the exchange relations of the housing market is that of the allocation of particular buyers to particular houses at specified locations. Therefore, a residential location model has to handle a far more difficult problem than that tackled by a standard market model which simply assigns gross total goods to undifferentiated buyers. We wish simply to model the market processes as they occur over space and time without making counterintuitive assumptions of market clearing solutions (fortunately for house buyers, the market is never cleared), or of 'equilibrium' or 'optimum' solutions where every household gets a bundle of housing goods in a location upon which it cannot improve. Where disequilibria occur so that *ex ante* market intentions are not realized *ex post*, we wish to represent them explicitly.

If we assume that all households have one worker in order to help us work out accounting relationships for the purpose of describing the general principles of this sort of model, we can identify all house-movers by workplace — either existing, in the case of those keeping the same job while they move house, or potential in the case of inmigrants to the region and those moving house and job simultaneously. Since jobs are identified by wages, we can therefore identify the incomes, actual or potential, of households. For each pair of potential buyers and sellers 'gross prices' are calculated from house sale price plus transport costs to the potential buyers.[6] We calculate which of the available houses can be afforded by buyers by comparing 'gross prices' with buyers' incomes minus their non-housing and potential transport expenditure.

Having estimated the quantities of the various types of *potential* buyers and sellers, actual sales would have to be modelled sequentially. As was the case with the proposed job market submodel, a random selection mechanism might be used to represent the actual sales of houses. Once a sale is made, the house is withdrawn from the market and so the available supply open to potential buyers, and the number of potential buyers remaining, are each reduced by one. The selection process would be continued until no more buyers and sellers could be paired. At the end of the time period we would be left with a number of new pairings of households and workers, and in recording these, the journey-to-work trip distribution would be updated. Those who could not buy or sell houses in the previous time period would remain in the pools of potential buyers and sellers and the model would attempt to allocate them in the next time period.[7] Therefore, the speed of operation of the market together with the excess demand and supply quantities, would have to be specified explicitly. Thus, there is no invocation of market-clearing solutions in the model: the buying and selling takes place as a continuous process.

It is interesting to note that a random allocation method such as this solves the problem of gravity models of satisfying destination constraints. At any one time, only a small number of people compete for a house (or destination). In order to satisfy the destination constraints, we have to select just one household from among the competing prospective buyers. In the gravity model and its disaggregated versions, the whole history of the competitive processes from which the present population obtained its present workplaces and residences is collapsed into the present, so that the process is misrepresented as one of simultaneous competition between all households. It is small wonder that this distorted conceptualization of market processes in space requires a clumsy iterative procedure (in the case of production-attraction constrained models) in order to satisfy the constraints.

4.8. SOME IMPLICATIONS OF THE RELATIVE SPACE MODEL

As we noted in Section 4.1, the chief interest of the model lies not in its possible operational details but in its encapsulation of a major conceptual shift away from static, absolute-space models, which generalize regularities among the contingent relations of urban systems towards models which generalize regularities among determining relations. As is usually the case with conceptual switches, we do not solve all the problems associated with the old approach because many of these are found to be inherently insoluble and result from asking the wrong questions, and the new approach presents us with a different set of questions and problems: indeed, we can frame the discussion of the implications of the relative space model in terms of the contrasting problems of the old and new approaches.

We can begin at the most general level by contrasting the ways in which existing models and the relative space model handle space, time and process. Gravity models, whether aggregate or disaggregate, present an utterly confused picture of space, time and process. In addition to their representation of space as absolute, doubly-constrained models misrepresent process and temporal development by assuming simultaneous competitive trip distribution, and singly-constrained models assume that *ex post* demand for travel and housing (or jobs) can be calculated without explicitly representing the housing (or job) supply, by means of the heroic assumption that demand creates its own supply.

In the relative space model, we correctly assume that creation of a supply of housing must logically be prior to the occupation of that housing, although expectations of future demand may have influenced that construction of the housing stock. Therefore, *ex post* spatial interaction is represented as being contingent upon the existing relative spatial distribution of activities such as homes and jobs and *ex ante* spatial interaction (estimated travel time and cost constraints) becomes merely one of several factors in trip-end choice: we do not invert the causality by making contingent spatial interactions determine spatial structure. Both trip distribution and migration take place in a relative space and are merely the spatial expression of processes in the housing and job markets. Thus, the model frees us from some of the confusion about the relationship between location and interaction created by gravity models.

Moreover, confidence in the relative space model is reinforced by its internally consistent *integration* of space, time and process; each of these three elements is modelled in such a way as to be inseparable from the other two. In order to represent *temporal* change correctly, we must also represent demand and supply *processes* as they operate in, and in turn define, a relative *space*. If we try to model any one of these elements in another way, perhaps using an absolute space concept, or an assumption of perfectly clearing markets, or of instantaneous equilibrium, we find that it contradicts the other two elements in such a way as to undermine the whole structure of the model; e.g. an assumption of instantaneously and perfectly clearing markets would make mis-specification of both the temporal and spatial dimensions of the housing system inevitable. Looking back on the general principles of the relative space model, it is clear that the integration of space, time and process is such that it becomes difficult to even speak of each element separately without referring to the other two. As Blaut argues:

> Relative space is inseparably fused to relative time, the two forming what is called the space-time manifold, or simply *process*. Nothing in the physical world is purely spatial or temporal; everything is process. . . . Pure space cannot even survive as an empirical abstraction. . . . Pure space is in fact relegated to pure mathematics, and *every empirical concept of space must be reducible by* a chain of definitions to a concept of process. (Blaut, 1961).

Although this has long been accepted in the comfortable isolation of methodological discussions, it has rarely been followed in actual modelling practice.

We can now recognize that some of the problems of gravity models with which we grappled in Chapter 3, are inherently insoluble. Curry's (1972) attack on gravity models for their lack of consideration of the effects of spatial autocorrelation can now be seen as being useful for criticizing the gravity model on its own ground — i.e. in using a concept of absolute space. Both spatial autocorrelation and the distance decay functions of gravity models, as absolute space statistics, abstract from social relations and represent their outward spatial expression as being capable of useful analysis on their own. This 'spatial separatist' approach makes it extremely difficult to provide causal analysis of patterns of location and spatial interaction. How can we determine (using this approach), the extent to which location and interaction patterns are determined:

(a) by peoples' tendencies to make trips of certain lengths (the distance decay or 'pure gravity effect')?

(b) by the spatial autocorrelation of origins and destinations? and

(c) how can we know to what extent the location of the trip-ends was determined by the same sorts of factors as those which govern (a)?

Clearly, if the discussion is couched purely in terms of spatial autocorrelation and 'gravity', we cannot provide satisfactory answers, and yet it is exactly these sort of questions which Curry tried to answer in a spatial separatist manner. Careful reading of Curry's important paper reveals the contradictions raised by this approach, in trying to separate (a) and (b). Thus, while Curry refers to the 'semi-mystical Newtonian analogy' of the gravity model (p. 134), he identifies gravity with (a), and yet admits, on p. 139, that it cannot be separated from the 'locational relations of jobs and homes'. He then tries to avoid this contradiction by defining 'pure gravity' as the sole determinant of travel when there is zero autocorrelation of uniform, unbounded distributions of origins and destinations (p. 139) — but even in this hypothetical limiting case, the *slope* of the distance decay function would be determined by the spacing of origins and destinations.

Such contradictions are insoluble in terms of a spatial separatist approach, for they exist only as technical problems *created* by the analyst through his own particular method of abstraction which ignores the processes by which the relative spatial distribution of activities and interactions comes into being. In view of this highly unrealistic and partial mode of abstraction it is hardly surprising that spatial autocorrelation and the value of the distance parameter in gravity models are not real world problems. The use of this kind of model is apparently based upon the profoundly mistaken, but widespread view among 'spatial analysts' that the spatial expression of social processes can be described by some mysterious 'mathematical or geometrical laws' that have an *identical* impact on the distribution of objects, irrespective of those social processes.[8] We may of course observe that negative exponential curves can be fitted to many real world distributions such as urban population density, but then without being able to work out what the values of parameters of such distributions ought to be *a priori*, and without empirical evidence of their universality, the discovery of such 'regularities' may amount to little more than the equivalent of observing that water tends to flow downhill (Harvey, 1969, p. 111).

However, as was shown in Section 3.4.6, as a simple matter of geometry, in view of the fact that urban development involves space-packing processes (Harvey, 1973, p. 172; Hägerstrand, 1973) and interactions between areas and points, it seems quite inconceivable that such spatial statistics could remain constant during a period of urban expansion. In short, spatial autocorrelation statistics and parameters in gravity models are nothing more than abstract spatial statistics of very limited substantive meaning.

If we reject approaches which concentrate on spatial relations to the exclusion of study of relevant social processes, we can forget about these problems. In the relative space model, although there are constraints which have a spatial expression, e.g. the limitations on areas of job or house search placed by work travel budgets, and the definition of the spatial dimensions of the housing and job markets, they are defined in process terms rather than pure-space terms and so we do not have to feed in any particular trip distance decay functions as inputs to the model. Instead, the processes in the housing and job markets reproduced in the model, themselves produce the trip distribution as an incidental output: distance-decay functions and spatial autocorrelation are of academic interest only.

Consideration of the implications of the relative space model forces us to face up to the question of the very possibility of forecasting urban development. In trying to formalize such a model, we might easily be tempted to increase its size beyond the limits of manageability. For example, it may seem necessary to represent social mobility explicitly in order to model the job market properly, and satisfactory representation of the housing market may require submodels of housing filtering and decay. In contrast, the Lowry model certainly has the advantage of being parsimonious, but it achieves this only by ignoring the 'openness' of the urban system, e.g. by completely omitting supply-side subsystems in housing and in the labour market: its parsimony is based upon contingent relations in the urban system, in abstraction from some of the most important determining relations. However, we are only just beginning the search for models based upon determining relations in urban systems, and so it is hardly surprising that we have yet to find out what 'modelling economies' can be made.

Nevertheless, there is a dilemma in that while there is often a great deal of order among the contingent relations (e.g. travel patterns), there is often apparently relatively little among the more fundamental determinants. For example, whereas it seems relatively straightforward to model household moves within an existing housing stock, it is much more difficult to model the construction of that stock. Since new construction involves decisions made by a very limited number of people at any one time and is greatly influenced by expectations of the future we have neither the regularity provided by large numbers of 'actors' nor any easily identifiable 'rationality' on which to base a model.

Aggregated equilibrium models have the drawback of being unable to enlighten us about urban problems because they neither refer to specific social groups nor identify disequilibria such as housing shortages and unemployment. In the relative space model we identify both explicitly. Therefore, it is possible that we may eventually be able to use such a model to look at particular urban problems; e.g. the extent to which low-paid workers find it difficult to compete in the housing market. Also, it is possible to have unemployment and labour shortages co-existing, either because the unemployed and the job vacancies are too widely separated spatially or because the vacancies are for particular types of work for which the unemployed are unsuited.

An important corollary of the relative space model's disequilibrium nature is that spatial organization, prices and wages can have an effect on overall efficiency and levels of activities, whereas they have none in existing models.[9] By admitting the possibilities that job vacancies will not be filled because of inaccessibility or insufficient wages and that households may not be able to move, given the level of house prices and number of houses for sale, we allow space and costs to affect overall urban system performance.

The ideas contained in the relative space model were only arrived at after an exhaustive attempt to refute existing urban models. Perhaps we could have reached the same destination by simply writing down how urban development takes place in space and time, ignoring the misleading abstractions of static, equilibrium, absolute space models. Also, a better source of ideas might have been urban gaming simulation models, in which the specification of space, time and process is generally correct. However, the latter tend to be thought of as a separate category of model and there has been no attempt to use them to challenge existing computer simulation models. Therefore, in view of the conspicuous absence of refutation in regional science, the particular route by which we arrived at the destination of the relative space model may prove useful, and in turn the relative space model itself may be of more use in pointing us in a new direction in urban modelling than as an alternative model in its own right.

NOTES: CHAPTER 4

1. Note that this inseparability of method and ontology is quite general; for example empiricists believe that events in the world are not governed by necessity and therefore their *method* does not rely upon looking for causal laws. Similarly, we should not expect two different ontologies to use the same method of investigation, nor two different methodologies to be applicable to the same ontology. Keat and Urry's recent book *Social Theory as Science* is very illuminating on this point.

2. This section draws heavily on the work of Holt and David (1966).

3. i.e. less than 1 year old.

4. The model deals only with private housing.

5. See e.g. Harvey (1974); Boddy, (1976); Duncan, (1976); and Pickvance (1976).

6. Gross prices are also used in the National Bureau of Economic Research: Detroit Prototype model (Kain *et al.*, 1973).

7. Very short time periods would be used to approximate the continuous process, as in the system dynamics technique of simulation modelling (Forrester, 1968).

8. Cf. Semevskiy, (1973).

9. See above, Chapters 2 and 3. Also Hägerstrand notes that 'We have not even given much thought to the evaluation of the performance of socio-economic systems as a function of their spatial arrangements.' (1973. p. 68).

CHAPTER 5

Economic Theory and Urban Modelling

5.1. INTRODUCTION: THE CRITIQUE OF NEOCLASSICAL ECONOMICS

The new discipline of regional science has its strongest intellectual ties with neoclassical economics. Much of the theory of the former is derived from the latter; Christaller's original central place theory is a prominent example (Christaller, 1966, chapter 1). Hence, a large part of our critique of regional science in general and urban modelling in particular is derived from the critique of neoclassical economics put forward by what may be losely termed the Cambridge economics school and its supporters. These critics have very diverse theoretical affiliations – post-Keynesian, neo-Ricardian, Marxist, neo-Marxist, or simply non-aligned, but they are united in their opposition to neoclassical economics and their advocacy of its replacement by political economy. Nevertheless, the conventional wisdom in economics often seems oblivious to this rising tide of opposition, while regional science also languishes in comfortable ignorance. Ironically, the volume of imports of neoclassical theory into regional science has been undergoing a minor resurgence recently, perhaps because, as Kaldor (1972) suggests, the neoclassical conceptual apparatus provides a prolific source of 'building-blocks' for the growing ranks of mathematical model-builders and econometricians.

It is the aim of this chapter to draw attention to the inadequacy of neoclassical, equilibrium economics, and in particular, the theory of demand – to show that it is *necessarily* based on counterintuitive assumptions and that it gives us grossly distorted representations of real world economic mechanisms.

As will become clear, the critique of spatial models and the recommended alternatives presented in Chapters 3 and 4 are directly analogous to the critique of neoclassical economics and the revival of political economy. Indeed, many of the arguments presented in the previous chapters were *direct transfers* of arguments from the critical literature in economics to the content of urban modelling. Just as utility theory and gravity models are compatible, non-trivial dynamic spatial models such as the relative space model are incompatible with neoclassical economics, but potentially compatible with an alternative political economy approach.

As is usually the case with inter-paradigm debates, each side prefers to conduct the argument on its own ground, and consequently many of the attacks fail to find a target and are brushed aside by the opposition which interprets them as peripheral to its main interests.[1] The main focus of interest in neoclassical economics is the operation of markets, of exchange. This interest is clearly reflected in the popular definition of economics as 'the study of the allocation of scarce resources between competing ends'. 'Pure', 'economic' relations are torn out of their sociological, political and historical context and analyzed in sterile isolation. In contrast, the main concern of political economy is much broader, encompassing production, accumulation and distribution – all examined explicitly *within* their social, political and historical context: exchange is demoted to a subordinate position.

The most powerful, damaging and best-known aspects of political economy's critique of neoclassical economics are the 'capital controversies'.[2] These controversies are particularly significant because they penetrate and demystify the innermost relations of the workings of capitalism – the relations between capital and labour and the nature of profits. However, given that neoclassicists are more concerned with markets than with production and capital accumulation, they have tended to carry on working within their own paradigm, relatively unruffled by these challenges. However, there is a lesser-known critique of neoclassical economics which is carried out on its own ground – in terms of the analysis of demand – supply relations and the operation of markets. It is this critique which provides the centre-piece for discussion here, for, as Kornai argues in his book *Anti-Equilibrium,*

> The schools of thought wishing to replace GE (general equilibrium, i.e. neoclassical) theory must not shy away from the territory where the latter is really at home. (Kornai, 1971, p. 221).

If we first bring down neoclassical theory on its own ground, our case for shifting to a new territory, that of political economy, will be all the more convincing. Therefore our method of criticism corresponds to that used in Chapters 3 and 4 against gravity models.

Before beginning a critique of the neoclassical 'laws' of supply and demand, certain misconceptions must be removed and clarifications made. It should be noted first that neoclassical economics is not merely the outcome of the 'marginalist revolution' (i.e. the study of economic movements 'at the margin' using calculus) as has often been implied. Underneath this superficial technical 'revolution', there are much more fundamental characteristics. These include beliefs in economic laws as being independent of specific historical, social and cultural circumstances, as being value-free, and in contradistinction to classical political economy, there is a belief in a subjective, as opposed to a cost-based theory of value (Dobb, 1973). Corresponding to these different facets of neoclassical economics, there are several different strategies we can follow in trying to refute demand–supply analysis. One popular strategy has been to start from the basis of ideology; e.g. Dobb (1973) and Robinson (1962) have interpreted neoclassicism's concentration on superficial market relations as a reaction to some of the unpalatably egalitarian implications of classical economic theory. Fascinating though this type of critique may be, we shall leave it to the students of the history of economic thought: not surprisingly, such unsavoury accusations as this have been dismissed by those for whom the ideology of value-free social science is above question.

Another popular line of attack is made from a practical standpoint regarding the utility of neoclassical theory, noting that it is of virtually no use to individuals and firms in making decisions. However, the approach taken here is to concentrate the attack on the *logical structure* of neoclassical models, and on their use of counterintuitive assumptions, and to show how, by changing some of the latter, the foundations of these models can be undermined. If it is true that neoclassical economists take a special pride in the *rigour* of their analysis, then they should be highly sensitive to this kind of criticism.

5.2. THE LOGIC OF DEMAND–SUPPLY ANALYSIS

Firstly, as was pointed out in the arguments used against utility theory and spatial interaction models, neoclassical economics tends to focus on the contingent relations of markets and to analyze these as if they represented the essence of their determining relations.

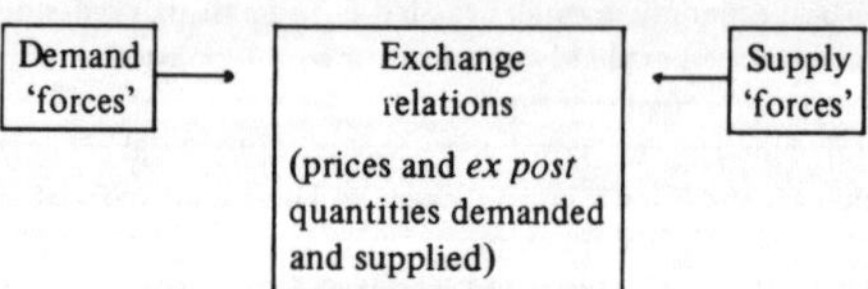

We know that the exchange relations represent the resolution of the demand and supply 'forces'. However, acceptance of the fact that there is a two-way causation between demand and supply can easily put us in a position of 'helpless relativism', where supply influences demand and demand influences supply. Neoclassical economics gets out of this trap by emphasizing one of the directions of causality (usually demand → supply) at the expense of the other (the role of supply is usually de-emphasized, e.g., by assuming it to be infinitely elastic, as in the perfect competition model). The crucial assumption which permits this bias towards treatment of the consumer as sovereign, is that all preferences are revealed in the market. This means that the exchange relations are assumed to hold all the necessary information about the demand forces. Thus, the exchange relations which in the real world are *contingent* upon semi-autonomous demand and supply forces, can be made to appear as the determining relations, and can be treated in abstraction from the more fundamental determinants which are excluded by means of *ceteris paribus* assumptions.

By excluding from their analysis the study of the social relations behind the market processes, neoclassical economists successfully blinkered themselves against any political implications of market behaviour, and in so doing, increased the academic isolation of economics from other social sciences. Having extracted the contingent exchange relations from their socio–political matrix, neoclassical analysis presumes too readily that they will also apply to novel or imperfectly known situations.[3] Since the exchange relations are assumed to hold all the necessary information, by specifying one of the elements of the system (usually *ex post* demand) as *given,* and by simple multiplication of this by the observed ratios of one element to another, the whole system can be derived.[4]

However, observation of the exchange relations obtaining in a market at a certain time merely provides us with 'a situation composed of a cluster of internally related elements and treated as being isolated' (Dobb, 1973, p. 8), which does not amount to an *explanation.* In order to achieve the latter,

> . . . the equational system must be made to tell us something *more*; and this 'something more' almost inevitably has a causal form, whether as complex mutual interaction of a set of variables or as the simpler type of uni-directional causal linkage. This is commonly done, in fact, even with what lay claim to be purely formal systems depicting a *catena* of interrelations and no more; an order of determination being implied as soon as some of the variables are treated as exogenously determined from outside the system, or else treated as constants, and hence specified as *data* . . . . and the others as being dependent on the internal relations of the system or as 'unknowns' awaiting a solution. (Dobb, 1973, pp. 8–9).

Such a procedure is no substitute for discovering the true directions of causality operating in a system, and it will invariably give quite spurious results, yet it is characteristic of neoclassical analysis and of course, it occurs widely in regional science in its use of demand-oriented models, as was shown in Chapter 2. The problems are usually ignored by assuming a static equilibrium in order to legitimize the procedure and by quickly setting the relations out in equation or diagram form in order to give the appearance of confidence and rigour.

Wherever there is two-way causation in a system, this procedure is invalid. Moreover, we cannot choose appropriate procedures for statistical estimation of such a system without taking into account the whole network of causal relationships (Bentzel and Hansen, 1954). Yet in using static equilibrium models we create these problems for ourselves. By collapsing dynamic processes into a single point of time we artificially create a model system characterized by interdependence between variables, even though such simultaneous interdependence does not exist in reality. In so doing, we forget that 'Time is a device to prevent everything from happening at once.'[5]

In commenting on one of the most popular static equilibrium models, the Walrasian model, which is characterized by complete simultaneous interdependency between variables, Bentzel and Hansen write,

> (A) static equilibrium system only expresses the *conditions* for an unspecified dynamic system to be in equilibrium, i.e. to repeat itself unchanged . . . . The interdependency between the undated variables in a Walras system should not be interpreted as saying that these variables are also determined simultaneously in time. This means that all the (undated) relationships entering a Walras system may be of no relevance when equilibrium does not exist . . . . Indeed, in most of the interdependent models which have actually been used for econometric research work, static equilibrium conditions seem to be the main *cause*[6] for the interdependency of the models . . . . Static equilibrium assumptions can at most be *special*[7] hypotheses and can never be accepted as a general argument for interdependency. (Bentzel and Hansen, 1954, p. 160).

To paraphrase the above argument – by setting up a static equilibrium model we lay a trap for ourselves. Having created a system of interdependencies, we find ourselves in a situation of helpless relativism, where everything affects everything else simultaneously. We can then usually only escape from this circularity to provide an 'explanation' by misrepresenting the causal structure, by assuming one element of the system to be exogenous and the rest derived from it.

Of course, the usual defence for equilibrium analysis is that it can serve as an approximation of a disequilibrium system or as a stepping stone towards the formulation of a more general disequilibrium theory.[8] As we have seen, equilibrium analysis is neither of these things; the assumption of equilibrium is *indispensable* because, only in an equilibrium system can the contingent exchange relations reproduce themselves at different times and hence hold all the information required to define the system. It is in this sense that we argue that neoclassical analysis must necessarily be propped up by the counterintuitive assumption of equilibrium coupled with tautological definition of variables such as 'jobs' and 'employment'.[9] Moreover, equilibrium models do not generally specify how a position of equilibrium can be reached. as one might expect of an ideal model which is supposed to provide a basis for generalization to disequilibrium systems. Kregel (1973, pp. 39—40) demonstrates that a price system in disequilibrium shows *no* logical tendency towards an equilibrium, so that it can now be seen that 'equilibrium analysis' is nothing more than a closed system of axioms referring only to a definitional 'knife-edged-equilibrium'.[10]

All models are based upon simplifying assumptions, but those of neoclassical economics are often quite plainly 'counterintuitive', and contradict rather than simplify our experience. Kaldor (1972) finds that the most sensitive *ceteris paribus* assumption of general equilibrium models – the assumption of constant returns to scale, is not only counterintuitive but also cannot be removed without falsifying the whole theoretical structure. Once increasing returns are allowed, we find that change can no longer be assumed to be determined exogeneously, but is engendered from within the economic system, so that actual states of the economy at any one period cannot be predicted except as a result of the sequence of events in previous periods which led up to it. Kaldor goes on to show how the implications of the removal of this key assumption challenge major parts of conventional economic theory and methodology.

5.3. TIME AND EXPLANATION IN ECONOMIC THEORY

While Kaldor uses a dynamic process to overthrow equilibrium analysis, Robinson, Shackle and Bliss concentrate on time itself.

> In equilibrium analysis, either the whole of future time is collapsed into today or else every individual has correct foresight about what all others will do and vice versa; it contradicts the essence of life lived in time, where the individual is always poised between an irrecoverable past and an uncertain future. (Robinson, 1972).
> But if an hypothesis is framed in terms of the position of equilibrium that would be attained when all parties concerned had correct foresight, there is no point in testing it; we know in advance that it will not prove correct. (Robinson, 1962, pp. 69–70).

Likewise the appeal to 'long-run equilibrium' is just a device for assuming that any amount of time can be used up: economies are always in the short-run.[11]

When we do consider time in economic behaviour, we must distinguish between time represented as a dimension – as a space of 'co-valid points' with no fundamental distinction between past and future – i.e. as it is normally conceptualized in natural science, and time in real life, where there is an asymmetry between an unchoosable past and an unknowable future (Shackle, 1972). Shackle argued that we should use the former concept only when we are modelling well-understood, repetitive patterns of behaviour among highly aggregated populations, e.g. in business cycle studies. For most subjects in economics we must face up to the fact that all economic behaviour is undertaken under uncertainty as to what the repurcussions will be, especially in terms of the behaviour of competitors. We can either accept that the individual's behaviour is governed by intentions which are private, subjective and unobservable and hence reduce the possibility of modelling such behaviour, or we can attempt to assume the position of an outside observer who is simultaneously informed of the intentions of the individuals being modelled (Shackle, 1967).

This latter approach offers the greatest promise for dynamic analysis. To operationalize it we require the familiar distinction between *ex ante* intentions and expectations, and *ex post* actual outcomes, for

> . . . that language of *ex ante* and *ex post* was the key which realised economic theory from its subservience to that conception of time which is a mere dimension where the distinction between past and future is meaningless. (Shackle, 1972, preface).

When this 'language' is used in conjunction with a technique known as 'sequence analysis',[12] developed by the Stockholm school of economists in the 1930s, we have a powerful tool for dynamic modelling. The idea behind sequence analysis is that,

(E)conomic development is generated by economic subjects' attempts to carry out their plans. These plans are determined by the expectations about the future of the economic subjects. Expectations are again dependent on the preceding development and are revised from time to time. Since, as a rule, not all individuals plans are compatible, some plans must break down. Therefore, the individually planned and realised magnitudes need not coincide. From this follows the well-known necessity of working with both *ex ante* and *ex post* magnitudes in economic theory. All changes in plans and expectations take place at the points of division between the periods; no such change takes place during a period. (Bentzel and Hansen, 1954, p. 156).

Figure 5.1 shows the procedure for sequence analysis diagrammatically.

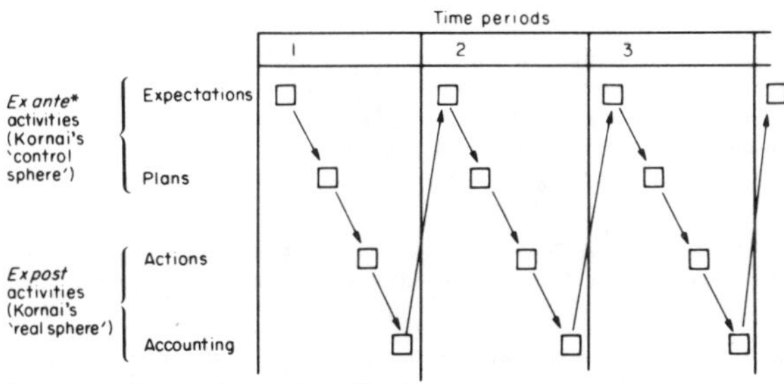

FIG. 5.1. Sequence analysis (based on Bentzel and Hansen, 1954).

Sequence analysis allows us to escape from the trap of helpless relativism induced by interdependencies which was described earlier, *without* misrepresenting the causal structure of the system being modelled. In each time period we have only one-way dependency, but no *ex ante* interdependency. To understand the intra-periodic relations of dependency we must distinguish between conditioned and unconditioned plans. Conditioned plans are functions of the outcome of one or more future events within the period (e.g. other people's pricing). When these events have taken place the conditioned plan becomes unconditioned and action results. Therefore there is an obvious affinity between the conceptions of 'conditioned plans' and 'causality'.

Even though many of the actions may be simultaneous, inter-dependency within a time period need not result. Any *joint* plans of two or more actors are treated as the plans of a *single* behaviour unit, thus ruling out interdependency. Sequence analysis encourages a proper representation of causal structure because it recognizes that two separate economic subjects *cannot* act interdependently at the same time unless there are negotiations between them – in which case they should not be treated as separate subjects. All reactions include time lags of some sort, and the appropriate length of time periods will vary according to the minimum response times.

The gravity model provides an excellent example of how static equilibrium assumptions *create* the problem of interdependence and we have already seen how doubly-constrained journey-to-work models give the impression of total interdpendency among all workers in their simultaneous competition for all jobs and all housing.[13] Moreover, we have seen how a dynamic disequilibrium model (the relative space model), can eliminate the problem of interdependence. The method by which this model represents the placing of options by buyers on houses for sale and the consequent sorting process corresponds directly to the sequence analysis method, with its distinction between conditioned and unconditioned plans; as options are placed on some of the houses for sale, the plans of the remaining prospective buyers become more unconditioned. In the case of owner-occupiers whose ability to buy a new house depends on selling their old one, the conditional nature of the market processes is even more obvious. Therefore, if we are prepared to look at real-world behaviour, in its true dynamic context instead of the misleading abstractions of equilibrium economics, we can avoid the pitfalls of interdependence.[14]

A market is a feedback system in which the feedback enables economic subjects to *learn* of the repercussions of their own and others' actions. This stimulus-response process, coupled with 'originative' behaviour[15] is characteristic of social systems, and models which ignore this, such as Walrasian models with their concept of 'pre-reconciliation' of the plans of economic subjects, are a negation of the essence of human behaviour.

Given neoclassical economics' mis-specification of the operation of markets in time, it is not surprising that Kornai found it impossible to build truly dynamic simulation models using neoclassical theory (Kornai, 1971, p. 300). The reasons for this are several. Firstly, the fact that equilibrium models collapse a succession of events into a single moment of time means that we are denied the principal clue for discovering the directions of causality, namely, the temporal ordering of events. Secondly, where there is a recognizable causal structure in neoclassical models, it usually contains (simultaneous) interdependencies. Thirdly, neoclassical models tend to be inadequately specified in terms of stocks and flows and consequently, the material effects of under- and over-supply and ineffective demand are simply not accounted for, even though the regulation of stock levels is an essential control variable of any production or marketing system (Kornai, 1971, pp. 299, 300, 364).

Fourthly, as Kornai, and Grossman (1974) have noted, the basic terms 'supply' and 'demand' are hopelessly underdefined and ambiguous. For example, 'supply' may mean:

(a) selling intentions;
(b) selling possibilities relative to constraints of stocks and buying intentions of buyers (actual *ex post* supply);
(c) the set of explored selling alternatives deemed implementable by the seller;
(d) that set of eligible selling alternatives which the seller would consider not only implementable but also acceptable from the point of view of his interests (Kornai, 1971, p. 238).

A similar set of definitions exists for 'demand'. Clearly, the required definitions have to be selected very carefully when formulating a correct model of a market, in order to prevent confusion. As we found in Chapter 2 in the critique of the Lowry model's economic base mechanism, the apparent validity of equilibrium demand—supply analysis rests upon the use of slippery, ambiguous definitions of 'supply' and 'demand'.

In view of the variety of different meanings of the basic terms, it is hardly surprising that the familiar Marshallian demand—supply curve diagram has been found lacking with respect to its temporal interpretation (Robinson and Eatwell, 1973, p. 162) and has been shown to deal only with superficial, first order market responses, ignoring the repercussions which undermine this form of analysis. For example, Shackle (1972) argues that it is difficult to imagine any movements along either curve which would not cause a shift in the other curve.

A fifth source of difficulties when trying to formulate a dynamic model using neoclassical theory is connected with the use of price as a control variable of a market. A prime aim of neoclassical and some classical theory was to demonstrate the internal logic and competence of 'The Price System' in controlling the economy, but in order to do so it had to invoke metaphysical and counterintuitive concepts such as Adam Smith's 'invisible hand' or Edgeworth's 'recontracting' or Walras' god-like 'auctioneer' or inappropriate mechanical analogies, such as Marshall's comparison of market equilibrium with the oscillations of a pendulum (Hines, 1971, p. 12; Lowe, 1965, p. 107). One of the most important results of the reinterpretation of Keynesian theory is that price, on its own, is not an adequate control variable for an economic system — either at the macro- or micro-level. Prices alone cannot both —

> ... *disseminate the information* necessary to coordinate the economic activities and plans of the independent transactors ... (and) *provide the incentives* for transactors to adjust their activities in such a manner that they become consistent in the aggregate. (Leijonhufvud, quoted in Hines, 1971, p. 11).

Economic actors can never obtain a set of prices which will obtain at future dates (Hines, 1971; Bliss, 1972), and neither present price- nor non-price information can guarantee perfect harmonization of the actions of separate economic actors because of the impossibility of perfect knowledge or perfect foresight and the existence of 'originative behaviour'. In the real world, where expectations, which are the bases of action, are usually inelastic, where demand is often reserved and supplies withheld during phases of unfavourable market conditions, and

where adjustments often incur costs themselves. prices are often the creatures rather than the
creators of economic behaviour.

5.4. ALTERNATIVE MODELS OF MARKET BEHAVIOUR

An acceptable alternative to neoclassical demand–supply analysis must include a clear
distinction between physical material flows and information flows. This assertion is echoed in
Forrester's system dynamics simulation technique (Forrester, 1961, 1968), in economics in
Kornai's distinction between a 'real sphere' and a 'control sphere', and in geography in
Langton's characterization of 'dualistic systems' (Langton, 1972). The explicit representation
of stocks and flows of materials together with information flows and 'originative' objectives in a
model would allow us to account for unsatisfied demand and unsold products. We could use
such a model to discover the extent to which activities are coordinated and 'equilibrium' would
become a matter for discovery, not presupposition. Moreover, we would even have to dispense
with the over-simplistic conceptual dichotomy of 'equilibrium' and 'disequilibrium'. In most
social systems there will be both positive and negative feedback loops, and some loops may
change sign under certain circumstances. The interaction over time of these loops determines
the dynamics of the system: to say that the system is simply either in 'equilibrium' or
'disequilibrium' is unenlightening.

The best-known alternative to the neoclassical models of price-fixing and market behaviour
is the Kaleckian model, which provides an explanation which is in much closer accord with our
real world experience. Kalecki (1971, Chapter 5) maintained that most fluctuations in demand
are absorbed through the 'dampening mechanisms' of stocks, and that firms responded to these
fluctuations primarily by varying output rather than by altering prices.[16] Price changes which
do occur result mainly from changes in costs of production. Firms generally operate below the
point of maximum practical capacity and, as has been found in many empirical studies, prime
costs (materials, wages and salaries) per unit of output tend to be stable. As the future is
uncertain, pricing policy can achieve profit maximization only very imperfectly. By a process of
trial and error, the firm finds a price approximating the highest which can be achieved without
drastically reducing its sales and marginal revenue. On the producer's side of the market,
competition through advertising is preferred to price competition as the latter reduces profits,
and on the consumer's side, constraints on the supply of information and ability to digest it,
coupled with the cost of travelling to different markets, make demand insensitive to all but
major price changes.

Kalecki demonstrated that the conditions in a market which permit a particular level of the
ratio of gross margins to the value of output to be realized, reveal the firm's *'degree of
monopoly'*.[17] There are clear similarities between this model and Bliss' housing market model
and Holt and David's job market model (see Chapter 4). In these cases the equivalent
trial-and-error mechanisms take the form of adjustments of the house sellers' *ex ante* prices and
the unemployed worker's acceptance wage. Kornai also emphasizes the importance of
adjustments of *ex ante* prices as functions of the length of the period of waiting for them to be
realized, and of expectations of future demand (Kornai, 1971, Chapter 18).

5.5. RATIONALITY AND ECONOMIC BEHAVIOUR

These 'anti-neoclassical' models recognize the importance of expectations and uncertainty in
governing behaviour without ducking behind the counterintuitive assumptions of 'perfect
foresight' or 'pre-reconsiliation'. They also perform a useful function in drawing us into a
discussion of some more general, but vitally important philosophical problems facing
model-builders. Most importantly, they lead us to question whether we can assume 'rational
behaviour' when every act is based on expectations in the face of uncertainty about the future.
Shackle (1967) goes as far as to question the use of the word 'uncertainty' in describing the
future, because it implies an already-existent body of facts which will not be altered by our
behaviour and about which we can be uncertain. Instead, he argues that we can only be rational

about the past, so that 'Time is a denial of the omnipotence of reason' (Shackle, 1972, p. 27), and 'To discern what specific action is rational is only useful *ex ante*, but is mostly only possible *ex post*' (Shackle, 1972, p. 84). The neoclassicists rejected time in order to retain rationality, and in so doing, misunderstood economic behaviour.

Shackle's acceptance of the limitations of rationality leads him to take a very pessimistic view of the *possibility* of economic modelling. This view is evident in his interpretation of Keynes' 'General Theory' – Keynes'

> ... ultimate thesis was brief and destructive. It declared that economic actions, most of all, the commanding activity of investment in durable facilities, were governed in their scale, character and timing by expectations, and that expectations can be transformed, and the 'confidence' which gives them their ascendancy can be dissolved by a breath of suggestion from 'the news', so that the size of the stream of general output, and the quantity of employment, rest upon the most mutable of all economic elements. Where in such a vision, is any place for theory which assumes that conduct can be rational, calculated, efficient and sure of success? Where is the basis of mechanistic, or 'hydraulic' determinism, which for orthodox analysts was the presupposition and *sine qua non* of analysis? Where is the mathematisation of economic theory? (Shackle, 1972, p. 224).

Shackle's challenge is no less relevant to urban modelling, and therefore requires an answer – before we go back confidently to calculating how many service jobs zone 26 will have, 15 years hence. As was acknowledged in the description of the relative space model (especially Section 4.6), some areas of human behaviour may exhibit too much novelty and irregularity to allow them to be generalized reasonably, and yet they may be too momentuous to be ignored.

Although some investment decisions which shape urban form may have been based on what Shackle would have considered a remarkably insubstantial rationality, we can take heart as model-builders by observing the very similarity of urban forms in the Western world, and the continuity of their development and of related types of economic behaviour. We must not allow the realization of the nature of life lived in time to make us resort to ideographic methods of study, where places and events are simply unique. The decision of a household to change house is only unique in a trivial sense, and the constraints of the existing structure of society at any one time are sufficient to severely limit any genuine novelty. Also, the expectations governing behaviour are commonly generated on the grounds of the belief that certain associations of events experienced in the past will be repeated in the future. Expectations of this sort (and they include formal forecasting models) are usually in some way self-fulfilling or, if the possible outcomes are highly undesirable, self-denying (Jahoda, 1973). In either and every case, man *creates* the future.

The very fact that we have to reiterate these truisms reveals the profundity of the delusions of much of social science and especially economics in trying to ignore them. Human behaviour cannot be reduced simply to a set of responses to stimuli, for there is an important sense in which behaviour is originative, in which it gives a thrust to the direction of change and the future (Shackle, 1974).[18] Economic theory which treats the 'market' as something to which people and institutions respond rather than as something created by them, or which legitimizes the behaviour of firms which refuse to invest because profits are low during a business slump, as being 'rational', interprets all behaviour as being of the response variety. As Keynes showed, profits can only be raised again after a slump by *originative actions* – by raising the level of investment so as to set a more constructive self-fulfilling prophecy in motion.

Acceptance of the importance of originative behaviour need not deny us the possibility of improving understanding through models, although it may limit their scope: the very fact that the past is unchangeable means that the existing structure will order the impact of originative behaviour in some way. Consequently, severe discontinuities in socio-economic development are rare in relation to the time scales dealt with in urban modelling. Perhaps then, we can best answer Shackle's challenge by asking another question – 'What is there so different about the present which will make the future much different from the past?'

5.6. CONCLUSION: TOWARDS POLITICAL ECONOMY

The implications of the critique of neoclassical economics for regional science and urban modelling are far-reaching. What at first appears as a harmless analytical aid – the assumption of equilibrium — leads us to make additional, supporting counterintuitive assumptions and enter a closed system of axioms, in which we find it impossible to understand disequilibrium development processes. Since equilibrium is the reference position we use to judge change, equilibrium analysis voids analysis of any other position (Kregel, 1973, p. 208). Of course, if we are not concerned about the correspondence of our models to the real world, we may find plenty of modelling work to do within the bounds of this closed system. Unfortunately, there is a depressing tendency for regional scientists to follow the lead of neoclassical mathematical economists in the elaboration of this fictional system, even managing to ignore the contradictions which the addition of space, with its inherent monopoly characteristics, introduces (Massey, 1974). For the sake of a once-promising new discipline, it is to be hoped that these neoclassical influences can be combatted before they become more deeply entrenched.

At the beginning of this chapter, we promised to attempt to bring down neoclassical economics on its own ground before showing that a shift of ground then becomes necessary, but most political economists would argue that this shift should go *beyond* our recommended (Kaleckian) models of market behaviour. Just as the relative space model would seem to rest rather uncomfortably between the levels of resolution of functionalist models and urban political economy, so the alternative market models proposed by Kalecki and Kornai rest between the levels of neoclassical models dealing with the 'superficial appearances' of economies, and political economic theory dealing with their structural determinants. Nevertheless, they are both important in that they demonstrate that the 'surface features' are inextricably tied to these 'inner relations'.[19]

We first argued that in neoclassical analysis, the determining relations of market processes are either left out or inverted and represented as contingent relations, all by means of the fatal 'revealed preference' assumption which renders *ex post* exchange relations as *self-explanatory*. Our answer was to separate out *ex ante* from *ex post* quantities and hence show how the latter are determined by, but need not equal, the former. If our prescriptions go no further than this, then we can be accused of voluntarism, for exchange now appears as the outcome of buyers' and sellers' 'wishes', wishes that are certainly partly independent of exchange relations, but which seem to come from nowhere. So what determines these *ex ante* quantities? What determines the determining relations of exchange, e.g. the decisions of builders to 'supply' housing, the decisions of people to acquire housing, the decisions of credit-lending institutions to finance house-buying?

For those involved in the provision of new housing, potential demand for the housing is no more than a necessary condition — it is certainly not a sufficient condition. The investment must also be profitable and the necessary finance must be raised. As students of the political economy of housing have at last realized, the operation of the housing market is not to be explained by examining exchange relations such as house prices and journey-to-work distances in isolation, but must be viewed in terms of its relations with finance capital as providers of credit for purchase of private housing and for construction of local authority housing (e.g. Lamarche, 1976; Duncan, 1976; Boddy, 1976; Gray, 1976; Pickvance, 1976; Harvey, 1973, 1974). Distinction must be made between use value and exchange value in order to explain the different behaviour patterns of the various groups involved. In the case of those institutions to which housing is an exchange value, profit-maximization governs decision-making, and so the means by which profits are maximized must be examined. For the purchaser, to whom housing is usually a use-value, access to credit is crucial. Set in this context, the contingent nature of effective demand and supply is clearly revealed. The issue of how many trips entering zone 13 come from zone 49, suddenly seems perversely unreal. Exactly, it is so. An equivalent argument can be made at the regional level. Countless studies have been made of regional multipliers, but these too refer only to surface relations. Regional input—output studies, besides compounding identification errors in their use of coefficients fitted to *ex post* exchange relations, say nothing about the causes of the inter-industry dependencies, they conceal the very things which bring about regional development — capital accumulation, profitability, movement of surplus, realization problems (cf. Murray, 1972; Harvey, 1975), and merely document the superficial effects of these inner processes.

Therefore, as is so often the case, methodological critiques suggest ontological shifts; the critique of the neoclassical *method* of analyzing markets also suggests that the preoccupation with markets is itself misplaced, and should be replaced by political economic studies which put exchange into a subordinate position relative to *production*, distribution and consumption.

NOTES: CHAPTER 5

1. For a good example of this see the Boddy–Evans interchange on economic theories and housing (Boddy, 1975, Evans, 1975).

2. See, for example, J. Robinson, 1964, 1965; Harcourt and Laing, 1971; Hunt and Schwartz, 1972; Nell, 1972; and see Appendix A.

3. As was shown in Chapter 3, the same argument applies to the switch from fitting a gravity model to an existing trip distribution to using it for the prediction of the location of activities.

4. This same procedure was found in the Lowry model's economic base mechanism, where the equivalent 'exchange relation' was the activity rate, (Chapter 2).

5. Bergson, quoted in Robinson (1962, p. iii).

6. Emphasis added.

7. Original emphasis.

8. For example, see Evans (1974, p. 21).

9. Cf. Section 2.1, the example of definition of variables in the economic base model.

10. Kaldor (1972) argues that the elaboration of this closed system and the acceptance of its 'stylized facts' has made the possibility of generalizing it to disequilibrium systems even more remote.

11. This answers Britton Harris' widely quoted assertion that the (alleged) existence of equilibrium tendencies in urban systems justifies the use of (long run) equilibrium models, for while there may indeed be such tendencies, there are certain to be counteracting positive feedback loops which prevent the hypothetical long-run equilibrium being reached. (Harris, 1968).

12. Also known as 'period analysis' (Baumol, 1959).

13. See above, Section 4.7.

14. Those familiar with the system dynamics technique of simulation will note its striking congruence with sequence analysis. System dynamics does not permit simultaneous equations and hence interdependence, and so it induces a correct representation of causal structure. System dynamics is therefore potentially compatible with non-neoclassical models of markets, e.g. that of Kornai (1971). (cf. Sayer 1975, Chapter 9).

15. Shackle (1974).

16. Firms dealing with raw material extraction or perishable goods are often exceptions, as they have limited possibilities for stockholding.

17. It is also of interest for regional science that this Kaleckian model is potentially compatible with central place theory, for the latter shows how space contributes to the 'degree of monopoly'. Paradoxically, central place theory was based on a neo-classical perfect competition economic model, but the addition of space turned it into a model of spatial monopolies!

18. For an interesting parallel, see Chomsky's devastating critique of B. F. Skinner's attempt to explain verbal behaviour by a stimulus-response model. The critique has many similarities with the Cambridge criticism of neoclassical economics, especially in Chomsky's discussion of the verbal equivalent of the *ex ante – ex post* distinction (Chomsky, 1959).

19. Sraffa's 'Production of commodities by means of commodities' performs this function of linking 'surface appearances' to structural determinants with great force, by showing that prices may be determined in the sphere of production and distribution rather than in exchange. (Sraffa, 1960).

CHAPTER 6

A Structuralist Synthesis

6.1. THE FUNCTIONALIST APPROACH

By now, it should be apparent that many of the faults of specific models which have been discussed all belong to the same category. Description of these faults for each model may therefore seem to have entailed some repetition of arguments, although it is hoped that each 'reprise' has been illuminating since it has been fashioned to a different set of circumstances. As these models of regional science and neoclassical economics share so many similar types of approaches, assumptions, and faults, we shall characterize them as belonging to the same 'paradigm'.[1] This paradigm is a positivist one, but more specifically it consists of four interrelated methodological elements — functionalism, behaviourism, instrumentalism, and spatial separatism, of which the first is the most dominant, and hence we shall denote the combination of all four by the blanket term — the 'functionalist approach'. Before defining these methodological elements in detail, we shall attempt to characterize the essence of the shared faults of the models and theories belonging to this paradigm.

It should also be clear that models such as neoclassical equilibrium demand—supply models or gravity models are *closed systems* defined by a set of mutually supporting axioms: they have become 'rigid mathematical crystals' which can only be accepted as correct or incorrect, with no intermediate case (Kornai, 1971, p. 367). We have attacked these 'crystals' on different facets — e.g. by reference to their conceptualization of the three elements of space, time and process, and have pointed to the necessary connections between each facet. Attempts to improve *parts* of these models (such as Curry's 'spatial analysis of gravity flows'), are useful for understanding the basic axioms, but also serve to heighten and expose their internal contradictions. Many regional scientists have acknowledged isolated criticisms of specific aspects of 'functionalist' models, but these criticisms have as yet failed to amount to a refutation because the necessary connections between the different facets have not been illuminated. Consequently, recommendations for solving the problems have been correspondingly piecemeal. If, on the other hand, we can demonstrate the structure of the network of mutually-supporting axioms, it becomes clear that progress may only be possible with a major act of demolition of this basic conceptual framework.

Perhaps one of the most general characteristics of the 'functionalist' approach is its concentration on the superficial aspects of a system of interest, as if they reveal at the present moment, all the information necessary to explain its existence and functioning. This approach is supported by the customary, and indeed indispensable assumption of equilibrium.

More importantly, 'functionalist' analysis tends to make its generalizations about empirical regularities existing among the *contingent relations* of the system being studied. A 'system' is usually defined as a set of elements together with their attributes and relationships between these elements. 'Functionalist' analysis usually restricts the definition of 'relationships' to the 'synchronic transformations', as they are known in structuralist jargon, i.e. the contingent relations obtaining at time *t*. (see Fig. 6.1.). In the context of the systems studied in regional science, examples of synchronic transformations are activity rates, prices, regular interaction patterns, physical distance separating activities, etc. While the synchronic transformations are largely *contingent* upon the existence of the elements, they also support and sometimes change the elements themselves.

As was very plain from the example of explanation in neoclassical economics (taken from Dobb, 1973, Chapter 1), functionalist models tend to assume that because we have some

measures of these transformations, we can simply treat one of the elements as exogenously
defined and, by simple mathematical operations, derive the whole system, so that the
contingent relations of the real world become the determining relations of the model. (see Fig
6.2.). It has been shown repeatedly that this procedure is quite spurious, though often
intellectually seductive to those whose prime interest is mathematical modelling *per se*. The
implicit assumption that the contingent relations are stable enables us to misrepresent economic
and urban systems as being in states of soothing, harmonious equilibrium. By feeding in
equilibrium assumptions and then 'proving' that the system is in equilibrium, we merely achieve
a satisfying *déjà vue* which short-circuits understanding.

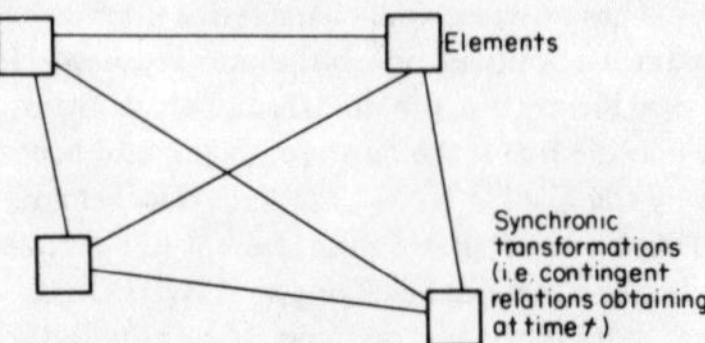

**FIG. 6.1. The system of interest of functionalist
analysis.**

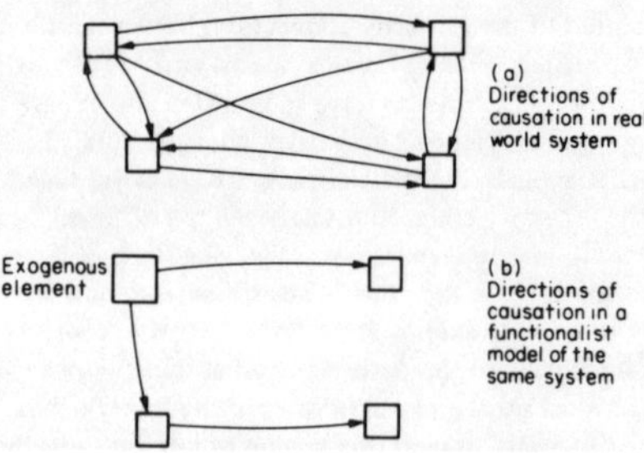

**FIG. 6.2. Identification/specification error in
functionalist analysis.**

The same type of major specification/identification error was found in the Lowry model's
assumption of a one-way direction of causation from jobs to population, while in the
singly-constrained gravity model it has a spatial expression (see above, Chapters 2 and 3). In
single causal chain models, such as Wilson's general urban model (1974), this type of error is
compounded several times over.

Jobs → Population → Housing

Single causal chain model

Other modelling procedures may invite similar errors. For example, the use of statistical
inference techniques such as regression analysis, to 'estimate' the structure of a model system in
which there are interdependencies, without incorporating prior knowledge of directions of
causation, invites similar spurious results of very uncertain interpretation.

As Bentzel and Hansen (1954) and Dobb (1973) show, causal structure cannot be deduced
simply from a study of a system state at one point in time — the elements and synchronic
transformations merely tell us what has to be explained. In economics, synchronic
transformations are usually *ex post* quantities which represent the resolution of conflicting

plans of economic subjects. The word 'conflicting' may appear too strong, until it is realized that, since each subject cannot know the intentions and actions of others in the future, there is bound to be some conflict of interests even if it is not openly antagonistic. Therefore '*Ex post* equilibria necessarily conceal their own origins' (Shackle, 1972, p. 162). Moreover, *ex post* equilibria are simply *definitional* equalities — they do not imply any real equilibrium of a system (Klappholz and Mishan, 1962).

Spatial equivalents of this argument raise important questions about the logic of analyzing spatial distributions and interactions in abstraction from the (non-spatial) socio-economic processes which create them. Studies of nearest-neighbour distances, distance decay functions, spatial autocorrelation, etc., in fact most of the 'geometric' school or 'spatial separatist'[2] approach in modern geography, concentrate almost entirely on synchronic transformations treated in isolation. Consequently, while these studies may find order in *appearances* — in the geometry of urban and regional systems, their utility for understanding the origins and functioning of those systems is limited.

It would of course be quite unfair to overstate this and say that spatial separatist studies have been of no use whatsoever. On the contrary, they have revitalized the formerly moribund discipline of geography and produced important insights on the nature of the space economy which have both enriched and challenged non-spatial literature in related subjects. Thus, it has already been proved to be a valuable approach for understanding formerly sparsely investigated aspects of spatial development. However, it is considered that its usefulness is primarily limited to this function of providing an *initial, outline* understanding of 'surface' phenomena. It is obviously important to appreciate that interaction is generally found to vary directly with mass and inversely with distance in a fairly regular manner, but it is unreasonable to expect that empirical regularity to provide more than a superficial understanding of the growth and functioning of socio-economic systems in space. In order to achieve the latter, an integration of space, time and process in the model would have to correspond in a more balanced manner to the integration that exists in human practice; to ignore space because economists traditionally ignore it, or to overemphasize space because, as a geographer one has a vested interest in it, would be to distort that reality, although such biases of functionalist approaches may have provided a useful starting point for breaking into the system of interest.

The use of statistical inference in much of social science and especially economics also belongs to the functionalist approach. Leontief (1971) provides an argument which links up Dobb's (1973) logical critique with a critique of the use of statistical inference in economics.

> As theorists we consruct systems in which prices, outputs, rates of saving and investment, etc., are explained in terms of production functions, consumption functions, and other structural relationships whose parameters are assumed, at least for argument's sake, to be known. As econometricians, engaged in what passes for empirical research, we do not try, however, to ascertain the actual shapes of these functions by turning up new factual information. We make an about face and rely on indirect statistical inference to derive the unknown structural relationships from the observed magnitudes of prices, outputs and other variables that, in our role as theoreticians, we treated as unknowns. (Leontief, 1971, p. 4).

Exactly the same sort of 'about-face' is made when we pass from the stage of specification of a gravity or Lowry-type model, where the spatial interaction parameters together with the activity rate and population-serving ratio, determine the population and service jobs by zone, to the stage of calibration where we estimate the former and take the latter as given. Clarkson (1963, p. 85) shows that this procedure does not conform to standard (deductive-nomological) models of scientific explanation. The econometric approach, and likewise calibration exercises in urban modelling, do not *test* models, but assume them to be true and then *fit* them to the data. They 'illustrate' or 'decorate' the theories, but do not provide support for the basic hypotheses (Kaldor, 1972, p. 123a). In the case of exercises in statistical inference

> ... the computation of correlation coefficients and fitting of regression lines should not be taken for a law-finding method as is so often the case in the behavioural sciences. When a linear regional model is assumed and the parameters computed from the data, the central law that is supposed to run through the 'noisy' (scattered) information is not found but assumed beforehand ... (M. Bunge, in Guelke, 1971, p. 41).

And so, models which rely heavily on calibration, such as Lowry-type and gravity models, are not validated in any sense by their being fitted to a certain region or city at a single point in time.[3] Calibration and validation are in some ways utterly opposed. The very fact that we have to rely upon 'tuning-up' every time we use such models suggests that they are theoretically deficient, but the fact that the calibration process also *covers up* these defects makes it difficult to establish any degree of empirical truth in the model or to falsify the model. Sometimes the theoretical structure is so distorted that absurd parameter values are assigned in calibration, as was the case with Cripps' and Cater's disaggregated residential location model (see above, Section 3.8.), but even then the response tended to be to patch up the model rather than to discover the faults in its theoretical structure. Within the wide range of possibilities where parameters are not wrongly-signed, there is usually no means of telling whether the values are 'reasonable' or not. By definition, the use of 'fudge-factors' in a model immediately renders its operation opaque. For this reason, Forrester (1968, pp. 8-9), argues that they should be excluded entirely from models and that all variables should be directly relatable to the actual processes being modelled.

In the case of gravity models, we have seen that the parameter values cannot, on *a priori* grounds, be stable for a situation in which spatial development is taking place (see above, Section 4.8.). Not surprisingly, the only true empirical test of the robustness of gravity models known to the author (in which a shopping model was fitted to one area, and then used to attempt to replicate the shopping patterns of another area, without any further calibration), produced a dismal failure (Roe, undated). Therefore, despite their popularity, despite the conventional wisdom which seems to regard a 'good fit' as adequate evidence of validity, the robustness and degree of confirmation of gravity/entropy-maximizing models is minimal. In the case of doubly-constrained models, their nature as *ex post rationalizations* (the constraints from which they are derived refer to *ex post* quantities), denies the possibility of using them to generate data other than those from which they are derived. Like utility theory and the theory of demand, gravity/entropy-maximizing models do not belong to empirical science.

Bailey (1975, p. 63) argues that functionalism's fundamental and dangerous error is its promotion of 'what *is*' to the level of 'what *must be*'. This statement may seem rather metaphysical when considered in isolation. However, when we recall the particular problems that we have discussed, we can demonstrate its truth. In the case of gravity models, we found that they assume that the trip distribution that *is* (as found in the calibration process) is the trip distribution that *must be* (because trip distribution becomes a determining relation in a single-constrained gravity model). In the case of the demand—supply models of neoclassical economics, we found that, by means of the equilibrium and revealed preference assumptions, we could interpret a *particular* observed set of contingent exchange relations as the exchange relations which *must* be. Functionalist models manage to misrepresent the *status quo*, to legitimize the *status quo*, and, in a forecasting situation, to extrapolate from this distorted representation of the *status quo*.

The trend towards building dynamic models in regional science has perhaps partly been a response to the vague recognition of specific instances of these 'functionalist fallacies'. However, this on its own is not enough to break free of the closed system of axioms, for we have seen that trivial and semi-trivial dynamic models share the same features, although they may help to make us more aware of some of the distortions of this mode of abstraction.

Figure 6.3 represents the network of mutually-supporting features and assumptions or 'closed set of axioms' of functionalist models in regional science diagrammatically. It attempts to summarize and lay bare the necessary connections between the major points of criticism covered in the foregoing chapters, and hence it hopefully constitutes the heaviest blow in our bid to overthrow the functionalist paradigm.

6.1.1. Methodological Summary: Functionalism, Behaviourism, Spatial Separatism and Instrumentalism

In the social sciences, economists and regional scientists generally rank low in terms of methodological awareness. Ironically, those who are least aware of the considerable methodological problems involved in the study of society, tend to be those who most confidently proclaim the 'scientific' nature of their own studies. Economists often think of their subject as the 'hardest' of the social sciences, but regard sociology, from which most of the major contributions to the philosophy of social science have come, as a 'soft' or 'unscientific' discipline. For many social scientists, there is only *one* type of science —

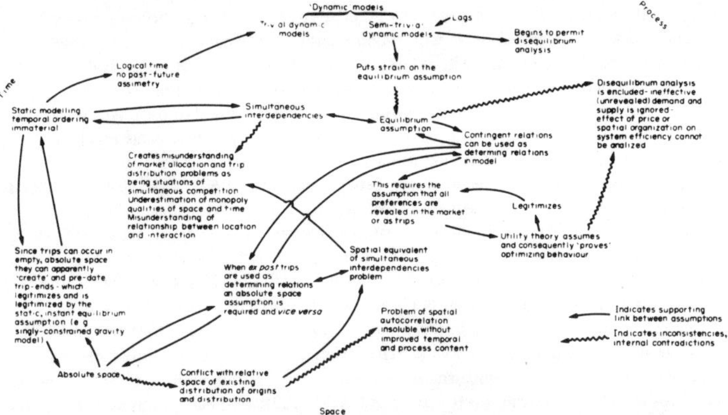

FIG. 6.3. A diagrammatic summary of part of the network of mutually-supporting assumptions of the functionalist approach (N.B. only a few of the total number of links are shown).

positivism, and all the rest is non-science. Positivist social science itself has been strongly challenged, e.g. Hollis and Nell (1975); Keat and Urry (1975); Giddens (1974), but the variants of positivism upon which regional science and neoclassical economics are founded — functionalism, behaviourism, and instrumentalism, are particularly heavily discredited. Regional scientists seem to be totally unaware of this, but as Bailey (1975, p. 59) observes, the critique and rejection of functionalism and behaviourism in sociology is now almost routine! Recently, in a series of geographical articles by Sack, spatial separatism has also been attacked (Sack, 1972, 1973, 1974). Given this undermining of the methodological foundations of what we have loosely termed the functionalist paradigm, it is worth summarizing the methodological characteristics of its components in order to underline the more substantive summary of the previous section.

Firstly, Functionalism, *in the strict sense*, is a branch of positivism which interprets the elements of social reality almost entirely in terms of their contribution to the functioning and maintenance of an observed social system. Most systems analysis is functionalism carried to an extreme and highly complex form. Questions of *origin* of the various elements of the system are either ignored or distorted by teleological interpretations. To take a simple example, housing is implicitly assumed to come into being merely to fulfil the function of meeting a demand for housing. (If only that were true!) In the crude forms of functionalism found in regional science, the possibility of the behaviour of elements being *dys*functional or contradictory is excluded. As we have seen, functionalism can be attacked on the grounds of logic and choice of assumptions, but it is essential to see the connections of this critique with the *ideological* critique of functionalism. For example, static equilibrium analysis is *doubly* deficient because it leads to logical absurdities, *and* it also legitimizes the *status quo* and obscures the possibilities for radical change of system structure. In looking at things only in terms of the way in which they happen to be functioning at the present time, functionalism makes what *is*, appear to be what *must* be, and smuggles in a conception of society as based on consensus and equilibrium, rather than on conflict and disequilibrium. (For fuller discussions, see Bailey, 1975; Andreski, 1974; Rex, 1961; Giddens, 1974; Keat and Urry, 1975).

Secondly, regional science is characterized by a crude form of Behaviourism. Behaviourism maintains that scientific explanations should refer only to observable behaviour. We should explain the occurrence of a particular social event, not by reference to unobservable motivations or expectations which cannot be directly verified, but to other observable events. There is, therefore, an implicit 'stimulus-response' form to explanation, which by-passes the realm of thought, or at least makes the latter unproblematic and mechanical. Economists' aversion to dealing with expectations and intentions and their absurd invention of the 'revealed preference' assumption can be interpreted as examples of behaviourism. Behaviourism's superficiality goes very harmoniously with functionalism's preoccupation with timeless functioning of social systems and lack of historical perspective. Another more insidious characteristic of behaviourism is its treatment of *socially*-produced relations or objects as mere 'things', in the same way that non-human objects of study are treated in the physical sciences. For example, in Alonso's theory of urban land use, rent is simply conceived as a technical 'thing' – no investigation or explanation is made of the social relations between landowner and tenant upon which the very existence of rent depends (Alonso, 1967). Again, behaviourism is doubly deficient; firstly for its treatment of selfconscious, purposive human behaviour in mechanical terms (e.g. Marshallian demand–supply analysis), and secondly, resulting from this, on ideological grounds, we can object to its profoundly reactionary reification of social practice. (For fuller discussions, see Rex, 1961; Keat and Urry, 1975; Bailey, 1975; Filmer *et al.*, 1972. Although the subject matter is a long way from regional science, Chomsky's celebrated demolition of Skinner's *Verbal Behaviour* is too good to miss (Chomsky, 1959).)

We have already commented on Spatial Separatism, and so we need do little more than indicate its relations with functionalism, behaviourism and instrumentalism. Clearest of all, are its affinities with behaviourism, for it maintains that the spatial aspects of physical phenomena can be understood in isolation from the real world temporal processes which brought them into being. Spatial separatists search for 'laws' which refer only to the observable *spatial* attributes of social phenomena – laws which are separate from those governing temporal processes, e.g. a spatial 'law' of distance-decay of spatial interaction which is independent of process 'laws' governing the social processes embodied in that spatial interaction.

The systems approach in geography can be seen as an alliance of functionalism and spatial separatism. Both tend to exclude questions of genesis, indeed modern geography's exaggeration of the importance of functional relations can be interpreted as an over-reaction against traditional geography's exaggerated emphasis of genetic explanation. Geographers paid some attention to the problems of 'system-closure', but chiefly in terms of the closure of purely *spatial* systems – i.e. functional regions. Urban modellers, having discovered that a high degree of closure could be achieved in the definition of the spatial extent of labour markets, seem to have neglected other imperfectly closed sectors. For example, systems models of residential location cut straight through the heart of the housing system, because they leave out any account of the construction of housing. Therefore the problem created by functionalism (system-closure) is inseparable from the problems created by spatial separatism – which, of course, is hardly surprising given the inseparability of space, time and process. (For fuller accounts, see Sack, 1972, 1973, 1974).

Instrumentalism is perhaps the most insidious of all these components of regional science's methodology, for it legitimizes all the others. Instrumentalists argue that models need only be 'useful', 'stimulating', 'intuitively-appealing', *computational devices* which generate correct predictions. We can only question the 'usefulness' of a model, not its truth, and its primary purpose is prediction rather than explanation. This view of the role of models obviously legitimizes such models as gravity or entropy-maximizing models in which there is no pretence that the mechanisms within the model, e.g. finding the maximally probable trip distribution, have any parallel in real world processes. The best-known advocate of instrumentalism is probably the economist, Milton Friedmann, but it is also very pervasive in geography;[4] indeed to justify using spatial separatist models one would have to invoke instrumentalism.

In the critical literature on methodology in the social sciences, instrumentalism is almost universally discredited. Models with incorrect assumptions can only be wrong or at least right for the wrong reasons. In the models that we have examined, even the slender justification of correct prediction falls away, because it has not been shown that they can predict successfully; they can only be *fitted* successfully. The critique in the preceding chapters could be interpreted as a documentation of the consequences of instrumentalism. One of the most damning conclusions was that the technical problems of (instrumentalist) entropy-maximizing models were artificially *created* by the use of a distorted 'mode of abstraction', and that attempts to find technical solutions to them within this same 'mode of abstraction' were utterly futile. Such technical problems as the interference of spatial autocorrelation in gravity/entropy-maximizing models do not correspond to real world problems.[5] Therefore, to avoid these artifical problems,

it makes sense to reject instrumentalism and base our models not on ingenious but empty
formalisms, but rather directly on 'human practice'. Compare, e.g. the empty abstractions of
residential location models with their metaphysical distance-decay functions, with the recent
research on the political economy of housing, with its direct reference to real world institutions
and problems. (e.g. compare Apps, 1971; Duncan, 1976; Boddy, 1976).

6.2. A STRUCTURALIST APPROACH[6]

The structuralist approach is in many ways the opposite of the functionalist paradigm. It
attempts to discover the causal structure, processes and origins which underlie the superficial
system state. It concentrates on the determining relations of systems to a much greater extent
than does functionalist analysis, even in situations where the contingent relations may be more
regular and observable. Structuralist analysis recognizes that several or most of the elements in
the system may have aspects of behaviour which are independent of what happens to other
elements, so that in the context of a single, small system, most of the variables are partly
endogenous and partly exogenous. Indeed, our denial of the possibility of perfect knowledge
and foresight requires that there will *always* be elements of independent behaviour.

The synchronic transformations reflect the extent to which the behaviour of the variables is
endogenous — they do *not* represent simultaneous interdependence among the variables (as this
is impossible in the real world), but rather they are the outcome of non-simultaneous two-way
causation as described above (see Chapter 5). It is only by investigating the aspects of
independent behaviour of the variables that we can determine appropriate equations of motion
(see Fig. 6.4.).

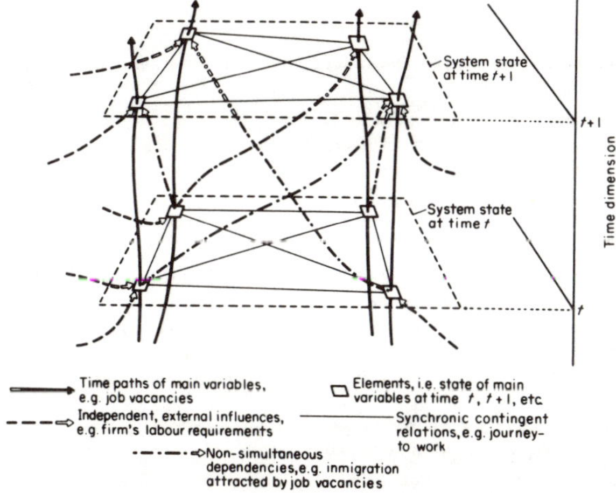

FIG. 6.4. The system of interest of structuralist analysis: diachronic change.

As Ward (1973) observes, in the context of economics, there is a paradox in that, while there
is a 'fundamental preconception' that everything depends on everything else, yet —

In practice (model) specification depends crucially on deciding that certain variables are *not* dependent on
certain others. (Ward, 1973, 262n).

We must not follow the functionalist route of assuming just one element to be exogenous for
the sake of analytical simplicity, but specify the degree of independence of *all* variables. This
may result in a model which can only be solved by simulation, but then, as we have seen,
mathematical elegance can often be bought only at the price of distorting the causal structure.

For example, in looking at the link between the demographic and economic sectors of an area, it would not do to concentrate entirely on migration, labour demand etc. as expressions of the causal relationships between the two sectors, as a basis for constructing a model. We must also include the elements of independent behaviour such as natural increase or changing productivity. Even *within* the elements of migration and labour demand, we will find that there are independent components, such as migration due to non-economic factors. In addition to this, we must specify the relations between the independent and dependent components of each sector, e.g. between migration rates and birth rates (see Fig. 6.5). It is also clear that the parameters of one system may be internal variables of a larger system within which it is nested.

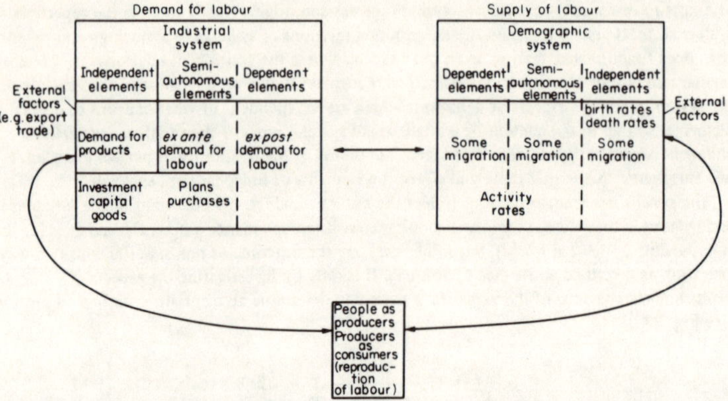

FIG. 6.5. Independent and dependent elements of the interaction of the 'supply and demand' of labour.

The structuralist approach allows *diachronic change*, (where system structure may change) to be modelled, in contrast to the restriction of functionalist trivial and semi-trivial dynamic models to modelling *synchronic change* —

> . . . systems must exist as an organised set of relationships, or as a 'structure', which 'behaves' to perform some function, during the process of which the original relationships are changed so that the system in effect becomes something else. (Langton, 1972, p. 136).

The constraining effect of present structure on future behaviour is usually sufficient to make diachronic change gradual and discontinuities rare. This is more simply expressed in D'Arcy Thompson's famous dictum that 'growth creates form and form limits growth'.

Only when there is synchronic change, i.e. when the system is in equilibrium, can the functioning and growth of the system be reduced to its internal transformations: otherwise, the transformations are *formative* (Langton, 1972; Piaget, 1973). Piaget goes further and argues that even when dealing with a real-world system which is unequivocally in equilibrium, we are not absolved from explaining how it came into existence.

> . . . the central problem of structuralism in the biological and human sciences is that of reconciling structure and genesis, since every structure involves a genesis and every genesis must be conceived as the (strictly formative) transition of an initial structure to a final structure. (Piaget, 1973, p. 24).

This 'central problem' is evaded by most urban and economic models. Studies which ignore how static equilibrium came into being are therefore apologetic as they legitimize the *status quo* by failing to show whether there is any alternative to the existing socio-economic framework (Dobb, 1973).

Some of the voluminous literature on systems theory and methodology has been consistent with this structuralist approach, e.g. Langton (1972). However, in practice, systems analysis has tended to concentrate excessively on functional explanation to the exclusion of genetic explanation. While the pitfalls of functionalist analysis stem from this gross imbalance of these two modes of explanation, the structuralist approach affirms their inseparability.

Piaget tries to show how structure, growth and functioning are connected in the context of economics by distinguishing between 'values of finality' or of means and ends, and 'values of yield', which relate to the costs and benefits of achieving and maintaining the values of finality. The two types of value are clearly highly related, but Piaget's distinction helps us to understand how imbalances between the two are resolved to produce structural change. The more open a system, and the further it is from equilibrium, the larger the imbalances between the two types of values and the weaker the connection between synchronic functioning and diachronic structural change. Therefore, it becomes still more clear, that it does not make sense to attempt to represent the growth of an open, disequilibrium system such as a city purely in terms of its present functioning, i.e. its spatial interaction and exchange relations.

This type of causal analysis is also useful for illuminating the roles of particular disciplines in understanding urban reality. The diagrams used in Fig. 6.2 can be reinterpreted for this purpose so that the 'elements' represent particular research viewpoints — e.g. urban studies centred around *planning*, or around *locational* patterns. Each element has a place in, or is an important aspect of, the urban 'totality', and as we found with particular variables in the models discussed above, each element has both links with others, and aspects of independence — e.g. spatial organization is an important problem for all economies regardless of whether they are feudal, capitalist or socialist, and yet the *particular* forms of spatial organization will reflect the different types of socio-economic relations encountered. However, as with functionalist models, there is a common tendency to overemphasize the importance of the element which happens to be taken as the viewpoint. For example, in some quarters, it has almost become accepted by the conventional wisdom that all urban research should be primarily relevant to *planning*. The apparent interdisciplinary nature of such studies often belies their onesidedness — other elements may be 'taken into account', but only insofar as they relate to planning — their independent aspects are largely ignored and too much of the responsibility for actual interactions is loaded onto the planning element. Thus, the relative importance of planning in determining urban development and functioning, may be exaggerated, and consequently policymakers may underestimate the power of forces outside their control. While it would be foolish to suggest that we cannot understand any part of an urban system until we understand the whole, it would be wise to keep the dangers of partial functionalist analyses in mind, and to attempt to locate the importance of particular aspects, such as planning or the spatial dimension, within a concept of the urban totality.

Figure 6.6, which is intended to be contrasted with Fig. 6.3, is a crude diagrammatic summary of the network of mutually- supporting assumptions and characteristics of the

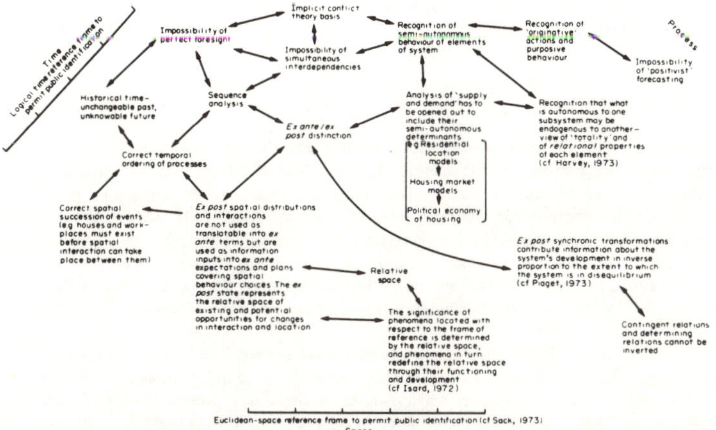

FIG. 6.6. A diagrammatic summary of the network of mutually-supporting assumptions of the 'structuralist' approach.

structuralist approach. Again, it is the 'mutually-supporting' aspect which is the most important, for many of the individual features have been advocated in isolation for some considerable time but their advocacy has been weakened by their isolation.

To some the cure may no doubt seem worse than the disease, for a structuralist approach may impel us to include far more in our models than we can handle, so that we may start from trying to understand some small subsystem, and in our search for a system closure which allows the determining relations to be included, end up modelling the entire urban system. This search process in itself may be a valuable heuristic exercise for discovering the position of certain urban problems within their wider context. It may, for instance, force us to the conclusion that urban problems are the outward expression of more fundamental social, economic and political problems and not simply aberrations of particular areas. Where a subsystem's behaviour is chiefly determined by variations in its external co-ordinates (and this may be the normal case), it might be wise to build generalized models of the larger systems which internalize these external co-ordinates first (and perhaps at the level of 'urban political economy'), in order to discover their range of variation, before building a partial model of the subsystem, and then running it against these variations.

This search for 'determining relations' does not necessarily entail an infinite regress: the regress ends at the level of macro-political economy. For example, to explain property development we have to include an examination of the flows of finance capital and investment in property. The particular market conditions and spatial distributions of individual cities are still important at this level, for the realization of this investment is dependent on the social manipulation of the inherent monopoly characteristics of space in those cities. At a still higher level, that of macro-political economy, investment in property is dependent on its expected rate of return as compared with other forms of investment, such as industrial investment. At every level, the prior historical development of the structure is crucial; e.g. the amount of funds available for investment, is, as Kalecki (1971) showed, dependent on past levels of spending and investment.

While it is important to keep in mind these relations which make up a rough schema of the 'totality' of which cities are a part, a structuralist model would not have to represent all of it. A subsystem could be modelled in a structuralist manner provided that all the autonomous aspects of the elements represented as such, i.e. as exogenous variables, rather than as functions of a single convenient 'determinant' such as consumer demand.

Thus, although the adoption of a structuralist approach may put heavier demands on model construction, it is more firmly grounded in human practice than is functionalist modelling; we represent urban development in terms of the actual processes of development instead of in terms of the consequences of those processes as they appear 'on the surface', in the form of day-to-day functioning.

6.3. CONCLUSION

One of the most basic causes of the inadequacy of the models we have criticized is the misguided attempt to make the 'soft' sciences 'hard', to equate 'science' with 'natural science' and therefore, to use an inhibiting methodology (positivism) based upon the idolatory of physics, which is quite inappropriate to the study of society.[7] Wright Mills attacked this type of social science, for its naive belief in the transferability of techniques from the natural sciences, for its tendency to substitute mathematical and statistical techniques for scholarly knowledge of society, for its tendency to ignore social structure in explaining behaviour and to invoke 'psychologism' by loading all the explanatory factors of behaviour onto individual 'preferences', (Wright Mills, 1959).

Nevertheless, the dominant impression given by the urban modelling literature is a confident one of research as the application and development of a reliable 'standard tool-kit' of models and techniques such as input—output, entropy-maximization, linear programming, etc.[8] The technocratic and highly formalized presentation of urban models as little more than internally consistent sets of equations, as if their degree of confirmation was on a par with those of physics, and with little or no discussion of choice of assumptions or mode of abstraction, militates against useful critical appraisal. As a result, in the case of planning models, the planner is rarely advised to ask whether the model's conceptualization of the city and urban life is appropriate — the validity of the mode of abstraction is largely taken for granted. All the planner is supposed to worry about are the secondary issues of zoning systems, data sources, calibration, etc.

One of the chief barriers to progress in regional science is the very thing which is least discussed by regional scientists, that is, the mode of abstraction — the choice of what should be studied, what should be left out, and how it should be conceptualized. Instead, it seems to be implicitly assumed that the adoption of mathematical techniques of analysis is all that is required, so that we need not worry about content and meaning. However, it is probably only possible to see the merits and problems of different modes of abstraction through critiques of particular models which exemplify them. Models, by definition, simplify reality, but always at the risk of distorting and obscuring it. The debates which have characterized urban modelling in its period of 'normal science' or consensus regarding the appropriate mode of abstraction have been highly technocratic and centred around 'secondary' issues of mathematical consistency and elegance, and practical application of models. These debates have rarely been addressed to the more fundamental issues of the interpretation of the meaning of the implicit and explicit assumptions of models — the foundations upon which the 'secondary' issues rest. Consequently, there has been very limited success in illuminating the gross distortions of the functionalist approach, although particular symptoms of its defects may have been noted in the form of what appear to be technical, isolated modelling problems.

This lack of study of the meaning and interpretation of models has resulted in a minimization of feedback from urban modelling to our general understanding of urban development. The modelling effort has been cut off from theoretical research on the nature and development of the space economy. If anything, urban modelling may have contributed to a *regress* in the understanding of urban systems, where 'paralysis-by-analysis' through over-use of Lowry and gravity models has led us to think of residential location urban development as being determined by contingent factors existing on the 'surface'. Intelligent laymen, with their (albeit fragmented) appreciation of the nature of housing, with its associations of land values, rents, mortgages, institutional structures, council house waiting-lists, etc., could be excused for being somewhat perplexed by the striking selectivity of perception of the urban modeller-'experts' with their curious obsession with journey-to-work and other contingent relations. The fear that urban modellers tend to learn more and more about their models and less and less about the real world has become all too true.[9]

As long as there is so little emphasis on refutation in regional science, and as long as models are treated as ends in themselves, rather than as means to the end of understanding the space economy, there is little prospect of improving this situation.

NOTES: CHAPTER 6

1. It is acknowledged that we are using the term 'paradigm' to denote a much smaller scientific community than would have been considered by Kuhn, who referred to the whole of social science as a pre-scientific paradigm.

2. Cf. Haggett, 1965; and Sack, 1974.

3. See, e.g. some of the models in Baxter, Echenique and Owers (1975), which refer to calibration runs as 'tests'.

4. Cf. Chorley and Haggett's *Models in Geography* (1967).

5. Likewise, Harvey and Chatterjee (1974, p. 22) argue that 'Economics do not stop working because of the aggregation problem'.

6. It is acknowledged that there are many varieties of 'structuralism' used in the social sciences. The approach adopted here follows that of operational genetic structuralism explained by Piaget (1970, 1973) and Harvey (1973). We do not refer to the more fashionable Althusserian structuralism!

7. See Georgescu-Roegen, 1971.

8. For example, see Wilson, 1974, pp. 71, 313.

9. Cf. Batty (1975).

References

ALONSO, W. (1967) A reformulation of classical location theory and its relation to rent theory, *Papers, Regional Science Association*, **19**, 23–44.

ANDRESKI, S. (1974) *Social Science as Sorcery*, Harmondsworth, Middlesex.

APPS, P. (1971) A residental model. 1. Theory, *Land Use and Built Form Studies*, W. P. 59, University of Cambridge.

BAILEY, J. (1975) *Social Theory for Planning*, Routledge and Kegan Paul.

BARRATT-BROWN, M. (1970) *What Economics is about*, Weidenfeld and Nicholson.

BATTY, M. (1969) The impact of a new town: an application of the Garin-Lowry model, *J. Town Planning Inst*, **55**, 428–435.

BATTY, M. (1970a) Models and projections of the space economy, *Town Planning Rev.* **41**, 121–147.

BATTY, M. (1970b) An activity allocation model for the Notts–Derby sub-region, *Regional Studies*, **4**, 307–332.

BATTY, M. (1971) Design and construction of a sub-regional land use model, *Socio-Economic Planning Sciences* **5** (2).

BATTY, M. (1972) Recent developments in land-use modelling: a review of British research, *Urban Studies* **9**, 151–178.

BATTY, M. (1973) A probability model of the housing market based on quasi-classical considerations, *Socio-Economic Planning Sciences* **7**, 573–598.

BATTY, M. (1975) In defence of urban modelling, *The Planner* **61**, 184–187.

BAUMOL, W. J. (1959) *Economic Dynamics: An Introduction*, (2nd edn), Macmillan.

BAXTER, R., ECHENIQUE, M. and OWERS, J. (eds.) (1975) *Urban Development Models:* Land Use and Built Form Studies conference proceedings, No. 3.

BAXTER, R. and WILLIAMS, I. (1973) The third stage in disaggregating the residential sub-model, *Land Use and Built Form Studies*, W. P. 66, University of Cambridge.

BENTZEL, R. and HANSEN, B. (1954) On recursiveness and interdependency in economic models, *Review of Economic Studies* **XXII**, 153–168.

BLACKBURN, R. (ed) (1972), *Ideology in Social Science: Readings in Critical Social Theory*, Fontana.

BLAUT, J. (1961) Space and Process, reprinted in W. K. D. Davies, (1972) *The Conceptual Revolution in Geography*, London.

BLISS, C. J. (1972) Prices, markets and planning, *Economic Journal* **82**, 87–100.

BODDY, M. (1975) Letter to the editor (Theories of residential location or castles in the air), *Environment and Planning A* **7**, 109–111.

BODDY, M. (1976) The structure of mortgage finance: building societies and the British social formation, *Transactions of the Institute of British Geographers New Series*, **1**, no. 1, 58–71.

CAREY, H. S. (1858) *Principles of Social Science*, Lippineott, Philadelphia.

CARROTHERS, G. A. P. (1956) An historical review of the gravity and potential concepts of human interaction, in Ambrose, P. (1969), *Analytical Human Geography*, Longman.

CARUSO, P. and PALM, R. (1973) Social space and social place, *Professional Geography* **XXV**, 221–225.

CASTELLS, M. (1972) *La Question Urbaine*, Maspero, Paris.

CHOMSKY, N. (1959) Review of 'Verbal Behaviour' by B. F. Skinner, *Language* **35**, 26–58.

CHORLEY, R. J. and HAGGETT, P. (eds) (1957) *Models in Geography*, Methuen.

CHRISTALLER, W. (1968) *Central Places in Southern Germany*, Prentice Hall, translated from 'Die Zentralen Orte in Suddeutschland' by C. W. Baskin.

CLARKSON, G. P. E. (1963) *The Theory of Consumer Demand: A Critical Appraisal*, Englewood Cliffs, New Jersey.

CLIFF, A. D., MARTIN, R. L. and ORD, J. K. (1974) Evaluating the friction of distance parameter in gravity models. *Regional Studies* **8**, 281–286.

COLE, C. L. (1973) *Microeconomics: A Contemporary Approach*, Harcourt, Brace, Jovanich.

CORDEY-HAYES, (1972) Dynamic frameworks for spatial models, W. P. 76, *Centre for Environmental Studies*, London.

CRIPPS, E. L. and CATER, E. A. (1972) The empirical development of a disaggregated residential location model: some preliminary results, in *Patterns and Processes in Urban and Regional Systems*, A. G. Wilson (ed.), pp. 114–145, (London Papers in Regional Section 3), Pion.

CRIPPS, E. L. and FOOT, D. H. S. (1969) A land-use model for sub-regional planning, *Regional Studies* **3**.

CURRY, L. (1972) A spatial analysis of gravity flows, *Regional Studies* **6**, 131–147.

DOBB, M. (1937) The trend of modern economics, reprinted in *A Critique of Economic Theory*, E. K. Hunt and J. G. Schwartz (eds.), pp. 39–82, Penguin, (1972).

DOBB, M. (1973) *Theories of Value and Distribution since Adam Smith, Ideology and Economic Theory*. Cambridge University Press.

DUNCAN, S. S. (1976) Research directions in social geography: housing opportunities. *Transactions of the Institute of British Geographers New Series* 1 no. 1, 10–19.
ECHENIQUE, M. *et al.* (1969) A spatial model of urban stock and activity, *Regional Studies* 3 281–303.
EDEL, M. (1975) Marx's theory of rent: urban applications, *Discussion Paper No. 38, Birkbeck College, London.*
EVANS, A. W. (1974) Economics and planning, in J. Forbes (1974) *Studies in Social Science and Planning,* Scottish Academic Press, Edinburgh.
EVANS, A. W. (1975) Theories of residential location or castles in the air – a reply, *Environment and Planning A* 7, 601–603.
FEYERABEND, P. K. (1975) *Against Method,* N. L. B.
FILMER, P., PHILLIPSON, M., SILVERMAN, D. and WALSH, D. (1972) *New Directions in Sociological Theory,* Collier Macmillan, London.
FORRESTER, J. W. (1961) *Industrial Dynamics,* M. I. T., Cambridge, Massachusetts.
FORRESTER, J. W. (1968) *Principles of Systems,* Wright-Allen Press, Cambridge, Massachusetts.
FRANK, A. G. (1967) *Capitalism and Underdevelopment in Latin America,* Harmondsworth.
GEORGESCU-ROEGEN, N. (1971) *The Entropy Law and the Economic Process,* Harvard University Press, Massachusetts.
GIDDENS, A. (1974) *Positivism and Sociology,* Heinemann.
GOLDNER, W. (1971) The Lowry model heritage, *J. Am. Inst. Planners* XXXVII, 100–110.
GRAY, F. (1976) Selection and allocation in council housing, *Transactions of the Institute of British Geographers New Series* 1 34–46.
GROSSMAN, H. I. (1974) The nature of quantities in market disequilibrium, *American Economic Review,* LXIV, 509–514.
GUELKE, L. (1971) Problems of scientific explanation in geography, *Canadian Geographer* XV, 38–53.
HAGERSTRAND, T. (1973) The domain of human geography, in *Directions in Geography,* R. J. Chorley (ed.), pp. 67–87.
HAGGETT, P. (1965) *Locational Analysis in Human Geography,* Arnold.
HANSEN, S. (1972) Utility, accessibility and entropy in spatial modelling, *Swedish Journal of Economics* 74 35–44.
HARCOURT, G. C. and LAING, N. F. (1971) *Capital and Growth,* Penguin, Harmondsworth.
HARRIS, B. (1968) Quantitative models of urban development, in H. S. Perloff and L. Wingo (eds.), pp. 363–412, *Issues in Urban Economics,* John Hopkins.
HARVEY, D. W. (1969) *Explanation in Geography,* Arnold.
HARVEY, D. W. (1973) *Social Justice and the City,* Arnold.
HARVEY, D. W. (1974) Class-monopoly rent, finance, capital and the urban revolution, *Regional Studies* 8, 239–255.
HARVEY, D. W. (1975) The geography of capitalist accumulation: a reconstruction of the Marxian theory, *Antipode* 7, no. 2, 9–21.
HARVEY, D. and CHATTERJEE, L. (1974) Absolute rent and the structuring of space by governmental and financial institutions, *Antipode* 6, no. 1, 22–36.
HINES, A. G. (1971) *On the Reappraisal of Keynesian Economies,* Martin Roberts.
HOLLIS, M. and NELL, E. (1975) *Rational Economic Man,* Cambridge University Press.
HOLT, C. C. and DAVID, M. H. (1966) The concept of job vacancies in a dynamic theory of the labour market, in *The Measurement and Interpretation of Job Vacancies,* pp. 73–110. NBER, New York.
HUNT, E. K. and SCHWARTZ, J. G. (eds.) (1972) *A Critique of Economic Theory,* selected readings, (Penguin Modern Economics Readings), Harmondsworth, Middlesex.
ISARD, W. (1960) *Methods of Regional Analysis,* M. I. T. Press, Cambridge, Massachusetts.
ISARD, W. (1972) Why is general relatively theory relevant to regional and other social sciences? in *Recent Developments in Regional Science* R. Funck (ed.), pp. 150–153, Pion.
JAHODA, M. (1973) Postscript on social change, in *Thinking About the Future,* Cole, H. S. D., Freeman, C., Jahoda, M. and Pavitt, K. L. R. (eds.), Chatto and Windus.
KAIN, J. F., INGRAM, G. and GINN, R. *et al.* (1973) *The National Bureau of Economic Research, Detroit Prototype, Urban Simulation Model,* NBER, New York.
KALDOR, N. (1972) The irrelevance of equilibrium economics, *Economic Journal* 82, 1237.
KALECKI, M. (1971) *Selected Essays on the Dynamics of the Capitalist Economy 1933–1970,* Cambridge University Press.
KAY, G. (1975) *Development and Underdevelopment: A Marxist Analysis.* Macmillan.
KEAT, R. and URRY, J. (1975) *Social Theory as Science,* Routledge and Kegan Paul.
KIRWAN, R. M. and MARTIN, D. B. (1970) The economic basis for models of the housing market, *Centre for Environmental Studies,* London WP 62.
KIRWAN, R. M. and MARTIN, D. B. (1971) Some notes on housing market models for urban planning, *Environment and Planning* 3, 243–252.
KLAPPHOLZ, K. and MISHAN, E. J. (1962) Identities in economic models, *Economica* 29, 117–128.
KORNAI, J. (1971) *Anti-Equilibrium, On Economic Systems Theory and the Tasks of Research,* North-Holland Publishing, Amsterdam.
KREGEL, J. A. (1973) *The Reconstruction of Political Economy: An Introduction to Post Keynesian Economics,* Macmillan, London.
KUHN, T. S. (1970) *The Structure of Scientific Revolutions* (2nd edn.), Chicago.
LAMARCHE, F. (1976) The economic foundations of the urban question, in *Urban Sociology: Critical Essays,* C. G. Pickvance (ed.), Methuen.
LANCASTER, K. (1969) *Introduction to Modern Micro-Economics,* Rand McNally.
LANGTON, J. (1972) Potentialities and problems of adopting a systems approach to the study of change in human geography, in *Progress in Geography,* R. J. Chorley, C. Board and P. Haggett (eds.), Arnold.
LE BOULANGER, H. (1971) Research into the urban traveller's behaviour, *Transportation Research* 5 113–125, Pergamon, Oxford.

LEE, C. (1973) *Models in Planning*, Pergamon, Oxford.
LEE, D. B. (1973) Requiem for large-scale models, *J. Am. Inst. Planners* **39**, 163–178.
LEONTIEF, W. (1971) Theoretical assumptions and non-observed facts, *American Economic Review* **61**, 1–7.
LOWE, A. (1965) *On Economic Knowledge*, Harper and Row, New York.
LOWRY, I. S. (1964) A model of metropolis, *Rand Corporation*, Santa Monica, California.
MAISEL, S. J. (1963) A theory of fluctuations in residential construction starts, *American Economic Review* **53**, 359–383.
MANDEL, E. (1968) *Marxist Economic Theory*, Vol. 1 and Vol. 2, Merlin Press.
MASSEY, D. B. (1974) Towards a critique of industrial location theory, *Centre for Environmental Studies, Research Paper 5.*
MURRAY, R. (1972) Underdevelopment, the international firm and the international division of labour, *Institute of Development Studies* at the University of Sussex, mimeo and in *Towards a New World Economy*, pp. 159–247, Rotterdam University Press, 1973.
NELL, E. (1972a) Property and the means of production: a primer on the Cambridge controversy, *The Review of Radical Political Economics* **IV**, no. 2, 1–27.
NELL, E. (1972b) Economics: the revival of political economy, in *Ideology in Social Science*, R. Blackburn (ed.), Fontana.
OLSSON, G. (1965) *Distance and Human Interaction*, Regional Science Research Institute.
PAELINCK, J. (1973) Book review of A. G. Wilson's, Entropy in urban and regional modelling, *Urban Studies* **10**, 280–281.
PFOUTS, R. F. (1960) *The Techniques of Urban Economic Analysis*, New York.
PIAGET, J. (1970) *Structuralism*, New York.
PIAGET, J. (1973) *Main Trends in Interdisciplinary Research*, George Allen and Unwin.
PICKVANCE, C. G. (1976) *Urban Sociology: Critical Essays*, Tavistock, London.
RAVENSTEIN, E. G. (1885) The laws of migration, *J. Royal Statistical Society* **48**, 52.
REX, J. (1961) *Key Problems of Sociological Theory*, Routledge and Kegan Paul.
ROBINSON, J. (1962) *Economic Philosophy*, Pelican, Harmondsworth, Middlesex.
ROBINSON, J. (1964) *Collected Economic Papers*, Vol. II, Blackwell, Oxford.
ROBINSON, J. (1965) *Collected Economic Papers*, Vol. III, Blackwell, Oxford.
ROBINSON, J. (1972) The second crisis of economic theory, *American Economic Review*, (papers and proceedings) **LXII**, 1–9.
ROBINSON, J. and EATWELL (1973) *An Introduction to Modern Economics*, McGraw-Hill.
ROE, P. (undated) Shopping models, *Building Research Establishment*, mimeo.
ROGERS, A. (1971) *Matrix Methods in Urban and Regional Analysis*, Holden-Day, San Francisco.
SACK, R. D. (1972) Geography, geometry and explanation, *Annals of the Associated American Geographers* **62**, 61–78.
SACK, R. D. (1973) A concept of physical space, *Geographical Analysis* **5**, 16–34.
SACK, R. D. (1974) The spatial separatist theme in geography, *Economic Geography* **50**, 1–19.
SAYER, R. A. (1974) A dynamic Lowry model, in *Urban Simulation: Models of Public Policy Analysis*, M. H. Whited and R. M. Sarly, (eds.), Sijthoff, Leiden.
SAYER, R. A. (1975) *Dynamic Spatial Models of Urban and Regional Systems*, unpublished D. Phil dissertation, University of Sussex.
SEMEVSKIY, B. N. (1973) Problems in the theory of geography in the section on geographic theory and model building at the 22nd International Geographical Congress, *Soviet Geographer* **14**, 625–633.
SENIOR, M. L. and WILSON, A. G. (1972) Disaggregated residential location models: some tests and further theoretical developments, *Department of Geography, University of Leeds*, WP 22.
SHACKLE, G. L. S. (1967) *Time in Economics*, North Holland Publishing, Amsterdam.
SHACKLE, G. L. S. (1972) *Epistemics and Economics: A Critique of Economic Doctrines*, Cambridge University Press.
SHACKLE, G. L. S. (1974) Decision: the human predicament, *Annals of the American Academy of Political and Social Science* **412**, 1–10.
SMITH, W. F. (1970) *Housing: the Social and Economic Elements*, Berkeley.
SRAFFA, P. (1960) *Production of Commodities by Means of Commodities*, Cambridge University Press.
STOUFFLER, S. A. (1940) Intervening opportunities: a theory relating mobility and distance, *American Sociology Review* **5**, 845–867.
STYLES, B. J. (ed.), (1968) *Gravity Models in Town Planning*, Mimeo, Lancaster Polytechnic.
THOMPSON, W. (1965) *A Preface to Urban Economics*, Resources for the Future, John Hopkins Press.
TURNER, C. G. (1971) The development of an activity allocation model for the British sub-region, *Urban Systems Research Unit*, WP8, University of Reading.
WARD, B. (1972) *What's Wrong with Economics?*, Macmillan.
WILSON, A. G. (1970) *Entropy in Urban and Regional Modelling*, Pion.
WILSON, A. G. (1971) A family of spatial interaction models, and associated developments, *Environment and Planning* **3**, 1–32.
WILSON, A. G. (1972) *Patterns and Processes in Urban and Regional Systems*, London Papers in Regional Science 3, Pion.
WILSON, A. G. (1973) Further developments of entropy maximising transport models, *Transportation Planning and Technology* **1**, 183–193.
WILSON, A. G. (1974) *Urban and Regional Models in Geography and Planning*, Wiley, London.
WRIGHT MILLS, C. (1959) *The Sociological Imagination*, Harmondsworth, Middlesex.

Policy and Politics, Vol. 14 No. 1 (1986), 93–106

EC ENVIRONMENT POLICY, LAND USE PLANNING AND POLLUTION CONTROL

R. H. Williams

In March, 1985, the Environment Council of the European Communities adopted a 'Directive concerning the assessment of the environmental effects of certain public and private projects' after many years of deliberation. This directive, also referred to as the Environmental Impact Assessment (EIA) Directive, represents a major step forward in implementing community environment policy, and is the first example of Community land use planning legislation to be incorporated into national physical planning systems (Luxembourg, 1985).

This paper discusses the rationale and scope of the Community environment policy and the place of the EIA directive within it; outlines the provisions of the directive itself and the changes resulting from the long period of negotiations prior to adoption; and discusses the process of incorporation into national planning legislation and potential impact of the directive.

Rationale of EC environment policy

There is no reference to an environment policy in the Treaty of Rome, but a Community environment policy has been in operation since 1973. It is based on the premises that the community needs to be concerned with the quality of life of its population, as well as economic integration and growth; that pollution tends by its very nature to cross national frontiers (acid rain being a most prominent example; cleansing the waters of the Rhine has also been a priority); and that there can be direct economic benefits from environment protection, especially in the agriculture, forestry, fisheries and tourism sectors and through the stimulation of clean technologies and manufacture of the necessary equipment (Commission, 1979). The legal basis for an environment policy rests on Articles 100 and 235 of the Treaty of Rome, concerned with harmonisation, and initiation of policies not otherwise specified in the Treaty (Williams 1984, Chapter 12).

Three Action Programmes on the Environment have been approved since 1973, embodying the elements of the community environment policy. These have covered the periods 1973–6, 1977–81 and 1982–6.

Environment policy principles

Two basic principles underlie the community environment programme: that the polluter should pay; and that prevention is better than cure.

A conflict of interest is likely to exist between the potential polluter, who may want to minimise profits, and regard costs of anti-pollution measures as being externalities to be avoided if possible, and the interests of the community or district suffering pollution. The principle that the polluter should pay for the costs of emission control or other anti-pollution measures and not regard these as externalities, outside his responsibility, has therefore been adopted in the environment programme, in the interests of those potentially affected by pollution (Commission 1979).

The willingness of the potential polluter to bear any additional costs imposed as a result of a requirement to adopt pollution control measures depends on where the economic interests of the developer lie. In the case of a locationally mobile or multi-national company, there is likely to be the temptation to propose an alternative location for a development where pollution control requirements may be less stringent and less expensive. This temptation is likely to be particularly strong if the alternative site offers equally good access to the same market. In Europe at present locationally mobile multi-site or multi-national firms can seek to avoid costs of anti-pollution measures by choosing a location in another member state of the EEC where the approval procedures are more easily satisfied and lower standards of environmental protection allowed to prevail. The developer nevertheless still has access to the same market, being within the common external tariff. In this way, pollution havens may emerge, and distortions of competition occur as firms have to comply with very different environmental standards, while competing in the same market (Williams 1983). It is therefore in the interests of the community and of member-states with high environmental standards, such as Federal Germany, to harmonise authorisation and control procedures throughout the EEC, in order to avoid economic disadvantage as a result of high national standards.

The common environmental assessment procedure now to be introduced is intended to have the effect of reducing the disparities in environmental standards between member states, by bringing all national authorisation procedures up to an acceptable minimum standard, in order to counteract any temptation to locate in a pollution haven. A location outside the EEC to avoid these controls would be against the economic interests of the developer since it would place its products in a disadvantageous marketing position outside the common external tariff and choice of location within the EEC would be based on other factors. Of course, a common procedure does not necessarily produce equality of environmental control of development throughout the area of its application, but it should alter the balance of forces in that direction.

The European scale of operation of the proposed procedure will greatly enlarge the geographical scale at which spatial variations in planning and pollution control might affect the distribution of industrial or other polluting activities. Blowers (1984) refers to the power of the environment protection movement to influence the distribution of industry and the creation of a new geography of industry, with pollution havens where pollution controls are being applied less strictly, for either political or procedural reasons, and to which polluting activities therefore tend to locate. Harmonisation of approval procedures on a European scale would have the effect of reducing procedural variations as a factor in location decisions within the EEC, but would not necessarily have any effect on variations due to differences in political attitude and political will to enforce strict pollution standards.

The first generation of environmental measures, contained in the First Action Programme on the Environment (Luxembourg 1973) were primarily remedial, designed to overcome specific problems and regulate or eliminate the discharge of toxic substances. These are described in the Second Report on the State of Environment (Commission, 1979). The great majority of the 58 legislative texts adopted prior to 1980 are of this type (Commission, 1980a). The second action programme 1977–81 (Luxembourg, 1977) introduced a new orientation. The main emphasis was directed away from remedial action in response to specific sources of pollution and specific industrial processes, and towards preventive measures.

The principle that prevention is better than cure was put forward because of the high cost of clearing up after major pollution. Dramatic evidence of this occurred after the Amoco Cadiz oil spillage, and the Flixborough and Seveso disasters. The latter created the political impetus for the adoption of a directive on the storage and use of dangerous substances in industrial plants, known as the Seveso directive (Luxembourg 1982).

The second action programme explicitly adopted the principle that 'prevention is better than cure' as a fundamental element in environment policy, on the basis that the policy should prevent 'the creation of pollution of nuisances at source, rather than trying to counteract their effects' (Luxembourg, 1977, P50). As Wood has demonstrated, the use of land use planning procedures is a major way in which this principle can be put into practice (Wood 1979).

Several proposals contained in the second action programme and

 Environment, Land Use and Urban Policy

 Policy and Politics

also in the third action programme are of a preventive type. In the latter they are related to the practice of land use planning more explicitly than ever before. As the third action programme puts it, 'Land in the Community is a very limited and much sought after natural resource. The way in which it is used very largely conditions the quality of the environment. Physical planning is therefore one of the areas where a preventive environment policy is very necessary and very beneficial' (Luxembourg, 1983, Art 26).

A very wide range of interests may be affected by physical planning measures of this sort since they are designed to control hypothetical future pollution. An emission control measure concerned with a specific substance or industrial process has a clearly defined impact on the industry in question, and the political debate on its acceptability is likely to be relatively self contained, involving interest groups concerned with the industry or process. In contrast, the range of interests potentially affected by the adoption of pollution control by preventive planning procedures is very much greater, and open ended because the extent of its impact is not precisely defined or wholly predictable. Consequently, the number of interest groups seeking to resist or dilute a preventive planning procedure, especially on a European scale, is considerable, and in certain cases includes national government department as well as non-government public and private bodies. In addition, there is by no means general public or political support for extending, or appearing to extend, the scope of town planning and environmental protection procedures, and proposed controls may be interpreted as placing further hurdles in the way of developers who are offering much needed jobs and economic stimulus. This was clearly demonstrated by the Danish veto on the directive during 1983-85 (see below), and is no doubt a factor in the UK government's luke-warm attitude.

In addition, all member states have already got a system of town and country planning (Williams 1984). Although these have broadly similar overall objectives, the differences between them both in procedures and in effective policies are very great, for a variety of legal constitutional and historic reasons. Some governments, notably our own, argue that they already have perfectly adequate procedures for environmental assessment and control in their existing codes of environmental protection legislation that is quite separate from town and country planning legislation. For these reasons, it is not surprising that the formulation of an acceptable land use planning measure, and its adoption, took a long time.

The Commission in its progress report (Commission 1980a) acknowledged as much. The technical complexity of many of the measures proposed, and limited staffing resources are identified as reasons for slow progress. Other reasons put forward include the existing variety of institutional and administrative procedures and responsibilities in the

Williams: *EC environment policy*   **97**

different member states, and the uncertainty of political will. The progress report refers to the need for political impetus if progress towards better environmental protection is to be achieved, referring to the fact that difficulties may sometimes arise if the 'political will is uncertain' and to 'the half-hearted political response to oil pollution at sea' (Commission 1980a P5). It is clear from the report that general preventive measures affecting potentially a wide range of interests, such as land use planning measures were among those where sufficient political support for progress was lacking at that time.

Subsequently, the electoral impact of environmental or 'Green' politics has increased significantly in several member states, and the 1984 European Parliament elections returned a Green political group to Parliament for the first time. When consulted on the proposed directive on environmental assessment of projects in 1981, the European Parliament wanted to strengthen its provisions considerably (Strasbourg 1981). It is to be expected that the present Parliament would take a more strongly environmentalist line than the previous Parliament as a result of the presence of a Green political group. Members of the Council of Ministers are also under increasing pressure to respond to environmental issues, whether or not they represent countries where environmentalists are winning Parliamentary seats.

The lack of progress in adopting land use planning measures to control pollution during the course of the second action programme on the environment has meant that many of the proposals envisaged then also found a place in the third action programme (Luxembourg 1983). However, certain changes of emphasis are apparent in the third programme. It places greater emphasis than earlier programmes on jobs, on a transectoral approach linked to the EEC's regional and industrial policies, co-ordination of specific anti-pollution measures, monitoring, co-operation with other national or international agencies, and with research, education and information exchange. It continues to emphasise prevention, but in doing so makes much more frequent and explicit reference to the role of physical land use planning. The argument that environmental protection is not a luxury to be afforded only in times of prosperity, but a necessary part of economic development at all times, is put forward more strongly than in earlier programmes.

Place of environmental assessment
The concept of environmental assessment of projects fits very well into the logic underlying the community environment policy. In essence, it is a procedure whereby the environmental consequences of a proposed development are assessed at the time when authorisation of the development is sought. The prospective developer is required to submit sufficient details of the proposal to allow the environmental consequences,

and the adequacy of any remedial measures, to be assessed prior to authorisation of the development. The authority competent to grant permission is required to assess the project, grant permission to develop only if it is satisfied that any adverse environmental consequences are alleviated as far as possible, and impose any necessary conditions to ensure that any circumstantial damage from the project is minimised, and the danger of subsequent pollution removed as far as possible. It is thus a procedure which embodies the principle that prevention is better than cure, and imposes on the developer the discipline of considering the environmental consequences of a proposed development at the time when it is in the developer's interest to pay for any necessary remedial measures in order to obtain authorisation for the development.

Environmental assessment need not necessarily be seen as an integral part of land use planning and control of development. It could be associated with separate environmental and public safety procedures, for instance. However, the normal arrangement will be for environmental assessment to take place alongside the existing procedures for authorisation of land use and development, in the case of the UK as part of the development control responsibilities of local planning authorities. It will, in fact, be the first example of the use of a physical planning procedure operating throughout the community as a means of pollution control.

Although the requirement to undertake environmental assessment is embodied in an EEC directive, the actual operation of the procedure is the responsibility of the authorities designated for this purpose by member states. This is in accordance with a guiding principle governing the operation of the community environment policy, namely that action should take place at the appropriate level of government ie local, regional, national or supra-national. In the UK it will be operated by local planning authorities, and a similar level of government is likely to be responsible elsewhere in the community.

The environmental assessment directive

The Commission's proposals are first outlined, the politics associated with the process of adoption are discussed, and then the differences apparent in the version finally adopted are indicated in order to illustrate the outcome of the bargaining process.

The proposed directive

In June, 1980 the Commission tabled a proposed directive 'concerning the assessment of the environmental effects of certain private and public projects' (Commission, 1980b). The version subject to this formal proposal was itself a product of a long series of studies and consultations over several years, generating numerous revisions of the draft.

This document consisted of a substantial explanatory memorandum, plus the Articles of the proposed text, and three Annexes. The Articles and Annexes are the parts which become Community legislation upon adoption.

The legal basis of the directive is Article 100 of the EEC Treaty, under which the Council may adopt objectives for the approximation of laws directly affecting the functioning of the common market.

The essence of the proposed directive is contained in Article 2: 'Member states shall adopt all necessary measures to ensure that, before any planning permission is given, projects likely to have a significant effect on the environment by virtue of their nature, size and/or location are made subject to an appropriate assessment of these effects, in accordance with the following Articles'.

A project can be a new development, or a modification, and the types of project covered by the proposal are listed in two of the Annexes. The first contained those for which a full assessment would be mandatory; and the second those for which a simplified version was to be sufficient.

Annex I includes a variety of processes in the iron and steel, chemical, rubber, cement, asbestos, and energy production industries, fuel and ore extraction, and major construction projects such as motorways, airports, intercity rail tracks and pipelines. Annex II includes agriculture and a number of other extraction and industrial processes.

The assessment is to refer to effects on the natural and built environments (Art 3), but no specific mention is made of social and economic impact. The developer is required to prepare, and submit with his application for planning permission, a detailed statement describing the proposal, assessing the impact, justifying the choice of site and alternatives considered together with non-technical summary for consultation purposes, (Art 6). Annex III indicates the scope of the information required. The competent authority, ie in Britain the local planning authority, would carry out the usual consultations, including the general public and, where appropriate, the competent authorities of another member state, (Art 7, 8). The submitted assessment is to be made public, as is a statement by the authority of the decision reached and why, its own opinion of the environmental effects of the project, and a synthesis of the opinions received (Art 9).

Considerable emphasis is given to public participation and to ensuring that the process is subject to public scrutiny. The cross-frontier consultations requirement is not necessarily irrelevant for the UK, for instance in the case of development near the English Channel creating development pressures on the opposite coast. More contentiously, if authorities in Denmark or Germany could establish a link between acid rainfall there and specific emissions in the UK, projects likely to cause such emissions could be subject to this procedure. Obviously, cross-frontier consultation is of more significance along land frontiers.

The type of project listed in Annex I is, in general, the type of project which would be subject to very detailed scrutiny by planning authorities in any event. Consequently, much if not all of the information required under this directive would be required by the local authority at some stage anyway, and it cannot be argued that this proposal corresponds to existing good practice, and will have the effect of levelling all authorities up to this standard. It will also, on occasions, have the effect of requiring certain forms of data to be assembled and made available to the public at an earlier stage in the process.

The scope of the proposed directive extended beyond the range of development which local planning authorities in the UK are themselves empowered to control. Several forms of development included in Annex I and in Annex II are projects which in several countries, including the UK, are the responsibility of government departments, statutory undertakers or nationalised industry, such as nuclear power stations, motorways, gas production from coal, new railways or airports, where 'deemed permission' and in some cases private Acts of Parliament are involved.

The directive would not have had the effect of devolving responsibility for these to local authorities, but it would impose duties in respect of public participation and public access to the assessment and reasons for the decision, which would create the opportunity for public scrutiny. Secondly, a number of agricultural projects were included in Annex II, although the agriculture sector is largely excluded from existing planning control. There is concern in several countries about the environmental and ecological consequence of modern farming techniques, hedgerow removal, land holding consolidation and similar changes, and the proposed directive would have had the effect of bringing these within a form of planning control. There is a paradox here, as Holdgate (1983) has pointed out: 'in recent decades it has been agricultural policy to maximise crop production and the EEC's agricultural policies have supported this trend' (p. 15). Thus one sector of EEC policy-making is potentially in conflict with another as the third Action Programme itself acknowledges (Luxembourg 1983 Art 26).

The impact of the directive, will, of course vary as a result of the different planning systems in operation. In Britain, development control operates on the basis of assessing each proposal on its merits, when it is put forward in the form of a planning application. A decision, to grant permission with or without conditions or refuse the application, is made by the elected members of the local planning authority on the basis of the information presented to them, and the assessment procedure should have the effect of improving the quality and scope of information on which judgement can be made.

Williams: *EC environment policy*   101

The majority of other member states of the EEC operate procedures for the control of development which do not provide for the degree of discretion to decide planning proposals that exists in Britain. The determination of an application for permission to build is, in principle, an administrative act in several countries. For instance in Federal Germany a proposal that conforms to an approved *Bebauungsplan* will automatically obtain permission, scrutiny being concerned with establishing conformity with the plan and with building regulations. In the Netherlands, planning and other laws are based on the principle of *Rechtstaat* or legal certainty for the citizen. Consequently, an approved development plan or *Bestemmingsplan* has the effect of automatically conveying permission for development which conforms to it. In fact, as Faludi and Hamnett (1979) have demonstrated, these systems are by no means as rigid and lacking in flexibility as a look at the legal position would indicate. Nevertheless, the advent of a procedure that explicitly requires a decision to be taken on the merits of the case as established in the assessment, and responses to it, represents a departure from the principle of certainty, introducing new discretionary controls and opening the way for political pressures to be exerted at this stage.

The process of adoption

The 1980 proposal was presented to the Council of Environment Ministers, who were required to consult national Governments, the European Parliament and the European Economic and Social Committee before they could take a decision on it. This process took place during 1980–82, as a result of which a revised proposal was prepared and submitted to the Environment Council in March, 1982 (Commission 1982). Widespread consultations and public debates took place during this time and some of these are referred to below to illustrate the ways in which different interest groups reacted to the proposal.

After the revised proposal was tabled, negotiation was in the hands of the Council of Ministers, the Committee of Permanent Representatives (Coreper) in Brussels and between individual Ministers and the national governments of which they were members. This period of negotiation, from 1982 to eventual agreement in March, 1985, was largely behind closed doors, although certain key features of the negotiations can be inferred.

In the British Parliament, the proposed directive was the subject of a short debate in the House of Commons following much more elaborate scrutiny in the House of Lords.

The evidence presented to the House of Lords Select Committee on the European Communities is the principle source available indicating considered responses and attitudes to the directives (House of Lords,

 Environment, Land Use and Urban Policy

 Policy and Politics

1981). Many organisations and interest groups took advantage of the opportunity to make representations to the Select Committee, or give oral evidence, and their final report is a very thorough analysis of the proposal, forming very favourable conclusions for those advocating adoption of the directive. The attitude of the Government in the subsequent Commons debate was markedly less enthusiastic.

On the issue of inclusion of agricultural and forestry projects the report illustrated the sides taken in this issue, with the Country Landowners' Association pressing for the total exclusion of this category of development, while the Countryside Commission welcomed it as 'a potentially very powerful instrument for projects and developments which at present fall outside development control' (Para 40).

One other major way in which the balance of political influence could be tilted rather more in favour of environmental interests is in respect of projects proposed by central government and statutory undertakers, especially, as the Lords report noted, in those cases where a Private or Hybrid Act of Parliament is necessary for authorisation of the project (Para 28). The requirements of the directive to prepare an assessment, and make it publicly available prior to authorisation, will create opportunities for informed public debate, and the presentation of opposing arguments by environmental interests, at an early stage in the authorisation process.

A consistent line of argument from both government and industrialists against the provisions of the directive concerns the question of standards and formalised procedures. There seemed to be an underlying fear that the directive is the product of an alien system, and would cause the imposition of fixed standards of environmental quality and rigid procedures to be followed. These fears were expressed by several witnesses to the House of Lords Committee, including the Department of Environment, the Association of Metropolitan Authorities and the Confederation of British Industry, all of whom indicated that they would prefer an informal code of practice rather than a directive. All accepted the desirability of environmental protection and pollution control but argued in effect that this was already achieved by existing legislation. However, it is difficult to see, from the text, any basis for these fears, or avoid the interpretation that these interests were seeking continuation of the *status quo* without any enforceable requirement for environmental assessment in order to preserve the existing balance of interests and freedom to develop.

The British Government was one of the less enthusiastic national governments, preferring to keep any directive as flexible as possible, taking the view that existing procedures were already adequate and seeking to keep to a minimum the list of projects for which some form of assessment is mandatory. This is contrary to the argument advanced above that the economic interests of a country with a relatively high standard of pollution control would be better served by adoption of the directive.

The European Parliament, in contrast, proposed modifications to the directive which would have significantly strengthened its provisions. Notable among these were proposed amendments extending the scope of the directive to include development plans, and to include agricultural and forestry projects within Annex I rather than Annex II. This would have had the effect of requiring a full mandatory assessment for all projects in these categories.

Following the presentation of revised proposals by the Commission, which took into account many of the representations made in March, 1982, (Commission 1982) much of the negotiations conducted by Coreper on behalf of the Council of Ministers was concerned with seeking a formulation whereby the British, and certain French, reservations could be accommodated within a directive which would also have sufficient substance to be acceptable to the more enthusiastic national governments. Such a formula was achieved by the end of 1983, raising expectations that the directive would be adopted then. However, the Danish Government exercised a veto on the proposal because it was undertaking a review of all land use planning legislation and did not want to be encumbered with any more. This veto remained until 1985, when it was lifted to allow adoption by the March 1985 Council, as Directive 85/337/EEC (Luxembourg 1985).

The directive as adopted

The text finally adopted shows a number of significant variations from the text of the Commission proposal. Article 1 excludes defence projects and any project authorised by a specific act of national legislation on the basis that the objectives of the directive would be achieved through the legislative process. Thus a potentially significant feature of the directive in respect of certain development projects promoted by Government has been removed.

An even more crucial change concerns Annexes I and II. Projects listed in Annex I are to be subject to a full assessment, although exemptions can be made by member states in exceptional cases (Art 2(3)). However, projects listed in Annex II, which includes agriculture, mineral extraction and non-nuclear power stations, *inter alia*, are to be subject to assessment 'where member states consider their characteristics so require' (Art 4(2)). Member states have therefore much greater freedom to exempt projects in Annex II than under the earlier proposals, in which Annex II projects were to be required to undergo a simplified assessment. In the latter case, projects in the category, including agricultural projects, would all have had to seek a form of planning authorisation.

It was also agreed to allow three years rather than two for national governments to take any necessary legislative steps to implement the directive, following notification. It will therefore become operative in July, 1988.

The impact of the directive

Although the final form of the Environmental Assessment Directive is now known, it is not possible to do any more than speculate on the extent to which it will achieve higher environmental standards of development, reduce pollution, and bring all parts of the Community up to an acceptable minimum standard of environmental planning and control. The text does allow for a considerable variation in interpretation by different member states, especially in respect of setting standards, criteria or thresholds for determining when assessment is required. Variations in the practice of granting exemptions under Article 2 (3) can also be expected.

Much will depend, of course, on the extent to which common standards are adopted at national or Community level. At present, it appears quite possible for a local authority determining planning applications requiring assessment to make exactly the same decision as they would have done without directive. However, the impact of its adoption would be much greater and more equality of environmental standards in different authorities would be achieved if common standards were to be adopted.

This relates to the question of harmonisation of conditions of development between member states of the EEC and to the question of pollution, both at the member state level and at the local authority level. The retention of the traditional pragmatic British approach of deciding each case on its merits depends on the political will of the authority to insist upon a satisfactory level of environmental impact and on the quality of advice given to it. In this situation there is a clear temptation for authorities to compete for development, and to take very different interpretations of the best interests of their authority. This is well illustrated by the cases described by Blowers (1984) and by the attitudes of Bedfordshire and Cambridgeshire referred to there. In this pragmatic situation, pollution havens would still be likely to occur in spite of the directive and little would be achieved. To achieve greater harmonisation and reduction of pollution havens, it will be necessary to develop common environmental standards in association with environmental assessment.

Early experience of implementing legislation requiring Environmental Impact Statements in the USA gave rise to fears that implementing this proposal would cause delays and increase developers' costs. However, there are indications that the consequence could in fact be to speed up the approval process and save money for the developer. In the case of major controversial proposals under present UK legislation extra information may well be requested by local planning authorities or the inspector at the public inquiry before any decision can be taken, thus causing delay. If an assessment is required as part of the normal application procedure, all necessary information should be assembled while the application is being prepared and subsequent delays could therefore be avoided. The best documented support for this point of view comes from the British Gas Corporation, who claim that they have saved a total of £30 million over ten years as a result of preparing full assessments of their projects prior to seeking authorisation, thus enabling the application to be considered more quickly (House of Lords 1981, P52).

Conclusions

The adoption of a form of environmental assessment of projects on a European scale could have a modest, but discernible effect in strengthening the hand of interests wishing to control pollution. It would extend the scope of planning control, and would create more opportunities for environmental interests to identify potential sources of pollution and for more effective pursuit of higher environmental standards by the competent authorities. It also provides the means whereby some harmonisation of standards and reduction of pollution havens could be achieved.

It will also be a step in the direction of strengthening the planning control systems of those member states, especially in southern Europe, where they are relatively weak.

However the proposed directive is by no means an environmentalists' charter, or wholly against the interests of developers, in spite of the general welcome from the environmental lobby and suspicion from developers and government interests.

Its significance lies in the fact that it is a major preventative measure, using land use planning methods, to be introduced on a European rather than national scale. Pollution is an international problem, and in the long run will need to be tackled at this scale. The proposed directive is only a first step and one can only speculate on its effectiveness, on the basis of reaction to date.

REFERENCES

Blowers, A. (1984) *Something in the air: corporate power and the environment,* London, Harper and Row.
Commission of the European Communities, (1979) 'State of the environment,' Second Report.
Commission of the European Communities, (1980a) 'Progress made in connection

with the environment action programme and assessment of the work done to implement it,' Com (80) 222 Final.

Commission of the European Communities, (1980b) 'Draft directive concerning the assessment of the environmental effects of certain public and private projects,' Com (80) 313 Final.

Commission of the European Communities, (1982) 'Proposal to amend the proposal for a Council Directive concerning the environmental effects of certain public and private projects,' Com (82) 158 Final.

Faludi, A, and Hamnett, S. (1979) *Flexibility in Dutch local planning,* Oxford, Dept., of Town Planning, Oxford Polytechnic WP 28.

Holdgate, M. W. (1983) 'Environmental policies in Britain and mainland Europe' in McRory, R. B. (Ed) *Britain, Europe and the environment,* London, Imperial College Centre for Environmental Technology.

House of Lords, (1981) 'Environmental assessment of projects,' Select Committee on the European Communities, 11th Report 1980–1, House of Lords Paper 69, HMSO.

Luxembourg (1973) Official Journal of the European Communities, C112, 20th Dec.

Luxembourg (1977) Official Journal of the European Communities, C139 13th June.

Luxembourg (1982) Official Journal of the European Communities, L230.

Luxembourg (1983) Official Journal of the European Communities, C46 17th Feb.

Luxembourg (1985) Official Journal of the European Communities, L175 5th June.

Strasbourg (1981) European Parliament Document 1 — 569/81 21st October.

Williams, R. H. (1983) 'Land use planning pollution control and environmental assessment in the EC. Environment policy,' *Planning Outlook* Vol. 26. No. 2.

Williams, R. H. (Ed) (1984) *Planning in Europe,* London: George Allen & Unwin.

Wood, C. M. (1979) 'Land use planning and pollution control' in O'Riordan, T. and D'Arge, R. C. (Eds) *Progress in resource management and environmental planning,* John Wiley.

Part IV
Urban Policy and the Environment

[16]

Urban Studies, Vol. 33, No. 1, 7–35, 1996

Urban Form, Energy and the Environment: A Review of Issues, Evidence and Policy

William P. Anderson, Pavlos S. Kanaroglou and Eric J. Miller

[Paper first received, February 1994; in final form, June 1995]

Summary. The spatial configuration of cities and its relationship to the urban environment has recently been the subject of empirical, theoretical and policy research. Because of the disciplines involved, relevant articles are scattered over a large number of journals. The objective of this paper is to put the issues in perspective by reviewing the basic concepts and relationships involved, and to evaluate critically the current state of knowledge about urban form, energy utilisation and the environment. The scope of the paper is limited to urban transport energy use and the associated emissions. Suggestions for further progress in the field are offered, with emphasis placed on integrated urban models as useful and policy-sensitive analytical tools.

1. Introduction

Recent concerns about the quality of urban environments, long-range and global environmental effects, the cost and security of energy supplies, and the environmental impacts of energy production have fostered a renewed interest in the investigation of energy demand behaviour and associated environmental emissions. Much of the investigation has focused on the technical characteristics of energy-using machinery such as vehicles, space conditioning systems and industrial processes. Still other research efforts have addressed related behavioural issues such as choice of transport mode and adoption of energy-conserving equipment. There has been relatively little research, however, on the broader question of how urban form affects energy demand and environmental emissions (Pisarski, 1991).

In free-market economies, urban form evolves as the outcome of locational decisions of many thousands of households, firms and public-sector agencies. There are therefore a variety of policy instruments that may be used to guide the evolution of urban form in the direction of reduced energy demand and environmental emissions. Urban form is primarily affected by transport policy and land-use policy. Transport policy is concerned with the provision of transport services on infrastructure that is almost exclusively owned and operated by the public sector (Rice, 1978). Transport authorities therefore have considerable power to design the configuration of infrastructure and set rules for its utilisation by private and public vehicles. By contrast, land-use services such as residential accommodation and commercial space are generally provided by the private sector, and the facilities and land

William P. Anderson and Pavlos S. Kanaroglou are in the Department of Geography, McMaster University, Hamilton, Ontario, L8S-4K1, Canada; Eric J. Miller is in the Department of Civil Engineering, University of Toronto, Toronto, Canada.

associated with them are generally privately-owned. Land-use authorities are therefore faced with a complex task of market intervention to achieve desirable outcomes. The very different nature of these two areas of policy and the general lack of coordination between them has limited the success of efforts to regulate urban form in most countries.

The current state of knowledge allows for some generalisations to be made about energy-efficient urban forms. Many questions, however, about the marginal effects of policy-induced changes in the existing pattern of land use and transport on energy demand and the environment remain unanswered. It is not clear, for example, whether adding to the road infrastructure reduces congestion and vehicle emissions, or if it leads to a more dispersed and inefficient pattern of land development (Downs, 1992). The goal of this paper is to review critically the literature that comprises the current state of knowledge about the effect of urban form on energy demand and the environment and to identify areas where further research is warranted.[1]

The remainder of this paper is divided into six sections. The next three sections set the problem in perspective, examine the currently held views about the concept of urban form, and examine recent findings on urban form trends. An overview of what is known about the link between urban form, energy utilisation and the environment is provided next. Following that, findings of the most influential empirical studies are critically evaluated. The last section delineates the areas within which future research is needed.

2. The Current Context

Concerns about the environmental consequences of human activities have been increasing since the 1960s. In addition, concern with the security of energy supply in the early 1970s gave rise to a critical re-evaluation of wasteful practices in such areas as transport, industrial processes and space conditioning. The two complementary goals

of environmental preservation and energy conservation resulted in a variety of new policies and regulations in the countries of the developed world. While the oil glut of the 1980s reduced the direct economic benefit of energy conservation efforts, previously unforeseen environmental problems—such as acid precipitation, ozone depletion and global warming—gave new urgency to the goal of controlling emissions. The rationale for energy conservation has shifted from reducing the risk for supply interruption to reducing the harmful environmental impacts of fuel consumption (Anderson, 1994).

The main instruments of energy and environmental policy have been 'technological fixes'. Alternatives to fossil-fuel-based energy supply have been promoted through subsidies, while emission- and fuel-efficiency standards have encouraged the development of efficient energy end use and pollution abatement technologies.[2] In order to respond adequately to the environmental challenges of the next century, however, it is likely that technological improvements will need to be augmented with some fundamental changes in the day-to-day patterns of human activity. Such changes could include reduction in household water use, recycling of wastes, acceptance of interior environments that are cooler in the winter and warmer in the summer, and reduced use of private automobiles. It is this last change which has received the greatest attention from planners and analysts (Lowe, 1990). Despite significant improvements in fuel efficiency and emissions, the rapid growth in automobile ownership, together with the increase in average auto trip lengths constitute perhaps the most pressing environmental threat of the current age.

Until recently, policies to curtail the environmental damages associated with automobile use have focused on vehicle technology and on transport systems design and management. According to Carley (1992), these policies will have limited success if they are not accompanied by a policy of integrated transport and land-use planning that facilitates a reduction in auto use. For example, the failure of multi-billion-dollar rapid transit projects in Washington DC and San Francisco significantly to alter travel behaviour is due to the fact that the increasing dispersion of residential patterns has reduced the accessibility of these systems to the average commuter over time. Thus, the relative locations of residences, workplaces, shopping and recreation areas, and transport infrastructure—i.e. the *urban form*—affects the ability and desire of individuals to choose alternatives to the automobile in meeting their transport needs.

Urban form may have a variety of other energy and environmental implications. For example, the compact residential spaces associated with a high-density city may have lower energy requirements for space conditioning and lighting than those of a more dispersed city, and their more clustered pattern may be more efficiently served by district heating. The suburban lifestyle may imply activities that affect air and water quality, such as use of lawnmowers, fertilisers and pesticides, and may be associated with increased levels of solid waste generation. Also, urban sprawl implies the permanent transfer of areas such as farms, woodlots, open spaces and ecologically sensitive areas to urban uses, and thus has a negative impact on renewable resources, water quality, recreational activities and biodiversity.

From a policy perspective, the issue of urban form is a complicated one. Naturally, the most desirable urban form cannot be determined solely on the basis of energy and environmental issues. Questions of personal safety, public and private costs, aesthetics and social interaction are equally prominent. Furthermore, even if an ideal form could be envisioned, it is not clear how it could be attained. This is because urban form is not simply designed and dictated by planners. Rather, it evolves over long periods as the outcome of constantly changing public policies and the locational preferences of firms and households. From a political perspective, a fundamental change in urban form, which will require a change in the lifestyles of many residents, may not be possible unless

there is a significant shift in public attitudes toward the environment (see Kuhn, 1992).

Before any progress can be made in this area, there are two lines of research that must be pursued. The first seeks to identify the relationships of the various components of urban form with energy consumption and environmental quality in quantitative terms. This is necessary in order to see whether changes to transport and land-use patterns are beneficial or not, and to identify those changes with the greatest potential impacts. The second line of research seeks to assess the effectiveness of using various policy instruments to promote changes in urban form, and thereby to achieve environmental goals. Neither of these can be adequately addressed through casual empiricism, but rather require use of the best available analytical methods from both the physical and social sciences.

3. Concepts of Urban Form

Urban form may be defined as the spatial configuration of fixed elements within a metropolitan region. This includes the spatial pattern of land uses and their densities as well as the spatial design of transport and communication infrastructure. Urban interaction refers to the flows of goods, people and information among different locations in the city. From the perspective of energy use and environmental emissions, the flows of people (commuters, shoppers, etc.) are most important, although flows of goods, especially by truck, also have significant impacts. While communications flows are not directly linked to energy use or emissions, they are important in that they may be substitutable for flows of people. (See further discussion in section 4.)

The urban spatial structure is a more comprehensive concept. According to Bourne (1982) it consists of three elements: the urban form, urban interactions, and a set of organising principles that define the relationship between the two. The key point here is that urban form has a profound influence on the flows within the city, but does not determine them completely. One can envision, for example, two very different commuting patterns that might overlay the same urban form: the first in which people commute short distances to employment districts close to their residences, and the second in which people make longer commutes, bypassing nearby employment districts for more distant ones. In the first instance, efficient commuting is the organising principle—people choose to live close to their jobs. In the second, some other principle, such as social or ethnic status and preference for locational amenities, may determine residential location (Giuliano and Small, 1993). In reality, a number of organising principles work simultaneously in determining urban spatial structure. An implication of this is that more efficient commuting patterns may be achieved without any change in urban form if people can be encouraged to place greater emphasis on efficiency in their locational decisions.

In order to understand different possibilities for urban form, urban analysts often refer to simple archetypal forms that might be expected to emerge under different circumstances (see Rice, 1978). Three such archetypal forms are illustrated in Figure 1. The best known of these is the concentric city, which is often associated with urban economic theory (see Papageorgiou, 1990). The focal point of this form is the central business district (CBD), which is the location with maximum employment density, the maximum number of trip ends and the maximum rent. Land uses are segregated into concentric zones around the CBD, based on the organising principle that those uses that put the greatest value on access to the CBD will command the most central locations.

The concentric form assumes a very dense transport network, so that straight-line distance is an adequate surrogate for travel impedance. A more realistic assumption is that the transport network consists of a smaller number of major routes that extend out from the CBD. In this case, we expect to see the radial city, in which sectors of intense land uses extend out from the CBD along major lines of transport, leaving areas of sparse

development between them. (A special case where there is only one transport line with the CBD located at its centre is called the liner city.) A characteristic of the radial form is that trips between points in different sectors must be made by way of the CBD—that is, there is a relatively low level of *connectivity* among locations in the city.

An archetypal urban form that has received increasing attention in recent years is called the multinucleated city.[3] Here the CBD has lost its dominance to a number of other foci distinguished as local maxima for employment density, trip ends and rent. This form is consistent with a more complex, hierarchical system of transport infrastructure where not all routes are oriented toward the CBD and therefore there is a higher overall level of connectivity in the city. Spatial interactions in such a city may flow in all directions and the simple relationship between land-use type and centrality dissolves.

These archetypal forms prove useful in thinking about energy and environmental issues in cities, but their usefulness is limited by their fundamentally static nature. It is important to recognise that no real urban form is determined by the circumstances that exist at one particular point in time, but rather it must reflect events, technologies, policies and preferences over the entire history of the city (see Adams, 1970). This is because certain long-lived elements of the urban form, such as buildings and infrastructure, continue to influence the spatial configuration of new elements for decades or even centuries (Wegener, 1986). In a word, urban form is *evolutionary*.

4. Trends in Urban Form

Changes in human settlement patterns during the twentieth century can be characterised as the outcome of two simultaneous spatial trends: the concentration of an increasing share of the population and economic activities into urban areas; and the dispersion of population and economic activities within urban areas. The first of these trends simply reflects the shift from an agrarian economy,

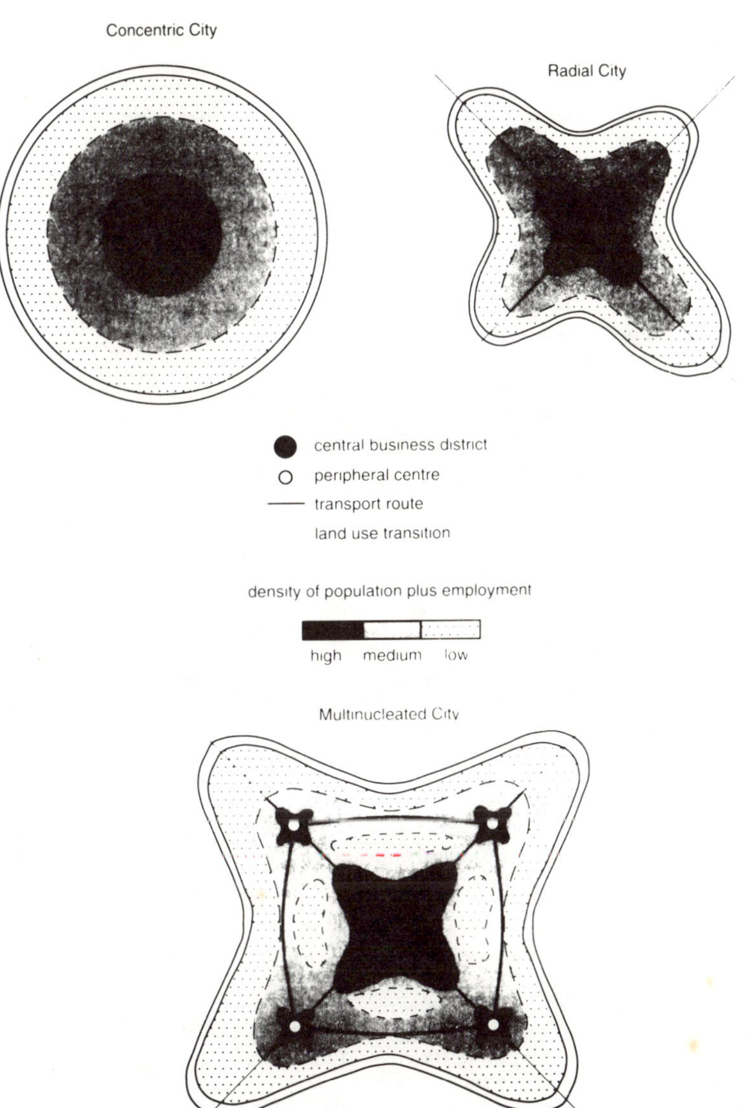

Figure 1. Archetypal urban forms.

in which most people are employed in resource-oriented activities, to an urban economy, in which most people are employed in activities that are more spatially clustered. This trend has been extant during most periods in recorded human history, but accelerated greatly during the past two centuries. It continues at a rapid rate in the developing world, but shows some sign of abatement in developed countries, where the population in urban areas is already over 75 per cent of the total (Beale, 1977; Vining and Kontuly, 1978).

The second trend, which is commonly referred to as urban sprawl, represents a fundamental transformation of urban form. It is characterised by

(1) an outward expansion of the metropolitan boundary that separates urban from rural land uses;
(2) a general decline in intensity of all forms of land uses, as measured by population and employment densities;
(3) transport networks that provided high connectivity among points, even in peripheral parts of the city; and
(4) the segregation of residential from other land uses, with the greater part of residences locating in peripheral suburbs.

Significant expansions of urban boundaries and the development of suburbs began to occur in many cities during the nineteenth century, due largely to contagious growth and the ability of rail transport to support more dispersed development along its corridors (see Lewis, 1991; Muller, 1986; Warner, 1978). However, rapid acceleration of urban sprawl is generally associated with the widespread adoption of automobile and truck transport, especially in the 1950s and 1960s. As a private and highly flexible mode of transport, the automobile provided its owner with the freedom to choose residential locations far removed from his or her workplace, and allowed for the development of residential areas without regard to their accessibility to public transport infrastructure. The shift from rail to truck transport allowed the accelerated development of businesses in the suburbs, initially in the retail sector but eventually in all economic sectors.

Many elements of public policy helped to promote suburbanisation. The most basic of these was the construction of major commuter roads connecting central areas with suburbs and of local roads to provide easy auto access to new housing surveys. As developers built modest homes on cheap land in the urban fringe, policies promoting home-ownership tended also to promote suburbanisation. They included direct subsidisation of mortgages or mortgage insurance, and elements of the tax code that favour home-owners relative to renters. These tax policies included deductibility of mortgage interest and exemption of residences from capital gains taxes. At the local level, zoning policies that excluded high-density development from suburban communities contributed to the continual expansion of the metropolitan boundary to accommodate increasing housing demand.

Until recently, the only major policies designed to retard urban sprawl have been those that come under the heading of urban containment. These policies, which are intended to prevent the transfer of agricultural land to urban uses and to preserve the rural way of life, have a long history in Europe, especially in the UK (Breheny, 1992). In North America, they have been much more prominent in Canada than in the US (Richardson, 1992). This may in part explain the slower pace of sprawl in Canada.

The idea of sprawl does not convey a complete picture of how urban forms have been changing. Returning to the archetypal forms in Figure 1, it is easy to imagine sprawl occurring within any of the three general types. In a purely concentric city, sprawl would simply involve an outward shift in the outer boundaries of all land-use zones over time, along with a reduction in densities. In a radial city, sprawl would be channelled along sectors that extend ever further away from the CBD. The multinucleated city is perhaps a more useful abstract type to consider in relation to sprawl, because the underlying processes of sprawl are consistent with a transition from a concentric or radial form to a multinucleated form. For example, the addition of population at increasingly long distances from the CBD creates a demand for retail and other services in the periphery of the city—thus the emergence of peripheral centres.[4] Also, peripheral centres tend to emerge where well-established radial transport corridors intersect with new circumferential routes. Thus, the effect of building such routes may be a transition from a radial to a multinucleated city. It is important to remember, however, that within the category of multinucleated forms there can be different degrees of sprawl, depending upon how tightly land-use activity is clustered around peripheral centres.

The trend to urban sprawl is evident in all affluent countries, but with significant variation. For example, the high rate of sprawl in North American cities as compared with European cities is well known. Within North America, Canadian cities exhibit a slower rate of sprawl than American cities, due in part to the continual supply of urban-oriented immigrants in Canada, the absence of the high crime rates that have driven many middle-class Americans from the central cities, and more proactive planning institutions in Canada[5] (Pressman, 1988).

What can be said about future directions in urban form? Long-term forecasting has never been an important activity in urban research, so there is little in the way of predictions about urban form in the twenty-first century. There are, however, some debates concerning the possible future urban forms that current developments in infrastructure and technology may support. For example, Wegener (1986) argues that decisions about the location and capacity of transport infrastructure have very long-term implications with respect to urban form. Based on his analysis of the Dortmund metropolitan area in Germany, he predicts that policies intended to curtail urban sprawl will have little effect because the infrastructure that is already in place was designed to support decentralisation. This effectively means that sprawl is built into the 'hardware' of the urban system, and is therefore very difficult to reverse.

There has been a lot of speculation about the impact of new technologies, especially telecommunications technologies, on urban form. It is generally acknowledged that the introduction of a new transport technology—the private automobile—brought on the age of urban sprawl. It has been argued by some that new telecommunications technologies such as telemarketing, conference calls, video telephones, fax machines and computer networks, may lead to an equally profound transformation. Telecommunications innovations are seen as 'friction-reducing' technologies that are capable of supporting decentralisation both at the metropolitan level and at the larger national level. From an energy and environmental perspective, this may have both positive and negative implications (Nilles, 1991). While telecommunications can reduce the energy consumption, congestion and pollution associated with using cars to commute and make business calls, the associated decentralisation of land use might lead to increasing automobile dependence for non-work trips, as well as other environmental problems associated with dispersed residential development.

Those who have given careful consideration to the relationship between telecommunications and spatial patterns have generally come to the conclusion that there is little evidence to support the contention that massive deconcentration will result (Gillespie, 1992; Janelle, 1986; Nijkamp and Salomon, 1989). The reluctance of both management and labour to adopt work-at-home practices, and the continuing need for face-to-face contact in many sectors will slow down the adoption of telecommunications innovations. Even in those sectors where they are adopted, they will not necessarily promote dispersion, because communications networks will continue to be focused on existing urban centres, and some technologies, such as 'smart buildings', may actually favour centralised operation.

Addressing the Canadian context specifically, Pressman (1988) argues that there are other trends that work against the decentralising tendencies of infrastructure and new technologies. These include demographic changes, such as general ageing and a move to smaller households, that call for more compact living spaces. Chinitz (1991) cautions against making strong inferences based on demographic trends, however, noting that in the US the locational preferences of demographic groups have been highly unstable over recent decades.[6]

5. Urban Form, Energy Consumption and the Environment

Energy Consumption

Energy conservation generally takes two forms: changes to the stock of energy using capital, such as boilers, vehicles, furnaces and appliances; and changes to the rate or intensity at which the capital is used. The first form entails the scrapping of old, energy-inefficient capital, the substitution of new, energy-conserving capital, and the retrofitting of existing capital to make it more efficient. The second form ranges from the complete curtailment of certain industries or activities with high energy intensities, to relatively minor adjustments, such as turning down thermostats.

Of all consumer goods, the automobile is the most massive user of energy. Furthermore, its exclusive dependence on gasoline as a fuel made it particularly vulnerable to the increases in petroleum prices in the 1970s. Thus, attempts by households to conserve costly energy began with the car (Yergin, 1979). It was relatively easy to achieve the first form of conservation. Compared to other types of energy using capital, cars have short lives, and therefore a significant substitution of energy-efficient cars into the vehicle stock was achieved within a few years.

The second form of conservation, as it applies to the automobile, is simply achieved through a reduction in driving. Most households were able to achieve some modest conservation of this type by combining trips, carpooling or cutting down on recreational driving. In North America, more radical conservation, up to and including a complete curtailment of automobile use for some or all trips, was only feasible to a limited number of households. This is because the juxtaposition of suburban residences with places of employment, shopping and recreation did not accommodate switching to more energy-efficient transport modes such as public transit or cycling. For most purposes, suburbanites had little choice but to drive. This gave rise to speculation that radical changes in urban form would be necessary to free suburban households from their dependence on the automobile in an era of expensive energy.

Making adjustments to urban form does not in itself constitute a direct energy conservation, but rather a facilitating strategy which makes a variety of conservation activities possible (Keyes, 1977). For example, changes in the relative positions of residences and workplaces make it possible for transport energy consumption to be reduced through reductions in average journey-to-work trip lengths and mode switching from cars to public transit. However, this reduction will only come about if individuals adjust their own behaviour—including their residential and mode choices—to take advantage of the opportunity. (Once again, urban form affects, but does not determine, urban spatial structure.) Given the uncertainty surrounding the link between urban form and energy use, it is not surprising that there have been considerable debates over the relative importance of land use and transport policies in a larger energy conservation strategy.

In the wake of the first petroleum crisis, results of a number of studies giving a broad range of estimates of the effectiveness of land use planning for energy conservation were published during the 1970s. The studies adopted a similar approach in that each proposed two or more hypothetical urban forms, or hypothetical patterns of growth for existing cities, and projected differences in aggregate energy consumption over a finite time-period. While these studies all employed significant amounts of real-world data, they cannot be viewed as empirical evidence, as they all represent informed estimates of what might happen, rather than measurements of what actually has happened. (Empirical studies are reviewed in section 6 below.)

The results of five studies are summarised in Table 1. The reductions reported in the final column represent the difference between each land-use scenario for which energy consumption estimates were made and the most energy-intensive scenario. The extreme variations in the magnitude of these reductions should be interpreted with some care, as they are based on very different types of assumptions.

The Council on Environmental Quality (1975) is a summary of a study commissioned in conjunction with the US Department of Housing and Urban Development. The full report is in Real Estate Research Corporation (1974). It was the most abstract of the studies, as it compared purely hypothetical urban forms designed to house a predefined number of people in a 'new town' setting. Three urban form scenarios were developed: low-density sprawl, high-density planned, and a combination scenario that included aspects of both. In addition to energy end-use, it compared these forms on the basis of public service cost, land consumption and pollution generation, and found significant differences on all counts. While this is one of the most frequently cited studies in the literature, it has been severely criticised on the basis of its simplistic assumptions and a perceived bias in favour of compact development (Windsor, 1979).

Roberts' (1977) study on the Washington DC metropolitan area was more practical in nature; first because it was based on spatial data for a real city, and secondly because it sought to address the possible outcomes of specific land-use planning proposals being considered by the Metropolitan Washington Council of Governments. He considered how an expected increase of 500 000 households over a 20-year period would be accommodated under different land-use planning regimes. These included the polar opposites of sprawl and dense centre, but also a sectoral development scenario and scenarios in which growth is concentrated around public transit and the circumferential Beltway road system. One interesting result here is that energy consumption under the transit-ori-

ented scenario was estimated to be quite similar to that under the dense-centre scenario, suggesting that planning principles other than compactness can accommodate significant energy conservation.[7]

Carrol's (1977) study addresses a quite different context as it deals only with one suburban component of the New York metropolitan area. Like the Washington study, it considered the energy implication of accommodating an increase in population under a base sprawl scenario and a clustered scenario consistent with proposed land-use planning restrictions for Nassau and Suffolk counties in Long Island. The very high reductions should be interpreted with caution, as they represent a difference in incremental, as opposed to total, energy use under the two scenarios. Their implication is that significant reductions in energy consumption can be achieved through quite localised clustering—as in a multinucleated urban form.

Edward's (1977) study used data on population, employment, trip generation rates, etc. for Sioux Falls, South Dakota, and applied them to an analysis of 37 hypothetical urban forms. Thus it is best thought of as an assessment of how much energy a city of the size and economic structure of Sioux Falls would consume under different spatial configurations. It is therefore not surprising that very extreme differences are observed between the most energy-efficient and least energy-efficient spatial scenarios. Edward's employed a sophisticated modelling framework which allowed him to examine the relationship between energy efficiency and other characteristics of urban form. He found that, for the most part, there is a trade-off between energy efficiency and overall accessibility, measured in terms of the time-cost of commuting. He concluded that the best hope of satisfying the need to reduce energy consumption while maintaining high levels of accessibility is to promote multinucleated forms, by which "proximity is provided as a substitute for mobility" (p. 53).

A much more pessimistic view of the potential for land-use planning to aid energy conservation was provided by Keyes (1977)

Table 1. Estimated impacts of land-use planning on energy consumption

Author	Study area	Time-horizon	Scenarios	Percentage reduction	
				Transport energy	Total energy
Council on Environmental Quality (1975)	Hypothetical city	Static comparison	1. Low-density sprawl 2. High-density planned 3. Combination	0.0 53.9 29.4	0.0 46.3 26.8
Roberts (1977)	Washington, DC (hypothetical growth patterns)	1973–92	1. Sprawl 2. Sectoral 3. Beltway-oriented 4. Transit-oriented 5. Dense centre	0.0 5.4 9.0 18.4 17.4	0.0 2.8 3.4 7.6 7.9
Carrol (1977)	Nassau and Suffolk counties, Long Island (hypothetical growth patterns)	1972–2000	1. Sprawl 2. Clustered	0.0 51.9[a]	0.0 19.0[a]
Edwards (1977)	Sioux Falls, SD (hypothetical patterns of existing population)	Static comparison	1. Least efficient 2. Most efficient	0 80 +	
Keyes (1977)	Aggregate of US regions (hypothetical growth patterns)	1972–85	1. Base case 2. Modified growth pattern		0.00 0.35

[a]Reduction in incremental energy use.

He argued that the scenarios used in some studies involve far too radical changes in planning practices to be politically feasible. Equally pessimistic in affecting urban form through municipal policy is Downs (1992) who argues in favour of regionally based policy. Based on more modest modifications of growth patterns that he considered to be realistic, Keyes projected that land-use changes could reduce energy consumption in the US overall by less than one-half of 1 per cent.[8] While this effect appears to be quite small, it is roughly equivalent to the effect of an 80 per cent increase in gasoline prices estimated in the same study. It is, however, less than one-fifth as large as the effect of a fairly modest improvement in overall vehicle fleet fuel efficiency.

While the results of these studies provide some valuable insights, they share two important shortcomings that limit their usefulness for policy analysis. First, most of them emphasise journey-to-work travel in estimating transport energy demand. Since most empirical studies indicate that non-work trips make up more than half of total trips, and since the propensity to use public transit is generally lower for non-work trips, they have a major impact on total transport energy use. Secondly, they are weak on modelling the behavioural responses of individual households to such things as price changes. Since changes in urban form generally facilitate rather than enforce energy-conserving behaviour, a more careful analysis of household decision-making is needed.

The broad variety of estimates in Table 1 probably has less to do with differences in methods than with differences in what the analysts consider to be realistically achievable changes in urban form. A related question is therefore whether high energy prices provide a sufficient incentive for households to make residential location decisions that will result in more efficient land-use patterns. Small (1980) addressed this question by estimating the financial benefit that the typical suburban household would gain through reduced energy consumption if it were to move to a more central location. His results indicated that even under assumptions of very high future energy prices, this benefit would be relatively small. Thus government fiat, rather than market incentives, will be needed to bring about more energy-efficient urban forms. Given the difficulties associated with such massive market interventions in the American context, he concluded that technological change to improve energy efficiency is a much more fruitful path to conservation than land-use planning. This sentiment is strongly echoed by Lave (1978) and others.

In addition to the debates over the potential of land-use planning to conserve energy, there is a fundamental debate over what type of urban form is most efficient. Based in large part on the Council of Environmental Quality study, the early conventional wisdom was that the most compact centralised form is the most energy-efficient. Later research, however, favoured a compact multinucleated form,[9] both because it may be as efficient as or more efficient than a centralised form, and because it provides a more realistic goal to work towards, especially in the North American context. Haynes (1986) reviewed a number of studies on land use and energy consumption, and found that most of those that argued strongly for centralised forms, like the Council on Environmental Quality, did not consider multinucleated forms at all. Those that did, generally found multinucleated forms to be preferable to centralised forms. Despite this body of research, a strong preference for centralised development is still prevalent among policy-makers (Breheny, 1992).

Perhaps this enduring preference for compact centralised forms stems from the fact that, while a well-designed multinucleated form accommodates energy-efficient behaviour, a centralised form enforces it. Within a multinucleated form it is still possible for individuals to commute long distances and make long shopping trips if they do not choose residences close to their workplaces or take advantage of nearby shopping centres. In a compact centralised form, the length of work and shopping trips one can possibly make are, by definition, minimised.

Giuliano and Small (1993) provide evidence of imbalance between place of residence and place of work in Los Angeles, a multinucleated city.

Environmental Concerns

The impacts of urban form on the environment are closely related to the impacts of urban form on energy consumption. This is because many important environmental pollutants such as sulphur dioxide (SO_2), carbon monoxide (CO) and nitrogen oxides (NO_x) are primarily produced by the chemical reactions occurring in fuel burning. Fuel use in automobiles is of increasing concern because in many cities the emissions associated with industrial sources are stable or declining, while emissions associated with vehicles are rising (Deelstra, 1992; Richardson, 1992). It should be pointed out, however, that sulphur dioxide emissions are not primarily attributed to fuel use in automobiles.

There are, however, reasons why the environmental impacts of urban form are different, and somewhat more complicated, than the associated energy impacts. For one thing, while it is generally true that any change that conserves energy also reduces pollution, there are important cases where the reverse is true.[10] Also, there are a number of environmental problems associated with urban form that are not directly energy-related. These include problems of solid and liquid waste disposal, water use, land degradation and some forms of industrial pollution. Finally, from the perspective of behavioural modelling, environmental issues generally involve more complex and intractable interactions and incentives than do energy issues.

To elaborate on this last point, prospects for energy conservation can generally be analysed through a model of private incentives. For example, we can assume that economy-minded firms and households will reduce energy consumption in response to a sufficiently large increase in energy price. Analysis therefore consists of determining the magnitude of the response, which forms of conservation households will adopt, and what level of price increase is necessary to achieve a desired reduction in energy consumption. With environmental problems, the analysis is not so clear-cut because incentives are not so closely linked with individual behaviour. For example, when a commuter is faced with a decision of whether to drive to work or take public transit, the cost of the extra pollution generated if she drives will not be borne exclusively by her, but rather it will be spread over the large number of people who must breathe the marginally more polluted air. Put differently, if she decides not to drive, she will reap only a small portion of the environmental benefit. Thus in economists' terms, pollution is an *externality* because its costs and benefits are not reflected in market valuations.

There is broad consensus in the literature on a number of principal links between urban form and environmental quality. The first is that the more energy-efficient forms are generally the more environmentally benign forms. Despite the fact that some energy-conserving technologies have undesirable environmental side-effects, it is generally true that energy-conserving behaviour has a positive environmental impact. The Council on Environmental Quality (1975) study concluded that the benefit of dense development in terms of pollution reduction is of comparable magnitude to its benefit in terms of energy conservation. Elements of urban form that discourage use of cars are especially desirable.

A second point of broad consensus is that it is desirable to preserve open spaces with relatively dense vegetation *within* urban areas. In addition to their recreational and aesthetic value, these spaces play a significant role in improving local air and water quality (Spirn, 1984). This point may imply some contradiction with arguments in favour of high-density development (Breheny, 1992). Orrskog and Snickars (1992) suggest that in order to address open space, it is necessary to distinguish between two concepts of density. The first is the 'loading' of human activity onto that land that is developed, and the second is the ratio of population to the total land area within the metropolitan boundary. A city in which population is concentrated into districts which are separated by ample open spaces would have a high density of the first type but a low density of the second type. Despite the low overall density, such an urban form has significant environmental advantages.

A third point of consensus is that urban development should be conducive to a reduction in liquid and solid waste production and consumption of water and non-renewable resources such as building material. In this regard, the transport and land-use link is a bit more tenuous, as it is principally the suburban lifestyle that is seen as a problem. Land-use issues are more directly involved when this point is extended to say that wastes should be recycled or disposed of within the metropolitan boundary.

In general, all of these points lead to the conclusion that the least-desirable form of urban development from an environmental perspective is low-density suburbanisation (Roseland, 1992). There is no consensus, however, on the most desirable form. In Europe, both the European Community and some national governments have established long-term land-use policy guidelines based on a very strict principle of compact centralised development. This strong position is being challenged on a number of counts. First, striving for the most compact possible urban form leaves little room for open spaces (Breheny, 1992). Secondly, given the uncertainty about both growth prospects and evidence on environmental impacts, such a unidimensional strategy is imprudent (Van der Valk and Faludi, 1992). And finally, such a doctrinaire position is insensitive to the question of what types of cities people prefer to live in (Banister, 1992). Some critics of the 'compact city' approach challenge the empirical evidence upon which it is based, especially the close link between density and energy consumption (see section 6).

Alternative strategies for environmentally sensitive urban development include carefully planned multinucleated forms, with em-

phasis on transit orientation, mixed land use, preservation of relatively large open spaces within the metropolitan boundary, and localised recycling, composting and waste disposal. In their analysis of the Stockholm region, Orrskog and Snickars (1992) observe that the traditional radial form allows for the preservation of open spaces which are large enough to maintain biological vitality at close proximity to built-up areas. They argue that construction of circumferential roads would be undesirable, as the accompanying development would break up open spaces. Breheny (1992), based on his research in the UK, argues that the new communities should be developed either close enough to major urban centres to allow efficient commuting on transit lines, or far enough away to preclude commuting. Development in intermediate areas leads to long-distance commuting. Van der Valk and Faludi (1992) argue for the designation of growth regions in the Netherlands which are large enough to be self-sufficient in public services and to provide employment opportunities to local residents, and for the prohibition of new development outside these regions. This form of 'concentrated deconcentration' is meant to deflect growth both from overcrowded urban areas and from agricultural land.[11]

Similar ideas are reflected in recent planning initiatives in North America. For example, a proposed land-use planning strategy for Berkeley, California, establishes a number of focal points for development within the low-density urban area. Circles are drawn around these points to establish zones that are small enough to be traversed by bicycle or on foot. All development is restricted to the zones, and over time land between them is reclaimed for open space (Roseland, 1992). This provides a strategy for transforming a pattern of urban sprawl into a relatively compact multinucleated form.

6. Empirical Evidence

While the studies in Table 1 made possible some informed speculation about urban form, energy and the environment, a number of recent studies provide more direct evidence by concentrating on what can be observed about existing cities. Most of these are comparison studies, where energy or environmental characteristics are observed across a group of cities, and the observed differences are related to differences in urban form.[12] Also, there have been a number of case studies focusing on individual cities and, for example, on differences in commuting patterns between people in different types of suburbs.

In addition to reviewing comparison and case studies, we also include a review of a recent study of energy and environmental implications of urban form in the Greater Toronto Area. While this study shares the somewhat speculative approach of the studies in Table 1, it also draws on a wealth of empirical information, and addresses land use and transport at a sufficiently detailed level to provide some specific planning guidance.

Comparison Studies

The simplest and most economical approach to assessing the significance of urban form is to collect data from the broad range of urban forms that can be observed in the real world and attempt to draw conclusions based on the values of relevant energy and environmental indicators. The difficulty with this approach is that the indicators may be affected by a variety of other factors such as climatic conditions, differences in economic variables such as prices, and differences in behaviour or preferences. The factors that affect environmental indicators such as air quality measures are particularly complex. For this reason, and because of the relative paucity of environmental data, all of the studies reviewed here concentrate on energy consumption. (See Table 2 for a list of the studies and some brief information about their contexts and findings.)

The most extensive, and by far the most frequently cited, of all studies linking energy consumption with urban form is by Kenwor-

thy and Newman (1990). Annual per capita gasoline use was observed for an international cross-section of 32 large cities: 13 in Europe, 10 in the US, 5 in Australia, 3 in Asia and 1 (Toronto) in Canada. Gasoline use in 1980 varied from a high of 75 510 MJ per capita in Houston, Texas, to a low of 1987 MJ per capita in Hong Kong. Although the US cities used, on average, about four times as much gasoline as the European cities, the average rate of growth in consumption was almost three times higher in Europe than in the US. Toronto, at 34 813 MJ per capita in 1980 was well below the US average, but well above the European, Asian and Australian averages.

Based on some simple regression analyses, Kenworthy and Newman concluded that the standard explanatory factors—differences in gasoline price, income and vehicle fleet efficiency—explained only about 40 per cent of the variance in gasoline demand. They found, however, that a very high proportion of the remaining variation can be explained by a simple measure of urban population density. Other indicators of urban form, such as road provision per capita and mode share of public transit, also showed strong statistical linkages with gasoline use. They concluded that urban population density is the single most important factor, and called for policies of 'reurbanisation' to reduce transport energy demand and the associated environmental problems.

While these results are frequently referenced by proponents of compact development, Kenworthy and Newman are not without critics. Gomez-Ibanez (1991) argues that their method of analysis is too crude to provide evidence of a causal link between density and automobile dependency. For example, their statistical model fails to account for the link between density and income, and therefore may underestimate the importance of the latter in explaining differences in gasoline demand. Gordon and Richardson (1989) object strongly to the policy prescriptions of reurbanisation and increased spending on transit. They point to the failure of most American transit projects and to the

Table 2. Comparison studies

Authors	Indicator variable	Comparison	Conclusions
Kenworthy and Newman (1990)	Per capita gasoline consumption	32 major cities from 4 continents	1. Urban density is a major determinant of energy consumption
Webster and Bly (1987)	Public transit ridership	100 cities in 16 countries	1. Car ownership key factor in transit use 2. Centralised employment promotes transit 3. Small cities less transit-accessible 4. Radial forms more transit-accessible
Mogridge (1985)	Transport energy by distance from CBD	Paris and London	1. Car ownership more important than urban form 2. Policy emphasis should be on fuel efficiency
Banister (1992)	Per capita transport energy use	4 size categories of British towns and 6 small British towns	1. Mid-sized towns more energy-efficient than London 2. Diversity of services and labour-force containment reduce energy use

efficiency losses that may result from the application of draconian land-use restrictions. Also, Breheny (1992) points out a number of flaws in the general argument that increasing density yields environmental benefits.

Furthermore, Kenworthy and Newman's results do little to resolve debates over compact centralised vs compact multinucleated forms. This is because it was only possible to collect consistent data on relatively crude measures of urban form (Banister, 1992). Therefore it was not possible to compare cities with similar overall densities, but different degrees of clustering. The term reurbanisation, as used by the authors, refers to density increases in the CBD. The possibility of efficient multinucleated cities with little or no wasteful commuting is entirely ignored. Yet, land-use patterns in the majority of the US cities, identified in the study as major gasoline consumers, are such that policies towards efficient multinucleation will likely be more effective (Gordon *et al.*, 1991).

Webster and Bly (1987) examined factors affecting public transit use in a cross-section of 100 cities in 16 countries. Although they do not measure energy consumption directly, this study is relevant given the high energy intensity of automobile travel relative to transit. Their results present a consistent pattern of declining transit use, due largely to increased car ownership in most cities, and factors that favour car travel relative to transit. They found that, except where there are heavy subsidies, average fares have been increasing in real terms, while average transit travel speeds have been declining due to reduced service levels. By contrast, automobile costs have been relatively stable, as dispersion of residences and businesses has counteracted the effect of increased congestion on average automobile travel speeds.

Changes in the distribution across the urban hierarchy and within urban areas has also worked against transit. In some countries, a shift of population from the largest cities to smaller cities is an important factor, as big cities generally have better average transit access. As for urban form, they concluded

that the suburbanisation of employment makes it more difficult for transit to serve commuters effectively. (Toronto is cited as an example of a city where healthy employment growth in the CBD has kept transit's share relatively high.) They also found that the form of suburbanisation matters. Specifically, cities like Paris and Stockholm with a radial pattern of growth in suburban communities located like 'beads on a string' along rail transit lines are better able to maintain transit share. Despite these conclusions, their cross-sectional regression model had low explanatory power, suggesting that a large number of unobserved factors affect transit choice.

A dissenting view on the importance of urban form is provided by Mogridge (1985). Based on a comparison of data for London and Paris, he concluded that car ownership rates are of far greater importance in explaining why per capita transport energy consumption is higher in Paris than are density measures or transit provision levels. Instead of using a gross measure of total energy consumption divided by population, Mogridge calculated energy consumption based on travel survey data and a model for estimating fuel consumption per trip. This allowed him to estimate per capita consumption for people who live at various distances from the CBD. He found that energy consumption rises with more peripheral residential location, but at about the same rate as car ownership. He concludes that policies to promote fuel efficiency will be more effective than land-use policies.

While Mogridge adopts some valuable methodological innovations, there are a number of reasons to question his overall conclusion. First, there is limited information in a comparison of Paris and London, since they are relatively similar in terms of energy consumption. (According to Kenworthy and Newman, fuel consumption in Paris is only 13 per cent higher than in London, as compared with Toronto, where it is 180 per cent higher.) Secondly, while Mogridge carefully measured all relevant indicators by categories of distance from the CBD, he did nothing to identify any radial or multinucleated structures in the two cities. Finally, the notion that it is car ownership rather than urban form that affects energy consumption neglects the possibility that car ownership may itself be affected by urban form.

Banister (1992) compared estimates of weekly transport energy consumption for different size categories of British cities. Contrary to expectations, London was relatively inefficient, compared with other urban places of over 25 000 population. This appears to contradict the conventional wisdom that those cities served by rail transit are relatively efficient, as most of the smaller cities only had bus transport. The reason appears to be that, despite its high density, London had more travel per person and a longer average trip length.

Banister also compared six small urban places in South Oxfordshire with populations varying from 100 to 10 000. He found that the largest town, despite having the largest number of trips per person, also had the lowest per capita energy consumption. So there would appear to be some economies of scale at the lower end of the city size range. While this analysis of small towns may seem irrelevant to large metropolitan areas, the basic principle underlying the results is not. Towns become more energy-efficient as they become more diversified in terms of services and reach a higher level of journey-to-work containment (i.e. a higher share of residents employed locally). A large metropolitan area might be similarly more efficient if it is made up of relatively self-contained sub-units.

A problem with the Mogridge study is that it only uses journey-to-work (JTW) data for calculating energy consumption figures. This is a general problem with such studies because JTW data are more readily available than non-work trip data. Banister (1992), who also makes use of discretionary trip data, points out that JTW trips make up an ever-shrinking share of total trips. For example, in the mid 1980s JTW made up 23 per cent of UK trips and 24 per cent of Dutch trips. JTW trips make up a greater share of total trips in the Greater Toronto Area, but

their share has shrunk from 43 per cent in 1964 to 38.4 per cent in 1986 (Transportation Tomorrow Survey, 1988). Assessing the determinants of the frequency, pattern and mode split of non-work trips should be given the highest priority in further empirical research on urban transport energy use.

Case Studies

A number of case studies have been conducted to assess the effect of aspects of urban form on transport energy use and its environmental implications in particular cities. Four studies are described below. Two of these studies (Newman and Kenworthy, 1988, and Prevedouros and Schofer, 1991) are primarily concerned with assessing the implications of travel behaviour of people in different parts of the city. The other two (May and Scheuernstuhl, 1991, and Barton, 1992) extend the analysis to consider the outcome of proposed transport policies. (Brief information on the case studies is provided in Table 3.)

In a study of the Perth metropolitan area, Newman and Kenworthy (1988) examined the link between road congestion and fuel consumption. From a policy perspective, their main purpose was to look critically at the proposition that increasing the overall road capacity can actually promote energy conservation by reducing congestion. (This is based on the fact that slow, stop and go driving greatly reduces the energy efficiencies of cars.) To address this question they assembled two disaggregate data sets. The first was a set of 'driving cycle' characteristics which was collected by driving specially metered cars through different parts of the city. This information was used to estimate energy consumption patterns in an engineering model. The second was a set of travel behaviour patterns for people who live in different areas, collected through travel diaries.

They found that, despite the energy saved per vehicle-km by driving on uncongested roads, those people whose residential loca-

24							WILLIAM P. ANDERSON *ET AL.*

Table 3. Case studies

Authors	City	Indicator variables	Data	Conclusions
Newman and Kenworthy (1988)	Perth, Australia	1. Fuel use per capita	1. Household travel diaries 2. Driving cycle data	1. Road expansion to reduce congestion increases energy use
Prevedouros and Schofer (1991)	Chicago, USA	1. Trips 2. Mode split 3. Average distance 4. Fuel use	1. Mail survey	1. Peripheral suburb residents take longer trips, use more fuel, have lower transit share 2. Trip generation depends on household characteristics rather than just location
May and Scheuernstuhl (1991)	Denver, USA	1. Travel demand characteristics 2. Emissions of 4 pollutants under 2 land-use scenarios	1. Household survey 2. Census data	Transport/land-use policies to promote transit will not reduce emissions because of: 1. increased congestion 2. longer average trip length
Barton (1992)	Bristol, UK	1. Transit ridership under LRT scenario	1. Travel survey	1. Introduction of LRT has little energy and environmental benefit without complementary land-use restrictions

tion exposed them to the least congestion used the most fuel on a per capita basis. This is because they tended to make more and longer trips. They inferred from this that locational factors have a greater impact on energy consumption than does congestion, and that a policy of expanding road capacity would lead to more, rather than less, fuel consumption. Thus, they concluded, a policy of more compact urban land-use planning is preferable as an energy-conservation strategy.

Prevedouros and Schofer (1991) examined variations in travel behaviour and energy consumption in the Chicago metropolitan area between people living in older suburbs that are close to the CBD and those in newer suburbs in the urban periphery. Based on the results of a mail survey, they found that a much higher percentage of older-suburbs' residents worked in the central city, and a correspondingly higher percentage commuted by public transport. However, even in the older suburbs, more than half of the JTW trips had suburban destinations. Despite the lower densities in the newer suburbs, the average level of congestion for trips originating there was roughly the same as in the older suburbs. Including both JTW and non-work trips, they found that residents of newer suburbs made longer trips and consumed more energy.

In terms of trip generation, however, their analysis suggested that variations in household characteristics between the older and newer suburbs were more important than any 'pure' locational effects. Thus, demographic and employment trends play a significant role in aggregate energy consumption. Specifically, younger people, people in households with a high ratio of cars to drivers, and women who are employed part-time have high numbers of daily trips.

These results have some important implications for the study of energy–urban-form relationships. The relatively long JTW trips indicate a poor matching of residences and workplaces in the newer suburbs. Thus, these studies provide no evidence of efficient multinucleation in the periphery, a finding that is re-enforced by Giuliano and Small (1993). Also, the importance of household characteristics in trip generation indicates that trends in urban form cannot be addressed in isolation from other social and economic trends.

May and Scheuernstuhl (1991) used a transport demand forecasting model for the Denver, Colorado, metropolitan area to assess the outcomes of different transport system scenarios on aggregate emissions of carbon monoxide, ozone, particulates and nitrogen dioxide. The model, which adopts a four-stage—trip generation, trip distribution, modal split, network assignment—methodology was calibrated on a combination of home-interview data and census data. It was applied to two scenarios describing what the Denver transport system might look like in 2010. The first, which essentially simulated current plans, included an expanded transit system, but also a system of circumferential highways overlaying the existing road network which is essentially radial. The second 'alternative' scenario excluded the circumferential highways, included high-occupancy-vehicle (HOV) lanes, and channelled growth in dense strips along the transit and highway systems. Both assumed the same rate of growth in population and employment.

As expected, the model predicted a greater concentration of trip origins and destinations for both work and non-work trips along the transit corridors and in the CBD, and a 27 per cent increase in transit use for the alternative scenario. However, the effect of the different scenarios on each of the four categories of emissions was small or negligible. This is because the average distance travelled per automobile trip, and the average level of road congestion, are both higher under the alternative scenario due to the reduced road network. Thus the improvements due to mode shifting are offset by increasing emissions in the remaining auto trips.

These results should be addressed with some caution. First, they apply to a metropolitan area that is overwhelmingly car-oriented, so the increase in transit represents only a tiny fraction of trips. Secondly, the methodology of translating transport systems data into emissions is relatively uncertain. (The authors note, for example, that the method does not do a good job of reproducing emissions.) Finally, as the authors point out, the potential transport–land-use interactions are only partially represented as the land-use differences between the two scenarios only relate to growth—there is no provision for relocation of existing households or businesses. Still, this is clear evidence that, despite the findings of Newman and Kenworthy (1988), the congestion factor cannot be ignored.

A more specific land-use planning initiative is examined in Barton's (1992) study of Bristol, UK. Like most North American cities, Bristol has had rapid increases in traffic congestion arising from suburbanisation and a rate of car ownership that is very high by British standards. In order to provide a rapid transit option that is relatively unaffected by automobile traffic, a light rail transit (LRT) has been proposed. In addition to saving commuters' time, the LRT system would reduce energy use and emissions because it is more energy-efficient even than the existing bus transit system.

Standard transport demand forecasting methods were used to project that construction of the LRT system would increase overall transit ridership by 18 per cent, and shift 30 per cent of the current bus trips to the more efficient LRT. These figures must be viewed in light of the fact that the majority of trips are by cars, so the 18 per cent transit increase represents only a 5 per cent decrease in car trips. Also, it is unlikely that even this 5 per cent reduction would be achieved, as the shift of a commuter from a car to transit frees up his or her car to be used by another household member for some other purpose. Thus a much larger shift to transit would be needed to have an important impact on energy use and emissions.

Barton makes a strong argument that public-transit infrastructure projects will not, in themselves, achieve environmental ends such as CO_2 reduction. They must be accompanied by an integrated approach to land-use and transport planning that restricts the use of cars and orients development to transit nodes. Also, park-and-ride arrangements, which have been shown to be effective in increasing transit ridership, may have undesirable consequences as they promote more peripheral residential development that is segregated from other land uses.

The Greater Toronto Area Study

The Greater Toronto Area (GTA) study (IBI Group, 1990) is a detailed analysis of the implications of urban development scenarios in Toronto and surrounding communities. The stated purpose of the study is not to predict future trends in urban form, but is, rather, an attempt to compare the relative merits of possible urban forms as a way of gaining insights that may be useful in policy formulation. Based on a set of assumptions about demographic and immigration trends, population growth in the GTA was projected to be 2m by 2021. Three urban-growth scenarios were designed, each of which envisioned a spatial configuration for the same enlarged population and a correspondingly enlarged employment base. These three urban form scenarios were then compared on a number of dimensions, including infrastructural requirements, public service costs, open space, energy use, environmental impacts and economic impacts.[13]

The three urban form scenarios are: spread; central; and nodal. The spread scenario is described as the *status quo* scenario. It assigns most of the growth in population to suburban regions, but assigns most of the existing employment growth to downtown Toronto and existing sub-centres, which is consistent with existing trends in the GTA. (Employment trends are more centralised than in most other North American cities.) The central scenario is consistent with the 'compact city' view of development, with the vast majority of growth in population confined to existing built-up areas. The third scenario, nodal, foresees a multinucleated form of development, with both population and employment concentrated around exist

Table 4. Land-use characteristics for GTA 2021 urban form scenarios

	Spread	Central	Nodal
Urbanised land as a percentage of total land	33.4	24.8	29.0
Percentage change over 1986	+ 59	+ 18	+ 38
Population/Total land (km^2)	836.1	836.1	836.1
	+ 61.5	+ 61.5	+ 61.5
Population/Urbanised land	249.8	3363	2874
	+ 0.9	+ 35.8	+ 16
New transport capital expenditures (1990 $m)			
Public transit	7164	14414	11579
Road	19928	13199	17043
Average JTW trip length (km)			
Transit	15.2	11.8	14.2
Road	14.9	13.9	14.4
Transit share	.26	.35	.29
Percentage change over 1986	+ 1.0	+ 40.0	+ 16.0

Source: IBI Group (1990).

ing urban nodes, some of which are at relatively long distances from the CBD.

Table 4 presents some basic characteristics for each of the three scenarios. Urbanised land includes all areas designated for residential, commercial, industrial, public facility or transport land use. It is interesting to note that *all* the scenarios assume increasing density and increasing transit use, and therefore there really is no 'business as usual' scenario that is consistent with current trends. This reflects an underlying assumption that relatively strict land-use control will be in force in Ontario over the next three decades.

Table 5 summarises some of the projected differences between the three scenarios on measures related to energy use and the environment. (Emissions and energy data for the transport sector only were published in the IBI report.) These measures were calculated by passing the transport demand characteristics projected in the 4-stage model into an engineering model that estimates energy input and emissions output as a function of vehicle cycle characteristics such as average speed, and assuming no progress in fuel efficiency or abatement technology. The information in this table basically indicates that urban form has a very significant effect on energy consumption and emissions. It also indicates, however, that urban form alone cannot meet environmental goals under circumstances of population growth. The 40 per cent increase in CO_2 emission under the most efficient land-use scenario is particularly sobering, given the often-stated goal of a 20 per cent reduction by early in the next century.

There is not sufficient space here to give adequate coverage to the methodologies and results of the GTA study. (The final report fills nine volumes!) Comparisons were made on a variety of measures of public service cost, public service accessibility, land preservation, and potential for green space generation and rehabilitation of contaminated soils. On most measures, either the central or nodal scenario was shown to be preferable. Thus, the results point clearly to the disadvantages of continued dispersal tendencies, but fail to determine any clear preference for centralised or multinucleated development.

The authors of the GTA study employed a broad range of methods in their analyses, including physical engineering models, gravity models, transport network models and models for estimating financial variables

28   WILLIAM P. ANDERSON *ET AL.*

Table 5. Energy and environmental outcomes of GTA 2021 urban form scenarios (all figures are percentage change over 1986 base)

	Spread	Central	Nodal
Total transport energy	+ 77	+ 47	+ 60
Per capita transport energy	+ 10	− 12	− 1
Total transport emissions			
CO	+ 54	+ 27	+ 44
CO_2	+ 75	+ 40	+ 59
HC	+ 67	+ 35	+ 53
NO_x	+ 131	+ 68	+ 97
Per capita transport emissions			
CO	− 5%	− 21	− 11
CO_2	+ 9%	− 13	− 1
HC	+ 3%	− 16	− 5
NO_x	+ 43%	+ 4	+ 22

Source: IBI Group (1990).

such as capital costs. It is fair to say, however, that the methodological framework did not employ many behavioural relationships. This precludes the simulation of many behavioural and economic processes that influence the evolution of urban form through time, and in particular precludes any assessment of policy instruments that provide financial incentives to make certain locational or transport choices, such as transit fares, energy prices, parking fees, road pricing or capital incentives to promote densification. Thus the analytical framework is well suited to its stated intention—the assessment of various impacts associated with possible future urban forms—but would be less appropriate as a framework for policy analysis.

Engineering Studies of Transport Energy and Emissions

Despite technological advances in fuel efficiency, the share of the transport sector in total energy end-use has been increasing in most countries. For example, in the UK, France and Germany there were significant decreases in industrial energy use between 1980 and 1990, but in all three cases transport energy use increased by at least 25 per cent.[14] Canada, by contrast, registered a small reduction in transport energy use during the same decade, although it continues to maintain a much higher per capita level than all countries except the US (OECD, 1992).

Transport is also responsible for a large and growing share of harmful environmental emissions. In Canada, the transport sector accounts for 75 per cent of emitted carbon monoxide (CO), 67 per cent of nitrogen oxides (NO_x, 49 per cent of non-methane hydrocarbons (HC) and 25 per cent of carbon dioxide (CO_2). Of this, the great majority is from road transport. Also, automobile air-conditioning systems are major sources of chlorofluorocarbons (CFCs) (OECD, 1991).

Due to the central importance of road transport in addressing energy and environmental issues, a large body of research has developed over the past decade to examine factors affecting fuel consumption and emission levels. (See, for example, Horowitz, 1982; Post *et al.*, 1984; USEPA, 1989; Vuchic, 1981; Waters, 1992.) A general finding is that three categories of factors come into play: vehicle characteristics; driving characteristics; and weather conditions.

Among vehicle characteristics that affect fuel efficiency, engine type and engine size are prominent. Diesel engines are from 5–25 per cent more efficient than comparable gasoline engines, and a 10 per cent reduction in engine size leads to a 3–4 per cent reduction in fuel consumption. Since matching transmission ratios with engine speed is an important factor in fuel economy, transmissions with more gears produce significant fuel savings. Also, the weight and aerodynamics of the vehicle are important. General technological improvements have led to significant rises in overall fleet efficiency, and there are a number of promising technologies on the horizon such as continuous variable transmissions and regenerative braking systems (Richardson, 1980, Gilmore, 1992).

Vehicle technologies that improve fuel efficiency generally reduce CO, HC and CO_2 emissions. However, some energy-saving characteristics, such as higher air–fuel ratios and combustion temperatures, actually increase NO_x emissions. The use of a catalytic converter in the exhaust stream, which is now mandatory in North America and much of Europe, is effective in reducing HC and CO, but not CO_2.

The relationships between energy efficiency, emissions and driving characteristics have been established by empirical studies that monitor cars in actual driving conditions (Post *et al.*, 1984; Waters, 1992). Most automobiles achieve their highest efficiencies while cruising at an optimal speed of about 60 kph. Efficiency is greatly reduced by the number of accelerations, decelerations and idles. Thus both traffic and driving behaviour come into play. Driving in congested traffic results in repeated accelerations and decelerations, long or frequent idle periods, and generally sub-optimal cruising speeds (Biggs and Akcelik, 1986; Watanatada *et al.*, 1987). In the absence of traffic, driving behaviour such as excessively rapid acceleration and driving too fast to take advantage of timed lights may reduce efficiency by 10–20 per cent (Weeks, 1981).

Driving characteristics generally affect emissions levels in an analogous fashion. HC, CO and CO_2 emissions are highest while the vehicle is accelerating, decelerating or idling. HC and CO per vehicle km travelled (VKT) decrease with speed, while CO_2 emis-sions are lowest at a consistent moderate speed. NO_x emissions, however, tend to increase with speed.

Cold weather conditions have been shown to have undesirable impacts on both energy efficiency and emissions. From the perspective of fuel consumption, the link is related to the amount of time it takes engines to reach efficient temperatures after cold starting, and the fact that transmission efficiency is adversely affected by low temperatures (Pearce and Waters, 1980; Williams *et al.*, 1985). Emissions of both CO and HC have been found to be higher in cold weather—first, because of low energy efficiency after cold starts and, secondly, because catalytic converters are less efficient at low temperatures (USEPA, 1989).

7. Directions for Future Research

An exploration of the literature on urban form, energy and the environment leads to two general conclusions. The first is that a better understanding of the process by which emissions are generated in an urban context is absolutely critical to the formulation of workable strategies to meet environmental targets. Effective policy interventions cannot be designed without better knowledge about the many individual choices concerning the mode, frequency and pattern of travel that give rise to aggregate traffic flows and congestion levels, and to the emissions that are associated with them. There is ample evidence to suggest that the urban form is an important influence and constraint on those choices.

The second conclusion is that our current level of understanding concerning the generation of urban emissions—and, in particular, the influence of urban form on them—is relatively weak. It is difficult to find consensus on even the most basic issues. Perhaps this is because, as compared with equally complex issues such as interregional migration or urban labour markets, the body of rigorous empirical work on urban form, energy and the environment is quite small. Thus, we would be hard pressed to make any recommendations concerning policy and we must resort to a call for more and better research.

There are many questions for which the literature still fails to provide consensus answers. We will focus on three here. The first and most fundamental question is whether land-use changes can really make a significant difference. If they cannot, policy efforts should be focused on technological fixes or on effective behavioural changes that do not involve land-use patterns. Some would argue that the cross-sectional evidence is sufficient to answer this question in the affirmative. It is one thing, however, to say that cities with different urban forms have different rates of energy consumption; it is quite another to say that a significant improvement can be achieved through realistic changes to the form of a particular city. It is probably fair to say that this debate boils down to what different observers consider to be realistic changes. To progress beyond this point, more behavioural work is needed to gauge the response of individual decision-makers to incentives that can be provided through policy. By this route, if observers can agree on what constitutes a realistic set of policy instruments, the associated changes in land use and transport choice become an empirical issue.

A second question concerns the role of congestion in determining transport energy consumption and emissions. The engineering research makes it clear that higher emissions and lower efficiencies are associated with driving cycles that include frequent accelerations, decelerations and idles. A relatively free flow of traffic seems therefore to be preferred. The response to reduced congestion, however, appears to be an increase in the number of kilometres driven. Thus from a behavioural perspective a certain amount of congestion may be necessary to restrain driving. The question is whether some optimal level of congestion is achievable, or whether other disincentives to driving, such as road pricing and fuel taxes, are more effective. This question can only be addressed within an analytical framework that includes both behavioural and engineering elements.

A third question concerns the magnitude of the role that public transport can play. Much of the literature seems to be predicated on a belief that public transport is the key to reducing transport energy use and emissions. Still, there are some who argue that, especially in the North American context, this emphasis is badly misplaced because—even under the most optimistic projections—transit trips constitute only a tiny fraction of the total trips. Cross-sectional evidence suggests that even in North America public transport can take up a very significant proportion of commuting trips where land-use patterns are appropriate to support it. It is important to note that the highest shares of transit ridership are found in cities like New York and Toronto where urban land development has been highly influenced by pre-existing patterns of rail infrastructure. Whether existing patterns of land use can be reformed for the improved support of an expanded system of public transport is quite another question. The key point is that it can only be addressed within a framework that integrates transport and land use.

Clearly, there is a great deal to learn about individual elements of transport and land-use systems, so more empirical case studies are needed. In order to address adequately questions such as the three above, however, we also need more sophisticated and comprehensive quantitative models. Models that are used for policy analysis fall into two general categories: prescriptive and descriptive models. Prescriptive models, which are sometimes called normative, optimisation or operations research models, are used in situations where both the interrelationships in a system and the objectives of the policy are well known.

Descriptive models, which are sometimes called positive or conditional forecasting models, do not attempt to define the best policy choice; rather, they attempt to predict in as comprehensive a manner as possible the outcomes of alternative policies. Thus their role is to provide information to the process of policy decision-making. These models are most applicable in a situation that is too complex to be represented adequately as a single optimisation problem. They generally include more stochastic and behavioural relationships than do prescriptive models. The best-known examples of descriptive models are the class of econometric forecasting models.

Since the evolution of urban form involves a number of distinct but highly interrelated processes, partial equilibrium models are inadequate. The most efficient way to develop more comprehensive quantitative models is to build on existing work in the class of descriptive models known as integrated urban models. They stem from the seminal work of Lowry (1964), who developed a model to predict residential and commercial land-use patterns based on an exogenous distribution of employment in manufacturing industries. The basic logic of this model was later extended to predict simultaneously land-use patterns and interzonal transport flows (Wilson, 1974; Mackett, 1990). In order to produce a more detailed representation of traffic patterns associated with land-use developments, Putman (1983, 1991) incorporated a network model that predicts flows and levels of congestion along specific links in the urban road network. Early integrated urban models incorporated little in the way of economic behavioural relationships. More recent specifications incorporate an urban land market with endogenous rents (Anas, 1986, 1990; Wegener, 1986). While most integrated urban models are descriptive in nature, there are also a number of prescriptive models that define land-use and transport patterns that maximise an aggregate social welfare function (Boyce, 1986; Prastacos, 1986; Putman, 1987; Rho and Kim, 1989).

In order to address questions about the energy and environmental impacts of urban form, the current generation of integrated urban models must be extended in two ways: first, to incorporate a range of policy instruments as exogenous variables; and, secondly, to interface with engineering models so that endogenous variables such as travel demand and changes in land use can be translated into aggregate energy demands and emissions. To incorporate more policy instruments, the models must include behavioural land-use and transport change functions with policy variables as arguments. Also, to see how individual responses translate into aggregate changes, the models should include system-wide equilibrium mechanisms, such as urban real estate markets and 'user equilibrium' network traffic assignments. Interfacing with engineering models will require a higher level of detail in the definition of land uses and vehicle stocks, and in the representation of network performance characteristics.

Notes

1. A comment on the scope of this paper is in order. We are interested in the energy and environmental impacts of general land-use patterns and transport system designs. There are, however, a large number of very specific issues of urban design which have important environmental implications but are outside the scope of this paper. These include such things as the placement of individual buildings on sites, the design and composition of parks and other green spaces, and the effect of construction on localised drainage patterns. (See for example, Spirn, 1984.)

2. The results of these efforts have been mixed: many new supply technologies have either proved economically infeasible or were found to produce their own environmental problems, while end-use and abatement technologies have produced significant environmental benefits. Current research indicates that the development of technologies to produce renewable fuels, especially from biomass, have enormous potential (Johansson *et al.*, 1992). On the demand side, however, the current rate of increase in energy efficiency due to improved technology and changes in economic structure is likely to decline (Schipper, 1992).

3. The terms multinucleated, polynucleated and polycentric are used interchangeably in the literature. Archetypal forms of the multinucleated city, complementary to that of Figure 1, are provided in Clark and Kuijpers-Linde (1994). For a compendium of recent research on the multinucleated city see Berry and Kim (1993).

4. Empirical studies suggest that during the first decade after a new housing area is devel-

32   WILLIAM P. ANDERSON *ET AL.*

oped, the percentage of its residents who work in the CBD tends to drop rapidly as employment opportunities in peripheral centres open up (Hutchinson and Kumar, 1990).

5. In a recent paper, Bourne (1989) attempted to draw some general conclusions about trends in Canadian urban form between 1971 and 1981. His results generally confirmed the most common preconceptions of trends toward urban sprawl, including a 'flattening out' of density gradients, increased spatial segregation by income class, and an increased mismatch between the location of residences and workplaces. Efficient commuting, it would seem, has not been a powerful organising principle in the development of urban spatial structure. Despite some clustering of employment around airports, regional malls and office parks, Bourne did not find compelling evidence for the emergence of a multinucleated urban form. This is in contrast to similar analyses on American cities. (See, for example, Greene, 1980.)

6. He points out, for example, that while large households were more likely than small households to choose suburban locations in the 1950s and 1960s, just the reverse was true in the 1970s.

7. It is worth noting that Roberts' dense-centre scenario assumes increasing suburbanisation of residences coupled with concentration of employment in the urban core. Since most empirical evidence indicates simultaneous suburbanisation of jobs and households, the reductions associated with all other scenarios are probably somewhat overstated.

8. These results were generated by a modelling system designed to assess President Nixon's 'Project Independence' energy initiatives.

9. We use 'compact centralised' to refer to a form where a high proportion of the population and employment is concentrated close to the CBD, 'compact multinucleated' to refer to a form where a high proportion is concentrated close to either the CBD or peripheral centres.

10. For example, some energy-conserving natural gas burning and automobile engine technologies actually increase production of NO_x (Anderson *et al.*, 1992; Hassounah and Miller, 1993).

11. This is in contrast to current Dutch planning guidelines, which restrict growth to established urban areas.

12. A recent study by Shukla and Parikh (1992) focuses on the effect of urban size, rather than urban form, on environmental quality. They compare various ambient pollution measures in an international cross-section of cities. While they find that some measures increase with city sizes up to about 4m, they conclude that there is no compelling argument for constraining city size as a means of pollution control.

13. The approach used to project the amount of transport infrastructure required in each scenario severely limits the range of transport outcomes. It was assumed that in each scenario sufficient infrastructure would be provided to maintain 1986 levels of transport service (average speed, frequency of trains, etc.). This precludes the possibility of significant changes in the overall level of congestion in the system.

14. On average, road transport makes up about 85 per cent of total transport energy consumption in the OECD countries.

References

ADAMS, J.S. (1970) Residential structure of Midwestern cities, *Annals of the Association of American Geographers*, 60, pp. 37–62.

ANAS, A. (1986) From physical to economic models: the Lowry framework revisited, in: B. HUTCHINSON and M. BATTY (Eds) *Advances in Urban Systems Modelling*. Amsterdam: North-Holland.

ANAS, A. (1990) A dynamic economic model of the regulated housing market, in: C.S. BERTUGLIA, G. LEONARDI and A.G. WILSON (Eds) *Urban Dynamics: Designing an Integrated Model*, ch. 7. London: Routledge.

ANDERSON, W. (1994) Energy and the environment: the new case for conservation, *Energy Studies Review*, 6(2), pp. 16–33.

ANDERSON, W., KLIMAN, M. and MACDONALD, R. (1992) Energy technology options for the 21st century: environment, economy, and society—a report on the Workshops, *Energy Studies Review*, 4, pp. 221–244.

BANISTER, D. (1992) Energy use, transport, and settlement patterns, in: M.J. BREHENY (Ed.) *Sustainable Development and Urban Form*. London: Pion.

BARTON, H. (1992) City transport: strategies for sustainability, in: M.J. BREHENY (Ed.) *Sustainable Development and Urban Form*. London: Pion.

BEALE, C.L. (1977) The recent shift of United States population to nonmetropolitan areas, 1970–75, *International Regional Science Review*, 2, pp. 113–122.

BERRY, B.J.L. and KIM, H. (1993) Challenges to the monocentric model, *Geographical Analysis*, 25(1), pp. 1–4.

BIGGS, D. and AKCELIK, R. (1986) An energy related model of instantaneous fuel consumption, *Traffic Engineering and Control*, 27(6), pp. 320–325.

BOURNE, L.S. (1982) Urban spatial structure: an introductory essay on concepts and criteria, in: L.S. BOURNE (Ed.) *Internal Structure of the City*, 2nd edn. New York: Oxford University Press.

BOURNE, L.S. (1989) Are new urban reforms emerging? Empirical tests for Canadian urban areas, *The Canadian Geographer*, 33(4), pp. 312–328.

BOYCE, D.E. (1986) Integration of supply and demand models in transportation and location: problem formulations and research questions, *Environment and Planning A*, 18, pp. 485–489.

BREHENY, M.J. (1992) The contradictions of the compact city: A review, in: M.J. BREHENY (Ed.) *Sustainable Development and Urban Form*. London: Pion.

CARLEY, M. (1992) Settlement trends the crisis of automobility, *Futures*, 24, pp. 206–218.

CARROL, T.O. (1977) Calculating community energy demand, in: R.J. BURBY and A. FLEMMING BELL (Eds) *Energy and the Community*. Cambridge: Ballinger.

CHINITZ, B. (1991) A framework for speculating about future urban growth patterns in the US, *Urban Studies*, 28, pp. 939–959.

CLARK, W.A.V. and KUIJPERS-LINDE, M. (1994) Commuting in restructuring urban regions, *Urban Studies*, 31, pp. 465–483.

COUNCIL ON ENVIRONMENTAL QUALITY (1975) The cost of sprawl in the USA, *Ekistics*, 239, pp. 266–272.

DEELSTRA, T. (1992) Western Europe, in: R. STREN, R. WHITE and J. WHITNEY (Eds) *Sustainable Cities: Urbanization and the Environment in International Perspective*. Boulder, CO: Westview.

DOWNS, A. (1992) *Stuck in Traffic*, Washington, DC: The Brookings Institution.

EDWARDS, J.L. (1977) The effect of land use on transportation energy consumption, in: R.J. BURBY and A. BELL (Eds) *Energy and the Community*. Cambridge: Ballinger.

GILLESPE, A (1992) Communications technologies and the future of the city, in: M.J. BREHENY (Ed.) *Sustainable Development and Urban Form*. London: Pion.

GILMORE, D.B. (1992) Fuel economy goals for vehicles with regenerative braking systems, *International Journal of Vehicle Design*, 13, pp. 125–133.

GIULIANO, G. and SMALL, K.A. (1993) Is the journey to work explained by urban structure?, *Urban Studies*, 30, pp. 1485–1500.

GOMEZ-IBANEZ, J.A. (1991) A global view of automobile dependence: review of "Cities and Automobile Dependence: An International Sourcebook" by P.W.G. NEWMAN AND J.R. KENWORTHY, *Journal of the American Planning Association*, 57, pp. 376–379.

GORDON, P. and RICHARDSON, H.W. (1989) Gasoline consumption and cities: a reply, *Journal of the American Planning Association*, 55, pp. 342–346.

GORDON, P., RICHARDSON, H.W. and JUN, M.J. (1991) The commuting paradox: evidence from the top twenty, *Journal of the American Planning Association*, 57, pp. 416–420.

GREENE, D. L. (1980) Urban subcentres: recent trends in urban spatial structure, *Growth and Change*, 11, pp. 29–40.

HASSOUNAH, M.I. and MILLER, E.J. (1993) *A perspective on transport-related pollutants and an assessment of current fuel consumption, emission, dispersion, and road assignment models*. Joint Program in Transportation, University of Toronto. (Prepared for Transportation Energy Division, Energy Mines and Resources, Canada.)

HAYNES, V.A. (1986) Energy and urban form: a human ecological critique, *Urban Affairs Quarterly*, 21, pp. 337–353.

HOROWITZ, J.J. (1982) *Air Quality Analysis for Urban Transportation Planning*. Cambridge, MA: MIT Press.

HUTCHINSON, B.G. and KUMAR, R.K. (1990) Modelling urban spatial evolution and transport demand, *Journal of Transportation Engineering*, 116, pp. 550–571.

IBI GROUP (1990) *Greater Toronto Area Urban Structure Concept Study*, 9 vols. Prepared for the Greater Toronto Coordinating Committee.

JANELLE, D.G. (1986) Metropolitan expansion and the communications–transportation trade-off, in: S. HANSON (Ed.) *The Geography of Urban Transportation*. New York: Guilford Press.

JOHANSSON, T.B., KELLY, H., REDDY, A.K.N. and WILLIAMS, R.H. (1992) Renewable fuels and electricity for a growing world economy: defining and achieving the potential, *Energy Studies Review*, 4(3), pp. 201–212.

KENWORTHY, J.R. and NEWMAN, P.W.G. (1990) Cities and transport energy: lessons from a global survey, *Ekistics*, 34(4/5), pp. 258–268.

KEYES, D.L. (1977) Land use and energy conservation: is there a link to exploit? in: R.J. BURBY and A. FLEMMING BELL (Eds) *Energy and the Community*. Cambridge: Ballinger.

KUHN, R.G. (1992) Canadian energy futures: policy scenarios and public preferences, *The Canadian Geographer*, 36, pp. 350–365.

LAVE, C.A. (1978) Transportation energy use: some current myths, *Policy Analysis*, 4, pp. 297–315.

LEWIS, R.D. (1991) The development of an early suburban industrial district: the Montreal ward of Saint-Ann, 1851–71, *Urban History Review*, 19, pp. 166–180.

LOWE, M.D. (1990) Alternatives to the automobile: transport for livable cities, *Ekistics*, 34(4/5), pp. 269–282.

Lowry, I.S. (1964) *A Model of Metropolis.* Santa Monica, CA: The Rand Corporation. RM-4036-RC.

Mackett, R.L. (1990) Comparative analysis of modelling land-use, transport interactions at the micro and macro levels, *Environment and Planning A,* 22, pp. 459–475.

May, J. and Scheuernstuhl, G. (1991) Sensitivity analysis for land use, transportation, and air quality, *Transportation Research Record,* 1312, pp. 59–67

Mogridge, M.J.H. (1985) Transport, land use and energy interaction, *Urban Studies,* 22, pp. 481–492.

Muller, P.O. (1986) Transportation and urban form: stages in the spatial evolution of the American metropolis, in: S. Hanson (Ed.) *The Geography of Urban Transportation.* New York: Guilford Press.

Newman, P.W.G. and Kenworthy, J.R. (1988) The transport energy trade-off: fuel efficient traffic vs. fuel efficient cities, *Transportation Research A,* 22A(3), pp. 163–174.

Nijkamp, P. and Salomon, I (1989) Future spatial impacts of telecommunications, *Transportation Planning and Technology,* 13, pp. 275–287.

Nilles, J.M. (1991) Telecommuting and urban sprawl: mitigator or inciter?, *Transportation,* 18, pp. 411–432.

OECD (1991) Environmental Data, in: *Compendium 1991,* Paris: OECD.

OECD (1992) OECD in figures, *The OECD Observer,* Supplementary to Issue No. 179.

Orrskog, L. and Snickars, F. (1992) On the sustainability of urban and regional structures, in: M.J. Breheny (Ed) *Sustainable Development and Urban Form.* London: Pion.

Papageorgiou, Y.Y. (1990) *The Isolated City State.* London: Routledge.

Pearce, T. and Waters, M.H.L. (1980) *Cold start fuel consumption of a diesel and a gasoline car.* TRRL Supplementary Report SR 636.

Pisarski, A.E. (1991) Overview, in: *Transportation, urban form, and the environment.* Transportation Research Board Special Report 231, National Research Council, Washington, DC.

Post, K., Kent, J., Tomlin, J. and Carruthers, N. (1984) Fuel consumption and emission modelling by power demand and a comparison with other models, *Transportation Research A,* 18, pp. 191–213.

Prastacos, P. (1986) An integrated land-use transportation model for the San Francisco region: 1. Design and mathematical structure, 2. Empirical estimation and results, *Environment and Planning A,* 18, pp. 307–322 and 511–528.

Pressman, N (1988) Technology and settlement form: a future scenario for Canada, *Transportation,* 14, pp. 295–309.

Prevedouros, P.D. and Schofer, J.L. (1991) Trip characteristics and travel patterns of suburban residents, *Transportation Research Record,* 1328, pp. 49–57.

Putman, S.H. (1983) *Integrated Urban Models.* London: Pion.

Putman, S H. (1987) Mathematical programming formulations of transportation and land use models: practical implications of recent research, *Transportation Research Record,* 1125, pp. 39–47.

Putman, S.H. (1991) *Integrated Urban Models 2.* London: Pion.

Real Estate Research Corporation (1974) *The Costs of Sprawl: Environmental and Economic Costs of Alternative Residential Development Patterns at the Urban Fringe.* Washington, DC: US Government Printing Office.

Rho, J.H. and Kim, T.J. (1989) Solving a three dimensional urban activity model of land use intensity and transport congestion, *Journal of Regional Science,* 29(4), pp. 595–613.

Rice, R.G. (1978) Evaluation of road and transit systems requirements for alternative urban forms, *Transportation Research Record,* 677, pp. 15–22.

Richardson, N.H. (1992) Canada, in: R. Stren, R. White and J. Whitney (Eds) *Sustainable Cities: Urbanization and the Environment in International Perspective.* Boulder, CO: Westview.

Richardson, R.M. (1980) Derivation of economy strategies for stepped ratio automatic transmission. Paper C355/80, in: *Proceedings of the Conference on Systems Engineering in Land Transport, The Institute of Mechanical Engineering.* London: Mechanical Engineering Publishers Ltd.

Roberts, J.S. (1977) Energy conservation and land use: prospects and procedures, in:R.J. Burby and A. Flemming Bell (Eds) *Energy and the Community.* Cambridge: Ballinger.

Roseland, M. (1992) *Toward Sustainable Communities: A Resource Book for Municipal and Local Governments.* Ottawa: National Round Table on the Environment and the Economy.

Schipper, L. (1992) Energy efficiency scenarios in the OECD countries—what to do when CO_2 comes calling, *Energy Studies Review,* 4(3), pp. 213–220.

Shukla, V. and Parikh, K. (1992) The environmental consequences of urban growth: cross national perspectives on economic development, air pollution, and city size, *Urban Geography,* 13(5), pp. 422–449.

Small, K.A. (1980) Energy scarcity and urban development patterns, *International Regional Science Review,* 5(2), pp. 97–117.

Spirn, A.W. (1984) *The Granite Garden. Urban Nature and Human Design.* New York: Basic Books.

TRANSPORTATION TOMORROW SURVEY (1988) *An Overview of Travel Characteristics in the Greater Toronto Area*. Prepared for the Toronto Area Transportation Planning Data Collection Steering Committee.

US ENVIRONMENTAL PROTECTION AGENCY (1989) *User's Guide to MOBILE5*. Vehicle Emissions Laboratory, Report No. EPA-AA-TEB-89-01, Ann Arbor.

VAN DER VALK, A. and FALUDI, A. (1992) Growth regions and the future of Dutch planning doctrine, in: M.J. BREHENY (Ed.) *Sustainable Development and Urban Form*. London: Pion.

VINING, D.R. JR and KONTULY, T. (1978) Population dispersal from major metropolitan regions: an international comparison, *International Regional Science Review*, 3, pp. 49–73.

VUCHIC, V.R. (1981) *Urban Public Transit Systems and Technology*. New Jersey: Prentice-Hall.

WARNER, S.B. (1978) *Streetcar Suburbs: The Process of Growth in Boston (1870–1900)*. Cambridge, MA: Harvard University Press.

WATANATADA, T., DHARESHWAR, A. and LIMA, P. (1987) *Vehicle Speeds and Operating Costs: Models for Road Planning and Management*. Baltimore: The Johns Hopkins University Press.

WATERS, M.H.L. (1992) *Road Vehicle Fuel Economy: State of the Art Review*. London: HMSO.

WEBSTER, F.V. and BLY, P.H. (1987) Changing patterns of urban travel and implications for land use and transport strategy, *Transportation Research Record*, 1125, pp. 21–28.

WEEKS, R. (1981) *Fuel consumption of a diesel and petrol car*. TRRL Report 964.

WEGENER, M. (1986) Transport network equilibrium and regional deconcentration, *Environment and Planning A*, 18, pp. 437–456.

WILLIAMS, T., RAMSHAW J. and SIMMONS, I. (1985) *Dynamometer tests of the efficiency of a van transmission system*. TRRL Research Report RR 10.

WILSON, A.G. (1974) *Urban and Regional Models in Geography and Planning*. Chichester: John Wiley.

WINDSOR, D. (1979) A critique of 'the costs of sprawl', *Journal of the American Planning Association*, 45, pp. 279–292.

YERGIN, D. (1979) Conservation: the key energy source, in: R. STOBAUGH and D. YERGIN (Eds) *Energy Future*, ch. 6. New York: Random House.

Urban Studies, Vol. 30, Nos. 4/5, 1993 775–796

Environmental Policy: The Quest for Sustainable Development

Andrew Blowers

From Chernobyl to Rio

With the catastrophe at Chernobyl in 1986, the world glimpsed the abyss—the destructive potential for global environmental pollution and degradation of modern industrial development. Six years later at Rio de Janeiro in 1992, the Earth Summit presented a programme for action to avert global environmental disaster based on the underlying principle of sustainable development. These two events mark a period during which the environment was fully established on the agenda of international policy-making. It has been a period of major political change. There has been the ending of the Cold War, the break-up of the former Soviet empire, the war in the Gulf and conflicts elsewhere, and the emergence of an array of new nation-states. The uneasy stability of the superpower has been replaced by an increasingly unpredictable world. As the vast arsenals of nuclear weapons were destroyed, there opened up the prospect of diverting resources into more creative, peaceful purposes. One of these was the environment.

In the advanced Western countries, public interest in the environment mounted. In eastern Europe and the former USSR, the urgency of the problems was underlined by the emerging evidence of grossly degraded and polluted areas. In the developing countries, problems of deforestation, desertification and resource depletion were also attracting greater attention. And the longer-term, but nonetheless apparently inevitable, threats from global warming and

ozone depletion underlined the global interest in environmental protection. At national, international and global levels, environmental policy achieved a higher priority and underwent vigorous development. At all levels, the notion of *sustainable development*, the *leitmotif* of the Brundtland Report in 1987, had become the accepted goal of policy at Rio five years later (World Commission, 1987).

It soon became clear that optimism must necessarily be qualified. Interest in the environment, though sustained, was not always translated into action in the face of more immediate and pressing economic concerns. The dissolution of the Soviet economic system, the problems of poverty in the developing world and the deepening recession in the West emphasised the competing priorities and inherent conflicts between environment and development. The eponymous process of balkanisation in areas such as former Yugoslavia (but also in other areas such as the Middle East) threatened to entangle countries in a series of regional conflicts. As the Gulf War had shown, such conflicts could do serious harm to sensitive ecosystems (Barnaby, 1991). Over all, the threat of nuclear proliferation was more alarming as the Soviet nuclear complex was dispersed and, if not restrained, would pose a far more imminent threat to world survival than the more publicised problems of global warming and ozone depletion. As the 1990s dawned, it was evident that progress on environmental

Andrew Blowers is Professor of Social Sciences (Planning), The Open University, Walton Hall, Milton Keynes MK7 6AA, UK.

policy, particularly at international level, would be slow, uneven and fraught with political conflict.

Environmental policy, touching as it does on almost every aspect of social life, raises an almost impossibly wide agenda for investigation and action. In this review, I shall take as my theme the quest for sustainable development, a speculative focus suitable for the last decade of the second milennium. My emphasis will be on contemporary political conflicts over the environment and the prospects for change. Environmental policy transcends conventional political boundaries and therefore I shall concentrate primarily on the broader international context which increasingly sets the parameters for policy-making at subsidiary national and regional levels. In particular, I shall focus on the political processes that have defined and shaped the environmental agenda over the past five years. As I see it they are:

(1) The process of uneven development, particularly between North and South which has focused attention on development and the need to prepare policies that incorporate environment *and* development as complementary, not conflicting, goals.

(2) The role of scientific evidence in defining the scale of problems, the grounds for conflict and the scope for solutions in environmental policy-making.

(3) The growing political importance of transboundary and global environmental impacts which have intensified conflicts of interest between states but have also stimulated processes of globalisation, the development of transnational political processes that challenge the nation-state.

In the first main part of the review, I shall discuss each of these in turn. In the second part, I shall examine the challenge posed by sustainable development to sovereignty and the market and the importance of equity in the development of policy. But, first, a little background is needed to provide the context for the discussion.

Contemporary Trends in Environmental Policy

Environment as a National Political Issue

During the latter part of the 1980s, the environment rose up the agenda of public concern in the West. In the UK, a peak was reached in 1989. A Department of Environment survey revealed that environment and pollution was regarded by 30 per cent of the population (unprompted) as one of the most important problems the government should deal with (up from 8 per cent only three years earlier), second only to health and social services with 32 per cent each (ENDS, 1989, p. 3). Around this time, too, an EEC survey found that over half the population (55 per cent) regarded protecting the environment and preserving natural resources as essential to economic development (OECD, 1991, p. 254). This public concern was reflected in a high poll for the Green Party in the European elections, with the highest being 15 per cent in the UK—though much of that was almost certainly a protest vote.

Following the Brundtland Report of 1987 (World Commission, 1987), national governments began to echo the theme of sustainable development in their policies and plans. For example, in 1989 the Dutch published their National Environmental Policy Plan, *To Choose or to Lose*, which affirmed that sustainable development was the main objective of environmental management (NEPP, 1989, p. 92). This plan, following the ideas set out in a major research report—*Concern for Tomorrow* (RIVM, 1988)—adopted five spatial scales (local, regional, fluvial, continental and global—see Figure 1) and established targets and identified the time-scales within which action must prove effective. The plan recognised the urgency of the task: "This requires a departure from the existing trend in our behaviour, which must bear fruit within the term of office of the existing governments" (p. 5). In passing, we may note

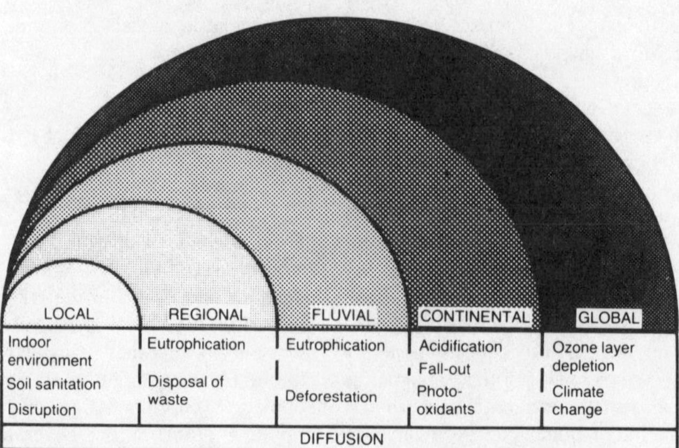

Figure 1. The 5-level model of the Dutch National Environmental Policy Plan. *Source:* Dutch NEPP.

"a strong tradition in Dutch planning to ignore the difference between intention and the realisation of policy" (van der Straaten, 1992, p. 47).

The Dutch plan became widely recognized as a model for environmental planning and management. The following year, the UK government issued its environmental White Paper, *This Common Inheritance*, which was a compendium of environmental principles, policies and prospects (HMSO, 1990). Though much criticised for its lack of commitments, targets or priorities, it was a remarkable document for a Conservative government hitherto genuflecting entirely to the principles of the unconstrained market. Although the belief in using the market was still strongly present, the White Paper also stressed the longer-term needs of future generations, the need for international co-operation, the importance of regulation, the adoption of the precautionary principle and a commitment to sustainable development. The White Paper was followed up in various ways, by identifying ministers in every department responsible for ensuring that environmental matters were considered as an integral part of policy-making; by guidance on the application of environmental considerations to policy (HMSO, 1991a); by annual monitoring reports to establish progress, review development and indicate priorities (HMSO, 1991b, 1992); and by the publication of detailed statistics on the state of the environment (Department of Environment, 1992a). Although the gap between rhetoric and action was much criticised, there was some evidence that government was beginning to recognise the importance of the 'environment' as an integral part of policy-making.

This recognition was evident in the legislation, notably in the Environmental Protection Act of 1990 which formalised the introduction of Integrated Pollution Control (IPC); the Water Act (1989) which privatised the water authorities and established the National Rivers Authority to provide environmental protection; and the Water Resources Act of 1991 which introduced statutory water-quality objectives. The principle of integrating functions will be taken a further step with the creation of an Environment Agency incorporating HMIP, the National Rivers Authority and the waste-regulation functions of the local authorities (Department of Environment, 1991).

The introduction of principles of integration and sustainability and the creation of new structures seemed fine but needed to be set against the realities of policy-making. The contradictions were everywhere apparent, for example in the massive road building programme to cater for a projected 83–142 per cent growth in traffic by 2025; or in the withdrawal of subsidy and cut-backs on investment in railways and the deregulation of buses; or in the evasion or slow adoption of certain European Environmental Directives; in the procrastination over retrofitting power stations to avoid sulphur pollution; in the deregulation of the land-use planning system and the promotion of support for market forces; or in the fragmentation of environmental conservation apparent in the splitting up of the Nature Conservancy Council; or in the vigorous defence of the nuclear industry despite dangers of radioactivity and proliferation. In their different ways, these and other policies reflected short-term political and economic pressures rather than the longer-term strategies required for sustainable development.

International Developments

The UK has been increasingly affected by policy-making at European and global levels. In Europe, the EC continued to promulgate and propose Directives adding to over 100 Directives in the course of implementation. The Maastricht Treaty embraced the principle that "Environmental protection requirements must be integrated into the definition and implementation of other Community policies" (European Communities, 192, p. 39). The EC's Fifth Environment Action Programme, with the thematic title *Towards Sustainability*, is a compendium of trends, objectives, targets, means and actions "intended to reflect a policy and strategy for continued economic and social development without detriment to the environment and the natural resources on the quality of which continued human activity and further development depend" (Commission of the European Communities, 1992). Agreements between neighbouring countries were reached to prevent pollution of the Rhine and the North Sea.

At the global level, there was international agreement to ban mining in Antarctica; the series of agreements (Vienna Convention, 1985; Montreal Protocol, 1987; and London Agreement, 1990) which led to the banning of CFCs to protect the ozone layer and the various agreements designed to restrict the trade in hazardous wastes (Basel Convention, 1989; Bamako Convention, 1991; and related EC Directives).

This process of global negotiation and agreement on environmental problems culminated at the Rio Summit which saw the adoption of 27 principles constituting a Declaration on Environment and Development, the first of which was "Human beings are at the centre of concerns for sustainable development". Over 150 nations signed a Framework Convention on Climate Change to tackle the problem of global warming and also a Convention on Biological Diversity. By consensus, the summit endorsed Agenda 21 an 800-page action programme covering every conceivable issue designed to set the programme of follow-up (United Nations, 1992). Although the Summit had been preceded by conflicts—especially between North and South over issues of responsibility and resources—Rio produced a number of positive features. It was a process engaging more governments than ever before and the participation of 6500 non-governmental organisations and 15 000 participants at their Global Forum. The involvement of NGOs had begun at the Bergen Conference on Sustainable Development in 1990. Despite the failure to reach agreements on certain issues—notably forests—and the USA's reluctance to enter into binding targets or to sign the Biodiversity Convention, Rio was a global endeavour at co-operation in the interests of mutual security. "It defined the new international values of equity and environment, linked them inseparably, and dramatised how powerfully they affect North–South relations" (Speth, 1992, p. 145). Rio should also be seen as a stage in a continuous process of developing policy and securing implementation.

The environment has now passed a threshold of public and political concern that makes it fully and permanently established as an issue of high priority on the national and international policy-making agenda. Although the environment is on the agenda, environmental policy-making is fraught with uncertainty and conflict. In the sections that follow, I will examine the political opportunities and constraints on environmental policy.

Part 1: The Political Context

Environment and Development—Contrasting Perspectives

At Rio, the contrasting attitudes to environmental problems between the rich and the poor countries (usually categorised as North and South, though this leaves the designation of the former communist bloc somewhat ambiguous) were at the heart of the political conflict over global environmental policy. In the North, the emphasis is on environmental problems and there is a tendency to see economic growth and environmental protection as mutually compatible, not contradictory aims of policy (Pearce *et al.*, 1989; Jacobs, 1991). Indeed, environmental protection is now seen as a spur to economic growth. "The largest and most technically advanced environment markets, and also environment industries, have developed in those countries with the most comprehensive and effective environmental regulations" (OECD, 1991). In the rich countries, environmental quality has become an integral aspect of the quality of life.

In marked contrast, the problems in the developing countries stem from underdevelopment and poverty. This was an underlying theme of the Brundtland Report: "Poverty reduces people's capacity to use resources in a sustainable manner; it intensifies pressure on the environment" (World Commission, 1987, p. 49). The "poor are forced to forgo the needs of the future to meet the needs of today" (Holmberg *et al.*, 1991, p. 32). Hence the issues that concern the South—poverty, food security, desertification—stand in stark contrast to the environmental preoccupations of the North. In the poor countries, environ-

mental inequality is a direct result of uneven development.

Environmental inequalities are, of course, partly determined by natural factors. It is perfectly obvious that deserts, some dense forests, tundra and mountainous regions are often inhospitable. Beyond the largely unoccupied wilderness areas, uneven development can, in part at least, be explained by differences in climate, resource endowments or accessibility resulting from natural and spatial factors. But, environmental determinism—though it cannot be altogether discounted—is often a relatively unimportant explanatory factor. Uneven development is not simply the product of natural factors; it is much more complex, involving historical, cultural and economic explanations that are the source of considerable academic debate and controversy (see, for example, Smith, 1991; Open University, 1992). It is, in short, a largely socially determined process.

Uneven development is a major source of conflict and, consequently, a major impediment to the achievement and implementation of environmental policy. It is at the heart of the conflict between North and South which has emerged, perhaps, as the critical political fault-line in the contemporary world. Put simply, the North tried to set an agenda to deal with environmental issues of ozone depletion, global warming, deforestation and biodiversity. The North wants the South to tackle population control and to halt the depletion of global assets such as tropical rainforests. By contrast, the South insisted on the linkage between environment and development; identified the North as most implicated in the squandering of global assets; and demanded that resources and technology be transferred in various ways to enable the South to cope with the environmental problems arising from underdevelopment. The South's position was put cogently and uncompromisingly by Dr Mahatir, Prime Minister of Malaysia:

If the rich North expects the poor to foot the bill for a cleaner environment, Rio

[will] become an exercise in futility . . . There will be no development if the poor countries are not allowed to extract their natural wealth. The only way for them to develop and yet avoid damage to the environment is for them to receive substantial material help (*Independent*, 5 June 1992).

Uneven development also affects the capacity of individual countries to deliver environmental policies. The poorer countries lack the scientific information-base, the monitoring capability and the administrative support essential to implementing agreements. Moreover, abiding by externally-induced environmental targets or deadlines is scarcely the highest priority for countries crippled by debt and poverty and, in some cases, riven by internal conflicts and lack of social cohesion. Even in a rich region such as the EC, there are frequently complaints about the unwillingness or inability of members to adhere to environmental policies. In the wider global context, it is difficult enough (as Rio has shown) to gain agreement on policies—let alone procedures for detailed implementation. Equity among the participants is the key to success (RIIA, 1991). Successful implementation will require pledge and review processes that are clear as to what is required of participants, significant in terms of the commitment to goals and verifiable through effective monitoring (Greene, 1991). The success or failure of environmental policy will depend, in part, on the quality and interpretation of the evidence, the subject of the next section.

Science and Policy

The evidence of environmental degradation. Within the advanced countries, environmental data provide a record of environmental degradation or improvement.[1] Such data have provided a basis for monitoring environmental change within countries and have stimulated conservationist policies. More recently, it has been the evidence of deterioration at the global level that has done most to force the environment up the international policy-making agenda.

In the past, there has been considerable disagreement among scientific experts over trends and their implications. The Club of Rome's Malthusian predictions of global catastrophe were savaged by academics, business people and public officials and quickly sank from sight (Buttel *et al.*, 1990). By contrast, the ozone hole and global warming have become universally accepted as palpable threats to the global ecosystem. In the case of ozone, the evidence was unmistakable. The Antarctic ozone 'hole' can reach up to four times the size of the US with depletion rates commonly at 40–50 per cent and occasional readings as high as 95 per cent. By 1992 there was evidence of 15–20 per cent depletion in ozone levels in the northern hemisphere. The cause—CFCs and other depleting chemicals such as halons—and the consequences—skin cancers and cataracts—are widely known and have been a spur to action.

In the case of global warming, too, there has been a remarkable scientific consensus. Overall estimates of global warming have been refined by the International Panel on Climate Change to 0.3°C per decade, giving a 1°C rise by 2030—a rate believed to be too high for adaptation by plant and animal communities. The implications have been forecast in terms of, for example, potential flooding in England and Wales (Department of Environment, 1992a, 1992b) (see Figure 2); agricultural change in Europe (Carter *et al.*, 1991); hunger in Africa (Downing, 1991); or water resource problems in the Middle East (Lonergan and Kavanagh, 1991). The acceptance of the inevitability of global change is, perhaps, striking; "for a notion that challenges the basis of modern industrialisation, global change has gained extraordinary respectability" (Buttel *et al.*, 1990, p. 60). It may be explained by the strength of the scientific consensus and the lack of any real dispute over the general climatic trends and their anthropogenic causes. The prominence of the issue stems from the existence of a scientific 'epistemic

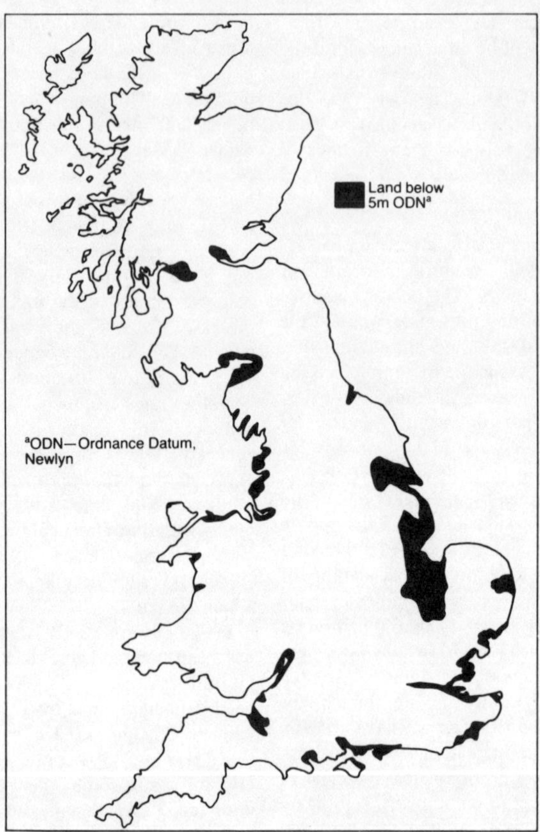

Figure 2. Areas where sea level increases could have a significant impact *GB. Source:* CCIRG, DOE: reproduced with the permission of the Controller of Her Majesty's Stationery Office.

community'—that is, "a network of professionals with recognized expertise and competence in a particular domain and an authoritative claim to policy-relevant knowledge within that domain or issue-area" (Haas, 1992, p. 3).

While there can be no doubt that scientific evidence has been instrumental in identifying issues for the environmental agenda, the evidence is often incomplete, provisional or uncertain. As a result, science has provided a basis for conflict between interests that impedes progress in policy-making. The evidence is problematic in several ways.

1. The problem of establishing cause and effect. For example, it is known that radioactivity causes certain cancers. There is a strong presumption but no conclusive proof that nuclear facilities are responsible for leukaemia clusters (e.g. Craft and Openshaw, 1987). The Black Report reached a qualified conclusion after an extensive investigation, noting that although there was an observed statistical relationship the possibility of a causal link was "not one that can be categorically dismissed, nor, on the other hand is it easy to prove" (Black, 1984). Similarly, the precise causes and effects of acid rain are difficult to identify. The scientific problem of cause and effect means it is difficult to establish responsibility for the externalities produced by polluting activities.

2. The problem of forecasting impacts. This is notably the case with global warming. While there is broad agreement on the general range of the uplift in average global temperature, there is considerable uncertainty about the incidence, distribution, timing or effects of the process (Idso, 1991; Mac-Cracken, 1991; Schneider, 1991). Thus, although it is a global process, the costs and benefits will be unevenly distributed. Some areas may gain a better climate or have the resources to mitigate impacts. For instance, in the US the costs of extra sea defences might be easily outweighed by improved crop yields from a better climate whereas, in parts of Africa, global warming might exacerbate the already severe problems of drought and food supply. Thus countries who perceive benefits may be unenthusiastic about providing support for countries who must bear the brunt of the harmful effects. This unevenness of the potential impacts could undermine a global approach to the problem such as has been initiated with the Convention signed at Rio. Indeed some commentators, taking a narrow regional view of impacts, have even interpreted the rise in temperatures in such terms as "the single best thing that could ever happen to the biosphere" (Idso, 1991, p. 181).

3. Uncertainty over the consequences of present actions and the risks imposed on future generations. The destruction of habitats is literally depriving the future of its natural assets. Only about 1 in every 100 plant species has been subject to scientific investigation and the proportion for animals is even smaller. The potential resources locked up in the earth's ecosystems are simply unknown and can only be realised over a long time-span. "Biological resources constitute a capital asset with great potential for yielding sustainable benefits, with new ways constantly being found in which they can contribute to sustainable development; for example, through new foods, pharmaceuticals and many other products" (UN, 1992, p. 67). If present trends continue, it is thought that up to 25 per cent of the world's species could be gone by the middle of the next century (IUCN *et al.*, 1991, p. 28).

The precautionary approach has become widely adopted in principle to protect the future against the harmful actions of the present. At Rio it was declared: "Where there are threats of serious or irreversible damage, lack of full scientific certainty shall not be used as a reason for postponing cost-effective measures to prevent environmental degradation" (Rio Declaration on Environment and Development, Principle). The difficulty is that it is sometimes better not to act for fear of committing irreversible damage at some time in the far-distant future. The uncertainty of effects may lead to a paralysis of policy or, more dangerously, a tendency to ignore or discount the future risks of present action.

4. Inadequacy of evidence and the problem of interpretation. As concern for the environment has grown, so more effort has been put into collating evidence showing trends in pollution, habitat degradation or resource depletion—evidence which is published in annual reports of monitoring statements (OECD, 1991; Department of Environment, 1992a; Brown *et al.*, 1991). Some records have long time-spans and are reliable. But, in general, collection of environmental data has been patchy and it is difficult to compare over time or between places. In some crucial areas, evidence is almost completely absent. For instance, in Africa south of the Sahara there is only one upper-atmosphere ozone-measurement station and there are no systematic measurements of greenhouse gases in the African continent. Consequently, in very crucial areas the quantity and quality of data are inadequate.

There is the additional problem that interpretation of evidence is wide open to manipulation by vested interests. It is generally acknowledged that the rich countries of the North are responsible for the major burden of polluting substances that threaten long-term survival. In terms of CO_2 emissions, the US produces 5 tonnes per head per year against an average of 0.2 tonnes in the developing countries. The OECD countries with about one-sixth of the world's population consume 11 times more fossil-fuel energy per head than the developing countries; are responsible for half the CO_2 output; produce three-quarters of the industrial wastes, four-fifths of hazardous wastes and have three-quarters of the world's cars which produce a cocktail of noxious emissions and contribute an increasing share of greenhouse gases. Furthermore, practically all the anthropogenic ozone-depleting substances are produced by the advanced industrialised countries. Not surprisingly, the developing countries argue that the rich countries must reduce their disproportionate claims upon the planet's limited resources and the regenerative capacity of its ecosystems.

In their defence, the rich countries argue that their share in polluting the planet is diminishing (by 2025 only one-third of CO_2 is forecast to come from OECD countries, for instance). The developing countries—with their burgeoning populations and demand on resources and energy—pose a looming threat which should be tackled now. A dialogue of the deaf has opened up, with each side interpreting the evidence in the most favourable light for their own purposes. The US, for example, has tried to shelter behind the composite index of greenhouse gases prepared by the World Resources Institute (McCully, 1991). By combining the gases in a single index, three developing countries (Brazil, India and China) are exposed as major contributors through deforestation, methane production, etc, while the USA is shown to have a smaller proportion of total emissions (18 per cent) compared to its share of CO_2 output (over one-fifth) with a stable output and therefore declining share by the year 2000. But this composite index nicely masks the fact that stability is achieved by a decline in CFCs while CO_2 output continues to rise. Further-

more, the index is favourable to the rich countries in other ways—it underestimates the lingering effect of CFCs; it is based on uncertain and selective data for methane and deforestation; and it neglects the feasibility of action which is much higher for gases produced in the richer countries. Finally, by implying a shared responsibility, the index provides the rich countries with an excuse to evade their prime responsibility for the problem and its solutions.

New evidence and interpretation can further complicate the picture. It is now argued that CFCs are less important than was thought since their contribution to global warming as a greenhouse gas is partly offset by their depletion of the ozone layer which promotes cooling. This certainly qualifies—if it does not altogether undermine—the US' argument that its contribution to reducing global warming from phasing out CFCs compensates for any increase in CO_2 outputs. This debate over the evidence demonstrates the ample scope for procrastination and conflict between interests which inhibits effective co-operation.

5. Science and politics. In attempting to understand the behaviour of ecosystems, science is confronting problems of enormous subtlety and complexity. At a fundamental level, there is controversy over the role and potential of natural processes. This debate has a metaphysical as well as a scientific dimension. There is the view, most evidently publicised through the Gaia hypothesis, of the earth as a living complex entity with a feedback system which maintains an optimal physical and chemical environment by active control—a process called 'homeostasis' (Lovelock, 1979, 1988). The Gaia hypothesis was originally propounded "as an alternative to that pessimistic view which sees nature as a primitive force to be subdued and conquered" (Lovelock, 1979, p. 12). But, the recuperative powers of the earth in the long-term certainly do not rule out catastrophe for human society in the short-term. As Lovelock puts it, "Anything that makes the world uncomfortable to live in tends to induce the evolution of those species that can achieve a new and more comfortable environment. It follows that, if the world is made unfit by what we do, there is the probability of a change in regime to one that will be better for life but not necessarily better for us" (Lovelock, 1988, p. 178). Critics of Gaia dispute that the earth is a self-regulating set of complex systems and argue instead that it is vulnerable to unanticipated, chaotic and catastrophic changes. But all sides seem to concur that human processes are perfectly capable of rendering the environment unsustainable for the human species.

Science cannot provide definitive answers. "Science is not knowledge, and never will be, but it is the advancement of knowledge" (Wiman, 1991, p. 245). Science depends on interpretation of evidence and judgement as to its significance. In the present state of the available evidence and the techniques of interpretation, much of the evidence on environmental processes may be ambiguous and uncertain. Therefore, scientific judgements will be provisional and revocable (Yearley, 1991a, 1991b). Evidence can be manipulated to serve particular interests. It is, therefore, important to understand the nature, terms and quality of evidence. There is a need to develop interdisciplinary approaches across the natural sciences and between the natural and social sciences to ensure greater understanding of the interaction of natural processes and the implications for social processes. This process has begun with an emphasis on Science for Sustainable Development in Agenda 21 at Rio and, for example, in the major research initiative on Global Environmental Change initiated by the UK's Economic and Social Research Council. Greater research and understanding will contribute to greater consensus on policy. Meanwhile, scientific uncertainty or disagreement can fuel the conflicts between interests which is the subject of the following section.

Conflict and the Common Interest

Local interests in conflict. Looked at in his-

torical perspective, it seems clear that policies for environmental conservation have been driven by self-interest whether of the individual, a class or the nation-state. There is room for qualifying this rather stark expression of a realist perspective as we shall see in a moment, but the notion that conflicts can be explained in terms of self-interest is a powerful, if not entirely persuasive, one. As Grove puts it: "If there is a single historical lesson to be drawn from the early history of conservation . . . it is that states can be persuaded to act to prevent environmental degradation only when their economic interests are shown to be directly threatened" (Grove, 1990, p. 13). This appears also to be true of class interests within industrial societies. As the scale of environmental problems has grown, so the focus of conflict has shifted. During the industrialisation of the 19th century it was fear of the outbreak of cholera or other epidemic disease from the squalid, malodorous and insanitary tenements of the urban poor that motivated the richer middle classes to introduce the venous–arterial system of sewers and piped water that improved health and removed the threat of rampant disease (de Swan, 1988). The class pattern was reflected in spatial social segregation.

By the 20th century, the attention of the privileged had switched from concern about public health to the protection of amenity. Environmental quality had become an integral aspect of the quality of life, a positional good to be cherished and defended against the incursions of the masses. But, as affluence became more common so the need to defend the environment against degradation or risk became more widespread. Local communities protested at the intrusion of locally unwanted land uses (LULUs) in greenfield locations (Popper, 1985). More and more these LULUs (e.g. radioactive-waste facilities, incinerators, petrochemical plants, waste-disposal facilities) became located in peripheral locations, characterised by geographical remoteness, economic marginality, environmental degradation, social homogeneity and political powerlessness

(Blowers and Leroy, forthcoming). This process became portrayed as an expression of NIMBYism—the defence of self-interest, whatever the costs imposed on other communities.

The realist explanation of the role of self-interest in promoting political conflict and resolution should be treated with some scepticism. At the local level, NIMBY is not simply an expression of self-interest. This assumes that facilities are wanted so long as they can be situated elsewhere. In practice, facilities are often opposed in principle, as unjustifiable anywhere. This has certainly been the case with protests against nuclear-waste facilities with many protestors arguing against the generic principles as well as the specific locations put forward (Blowers *et al.*, 1991; Lidskog and Elander, 1992). In practice protests often convey a mixture of motivations, a blend of self-interest, pragmatism and altruism, and they are essentially pleas for greater involvement, participation and control over decisions that affect local people (Wolsink, 1993).

National interests in conflict. Until relatively recently, the negative externalities of industrialisation were localised. The distribution was inequitable falling upon poorer groups within a city or region. As the scale of technology has increased, the inequitable distribution occurs between countries. Externalities are exported to other countries in the form of pollution of the Rhine or North Sea or acid rain arising from tall stacks designed to dilute and disperse localised pollution. Global pollution from greenhouse gases or CFCs is different since it is virtually undiscriminating in its impact. All are threatened and none can ultimately escape.

From a realist perspective, it would appear that the predictions of the Tragedy of the Commons are coming true. So long as an individual country continues to gain from a polluting activity it will continue production regardless of the impact on the carrying capacity of the environment. Hardin argues that, under assumptions of a free market, this

incentive for individual countries to pollute the global commons continues until well beyond the point when global deterioration sets in and may become irreversible (Hardin, 1968).

Global warming illustrates the point. Its onset is imperceptible but inevitable. It poses a Catch-22 for policy-makers as outlined by Prins: "when you don't see it, you could still act to prevent it but it is denied status by 'realist' politics so you can't; when you do see it and it is granted status and you could act, you probably can't because natural processes have passed a point of no return" (1990, p. 729). Latterly, as recognition has dawned of the global span of pollution so self-interest has fused with a common interest in environmental protection and has, at last, created the political environment for negotiation and agreement. To avert catastrophe it is necessary to adopt the precautionary principle—that is, to act "where there are good grounds for judging either that action taken promptly at comparatively low cost may avoid more costly damage later, or that irreversible effects may follow if action is delayed" (HMSO, 1990, p. 11). It is the mutual interest in survival that has prompted international agreements on ozone and global warming. While there is clearly conflict between national interests, there is also a genuine and growing transnational interest in environmental conservation and protection.

The nation-state is a universal form of organisation which has the administrative complexity to develop policy, the legitimate government to make binding decisions, the economic resources to carry them out and the coercive power to enforce them (Giddens, 1985). Within its own territory, the state can manage the physical environment as it chooses. At the same time, the state is capable of creating transboundary pollution that inflicts negative externalities on other states. In a real sense, states can invade the sovereign territory of others who may be incapable either of defence or retaliation. Where it is in the mutual interests of states to do so, solutions must be found by agreement. In essence, it is state interests that are paramount. This is certainly the way political leaders appear to think and speak. For example, President Bush, for once, made his position unequivocally clear on his arrival in Rio, declaring, "I am determined to protect the environment, and I am also determined to protect the American taxpayer. The days of the open cheque book are over" (*Independent*, 12 June 1992).

From a purely realist perspective, it follows that the nation-state is both the cause of and the solution to the world's environmental problems. Agreements need to be forged among the nation-states which have the capability to regulate, monitor, verify and enforce. Again, there are grounds for criticising a realist perspective based entirely on the promotion of self-interest. In the first place, it is not always clear where a nation-state's real interests lie. Very often, the state's interests are difficult to foresee clearly and to calculate. Secondly, states are not simply unitary organisations with a single-minded consensus on interests. They are themselves composed of *congeries* of different, frequently-conflicting interests. These interests are expressed in terms of class, politics, regions, ethnic groups, cultural affinities and so on. At different times, the state's interests will reflect different aspects of its many interests providing different emphases. For example, in environmental policy there is bound to be a shift in the expression of the US's interests with the change in the Presidency in 1993.

A third reason for qualifying the role of the nation-state is that the capability of states to develop and deliver policies varies considerably. Many states simply lack the resources, the bureaucracy or even the motivation to ensure that policies are implemented. Supranational governmental organisations (e.g. UNCEP, the EC's Environmental Commission) as well as NGOs have raised awareness and influenced policy-making that extends beyond the boundaries of the nation-states. In practice, the developments in environmental policy-making cannot be explained simply as an expression of balancing competing interests, though that

is clearly a necessary condition for success. Rather, environmental policy is an outcome of a dynamic and developing process of interaction between a wide diversity of interests not simply confined to the environment. Complicated trade-offs between environmental, security, economic and other policies may be necessary. For instance, it is becoming clear that the USA cannot stand aside from the debate about sustainable development since its fundamental interests are involved. Speth makes the point explicit

> If population growth continues to outpace the creation of new jobs, if pressures on resources mount and growth proves unsustainable, if social and ethnic tensions increase, the effects could be felt in many spheres—from the collapse of governments to the adoption of authoritarian measures, to waves of ecological refugees, to civil unrest and regional conflict (Speth, 1992, p. 153).

Looked at in this broad sense, conflicts over environment are an aspect of more general conflicts, an integral element in an interlocking system of policy-making to ensure economic, environmental and social survival. Sustainable development is therefore not simply an environmental objective, but a fundamental principle relevant to all areas of policy at local, national and global levels. In the second part of the review, I turn to the changes that will be necessary if the challenge of sustainable development is to be met.

Part 2: Sustainable Development —the Necessary Conditions

The Political Implications of Sustainable Development

Sustainable development has been criticised as a catch-all offering different meanings to different interests. It has been adopted enthusiastically by environmentalists and is now a commonplace in official reports and a slogan for politicians. Business has enthusiastically embraced it to help legitimate its activities

(WICEM II, 1991). At an intellectual level, Redclift has warned that sustainability obscures "the contradictions that 'development' implies for the environment. Instead of bringing intellectual rigour to the discussion of environment and development, we frequently encounter moral convictions as substitutes for thought" (Redclift, 1987, p. 2).

It would be a mistake to dismiss sustainable development as mere platitude or just the fashion of the day, soon to disappear—like the concern about 'limits to growth' of an earlier era. For one thing, many of the issues—the depletion of resources, the growth of population, the increase of pollution, the degradation of soil, habitats and species—are recurrent themes. They threaten the planet's overall carrying capacity and the ability of its ecosystems to regenerate themselves. By linking development and environment, the needs and aspirations of the developing world have been incorporated. It has become apparent that environmental issues cannot be dealt with in isolation—"they are interdependent parts of a greater whole, and that whole is the overarching and problematic question of the relationship between humans and nature; and between humans and humans" (Dovers and Handmer, 1992). Strenuous efforts are being made to define, interpret and introduce sustainable development at local, national and global levels. Sustainable development is already passing from being just a vague concept (Redclift, 1991, p. 36; Holmberg *et al.*, 1991, p. 6) to becoming a set of objectives and policies requiring implementation.

On the other hand, it is by no means clear that the implications of sustainable development are fully recognised. The oft-quoted Brundtland definition suggests that more than marginal adaptation is needed for survival:

> Sustainable development is development that meets the needs of the present without compromising the ability of future generations to meet their own needs (World Commission, 1987, p. 8).

This involves a wholesale shift from resource exploitations to conservation, a redistribution of wealth from rich to poor in order to meet needs, and a withdrawal from those activities which could harm future generations (Blowers, 1992a). This is a very tough set of propositions which have been but simply grasped by policy-makers engaged on programmes for sustainable development.

It is now widely assumed that the pace of environmental degradation is such that, if it is not arrested, catastrophe will—gradually or suddenly—overwhelm the earth's ecosystems. There has been an unprecedented attempt to grapple with global environmental problems which reached its apotheosis at Rio de Janeiro. Rio demonstrated just how far there was to go in understanding the problems, devising appropriate solutions and overcoming the conflicts between states and interests that threaten to subvert the implementation process. Sustainable development poses a challenge to the most entrenched bastions of contemporary political and economic organisation. It challenges the notions of sovereignty, the free market and the prevailing inequitable distribution of resources.

The Role of the Nation-state

Sovereignty and the role of the nation-state. An interesting development in recent years has been the development of a new framework for environmental policy-making that extends well beyond the frontiers and capabilities of individual nation-states. Transnational political processes have developed that challenge the nation-state. This process may be described as *globalisation*.

Globalisation is characterised by the development of organisational forms which transcend the nation-state. These are of three kinds. There are, first, the *intergovernmental organisations* (IGOs) which seek to identify common interests between states, often on a global scale. For example, the United Nations Environment Programme seeks to develop common environmental strategies and played the key role in promoting the UN Conference on Environment and Development at Rio and in brokering international conventions and agreements. The Global Environmental Facility (GEF) was established in 1991 as a fund managed by the World Bank to support the efforts of developing countries to meet the obligations of the various conventions. Many IGOs affect the environment—although the environment is not specifically within their remit. Examples of these are the Food and Agriculture Organisation, the General Agreement on Tariffs and Trade or the International Atomic Energy Agency. The World Bank and multilateral development banks have been much criticised for the adverse environmental impacts of development projects which they have funded (Bramble and Porter, 1992). It is clear that IGOs possess considerable power and provide a challenge to the sovereignty of the nation-state.

A second kind of transnational organisation is the *multinational corporation* (MNC) whose operations often have a global reach. They have a major stake in the exploitation of the earth's major economic physical resources of energy (notably oil), minerals, timber and some commercial agricultural products. They can move investment capital around the globe and have a major influence on governments which are, to some extent, dependent upon them (Lindblom, 1977). While they are bound by environmental regulations, they will also indicate clearly to governments what they consider to be the extent of the regulation they will find tolerable. Therefore, MNCs are, in certain respects, beyond the control of individual governments.

Non-governmental organisations (NGOs) constitute a third form of transnational organisation. NGOs encompass an enormous diversity ranging from small, localised NGOs, through national bodies, up to international NGOs. They cover a wide variety of issues. As well as NGOs directly concerned with the environment, there are all kinds of NGOs engaged in such fields as development, human rights, women's concerns, youth, etc, which frequently have an indirect bearing on the environment. The Global Forum in Rio was the most visible expression of the multitude of NGOs concerned with the environment. NGOs vary in their orientation, organisation and culture, and in their strategies and techniques for achieving influence. In relation to the state, NGOs may seek to complement state provision, to reform the state by representing specific interests, or to oppose the state's policies (Clark, 1991). In respect of environmental issues, NGOs exhibit all three strategies. They are increasingly significant in drawing attention to problems, mobilising opinion and lobbying for specific policies. Some of the biggest NGOs such as Friends of the Earth or Greenpeace have built up global networks, developed counter expertise and displayed skilful use of the media. The attempts to establish development as the key theme on the environmental agenda have been substantially the work of NGOs, especially those speaking for Third World interests.

Sovereignty and subsidiarity. In different ways IGOs, MNCs and NGOs are components of the process of 'globalisation'. Through complex and dynamic interactions, environmental policy-making is mediated at supranational level and, consequently, the sovereignty of individual nation-states is compromised. The development of supranational authority in Europe has led the dramatic debate about *subsidiarity*. This was broadly defined in the Treaty of Maastricht as a process "in which decisions are taken as closely as possible to the citizen". The UK has interpreted subsidiarity purely in terms of *national* interest and the focus of attention has been on economic and monetary union rather than on environmental policy.

Subsidiarity has been invoked to justify leaving areas of environmental policy-making to individual states without interference from the EC. This reflects, for example, the irritation felt about EC intervention in UK land-use decisions (e.g. road schemes) and over breaches of the drinking-water-quality directive. Cases would need to be decided against the precept that "action should be taken at community level only where it would be more appropriate than action at national or local level" (ENDS, 1992, p. 14). The transboundary nature of environmental processes suggests that community-wide environmental policy-making is likely to be justified in most cases. In addition, the concept of a single common market requires a level playing-field in which environmental policies (among many others) should not advantage one country as against others.

The debate over sovereignty and subsidiarity has focused on the power of the nation-state. What has been neglected is the sub-national level. Indeed, with the increasing centralisation occurring in some states, and noticeably in the UK, the power of local government has been much diminished. Deregulation of land-use planning combined with severe financial restraint and controls, together with the privatisation of certain functions (e.g. waste disposal) combined with emphasis on the market, have reduced local government's effective powers over the environment relative to central government and developers. The absence of an effective and elected regional tier of government in the UK, including greater autonomy for the nation-regions of Scotland and Wales, is a further restraint on any devolution of powers.

It is at the sub-national level that environmental movements are particularly strong and effective. Local environmental action groups developing as a spontaneous response to external threat have frequently been successful—though frequently if unfairly criticised for their self-interested NIMBY motives. Conservation groups, often linking up with established NGOs, have done much to arrest the tide of destruction of landscapes, habitats and species; they have campaigned against polluting and hazardous activities; and they have promoted the case for more sustainable forms of development. A relatively new feature has been the development of coalitions of action groups able to invoke traditional patterns of community and local identification and able to cut across modern class-based social patterns (Blowers and Leroy, forthcoming). Such coalitions can potentially operate across state frontiers. A good example of this newly-emerging form of environmental movement is provided by the protests against nuclear-waste repositories (Blowers *et al.*, 1991).

In the case of environmental policy national sovereignty is challenged both from above and below. The interaction and integration of policy making from local through to national and up to global level is a feature of environmental issues. Another feature is the extent to which policy making and implementation has become dependent on the market.

The Market, the Environment and the Role of Intervention

The triumph of the market. At the end of the 1980s, it appeared that market capitalism had achieved a universal triumph. In the developed countries of the West, the market was hailed as the source of efficiency and economy and, consequently, the prescription for economic growth. In many countries, whatever the orientation of the party in power, the market was encouraged through deregulation, privatisation and the removal of subsidies and barriers to trade. In the UK, especially, the process has been deeply entrenched through 14 years of Conservative government. Large areas of the public sector have been either privatised or invested with regimes of cost accounting, competition and contracting out.

Internationally, the market and free trade have been dominant economic forces over the past decade. As the state centralism imposed by communist regimes disintegrated, the market offered a natural—if immediately painful—route to prosperity. The EC became a single internal market in 1993, though some barriers remained. The Uruguay Round of the General Agreement on Tariffs and Trade (GATT), despite conflicts over certain goods, basically espouses the doctrine of international free trade. This is regarded as an unquestioned benefit to all trading partners, paving the way through increased growth and resources that will support the environmental improvements that ensure sustainable development. Agenda 21 affirms that "Trade liberalisation should be pursued across economic sectors so as to contribute to sustainable development" (UN, 1992, p. 24). There appears to be a universal political rhetoric that the development of market forces is a means—indeed, the means—to ensure the ultimate protection of the environment.

As might be expected, this view is challenged by Marxist theorists who hold that capitalist economic development is the fountain-head of uneven development with its pattern of dominance and development. Capitalism wrecks the environment through flows of trade, investment and aid that encourage the exploitation and waste of resources, pollution and destruction of the ecosystems. The answer for Marxists is "a social, economic and cultural revolution that abolishes the constraints of capitalism and, in so doing, establishes a new relationship between the individual and society and between people and nature . . ." (Gorz, 1980, p. 4). The rhetoric of revolution is captivating, though the pathway to transformation is unclear.

What is interesting is that a critique which accepts that market capitalism is responsible for environmental degradation is now widely shared and beginning to influence political thinking. Economists of various leanings have emphasised the existence of ultimate limits to growth set by the finite stock of non-renewable resources and the capacity of the atmosphere, earth and oceans to absorb the burdens of production and pollution now being imposed upon them (Pearce *et al.*, 1989; Redclift, 1987; Daly and Cobb, 1989; Jacobs, 1991). Environmental assets should not be regarded as free goods, but should be properly valued. GNP is an inadequate measure of development, "since it treats sustainable and unsustainable production alike and compounds the error by including the costs of unsustainable economic activity on the credit side, while largely ignoring processes of recycling and energy conversion which do not lead to the production of goods or marketable services" (Redclift, 1987,

p. 16). Some argue that solutions should be sought through the market—that once a proper valuation is secured, it will, in principle, be possible to devise means of intervention in the market that will ensure patterns of sustainable development (Pearce *et al.*, 1989). Opponents contend that it would be difficult to value future unknown environmental resources (e.g. forest habitats) or those whose scarcity value increases over time or to recognise the possible changes in the evaluation of resources by different societies over time.

As this thinking develops, so governments have begun to examine a wide range of market-based economic measures (taxes, incentives, pollution permits, recycling credits, and so on) designed to protect resources, prevent pollution and encourage sustainable forms of technology. Business has turned its attention to life-cycle analysis of products, use of sustainable resources and new technologies designed to reduce environmental impacts. In both government and industry, regulatory instruments are adopted as a necessary complement to market mechanisms. The Conservative government is comfortable with the idea that regulation is necessary; just as, conversely, the Labour Party has accepted the importance of the market in the prosecution of environmental policy (The Labour Party, 1990).

The case for intervention. Paradoxically, this convergence in political thinking on the appropriate approach to environmental policy may prove detrimental to the cause of environmental protection. In the first place, lack of political conflict and a presumed consensus reduces the political visibility of the environment. The environment is securely on the agenda but it becomes less of a priority than those issues over which there is conflict. This point was certainly evident in the British general election of 1992 when the environment received little attention compared to the big issues of the economy, the health service and even the constitution (Carter, 1992). Important though it undoubtedly was for the longer term, the Rio Earth

Summit was scarcely recollected in the popular imagination (as reflected by journalists and politicians) as an event of great signficance when compared to the world recession, conflicts in Bosnia, the changing Presidency in the US or the future of the Maastricht Treaty. The urgency about environmental problems undoubtedly felt by some politicians, NGOs and environmentalists has not yet conveyed itself to the wider public audience.

The political consensus over environmental management has another unfortunate consequence: it stifles debates over policy options. The pervasive belief in a market solution tempered by necessary regulation denies debate about the need for far more interventionist strategies. The idea and practice of planning as a process of economic and environmental management has suffered a virtual eclipse in recent years. Right-wing ideologies attacked the controls, subsidies and bureaucratic structures associated with state planning as evidence of waste, inefficiency and inflexibility. The supremacy of the market seemed to be vindicated by the collapse of the Soviet state planning system and the subsequent revelations of appalling environmental catastrophes it spawned. The inadequacies of the market as the primary vehicle for delivering a sustainable environment were ignored.

The major failing of the market, in relation to the environment, is that it is concerned with short-term economic criteria placing an emphasis on growth achieved through comparative advantage. As specialisation develops, those areas unable to compete become impoverished and, elsewhere, the environment becomes degraded through the pollution, waste or resource depletion associated with overexploitation. The market fails to take account of externalities which impose unwanted or unforeseen costs on third parties (individual, communities or countries). Moreover, the market promotes the private interest over the public and ignores or discounts the interests of future generations. Finally, the market values resources in respect to their use in production and does not account for the costs of depletion of non-renewable resources. For these various reasons, the market intrinsically cannot deal with the long-term conservation of the environment. Intervention becomes necessary to deal with market failure.

Concern for the environment may revive political interest in the merits of planning. It is important to recognise that planning for sustainability "stands in contrast to the operation of market forces, but it does not preclude the existence of markets" (Jacobs, 1991, p. 125). The essential characteristic of planning is that goals or outcomes are specified by the planning authority, be it local, state or international. In order for the desired goal to be achieved, a planning process will need to identify targets, specify methods for achieving them and possess the capability for monitoring and evaluating outcomes and, where necessary, the sanctions necessary to secure compliance. This process, even if only in a residual form, may be observed in the ozone protocols where targets have been set to be achieved through the phasing out of ozone-depleting chemicals supported by financial funds to assist the compliance of poorer countries. In the case of the climate convention, only the first stage—the setting down of targets—has been reached.

An environmental planning system in which the market is subordinate to long-term environmental criteria appears, in the early 1990s, to be a distant possibility. But as environmental factors impinge more and more on economic policy-making, so the need for a planned approach to resource conservation and pollution control will become evident. A shift towards greater intervention through what might be termed 'environmental planning' to defend the environment can be predicted over the coming decade. Even in the most ideologically committed market economies, environmental constraints will begin to impinge more on policy-making. For example, in the UK the creation of the Environment Agency represents a further step in the direction of integrating environmental protection bodies (Department of

Environment. 1991). While remaining chary about the role of regulation, the government is conducting intensive research into the use of economic instruments to ensure that "environmental costs are taken into account in decision-making in the same way as other costs" (HMSO, 1992, p. 34). The rudiments of a more interventionist approach to environmental policy-making, albeit still clothed in market philosophy, are beginning to emerge.

Environmental planning may develop in various ways. In principle, it will reflect an emphasis on the longer term through the *precautionary* approach; it will be a *strategic* process dealing with the environmental implications of sectoral policies; it will *integrate* spatial economic planning, land-use planning and environmental protection; and it will *co-ordinate* policies at different governmental levels through the development, monitoring and implementation of plans at different levels of government from the local, through the regional, to the national and international levels. These plans will set out the goals, time-scales and targets to be achieved. The justification for environmental planning for sustainability and an indication of how it would work in practice have begun to be set out by academics and professional planners (Jacobs, 1991; Blowers, 1992b and 1992c).

Equity and the Principle of Compensation

It was argued earlier that environmental policy goals will be difficult to establish, let alone achieve, unless fundamental inequalities are tackled. This involves providing compensation to those communities who experience the environmental costs of economic development; preventing over-exploitation of resources and environmental deterioration in poorer countries; improving environmental conditions in areas already suffering degradation; preventing or ameliorating transboundary impacts of pollution and risks; and ensuring that the present generation does not rob or imperil the future. These are the preconditions needed to ensure the third principle of the Rio Declaration: 'The right to development must be fulfilled so as to equitably meet developmental and environmental needs of present and future generations'.

Environmental risks and degradation have become concentrated in communities that were earlier defined as 'peripheral'. Within the advanced industrial countries, hazardous activities are found in what may be called 'pollution havens' such as petrochemical complexes or 'nuclear oases' such as Sellafield in the UK or Hanford in the US (Blowers *et al.*, 1991; Loeb, 1986; McSorley, 1990). A process of peripheralisation may be perceived, strengthening over time, whereby peripheral communities are created and reinforced by the power of communities to prevent unwanted land uses, combined with the powerlessness of peripheral communities to resist them (Blowers and Leroy, forthcoming). A similar process may be observed at international level, where polluting and hazardous industrial activities are found in various developing countries. It must be emphasised that peripheral communities are primarily economically determined. Industries have developed and remain in those locations that have become dependent upon them. Therefore, environmental degradation is a consequence rather than a cause of peripheralisation. There is little evidence to suggest that dirty activities migrate to pollution havens primarily to avoid environmental regulations.

In the developed countries, it is becoming increasingly difficult to extend hazardous activities at existing sites and virtually impossible to establish them in new greenfield locations. Compensation in various forms is becoming a political expedient as well as a moral principle. Compensation can take a variety of forms including economic incentives (tax concessions, infrastructure provision, economic development and training programmes) and participation in decision-making affecting the community. Indeed, research into siting nuclear facilities undertaken in the US and Canada indicates that shared power and some local control over decisions is regarded as more important for the local community than any other form of compensation or incentive (Solomon and Cameron, 1985; Siting Process Task Force, 1987, 1990). At the international level, it is also clear that countries will increasingly resist becoming dumping grounds for industrial and hazardous wastes. The Bamako Convention banning the import of hazardous wastes illustrates the power of collective action among developing countries.

The principle of compensation will be necessary to protect the global environment. Pressures will grow on the rich both to reduce their own excessive demands on the global environment and to provide finance and technology to enable sustainable development in the poor countries. Debt-for-nature swaps, technology transfer and the Global Environmental Facility are early if modest indications of some redistribution of resources to promote environmental goals.

This process may have to go further. Certain global resources will have to be conserved to protect the environment. But, nations are unlikely to waive their sovereign rights to develop their territory unless they are fully compensated for doing so. Developing countries are clearly unprepared to make unilateral sacrifices to save the global commons. If it is necessary in the common interest to withold certain global assets such as tropical forests from exploitation, then it is equally justifiable to provide greater access to the resources of those areas that are exploited. Resources in both developed and developing worlds are arguably the property of the global community whether exploited now or held in reserve to protect the environment and to pass on to future generations (Luper-Foy, 1992). To put it simply, if Brazil is expected to conserve its rainforest, the USA might equally be expected to share more widely the benefits of exploiting its resources—or, alternatively, to transfer some of its wealth in the interests of sustainable development.

This principle of global property rights argues that sovereignty does not confer on individual countries a right to exploit their territory as they please. It applies equally to the problem of transboundary pollution. There can be no justification for one country inflicting gratuitous damage on its neighbours. Where damage occurs, compensation is appropriate—though in the case of certain hazards, such as radioactivity, it is difficult to envisage any appropriate compensation. Some countries are too poor to provide compensation or to prevent transboundary effects without help. For example, it is well known that nuclear reactors of Soviet design in Russia, the Ukraine and Eastern Europe are potentially unsafe, but if they were shut down, power supplies would be cut off over large areas. These countries lack the resources to upgrade their reactors. Therefore technological and financial assistance from the West may be necessary if the threat of further widespread radioactive leakages is to be averted.

Finally, there is the obligation of the present to future generations; the principle of inter-generational equity. This does not mean handing on the environment as it is, since much of it is heavily degraded anyway, but rather avoiding actions that will deprive the future of environmental assets. In some cases, present benefits from technological development (e.g. toxic and radioactive waste) are responsible for inevitable future risks. Where future hazards are unavoidable then we are obliged to mitigate the risks through research and appropriate technology and to provide resources for the future management of hazardous sites. The problem of securing the future while maintaining present development is at the heart of the quest for sustainable development. Neither the present nor the future environment can be sustained unless equity is at the core of policy.

Postscript

Over the past five years or so, the environment has become established as a key area of policy-making. Scientific analysis and evidence has had a significant impact on policy. The need for greater integration of environment into all areas of policy-making has been recognised. The environment has assumed greater importance in political debates at all levels. There has been greater public interest.

The widespread participation of citizens' groups and NGOs is a trend that is likely to have major influence on setting the environmental agendas over the next decade. Governments at all levels have responded to the growing alarm at the threats posed to health and survival by the gross exploitation of our natural resources. Within the UK, the environment has been the subject of comprehensive legislation and a major White Paper; in the EC, it has been a prominent and, on the whole, successful area of policy-making; and, at the international level, there has been an impressive series of agreements culminating in the Rio Earth Summit in 1992. Consensus on the importance of the issues reigns.

Though now well established on the policy agenda, the environment has not yet secured its place alongside the quotidian preoccupation with economic management. Indeed, the interdependence of economy and environment is barely recognised and the practical integration of the environment into all sectors and levels of policy-making is still a distant prospect. The environment remains a somewhat tangential issue, a matter of vague forebodings but, as yet, the social and economic implications of the quest for sustainable development have still to be fully appreciated. When they are, the consensus may well dissolve into a conflict over resources as powerful interests and countries seek to acquire or defend a bigger share of resources. The seeds of discord are already sown.

International attention has been focused on the relatively distant dangers of deforestation, global warming, ozone depletion. Future security lies in present action. A set of principles, some significant agreements and a programme for future action (Agenda 21) were established at Rio, evidence of the growing sense of urgency and commitment to the desirable if unspecific goal of sustainable development. But, the more immediate threat to global survival posed by nuclear proliferation has excited much less attention.

Herein lies the biggest danger. The prospects of a nuclear exchange did not subside with the end of the Cold War. If anything, the danger of nuclear conflict has increased with plutonium accumulating from reprocessing operations in the UK and France; large stockpiles from production and dismantling of nuclear weapons in the USA and the former USSR; and the development of a nuclear-weapons capability in several countries. The problem of proliferation demands the most urgent attention alongside the other global environmental issues; otherwise the quest for sustainable development may be in vain.

Notes

1. For example, in the UK national data identify the extent of the degradation and the loss of habitats and species. The area of moorland has shrunk by 20 per cent since the 1940s, much of the lowland heath has been converted to farming, about 40 per cent of unintensified grassland has gone, with significant losses also of fens and wetlands, a net loss of 25 000 km of hedgerows—all taking with them the loss of wildlife (Department of Environment, 1992a). There has been a slight deterioration in water quality in England and Wales since 1980 and levels of NOX rose 35 per cent in five years (1986–91) while carbon monoxide has risen by a third since 1980. On the other hand, levels of sulphur dioxide and black smoke have declined.

   In the EC countries, environmental improvements brought about by the reductions in sulphur dioxide, CFCs, particulate and lead in the atmosphere must be measured against the failures, the increasing CO_2 burdens, rises in NOX, the deterioration of soil quality in some areas, groundwater pollution and pressures on endangered species and their habitats.

References

BARNABY, F. (1991) The environmental impact of the Gulf war, *The Ecologist*, 21(4).

BLACK, D. (1984) *Investigation of Possible Increased Cancer in West Cumbria*. Report of Independent Advisory Group Chaired by Sir Douglas Black. London: HMSO.

BLOWERS, A. (1992a) Sustainable urban development: the political prospects, in: M. BREHENY (Ed.) *Sustainable Development and Urban Form*, pp. 24–38. European Research in Regional Science. Pion: London.

BLOWERS, A. (1992b) Planning a sustainable future: problems, principles and prospects, *Town and Country Planning*, 61(5), pp. 132–135.

BLOWERS, A. (1992c) Planning for a sustainable city, *Streetwise*, 10, pp. 3–10.

BLOWERS, A. and LEROY, P. (forthcoming) *Power, politics and environmental inequality: a theoretical and empirical analysis of the process of 'peripheralisation'*. Paper first presented at International Sociological Association Symposium on *Current Developments in Environmental Sociology*, Woudschoten, Netherlands, June 1992.

BLOWERS, A., LOWRY, D. and SOLOMON, B. (1991) *The International Politics of Nuclear Waste*. London: Macmillan.

BRAMBLE, B. and PORTER, G. (1992) NGOs and the making of US policy, in: Business Council for a Sustainable Development (Ed.) *Changing Course: The Global Business Perspective on Development and the Environment*, pp. 325–353. Cambridge: MIT Press.

BROWN, L.R. *et al*. (1991) *State of the World 1991*. London: Earthscan.

BUTTEL, F.H., HAWKINS, A.P. and POWER, A.G. (1990) From limits to growth to global change: constraints and contradictions in the evolution of environmental science and ideology, *Global Environmental Change*, 1, pp. 57–66.

CARTER, N. (1992) Whatever happened to the environment? The British General Election, 1992, *Environmental Politics*, 1, pp. 442–448.

CARTER, T.R., PORTER, J.H. and PARY, M.L. (1991) Climatic warming and crop potential in Europe: prospects and uncertainties, *Global Environmental Change*, 1, pp. 291–312.

CLARK, J. (1991) *Democratising Development: The Role of Voluntary Organisations*. London: Earthscan.

COMMISSION OF THE EUROPEAN COMMUNITIES (1992) *Towards Sustainability*. A Eureopean Community Programme of Policy and Action in relation to the Environment and Sustainable Development, Brussels, March.

CRAFT, A. and OPENSHAW, S. (1987) Children, radiation, cancer and the Sellafield nuclear reprocessing plant, in: A. BLOWERS and D. PEPPER (Eds) *Nuclear Power in Crisis*, pp. 244–271. London: Croom Helm.

DALY, H. and COBB, J. (1989) *For the Common Good*. London: Green Print.

DEPARTMENT OF ENVIRONMENT (1991) *Improving Environmental Quality*. Consultation Paper. London: HMSO.

DEPARTMENT OF ENVIRONMENT (1992a) *The UK Environment*. London: HMSO.

DEPARTMENT OF ENVIRONMENT (1992b) *Land Use Planning Policy and Climate Change*. London: HMSO.

DOVERS, S. and HANDMER, J. (1992) Uncertainty, sustainability and change, *Global Environmental Change*, 2, pp. 262–276.

DOWNING, T.E. (1991) Vulnerability to hunger in Africa: a climate change perspective, *Global Environmental Change*, 1, pp. 365–380.

ENDS (ENVIRONMENTAL DATA SERVICES) (1989) *Report 176*. September.

ENDS (ENVIRONMENTAL DATA SERVICES) (1992) *Report 209*. June.

EUROPEAN COMMUNITIES (1992) *Treaty on European Union*. Maastricht Treaty, CM1934. London: HMSO.

GIDDENS, A. (1985) *The Nation-state and Violence*. Polity Press: Cambridge.

GORZ, A. (1980) *Ecology as Politics*. Boston: South End Press.

GREENE, O. (1991) *Building a global warming regime: the significance of verification and confidence building measures*. Paper to Conference on *International Arrangements for Reaching Environmental Goals*, Strathclyde, September.

GROVE, R. (1990) The origins of environmentalism, *Nature*, 345, pp. 11–14, 3 May.

HAAS, P.M. (1992) Introduction: epistemic communities and international policy coordination, *International Organization*, 46, pp. 1–36.

HARDIN, G. (1968) The tragedy of the commons, *Science*, 162, pp. 1243–1248.

HMSO (1990) *This Common Inheritance*. CM 1200. London: HMSO.

HMSO (1991a) *This Common Inheritance, The First Year Report*. CM 1655. London: HMSO.

HMSO (1991b) *Policy Appraisal and the Environment, a guide for government departments*. London: HMSO.

HMSO (1992) *This Common Inheritance, The Second Year Report*. CM 2068. London: HMSO.

HOLMBERG, J., BASS, S. and TIMBERLAKE, L. (1991) *Defending the Future: A Guide to Sustainable Development*. London: IIED/Earthscan.

IDSO, S.B. (1991) Carbon dioxide and the fate of Earth, *Global Environmental Change*, 1, pp. 178–182.

IUCN, UNEP and WWF (1991) *Caring for the Earth: A Strategy for Sustainable Living*. Gland, Switzerland.

JACOBS, M. (1991) *The Green Economy*. London: Pluto Press.

LABOUR PARTY, THE (1990) *An Earthly Chance*.

LIDSKOG, R. and ELANDER, I. (1992) Reinterpreting locational conflicts: NIMBY and nuclear waste management in Sweden, *Policy and Politics*, 20, pp. 249–264.

LINDBLOM, C.E. (1977) *Politics and Markets: The World's Political-Economic Systems*. New York: Basic Books.

LOEB, P. (1986) *Nuclear Culture*. Philadelphia: New Society Publishers.

LONERGAN, S. and KAVANAGH, B. (1991) Climate change, water resources and security in the Middle East, *Global Environmental Change*, 1, pp. 272–290.

LOVELOCK, J. (1979) *Gaia: A New Look at Life on Earth*. Oxford: Oxford University Press.

796   ANDREW BLOWERS

LOVELOCK. J. (1988) *The Ages of Gaia: A Biography of our Living Earth.* Oxford: Oxford University Press.

LUPER-FOY. S. (1992) Justice and natural resources. *Environmental Values*, 1, pp. 47–64.

MACCRACKEN. M.C. (1991) Comment on 'Carbon dioxide and the fate of Earth' by Sherwood B. Idso, *Global Environmental Change*, 1, pp. 266–268.

MCCULLY. P. (1991) Discord in the greenhouse: how WRI is attempting to shift the blame for global warming, *The Ecologist*, 21, pp. 157–165.

MCSORLEY. J. (1990) *Living in the Shadow.* London: Pan Books.

MEADOWS, D., *et al.* (1972) *The Limits to Growth.* Earth Island.

NEPP (NATIONAL ENVIRONMENTAL POLICY PLAN) (1989) *To Choose or to Lose.* Second Chamber of the States General, The Netherlands.

OECD (1991) *The State of the Environment.* Paris: OECD.

OPEN UNIVERSITY (1992) *Third World Development.* Course U208. Milton Keynes: Open University.

PEARCE, D., MARKANDYA, A. and BARBIER, E. (1989) *Blueprint for a Green Economy.* London: Earthscan.

POPPER, F.J. (1985) The environmentalist and the LULU, reprinted in: R. LAKE (Ed.) (1987) *Resolving Locational Conflict*, pp. 1–13. New Jersey: Rutgers University.

PRINS, G. (1990) Politics and the environment, *International Affairs*, 66, pp. 711–730.

REDCLIFT, M. (1987) *Sustainable Development: Exploring the Contradictions.* London: Routledge.

REDCLIFT, M. (1991) The multiple dimensions of sustainable development, *Geography*, 76, pp. 36–42.

RIIA (ROYAL INSTITUTE OF INTERNATIONAL AFFAIRS) (1991) *Pledge and Review Processes: Possible Components of a Climate Convention.* Report of a workshop, London, August.

RIVM (1989) *Concern for Tomorrow, A National Environmental Survey 1985–2010.* National Institute of Public Health and Environmental Protection, Bilthoven, The Netherlands.

SCHNEIDER. S.H. (1991) Why global warming should concern us, *Global Environmental Change*, 1, pp. 268–271.

SITING PROCESS TASK FORCE (1987) *Socially responsive impact management: a discussion paper.* Report to the Siting Process Task Force on low-level radioactive waste disposal, Energy, Mines and Resources, Canada, October.

SITING PROCESS TASK FORCE (1990) *Opting for co-operation.* Report of the Siting Process Task Force on low-level radioactive waste disposal, Energy, Mines and Resources, Canada.

SMITH, P. (1991) Global development issues, in: P. SMITH and K. WARR *Global Environmental Issues*, pp. 203–242. London: Open University/Hodder and Stoughton.

SOLOMON, B. and CAMERON, D. (1985) Nuclear waste repository siting: an alternative approach, *Energy Policy*, 13, pp. 564–580.

SPETH, J. (1992) A post-Rio compact, *Foreign Policy*, 88, 145–161.

STRAATEN, J. VAN DER (1992) The Dutch National Environmental Policy Plan: to choose or to lose, *Environmental Politics*, 1, pp. 45–71.

SWAAN. A. DE (1988) *In Care of the State.* Cambridge: Polity Press.

UNITED NATIONS (1992) *The Global Partnership for Environment and Development: A Guide to Agenda 21.* UNCED, Geneva, April.

WICEM II (1991) Official Report, Second World Industry Conference on Environment and Management, in: *Environment Strategy Europe*, pp. 71–107. London: Campden Publishing.

WIMAN, B.L.B. (1991) Implications of environmental complexity for science and policy: contributions from systems theory, *Global Environmental Change*, 1, pp. 235–247.

WOLSINK, M. (1993) Entanglement of interests and motives in facility siting: the not-in-my-backyard theory. (draft).

WORLD COMMISSION ON ENVIRONMENT AND DEVELOPMENT (1987) *Our Common Future.* The Brundtland Report. Oxford: Oxford University Press.

YEARLEY, S. (1991a) *The Green Case.* London: Routledge.

YEARLEY, S. (1991b) Greens and science: a doomed affair?, *New Scientist*, 13 July, pp. 37–40.

[18]

Planning, Politics, and the Environment

John Friedmann

[In this commentary John Friedmann outlines a six-point approach to environmental planning. Two responses follow.]

I intend to present here a series of propositions about environmental planning under the special circumstances prevailing in the United States. The propositions I will defend apply to metropolitan regions—and to people's life spaces contained within them. There are larger scales that must engage our thinking about the environment: national, multinational, and global. But for now I would like to leave these larger dimensions of the problem aside. Let us concentrate on the setting for the politics of daily life. In the United States, this setting is the metropolitan region or, as we may also call it, the daily urban field.

Proposition 1

A good, that is, a life-supporting and life-enhancing environment in metropolitan regions calls for a reduction in the long-term rate of capital accumulation and, thus, of regional economic growth.

Comment

This is a bold statement that we will shortly need to limit and modify. Although the relation between economic growth and environmental quality is not as straightforward as the proposition implies, it is difficult to escape the conclusion that a relation, however circuitous, exists. And so I want to begin with it.

Terms like "life-supporting" and "life-enhancing" are purposely vague, to allow for different interpretations. Deriving standards from them is a political exercise. I use "environment" in an inclusive sense, referring to the air we breathe, the water we drink, the recreational spaces we enjoy, the sense of security and tranquillity we experience in our daily life. Such an environment is either relatively healthful or harmful to health. Why, then, should we argue that a good and healthful environment requires a reduction in the long-term rate of regional economic growth?

Let me put the matter as simply as possible. The value of production can be translated into a measure of density (e.g., so many dollars per square kilometer). An increase in production will therefore increase the density of production within a given region. Proposition 1 declares that indicators of environmental quality are likely to decline with long-term increases in the density of regional production.

Like all statements of this sort, this one depends for its validity on "all other things being equal." There will be variations depending on local conditions, on the existing long-term rate of economic growth, on the sources of this growth (whether generated by different branches of manufacturing or office employment, for example), and on the actual location of the production facilities within the region. Also, indicators of environmental quality will respond differently to different measures of economic growth. But these are essentially refinements. The proposition relating growth in production to environmental quality would appear to hold in a general way.

This relationship has long been understood, of course. It is the main reason why zoning ordinances in the United States try to keep production out of residential, usually higher-income, areas. It is also the reason why, in rapidly growing regions, such as Los Angeles, the slow-growth movement has become the hottest political issue of the 1980s. The thrust of this movement is to slow down the rate of investment in production (and sometimes even residentiary construction) in neighborhoods and urban sectors that are especially threatened by the dysfunctional consequences of growth. Its object is to achieve what is called "planned growth."

Having said all this, I must now introduce an important qualification. Some metropolitan areas in aging industrial regions are, in fact, suffering from the reverse of the problem indicated: their environment is deteriorating as the density of production *declines*. This phenomenon, especially noticeable in cities of the northeastern United States, suggests that, relative to the quality of the environment, there may be a growth rate that is *optimal*. Proposition 1 must therefore be modified substantially. It holds only for those regions where the rates of capital accumulation and of growth *exceed* the optimum. Although the quantitative determination of a rate optimal in terms of environmental conditions may be difficult, we may assume it to be greater than zero and not greater than the region's capacity successfully to adjust to its growth. *Growth management thus becomes an important part of the equation.*

Proposition 2

A reduction in the rate of economic growth can be achieved in two ways: either by an equitable reduction of individual (household) consumption expenditures (meaning higher taxes for urban infrastructure and an improved environment) or by shifting the bulk of environmental costs, such as foul air, excessive noise, toxic wastes, deteriorating social infrastructure, and arduous commutes, to those parts of the population who, being poor, are least able to defend themselves.

Comment

Limited evidence suggests that it is largely the second alternative that is being chosen in American cities. Overall, metropolitan growth rates have been brought down from their high levels in the 1960s and early 1970s to the present slow-to-moderate rates, but in ways that are highly uneven. Although open unemployment is quite low in the United States at present, the average weekly wage has declined in real purchasing power, and more and more jobs are classified as requiring only unskilled or semi-skilled labor, commanding wages that are at and even below the official minimum. Professional work, on the other hand, has been reaping premium fees, and this new affluence of an upwardly mobile professional class has given rise to the social phenomenon of the so-called Yuppies (young urban professionals). Yuppies enjoy a growing percentage of an economic pie that, although no longer growing at the spectacular rates of 20 years ago, in overall terms scores very high rates in selected sectors of the emerging information society. What we are observing, then, is a gradual polarization of income classes, with the famous "middle class" uncertain of its future and poised on the edge of economic decline.

Now the newly affluent, constituting between 15 and 20 percent of metropolitan populations, are in fact able to buy themselves a more healthful environment (garden villas in privileged, protected suburbs, vacations in remote and unpolluted regions) and are also prepared to bring political pressure to bear on city authorities to slow down the rate of growth in certain neighborhoods, impose pollution fees, or shift new infrastructure investments (a solid-waste incineration plant, for example) into locations where they are least likely to interfere with their own sybarite pleasures.

Of course, "slow growth" policies and, more generally, environmental strategies of the sort described are often resisted by working class people and minorities and, from a Yuppie perspective, may not always be successfully implemented. This leads me to my third proposition.

Proposition 3

The alternatives I have described—equitable reduction in household consumption or uneven development favoring the new professional classes—are intensely political. A simple and straightforward application of technical norms is therefore unlikely to have the desired impact on the rate of economic growth and/or the distribution of environmental costs.

Comment

An interesting environmental politics is developing in the United States. On one hand, there are the Yuppie liberals with their concern—pitched in highly emotional language—for a more healthful environment largely for themselves. On the other hand, we find working class people, both white and minority, who are fighting for jobs (correctly seen as depending on continued high economic growth) in an "unholy" alliance with the capitalist class of developers and industrialists for whom dynamic growth translates into profits.

This class struggle setting is further complicated by three features specific to urban politics in the United States. To begin with, our metropolitan regions are divided into multiple government jurisdictions that, because they are jealous of their own autonomy, are reluctant to join in coordinating their efforts. Thus, growth might be kept out of one area but welcomed by a neighboring city that has much the same material (locational) advantages. But environmental degradation does not necessarily stop at the city line, and though the first area may have kept out "growth," it may not, in fact, have stopped pollution, which could spill across the municipal boundary into its own area. (There are other growth effects that spread throughout the urban field as a result of input-output linkages.)

A second feature unique to American city politics is that city politicians, though financially supported by upper income groups, especially the capitalist or business class, depend on the popular vote for their survival. The class struggle over the environment thus takes place on the terrain of the local state, and the outcome is not always a foregone conclusion.

Finally, because environmental improvements—such as rebuilding a sewage treatment system to accommodate growth, or constructing a rail rapid transit system to relieve congestion on freeways and surface streets—must be paid for out of the public purse, the well-off sectors of the population must agree to an increase in taxes and/or public indebtedness. And although they may be eager to enjoy the benefits of a healthful environment, they may not be prepared to pay for these improvements (via special assessments, increased property taxes, bond issues, etc.). The problem is, in part, individual mobility. Well-to-do households can move to new locations that offer a better quality of life *without* having to pay more taxes, at least in the short run. (This may help explain the enormous growth of suburban regions, such as Orange County, in southern California.)

In a situation so highly charged with class politics, it is impossible to remain neutral. And yet, at issue is the quality of the physical environment, which ideally is something to be enjoyed by all sectors of the population, rich and poor alike. If this much is granted, what are the implications for planning? This leads me to my fourth proposition.

Proposition 4

A form of planning that seeks to improve the quality of the environment for the whole population will become

COMMENTARY

increasingly politicized. No matter what position plan-
ners take in an argument concerning environmental
policy, they are certain to antagonize important segments
of the population. In their search for political support of
democratic policies capable of being carried out, plan-
ners will need to turn to those groups that are prepared
to support greater equity in the distribution of costs and
benefits from reduced household consumption. Politi-
cally, they will need to turn to the so-called New Left of
social movement activists.

Comment

What would this involve? To begin with, we must recognize that planners—American planners, at least—have
little if any political power in the conventional sense.
They do exercise administrative control over zoning, and
they can sometimes gain access to the public media. But
they are rarely able to "control" political outcomes. (I
am tempted to put this even more strongly. American
planners are *never* able to control political outcomes.)
But having acknowledged this, it remains to consider the
nature of the political game, which always involves some
sort of compromise or trade-off. In the fragmented urban
field of the large American city, environmental issues
cannot be dealt with as integrated wholes; they must be
attacked on a piecemeal, catch-as-catch-can basis. Issues
present themselves as locally differentiated, and even
though environmental effects may not be stopped by administrative boundaries, problems attendant to environmental quality, including the long-term goal of reducing
economic growth, require local citizen mobilizations.
It is at this level of local mobilization that planners
must aim.

The first and most important lesson to be drawn from
this analysis is that environmental planning (which involves questions not only of the physical environment
but also of investment and production, the quality of life,
and the distribution of costs and benefits among different
sectors of the population) *has to become decentered and*
prepared to enlist citizen power. Given the "unholy"
alliance between the working class and the capitalist class
in the sensitive question of growth versus the quality of
the environment, a "turn to the Left" fails to provide
clear-cut criteria of what to do. Working class demands
for more jobs and better pay are certainly legitimate, but
so is their claim—you might even call it a right—to a
healthful environment. But how to combine these two
"rights" in a situation that appears to be inherently contradictory?

The most obvious solution to this quandary is suggested
by the possibility of trade-offs between economic growth
(e.g., jobs) and collective facilities and services (such as
child-care centers, police protection, subsidized transit,
housing subsidies, community colleges) that would upgrade the quality of life in working class communities.
Such trade-offs are extremely difficult to achieve but are
often possible, especially when their costs can be shifted
"to the other side"—the capitalist class and the Yuppies.

Planning trade-offs may seem far away from environmental concerns, but they are in fact the most realistic
way to cut through the political entanglements of environmental alliances. However, we should note that such
trade-offs, to be politically effective, must be made at
extremely local levels *where their benefits can be inter-*
nalized by the relevant populations.

Decentering planning to the level of people's life
spaces, however, is not enough unless the relationship
between planners and citizens can also be restructured.
Planners enjoy official power and citizens enjoy citizen
power, which is basically the vote and the right to pe-
tition. This is an uneven relation that leaves planners
with trump cards in hand. Planners may not have much
power overall (especially when issues have become politicized); nevertheless, they are part of the state bureaucracy and carry their authority as emblem. Restructuring
the relation of planner to citizen means, therefore, to
mobilize citizen power around specific issues; *it means*
to encourage a process of citizen empowerment.

Planners, though they don't do so now, could play a
role in this movement of citizen empowerment. They
could, for example, provide funding to organized citizen
groups that engage in their own (counter) planning for
local improvements. They could engage in joint planning
exercises within the life space of local neighborhoods.
They could engage in environmental education and the
development of environmental information systems to
which citizens have easy access.

A revitalized neighborhood planning, however, which
is what both decentering and citizen empowerment implies, would need to be reintegrated into the daily urban
field that is the economic space on which people depend
for their livelihood. (In the United States, metropolitan-
wide planning used to be done through so-called councils
of government, but, with the loss of federal revenues for
urban programs, the institution has gone into precipitous
decline.)

Finally, social mobilization at local levels needs to be
backed by mobilization around policy issues that require
national and even international resolution. A global capitalism requires a global approach to the environmental
question.

Proposition 5

Counterpart to a decentered planning for an improved
environment is a strong central authority, powerful
enough to carry out equitable policies of redistribution.
Redistribution cannot be decentered. Only a central state
has the requisite policy instruments to ensure distributive
justice in environmental management.

Comment

In the eagerness to "decentralize" planning to neighborhood levels, the ancient principle of central redistribution must not be forgotten. Indeed, in the "rightist"

COMMENTARY

version of decentralization (known as the "new localism") redistribution is purposely left out of consideration in order to create the illusion that Left and Right have finally overcome their traditional antagonisms in a rediscovery of the consensual community. Much of the legitimacy of central authority derives, however, from the ability of central governments to redistribute the wealth of the "community" more equitably or at least to ensure that the basic needs of citizens are being met. Central government is indeed the only mechanism through which income redistribution and, therefore, social justice, become possible in complex class societies. (Wealth is another matter. Its redistribution may require revolutionary change.)

This much may be granted. But which central state has the power to intervene effectively in the distribution of income? Is it the municipality? Its financial resources are exceedingly limited. Is it the daily urban field? As a region, it lacks central authority. Is it the state (as in the state of California)? And, finally, is it perhaps the federal government? By a tradition that goes back to the American New Deal of the 1930s, it is the federal government that is charged with primary responsibility for ensuring social justice in America. But experience with the War Against Poverty in the 1960s showed that the federal government's ability to guide local developments in the interest of social justice is far from subtle. Even when federal assistance was channeled through so-called councils of government at the metropolitan level, most urban programs, when measured by their intentions, turned out to be sorry failures. As someone aptly described the effect, when it comes to acting locally, the federal government is like a bulldozer.

But perhaps my question is misguided and the search for an appropriate central state is less important than a search for a new politics of redistribution, implying political mobilization at all levels, from urban neighborhoods to the national (and even international) arena. Redistribution used to be thought of as a result of class politics, and so it is. But it is also something more, since the place of redistribution has shifted from the workplace, the traditional site of class struggle, to the neighborhoods and life spaces of large, multi-ethnic urban regions. Here there are additional concerns besides merely wages and conditions of work, and there are other actors. Women play a major role in community organization. Different ethnic groups have different political agendas. Questions of social reproduction loom larger in the neighborhood than in the working class politics of the past. Environmental activists are writing a new political agenda.

The process of citizen empowerment, which is necessary for improving the quality of the environment, and in which planners have a significant part, can lead—though it may not—to a process of social learning that will, over time, create the basis for a new politics of redistribution, because the question of redistribution is fundamental to a working out of environmental agendas.

And so I come to my final proposition.

Proposition 6

The preceding propositions point to far-reaching implications for the education of planners and, more specifically, environmental planners.

Comment

Traditional planning education stressed—perhaps I should say, still stresses—planners' technical expertise. Planning is understood primarily as a technical function auxiliary to politics; it is this that has ensured its legitimacy as a profession. (Some planners still fancy themselves as standing *above* politics; but that is another matter.) The kind of planning for a healthful environment that has been the subject of this discussion is inherently a political form of planning. Rather than being viewed as a technical appendix to politics, planning and specifically planning for the environment must be conceived to its very core as an activity in which expertise and politics are linked.

Given this new understanding of planning, what shall we say then of its praxis? A three-fold division suggests itself. The praxis of planning divides into *technical, moral,* and *utopian* dimensions. The first dimension answers to the question of how we can best achieve the ends we seek. The second answers to the question of how we shall live with one another. It is fundamentally a question of social and environmental ethics. And the third addresses the long-term future and our vision of what life for all of us might be like. It is what inspires us beyond the mundane affairs of politics. Utopian visions enshrine our hopes.

Once we accept this three-fold division of the praxis of planning, where the moral dimension is clearly the most salient, but where all dimensions must work in concert, a different education from that to which we have become accustomed suggests itself.

New concepts and new meanings must be explored. These include life space, citizen power, joint and counterplanning, environmental education, social learning, redistributive justice in relation to the environment, the politics of redistribution, and mediation and negotiation processes. An environmental planning understood as a dynamic social and political process must come to rest on an ideological—or, if you will, philosophical—foundation. Lacking such a foundation, planners' praxis will teeter from one pragmatic issue to another, like a rudderless ship. An appropriate ideology—which is still far from having been worked out in the United States, though the West German Greens seem to come a bit closer to what's required—would need to address such questions as the global economy, participatory democracy, basic human rights, the relations of rich countries to poor, relations between humans and the natural environment, obligations toward future generations, the importance of meaningful work, collective self-empowerment and social movements, and the role of the state. It is a large and ambitious agenda that is almost certainly going to preoc-

COMMENTARY

cupy us in the decades ahead. Planners must learn to address these issues.

In its broadest terms, planning may be seen as an education for public life. But because public life in our time lies largely in shambles, we must not only educate for public life (open to all citizens and requiring global responsibilities) but also work toward a reconstruction of the very meaning of what is public. This may well be done in contexts other than planning itself. But it is also a responsibility of planners who necessarily work in the public domain. We need urgently to address the question of a public philosophy.

AUTHOR'S NOTE

This commentary was presented as a talk at the Second International Congress of the Association of European Schools of Planning (AESOP), University of Dortmund, Germany, November 10–12, 1988.

Friedmann is professor of urban planning at the University of California, Los Angeles. His most recent book is *Life Space and Economic Space: Essays in Third World Planning* (Transaction 1988). He received the Distinguished Educator Award from the AICP in 1988.

Growth Management from an Economist's Perspective

Benjamin Chinitz

Let's begin looking at John Friedmann's six propositions with the fundamental premise that, in common circumstances, rapid long-term economic growth in metropolitan regions can be achieved only at the cost of environmental quality. I accept Friedmann's all-inclusive definition of *environment* as appropriate to the argument. But what does he mean by economic growth?

"There he goes again . . . ," the *JAPA* reader may be thinking; the economist going after the planner for taking liberties with a sacred economic concept. I plead guilty, and I have to do it.

Friedmann tips his hand in Proposition 1 by equating

growth with capital accumulation. That is only one source of economic growth. There are at least two other major sources of growth. One is "labor accumulation"—the growth of the labor force in sheer numbers and "quality." A second is the famous "residual" in the growth equation. This is generally assumed to reflect technological progress that increases total factor productivity, namely, the output a given quantity of capital and labor will produce.

Does Friedmann want to ignore economic growth that results from the growth of the labor force and technological progress? Surely, labor force growth, typically accompanied by or resulting from population growth, is a major threat to environmental quality.

Let me rephrase the question. Is it aggregate growth (the metro GNP) that threatens environmental quality or is it (also) growth per capita?

Ultimately, Friedmann allows for both when he speaks of density of production, which he defines as "so many dollars per square kilometer." But this does not totally dispel the ambiguity and the confusion. I would offer the proposition that the malaise about growth is caused by both kinds of growth: too many people and/or too much money generate too much congestion, too much pollution, and so forth. If we were to freeze per capita income in California we would still "worry" about the prospect of adding another 5 million people to the state by the year 2000. In Massachusetts, with a relatively stable population, we worry about the negative environmental effects of rapidly rising incomes.

Nevertheless, from the perspectives of both the politics and economics of growth management, these are radically different situations.

Friedmann, himself, hints at other problems with Proposition 1 with his various qualifications to the general theorem. One crucial issue he does not deal with is geographic size. The focus on "density" suggests fixed boundaries. But economic growth in metropolitan regions is almost always accompanied by spatial expansion. When he speaks of "optimal" rates of growth, is he also thinking of optimal city size. Or is the optimal rate of growth a function of the size of the region?

Despite all these qualms (some would say quibbles) I firmly believe that Friedmann's Proposition 1 retains its fundamental validity and serves well (as amended) as a point of departure for the rest of the argument.

Now, let us turn our attention to Proposition 2, which is absolutely central and crucial to Friedmann's major message.

Again we need to raise basic questions and clarify ambiguities.

Friedmann first equates a retardation of economic growth with a decline in per capita consumption expenditures induced by higher taxes devoted to public spending on infrastructure and other environmental protection investments. Here is where Friedmann's treatment of the concept of economic growth gets him into serious trouble to the point of contradicting and undermining Proposition 1.

While we tend to relate or even equate the standard of living (as measured by consumption expenditures) to rates of economic growth, the two are not equivalent. When we go to war and devote 50 percent or more of the GNP to military purposes, our standard of living, as signified by goods and services available for private consumption, may stagnate or decline while the rate of economic growth as measured by the GNP accelerates.

Friedmann is defining a change in the composition of the product—less private, and more public—as a retardation of the rate of economic growth. Moreover, he is suggesting the kind of change in product mix that could be viewed as a growth management strategy—that is, maintain growth, depress consumption, invest in infrastructure. A reduction in consumption will help in two ways. It will reduce shopping traffic, the generation of garbage, and other environmental negatives. It will also release the resources required to invest in infrastructure and other means to protect the quality of life.

(An important caveat: the economic activity associated with these beneficial investments is itself a source of concern in relation to environmental quality. Take, for example, the horrifying prospect in Boston of ten years of construction of the depressed central artery, the third harbor tunnel, and the waste treatment plants in the harbor.)

The second part of Proposition 2 is also troublesome. We do not achieve "[a] reduction in the rate of economic growth" by "shifting the bulk of environmental costs . . . to those parts of the population who, being poor, are least able to defend themselves."

Just as the rate of economic growth is not defined by the rate of growth of private consumption, so is it unrelated to issues of equity—namely, the distribution of benefits and costs. Growth management by and for the wealthy, which preserves their affluence while protecting them against environmental degradation, is not what I look for in public policy addressed to growth, but I would not and cannot describe that policy as one way of reducing economic growth.

I have no problem with Friedmann's Propositions 3 through 6, as long as we are clear that we are not talking about alternative strategies for reducing the rate of economic growth. There is no doubt that, if planners are to be effective participants in the growth management process, their training must embrace the art of politics along with the relevant sciences and technologies. That conclusion is independent of the definition of the goals, on which Friedmann and I seem to have some differing views.

Chinitz, an urban economist, completed his doctoral work at Harvard in 1956. As professor, author, consultant, and public servant, he has focused his attention on the factors that produce growth or decline in urban areas and regions, and the role of public policy and local initiatives in affecting these trends. In September 1987, Chinitz was appointed director of research at the Lincoln Institute of Land Policy in Cambridge, Massachusetts.

The Environment as Common Ground
Learning from Practice

Hilda Blanco and Michael Neuman

We welcome John Friedmann's theoretical insights on planning, politics, and the environment, and we agree with many of his theses—the importance of the new wave of growth management, the salience of issues of fairness, the idea that planning is an inherently political enterprise. Our experience in developing New Jersey's state-wide growth management plan has focused many of these issues for us, and has thrown into question some of the assumptions and dichotomies upon which Friedmann relies.

Proposition 1

On the inverse relationship between environmental quality and economic growth. This seems a self-evident proposition, if we assume that there is no alternative to our economic system under which environmental impacts are treated as externalities. In a system that fosters sustainable production and distribution processes—the direction in which our societies must turn if we are to survive as a species—this proposition would not hold. Although we are far from being a sustainable society, leading development trends recognize the value of environmental quality for economic growth. For example, the services and information sectors seek out locations with high quality environments.

Proposition 2

On the inverse relation between investment in infrastructure and the environment and a reduction in consumption and economic growth. Friedmann assumes that taxes will finance infrastructural and environmental improvements. While this assumption reflects the status quo, there are at least two alternatives. The first is an array of exaction techniques that aim to apportion the costs of growth equitably between the public and the agents of growth. The second alternative is the practice of enlightened self-interest. As we learn to accept that over the long run it is cheaper and more healthful to use sustainable economies, we will wean ourselves away

COMMENTARY

from short-term, profit-maximizing economies and their inevitable, and high, external environmental costs.

Proposition 3

On the prominence of political and equity issues in growth management. We agree with Friedmann here. Political and equity issues are of paramount importance in growth management. However, environmental quality has deteriorated to the point that it affects nearly everyone. Reviving the old environmentalists-versus-working-class debate is no longer pertinent. It is the broad middle and working classes that are caught in the daily traffic congestion in urban and suburban roads, and that feel the pinch of skyrocketing municipal services. In New Jersey, it is not the "New Left," but broad-based groups, such as the League of Women Voters, New Jersey Future, New Jersey Business and Industry Association, and numerous environmental groups that are proponents of the state planning process. The challenge to planners is to balance the varied claims of the public interest and at the same time to protect effectively our land, water, and air for future generations. This balancing suggests a new role for planners as mediators of the public interest. In New Jersey the state planning process calls for extensive public dialogue involving all levels of government and all private interests. One estimate suggests that 100,000 persons may participate directly in this undertaking. The Preliminary State Plan serves as a "single-text negotiating" document on which all discussion is focused. State planners assume roles of process facilitators, advancing the multi-interest debate.

In New Jersey equity issues have surfaced in at least three important ways: (1) in the competing claims for public investment from the older industrial cities and their surrounding suburbs and the newly developing suburban and rural areas; (2) in the affordable housing area; and (3) in the controversy generated by the strategy to limit development in some areas and concentrate it in others. Our experience thus far shows that the choices are not clear-cut. The stereotyped opposites of "cities and suburbs" and "poor and affluent" serve large-scale planning poorly, if at all. Instead, a responsible planning strategy must efficiently utilize and build upon existing resources and settlement patterns, simultaneously preserving environmental resources for the future. At the same time, it must distribute equitably the benefits and costs of growth, both geographically and demographically.

Overall, these goals called for a differentiated development strategy, one that concentrates public investment in central places throughout the state. This approach ensures economies of scale in infrastructure provision, and conserves undeveloped lands. Part of the strategy is also aimed at achieving a better geographic balance of jobs and housing and at providing a mix of housing types, to remedy the current mismatch of jobs and housing in many parts of the state and to increase the supply of affordable housing throughout the state. These central places include the older urban centers, new centers along major transportation corridors, and smaller-scale towns, villages, and hamlets.

This overall strategy to organize development into communities of place of different scales and character also posed another equity issue. What about the property owners, including struggling farmers, in those areas of the state that the state plan indicates should be sparsely developed? Should the plan make some provision for mitigating the loss in value of their property? On the reverse side of the coin, how should the windfalls of those property owners in areas designated as growth centers be addressed? As a result of the state planning process, an emerging consensus is advocating a statewide transfer-of-development-rights program whereby developers of new communities would buy development rights from the landowners in those areas where development rights are limited.

Propositions 4, 5, and 6

On centralization versus decentralization of planning and the redistribution of resources. Environmental issues in planning cannot be dealt with adequately on an exclusively centralized or decentralized basis. The New Jersey experience has taught us that the challenge facing planners is the design of intergovernmental systems where each level of government exercises its significant and appropriate functions, and where all levels of government cooperate to mutually strengthen their individual roles. Friedmann advocates the strategy of the New Left, which calls for decentralizing planning to extremely local levels. But the cumulative impacts of growth and development that we are beginning to experience—acid rain, the greenhouse effect, ozone depletion, deforestation, traffic jams, and water pollution—are all results of decentralized decisions. What guarantee is there that local communities will be less parochial in pursuing their narrow self-interest than the private sector has been? On the contrary, there is ample evidence that local municipalities cannot adequately deal with undesirable land uses (witness the NIMBY syndrome) and with environmental impacts of greater than local significance. State planning efforts in the past two decades have been motivated by the recognition of this fact.

Environmental problems require a sophisticated integrated response that involves both centralized and decentralized functions. Friedmann notes that a strong central authority is needed to redistribute resources. He notes the failure of the federal government and of councils of government to carry out this function. But he bypasses the potential role of states in both planning and redistribution.

In particular, on the issue of planning, the New Jersey experience provides a new model. New Jersey, through its planning process, is evolving a sophisticated system whereby the state provides leadership through its growth management plan, as well as financial and technical sup-

COMMENTARY

port to implement it. Hence, the state plan sets the framework for regional and local planning. Regional planning, dealing as it does with interjurisdictional concerns, requires a state framework that recognizes and empowers such planning. One of the major thrusts of the New Jersey Plan is thus to strengthen the planning capability of county governments, as the prime administrators of regional planning, as well as to enable the establishment of other interjurisdictional regional entities as required for planning purposes. Finally, local planning in this system retains its jurisdiction over those development issues that have no significant regional impacts.

The centerpiece of this intergovernmental system of planning is an educational and political process of coordination and accommodation called "cross-acceptance." Cross-acceptance involves state agencies, counties, and municipalities in a process of comparing and negotiating their policies and regulations in an effort to achieve consistency and compatibility. Cross-acceptance ensures give and take among all participants. The final state plan will reflect the input that municipalities and counties offer in cross-acceptance.

We agree with Friedmann that planning is an inherently political enterprise. But the old class divisions and special interests that still dominate political discourse do not do justice to the environmental problems that confront our societies. The erosion of environmental quality affects the housewife and the commuter, the poor and the affluent, the developer, the businessman, the cities, the suburbs, and the rural areas. The challenge for planning in our day is to capitalize on these common problems in designing educational and collaborative processes that provide meaningful participation truly empowering people by enabling them to deal effectively with common problems and concerns. By uncovering this common ground of environmental concerns, we will be taking a step toward revitalizing our public domain.

Blanco is an assistant professor in the Department of Urban Affairs and Planning at Hunter College. She earned her doctorate in city and regional planning from the University of California, Berkeley, and was formerly with the New Jersey Office of State Planning. Neuman, AICP, is a coastal planning manager with the New Jersey Office of State Planning. He earned his master's degree in city and regional planning at the University of Pennsylvania.

[19]

The metabolism of cities

Herbert Girardet

In this Chapter, Herbert Girardet adopts a global view of the future of the city, examining the demands which cities place upon soil fertility and other natural resources and their environmental outputs in the form of solid wastes and air pollutants. He shows that the linear processes by which cities transform environmental resources into waste products is disruptive of the planet's life support systems. As such, a new approach is urgently needed to reorganize the metabolism of cities so that it is more 'circular' and recycles resources to maintain an ecological balance. Girardet lists some of the practical measures which will need to be adopted internationally but should particularly be adopted in the more affluent nations which both cause much of the problem and have the resources to deal with it.

Herbert Girardet graduated from the London School of Economics with a degree in social anthropology. Since 1976 he has specialized in cultural ecology and has written many articles on the human impact on this planet. He has appeared in numerous radio and TV broadcasts in Britain and West Germany. He organized and researched 'Far From Paradise', a seven-part BBC TV series concerned with the history of human impact and the present state of our planet. He co-authored the book of the series. In 1987 he wrote Blueprint for a Green Planet, *with John Seymour, and was consultant on programmes based on the book which were produced for television. He is currently producing 'Jungle Pharmacy' for Central TV and has been commissioned to write a book,* Closing the Circle, *on the long-term ecological consequences of industrial processes.*

Ancient Rome, at the height of its power, obtained much of the grain needed to feed its citizens from North Africa. Its freight ships crisscrossed the Mediterranean laden with the produce of its colonies. As its own land grew tired, and ever more farmers were turned into soldiers, the insatiable appetite of the metropolis could be met only with foodstuffs grown, or robbed, further and further afield.

The metabolism of cities

The role of North Africa as the bread-basket of Rome had profound ecological consequences:

1) As forests were turned into farmland a massive loss of wildlife habitat occurred.

2) Large-scale deforestation resulted in soil erosion and moisture loss from the environment which is still felt today.

3) The export of wheat and other foodstuffs was also an export of soil nutrients, never to be returned. Thus the soil fertility of much of North Africa was shoved through the stomachs of the Romans into the Mediterranean.

Rome, before its decline, reached a population of about 1 million people. At that time it was, by far, the largest – and most powerful – city in the world. Today, just under 2,000 years later, nearly half the world's 5 billion people live in cities; never has urban growth been as rapid as it is today. Everywhere small farmers are leaving – or are forced to leave – the land. Usually relatively self-reliant peasants or herdsmen with a self-interest in caring for the land that feeds them are turned into consumers of cash-crops, as they adopt – or are forced to adopt – their new urban life-style.

We all need food every day, but every meal represents an export of plant nutrients from the land where it was grown, never to be returned. And where does the precious waste end up? Well, in the sea, eventually. This one-way traffic in soil fertility, first practised by the Romans, has now reached global proportions.

In the nineteenth century, when a new world metropolis, London, grew by leaps and bounds, its 'sewage problem' was solved by building an extensive drainage system. The motto was: out of sight, out of mind. As in Rome, the sewage was disposed of into the sea, and not returned to the land. In order to keep Britain's farm land fertile, guano (bird droppings) were shipped over the Atlantic from Chile.

When the guano ran out, scientists came up with artificial fertilizers. Never mind the sewage, they said, we have mineral fertilizers – nitrate, phosphate, potash – in bags. The victory of these mineral fertilizers was overwhelming and, thus, sewage systems in cities all over the world continue being constructed as disposal rather than as recycling systems. Disposal, not recovery, continues to be the brief of most sewage engineers. Thus, much of the fertility of the world's farmland that feeds the teeming billions in the cities ends up in rivers, and finally, in the sea.

Liquid wastes

Because sewage is considered a nuisance, not an asset, it may as well be mixed with whatever else needs to be flushed out – cleaning fluids, disinfectants, chlorinated hydrocarbons, heavy metals, an all the other

Herbert Girardet

poisons we now routinely discharge from our households and factories. The Romans didn't do *that,* but we do, and we hardly bat an eyelid. Add a few million gallons of oil every year and you end up with the kind of potent brew that fish now have to cope with in coastal waters world-wide. And, of course, add fertilizers – nitrate, phosphate, potash – from farmland, half of which are not absorbed by the food plants but leached into the ground-water and, eventually, washed out into the sea. And add slurry from our factory farms, much of it originally imported as animal feed from distant lands, and you have another one-way transport of plant nutrients from the farmland to the sea.

In the 1960s and 1970s there was growing concern about the eutrophication of *lakes* in heavily urbanized regions of Europe and North America: that is, loss of oxygen in the surface waters as a result of overfeeding with plant nutrients from sewage, fertilizers and slurry. Lake Erie, in particular, made the headlines. The problems have not really gone away, though some lakes have been improved by the installation of sophisticated sewage works or, even, by pumping oxygen into the water at great expense.

In the 1980s there is growing concern about *costal waters.* The landlocked seas, in particular, such as the Baltic and the Adriatic, are a real worry. Next on the list is the North Sea where eutrophication now occurs every summer in places like the German Byte. Rivers like the Rhine, the Thames, the Elbe, and the Wester all carry huge quantities of plant nutrients with them. (The Rhine alone transports enough nitrates every year potentially to meet the requirements of the whole of Dutch agriculture.) The over-supply of plant nutrients causes the excessive growth of algae and plankton. They are a sort of poisoned bait to the fish because of the ever more varied cocktail of toxins with which they are laced. These are heavily implicated in the rapid increase in fish diseases, notably ulcers and cancers, that have been observed in coastal waters in recent years.

Modern urban metabolism

Contemporary cities have a much more complex metabolism than their ancient predecessors like Babylon, Carthage, Athens or, indeed, Rome. Their impact was largely confined to forests (extraction of timber and firewood), soil (removal of nutrients, erosion, and salination) and water (long range aquaducts, sewage disposal). The archaeologists who excavated these ancient cities did not find any plastics, toxic waste or, indeed, radioactive substances in the rubbish dumps they examined!

In contrast, every inhabitant of a modern western country (typical level of urbanization being 80 to 90 per cent) generates around 2 tons of rubbish per year: 1 ton of domestic refuse and 1 ton of factory waste

172

The metabolism of cities

from the industrial products we all purchase. Future archaeologists investigating the waste dumps of late twentieth-century cities will be astounded at the sheer volume of artefacts, as well as the bizarre mixture of materials, that we saw fit to use and, indeed, to dispose of.

Urban and industrial rubbish dumps piled up over recent decades pose an environmental hazard whose scale is, as yet, inadequately understood. It is becoming quite apparent now that 'ordinary' domestic rubbish is far from harmless. The problems range from seepage of potentially toxic liquids like disinfectants, wood preservatives, cleaning fluids, used motor oil and medicines left in part-filled containers, to corrosion of discarded batteries and the accidental incineration of plastics. Waste dumps invariably give off toxic fumes as they catch fire, which they often do.

Factory wastes, an essential ingredient of our consumer way of life, are often deposited in the same dump as household rubbish and greatly add to its pollution potential. In one area of the USA alone, in New Jersey, where the problem of waste dumps has been investigated quite thoroughly, hundreds of mixed waste dumps have been found to leach all manner of potent poisons into the groundwater. In West Germany similar problems have now been unearthed in many places. In Hamburg the notorious Georgswerder dump leaked a great variety of pesticide residues, heavy metals, solvents, and other toxic factory wastes and is having to be sealed at huge expense.

The Age of Fire

Air pollution, too, is predominantly a problem of modern urban/industrial society. Coal mining, when it got into full swing in Britain, and then in Germany, in the nineteenth century, made available unprecedented amounts of carbon coumpounds for the purposes of combustion. As fire was tamed into motion power it came to replace muscle power in most of its 'heavy duty' applications – traction, transport, farming, and factory production.

Probably the most significant environmental impact of urban/industrial civilization is the large-scale transfer of carbon from geological deposits into the atmosphere, in the form of carbon dioxide. In the last 100 years the CO_2 content of the atmosphere has increased from 265 to 345 ppm, or by 30 per cent. It is going up by 1.5 parts per million every year. That doesn't sound so much, but few atmospheric scientists now doubt the reality of the greenhouse effect and expect dramatic environmental consequences in the next century. At the present time, however, it is the other by-products of combustion which are the most immediate cause for concern, notably sulphur and nitrogen oxides.

Since the early 1980s it has becoming increasingly clear that air pollution is by no means a problem of the past, as had been assumed

Herbert Girardet

when the worst city smogs had been tackled after the introduction of the 'clean air acts' in Britain and elsewhere in Europe and America. The combination of the use of smokeless coal by urban households and the construction of new power stations with tall stacks fitted with dust filters was thought to be the solution to the air-pollution problems of the industrialzed countries. But not so.

By the early 1980s the horror stories of dying trees in Germany and Czechoslovakia were beginning to hit the headlines of the international press. Since then, most European countries have reported serious damage to forests, with the statistics showing a further decline every year. Most countries in central Europe concluded by the end of 1987 that over 50 per cent of their trees were sick, or indeed, dying. Virtually everywhere, with the exception of Britain, air pollution is considered as the primary cause of forest decline.

Sulphur dioxide from power station and factory chimneys, as well as nitrogen oxides from these chimneys and from car exhaust pipes, are overwhelmingly implicated as the main culprits. In addition, some 3,000 'new', man-made, gases in trace quantities add to the cocktail of pollutants which is now permanently present in the air we all breathe. All living beings in the Northern hemisphere are now exposed to these to varying degrees.

The new gases range from seemingly harmless and stable compounds to highly phytotoxic chlorinated hydrocarbons. There is growing concern about the synergistic effect of these new substances reacting with each other under varying climatic conditions. Throughout the industrialized world millions of dollars are now spent on experimental research to try to understand the chemistry of trace gases, their reaction with each other, their persistence in the atmosphere, and their impact on the sensitive tissues of living matter.

It is becoming increasingly clear that it is not just trees that are affected by air pollution but that crops are damaged too. For instance, research in Switzerland has shown that low level ozone, generated by reactions between nitrogen oxides, hydrocarbons, and oxygen in the presence of sunlight, causes a reduction in crop yields of up to 10 per cent. Of course, there is no doubt now that ozone is also a major culprit in forest decline.

The beneficial layer of ozone right at the top of the atmosphere, on the other hand, which protects the Earth from excessive exposure to ultraviolet light, is being corroded by another group of man-made gases – CFCs or chlorinated fluoro-carbons – which are still widely used as propellants in spray cans, as foaming agents in polyurethane foams and as coolants in fridges, freezers, and air conditioners. All of these are ingredients of the urban, convenience oriented, life-style that we have come to take for granted.

The metabolism of cities

Third World cities

The phenomenal growth of Third World cities in recent years has led to a pattern of environmental damage similar to that experienced in the industrialized northern hemisphere. This applies to all the types of impact already mentioned in this chapter.

Deforestation in the south is preceding at an unprecedented speed. Tropical forests in Asia, South America, and Africa are under enormous pressure as a result of growing demand for farm land and land for cattle ranching, space for new open-cast mines, and for gigantic hydro-electric schemes to supply the new industries and the expanding cities with electricity.

The Third World countries continue to supply the consumers in the cities of the industrialized nations with raw materials – including timber, ores, oil, and coal. The pressure on their fragile environments as a result of their own urbanization is thus even more dramatic. Tropical forests are now shrinking at a – literally – breathtaking rate with, as yet, uncalculable consequences for the world's climate. Genetic depletion, too, has reached unprecedented levels – with insects, plants, and mammals, never investigated by science, disappearing as the forests go up in smoke or succumb to the chain-saw. And with the forests go the forest cultures: the intricate knowledge of the forest habitat accumulated by jungle dwellers over millennia of experimentation with food and medicinal plants being lost as rapidly as the forests themselves.

The one-way traffic of plant nutrients from rural areas to the new mega-cities like Calcutta, Seoul, Singapore, Mexico City, São Paulo, or Lagos is causing a severe depletion of soil fertility. Ranches established on the thin tropical forest soils of Amazonia, Central America or South East Asia tend to lose their viability within 10 years or so. Soil temperatures rise as the protective forest cover is removed, soil erosion is vastly increased by the same process, and the depletion of plant nutrients (particularly phosphates) as a result of the export of animal carcasses to urban markets, causes a permanent loss of soil productivity.

The coastal waters of Third World countries with rampant urban growth a now visibly laden with soil as a result of inland deforestation. In addition, they are increasingly polluted with both sewage and household/industrial chemicals. Since sophisticated sewage works which can cope with all types of water pollutants are very expensive indeed, it is likely to take a long time before these environmental problems now afflicting Third World cities are likely to be tackled.

However, the very poverty of Third World cities tends to result in a

Herbert Girardet

much more frugal use of non-renewable resources. Recycling of metals, paper, and plastics by the poorest of the poor on rubbish tips is a well-established procedure in cities as far apart as Cairo, Calcutta, or Rio de Janeiro. It is unfortunate that sheer poverty, rather than deliberate environmental policy, is presently the main incentive to this husbanding of resources.

The traffic explosion of cities world-wide is, of course, the major reason for unprecedented air pollution problems. Whilst these have been tackled to some extent by cities in rich countries like the USA and Japan, Third World countries simply cannot afford to curb emissions. The permanent smog over Mexico City with its population of now well over 20 million is a case is point. The chronic bronchial problems of a large proportion of its population are a notorious reality.

Closing the circle

The metabolism of modern cities as manifested at present – their throughput of food stuffs, forest products, fossil fuels and mineral resources – is demonstrably disruptive of the planet's life support systems.

The evidence for this statement is now readily available. Nevertheless, global urbanization is, if anything, accelerating. Industrial development and output growth is continuing apace. Less environmentally damaging cultures whose life-styles are based on long-term sustainable use of renewable resources are everywhere under attack. This applies to tribal groups of hunter-gatherers as well as to pastoral nomads and small-scale farmers world-wide. Urbanization in conjunction with the industrialization of agriculture for urban markets are the prime cause.

But, fortunately, growing minorities of city dwellers – even in the Third World – are becoming aware of the boomerang effect of unchecked urban-industrial growth. Self-interest is, obviously, a powerful motivating force for change and, as it is becoming apparent that we are on a collision course with all the life-support systems of this, our home planet, it is clear that all our futures are also at stake. The process of urbanization is likely to continue but how can its profound environmental destructiveness be reversed? If we can find answers to this question we shall be on the right track.

The most profound problem we are up against lies in the linearity of the development process we are engaged in. Nutrients are taken from the land as food is grown, never to be returned. Timber is felled for building materials or pulp and all too often forests are not replenished. Raw materials are extracted, processed, and combined into consumer goods that end up as rubbish which can not be beneficially rearbsorbed

The metabolism of cities

into living nature. Fossil fuels in unprecedented quantities are minded or pumped out from rock strata; they are refined and burned and thus released into the atmosphere. All in all, our present urban-industrial civilization is vastly accelerating the process of *entropy* with, as yet, hardly imagined consequences for the future of life on earth.

To undo the damage already done, and, indeed, to prevent further ravages, a great leap of the imagination, a profound act of collective will-power is called for. Of course, the ecology movement has drawn our attention to the issues at stake for some time now and nobody can claim that 'we didn't know'.

Cities are for people – or supposed to be – and all of us have to realize that our future, or, more precisely, that of our children, is at stake. To make the cities (our homes) ecologically viable must thus become our utmost priority. All living beings are profoundly concerned about the future of their own offspring and act accordingly: except, it seems, us – urban man and woman.

It is true that there has been growing concern about the physical fabric and appearance of cities in recent years. The slogan of the 'greening of the cities' has been catching on, but all too often it has mainly meant creating more green spaces and planting more trees just to improve the look of the place. It is, of course, crucially important to create a pleasant, greener urban environment for people to live in. But surely that can only be a start. Much more profound changes in the urban metabolism are required in order to make them ecologically viable, not just environmentally pleasant.

It will be crucially important to reorganize the whole metabolism of cities, the throughput of raw materials, energy, consumer goods, and the generation and treatment of waste from the perspective of long-term ecological viability. We simply cannot afford to continue with a pattern of input and output which makes the routine production of poisonous, life-damaging wastes a 'normal' activity.

This is not the place to go into great technical or organizational detail as regards the reorganization of the urban metabolism. I have attempted some of that in another book.[1] However, it may be useful to end this section by indicating in diagrammatic form how the 'urban metabolism' behaves at present and what a profound re-organization, according to ecological criteria, might seek to achieve (see Fig. 8.1).

The *'linear'* model of production, consumption and disposal, according to which our cities function at present, is not in the least concerned with the ecological viability of cities. Input and output are considered as unrelated. Food, fuels, construction materials, forest products and processed goods come from somewhere, never mind where, and when we are finished with them they are discarded never mind how. This system is profoundly different to nature's own circular

Herbert Girardet

metabolism. In nature every output is also an input which renews, and thus sustains, life. The urban metabolism is its present form, on the other hand, being linear in character, is profoundly disruptive of natural cycles. It thus accelerates entropy and undermines the dynamic balance of life on earth. As we are approaching the urbanization of the majority of the world population, this trend has massive implications for the well-being of the world's forests, soils, water courses, oceans, and for the composition of the very air we breathe.

Figure 8.1 Present (linear) and future (circular) urban metabolism

(a) *Present linear urban metbolism*

Input		Output
Food Fuels/energy Processed goods Timber/paper Building materials	→ City →	Sewage Exhaust gases Household/factory wastes (liquid and solid) Wanton disposal

(b) *Future circular urban metabolism*

Input		Output
Food production →	City	← Processed goods
Fertility returned ← (sewage recycling)		→ Recycled materials (minimized pollution)
Clean energy → (minimal use)		← Timber/pulp from sustainable forests
Production of gypsum ← by sulphur scrubbers, used in construction		→ Large-scale tree planting for uptake of surplus CO_2

Housing stock (use of lasting, sustainable building materials)

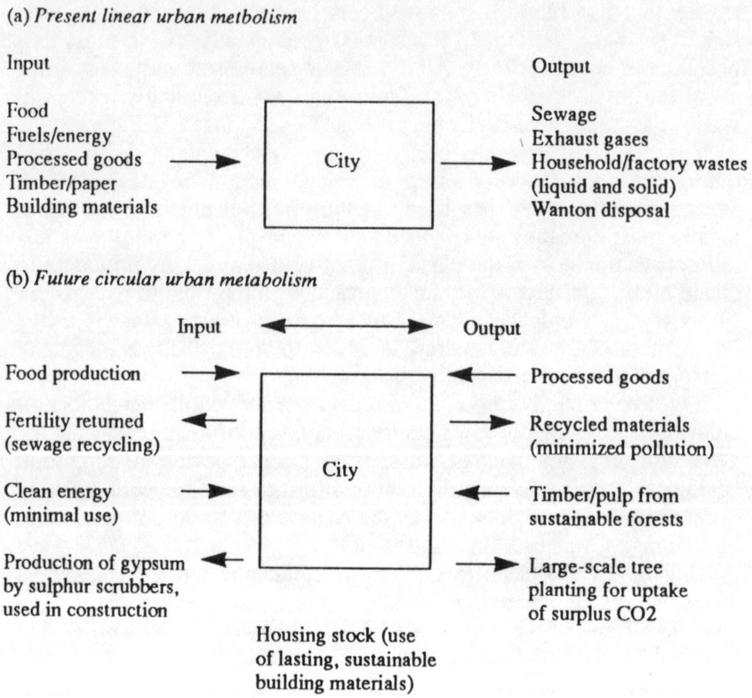

Worldwide urbanization can be ecologically viable only if the urban metabolism is designed to be essentially 'circular', (i.e. if it is assured that every output can also be an input). Sewage systems would have to cease being simply disposal systems for that noxious mixture of household and factory wastes. Sewage works would have to be designed to function as fertilizer factories rather than as disposal systems for unwanted, and often toxic, discharges. Liquid chemical wastes from factories would have to be intercepted, rather than released in the somewhat uncontrolled way which

The metabolism of cities

is common practice at present. Sooner, rather than later, the routine use of highly toxic materials in factory production would have to be examined.

Household and factory rubbish would have to be regarded as an asset rather than a nuisance. Detailed studies have shown that up to 80 per cent of the rubbish we discard at present could be re-cycled back into useful products. In this and other respects the poor people of the new, giant cities of the Third World have a great deal to teach us. But in the rich countries it is considered by urban authorities not to be economically viable to re-cycle more than a small proportion of our waste. But it is becoming all too clear now that ecological viability is a far more important criterion, as pollution problems are taking on increasingly unmanageable proportions.

The vast energy input required by conurbations is another case in point. It is only too evident now that the generation of CO_2, SO_2, NO_x and hydrocarbons by power stations, factories, household, and vehicles has reached totally unacceptable levels. Energy efficiency and, indeed, the avoidance of energy use must now be considered as policy priorities if further environmental damage by air pollution is to be avoided. This is becoming a particularly pressing issue as Third World coutries are beginning to plan for similar levels of energy use as the rich countries.

Technology to improve energy efficiency has made great strides in recent years. The same goes for 'clean energy technology'. Sulphur rich fumes, for instance, can now be cleaned by scrubbers fitted to power stations. The gypsum produced by injecting lime into the stream of flue gases is, potentially, a most useful building material.

The massive release of CO_2 into the atmosphere as a by-product of combustion can ultimately be absorbed only by tree planting on a huge scale on the barren lands of the earth which have expanded with the growth of cities worldwide. Today we are causing desertification on an unprecedented scale. Who is it who said that deserts are the footsteps of man on earth. Those of urban man in the late twentieth century are vastly larger than those of any of our predecessors. Are we prepared to reforest large parts of the earth and thus to contain deserts while tackling the CO_2 problem we have created at the same time?

If we want to enjoy the benefits of urban life we must also take responsibility for the impact of the urban metabolism on the living fabric of the earth. After all, it simply represents the sum total of our consumption and discharges which are part of our day-to-day way of life. Closing the circle – that is, re-designing the urban metabolism to make it truly compatible with the processes of the living world – is a responsibility we cannot shirk. A barren and poisoned planet is surely not what we wish to leave behind. It is up to all of us to assure that a reversal of current practices is initiated without delay. Re-designing the urban metabolism, as cities are becoming the home of most of us on this planet, is now a key priority.　　　　　[179]

Note

1.　Seymour, John and Girardet, Herbert (1987) *Blueprint for a Green Planet,* London: Dorling & Kindersley.

　　　　　[180]

[20]

KEVIN LYNCH

The Pattern of the Metropolis

THE PATTERN OF URBAN DEVELOPMENT critically affects a surprising number of problems, by reason of the spacing of buildings, the location of activities, the disposition of the lines of circulation. Some of these problems might be eliminated if only we would begin to coordinate metropolitan development so as to balance services and growth, prevent premature abandonment or inefficient use, and see that decisions do not negate one another. In such cases, the form of the urban area, whether concentrated or dispersed, becomes of relatively minor importance.

There are other problems, however, that are subtler and go deeper. Their degree of seriousness seems to be related to the particular pattern of development which has arisen. To cope with such difficulties, one must begin by evaluating the range of possible alternatives of form, on the arbitrary assumption that the metropolis can be molded as desired. For it is as necessary to learn what is desirable as to study what is possible; realistic action without purpose can be as useless as idealism without power. Even the range of what is possible may sometimes be extended by fresh knowledge of what is desirable.

Let us, therefore, consider the form of the metropolis as if it existed in a world free of pressures or special interests and on the assumption that massive forces can be harnessed for reshaping the metropolis for the common good—provided this good can be discovered. The question then is, how should such power be applied? We must begin by deciding which aspects of the metropolitan pattern are crucial. We can then review the commonly recognized alternative patterns, as well as the criteria that might persuade us to choose one over another. Finally, we may hope to see the question as a whole. Then we will be ready to suggest new alternatives and will have the means of choosing the best one for any particular purpose.

KEVIN LYNCH

The Critical Aspects of Metropolitan Form

There are at least three vital factors in our judging the adequacy of the form of the metropolis, once its total size is known. The first of all is the magnitude and pattern of both the structural density (the ratio of floor space in buildings to the area of the site) and the structural condition (the state of obsolescence or repair). These aspects can be illustrated on a map by plotting the locations of the various classes of density ranging from high concentration to wide dispersion, and the various classes of structural condition ranging from poor to excellent. Density and condition provide a fundamental index of the physical resources an urban region possesses.

A second factor is the capacity, type, and pattern of the facilities for the circulation of persons, roads, railways, airlines, transit systems, and pathways of all sorts. Circulation and intercommunication perhaps constitute the most essential function of a city, and the free movement of persons happens to be the most difficult kind of circulation to achieve, the service most susceptible to malfunction in large urban areas.

The third factor that makes up the spatial pattern of a city is the location of fixed activities that draw on or serve large portions of the population, such as large department stores, factories, office and government buildings, warehouses, colleges, hospitals, theatres, parks, and museums. The spatial pattern of a city is made up of the location of fixed activities as well as the patterns of circulation and physical structure. However, the distribution of locally based activities, such as residence, local shopping, neighborhood services, elementary and high schools, is for our purpose sufficiently indicated by mapping the density of people or of buildings. Hence, if we have already specified structural density and the circulation system, the remaining critical fact at the metropolitan scale is the location of the city-wide activities which interact with large portions of the whole.

When we come to analyze any one of these three elements of spatial pattern, we find that the most significant features of such patterns are the grain (the degree of intimacy with which the various elements such as stores and residences are related), the focal organization (the interrelation of the nodes of concentration and interchange as contrasted with the general background), and the accessibility (the general proximity in terms of time of all points in the region to a given kind of activity or facility). In this sense, one might judge that from every point the accessibility to drugstores was low,

80

uneven, or uniformly high, or that it varied in some regular way, for example, high at the center and low at the periphery of the region. All three aspects of pattern (focal organization, grain, and accessibility) can be mapped, and the latter two can be treated quantitatively if desired.

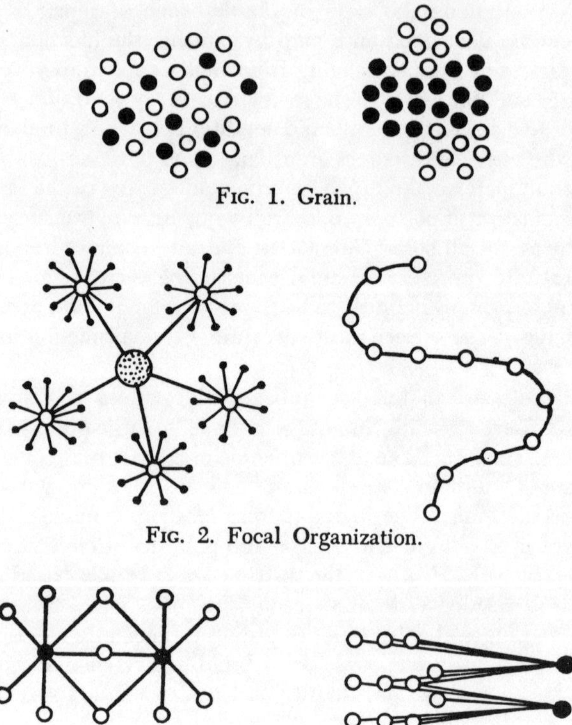

Fig. 1. Grain.

Fig. 2. Focal Organization.

Fig. 3. Accessibility.

It is often said that the metropolis today is deficient as a living environment. It has suffered from uncontrolled development, from too rapid growth and change, from obsolescence and instability. Circulation is congested, requiring substantial time and a major effort. Accessibility is uneven, particularly to open rural land. The use of facilities is unbalanced, and they become increasingly obsolete. Residential segregation according to social groups seems to be growing, while the choice of residence for the individual remains restricted and unsatisfactory. The pattern of activities is unstable, and running

81

KEVIN LYNCH

costs are high. Visually, the city is characterless and confused, as well as noisy and uncomfortable.

Yet the metropolis has tremendous economic and social advantages that override its problems and induce millions to bear with the discomforts. Rather than dwindle or collapse, it is more likely to become the normal human habitat. If so, the question then is, what particular patterns can best realize the potential of metropolitan life?

The Dispersed Sheet

One alternative is to allow the present growth at the periphery to proceed to its logical conclusion but at a more rapid pace. Let new growth occur at the lowest densities practicable, with substantial interstices of open land kept in reserve. Let older sections be rebuilt at much lower densities, so that the metropolitan region would rapidly spread over a vast continuous tract, perhaps coextensive with adjacent metropolitan regions. At the low densities of the outer suburbs, a metropolis of twenty million might require a circle of land one hundred miles in diameter.

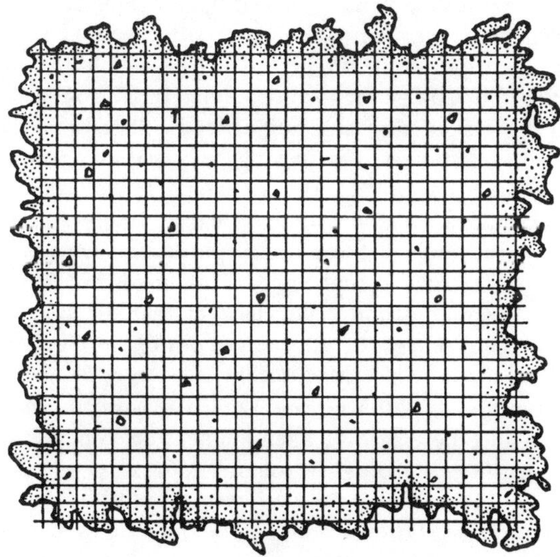

FIG. 4. The Dispersed Sheet.

The old center and most subcenters could be dissolved, allowing city-wide activities to disperse throughout the region, with a fine

The Pattern of the Metropolis

grain. Factories, offices, museums, universities, hospitals would appear everywhere in the suburban landscape. The low density and the dispersion of activities would depend on and allow circulation in individual vehicles, as well as a substantial use of distant symbolic communication such as telephone, television, mail, coded messages. Accessibility to rural land would become unnecessary, since outdoor recreational facilities would be plentiful and close at hand. The permanent low-density residence would displace the summer cottage.

The system of flow, concerned solely with individual land (and perhaps air) vehicles, should be highly dispersed in a continuous grid designed for an even movement in all directions. There would be no outstanding nodal points, no major terminals. Since different densities or activities would therefore be associated in a very fine grain, the physical pattern similarly might encourage a balanced cross-section of the population at any given point. Work place and residence might be adjacent or miles apart. Automatic factories and intensive food production might be dispersed throughout the region.

Frank Lloyd Wright dreamed of such a world in his Broadacre City.[1] It is this pattern toward which cities like Los Angeles appear to be moving, although they are hampered and corrupted by the vestiges of older city forms. Such a pattern might not only raise flexibility, local participation, personal comfort, and independence to a maximum, but also go far toward solving traffic congestion through the total dispersion and balancing of loads. Its cost would be high, however, and distances remain long. Accessibility would be good, given high speeds of travel and low terminal times (convenient parking, rapid starting); at the very least it would be evenly distributed. Thus communication in the sense of purposeful trips ("I am going out to buy a fur coat") might not be hindered, but spontaneous or accidental communication ("Oh, look at that fur coat in the window!"), which is one of the advantages of present city life, might be impaired by the lack of concentration.

Although such a pattern would require massive movements of the population and the extensive abandonment of equipment at the beginning, in the end it might promote population stability and the conservation of resources, since all areas would be favored alike. It gives no promise, however, of heightening the sense of political identity in the metropolitan community nor of producing a visually vivid and well-knit image of environment. Moreover, the choice of the type of residence would be restricted, although the choice of facility to be patronized (churches, stores, etc.) might be sufficiently wide.

KEVIN LYNCH

The Galaxy of Settlements

We might follow a slightly different tack while at the same time encouraging dispersion. Instead of guiding growth into an even distribution, let development be bunched into relatively small units, each with an internal peak of density and each separated from the next by a zone of low or zero structural density. Depending on the transport system, this separation might be as great as several miles. The ground occupied by the whole metropolis would increase proportionately; even if the interspaces were of minimum size, the linear dimensions of the metropolis would increase from thirty to fifty percent.

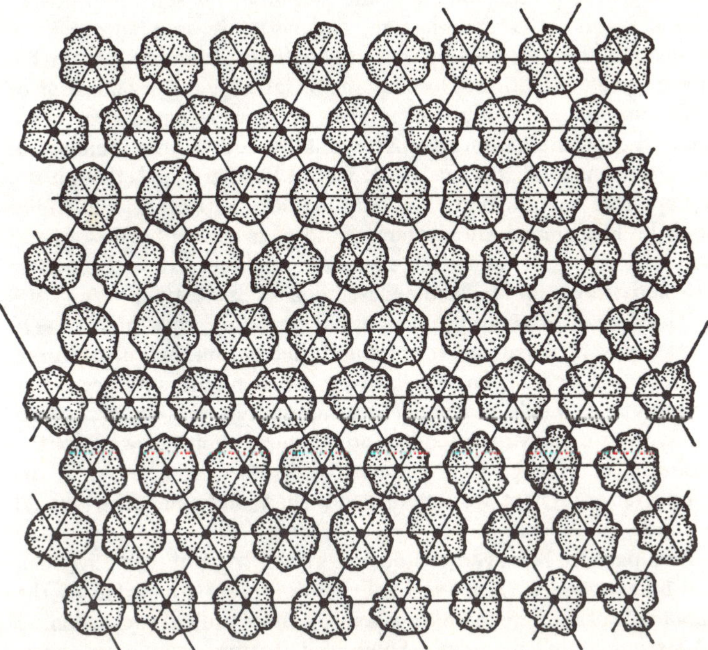

Fig. 5. The Galaxy.

City-wide activities could also be concentrated at the density peak within each urban cluster, thus forming an over-all system of centers, each of which would be relatively equal in importance to any of the others. Such a metropolitan pattern may be called an "urban galaxy." The centers might be balanced in composition or they might

84

vary by specializing in a type of activity, so that one might be a cultural center, another a financial center.

The system of flow would also be dispersed but would converge locally at the center of each cluster. It might be organized in a triangular grid, which provides such a series of foci while maintaining an easy flow in all directions over the total area. Since median densities remain low, while the centers of activity are divided into relatively small units, the individual vehicle must be the major mode of transportation, but some supplementary public transportation such as buses or aircraft running from center to center would now be feasible.

While it retains many of the advantages of the dispersed sheet, such as comfort, independence, and stability, this scheme probably enhances general communication, and certainly spontaneous communication, through creating centers of activity. It would presumably encourage participation in local affairs by favoring the organization of small communities, though this might equally work against participation and coordination on the metropolitan scale. In the same sense, the visual image at the local level would be sharpened, though the metropolitan image might be only slightly improved. Flexibility might be lost, since local clusters would of necessity have relatively fixed boundaries, if interstitial spaces were preserved, and the city-wide activities would be confined to one kind of location.

The factor of time-distance might remain rather high, unless people could be persuaded to work and shop within their own cluster, which would then become relatively independent with regard to commutation. Such independent communities, of course, would largely negate many metropolitan advantages: choice of work for the employee, choice of social contacts, of services, and so on. If the transportation system were very good, then "independence" would be difficult to enforce.

This pattern, however, can be considered without assuming such local independence. It is essentially the proposal advocated by the proponents of satellite towns, pushed to a more radical conclusion, as in Clarence Stein's diagram.[2] Some of its features would appear to have been incorporated into the contemporary development of Stockholm.

The pattern of an urban galaxy provides a wider range of choice than does pure dispersion, and a greater accessibility to open country, of the kind that can be maintained between clusters. This pattern has a somewhat parochial complexion and lacks the opportunities for intensive, spontaneous communication and for the very specialized activities that might exist in larger centers. Local centers, too, might develop a monotonous similarity, unless they were given some specific individuality. That might not be easy, however, since central activities tend to support and depend on one another (wholesaling and entertainment, government and business services, headquarters offices and shopping). A compromise would be the satellite proposal proper: a swarm of such unit clusters around an older metropolitan mass.

The Core City

There are those who, enamored with the advantages of concentration, favor a completely opposite policy that would set median structural densities fairly high, perhaps at 1.0 instead of 0.1; in other words, let there be as much interior floor space in buildings as there is total ground area in the city, instead of only one-tenth as much. If we consider the open land that must be set aside for streets, parks, and other such uses, this means in practice the construction of elevator apartments instead of one-family houses. The metropolis would then be packed into one continuous body, with a very intensive peak of density and activity at its center. A metropolis of twenty million could be put within a circle ten miles in radius, under the building practice normal today.

Fig. 6. The Core.

Parts of the city might even become "solid," with a continuous occupation of space in three dimensions and a cubical grid of transportation lines. (The full application of this plan could cram a metropolis within a surprisingly small compass: twenty million people, with generous spacing, could be accommodated within a cube less than three miles on a side.) Most probably there would be a fine grain of specialized activities, all at high intensity, so that apartments would occur over factories, or there might also be stores on upper levels. The system of flow would necessarily be highly specialized, sorting each kind of traffic into its own channel. Such a city would depend almost entirely on public transport, rather than individual vehicles, or on devices that facilitated pedestrian movement, such as moving sidewalks or flying belts. Accessibility would be very high, both to special activities and to the open country at the edges of the city. Each family might have a second house for weekends; these would be widely dispersed throughout the countryside and used regularly three or four days during the week, or even longer, by mothers and their young children. The city itself, then, would evolve into a place for periodic gathering. Some of the great European cities, such as Paris or Moscow, which are currently building large numbers of high-density housing as compact extensions to their peripheries, are approximating this pattern without its more radical features.

Such a pattern would have an effect on living quite different from that of the previous solutions. Spontaneous communication would be high, so high that it might become necessary to impede it so as to preserve privacy. Accessibility would be excellent and time-distance low, although the channels might be crowded. The high density might increase discomfort because of noise or poor climate, although these problems could perhaps be met by the invention of new technical devices. As with the previous patterns, the choice of habitat would be restricted to a single general type within the city proper, although the population could enjoy a strong contrast on weekends or holidays. The nearness of open country and the many kinds of special services should on the whole extend individual choice. Once established, the pattern should be stable, since each point would be a highly favored location. However, a very great dislocation of people and equipment, in this country, at least, would be required to achieve this pattern.

Such a metropolis would indeed produce a vivid image and would contribute to a strong sense of the community as a whole. Individual participation, on the other hand, might be very difficult. It is not clear how running costs would be affected; perhaps they would be lower because of the more efficient use of services and transportation, but initial costs would undoubtedly be very high. The segregation of social groups, as far as physical disposition can influence it, might be discouraged, although there is a level of density above which intercommunication among people begins to decline again. Certainly this solution is a highly rigid and unadaptable one in which change of function could be brought about only by a costly rearrangement.

The Urban Star

A fourth proposal would retain the dominant core without so drastic a reversion to the compact city. Present densities would be

KEVIN LYNCH

kept, or perhaps revised upward a little, while low-density development at the outer fringe would no longer be allowed. Tongues of open land would be incorporated into the metropolitan area to produce a density pattern that is star-shaped in the central region and linear at the fringes. These lines of dense development along the radials might in time extend to other metropolitan centers, thus becoming linear cities between the main centers. The dominant core, however, would remain, surrounded by a series of secondary centers distributed along the main radials. At moderate densities (less than the core pattern, and more than the sheet), the radial arms of a metropolis of comparable size might extend for fifty miles from its own center.

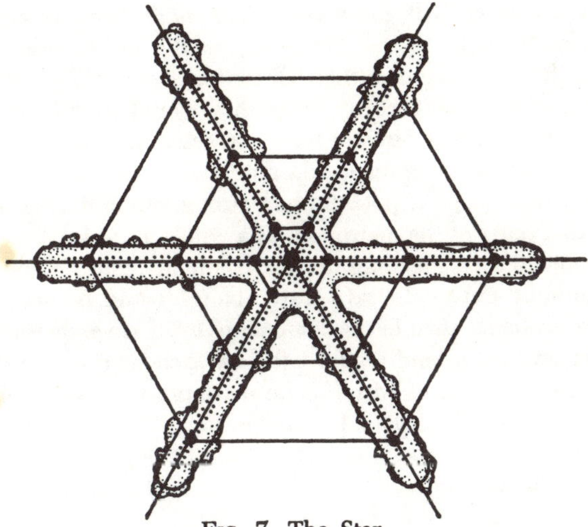

Fig. 7. The Star.

The metropolitan center of the star pattern would again contain the most intensive types of city-wide activity. Elsewhere, either in the subcenters or in linear formations along the main radials—whichever proved the more suitable—these activities would be carried on at a less intense level. The system of flow would logically be organized on the same radial pattern, with supplementary concentric rings. An efficient public transportation system of high capacity could operate along the main radials, whereas the ring roads could accommodate public transit of lower intensity. To some degree, travel by individual vehicles, although discouraged for centrally bound flows, would be practicable in other directions.

This pattern is a rationalization of the manner in which metropolitan areas were developing till the individual vehicle became the usual means of travel. It is the form the city of Copenhagen has adopted as its pattern for future growth;[3] Blumenfeld has discussed it at length.[4] This form retains the central core with its advantages of rapid communication and specialized services yet permits the location of other kinds of major activities. Lower residential densities are also possible. Individual choice should be fairly wide, both in regard to living habitat, access to services, and access to open land— this land lies directly behind each tongue of development, even at the core, and leads continuously outward to rural land.

Movement along a sector would be fairly fast and efficient, although terminals at the core might continue to be congested and, with continued growth, the main radials might become overloaded. Movement between sectors, however, would be less favored, especially in the outer regions; there distances are great, transit hard to maintain, and channels costly, since they would span long distances over land they do not directly serve. Accessibility to services would be unequal as between inner and outer locations.

The visual image is potentially a strong one and should be conducive to a sense of the metropolis as a whole, or at least to the sense of one unified sector leading up to a common center. Growth could occur radially outward, and future change could be accomplished with less difficulty than in the compact pattern, since densities would be lower and open land would back up each strip of development. The principal problems with this form are probably those of circumferential movement, of potential congestion at the core and along the main radials, and of the wide dispersion of the pattern as it recedes from the original center.

The Ring

In the foregoing, the most discussed alternatives for metropolitan growth have been given in a highly simplified form. Other possibilities certainly exist—e.g., the compact high-density core pattern might be turned inside out, producing a doughnut-like form. In this case the center would be kept open, or at very low density, while high densities and special activities surround it, like the rim of a wheel. The principal channels of the flow system would then be a series of annular rings serving the high-intensity rim, supplemented by a set of feeder radials that would converge at the empty center. In fact, this is essentially a linear system, but one that circles back on itself and is bypassed by the "spokes" crossing the "hub." This system is

KEVIN LYNCH

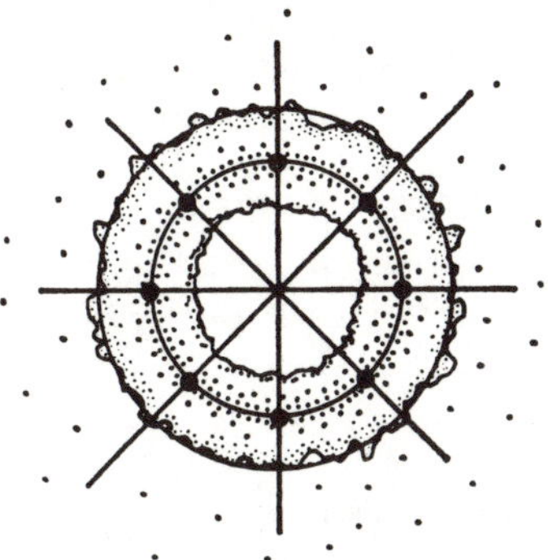

Fig. 8. The Ring.

well-adapted to public transportation, both on the ring roads and the cross radials, while individual vehicles might be used for circulation outside the rim.

Densities within the rim would have to be rather high, while those beyond the rim could be low. A system of weekend houses might also be effectively employed here. The central area could either be kept quite open or devoted to special uses at low densities. City-wide activities could be spotted round the rim in a series of intense centers, supplemented by linear patterns along the annular roadways. There would be no single dominant center but rather a limited number of strong centers (an aristocracy rather than a monarchy). These centers might also be specialized in regard to activity—finance, government, culture, etc.

This pseudo-linear form, like the radial tongues of the star plan, has the linear advantages: a high accessibility, both to services and to open land; a wide choice of habitat and location of activities; and a good foundation for efficient public transit. Congestion at any single center is avoided, yet there is a high concentration. In contrast to the galaxy or satellite form, the variety and strong character inherent in the specialized centers would have some hope of survival because of the relatively close proximity of these centers.

The visual image would be strong (though perhaps a little confusing because of its circularity), producing a particularly clear impression of the centers around the rim, in contrast to the central openness, and of their successive interconnections. The whole metropolis would seem more nearly like one community. One of the most difficult problems would be that of growth, since much develop-

90

ment beyond the rim would soon blur the contour and require a new transportation system. A second concentric ring might be developed beyond the first, but it would negate some of the advantages of the first ring and would demand massive initiative by the central government to undertake its development. Another difficulty would be that of control. How can the belts of open land or the accessible center be kept free of building? Even if this problem were solved satisfactorily, a dilemma is also likely to arise in regard to the size of the ring: should it be small enough for the major centers to be in close proximity to one another or big enough to allow all the residences and other local activities to be related to it?

One classic example of this form exists, although on a very large scale—the ring of specialized Dutch cities that surround a central area of agricultural land, Haarlem, Amsterdam, Utrecht, Rotterdam, The Hague, and Leiden. This general pattern is now being rationalized and preserved as a matter of national policy in the Netherlands. In our own country, the San Francisco Bay region appears to be developing in this same direction.

The ring tends to be rather rigid and unadaptable as a form. It would require an extreme reshaping of the present metropolis, particularly with regard to transportation and the central business district; but it might dovetail with an observable trend toward emptying and abandoning the central areas. The plan could be modified by retaining a single major center, separated by a wide belt of open space from all other city-wide activities to be disposed along the rim. It may be noted that this use of open land in concentric belts ("green belts") is exactly opposite to its use as radial tongues in the star form.

The Objectives of Metropolitan Arrangement

Many other metropolitan forms are hypothetically possible, but the five patterns described (the sheet, the galaxy, the core, the star, and the ring) indicate the variation possible. One of the interesting results of the discussion is to see the appearance of a particular set of values as criteria for evaluating these forms. It begins to be clear that some human objectives are intimately connected with the physical pattern of a city, while others are very little affected by it. For example, there has been little discussion of the healthfulness of the environment or of its safety. Although these factors are influenced by the detailed design of the environment, such as the spacing of buildings or the provision for utilities, it is not obvious that the specific metropolitan pattern has any significant effect on them so long

KEVIN LYNCH

as we keep well ahead of the problems of pollution and supply. Psychological well-being, on the other hand, may be affected by the shape of the urban environment. But again, we are too ignorant of this aspect at present to discuss it further.

We have not referred to the efficiency of the environment in regard to production and distribution. This represents another basic criterion that probably is substantially affected by metropolitan pattern, but unfortunately no one seems to know what the effect is. "Pleasure" and "beauty" have not been mentioned, but these terms are nebulous and hard to apply accurately. A number of criteria have appeared, however, and it may well be worth while to summarize them. They might be considered the goals of metropolitan form, its fundamental objectives, either facilitated or frustrated in some significant way by the physical pattern of the metropolis.

The criterion of choice heads the list. As far as possible, the individual should have the greatest variety of goods, services, and facilities readily accessible to him. He should be able to choose the kind of habitat he prefers; he should be able to enter many kinds of environment at will, including the open country; he should have the maximum of personal control over his world. These advantages appear in an environment of great variety and of fine grain, one in which transportation and communication are as quick and effortless as possible. There may very likely be some eventual limit to the desirable increase of choice, since people can be overloaded by too many alternatives, but we do not as yet operate near that limit for most people. In practice, of course, to maximize one choice may entail minimizing another, and compromises will have to be made.

The ideal of personal interaction ranks as high as choice, although it is not quite so clear how the optimum should be defined. We often say that we want the greatest number of social contacts, so as to promote neighborliness and community organization, minimize segregation and social isolation, increase the velocity and decrease the effort of social exchange. And yet, while the evils of isolation are known, we are nevertheless beginning to see problems at the other end of the scale as well. Too much personal communication may cause breakdown, just as surely as too little. Even in moderate quantities, constant "neighborliness" can interfere with other valuable activities such as reflection, independent thought, or creative work. A high level of local community organization may mean civic indifference or intergovernmental rivalry when the large community is involved.

In this dilemma, a compromise could be found in saying that potential interaction between people should be as high as possible, as long as the individual can control it and shield himself whenever desired. His front door, figuratively speaking, should open on a bustling square, and his back door on a secluded park. Thus this ideal is seen as related to the ideal of choice.

Put differently, individuals require a rhythmical alternation of stimulus and rest—periods when personal interchange is high and to some degree is forced upon them, to be followed by other periods when stimulus is low and individually controlled. A potentially high level of interaction, individually controlled, is not the whole story; we also need some degree of spontaneous or unpremeditated exchange, of the kind that is so often useful in making new associations.

The goal of interaction, therefore, is forwarded by many of the same physical features as the goal of choice: variety, fine grain, efficient communication; but it puts special emphasis on the oscillation between stimulus and repose (centers of high activity versus quiet parks), and requires that communication be controllable. In addition, it calls for situations conducive to spontaneous exchange. Storehouses of communication, such as libraries or museums, should be highly accessible and inviting, their exterior forms clearly articulated and expressive of their function.

These two objectives of choice and interaction may be the most important goals of metropolitan form, but there are others of major importance, such as minimum first cost and minimum operating cost. These seem to depend particularly on continuous occupation along the major transportation channels, on a balanced use of the flow system, both in regard to time and direction of flow, a moderately high structural density, and a maximum reliance on collective transport.

Objectives of comfort, on the other hand, related principally to a good climate, the absence of distracting noise, and adequate indoor and outdoor space, may point either toward generally lower densities or toward expensive ameliorative works, such as sound barriers, air conditioning, and roof-top play areas. The important goal of individual participation may also indicate lower densities and an environment that promotes an active relation between an individual and his social and physical milieu, thus giving him a world that to some extent he can manage and modify by his own initiative.

We must also consider that the urban pattern will necessarily shift and expand, and therefore it is important to ask whether the adjustment to new functions will be relatively easy, and whether growth, as well as the initial state, is achievable with a minimum of control and central initiative and intervention. Adaptability to

KEVIN LYNCH

change seems to be greater at lower densities, since scattered small structures are readily demolished or converted. Both an efficient transport system and some form of separation of one kind of activity from another are also conducive to flexibility. Discontinuous forms like the galaxy or the ring require special efforts to control growth, for these patterns raise problems such as the appearance of squatters and the preservation and use of intervening open land.

Stability is a somewhat contradictory goal; it takes into account the critical social and economic costs of obsolescence, movement of population, and change of function. It is very possible that stability in the modern world will be impossible to maintain, and it runs counter to many of the values cited above. Yet stability may be qualified in this light: if change is inevitable, then it should be moderated and controlled so as to prevent violent dislocations and preserve a maximum of continuity with the past. This criterion would have important implications as to how the metropolis should grow and change.

Finally, there are many esthetic goals the metropolis can satisfy. The most clear-cut is that the metropolis should be "imageable," that is, it should be visually vivid and well structured; its component parts should be easily recognized and easily interrelated. This objective would encourage the use of intensive centers, variety, sharp grain (clear outlines between parts), and a differentiated but well-patterned flow system.

The Relation of Forms to Goals

We have now treated a number of objectives that are crucial, that are on the whole rather generally accepted, and that seem to be significantly affected by the pattern of the metropolis: the goals of choice, interaction, cost, comfort, participation, growth and adaptability, continuity, and imageability. Other goals may develop as we increase our knowledge of city form. What even these few imply for city form is not yet obvious; moreover, they often conflict, as when interaction and cost appear to call for higher densities, while comfort, participation, and adaptability achieve optimal realization at lower levels. Nevertheless, we have immediate decisions to make regarding the growth of urban areas, and if we marshall our goals and our alternatives as best we can, we can the better make these decisions.

The clarifying of alternatives and objectives has an obvious value, for this will permit public debate and the speculative analysis of the probable results of policy as related to any given form. Yet this kind of approach will soon reach a limit of usefulness unless it is sup-

94

The Pattern of the Metropolis

ported by experimental data. Such experimentation is peculiarly difficult in regard to so large and complex an organism as a metropolis. To some degree we can form judgments drawn from such different urban regions as Los Angeles, Stockholm, and Paris, but these judgments are necessarily distorted by various cultural and environmental disparities. Possibly we can study certain partial aspects of city form, such as the effects of varying density or the varying composition of centers, but the key questions pertain to the metropolitan pattern as an operating whole. Since we cannot build a metropolis purely for experimental purposes, we can only build and test models, with some simplified code to designate pattern. By simulating basic urban functions in these models, tests might be run for such criteria as cost, accessibility, imageability, or adaptability. Such tests will be hard to relate to the real situation, and it is difficult to see how certain objectives (such as interaction or participation) can be tested, yet this technique is our best current hope for experimental data on the implications of the total metropolitan pattern.

Dynamic and Complex Forms

Until we have such experimental data, what can we conclude from our imaginary juxtaposition of metropolitan form and human goals? Each of the alternatives proposed has its drawbacks, its failures in meeting some basic objectives. A radical, consistent dispersion of the metropolis appears to restrict choice, impair spontaneous interaction, entail high cost, and inhibit a vivid metropolitan image. A galaxy of small communities promises better, but would still be substandard as regards choice, interaction, and cost, besides being harder to realize. A recentralization of the metropolis in an intensive core appears to entail almost fatal disadvantages in cost, comfort, individual participation, and adaptability. The rationalization of the old metropolis in a star would work better if central congestion could be avoided and free accessibility maintained, but this form is less and less usable as size increases. The ring has many special advantages but raises great difficulties in cost, adaptability, and continuity with present form.

Of course, these are all "pure" types that make no concessions to the complications of reality and they have been described as though they were states of perfection to be maintained forever. In actuality, a plan for a metropolis is more likely to be a complex and mixed one, to be realized as an episode in some continuous process, whose form involves rate and direction of change as well as a momentary pattern.

For example, let us consider, on the basis of the little we know, a

KEVIN LYNCH

form that might better satisfy our aspirations, if we accept the fact of metropolitan agglomeration: this form is in essence a variant of the dispersed urban sheet. Imagine a metropolis in which the flow system becomes more specialized and complex, assuming a triangular grid pattern that grows at the edges and becomes more specialized in the interior. Many types of flow would be provided for. Densities would have a wide range and a fine grain, with intensive peaks at junctions in the circulation system and with linear concentrations along major channels, but with extensive regions of low density inside the grid. Through the interstices of this network belts and tongues of open land would form another kind of grid. Thus the general pattern would resemble a fisherman's net, with a system of dispersed centers and intervening spaces.

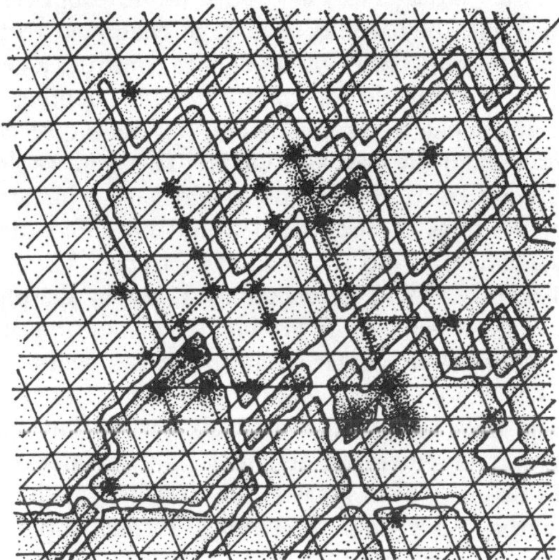

FIG. 9. The Polycentered Net.

City-wide activities would concentrate in these knots of density, which would be graded in size. In the smaller centers the activities would not be specialized but the larger centers would be increasingly dominated by some special activity. Therefore the major centers would be highly specialized—although never completely "pure"—and would be arranged in a loose central cluster, each highly accessible to another.

A metropolis of twenty million might have, not one such cluster, but two or three whose spheres of influence would overlap. These

96

The Pattern of the Metropolis

clusters might be so dense as to be served by transportation grids organized in three dimensions, like a skeletal framework in space. Elsewhere, the network would thin out and adapt itself to local configurations of topography. This general pattern would continue to specialize and to grow, perhaps in a rhythmically pulsating fashion. With growth and decay, parts of the whole would undergo periodic renewal. Such a form might satisfy many of the general criteria, but each particular metropolis is likely to encounter special problems. Even so, the description illustrates the complexity, the indeterminacy, and the dynamic nature of city form that are inherent in any such generalization.

Perhaps we can make such a proposal more concrete by stating it as a set of actions rather than as a static pattern. If this were the form desired, then the agencies of control would adopt certain definite policies. First, they would encourage continued metropolitan agglomeration. Second, they would begin to construct a generalized triangular grid of channels for transportation, adapting its interspacing and alignment to circumstances, but aiming at raising accessibility throughout the area as a whole. This grid would provide for many different kinds of flow and would have a hierarchy of its own—that is, the lines of circulation would be differentiated with respect to the intensity and speed of their traffic. Third, peaks of activity and density would be encouraged, but in sharply defined areas, not in rings whose density gradually declines from the center. The present metropolitan center would be encouraged to specialize and thus loosen into a cluster, while one or two major rival centers might develop elsewhere in the network, rather than allowing a general dispersal of city-wide activities. Such major specialized centers might be given even greater local intensity, with multi-level circulation, perhaps as a three-dimensional system of public rights-of-way.

Fourth, every effort would be made to retain, acquire, or clear a system of linked open spaces of generous size that pervaded the network. Fifth, a wide variety of activities, of accommodation and structural character, dispersed in a fine-grained pattern, would be encouraged. Once the concentration of special activities and the arrangement of higher densities in centers and along major channels had been provided for, then zoning and other controls would be employed only to maintain the minimum grain needed to preserve the character and efficiency of the various types of use and density, and large single-purpose areas would be avoided. Sixth, the form of centers, transportation channels, and major open spaces would be

KEVIN LYNCH

controlled so as to give as vivid a visual image as possible. Seventh, the agency would be committed to continuous rebuilding and re-organization of successive parts of the pattern.

Such a set of policies would mean a radical redirection of metro-politan growth. Whether this plan is feasible or worth the cost would require serious consideration. Even if this pattern were chosen, there would still be many crucial questions of relative emphasis and timing to be weighed. If life in the future metropolis is to be worthy of the massive effort necessary to build it, the physical pattern must satisfy human values. The coordination of metropolitan development, how-ever obligatory, will not of itself ensure this happy result. Coordi-nation must be directed toward some desired general pattern, and, to define this, we must clarify our alternatives and the goals they are meant to serve.

REFERENCES

1 Frank Lloyd Wright, "Broadacre City," in *Taliesin*, October 1940, vol. 1, no. 1.

2 Clarence Stein, "City Patterns, Past and Future," *Pencil Points*, June 1942.

3 *Skitseforslag til egnsplan for Storkobenhaven:* Copenhagen regional plan. Summary of the preliminary proposal, 1948-1949, with list of contents and notes explaining all illustrations of the preliminary proposal, translated into English.

4 Hans Blumenfeld, "A Theory of City Form," *Society of Architectural Historians Journal*, July 1949.

[21]

Economics and "Sustainability": Balancing Trade-offs and Imperatives

Michael A. Toman

ABSTRACT. *The concept of "sustainability" has been increasingly invoked in scholarly and public policy debates. Discussion has been hampered, however, by uncertainty and lack of uniformity in the meaning of sustainability. This paper seeks to identify some common ground among economists, ecologists, and environmental ethicists. Two issues seem salient: requirements for intergenerational equity and the definition of "social capital" to be provided to future generations. A concept of "safe minimum standard," which has received at least some recognition in the ecology, philosophy, and economics literatures, may provide the beginnings of a common ground for debate about sustainability. (JEL Q2)*

I. INTRODUCTION

The concept that use of natural resources, environmental services, and ecological systems somehow should be "sustainable" has become one of the most widely invoked and debated ideas in the area of resource and environmental management. It was a basic theme in the 1992 "Earth Summit," the United Nations Conference on Environment and Development (UNCED), and in the World Bank's 1992 *World Development Report* on environment and development. It is an issue discussed not just in professional journals but also in newspaper articles and in basic textbooks (see, e.g., Pearce and Turner 1990 and Tietenberg 1992). It is a principle behind the founding of a professional organization, the International Society for Ecological Economics, many of whose members question the sufficiency or even the validity of conventional economic approaches to resource and environmental management problems.

Despite the frequency with which the term is invoked, the concept of sustainability remains surprisingly ambiguous. It is clear from examining various usages of the term that writers have very different meanings in mind.[1] For example, the use of the term in the 1992 *World Development Report* seems to refer primarily to the application of existing neoclassical principles of efficient resource and environmental management in developing countries. This is very different than the ideas expressed by Herman Daly (see, e.g., Daly 1990, 1991), who argues that use ("throughput") of energy and materials must be sharply curtailed to avoid ecological catastrophe. Sustainability also is interpreted very differently by many economists, who see the natural environment as one of many fungible assets that can be deployed in satisfying human demands, and by many ecologists and ethicists, who express greater concern for both ecological integrity and the interests of future generations (compare Ehrlich 1989 and Solow 1993a, 1993b, for example).

The goal of this paper is to provide some vocabulary and grammar that may be useful for this ongoing debate among economists, ecologists, and ethicists. We begin, as do many others, with the statement about sustainability from the report of the "Brundt-

---

Senior Fellow, Resources for the Future.

Earlier versions of this paper were presented at meetings of the International Society for Ecological Economics and the American Economic Association, and at seminars at the World Bank, the Agency for International Development, and the University of Maryland. I owe a large debt to Pierre Crosson, Bryan Norton, and John Pezzey, whose insights played a substantial role in clarifying my understanding of the issues raised in the paper. I also appreciate helpful conversations with Geir Asheim, Doug Bohi, Allen Kneese, and Jeff Krautkraemer, and perceptive comments by Tom Tietenberg, Scott Gordon, Tim Brennan, and an anonymous referee on earlier drafts.

[1]See also Pezzey (1989) and Pearce, Markandya, and Barbier (1989), who catalogue scores of sometimes vague and conflicting sustainability definitions. Dixon and Fallon (1989) discuss how sustainability has been transformed from a condition on steady-state management of specific resources to an expression of broad ecological concerns.

Land Economics • November 1994 • 70(4): 399–413

land Commission," the World Commission on Environment and Development (WCED). That report described sustainable development as "development that meets the needs of the present without compromising the ability of future generations to meet their own needs" (WCED 1987, 43). The threat to future generations perceived in the report arise from potentially large-scale and irreversible degradation of natural systems in the course of global economic development, particularly in poorer countries.

The Brundtland statement thus focuses attention on two issues that seem to be central themes in any conception of sustainability: the nature of the current generation's responsibility to future generations, and the degree of substitutability between "natural capital" and other forms of social capital—physical investment and investment in knowledge and institutions as embodied in human capital.[2] The next two sections of the paper examine alternative views on these two issues to show how they lead to different conceptions of sustainability. In the fourth section of the paper these alternative conceptions are related to each other through a "two-tier" model of resource management based on the idea of "safe minimum standard." The fifth and last section of the paper contains concluding remarks.

II. INTERGENERATIONAL FAIRNESS

There is an enormous literature, spanning over two millennia, on concepts of distributive justice including fairness across generations. Unfortunately, there is not yet a conception of distributive justice that commands wide intellectual support. Nevertheless, there are several points of view that have attracted considerable attention in discussions of sustainability.[3] The discussion that follows emphasizes issues of intergenerational fairness even though these issues cannot be entirely divorced from the subject of the next section, substitution possibilities among components of society's wealth endowment.

One fundamental partitioning of justice concepts separates theories based on maximization of an independently defined good (teleological theories) from theories based more on innate rights and obligations (deontological theories). A further categorization can be made based on theories that emphasize the current generation and its immediate descendants—"presentist" theories—and theories that put greater emphasis on the "further future." Yet another distinction, particularly in nonpresentist theories of justice, concerns justice concepts that emphasize individuals and more "organicist" conceptions that put greater weight on community interests.

The typical criterion of discounted intertemporal welfare maximization in applied welfare economics occupies one point in the continuum of alternative justice conceptions. This criterion not only emphasizes preference satisfaction over rights; it also is highly presentist, since with *any* positive intergenerational discount rate the welfare of individuals living one generation in the future is scarcely relevant to current decision making. Many writers have suggested that the presentist focus of the present-value (PV) criterion implies an influence of the current generation over the circumstances of its more distant descendants that seems, at least intuitively, to be ethically questionable (Kneese and

---

[2]In emphasizing these themes we are placing ourselves within the anthropocentric stream of debate about sustainability, in which the needs and wants of people are central, as opposed to an "ecocentric" perspective that asserts the intrinsic worth of the natural environment. We also are sidestepping, without in any way minimizing, the issue of how the state of the environment may be connected to income distribution within generations—in particular, connections between poverty and environmental degradation. See Pearce, Barbier, and Markandya (1990) and World Bank (1992) for discussion of these issues. Finally, we consider sustainability primarily in the context of resource management to meet identified human needs, as opposed to the broader "co-evolutionary" perspective discussed in Norgaard (1988), which emphasizes the mutual interactions between social actions and goals.

[3]See Pearce and Turner (1990, chap. 15) for a compact summary; Pezzey (1992) provides a wide-ranging survey of motivations for considering sustainability.

Schulze 1985; Norton 1982, 1984, 1989; Parfit 1983b; Page 1977, 1983, 1988).

The debate over the ethical implications of the PV criterion is long-standing and involves a number of considerations that often seem to be misunderstood. One basic issue in this debate is the relationship between the PV criterion and the broader concept of intergenerational economic efficiency as defined by the Pareto criterion, which requires only that it be impossible to improve the welfare of members of one generation without reducing the welfare of members of some other generation. This notion of "no waste" seems desirable in any intergenerational welfare criterion, at least to those who give some weight to the importance of individual preference satisfaction. The difficulty with the PV criterion thus is not that it requires Pareto efficiency, but rather that it puts weight on the welfare of the current generation in the social welfare function that some regard as excessive.

As Page (1977, 1988) points out, there are infinitely many intergenerational social orderings consistent with the Pareto principle that allow for different sets of intergenerational welfare weights without the "dictatorship" of the current generation embodied in the present value criterion. A number of analysts have explored other social welfare criteria that preserve the Pareto principle without imposing the preferences of the current generation on future generations.[4]

This issue has been carefully considered in a series of papers by Howarth and Norgaard (see Howarth and Norgaard 1990, 1992, 1993 and Howarth 1991a, 1991b). Using an overlapping generations framework, they argue that the problem of intergenerational equity must be viewed as a problem of ethics that is distinct from economic efficiency in the Pareto sense. They further argue that the intergenerational equity problem should be approached as one that involves a fair distribution of property rights between current and future generations. This argument is a simple but powerful intergenerational extension of a standard result in welfare economics: "The choice of distribution of income is the same

as the choice of an allocation of endowments, and this in turn is equivalent to choosing a particular welfare function" (Varian 1984, 209; see also Bromley 1989). In particular, Howarth and Norgaard show that while purely "egoistic" utility concerns will motivate some savings to benefit the (short-term) future (since people live more than one period and may also have concerns for their own immediate descendants), purely egoistic savings will not in general be adequate to optimize a social welfare function that includes more altruistic concerns (e.g., the well-being of the entire next generation or individuals further into the future). Howarth's and Norgaard's arguments also have important implications for analyses of environmental valuation, discount rates, and policy design (e.g., pollution taxation), since all of these are affected by the income distribution.

Howarth and Norgaard do not investigate the range of intergenerational social welfare functions that might plausibly be invoked in connection with intergenerational equity. In their analysis they are concerned primarily with the egalitarian "maximin" criterion discussed below as an alternative to maximizing the present value of utility streams.[5] In addition, trying to achieve intergenerational equity solely through savings that transfer endowments across

---

[4] See in particular Page (1977), Pearce (1983), and Burton (1993) for discussions of intergenerational discounting. These analyses suggest that a positive discount rate to reflect the growth of the economy is compatible with a zero rate of pure time preference in the social welfare function on ethical grounds. The arguments in Sandler and Smith (1976, 1977, 1982), Bishop (1977), and Cabe (1982) indicate that the assumption of a uniform discount rate may not be consistent with intertemporal Pareto efficiency, particularly with intertemporal public goods.

[5] Howarth (1992) derives this social welfare criterion from a more restricted maximin ethic between just parents and their children. He shows that if parental altruism extends only to the direct *consumption* of the next generation, there is no assurance that utility levels will be maintained or increase over time; but if the current generation is concerned about the capacity of its descendants to exercise *their* bequest motive as well, the result is concern about the equity of welfare across all generations.

generations may not always be effective. Randall and Farmer (1993) argue that when the two-generation analyses of Howarth and Norgaard are extended to a setting with three or more generations, a kind of Coasian result obtains: the ultimate equilibrium allocation is not that sensitive to the initial distribution of property rights. Randall and Farmer argue for an approach to sustainability based on preservation rules like the safe minimum standard discussed subsequently in this paper.

The problem of intergenerational equity has received considerable attention in the economics literature through the application of a Rawlsian (1971) "maximin" concept of intergenerational rights (see, e.g., Solow 1974, 1986 and Norton 1989, as well as the work by Howarth and Norgaard cited above). The Rawlsian approach has been criticized as posing too harsh a trade-off between equity and welfare maximization, since a strict application of the Rawlsian criterion leads to the outcome that all generations must be equally well (or badly) off—that is, there is no scope for the current generation to pursue improvements in future conditions. However, more recent analyses of the Rawlsian social welfare problem suggest that this trade-off need not be so harshly drawn. In particular, Asheim (1988, 1991) shows that when individual preferences include some altruistic concern for immediate descendants, but there is also a social agreement to follow a Rawlsian ethic involving concern for the indefinite future, it is possible within the context of social welfare maximization to have economic growth coupled with a requirement that future generations be no worse off than the present.

As Pezzey (1989, 1994a) points out, there are a number of alternatives to the maximin criterion for social welfare orderings that could be used to reflect intergenerational equity concerns. Pezzey (1994b) analyzes in some detail the implications of a criterion based on the maximization of the present value of per-capita utility subject to an ethical constraint that per-capita utility not decline over time. Like Asheim, Pezzey finds that this criterion allows for concern

for future welfare without necessarily sacrificing all growth possibilities. A weaker version of this criterion would accord intergenerational equity (as indicated by nondeclining utility over time) some *finite* weight in the social welfare function, allowing for well-defined trade-offs between maximum present value and fairness (see, e.g., Broome 1992).

The discussion thus far has concerned mainly individualistic conceptions of what is good or right. Even the individualistic point of view gives rise to deep controversy. On the one hand, critics raise objections to the capacity of utilitarianism, or even the concept of human preferences, to adequately describe human interests (see, e.g., Sen 1982; Parfit 1983b; Sagoff 1988; and Norton 1992).[6] Defenders of deontological theory, on the other hand, point out the difficulties in assigning rights to future generations (e.g., Broome 1991). Even those who do not necessarily espouse utilitarianism agree that there are some deep logical difficulties in assigning standing to "potential" future persons whose circumstances not only are largely unknown to the present generation but also are endogenous to the set of choices made by the current generation (see, e.g., Baier 1984; Barry 1977; Golding 1972; Passmore 1974; and Parfit 1983a).

One approach to this problem has been the development of organicist arguments that invoke an obligation to the entire context of future human life—the species as a whole, and the ecological systems that surround it—rather than just to potential future individuals (see, e.g., Leopold 1949; Lovelock 1988; Callicott 1989; Norton

---

[6] Some critics argue that the conventional approach to specifying preference orderings in economics is deficient on both empirical and moral grounds, since it does not distinguish "lower" or "higher" impulses, or "self-interest" and "community-motivated" interests. The solution, it is argued, is some hierarchical representation of preferences. However, Brennan (1989) argues that this approach does not really solve any problems associated with conventional preference reasoning in economics; and in particular, that moral deficiencies associated with the outcomes of economic logic should be directly confronted as such, rather than attempting to reframe that logic.

1982, 1986, 1989; Page 1983, 1991; Nash 1989; Weiss 1989). This "stewardship" perspective emphasizes the safeguarding of the large-scale ecological processes that support all facets of human life, from biological survival to cultural existence. The stewardship perspective does not deny the relevance of human preferences, but it asserts the existence of larger societal concerns that members of society will feel (in varying degrees) beyond individualistic preferences.

The organicist position raises the interesting and as-yet unanswered question of whether there are important social values that simply cannot be captured in an individualistic resource valuation, no matter how broad and sophisticated the valuation methods are. The difficulty in addressing this issue is that the two perspectives are based on different fundamental axioms. The organicist position seems to avoid some of the difficulties in extending individualistic fairness concepts to intergenerational circumstances. On the other hand, a nonindividualistic perspective is a two-edged sword in that many of humankind's most cherished economic, political, and other social institutions derive fundamentally from giving high respect to individual rights. Organicism without constraints leads to supremacy of the group over the individual, a form of social order that history shows to be very dangerous and destructive. The two-tier system described subsequently in the paper seeks to provide a venue for considering the balance between individual trade-offs and social imperatives.

III. RESOURCE SUBSTITUTABILITY

Assuming one accepts some obligation to consider the well-being of future generations, what bundles of social capital should succeeding generations make available to their descendants? The answer to this question depends critically on one's assumptions regarding the degree of substitutability between the services provided by natural capital (material resources, waste absorption, other ecological functions, aes-thetic and cultural values) and other forms of capital (plant, equipment, knowledge, skills, social institutions).

One view, to which many economists would be inclined, is that all resources are relatively fungible sources of well-being. This view appears to be influenced heavily by a number of classic and more recent applications of aggregate growth models with natural resources. A number of familiar theorems come out of this literature. In the standard growth model without natural resource constraints, the modified Golden Rule indicates that per-capita consumption and utility will grow over time provided the economy is not already saturated with capital. Clearly, sustainability presents no challenge in this world, even with positive discounting of future utilities. The same outcome obtains with natural resources provided these resources are in some sense "augmentable"—capable of being renewed or of having damages offset by compensatory investments (for a recent exposition of this see van Geldrop and Withagen 1993). Even with exhaustible resources or some other irreversible degradation of the services provided by the natural environment (such as accumulative pollution), it is possible for consumption and welfare to grow if there is sufficient substitutability between natural resources and capital accumulation, or technical progress sufficient to offset the depletion/degradation of natural resource services (Dasgupta and Heal 1974; Solow 1974, 1986; Stiglitz 1974; Baumol 1986; Dasgupta and Mäler 1991; see also the surveys in Asheim 1989, Pezzey 1992, and Toman, Pezzey, and Krautkraemer forthcoming).

From this point of view, then, large-scale damages to ecosystems such as degradation of environmental quality, loss of species diversity, or destabilization from global warming are not intrinsically unacceptable. The question is whether compensatory investments for future generations in other forms of capital are feasible and are undertaken. This is the essence of the argument advanced by Solow (1986) and Mäler (1991), based on previous work by Hartwick (1977), that investments of resource rents in other forms of capital provide the means to sustain consumption possibilities over time. Investments in human knowledge, techniques of production and social organization are especially pertinent in humankind's efforts to outrace any increases in the scarcity of services provided by the natural environment.[7]

An alternative view, embraced by many ecologists and some economists, is that such compensatory investments often are infeasible as well as ethically indefensible. Physical laws are seen as limiting the extent to which other resources can be substituted for scarce natural resources or ecological degradation. In particular, physical capital cannot be substituted for scarce energy without limit because there are minimum energy requirements for accomplishing any transformation of matter. In addition, because matter is conserved, waste is an inherent part of any economic activity; and natural limits may constrain the capacity of the environment to process these wastes.[8] Healthy ecosystems, including those that provide genetic diversity in relatively unmanaged environments, offer resilience against unexpected changes that preserve options for future generations.[9] For natural life-support systems no practical substitutes are possible, and degradation may be irreversible. In such cases (and perhaps in others as well), compensation cannot be meaningfully specified.[10]

The question of physical scale is central to this debate. If substitutability is relatively easy, then the total scale of human activity relative to the natural environment is of limited significance relative to efficient use of resources and, depending on one's ethical perspective, the adequacy of society's total savings for the future. The notion of "carrying capacity," so often invoked in sustainability debates, then would be at most ephemeral and at worst meaningless outside its traditional ecological usage. Critics of this view turn the entire argument around by claiming that physical limits cannot be ignored and then putting much more emphasis on scale issues (see, e.g., Goodland, Daly, and El Serafy 1991 and Costanza 1991).

A related issue that sometimes is overlooked is the distinction between local and global impacts when considering substitution possibilities. Local resource depletion and ecological degradation, while often having serious consequences, may be more easily compensated for by trade, economic diversification, and migration than regional

---

[7]As pointed out recently by Asheim (1994) and Pezzey (1994b), Hartwick's reinvestment rule has been widely misinterpreted as an instant test of the future sustainability of an arbitrary economy. Although an economy with constant utility over time must satisfy the Hartwick Rule (as Hartwick proved), observing that investment currently happens to be greater than or equal to the resource rent measured at market prices does *not* imply that at least the current level of utility can be maintained by imposing Hartwick's Rule from now onwards. The intuition behind this result is that an economy which is depleting its natural resources too fast for sustainability will drive resource prices and hence resource rents too low, and investment at such a level does not ensure sustainability. The correct indicator of permanent sustainability would be resource rents as measured by shadow prices which reflect the sustainability constraint (which includes the constraint of the current resource stock). This poses a challenge for those interested in developing empirical indicators of sustainable development.

[8]Concern over these issues in the economics literature has been expressed by Ayres and Kneese (1969), Kneese, Ayres, and d'Arge (1971), Ayres and Miller (1980), Perrings (1986), Anderson (1987), Barbier and Markandya (1990), Gross and Veendorp (1990), Victor (1991), Daly (1992), Townsend (1992), and Common and Perrings (1992), see also the survey in Toman, Pezzey and Krautkraemer (forthcoming).

[9]A related argument at the macro level is that environmental quality may complement capital growth as a source of economic progress, particularly for poorer countries (Pearce, Barbier, and Markandya 1990).

[10]The importance of the substitutability issue can be illustrated in connection with the debate over allocating responsibility for greenhouse gas control. If one accepts the view that investments in adaptation to climate change have limited scope for effectiveness, then the atmosphere's capacity to absorb greenhouse gases also is a depletable resource with limited substitution potential. In this case cumulative past greenhouse gas emissions can be a simple metric for assessing a fair distribution of control obligation: greater cumulative emissions by industrialized countries imply greater responsibility. However, if one sees the investment in economic productive capacity and thus in global adaptive capacity by industrial nations as having provided significant benefits that do compensate for depletion of the atmosphere's capacity for greenhouse gas absorption, then the responsibility of industrialized countries is less clear-cut.

or global adversities. On the other hand, trade distortions (e.g., discrimination against manufactured exports by developing countries) may limit national capacities to develop sustainably, and individual countries may appear to develop sustainably by "exporting" unsustainable resource use to other nations that supply materials.

The discussion in this section and the previous one suggests that, at the risk of some caricature, three alternative polar conceptions of sustainability can be identified:

1. *Neoclassical presentism.* This position does not place much emphasis on sustainability as an issue distinct from efficient resource use. The standard present value criterion is adopted for intergenerational welfare comparisons, and natural capital scarcity is assumed to be remediable (given appropriate price signals and incentives) through substitution and technical advance.
2. *Neoclassical egalitarianism.* This view is the same as (1) with respect to assumptions about managing natural capital scarcity, but it also maintains a concern about a potential shortfall in total savings for the future that is not encompassed in the present value criterion.
3. *Ecological organicism.* In contrast to (1) and (2), this view emphasizes limits on substitution between natural capital and other assets. Like (2), this view includes a concern for intergenerational fairness, but that concern is not entirely individualistic; it also encompasses concerns for ecological systems and the human species as a whole.[11]

To be sure, views on sustainability that are composites of these positions also can be defined. The model discussed in the next section allows for a continuum of views about intergenerational fairness and resource substitutability.

IV. AN EXTENDED "SAFE MINIMUM STANDARD"

In this section a simple conceptual framework is outlined that can be used in considering how individualistic resource trade-offs might be balanced against social imperatives for safeguarding against large-scale, irreversible degradation of natural capital. The framework is not intended to imply a specific decision rule. Instead, its purpose is to indicate the implications of different sustainability conceptions and to provide some common ground for consideration of differences in conceptions among economists, ecologists, and ethicists. In broad outline, the framework is a two-tier system in which standard economic trade-offs (market and nonmarket) guide resource assessment and management when the potential consequences are small and reversible, but these trade-offs increasingly are complemented or even superseded by socially determined limits for ecological preservation as the potential consequences become larger and more irreversible. The framework is an extension of the logic of safe minimum standard promulgated by Ciriacy-Wantrup (1952) and Bishop (1978). Variants of this two-tier approach have been suggested by a number of writers from different disciplines (see, e.g., Norton 1982, 1992; Page 1983, 1991; and Randall 1986).

To begin the discussion, suppose for simplicity that all potential human impacts on the natural environment can be characterized by their prospective "cost" and "irreversibility." Prospective cost can be interpreted in several ways. It can be thought of as an (individualistic) economic measure of expected opportunity cost, as an ecological measure of predicted physical impact, or as some hybrid of individualistic or organicist concerns including social values like political freedom and justice. The

---

[11] It would be possible to identify a fourth position, ecological presentism, but this view could be internally contradictory and in any event it seems to hold little interest.

framework does not require a particular definition of cost, though some precision on what is counted as a cost is needed in practice when interpreting alternative conceptions of the safe minimum standard.

Similarly, irreversibility can be seen in terms of an ecological assessment of system function or as an economic construct involving the feasibility of restorative or compensating investment. Economic irreversibility here is taken to be the same as nonsubstitutability. Of course, considerable uncertainty exists regarding both the cost and irreversibility of particular human impacts. This uncertainty is in fact central to the concept of safe minimum standard.

One question that needs to be addressed is why two metrics are needed for gauging impacts and determining social responses. Economists are accustomed to valuing consequences of irreversibility in an uncertain setting (see, e.g., Krutilla 1967; Krutilla and Fisher 1985; and Fisher and Hanemann 1987), so this dimension to some extent is redundant. Indeed, the prospective cost measure could be thought of as including premiums reflecting risks that can be monetized. The concept of systemic scale in ecological research also may forge links between the severity and irreversibility of impacts (Norton and Ulanowicz 1992). This research suggests that damages to ecological systems that are larger in spatial scale or higher up in the hierarchy of natural processes—more complex, consisting of more component subsystems—is both more harmful and harder to reverse because of the complexity and slower time of adaptation in these systems.

Nevertheless, there are reasons for distinguishing the metrics. Monetizing all irreversibility suggests that compensatory investment for any environmental degradation is feasible and ethical.[12] This seems debatable, as already noted. Analytically, it rules out by assumption the ecological organicist position on sustainability defined above. To avoid this, we must retain both the cost and irreversibility dimensions.

The cost and irreversibility dimensions can be brought together in a single "sample universe" as shown in Figure 1.[13] Individu-

als can, in this theory, locate different impacts on the natural environment (e.g., a 5-degree global mean temperature rise or a 50 percent loss of tropical forest) in the square, depending on their own assessments of cost and irreversibility. Because of uncertainties, these assessments will reflect subjective judgments including attitudes toward known or potential risks (in other words, the cost and irreversibility assessments generally will not reflect just subjective mean or median values). Individual judgments inherently will reflect not just factual information but also personal values about the nature of the obligation to future generations. A variety of social institutions, notably the political process, education, and mass communication, presumably generate some synthesis of individual impact assessments at the societal level. The synthesis is dynamic in that it reflects a variety of forms of social learning (e.g., improvements in production technique and social organization).

We can now combine this construct with an extension of the safe minimum standard logic to indicate how individualistic tradeoffs and social imperatives regarding the natural environment might be balanced. The safe minimum standard originally was developed in the context of individual species preservation (see Bishop 1978 and Ciriacy-Wantrup 1952). The logic in this setting is that standard benefit-cost comparisons may be inadequate if the long-term cost of species loss is highly uncertain (in the Knightian sense of having probabilities that are difficult to gauge) but possibly quite substantial. Proponents of a safe minimum standard argue that with low information but high potential asymmetry in the loss function, the evenhanded assessment of benefit-cost analysis should give way to a greater presumption in favor of species

---

[12] This discussion leaves aside important practical problems of measurement that arise in any approach to irreversibility.

[13] This diagrammatic approach was originally developed by Bryan Norton (see Norton 1992). The figure shown here is an adaptation of Norton's schema.

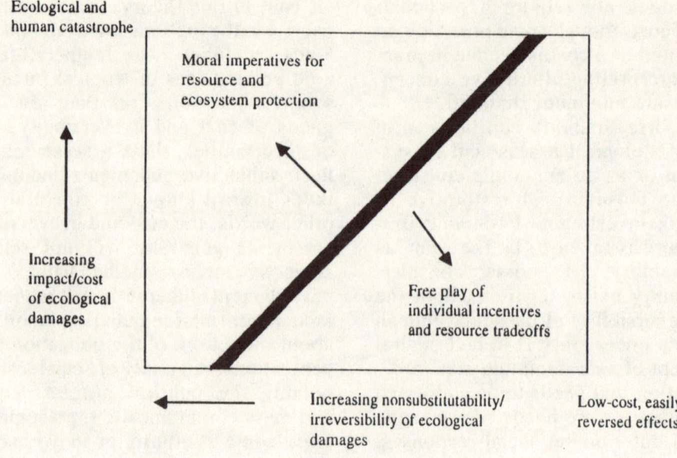

FIGURE 1

ILLUSTRATION OF THE SAFE MINIMUM STANDARD
FOR BALANCING NATURAL RESOURCE TRADE-OFFS
AND IMPERATIVES FOR PRESERVATION

preservation unless society judges that the cost of preservation is "intolerable."[14]

In Figure 1 we extend this logic to a continuum of potential impacts on the natural environment in the following way. First, impacts in the lower-right portion of the box involve both modest cost and a high degree of reversibility. In this area there is little threat of substantial lasting damage to the interests of future generations, and it is reasonable to rely upon individualistic valuations and trade-offs as reflected in benefit-cost analysis. Individual incentives for efficient resource use can be achieved through markets and incentive-based policies to correct "conventional" externalities.

Toward the upper-right corner of the box the costs become higher but still are relatively reversible. Here the primary concern in addition to efficient resource use might be to ensure that the current generation meets obligations to the future through general compensation for environmental degradation. On the other hand, impacts located toward the lower-left corner of the box are relatively irreversible but low in cost, so

they presumably can be absorbed without too much detrimental effect on the future.

It is in considering impacts toward the upper-left corner of Figure 1 that the safe minimum standard assumes prominence. Here the long-term costs are likely to be high and substitution options likely to be low, making the impacts irreversible. Moreover, uncertainty is likely to be substantial since the impacts in question involve large-scale ecological systems and functions that remain poorly understood.

Under these conditions even individualistic, presentist valuations can provide a considerable impetus toward resource preservation. However, the logic of the safe minimum standard suggests that this impetus alone may not fully satisfy reasonable obligations to future generations, particularly when the negative effects involve

---

[14] See Bishop (1979) and Smith and Krutilla (1979), as well as Castle and Berrens (1993) for further discussion of the distinction between the safe minimum standard and benefit-cost analysis. This reasoning is another way of highlighting the need for considering cost and irreversibility as distinct metrics of impact.

408 *Land Economics* *November 1994*

large-scale ecological systems and long gestation periods. One can imagine that the closer one moves to the northwest corner of the box, the more entirely individualistic valuation ciriteria are supplemented by other expressions of community interest in the form of a priori social rules of a "constitutional" nature for preserving natural capital. This is illustrated by the fuzzy demarcation line in Figure 1. Such socially determined criteria could be changed if the members of society deem the cost of preserving natural capital to be excessive, but a higher burden of proof would be placed on arguments favoring acceptance of high-cost, irreversible impacts than on acceptance of smaller impacts.

As already noted, individual perceptions of natural impacts and thus individual assessments of where the fuzzy line should be located depend strongly on individual values and knowledge. Figure 1 can be used to illustrate the different positions on sustainability summarized in the previous section of the paper. Generally speaking, ecologists with a primary concern for natural function and resilience might be more inclined than economists to emphasize the irreversibility dimension and to draw a more vertical fuzzy line, limiting even lower-cost irreversible effects; economists with greater concern for cost and more confidence in substitutability might be more inclined toward a horizontal line. Neoclassical presentists might put little or no area to the northwest of the dividing line (or even dismiss the whole construct), while ecological organicists would take a contrary view. Neoclassical egalitarians might take a middle ground, drawing a close to horizontal line but placing more area above it to limit high-cost burdens on future generations.

It should be emphasized again that there is a distinct difference between the safe minimum standard approach and the standard prescriptions of resource and environmental economics, which involve getting accurate valuations of resources in benefit-cost assessments and using economic incentives to achieve efficient allocations of resources given these valuations. Whether a resource-protection criterion is estab-

lished through application of the safe minimum standard concept or entirely by trade-offs through cost-benefit analyses, that criterion can be achieved cost-effectively by using economic incentives. However, for impacts on the natural environment that are uncertain but may be large and irreversible, the safe minimum standard posits an alternative to relying just on comparisons of expected economic benefits and costs for developing resource-protection criteria.[15] It places greater emphasis on scale issues involving potential damages to the natural system than on the sacrifices experienced from curbing ecological impacts, which are seen as likely to be smaller and more readily reversible. On the other hand, the arguments in this section do not require that either the safe minimum standard as a social decision rule, or individual preferences for environmental preservation, be rigidly hierarchical. The safe minimum standard can be seen as a social compact for expressing agreed-upon moral sentiments in the face of high ecological uncertainty and potential loss asymmetry, even with egoistic consumption, bequest, and time preferences that are entirely neoclassical.[16]

The arguments in this section are somewhat similar to those developed by Vatn and Bromley (1994) regarding environmental decision making and economic valuation. Briefly, these authors argue that large-scale environmental assets or risks are inherently difficult to value meaningfully in a conventional economic sense. This is not just because of limited information about these assets and risks, which causes individual preferences to be poorly defined, but also because large-scale environmental con-

---

[15] See also Pezzey (1989, 1994a), who shows with a simple example that efficient management of externalities over time may not generate sustainable welfare distributions.

[16] Tim Brennan suggests (in private communication) that the safe minimum standard also can be seen as a social decision strategy that economizes on costly information-gathering and enforcement activities relative to theoretically preferred marginal evaluations and policies.

siderations are bound up in social mores that condition individual preferences. Vatn and Bromley argue that people must be seen as dualistic, behaving as citizens as well as consumers, and that many social institutions for environmental management—including the norms surrounding government of the environment—must be seen as ways that societies have attempted to circumvent the informational and "contextual" problems surrounding individualistic valuation. This point of view justifies in particular the imposition of safe minimum standards determined through political discourse and other complex social processes.

V. CONCLUDING REMARKS

Sustainability ultimately is intimately wrapped up with human values and institutions, not just ecological functions. An entirely ecological definition of sustainability is inadequate; guidance for social decision making also is required. It must be recognized that human behavior and social decision processes are complex, just as ecological processes are. At the same time, economic analysis without adequate ecological underpinnings also can be misleading. The sustainability debate also should remind economists to carefully distinguish between efficient allocations of resources—the standard focus of economic theory—and socially optimal allocations that may reflect other intergenerational (as well as intragenerational) equity concerns.

The tension between ecological and economic perspectives on sustainability suggests several ways in which both economists and ecologists could adapt their research emphases and methodologies to make the best use of interdisciplinary contributions. For ecologists, the challenges include providing information on ecological conditions in a form that could be used in economic assessment.[17] Ecologists also must recognize the importance of human behavior, particularly behavior in response to economic incentives—a factor often given short shrift in ecological impact analyses. Economists for their part could ex-

pand analyses of resource values to consider the function and value of ecological systems as a whole, making greater use of ecological information in the process. Both methodological research and case studies are needed to synthesize ecological and economic perspectives. Research by economists and other social scientists (psychologists and anthropologists) also could help to improve understanding of how future generations might value different attributes of natural environments.

From the standpoint of economic theory, an important direction for further research is the consideration of how both physical limits and ethical constraints on resource use may affect the time paths and shadow values of natural capital stocks, relative to the results found in standard theory. The literature on economic growth with natural resources is beginning to address these issues, and there is a lot of basic methodology that can be exploited for this purpose.[18]

One example is the work by Asheim (1988, 1991) and Pezzey (1989, 1994a, 1994b) alluded to earlier. Asheim shows that if we accept the idea of two-tiered social preferences, in which individuals have limited altruism for the next generation but also subscribe to a broader conception of intergenerational social justice, socially preferred outcomes can promote justice without sacrificing growth. In particular, this argument provides a more basic justification for the criterion of nondecreasing utility assumed in Pezzey's sustainability analysis.[19]

Another set of examples concerns the issue of resource substitution. A number of

---

[17]Carpenter (1992) argues that the current state of biophysical measurement for assessing the sustainability of human impacts on ecological systems is too weak to effectively operationalize the concept of natural capital; only gross unsustainability can be detected.

[18]For further discussion see Toman, Pezzey, and Krautkraemer (forthcoming).

[19]Because of the obvious importance of uncertainty in dealing with long-term environmental change, for a complete analysis it is necessary to explicitly reflect this uncertainty in social welfare orderings. This issue is tackled in Asheim and Brekke (1993).

papers have explored the consequences for present-value-maximizing paths of including stocks in utility functions as a reflection of some sort of "amenity" value (see, e.g., Krautkraemer 1985, 1988 and Tahvonen and Kuuluvainen 1993). In these analyses, preservation of some positive level of environmental attribute is not assured; achieving preservation in the steady state requires some combination of large initial capital accumulation and unbounded disutility from environmental degradation. Barbier and Markandya (1990), in particular, consider the consequences of requiring a threshold level of environmental preservation to stave off irreversible environmental disaster. Common and Perrings (1992) go further in discussing the basic differences between economic and ecological sustainability, and the difficulties in bringing these ideas together in a single model.

Despite its continued abuse as a buzzword in policy debates, the concept of sustainability is becoming better established as a consequence of studies in economics, ecology, philosophy, and other disciplines. With a better understanding of the interdisciplinary theoretical issues, and a better empirical understanding of both ecological conditions and social values, sustainability also can evolve to the point of offering more concrete guidance for social policy.

References

Anderson, C. L. 1987. "The Production Process: Inputs and Wastes." *Journal of Environmental Economics and Management* 14 (Mar.):1–12.

Asheim, G. B. 1988. "Rawlsian Intergenerational Justice as a Markov-Perfect Equilibrium in a Resource Technology." *Review of Economic Studies* 55 (July):469–84.

———. 1989. "Intergenerational Conflicts in the Management of Natural and Environmental Resources: Sustainability in a Growth-Theoretic Perspective." Center for Applied Research, Draft Manuscript, Norwegian School of Economics and Business Administration (Oct.).

———. 1991. "Unjust Intergenerational Allocations." *Journal of Economic Theory* 54 (Aug.):350–71.

———. 1994. "Net National Product as an Indicator of Sustainability." *Scandinavian Journal of Economics* 96 (June):257–65.

Asheim, G. B., and K. A. Brekke. 1993. "Sustainability When Resource Management Has Stochastic Consequences." Central Bureau of Statistics, Discussion Paper No. 86, Oslo (Mar.).

Ayres, R. U., and A. V. Kneese. 1969. "Production, Consumption, and Externalities." *American Economic Review* 69 (June): 282–97.

Ayres, R. U., and S. Miller. 1980. "The Role of Technological Change." *Journal of Environmental Economics and Management* 7 (Dec.):353–71.

Baier, A. 1984. "For the Sake of Future Generations." In *Earthbound: New Introductory Essays in Environmental Ethics,* ed. T. Regan. New York: Random House.

Barbier, E. B., and A. Markandya. 1990. "The Conditions for Achieving Environmentally Sustainable Development." *European Economic Review* 34 (May):659–69.

Barry, B. 1977. "Justice Between Generations." In *Law, Morality, and Society: Essays in Honour of H. L. A. Hart,* eds. P. M. S. Hacker and S. J. Rax. Oxford: Clarendon Press.

Baumol, W. J. 1986. "On the Possibility of Continuing Expansion of Finite Resources." *Kyklos* 39:167–79.

Bishop, R. C. 1977. "Intertemporal and Intergenerational Pareto Efficiency: A Comment." *Journal of Environmental Economics and Management* 4 (Sept.):247–57.

———. 1978. "Endangered Species and Uncertainty: The Economics of the Safe Minimum Standard." *American Journal of Agricultural Economics* 60 (Feb.):10–18.

———. 1979. "Endangered Species, Irreversibility and Uncertainty: A Reply." *American Journal of Agricultural Economics* 61 (May): 376–79.

Brennan, T. J. 1989. "A Methodological Assessment of Multiple Utility Frameworks." *Economics and Philosophy* 5:189–208.

Bromley, D. W. 1989. "Entitlements, Missing Markets and Environmental Uncertainty." *Journal of Environmental Economics and Management* 17 (Sept.):181–94.

Broome, J. 1991. *The Intergenerational Aspects of Climate Change.* Bristol, UK: University of Bristol.

———. 1992. *Counting the Cost of Global Warming.* Cambridge: White Horse Press.

Burton, P. S. 1993. "Intertemporal Preferences

and Intergenerational Equity Considerations in Optimal Resource Harvesting." *Journal of Environmental Economics and Management* 24 (Mar.):119–32.

Cabe, R. A. 1982. "Intertemporal and Intergenerational Pareto Efficiency: An Extended Theorem." *Journal of Environmental Economics and Management* 9 (Dec.):355–60.

Callicott, J. B. 1989. *In Defense of the Land Ethic*. Albany: State University of New York Press.

Carpenter, R. A. 1992. "Can Sustainability Be Measured." Paper presented at the 2nd Meeting of the International Society for Ecological Economics, Stockholm, Sweden, Stockholm University, August 3–6.

Castle, E. N., and R. P. Berrens. 1993. "Endangered Species, Economic Analysis, and the Safe Minimum Standard." *Northwest Environmental Journal* 9:108–30.

Ciriacy-Wantrup, S. V. 1952. *Resource Conservation*. Berkeley: University of California Press.

Common, M., and C. Perrings. 1992. "Towards an Ecological Economics of Sustainability." *Ecological Economics* 6 (July):7–34.

Costanza, R., ed. 1991. *Ecological Economics: The Science and Management of Sustainability*. New York: Columbia University Press.

Daly, H. 1990. "Toward Some Operational Principles of Sustainable Development." *Ecological Economics* 2 (Apr.):1–6.

———. 1991. "Ecological Economics and Sustainable Development: From Concept to Policy." Environment Department Working Paper No. 1991–24, The World Bank.

———. 1992. "Is the Entropy Law Relevant to the Economics of Natural Resource Scarcity?—Yes, of Course It Is!" *Journal of Environmental Economics and Management* 23 (July):91–95.

Dasgupta, P. S., and G. M. Heal. 1974. "The Optimal Depletion of Exhaustible Resources." In *Review of Economic Studies, Symposium on the Economics of Exhaustible Resources*. Edinburgh, Scotland: Longman Group Limited.

Dasgupta, P. S., and K.-G. Mäler. 1991. "The Environment and Emerging Development Issues." In *Proceedings of the World Bank Annual Conference on Development Economics 1990*. Washington, DC: The World Bank.

Dixon, J. A., and L. A. Fallon. 1989. "The Concept of Sustainability: Origins, Extensions, and Usefulness for Policy." *Society and Natural Resources* 2:73–84.

Ehrlich, P. R. 1989. "The Limits to Substitution: Meta-Resource Depletion and a New Economic-Ecological Paradigm." *Ecological Economics* 1 (Feb.):9–16.

Fisher, A. C., and W. M. Hanemann. 1987. "Quasi-Option Value: Some Misconceptions Dispelled." *Journal of Environmental Economics and Management* 14 (June):183–90.

Golding, Martin P. 1972. "Obligations to Future Generations." *The Monist* 56:85–99.

Goodland, R., H. Daly, and S. El Serafy, eds. 1991. "Environmental Sustainable Economic Development Building on Brundtland." Environment Department, Environment Working Paper No 46, The World Bank (July).

Gross, L. S., and E. C. H. Veendorp. 1990. "Growth With Exhaustible Resources and a Materials-Balance Production Function." *Natural Resource Modeling* 4 (Winter): 77–94.

Hartwick, J. M. 1977. "Intergenerational Equity and the Investing of Rents from Exhaustible Resources." *American Economic Review* 67 (Dec.):972–74.

Howarth, R. B. 1991a. "Intergenerational Competitive Equilibria under Technological Uncertainty and an Exhaustible Resource Constraint." *Journal of Environmental Economics and Management* 21 (Nov.):225–43.

———. 1991b. "Intertemporal Equilibria and Exhaustible Resources: An Overlapping Generations Approach." *Ecological Economics* 4 (Dec.):237–52.

———. 1992. "Intergenerational Justice and the Chain of Obligation." *Environmental Values* 1 (Summer):133–40.

Howarth, R. B., and R. B. Norgaard. 1990. "Intergenerational Resource Rights, Efficiency and Social Optimality." *Land Economics* 66 (Feb.):1–11.

———. 1992. "Environmental Valuation under Sustainability." *American Economic Review* 82 (May):473–77.

———. 1993. "Intergenerational Transfers and the Social Discount Rate." *Environmental and Resource Economics* 3 (Aug.):337–58.

Kneese, A. V., and W. D. Schulze. 1985. "Ethics and Environmental Economics." In *Handbook of Natural Resource and Energy Economics*, Vol. 1, eds. A. V. Kneese and J. L. Sweeney. Amsterdam: North-Holland.

Kneese, A., R. Ayres, and R. d'Arge. 1971. *Economics and the Environment*. Baltimore, MD: Johns Hopkins University Press for Resources for the Future.

Krautkraemer, J. A. 1985. "Optimal Growth, Resource Amenities and the Preservation of Natural Environments." *Review of Economic Studies* 52 (Jan.):153–70.

———. 1988. "The Rate of Discount and the Preservation of Natural Environments." *Natural Resource Modeling* 2 (Winter): 421–37.

Krutilla, J. V. 1967. "Conservation Reconsidered." *American Economic Review* 54 (Sept.):777–86.

Krutilla, J. V., and A. C. Fisher. 1985. *The Economics of Natural Environments: Studies in the Valuation of Commodity and Amenity Resources*, 2d ed. Washington, DC: Resources for the Future.

Leopold, A. 1949. *A Sand County Almanac*. New York: Oxford University Press.

Lovelock, J. 1988. *The Ages of Gaia*. New York: Norton.

Mäler, K.-G. 1991. "National Accounts and Environmental Resources." *Environmental and Resource Economics* 1:1–16.

Nash, J. A. 1989. "Ecological Integrity and Christian Political Responsibility." *Theology and Public Policy* 1 (Fall):32–48.

Norgaard, R. B. 1988. "Sustainable Development: A Co-Evolutionary View." *Futures* 20 (Dec.):606–20.

Norton, B. G. 1982. "Environmental Ethics and the Rights of Future Generations." *Environmental Ethics* 4 (Winter):319–30.

———. 1984. "Environmental Ethics and Weak Anthropocentrism." *Environmental Ethics* 6 (Summer):131–48.

———. 1986. "On the Inherent Danger of Undervaluing Species." In *The Preservation of Species*, ed. B. G. Norton. Princeton, NJ: Princeton University Press.

———. 1989. "Intergenerational Equity and Environmental Decisions: A Model Using Rawls' Veil of Ignorance." *Ecological Economics* 1 (May):137–59.

———. 1992. "Sustainability, Human Welfare, and Ecosystem Health." *Environmental Values* 1 (Summer):97–111.

Norton, B. G., and R. E. Ulanowicz. 1992. "Scale and Biodiversity Policy: A Hierarchical Approach." *Ambio* 21 (May):244–49.

Page, T. 1977. *Conservation and Economic Efficiency*. Baltimore, MD: Johns Hopkins University Press for Resources for the Future.

———. 1983. "Intergenerational Justice as Opportunity." *Energy and the Future*, eds. D. MacLean and P. G. Brown. Totowa, NJ: Rowman and Littlefield.

———. 1988. "Intergenerational Equity and the Social Rate of Discount." In *Environmental Resource and Applied Welfare Economics*,

ed. V. K. Smith. Washington, DC: Resources for the Future.

———. 1991. "Sustainability and the Problem of Valuation." In *Ecological Economics: The Science and Management of Sustainability*, ed. R. Constanza. New York: Columbia University Press.

Parfit, D. 1983a. "Energy Policy and the Further Future: The Identity Problem." In *Energy and the Future*, eds. D. MacLean and P. B. Brown. Totowa, NJ: Rowman and Littlefield.

———. 1983b. "Energy Policy and the Further Future: The Social Discount Rate." In *Energy and the Future*, eds. D. MacLean and P. B. Brown. Totowa, NJ: Rowman and Littlefield.

Passmore, J. 1974. *Man's Responsibility for Nature*. New York: Scribner's.

Pearce, D. W. 1983. "Ethics, Irreversibility, Future Generations and the Social Rate of Discount." *International Journal of Environmental Studies* 21:67–86.

Pearce, D., and R. Turner. 1990. *Economics of Natural Resources and the Environment*. Baltimore, MD: Johns Hopkins University Press.

Pearce, D., A. Markandya, and E. Barbier. 1989. *Blueprint for a Green Economy*. London: Earthscan.

Pearce, D. W., E. Barbier, and A. Markandya. 1990. *Sustainable Development: Economics and Environment in the Third World*. London: Earthscan.

Perrings, C. 1986. "Conservation of Mass and Instability in a Dynamic Economy-Environment System." *Journal of Environmental Economics and Management* 13 (Sept.):199–211.

Pezzey, J. 1989. *Economic Analysis of Sustainable Growth and Sustainable Development*. World Bank, Environment Department Working Paper No. 15. Now reprinted as Pezzey, J. 1992. *Sustainable Development Concepts: An Economic Analysis*. World Bank Environment paper No. 2. Washington, DC: World Bank.

———. 1992. "Sustainability: An Interdisciplinary Guide." *Environmental Values* 1 (Mar):321–62.

———. 1994a. "Sustainability, Intergenerational Equity, and Environmental Policy." Draft manuscript, University College London (April).

———. 1994b. "The Optimal Sustainable Depletion of Nonrenewable Resources." Draft manuscript, University College London (May).

Randall, A. 1986. "Human Preferences, Economics, and the Preservation of Species." In *The Preservation of Species*, ed. B. G. Norton. Princeton, NJ: Princeton University Press.

Randall, A., and M. C. Farmer. 1993. "Policies for Sustainability: Lessons from an Overlapping Generations Model." Draft manuscript, Columbus: The Ohio State University (Jan.).

Rawls, J. 1971. *A Theory of Justice.* Cambridge: Harvard University Press.

Sagoff, M. 1988. *The Economy of the Earth.* New York: Cambridge University Press.

Sandler, T., and V. K. Smith. 1976. "Intertemporal and Intergenerational Pareto Efficiency." *Journal of Environmental Economics and Management* 2 (Feb.):151–59.

———. 1977. "Intertemporal and Intergenerational Pareto Efficiency Revisited." *Journal of Environmental Economics and Management* 4 (Sept.):252–57.

———. 1982. "Intertemporal and Intergenerational Pareto Efficiency: A Reconsideration of Recent Extensions." *Journal of Environmental Economics and Management* 9 (Dec.):361–65.

Sen, A. K. 1982. "Approaches to the Choice of Discount Rates for Social Benefit—Cost Analysis." In *Discounting for Time and Risk in Energy Policy*, eds. R. C. Lind et al. Washington, DC: Resources for the Future.

Smith, V. K., and J. V. Krutilla. 1979. "Endangered Species, Irreversibilities, and Uncertainty: A Comment." *American Journal of Agricultural Economics* 61 (May):371–75.

Solow, R. M. 1974. "Intergenerational Equity and Exhaustible Resources." In *Review of Economic Studies, Symposium on the Economics of Exhaustible Resources.* Edinburgh, Scotland: Longman Group Limited.

———. 1986. "On the Intergenerational Allocation of Natural Resources." *Scandinavian Journal of Economics* 88 (June):141–49.

———. 1993a. "An Almost Practical Step Toward Sustainability." *Resources Policy* 19 (Sept.):162–72.

———. 1993b. "Sustainability: An Economist's Perspective." In *Selected Readings in Environmental Economics*, ed. R. Dorfman and N. Dorfman, 3rd ed. New York: Norton.

Stiglitz, J. 1974. "Growth with Exhaustible Natural Resources: Efficient and Optimal Growth Paths." In *Review of Economic Studies, Symposium on the Economics of Exhaustible Resources.* Edinburgh, Scotland: Longman Group Limited.

Tahvonen, O., and J. Kuuluvainen. 1993. "Economic Growth, Pollution, and Renewable Resources." *Journal of Environmental Economics and Management* 24 (Mar.):101–18.

Tietenberg, T. 1992. *Environmental and Natural Resource Economics*, 3rd ed. New York: Harper Collins.

Toman, M. A., J. Pezzey, and J. Krautkraemer. Forthcoming. "Neoclassical Economic Growth Theory and 'Sustainability'." In *Handbook of Environmental Economics*, ed. D. W. Bromley. Oxford: Basil Blackwell.

Townsend, K. N. 1992. "Is the Entropy Law Relevant to the Economics of Natural Resource Scarcity? Comment." *Journal of Environmental Economics and Management* 23 (July):96–100.

van Geldrop, J., and C. Withagen. 1993. "Natural Capital and Sustainability." Draft Manuscript, Department of Mathematics and Computing, University of Technology, Eindhoven, Netherlands.

Varian, H. 1984. *Microeconomic Analysis*, 2d ed. New York: Norton.

Vatn, A., and D. W. Bromley, 1994. "Choices without Prices without Apologies." *Journal of Environmental Economics and Management* 26 (Mar.):129–48.

Victor, P. A. 1991. "Indicators of Sustainable Development: Some Lessons from Capital Theory." *Ecological Economics* 4 (Dec.): 191–213.

Weiss, E. B. 1989. *In Fairness to Future Generations.* Dobbs Ferry, NY: Transnational Publishers.

World Bank. 1992. *World Development Report 1992: Development and the. Environment.* New York: Oxford University Press.

World Commission on Environment and Development (WCED). 1987. *Our Common Future.* New York: Oxford University Press.

Part V
Sustainable Cities

[22]
Sustainable cities: transport, energy, and urban form

D. Banister, S. Watson and C. Wood

Abstract

This paper extends the debate over the ideal of the sustainable city, particularly as it relates to transport, by providing empirical evidence, from five case-study cities in the United Kingdom and one in the Netherlands on the links between urban form and energy consumption in transport. It also links energy use measures to the physical, economic, and social structure of the city to determine whether there are significant relationships. Energy-use measures combine all the characteristics of travel (mode, distance and frequency), together with occupancy, to give a new set of composite measures of travel. The conclusions reached are mixed in that significant relationships have been found, principally between energy use use in transport and physical characteristics of the city, such as density, size and amount of open space. But compatability problems make it difficult to establish definitive relationships.

1   Background to the debate

The United Kingdom is committed to the agreements made at the Rio Summit and a UK Strategy on Sustainable Development was published in January 1994 (DoE, 1994a), followed by a guidance document (March 1994) on transport (DoE, 1994b). This gives local authorities strong advice on the means to reduce the growth in length and number of motorized journeys, to encourage the use of alternative means of travel which has less environmental impact, and to reduce the reliance on the car. Although there has only been a modest growth in the number of trips in the United Kingdom from 18.4 trips per person per week in 1973 to 21.0 trips per person per week in 1990 (+14 per cent), the growth in average trip length has been substantial, from 7.5 km to 9.5 km (+27 per cent – this figure includes all short walk trips). The net result has been a phenomenal growth in travel of 45 per cent (from 133 km to 199 km per person per week). In addition, this growth has mainly been in car use with the modal proportion increasing from 46 per cent to 57 per cent, with public transport use declining from 13 per cent to 10 per cent over the period 1973–90. The government's principal response has been to raise fuel duty by 5 per cent in real terms each year (from 1993) to meet the Rio stabilization targets. They argue that targets to stabilize CO_2 emissions will be met by action in all sectors, including transport. However, there is little evidence that real petrol price increases have reduced the demand for travel by car in the short term. Longer term readjustments may result in more efficient vehicles being purchased.

Previous research (Banister, 1992; 1996; Banister and Banister, 1995) has used UK National Travel Survey data (DoT, 1988) to establish distance travelled per person per week and primary energy consumption for each mode of transport and for four types of area in the United Kingdom. Here, the intermediate-sized settlements, over 25 000 but smaller than London, seemed to be the least energy intensive in transport terms. The 1981 Census journey-to-work patterns have also been analysed for the 403 districts in England and Wales. Although the journey to work accounts for only 20 per cent of all journeys made, it has allowed clear spatial patterns of energy use in transport to be established. The energy-intensive commuter area of the Southeast of England around London is dominant, but other areas in the West Midlands and the North are also [125] energy intensive, reflecting long journeys to work by car and rail. The inner London boroughs and the 28 nonmetropolitan districts with high population densities (over 21 persons per hectare) were the locations where least energy was used.

From this research two main conclusions have emerged. One relates to the development of a new measure of energy use in transport. Although trips give one measure of travel, energy use allows the three main dimensions of travel to be combined in one composite measure. Energy use is a function of mode used, distance travelled, and frequency of trip. It can also be modified by vehicle occupancy to give energy use per passenger kilometre rather than vehicle kilometre. If any one of these four variables changes, so does the energy use. The second conclusion is that analysis needs to be carried out at a more local level than the city as there may be as much variation within cities as between cities. In this paper we report on a comprehensive set of results for a range of British cities where calculated energy use in transport has been related to the physical, economic, and social structure of the city to determine whether there are significant relationships. The work builds upon the considerable research carried out in the United Kingdom (for example, Breheny, 1993; 1995a; 1995b; Frost *et al.*, 1994; Owens and Rickaby, 1992; Rickaby, 1991), and the broader international debate (for example, Bae and Richardson, 1994; CEC, 1992; Gordon and Richardson, 1989; Gordon *et al.*, 1991; Naess *et al.*, 1993; 1994; Newman and Kenworthy, 1989a; 1989b).

2   The selection of case studies and research methodology

Five UK case-study cities have been selected: the large, industrial city of Liverpool (population 450 000); the provincial centre of Leicester (270 000); the low-density archetype of Milton Keynes (170 000); the small historic city of Oxford (124 000), with notable progressive transport policies in operation; and the market town of Banbury (30 000). Each of the areas represents a different size, urban type and urban configuration. They also represent an interesting range of planning and transport policies. In addition, one overses case study has been carried out in the Dutch new town of Almere (with a population of 85 000 and contrasting markedly with Milton Keynes). The two main areas of the research has been to establish which size of settlement is most efficient in transport and energy terms, and to link energy-use measures to the physical, economic, and social structure to determine whether there are significant relationships.

The primary requirements for an analysis of passenger energy use are details of trips for all purposes by mode, distance, and frequency – from travel diaries completed by people living in an urban area and those entering and leaving it. This is supplemented by public transport timetable information for the given area. Average energy-consumption figures for different modes of transport have been calculated from national figures (Table 1), and these figures can be adapted to local conditions through the use of local occupancy levels.

In an ideal world, primary data collection would allow direct comparison to be made between cities. However, life is not ideal and we have to rely on secondary data sources. The question is then modified to whether comparable analysis can be squeezed out of past surveys (Table 2). Once the travel, census, and other local data have been placed on a comparable basis, relationships are established through correlation and regression between energy consumption and three groups of measures of urban form: physical, economic, and social (Table 3). In each case, empirical analysis can focus on the city or town as the unit of study or on the social or economic disaggregation provided that the travel and energy consumption data are available at the appropriate level. The empirical relationships established for one city or town can be compared with those from the other case studies. [126]

The methodology used here is similar to that being developed independently at the Norwegian Institute of Urban and Regional Research (see Naess, 1993; Naess *et al.*, 1993; 1994). The analysis of the relationships between the different variables and the use of energy in transport has been through contingency table and correlational analysis. This has identified bivariate relationships, and stepwise regression analysis has been used to explain the measure of energy use – energy use per trip, energy use per person and energy use per kilometre. The methodology described above was followed in all our case-study areas. The results derived from this analysis have enabled tentative suggestions to be made about the relationship between urban form and transport energy use. [127]

3　The Results

3.1　Liverpool

Liverpool is the largest city studied and forms part of the Merseyside Metropolitan Area. Over the last twenty years the local economy has been restructured as the traditional shipbuilding and manufacturing industries have been replaced by commercial and service sector industries. Car ownership has been below national averages (63 per cent) with 43 per cent of households owning cars in Liverpool and 55 per cent of households in Merseyside. The city and metropolitan areas are characterized by high levels of rented accommodation (49 per cent in Liverpool and 37 per cent in Merseyside), and by high levels of [128] unemployment (20 per cent in Liverpool and 15 per cent in Merseyside). Public transport is used by nearly 30 per cent for the journey to work, and walking is still important for local journeys.

The analysis in Liverpool is based on a sample of a major transport study carried out in 1988 (Table 2) and the data have been aggregated into the five districts in Merseyside

Table 1.   Modal primary energy consumption figures

Mode	Seats or spaces	Energy consumption, MJ per:		
		vehicle km	seat km	passenger km
Rail:				
Inter City electric	564	316	0.56	1.4
Inter City diesel	490	210	0.43	1.1
Suburban electric				
25 kV AC	300	132	0.44	2.0
750 V DC	386	111	0.29	1.3
Suburban diesel	146	73.6	0.50	2.3
Average 'BR'	377	168	0.54	1.6
London Underground	555	141	0.25	1.7
Average	407	164	0.41	1.6
Light Rail	265	79.8	0.30	0.91	1.20
Bus:				
Double decker	74	18.5	0.25	0.75	1.25
Single decker	49	17.5	0.36	1.07	1.79
Average 'big bus'	62	18.0	0.29	0.87	1.45
Minibus	20	8.0	0.40	1.20	1.20
Average bus	48	14.7	0.34	0.92	1.53
Express coach	46	15.0	0.33	0.98	1.63
Car:				
Small petrol (1.11)	4	2.6	0.65	1.5
Large petrol (2.91)	4	5.3	1.33	3.0
Small diesel (1.81)	4	2.3	0.58	1.3
Large diesel (2.51)	4	3.3	0.83	1.9
Average	4	3.3	0.83	1.9
Other:				
Motorcycle	2	1.9	0.95	1.7
Moped	1	1.5	1.50	1.5
Average	1.3	1.6	1.33	1.6

Notes:

The modal primary energy consumption figures are measured in megajoules (MJ) and they include energy use in maintenance.

The capacity figures for London Underground and light rail refer to passenger spaces rather than seats. The derivation of these figures is explained, together with a review of other published sources, in Wood (1994).

Average figures for cars and motorcycles or mopeds are weighted according to national (GB) fleet sizes (DoT, 1993). Occupancy figures are as follows: Inter City electric and diesel = 40 per cent, Suburban = 22 per cent, London Underground = 15 per cent, Light Rail = 33 per cent (left column) and 25 per cent, and bus = 33 per cent (left column) and 25 per cent, and bus = 33 per cent (left column) and 20 per cent. Car occupancy figures are a weighted average of 1.76 (work = 1.2 and nonwork = 1.85). Occupancy for motorcycle is 1.11 and for moped is 1.00. 'BR' refers to train services run and formerly run by British Rail.

Source: based on Banister, 1994; and adapted from ACEC, 1976; Howard, 1990; Hughes, 1993; Wood, 1994, Wood et al., 1994.

Table 2.   List of data sets

Title	Nature of survey	Sample size	Mode	Limitations of survey	Date	Source
Liverpool	household	1490 trips	all	individual trip distance calculated from trip matrix by ward through shortest distance algorithm	1988	Merseyside Information Services (MIS, 1988)
Leicester	household	1196 trips	vehicle only	distance matrix absent for intrazonal trips. No walk or cycle – so energy figures higher than actual. Incompatibility between transport and administrative zones	1988	Greater Leicester Transportation Study (MVA, 1988)
Milton Keynes	household	1274 trips	all	detailed survey, but only carried out for Linford Ward	1990	TEST (1991)
Almere	household	about 1000 trips	all	detailed household survey, comparable with Milton Keynes (Linford Ward)	1990	TEST (1991)
Oxford	roadside interviews	4828 trips across 5 cordons	all	trips not assigned to household location – sorted by home or origin and destination. No intrazonal trip or energy figures	1991	Buchanan and Partners (1992) for Oxford City Council
Banbury	household	3000 households	all	only weekday morning peak trips. No leisure or shopping trips. No appropriate distance matrix so distances calculated on travel time or speed	1993	Cherwell District Council for Oxford City Council (OCC, 1993)

Table 3.   Definitions of the physical, economic and social variables used

Variable	Definition
Physical	
Density	Persons per hectare
Open space	Percentage not built up
Size	Hectares
Compactness	Maximum length to width ratio
Population	Population 1991
Economic	
Employment	Number of persons working in area
Car ownership	Cars per household
Unemployed	Percentage not working and actively seeking work
Jobs/population	Ratio of jobs to population
Social	
SEG	Percentage of household heads in socioeconomic group (SEG) A
Housing tenure type	Percentage owner-occupied
Household size	Persons per household
Young	Percentage under 17 years
Elderly	Percentage of pensioners
Household composition	Percentage of households with more than 2 children under 16 years
Housing type	Percentage terraced

(Table 4). Full information has been obtained for households, and all trips made by all modes and for all purposes are covered. It has provided the fullest information from all the case-study locations. However, individual trip distance has had to be calculated from the trip matrix and this has been calculated on a ward basis for shortest distance. This means that the distances are shorter than actual distances, and that journeys outside the metropolitan area are not included in the data set. The Merseyside conurbation does seem to have the characteristics of an energy-efficient urban form, at least in transport terms, as the proportions of walk trips and bus trips are both high (32 per cent and 17 per cent, respectively; see Table 5). It also illustrates the necessity of having all trips included in the analysis as it is the longer trips outside the metropolitan area which are the most energy intensive. The average trip lengths within the city are short, about 40 per cent of the Leicester and Oxford levels and 25 per cent of the Banbury levels. [129]

In the Merseyside conurbation significant relationships have been found (at the 95 per cent level) between energy use per household and tenure (percentage owner-occupied), housing type (percentage terraced) and car ownership (Table 6). It seems that within the Merseyside conurbation the generally low levels of car use and short trip lengths can be explained by housing and car-ownership variables. Similarly, at the individual level there are strong

Table 4. Energy-use data for Merseyside

| | Trip distance (km) | | Trips | Energy use (MJ) per: | | |
	longest	average		trip	household	person
Merseyside		3.26	1490	4.96	27.17	15.27
Knowsley	13.5	3.37	125	4.83	27.46	20.83
Liverpool	30	3.19	407	4.69	21.22	13.08
St Helens	18.6	3.29	336	4.71	25.92	13.40
Sefton	29	3.58	382	5.87	32.98	17.65
Wirral	14	2.75	240	4.39	33.98	16.45

correlations with energy use per person and age, household size, and household composition (all significant at the 80 per cent level). In the other cities, physical variables have emerged as significant, but in Merseyside this has not been the case. The Merseyside data have permitted only within-conurbation movements to be recorded as it is here that the socioeconomic variables become more important (Table 6). Although there was a substantial variation in density and size between the five districts in Merseyside, neither has emerged as a significant variable in the correlation analysis. The only significant relationship (at the 75 per cent level) was found between density and energy use per household.

In all cases, the signs on the correlations are appropriate as car ownership, as the proportion of owner-occupied properties, as the proportion of young people, as household size and household composition (households with more than two children under 16 years) increases, so does energy use per household and per person. Similarly, as the proportion of non-car-owning households, the proportion of elderly, and the proportion of terraced houses in the area increases, so the level of energy use per household and per person decreases. There was also a positive correlation between energy use per household and population change (significant at the 90 per cent level). The interpretation here is that the smaller the change in population (1981–91), the greater the use of energy per household. Those districts which had lost least population are [130] those which have higher car ownership levels and energy use. It is the inner-city districts which have lost most population whilst the peripheral districts have maintained population levels.

Table 5. Model split (%) in Merseyside

	Walk	Bicycle	Car driver	Car passenger	Rail	Bus	Other
Knowsley	28.2	0.0	32.3	6.7	4.0	28.2	0.6
Liverpool	40.0	2.0	23.8	10.3	2.5	18.9	2.5
Sefton	25.7	2.6	34.6	16.2	4.7	10.7	5.5
St Helens	30.4	1.2	30.7	12.8	2.7	22.3	0.0
Wirral	32.5	0.8	32.5	16.3	2.1	10.4	5.4
Merseyside	32.0	1.6	30.2	13.0	3.2	17.0	3.0

Table 6.   Correlations between variables

Variable	Correlation	Significance (%)
Energy use per trip		
Trip length	0.8207	95
Energy use per household		
Population change	0.7192	90
Car ownership	0.7557	92
No car ownership	−0.7557	92
Tenure	0.8254	95
Housing type	−0.8987	98
Trips per household	0.8130	95
Energy use per person		
Young	0.6577	85
Elderly	−0.6639	85
Household size	0.6517	85
Household composition	0.7017	82
Trips per person	0.8538	97

In the Merseyside conurbation, energy use per household is highest in the Wirral and Sefton, and lowest in Liverpool, but trips per person were highest in Knowsley (4.31 trips per person). Energy use per trip was similar in all districts (except Sefton), reflecting a similarity in average trip lengths and modal split (Table 5). Liverpool has the highest level of walk (40 per cent), which results in lower levels of energy use overall, even though trip lengths and trip rates are similar to those found elsewhere. The highest levels of energy use per household in Wirral and Sefton reflect the larger household sizes and the greater use of the car (Table 5). In these two districts, car accounts for about half the trips, whereas the average for Merseyside is 43 per cent. The overall patterns reflect these differences and those locations making the highest numbers of trips are not necessarily those that use the most energy in tranport – this pattern also relates to mode and trip distance.

The Merseyside data are interesting and the results are different from those in the other case-study locations. The data limitations make stronger conclusions difficult, but further analysis is warranted as the metropolitan area demonstrates the potential for low energy use in transport. However, this may in part be explained by the traditionally low levels of car ownership in Liverpool and a high level of public transport use and movement by foot.

3.2   *Leicester*

Leicester, with a population of some 300 000, has followed transport and land-use policies designed to take consideration of environmental objectives. It has been designated the first Environmental City in the United Kingdom, and it has adopted an Energy Action Plan and a Transport Choice Strategy. In planning for a sustainable transport system, it is important that all modes of transport are coordinated and the Central Leicestershire Transport Strategy

Table 7. Energy-use data for Leicester and surrounding districts

	Trip distance (km)	Trips	Energy use (MJ) per:		
			trip	household	person
Leicester	5.89	3700	10.55	52.32	18.62
Oadby	6.94	1096	13.63	108.22	37.84
Harborough	13.17	990	25.88	125.00	48.63
Blaby	7.85	292	15.12	93.90	35.70
Charnwood	12.72	288	24.63	118.22	42.29
Overall	9.31	6366	17.96	99.53	36.62

(LCC, 1990) sets out a series of options and adopts a Transport Choice option where high-quality, attractive, and efficient public transport systems must be provided to attract potential and actual car users. It links in closely with the County Structure Plan and the Environmental Strategy. Leicester was selected as an example of a typical medium-sized UK city with high-quality 'green credentials' (Banister *et al.*, 1994).

The analysis was carried out on the City of Leicester and for the four districts which surround the city (Tables 2 and 7). Average trip lengths increase from 6 km in the City of Leicester and Oadby and Blaby (the two most urban districts) to over 12 km in Charnwood and Harborough. The energy use per trip reflects the trip distance, but energy use per household and per person show a greater range (Table 7). Leicester City has substantially lower levels of energy use and this reflects both shorter journey lengths and a lower trip rate per person (1.76 trips per person as compared with the sample average of 1.93). The omission of bicycle and walk trips may also be relevant as these trip rates are likely to be higher in urban areas than in the more rural districts. Outside Leicester, the pattern of energy use in the four districts is similar both at the individual and at the household levels.

Correlation analysis has been carried out for energy per trip and energy use per person (Table 8). Three significant variables emerge from the energy-use-per-trip correlations. The relationship with trip length is to be expected, but it also relates to the density and size of the area. This reinforces the observations already made on the differences in trip patterns between the City of Leicester and the other districts. [131] Energy use per trip increases with trip length and size of area, and decreases as density increases.

Energy use per person is again linked with density of urban area, and also with car ownership, unemployment, the proportion of young people, socioenonomic group (SEG) and household composition. Positive links between energy use per person are found with levels of car ownership and proportion of household heads in SEG A. Less energy per person is used by the young (under 17 years), by the unemployed, by those households with more than two children and by those living in high-density areas.

From the Leicester data, the importance of density and size of area is clear in terms of energy use per trip. But this has to be placed within the wider context of the socioeconomic characteristics of the population. The number of trips made, the modes used, and the distances travelled are clearly related to the social composition of the population and these links are

Table 8.   Energy-use correlations in Leicester

Variable[a]	Mean value	Correlation	Significance (%)
Energy use per trip			
Trip length (km)	9.47	0.997	99
Density (ha^{-1})	14.26	−0.837	96
Area size (ha)	21 983	0.877	97
Energy use per person			
Young (%)	23.14	−0.8677	95
Car ownership	1.058	0.8657	95
Unemployment (%)	5.34	−0.8767	95
SEG (%)	16	0.8367	80
Household composition (%)	4.9	−0.8269	85
Density (ha^{-1})	14.26	−0.8986	99

Note: [a] See Table 3 for definitions.

reflected in the figures for energy use per person. These relationships seem clearer in the Leicester case than elsewhere, and may reflect the absence of walk and cycle trips from the data set.

3.3   Milton Keynes

The Milton Keynes data, collected by TEST in 1990 (Roberts and Wood, 1992; TEST, 1991), was the most detailed data set, using a 24-hour, 7-day, all-mode travel diary with distance included. In many ways it offered the definitive survey for this study. The data were only available for a small part of the city, but comparable census information shows that it is representative for the whole of Milton Keynes. Linford Ward is centrally located within the Borough of Milton Keynes, with a population of 19 000, about 10 per cent of the total Milton Keynes population. It nearly doubled its population over [132] ten years (1981–91), but in most other respects reflects the socioeconomic structure of Milton Keynes (Table 9).

Milton Keynes is a new town built on a designated site of 9000 ha with an eventual population of 250 000. Since 1967 is has formed the most rapidly growing district in Great Britain as its population has grown from 40 000 (1969) to 173 000 (1991). The original Master Plan aimed for a balance of housing and employment so that the city could be self-contained without large numbers of people needing to commute in or out (MKDC, 1992). The city was built around a 1 km grid of main roads serving dispersed land uses to allow freedom of movement by car and other forms of transport. Within this grid stands the city centre which acts as a geographical focus around the railway station. Residential areas were grouped into neighbourhoods with local activity centres, and pedestrian and cycle routes were segregated from the main roads. The grid system was adjusted in certain locations to allow linear parks to take advantage of natural features such as river valleys. Overall, Milton Keynes is a low-density city where most travel is undertaken by car. However, as land uses are mixed and

Table 9.   Data for Milton Keynes Borough and Linford Ward

Variable[a]	Milton Keynes	Linford
Population	172 969	18 990
Population change, 1981–91 (%)	39.1	91
Young (%)	27.9	27.6
Elderly (%)	11.7	9.6
Car ownership	1.1	1.1
Persons with no car (%)	25.1	23
Housing tenure (%)	69.2	69.3
Unemployment (%)	8.4	7.7
SEG (%)	17.1	21.0
Household size	2.6	2.7
Housing type (%)	36.3	36.43
Household composition (%)	6.5	
Area (ha)	30 851	693
Density (ha^{-1})	5.6	27.72
Open space (%)	73	10.14
Compactness	1.5	1.16
Employment	85 234	6620
Major supermarkets[b]	81	5
Schools	97	9
Leisure centres	44	4

Notes:
[a] The variables are as defined in Table 3, except that 'young' is the percentage under 18 years.
[b] Major supermarket chains represented by: Budgens, Co-op, Gateway, Kwiksave, Safeway, Sainsbury and Tesco.

based on neighbourhood planning principles, it would be expected that trip lengths should be short.

In a survey carried out by Milton Keynes Borough Council (1990), it was found that 60 per cent of the residents of Milton Keynes actually worked in the city. Most of the out-commuting was to the area to the north of the borough (15 per cent) and to London (9 per cent). Nearly three quarters of the respondents (1045) travelled to work by car and a further 10 per cent walked to work. Only 12 per cent used public transport (7 per cent rail and 5 per cent bus). Data were not collected on journey length, but over 65 per cent of the sample took less than 15 minutes to get to work and a further 10 per cent took more than one hour to travel to work. For other trip purposes (for example, retailing), Milton Keynes seemed to be self-contained with over 89 per cent of trips being made within the borough for food shopping. Car-ownership [133] levels are high with over 79 per cent of households having the use of a car or van (34 per cent had more than one vehicle). These levels are much higher than national car-ownership levels of 63 per cent (1987) and those found elsewhere in the South East (69 per cent in 1987).

For Linford Ward there were 1274 trips made in 195 households (6.53 trips per household)

Table 10.   Linford Ward travel data summary (1990)

Mode	Trips number	%	Purpose	Trips number	%
Foot	213	17.6	Work	201	19.6
Bicycle	73	6.0	Education	25	2.4
Bus	56	4.6	Health	23	2.2
Car	816	67.3	Shopping	296	28.8
Other[a]	54	4.5	Sport	74	7.2
			Leisure	132	2.9
			Social	226	22.0
			Other	48	4.7
Total	1212		Total	1025	

Note: [a] Includes coach, rail, taxi, motorcycle, van, minibus.

with 347 individuals responding to the survey (3.67 trips per person). In addition to the full trip information for all journeys (including short walk), there were data available on individual and household characteristics. As data were not available for all wards in Milton Keynes, the between-wards comparison carried out with the other case-study towns was not possible. An individual analysis was carried out on the variation in energy use per trip within the Linford Ward (Table 10). Energy use per trip was calculated in the same way as for the other case-study towns, but on a vehicle-kilometre base. This allowed the analysis to use actual occupancy values for each individual trip rather than taking averages. Correlation and regression analysis was carried out for a range of individual independent variables against the dependent variable of energy use per trip. This analysis was carried out on an individual basis (473 trips with complete information) and for data grouped by energy use per trip (18 categories).

For the individual analysis, energy use per trip is correlated with sex (significant at the 99 per cent level) and with occupation and age (significant at the 95 per cent level). The best-fit regression equation produced a reasonable result ($R = 0.225$), with sex and main purpose being the two main determinants of energy use per trip. The mean level of energy use was 13.4 MJ per trip. The interpretation here has to be careful, even though the variables used were all significant and the signs are also consistent. The data suggest that males use more energy per trip and that purposes such as work, education and shopping are more energy intensive than leisure and social trips.

For the grouped analysis, energy use per trip is correlated with sex and occupation (significant at the 99 per cent level), and with the main purpose and driving licence (significant at the 95 per cent level). The best-fit regression equation produced a good fit ($R = 0.874$) with sex, age and purpose being the main explanatory variables. As with the individual analysis, men in the older age groups with work-based activities tended to use most energy per trip, whereas younger people (particularly women) used less energy per trip for leisure and social purposes. Those with driving licences also used more energy per trip.

Within Linford Ward, there is a substantial variation in energy use per trip. About 34 per cent of trips were made by walk and bicycle and only used renewable forms of energy. For the remaining 66 per cent of trips by motorized forms of transport, the average energy use [134] was 22.6 MJ per trip. The overall energy use was 15.1 MJ per trip (slightly different from the level previously stated of 13.4 MJ per trip as there were different numbers in the two samples). The levels of energy use in Linford come within the mid-range of the districts and wards in the other cities, but it is one of the central wards in Milton Keynes and so may have slightly lower figures than the borough as a whole. However, the most interesting conclusion is the variability in the data and the range of energy use per trip. The vast majority of trips do not use much energy, with some 84 per cent below the average 15.1 MJ per trip figure – the 50 per cent level is only 4.1 MJ per trip and the 75 per cent level is 10.8 MJ per trip. The 181 trips using more than 15.1 MJ per trip threshold have an average energy use of 72.4 MJ per trip. So 24 per cent of the motorized trips use 78 per cent of the total energy. It is these long-distance car trips which have produced the heavily skewed distribution of values.

3.4 Almere

Almere in the Netherlands is a new settlement (85 000) which has a fully integrated transport and land-use system with a clear emphasis on cycling and public transport (Table 11). It is a linear city structured around three main centres in a polynucleated pattern. The new town has been built on reclaimed land in the IJsselmeer and it forms part of the national strategy to direct housing away from the green heart of the Netherlands to the northern and central parts of the country. Development initially took place in Almere Haven and it is now focused in Almere Stad. The original plan followed a 'cauliflower' layout in Almere Haven, but the more recent developments in the other two parts of the city follow the 'grid' pattern. [135]

The transport network is designed to maximize the use of sustainable forms of transport, with the land-use system providing services in locations accessible to the residential neighbourhoods. The town is centred on the railway station (opened in 1987) which provides a frequent service (4 trains per hour) to the main employment centre of Amsterdam (30 km away) and 2 trains per hour to Schipol and Den Haag. Two new suburban stations have been built (1987) and a further three are planned as the town expands (Verzetwijk opened in 1995). The main commercial and business centres are located at each of the accessible rail stations. A comprehensive network of bus-only streets leads away from the stations to the rest of the town, with cycle paths and footpaths forming an integral part of this network. At every external link to the town there is a car-pool area (both for cycles and for cars) which provides facilities for those arriving and leaving the town.

Housing density is designed to be high, but there are large recreational areas surrounding the town and open spaces within each neighbourhood. Each district is within a radius of about 2 km of its centre, where there is a range of retail and service facilities. Neighbourhoods contain a local primary school and a more limited range of shops. The town does not prohibit car ownership, but there is high use of noncar modes. The plan allows for 3000 new houses per year to be built (1995–2005), with Almere Stad and Almere Buiten being completed by 2000. Development will then take place in Almere Poort. The original Almere Structure Plan proposals suggested that 90 per cent would live and work in the Almere area, but a 60 per cent target may be more realistic.[1]

Table 11.   Data for Almere in the Netherlands

Variable	Almere	Almere Haven	Almere Stad	Almere Buiten
Population	84 920	22 686	45 786	16 026
Population change (% 1981-91)	322.1	52.7	880.0	[a]
Young (% under 15)	25.5	23.8	27.0	26.2
Elderly (% pensionable age)	7.7	9.7	6.6	7.1
Housing tenure (% owner-occupied)	42.0	32.9	45.0	43.3
Unemployment (% of local labour force)	8.5	—	—	—
Household size (persons per household)	2.57	2.57	2.59	2.50
Proxy for low income (% social rent housing)	41.8	57.9	35.4	40.9
Area (ha)	13 975	645	2484	1586
Density (residents ha^{-1})	6.1	35.2	18.4	10.1
Housing density (houses ha^{-1} in housing areas)	96.4	70.6	109.4	113.9
Open space (% area not built up)	71.3	14.5	24.3	57.4
Employment	20 250			
Retail daily goods (m^2 of retail space)	20 482	5133	12 917	2342
Retail nondaily goods[b] (m^2 of retail space)	55 286	6947	29 330	1446

Notes:
[a] The population of Almere Stad has increased from 5202 (1981) to 45 786 (1991), and that of Almere Buiten has increased from nothing in 1981 to 16 026 (1991).
[b] In addition, Doe Mere has 17 507 m² of retail space, mainly do-it-yourself shops.

Local accessibility in Almere is high with a large proportion of work trips being made by bicycle in Almere Stad (55 per cent). The proportion of shopping trips being made by walk and bicycle is even higher (75 per cent) to the local centres of Almere Haven and Almere Buiten. This proportion falls when longer journeys are made to Almere Stad, the main shopping centre (10–24 per cent by walk or bicycle). The planning approach, which combines dencentralized shopping centres with high levels of self-sufficiency in the individual centres, has led to short journey lengths and a high use of walk and bicycle modes (Hofstra Verkeersadviseurs, 1991).

Almere has followed a very different strategy from that in Milton Keynes. The TEST (1991) report compared the two cities form published data and from a small-scale [136] household survey (Tables 2 and 12). As expected, there is a much greater use of the bicycle and substantially lower levels of car ownership in Almere. Trip lengths are slightly longer in

Table 12. A comparison of survey data for Linford Ward (Milton Keynes) and Almere Haven (Almere)

	Linford Ward	Almere Haven
Population	18 990 (1990)	22 686 (1991)
Cars per household	1.37	0.94
Cars per adult	0.64	0.49
Licence holdership (%)	77	71
No car (%)	6.4	21.3
More than two cars (%)	39.3	14
Car essential (%)	71	52
Car not essential but want to keep (%)	16.9	29.9
Car journeys (%)	59.4	34.6
Bike journeys (%)	5.8	27.5
Walk journeys (%)	17.7	20.7
Bicycles per household	1.79	3.2
Bicycles per adult	0.5	1.15
Bicycles per child	0.7	0.83

Source: TEST, 1991.

Linford (7.2 km) than those in Almere Haven (6.9 km), but work trips in Almere Haven (17.7 km) are substantially longer than those in Linford (13.2 km). As noted earlier, there is a substantial level of self containment for the journey to work in Milton Keynes (60 per cent), but in Almere out-commuting has increased from 60 per cent in 1980 to 71 per cent in 1990.

3.5 Oxford

In Oxford there have been considerable pressures to build more roads to meet the growth in car use and the increased traffic congestion, but the City Council has resisted those pressures and developed an interesting set of alternative transport policies which have been implemented over the last 20 years (Banister *et al.*, 1994, p. 34). Oxford is a historic university city, with its urban form protected both internally (there are approximately 1000 listed buildings within the city, Jones, 1989) and externally (since the introduction in 1967 of a 7 km green belt around the city). This has meant that there has been a severe limit to the amount of open space available for new development. In addition, the growth in travel demand from existing employment, retail, and office land uses, as well as tourism and leisure activities, has resulted in longer journey distances from outside the constrained city centre.

The data set used in Oxford was part of the Oxford Transport Study carried out by Buchanan and Partners (1992). It consisted of three surveys – of vehicles passing through five cordons around the city centre, users of city-centre bus stops, and park-and-ride users. The data allowed energy figures to be calculated for only one trip, and as the survey questionnaire did not assign the trip to a household, the data had to be sorted by 'home' destination and origin purpose. In the distance matrix intrazonal trips were calculated as zero thus eliminating these trips from the energy equation. The transport zones were not directly coterminous with administrative or physical boundaries in Oxford, so some approximation was necessary to assign transport zones to the wards.

The energy analysis has included car, bicycle and walk, and other modes. Energy use per trip is correlated in a positive manner with trips made by car and by car ownership (Tables 13 and 14), and in a negative manner with employment in the area, the amount of open space and the ratio of jobs to population. As employment increases in an area, the use of energy per trip decreases. Similarly, as the ratio of jobs to population increases (a measure of job containment), energy use per trip decreases. [137] The anomaly here is the open-space variable, where an increase in open space has resulted in less energy being used; there is no clear explanation for this result.

Where energy use per kilometre is correlated with the range of socioeconomic variables, positive relationships are found with the use of the car mode and the proportion of young people in the area. Negative relationships are found with use of the bicycle and the proportion of households with no car. All the results quoted are significant at the 90 per cent level.

However, the only physical variable to emerge as significant has been the amount of open space, but even here there is a question mark against the sign of the correlation coefficient. Employment data seems important in explaining energy use per trip, but these results may have reflected the nature of the survey which recorded only one trip and so has not reflected the full range of travel activities in Oxford.

3.6 Banbury

Banbury is a small market town situated north of Oxford with approximately 30 000 inhabitants. Both in terms of population and physical size Banbury was the smallest of the study areas. Its current structure and form were not as much of interest in planning terms as its future role, as the area has been identified as one of Oxfordshire County Council's (OCC,

Table 13.   Transport energy use in Oxford

	Trip distance km	Trips[a]	Energy used per trip (MJ)	Modal split (%)		
				car	bike + walk	other
Oxford	8.33	4828	16.03	67.5	25.8	6.7
Centre	5.18	458	6.07	37	58	5
West	5.05	788	6.74	45	50	5
North	5.43	837	8.94	63	33	4
East	6.57	404	10.74	67	26	7
South	7.59	528	12.22	65	25	10
Others	13.91	1813	28.15	88	4	8
Five areas[b]	5.82	3015	8.74	55.2	38.9	5.9

Notes:
[a] Intrazonal trips were excluded as it was not possible to put a distance on them.
[b] These are the five areas excluding 'others'.

Table 14.   Key relationships in Oxford

Variable[a]	Mean value	Correlation	Significance (%)
Energy use per trip			
Employment	17 106	−0.876	97
Trips made by car (%)	55.4	0.911	98
Open space (%)	49.4	−0.871	97
Car ownership	0.76	0.736	92
Ratio of jobs to population	0.836	−0.776	93
Energy use per kilometre			
Bicycle (% by bike)	38.4	−0.966	99
Car (% by car)	55.4	0.990	99
No car (%)	39.2	−0.914	98
Young (%)	17	0.763	93

Note: [a] See Table 3.

1992) growth towns. To take pressure off Oxford City, Banbury is required to provide 4400 new dwellings in the current Structure Plan period (1986–2001). This has promoted debate within the local authority. Cherwell District Council, and between the district and county as to the location of this housing and associated infrastructure. The data used were from the Banbury Transport Study which was commissioned by Oxfordshire County Council to assess Banbury's growing transport needs (OCC, 1993). This study (1992/93) involved a household questionnaire, and 20 per cent of all households responded, providing a travel diary for all trips by all household members in 3000 households.

There were two problems with this data set. First, the travel diary recorded only weekday morning peak trips (as its primary function was to calibrate a SATURN model). Most of the leisure and shopping trips were omitted. Second, the distance matrix associated with the data could not be used and distances were calculated by relating travel time to average speed for each mode used (Table 2).

Table 15.   Banbury summary results for the morning peak (07.00–10.00 AM)

	Trip distance (km)	Trips	Energy use (MJ) per:		Modal split (%)		
			trip	household	car	walk + bike	other
Banbury	14.95	4073	29.14	56.88	67.27	27.02	5.70
Calthorpe	14.84	727	28.78	57.96	65.33	29.71	4.96
Easington	14.69	996	29.16	58.92	72.38	23.09	4.53
Grimsbury	18.59	585	36.85	68.43	70.94	24.10	4.96
Hardwick	14.56	816	28.41	50.73	68.17	24.47	7.36
Neithorp	13.28	398	24.63	47.82	55.77	34.42	9.81
Ruscote	13.25	551	25.57	50.14	63.70	32.12	4.18

Table 16. Transport energy use in Banbury

Variable	Mean value	Correlation	Significance (%)
Energy use per trip			
Trip length (km)	14.86	0.994	99
Modal split car (%)	66	0.706	94
Modal split bike + walk (%)	28	−0.702	94
Density (ha^{-1})	33.2	−0.756	96
Open space (%)	59	0.863	98
Size of area (ha)	348	0.896	99
Energy use per person			
Employment	3249	0.941	99
Distance (km)	14.86	0.993	99
Household size	2.5	−0.807	97
Density (ha^{-1})	33.2	−0.764	96

Despite these shortcomings, analysis was carried out on a ward-by-ward basis. With the base data for Banbury and the energy use data for the wards (Table 15), significant results were produced from the correlation analysis (Table 16). Energy use per trip is positively correlated with trip length, proportion of modal split by car, the amount of [138] open space, and the size of the area. Negative correlations are found with increasing density and the proportion of modal split by cycle and walk. All of these relationships are intuitively plausible and have the correct signs. Similarly, energy use per person is negative correlated with household size and density and positively correlated with employment and average trip distance. All of these relationships are sound with the exception of that for employment. It seems that energy use per person should be negatively correlated with employment as journey distance to work should be lower if there was local employment. The explanation seems to be that there is a job mismatch in Banbury as local jobs are not taken by local people. There is out-commuting from Banbury to other employment centres.

4 The verdict from the case studies

4.1 Findings

1. Substantial empirical and analytical progress has been made to provide real data and values for a range of UK cities on energy use in transport and the links with urban form. Much of the evidence cited in the past has been based on intuition rather than fact.

    (a) The results have supported the importance of *density* as a key variable, but has drawn attention to the problems of the exact measurement of density. A simple gross measure has been used here (persons per hectare). If a slightly different measure is used, such as persons per unit of built-up area or residential density in housing areas, then different figures emerge (for example, compare the results for Almere).

(b) *Amount of space*, defined as the percentage of the urban area not built up, has been identified as a significant new variable (Oxford and Banbury). [139]

(c) *Size of urban area* has also proved important in some case studies (Leicester and Banbury).

(d) *Employment, car ownership and socioeconomic group* are the most important social and economic variables.

(e) *Mixed land uses and concepts of self-containment* are most important in reducing energy consumption in transport, but local jobs and local facilities must be suitable for local residents, otherwise long-distance energy-intensive movements will be made. This mismatch seemed to be apparent in Banbury, but also in the other case studies where the levels of self-containment were low, particularly for work activities.

Other variables were significant in different locations, but no overall pattern has emerged. All these relationships need further analysis if this complex picture of urban form and its associated patterns of energy use in transport are to be unravelled.

2. The vast majority of trips do not use much energy. For example, in Milton Keynes some 24 per cent of the motorized trips use 78 per cent of the total energy. It is these long-distance car trips which have produced the heavily skewed distribution of values. Further analysis is required on these long-distance energy-intensive journeys. In some cases, these journeys could be made by public transport, but in many cases they may be work-related or business-related activities being carried out in company cars.

3. Overall, there has been a remarkable consistency in levels of energy use in the case-study locations as compared with the national figures derived from the National Travel Surveys (DoT, 1988). All the calculated figures are similar (Table 17). Banbury has higher than expected figures, but Milton Keynes (Linford Ward) has not emerged as energy intensive as might have been expected.

4. The data used here relate to all trip purposes by all modes. Most previous research has concentrated on the journey to work, yet this purpose now accounts for only 20 per cent of all travel. The main growth in trip making is taking place for leisure activities and shopping. These activities are more dispersed than work activities, less routinized, and more dependent on the car (Banister and Banister, 1995).

5. It is extremely difficult to make comparisons between cities as the data sets are different (Table 2). However, with careful use of secondary sources, it is possible to obtain clear relationships within cities and to begin to draw broader conclusions about the real links between transport, energy use, and urban form.

4.2 Implications

1. In this research we have tried to produce links between urban form and energy use in transport. However, the data are still a real problem and it has proved extremely difficult to obtain consistent data sets, either within towns (linking transport data with census, employment, and other data sets) or between towns (different types of travel surveys). Ideally, a comprehensive travel data set is needed rather than travel surveys which have been designed for other purposes. This would be a 24-hour, 7-day household survey, including all modes, all trips, and all household members. This data set needs to be made

Table 17.   Comparison of figures calculated from the National Travel Survey 1985/86 and town surveys (figures are given in MJ per person per week)

Type of area	National Travel Survey	Figures from survey data	
London	248		239
Urban	234	Liverpool	107
Intermediate	308	Leicester	263 (130)
		Milton Keynes	344
		Oxford	330 (180)
		Banbury	440
Rural	384	South Oxfordshire	389
Overall	269		

Notes:
Figures for each of the survey areas are given as averages and the figures for London come from Newman and Kenworthy (1991).
The National Travel Survey figures come from Banister (1992).
Liverpool includes only the internal trips within the Metropolitan area and the distances are the minimum ones as they are calculated from crow-fly distances.
Leicester covers Leicester city (130 MJ) and the surrounding districts.
Milton Keynes includes only the central ward of Linford.
Oxford data were taken from a cordon survey (figure in parentheses) and so there are no direct measures of trips per person, but the figure given is the best estimate based on the assumption of 2.94 trips per person.
Banbury data were collected for the morning peak and so there is no direct measure of trips per person, but the best estimate is given, based on the assumption of 2.94 trips per person per day. [140]

    comparable to the social-economic and physical data requirements, particularly the geographical areas so that the travel data can be related to census and other information.

2. Results from previous research show that we need: more detailed appraisal than at national or regional levels (Banister, 1992); analysis of the variation within a city and within a city region; results that are of practical use to local authorities; a scale which provides an understanding of the external and internal workings of a city or region.

3. In this research we have addressed some of these issues and suggest that further studies should: encompass a number of spatial scales; address the city within its region, perhaps using travel-to-work areas as the most useful boundary, and should certainly not be cut off at arbitrary administrative boundaries; examine the communities within the city, examining behaviour of similar households, or groups; generate comparable data sets so that assessment can be made across a range of scales and potential causal factors; question the nature and measurement of density, the importance of net versus gross densities; use easily accessible and compatible figurres to represent the number of facilities. In addition, socioeconomic and physical data sets need to be easily transcribed into the transport survey zones. Travel information should relate to the entire catchment area if a complete picture is to be obtained. The appropriate scale for analysis is the city with its region as this is the domain of the local authority.

The land-use system has not traditionally been seen as a major player in achieving urban sustainability. Yet the empirical relationships obtained here do show sufficient consistency to indicate that actions taken in the planning and transport sectors could help achieve sustainability objectives. The physical relationships have consistently emerged as significant. Higher density urban areas may help reduce the need to travel, but this has to be balanced against the availability of open space. Social and economic factors are also significant, but the levels of car ownership and socioeconomic group may reflect income levels and the higher propensity of more affluent car owners to travel longer distances by energy-consumptive modes. Even though sound and consistent statistical relationships have been established for each city, this does not imply causality. Our understanding of the links between transport, energy, and urban form are an essential component of achieving a greater clarity in the levels of analysis and policymaking. The next step is to establish a clearer theoretical and practical framework within which that causality can be established. Only then will be able to conclude in a substantive way that the objective of a sustainable city can or cannot be achieved through land-use policies. [141]

Acknowledgements

This paper is based on the final report for the EPSRC project on the Relationship Between Energy Use in Transport and Urban Form which is available from the authors. We are grateful to the Research Council for funding this project and for important inputs from other researchers at the Bartlett School of Planning, University College London – Marina Van Geenhuizen, Alberto Bounous, Ricardo Esteves and Paulo Camara. We would also like to thank all the local authorities covered in this research who gave both time and data to make the project analysis possible – Merseytravel and the Merseyside Information Service, Leicestershire City Council, TEST and the Open University, Milton Keynes Borough Council, Oxfordshire County Council and Almere Community Council. Useful comments were received from two referees on streamlining the paper.

Note

1. Interview of H. De Heji, by M. Van Geenhuizen and D. Banister in Almere Stad Community Offices, 27 September 1994.

References

ACEC (1976) 'Passenger transport: short and medium term considerations', Energy Paper 10, Advisory Committee on Energy Consumption, Department of Energy (HMSO, London).

Bae, C.H.C. and Richardson, H.W. (1994), 'Automobiles, the environment and metropolitan spatial structure', Lincoln Institute of Land Policy, Cambridge, MA.

Banister, D. (1992), 'Energy use, transport and settlement patterns', in M.J. Breheny (ed.) *Sustainable Development and Urban Form*, London: Pion, 160–81.

Banister, D. (1994), 'Energy consumption in transport: trends, policy alternatives and analysis methods', paper presented at the EU THERMIE JUPITER Evaluation Working Group Meeting, Patra, Greece, June; copy available from the author.

Banister, D. (1996), 'Energy, quality of life and the environment: the role of transport', *Transport*

Reviews, **16**(1), 23–35.

Banister, D. and Banister, C. (1995), 'Energy consumption patterns in transport in Great Britain: macro level estimates', *Transportation Research A*, **29**(4), 21–32.

Banister, D., Watson, S. and Wood, C. (1994), 'The relationship between energy use in transport and urban form', WP10, Planning and Development Research Centre, University College London, London.

Breheny, M. (ed.) (1993), 'The compact city', *Built Environment*, **18**(4) special issue.

Breheny, M. (1995a), 'Counterurbanisation and sustainable urban forms', in J. Brotchie, M. Batty, P. Hall and P. Newton (eds), *Cities in Competition: The Emergence of Productive and Sustainable Cities for the 21st Century*, Melbourne: Longman Cheshire, 402–29.

Breheny, M. (1995b), 'Urban densities and sustainable development', paper presented at the Institute of British Geographers Annual Conference, University of Northumbria at Newcastle, January; copy available from the author, Department of Geography, University of Reading, Reading.

Buchanan and Partners (1992), 'Oxford Transport Study. Phase 1 report of issue and options', report for Oxfordshire County Council, Buchanan and Partners, 59 Queen's Gardens, London W2 3AF.

CEC (1992), 'Toward sustainability: a European Community programme of policy and action in relation to the environment and sustainable development', COM 92(23), Commission of the European Communities, Brussels.

DoE (1994a), *Sustainable Development: The UK Strategy*, Department of the Environment, London: HMSO.

DoE (1994b), *Planning Policy Guidance 13: Transport*, Department of the Environment, London: HMSO.

DoT (1988), *National Travel Surveys: 1985/86 Report*, Department of Transport, London: HMSO.

DoT (1993), *Transport Statistics Great Britain 1993*, Department of Transport, London: HMSO.

Frost, M., Linneker, B. and Spence, N. (1994), 'Estimating the passenger energy efficiency of different transport modes: the sensitivity of worktravel energy use to vehicle occupancy rates', unpublished mimeo, Department of Geography, London School of Economics, London.

Gordon, P. and Richardson, H. (1989), 'Gasoline consumption and cities: a reply', *Journal of the American Planning Association*, **55**, 342–6.

Gordon, P., Richardson, H. and Jun, M.J. (1991), 'The commuting paradox: evidence from the top twenty', *Journal of the American Planning Association*, **57**, 416–20.

Hofstra Verkeersadviseurs (1991), 'Almere perspectief 2015 (Deelstudie Verkeer en Vervoer)', Groningen: Hofstra Verkeersadviseurs.

Howard, D. (1990), *Energy, Transport and the Environment*, Transnet, 16 Warren Lane, London SE18 6BW.

Hughes, P. (1993), *Personal Transport and the Greenhouse Effect: A Strategy for Sustainability*, London: Earthscan.

Jones, P. (1989), 'Oxford – an evolving transport policy', *Built Environment*, **15** (3, 4), 231–42. [142]

LCC (1990), 'Central Leicestershire Transport Strategy', Leicestershire County Council, County Hall, Glenfield, Leics LE3 8RJ.

Milton Keynes Borough Council (1990), 'Milton Keynes Borough Council Household Survey 1990', unpublished mimeo, Milton Keynes Borough Council, Civic Offices, 1 Saxongate East, Central Milton Keynes MK9 3EJ.

MIS (1988), 'County Wide Transport Survey', Merseyside Information Services, Royal Liver Building, Suite 301, Pier Head, Liverpool 2.

MKDC (1992), 'The planning of Milton Keynes', report produced by Chesterton Consulting for Milton Keynes Development Corporation, Saxon Court, 502 Avebury Boulevard, Saxongate East, Central Milton Keynes MK9 3HS.

MVA (1988), 'Greater Leicester Transportation Study', MVA Consultancy, 115 Shaftesbury Avenue, London WC2H 8WD.

Naess, P. (1993), 'Transportation energy in Swedish towns and regions', *Scandinavian Housing and Planning Research*, **10**, 187–206.

Naess, P., Larsen, S.L. and Roe, P.G. (1994), 'Energy use for transport in 22 Nordic towns', NIBR report 1994:2, Norwegian Institute of Urban and Regional Research, Oslo.

Naess, P., Roe, P.G. and Larsen, S.L. (1993), 'Who use most energy for urban travels and where do they live? The use of the private car and public transport in 30 residential areas in Greater Oslo'.

NIBR report 1993:22, Norwegian Institute of Urban and Regional Research, Oslo.

Newman, P. and Kenworthy, J. (1989a), *Cities and Automobile Dependence - An International Sourcebook*, Aldershot, Hants: Gower.

Newman, P. and Kenworthy, J. (1989b), 'Gasoline consumption and cities: a comparison of US cities with a global survey', *Journal of American Planning Association*, **55**, 24–37.

Newman, P. and Kenworthy, J. (1991), 'Transport and urban form in 32 of the world's principal cities', *Transport Reviews*, **11**, 249–72.

OCC (1992), 'Oxfordshire Structure Plan', Oxford County Council, Department of Planning, Speedwell House, Speedwell Street, Oxford OX1 1SD.

OCC (1993), 'Banbury Transport Study', Oxford County Council, Department of Planning, Speedwell House, Speedwell Street, Oxford OX1 1SD.

Owens, S. and Rickaby, P. (1992), 'Settlement and energy revisited', *Built Environment*, **18** (4), 242–52.

Rickaby, P. (1991), 'Energy and urban development in an archetypal English town', *Environment and Planning B: Planning and Design*, **18**, 153–75.

Roberts, J. and Wood, C. (1992), 'Land use and travel demand', paper presented at the PTRC Annual Conference, Manchester, September; copy available from Chris Wood.

TEST (1991), 'Changed travel, better world?', now available from Transport 2000, Walkden House, 10 Melton Street, London NW1 2EJ.

Wood, C. (1994), 'Passenger transport energy use and urban form', background paper, The Bartlett, University College London, London.

Wood, C., Watson, S. and Banister, D. (1994), 'A framework for assessing the impact of urban form on passenger transport energy use', paper presented at the PTRC Annual Conference, Manchester, September; copy available from the authors. [143]

[23]

Planning the Sustainable City Region

Michael Breheny and Ralph Rookwood

INTRODUCTION

Levels of intervention

Previous chapters have made it clear that, in order to achieve a more sustainable world, radical policies will have to be introduced at a variety of spatial and governmental levels. At inter-governmental level, agreements on environmental protection are required. At the national government level, legislative and fiscal changes, plus general example setting, could make a profound contribution to sustainable development. Finally, at the local government and local agency level – which in the UK covers all bodies from the regional to the very local – there are many positive actions that can be taken, some of which have been described earlier in this report.

These levels of possible intervention are increasingly difficult to achieve as we move from the local to the global. It is therefore encouraging that it has been at the international level that some of the earliest initiatives have been taken – in response to world-wide concern at the dangers posed by global warming – requiring implementation at national and local levels. Uneven though action 'on the ground' has been, it is also encouraging that many initiatives have been taken at a variety of levels in response to localised perceptions and opportunities, without necessarily waiting for direction 'from above'. Progress in practice is dependent on action at all three levels, preferably more or less simultaneously in order to minimise the risk of 'too little, too late'.

Whereas previous chapters have called for action at all three levels, as appropriate, this chapter has a narrower focus: to consider the implications for the shaping or reshaping of our physical environment, for the decisions that are being made daily about developments in both town and country, and for the planning system that exists in Britain to guide those decisions in line with approved objectives. Planning objectives have always included environmental protection and improvement in some form – usually to safeguard or enhance local (mainly urban) living conditions – but until recently these objectives have rarely included much about safeguarding the natural world. Now that the vital importance of the latter has been recognised, it is important to see what changes in planning objectives are necessary for this purpose. These changes necessarily relate mainly to the sub-national level, where policy meets design and where objectives are given their physical form.

This chapter focuses, then, on this sub-national level of intervention. It ranges from the regional to the local and tries to blend them together in an effort to indicate appropriate environmental policies across a multiplicity of circumstances: from central cities to remote rural areas. The whole we call the 'Social City Region'. Although different approaches are appropriate at different spatial scales and in different governmental circumstances, it is essential that they are both devised and implemented in an integrated, complementary fashion.

Policy initiatives that fit into this integrated approach have been put forward in each of the sectoral chapters. This chapter takes a different 'cut' at the problem by putting forward recommendations of two kinds:

1. those that link sectors by referring to appropriate sets of strategic urban and rural policies; and
2. those that relate to the institutional and governmental changes that may be required to deliver policies.

SUSTAINABLE TOWN/SUSTAINABLE COUNTRY POLICIES

It is clear that a major strategic factor determining sustainability is urban form; that is, the shape of settlement patterns in cities, towns and villages. In principle, it is obvious that urban form will affect patterns of private transport, which in turn will affect fuel consumption and emissions. By the same token, the viability and patronage of public transport facilities, and also consumption and emissions, will be affected by urban form. Such form may also affect rates of conversion of land from rural to urban uses and, by extension, the loss of habitats for flora and fauna. Certain urban forms and types of changes to those forms might also involve the loss of green spaces and habitats within urban areas.

It seems obvious, then, that urban form at all scales may be a significant determinant of the prospects for sustainability. It is also obvious, again in principle, that environmentally desirable urban forms may be less desirable in economic and social terms. The implication is that trade-offs have to be made. For example, higher urban densities may lower overall quality of life. Medium to low density housing has long been the preferred choice of many in the UK. Although the European Commission may denigrate the idea of suburban living, it remains the ideal for many people. There may also be a conflict between high urban densities and the desire to 'green the city'.

Urban form and sustainability are thus linked in principle; but is it possible to argue with any degree of certainty that some types of urban form are more sustainable than others? Debate on the issue[1,2] has tended to focus only on large cities. However, this is not sufficient. At each scale in the urban hierarchy, sustainability requires specific initiatives. But for maximum effect, these initiatives need to be co-ordinated. This is why the question of appropriate measures is addressed here in a multiplicity of situations.

THE CONTEXT FOR SUSTAINABLE URBAN DEVELOPMENT

Before pursuing these issues about urban form and sustainability any further, it would be wise to take stock of the major trends in the UK that are currently determining patterns of urban change. It may be that some of these are so powerful that policies that aim to reverse them are doomed to failure. The question may be: how can trends be best manipulated to move towards more sustainable forms of urban development?

The restructuring of industry, the decline of the older industrial cities and the growth of new activities in cleaner and rural environments have been touched on in Chapter 8. Together with the dispersal of population into villages and small towns, these trends are well recorded; but their implications are often resisted by many who wish to sustain the size of cities or protect the countryside from intrusion. However, the trends of the last 30 years have built a disproportionate potential for growth into a large part of the rural lowlands of Britain.

Census data, presented by a typology of districts, show these trends very clearly. The typology adopted by the Office of Population, Censuses and Surveys (OPCS) extends from the largest metropolitan districts to the most remote rural areas at the extremes[3]. The population change figures for each of these types are given in Table 9.1 for the three decades from 1961 to 1991. The table records the persistent drift of people away from the metropolitan areas and, since 1981, from the industrial districts of Wales and Northern England to the smaller towns and rural areas.

Table 9.1   *Population change, 1961–91, for types of area in England and Wales*

	1961–71		1971–81		1981–91	
	000s	**%**	**000s**	**%**	**000s**	**%**
England and Wales	2,629	5.7	262	0.5	−57	0.1
Greater London Boroughs						
Inner	−461	−13.2	−535	−17.7	−147	−5.9
Outer	−81	−1.8	−221	−5.0	−171	−4.2
Metropolitan Districts						
Principal cities	−355	−8.4	−386	−10.0	−258	−7.4
Others	412	5.5	−160	−2.0	−327	−4.2
Non-metropolitan Districts						
Large cities	−41	−1.4	−149	−5.1	−98	−3.6
Smaller cities	38	2.2	−55	−3.2	5	0.3
Industrial Districts						
Wales and Northern Regions	118	1.3	42	1.3	−72	−2.1
Rest of England	342	5.0	158	5.0	59	1.8
New Towns	337	21.8	283	15.1	133	6.1
Resort and Retirement	3461	2.2	156	4.9	174	5.2
Mixed and Accessible Rural						
Outside SE	6272	1.9	307	8.8	156	4.1
Inside SE	9602	2.1	354	6.8	162	2.9
Remote Largely Rural	399	9.7	468	10.3	328	6.4

Source OPCS (1992), 1991 Census

This process of decentralisation of population, and also jobs, is the major postwar geographical trend in the UK, as in many Western countries. Some commentators suggest that this process is so strong that it constitutes 'counter-urbanisation'; that is, not simply a process of extended suburbanisation but a clear rejection of urban living. Some researchers had suggested that this process was being reversed in the 1980s, with a 'return to the city'. However, the 1991 Census preliminary results show that the decentralisation process in the UK is clear and persistent. As Figure 9.1 shows, there is a neat inverse correlation between population growth and population size over the 1981–91 period. The larger the city, the greater the population losses; the more remote the area, the greater the gains.

There is also a social dimension to these losses and gains: this process has had a polarising social effect by leaving behind in the inner cities those with the poorest life chances – the poor, the unemployed, the low skilled, the elderly and minority ethnic groups. The corollary is that areas gaining from decentralisation tend to have become even more solidly middle class, relatively affluent and environmentally defensive. There are progressive exceptions to this pattern, such as the post-war new towns, which have provided a high quality of life to working class in-migrants from the large conurbations.

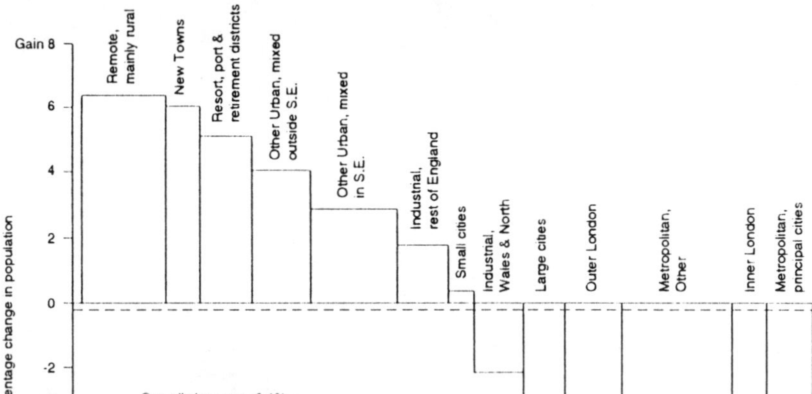

Source OPCS (1992)

Figure 9.1 *The relationship between population growth and population size, 1981–91*

The decentralisation process, then, has important linked economic and social dimensions. In considering the environmental consequences of this process, these must not be forgotten.

The effects of these decentralising changes on the population geography of England and Wales is very marked. Figure 9.2 shows population change by district in England and Wales for the period 1981–91. The areas of fastest growth are concentrated in non-metropolitan Southern and Central England. Thirty years of shifting population has been accompanied by parallel shifts in employment and a strengthening of recipient local economies. Although these areas have been hit severely by the current recession, there is a generally held assumption that they will nevertheless prosper relatively when the economic climate improves.

The result is that the greatest potential for growth lies in the shires of Central and Southern England, in an area extending from Cornwall to Lincolnshire and from Kent to Shropshire. Department of Environment household projections, which take some account of likely migration, suggest that over the twenty years 1991–2011 these same counties will have the highest rates of household growth in the country.

At a finer geographical scale, Breheny, Gent and Lock[1] have also considered this question of the future location of development. They begin by reviewing recent evidence on the proportion of housing development that has taken place as urban infill. Survey evidence suggests that this proportion varies across the country between 30 per cent and 60 per cent of all housing. They suggest that a reasonable assumption in the future is that, on average, up to 50 per cent of future housing development will take place within existing urban areas. This assumes continued containment policies. Possibly, this figure will be an over-estimate if current concerns over 'town cramming' become more widespread.

All these projections must be treated with caution, of course, but there seems little doubt that, for another generation at least, new development will continue to be focused

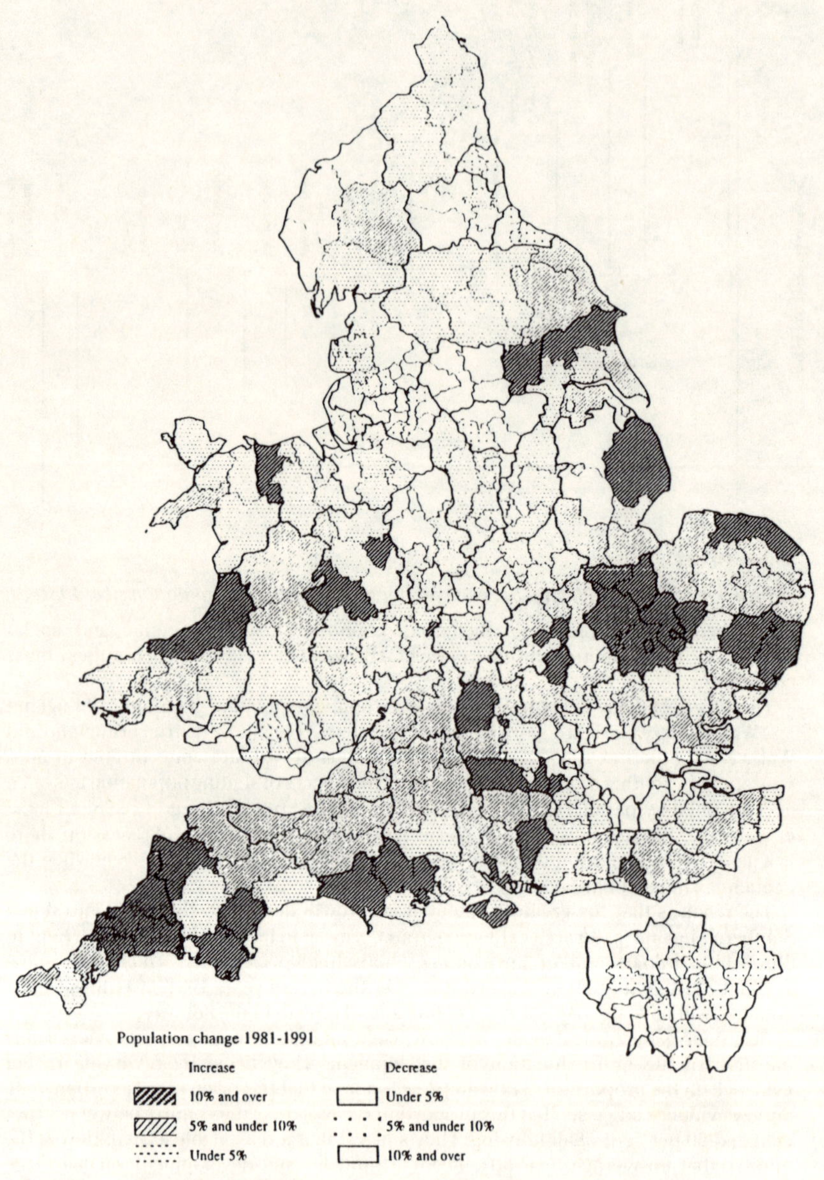

Figure 9.2   *Population growth for districts of England and Wales, 1981–91*

on the lowlands of Southern and Central England, and that within this area much of the pressure will be on greenfield sites in the countryside rather than urban sites.

THE COMPACT CITY PROPOSAL

All this evidence is important to the debate on urban form and sustainability. However, it is particularly important because it casts doubt on a solution to the urban form issue that has gained considerable support: the notion of the 'compact city'. The European Commission, for example, has argued that the high density, mixed use, city is likely to be energy efficient because it reduces travel distances and maximises prospects for public transport provision. In addition, the Commission argues, the compact city provides a superior quality of life for its residents. Suburban development, pejoratively referred to as 'sprawl', creates both high energy consumption and an inferior quality of life.

The Commission's view is a radical one. It suggests that future urban growth should be accommodated within the boundaries of existing urban areas: '...avoid escaping the problems of the city by extending its periphery; solve its problems within existing boundaries'. The compact city solution is also espoused by Friends of the Earth[5] and by other commentators such as Sherlock.[6] This view has been challenged on a number of grounds.[7] Some researchers doubt the superiority of the compact city on energy consumption grounds, arguing that decentralisation of jobs and houses has reduced journey lengths and that congestion in urban areas offsets any gains resulting from shorter journeys. One definite problem with the compact city proposal is that it requires a complete reversal of the most persistent trend in urban development in the last 50 years; that is, decentralisation. As demonstrated above, this 'Canute-like' proposal would simply be impossible to achieve, regardless of whether it is desirable or not.

At the other extreme are proposals for further decentralisation, both physical and institutional. Lower density alternatives to the compact city are proposed, on the very 'quality of life' grounds that the European Commission espouses. The proponents of this approach[8] point to the substantial decentralisation from cities as evidence of the problem of high density urban living. They assume that large tracts of surplus agricultural land are now available for development. They argue that improved telecommunications will facilitate much more localised activities and obviate the need for much of the travel that we see today. It is also argued that decentralised low densities provide environmental gains in terms of the use of ambient sources of energy and home food production. Others suggest that technical breakthroughs, particularly in the form of electric cars, will solve many of the energy consumption and emission problems. Some see an opportunity for decentralised living based on a return to 'rural values'.[9]

THE SOCIAL CITY REGION

The TCPA has strong reservations about all such extreme solutions. They are usually impracticable, unrealistic and undesirable. Even though each may have some merits, as comprehensive solutions they are entirely inappropriate. A detailed critique of these extremes has been argued elsewhere, but it will suffice simply to demonstrate their inadequacies.

The compact city solution is naively based on the idea that urban decentralisation, which has been the dominant urban trend in all Western countries since 1945, can suddenly be stopped and then reversed. Policies of urban containment will no doubt continue to be appropriate, but they must be realistic. This solution also fails to accept that sustainability must balance environmental and other aspirations. There is little point in creating an alienated community for the sake of energy conservation from high densities. The alternative decentralised solution is also based on naive assumptions. If it worked, it would be undermined. Large numbers of people seeking the rural 'good life' would destroy the very idea. Likewise, it is unrealistic to assume that by growing their own vegetables and having fax machines, people would stop travelling. Such a solution might also be socially regressive, condemning the poor to remain in the increasingly undesirable cities as everyone else leaves for the countryside.

Many of the arguments about the role of urban form in increasing sustainability are technical in nature. To some degree the various assertions are empirically testable. However, results are to date rather inconclusive. Nevertheless, sufficient evidence and experience is available to suggest that certain policy stances on urban form can be adopted. One line of argument says that in the absence of clear evidence about the relationship between urban form and energy consumption, and in the absence of any clear view on the prospects for new technologies, a robust policy stance should be adopted in the short term. This is the approach supported by the TCPA: to move towards greater sustainability while ensuring that no harm is done; a version of the 'precautionary principle'. In these circumstances, any attempt to prescribe some simple, single over-riding policy (such as the high density compact city) in order to reduce the impact of urban areas on natural ecosystems is unrealistic and incapable of successful implementation. What must be addressed is the whole inter-dependent regional complex – here christened the Social City Region, adapting the terminology used by Ebenezer Howard. What must be developed, in pursuit of future sustainability, is a whole set of distinctive policies attuned to the varying conditions and environmental potential of the different parts of the region but complementary and mutually reinforcing.

This message is therefore necessarily more complex than the 'compact city' prescription for the way forward – necessarily because the modern industrial world is much too diverse for simplistic rules. However, we recognise that some short formulation is necessary to encapsulate the main essentials of our alternative approach. We therefore propose that the basic principle to be followed in developing planning policies for future development in accordance with sustainability principles should be expressed as follows.

Recommendation

In planning for new development and in reshaping or adapting existing development in order to achieve long-term sustainability and a healthy relationship with the natural environment, the basic unit for the development of appropriate environmental standards shall be the whole of the Social City Region, varying the standards (for example for densities, urban form or transport systems) to suit differing conditions, while ensuring that policies are complementary and that the sum total for the region as a whole contributes to the realisation of the approved sustainability objectives.

To meet these varying conditions, we propose that a variety of approaches be considered to suit particular settlement types within the overall Social City Region. These proposed sets of ideas as to what might be appropriate in a multiplicity of circumstances we have called the 'MultipliCity' approach to sustainability.

It would be possible to produce a very lengthy classification of these settlement types in order to put forward proposals for each. However, in the interests of manageability, we suggest a six-fold typology, all components of the Social City Region itself. This is listed in Table 9.2, with typical areas given to indicate what we have in mind in each case.

Table 9.2 *Classification of the components of the Social City Region*

Area Type	Example
Social City Region	Greater Manchester, Strathclyde
1. City – centres	Glasgow, London
2. City – inner area	Handsworth, Birmingham; St. Ann's, Nottingham
3. City – suburbs	Sutton, London; Jesmond, Newcastle
4. Small towns and new communities	Henley, Clitheroe
5. Mixed urban-rural	Oxfordshire, North Yorkshire
6. Remote rural areas	West Scotland, Northumberland

This typology in types 1 to 6, from large inner city to remote rural areas is, in effect, a simplification of the OPCS classification of Urban Areas discussed earlier.

The following sections look in more detail at some of the principal changes needed in order to achieve future sustainability, first taking the region – the Social City Region – as a whole and then examining each of the six settlement types separately.

CHANGES NEEDED FOR FUTURE SUSTAINABILITY

A number of powerful forces have combined to disperse urban development widely throughout extensive regions, the various parts of which are heavily inter-dependent and strongly inter-acting. These forces include the specialisation and large-scale concentration of modern production, the reliance for distribution on fewer and larger warehouses and large long-distance lorries, the development of convenient long-distance commuter rail services, the increased speed and availability of information technology and communication systems, the failure of the property market and the planning system to maintain sufficient affordable housing close to workplaces, and the decline in the environmental quality of large cities for both living and working.

This wide dispersal of urban development means that strategies for controlling future physical development, whether in town or country and whether for sustainability objectives or not, must be capable of adapting to a wide range of local conditions and must provide not only for improved design of new development but also for the reshaping of existing urban areas. The short time available for successfully avoiding environmental catastrophe means that the latter are of particular importance, since this is where the majority of people will be living during the few decades in which the widespread conversion to sustainability standards must be achieved.

In the sections that follow we set out briefly what we consider to be the principal changes in development strategies that will be needed in the various parts of the city region, in order to achieve the reduced environmental impact which is essential if cities and their dependent areas are to stop inflicting further damage on the natural environment at a rate and scale that cannot be accommodated. In effect, this means broadening the objective of the existing physical planning system – which has been to control 'development' (as statutorily defined) so as to achieve certain aims *within* our built environment – to include the relationship *between* this built environment and the world of natural ecosystems. These strategies for urban and rural development still concern the ways in which, firstly, we design and construct our built environment and, secondly, we manage and use our physical infrastructure; but the criteria for making policy choices must now include the objectives for natural resources, energy, pollution and waste, and their implications for buildings, production and transport as set out in earlier chapters.

Some measures are, of course, common to all parts of the city region, such as:

- reductions in pollution and waste
- greater efficiency in using energy and scarce materials
- more environmentally friendly transport systems
- minimising the separation of homes from jobs and services.

Other measures differ widely according to circumstances, for example:

- densities reduced in some areas but increased in others
- activities decentralised from some locations but more tightly clustered in others
- the need to replace buildings by greenery in some areas but to do the reverse in others.

Nevertheless, in spite of these differences in what will be most appropriate in particular local circumstances, there are certain objectives which must guide all future development if an acceptable rate and scale of progress – taking the region as a whole – are to be achieved. The main objectives are given in Box 9.1.

BOX 9.1 The Social City Region: Changes needed for future sustainability

NATURAL RESOURCES

1. Increased biological diversity, including positive measures for encouraging wildlife.
2. Big increase in biomass (trees and other green plants) in both town and country.
3. Replacement instead of depletion of groundwater reserves and good quality topsoil.
4. Much greater use and production of renewable materials in place of scarce finite ones.

LAND USE AND TRANSPORT

5. Shorter journeys to work and for daily needs.
6. Much higher proportion of trips by public transport.
7. More balanced public transport loadings to minimise fuel consumption.
8. Greater local self-sufficiency in non-speciality foods, goods and services.
9. More concentrated development served principally by public transport.

ENERGY

10. Greatly reduced consumption of fossil fuels.
11. Increased production from renewable sources; eg sun, wind, tides and waves.
12. Reduced wastage by better insulation, more use of CHP, local power generation.
13. Form and layout of buildings better designed for energy efficiency.

POLLUTION AND WASTE

14. Reduced emission of pollutants, especially from industry, power stations and transport.
15. Comprehensive measures to improve the quality of air, water and soil.
16. Reduction in total volume of waste stream.
17. Greater use of 'closed cycle' processes.
18. Much greater recovery of waste materials through recycling.

CHECKLIST FOR MONITORING PROGRESS

1. Pollution reduced by:
   a) establishing the environmental capacity of the region for emission of pollutants;
   b) refusing permission for any development that would result in the total volume of emissions exceeding the regional capacity;
   c) setting up inducements and penalties to cut existing emissions.

2. Natural resources conserved by:
   a) encouraging rehabilitation rather than redevelopment;
   b) stimulating regional production of renewables to replace finite non-renewables;
   c) adopting conservation measures to save topsoil.

3. Total volume of waste stream reduced by measures such as:
   a) reducing business rates for firms using 'closed cycle' processes;
   b) introducing graduated charges for waste collection.

4. Increased recycling of most waste materials including:
   a) recovery of scarce inorganic materials for reuse;
   b) composting of organic wastes.

5. Reduced energy consumption and increased percentage from renewables by:
   a) programme for raising energy efficiency of all buildings to at least minimum sustainability standards;
   b) increased use of solar gain;
   c) greater use of combined heat and power systems;
   d) development of wind farms and wave power.

6. Major increases in biomass, both urban and rural, by:
   a) more community forests and other rural tree planting;
   b) protection of existing urban open space and creation of new open space in areas of deficiency;
   c) additional urban tree planting and other green vegetation;
   d) gardens on flat rooftops;
   e) more green areas in new development projects.

7. Regional water supplies augmented and consumption reduced by:
   a) tree planting to maximise rainwater retention in watersheds;
   b) metering consumers with graduated charges favouring low consumption;
   c) applying 'closed cycle' methods to water use;
   d) separating 'grey' water for filtering and return to groundwater reserves;
   e) reducing urban run-off by use of more permeable paving, providing natural channels and lagoons in place of closed drains.

8. Urban decentralisation and dispersal reduced by:
   a) greening and decongesting inner cities;
   b) making inner city housing more attractive by eliminating excessive densities, designing for 'defensible space';
   c) increasing average densities in city suburbs and small towns;
   d) using more concentrated forms for new development.

9. Commuting distances reduced by:
   a) more local production to meet local needs
   b) local employment to match local skills;
   c) more telecommunication-based home-working, especially in rural areas;
   d) more mixed development;
   e) more housing in major employment centres;
   f) more complementary development in adjoining small towns to reduce reliance on distant large cities;
   g) building balanced new communities.

10. Public transport made more attractive and economic by:
    a) concentrating more mixed-use development at public transport nodes;
    b) co-ordinating land use and public transport to achieve more balanced commuter flows;
    c) creating more dedicated public transport routes;
    d) improving frequency and reliability of services;
    e) raising densities to complement improved public transport.

11. Road traffic reduced by:
    a) locating new development so as to reduce travel demand;
    b) using opportunities to reshape urban areas to reduce private motorised trips;
    c) refusing permission for new car-based out-of-town retailing and business parks;
    d) pricing road use on congested routes;
    e) reducing car parking provision and increasing charges where public transport available;
    f) more pedestrian-priority areas.

Figure 9.3   *The social city region*

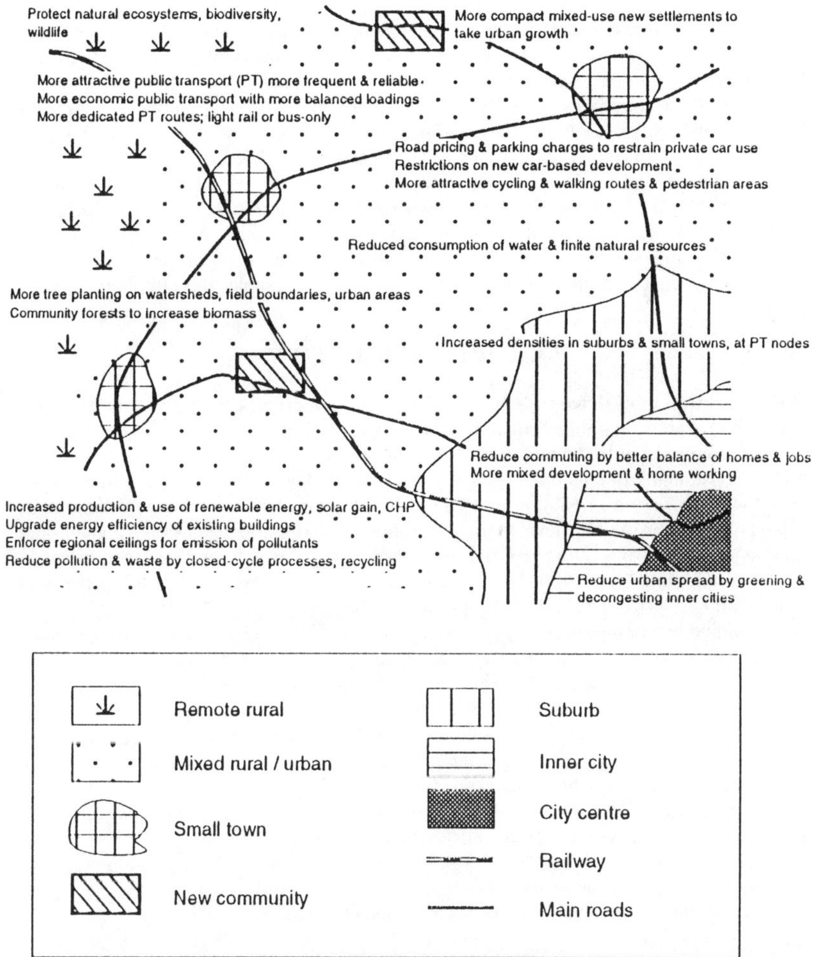

CITY CENTRES

Although often surrounded by declining inner areas, many city centres remain as important business and entertainment hearts to large city regions. Because of the intense activity and traffic that this generates, city centres are major foci for energy consumption and pollution. Because of their dominance, city centres also have a major bearing on the prospects for future sustainability of their city regions. The general decline in the environmental quality and ease of access in cities – both cores and inner areas – has been a major 'push' factor in the profound process of decentralisation that is so central to the sustainability debate. If cities can be revived and be seen again as desirable places in which to live and work, thus reducing the wider dispersal of urban areas, they will go a long way to reducing energy consumption and pollution. Conversely, if the improved environmental standards required for long-term sustainability are achieved, this will in itself make the city centres more desirable.

LAND USE AND TRANSPORT

The concentration of different activities in city centres creates the ideal conditions for maximum reliance on public transport, walking and cycling. All these are impeded by the present scale of road traffic and congestion; the result is excessive fuel consumption, air pollution damaging to health and buildings, wasteful delays and unreliability in business and other trips, poor accessibility, and a degraded street environment. The present pattern of land uses results in a high level of trip generation due to the squeezing out of housing and service industries from central areas, causing heavy reliance on long-distance journeys to work and additional road traffic for servicing and deliveries. Any attempt to curtail road traffic through pricing (either road pricing or higher parking charges) needs to be accompanied by changes in land use designed to reduce trip generation by, for example, dramatically increasing housing within and adjoining central areas or much more provision for mixed uses, thus allowing closer proximity of a wide range of support services to their principal customers. Decentralisation of some central area activities to major multi-purpose sub-centres would also be helpful, leading to improved accessibility and providing scope for the necessary central area restructuring and contributing to more economical public transport through more balanced loading.

Combined with these land-use adjustments, a comprehensive programme for improved traffic management – including more attractive and efficient public transport, reductions in car parking, more extensive pedestrian-priority areas, well-designed cycle and pedestrian routes made attractive by high-quality paving and street furniture, more trees and other greenery – would reduce pollution levels and sustain long-term viability.

NATURAL RESOURCES

These are significant both in terms of the value of natural features within the city and of the demands made by city development on resources imported from elsewhere. Parks, riversides and other water features, trees, 'green architecture' and wildlife contribute greatly to the attraction and health of cities, as both history and property values show. The greening of the city, especially the city centre, is one of the major lessons that the past has to teach us about how to enhance the value of cities as places in which to live and work. Further greening has the environmental merits of carbon dioxide absorption and the maintenance of flora and fauna and so on; it also has the merit of making city cores more attractive to residents and hence assisting the reversal of the process of out-migration.

City centres are by their nature major consumers of investment capital and natural resources and must make their contribution to the conservation of scarce world resources by reducing their demands wherever possible. Redevelopment should be refused except in those cases where a positive net contribution to sustainability objectives can be achieved by, for example, lower consumption of energy and non-renewable materials.

ENERGY

City centres are large-scale intensive users of energy within buildings, particularly in offices and shops. They must therefore play a major role in implementing effective energy conservation policies in existing buildings, encouraged and assisted by a comprehensive programme of incentives and penalties, technical advice and public exhortation. Integrated environmental planning and building regulations should require all new buildings to be substantially more energy efficient. Rydin[10] explains the relationship between commercial logic and conservation measures in the property industry. Such an understanding is needed if planning policies are to be effective in persuading developers to achieve net reductions in energy consumption. New forms of building – shape, orientation, cladding and glazing – will be needed to maximise solar gain and the use of renewable energy. CHP systems must be used in business and residential developments wherever possible.

WASTE

Commercial activities in urban cores produce large quantities of waste, much more of which must be recycled. Companies must be persuaded through appropriate regulations and differential charging to reduce the volume of waste and to assist recycling through separating waste products before collection. Given the large scale, local authorities must be responsible for collection and recycling jointly with any regional agencies.

Box 9.2 City centres: changes needed for future sustainability

CHECKLIST FOR MONITORING PROGRESS

1. More attractive for living as well as working.
2. Less dependence on long journeys to work.
3. Increased amount of affordable housing relative to total employment.
4. Selective decentralisation of employment.
5. Improved quality of housing through, for example, reduction of excessive densities and redesigning for 'defensible space'.
6. Greener, with more natural features, especially trees and water.
7. Augmenting local open spaces to meet shortages.
8. Exclusion of non-essential road vehicles.
9. Improved access by high-quality public transport.
10. Reduced car parking with priority for essential users.
11. Progressive reduction in road congestion and traffic delays.
12. Greater self-sufficiency of local areas for daily servicing.
13. Increasing the provision of more continuous and attractive cycling and pedestrian routes.
14. Increasing pedestrian-only and pedestrian-priority areas.
15. Better energy-efficiency standards in all buildings; greater use of solar gain.
16. Reduced consumption of fossil fuels; more use of CHP.
17. Reduction of total waste stream and greater percentage recycled.

Planning for a Sustainable Environment

Figure 9.4   *City centres*

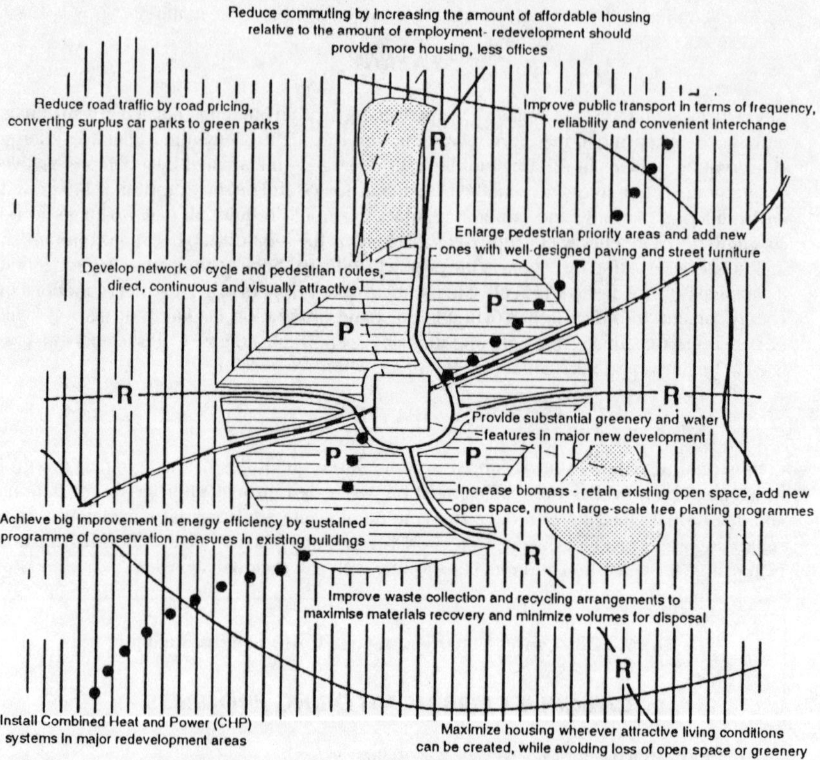

THE INNER CITY

In many respects, inner city areas may pose the greatest complexities for the application of sustainability criteria. In terms of proximity to central area employment, high housing densities, mixture of housing and other land uses, lower car ownership ratios and greater use of public transport, they would appear even in their present form to exhibit more fully than other areas the characteristics necessary for future sustainability. Yet of all the six area types discussed here, inner cities have over recent decades proved to be the least popular locations for living and working.

The lesson is clear: their compactness, higher densities and proximity to work and public transport will have to be combined with other qualities – or possibly give way at least partially to other qualities – if these areas are to be made sufficiently attractive to reduce the pressures for urban dispersal.

These are the areas where getting the balance right will be critical in creating a desirable living environment, giving precedence to measures such as 'greening' – with more open space and more trees and more provision for natural flora and fauna – traffic calming and the exclusion of through traffic, and the creation of safe areas for children's play and walking. The over-riding aim in many of these areas will have to be the steady elimination of those factors which have been driving people out and, in the process, destroying the community spirit and self-help networks which are also important components of a sustainable home environment. In some areas, this may well mean that housing densities must drop or the mixture of uses be reduced to eliminate incompatibilities, contrary to the sustainability policies appropriate elsewhere.

LAND USE AND TRANSPORT

Because of their existing compactness and complexity, alterations to the inner city structure will need especially careful design to suit local circumstances. Typically, the emphasis is likely to be on correcting the deficiency in local community facilities, reducing overcrowding, and improving the design of housing areas to provide more attractive surroundings and more 'defensible space'; the net effect will probably be some overall reduction in housing densities, even though some individual sites may be suitable for an increase. Some regrouping of business uses may be necessary to eliminate nuisance and to provide the more up-to-date operating conditions which are essential if the mixed-use character of these areas is to be maintained.

One objective of any such regrouping will be improved accessibility; but new traffic management schemes must be designed to reduce the blight of excessive road traffic. Through traffic will have to be rerouted and traffic calming measures widely used to create larger areas with safer, quieter streets and less polluted air. Networks of safe and attractive routes for walking and cycling then become easier to develop, adding to accessibility and further reducing the need for motorised trips. These restraints on road traffic must be accompanied by major improvements in public transport – in frequency, reliability and ease of transfer – with more use of electric vehicles, both buses and trams, to further reduce noise and pollution.

Where existing buildings are too old and decayed for rehabilitation to be practicable or desirable, urban renewal schemes must be used to introduce better environmental practices, replacing old polluting factories and energy-inefficient housing and providing improved routes for public transport. Proposals for 'urban villages' – developed on large derelict sites – offer the prospect of dramatic rejuvenation of parts of inner city areas. Such 'implants' are intended to provide all the characteristics – jobs, housing, recreation, local identity, quality of life – of viable communities in previously depressed, and often dying, areas. However, where sites have been derelict long enough to become wildlife habitats, this rare asset of nature near the heart of the city may best serve sustainability objectives by being retained to offset any local open space deficiency.

NATURAL RESOURCES

Because of the typical lack of open space and greenery throughout large parts of old inner city areas, every redevelopment scheme needs to make some provision for trees and other vegetation to add visual delight and to help increase the total biomass in the city. The use of permeable paving materials around new planting will help maintain it as well as reducing excessive rainwater run-off. In addition, more use could be made of open rainwater channels leading to streams and ponds in open spaces as part of the growing network of natural features that is needed for 'greening the city'. The reduction in road traffic will provide space for many more tree-lined streets, especially in areas that have re-acquired a sense of local identity and community.

ENERGY CONSERVATION

Since these are the areas where age and obsolescence often combine to require either complete redevelopment or major rehabilitation works, there will be scope both for reducing total demand for energy by requiring all such schemes to incorporate the best standards for heat-conserving insulation, and for increasing the share of renewable energy by maximum use of passive solar gain and combined heat and power.

Box 9.3 The inner city: changes required for future sustainability

CHECKLIST FOR MONITORING PROGRESS

1. Residential areas becoming more attractive through being less congested, greener, cleaner, quieter and safer.
2. Residential areas increasingly freed from through traffic, protected by traffic calming for local traffic.
3. Reduction in excessively high densities and additional local open space in areas of worst deficiency.
4. Improvements in design of mixed use areas to reduce nuisance and improve access and facilities for small businesses.
5. Increased variety in housing types, tenures and prices, attracting a wider range of income levels.
6. Better provision of community and leisure facilities, available to both local residents and employees.
7. Developing policies revised to provide for compactness and maximum accessibility to jobs and leisure opportunities while also creating attractive living and working conditions.
8. Improved frequency and reliability of public transport, both bus and light rail.
9. Expanding network of attractive routes for cycling and walking.
10. Active programme for major expansion of trees and other vegetation; protection and enhancement of natural features.
11. Increasing percentage of buildings adapted to reduce energy consumption, reduce heat loss and make more use of solar gain.
12. Development of CHP as part of redevelopment schemes; reducing dependence on external sources of power.
13. Reduction of total waste stream from housing and businesses.
14. Collection, separation and disposal of waste, arranged to maximise percentage of waste materials recovered and recycled.

Planning for a Sustainable Environment

Figure 9.5   *The inner city*

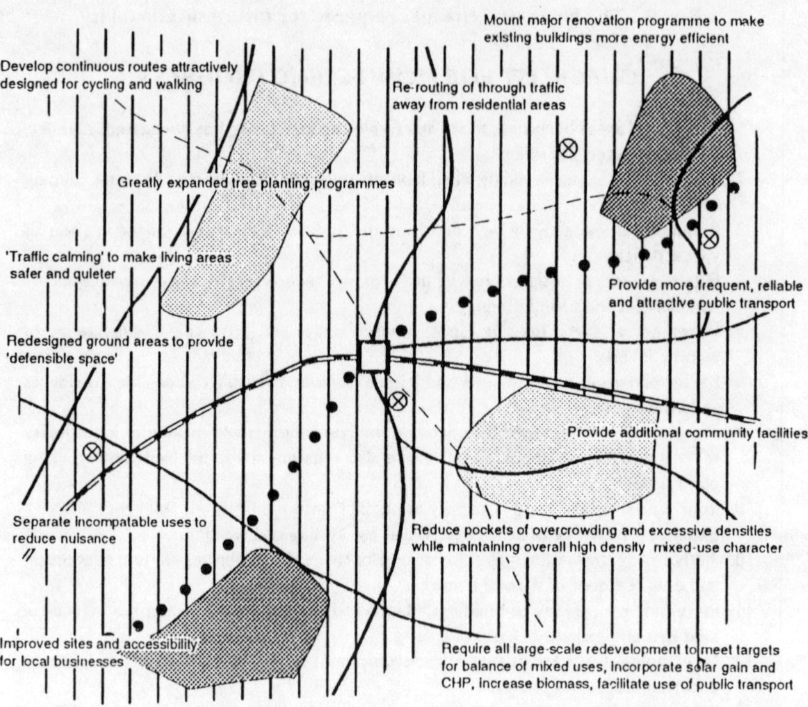

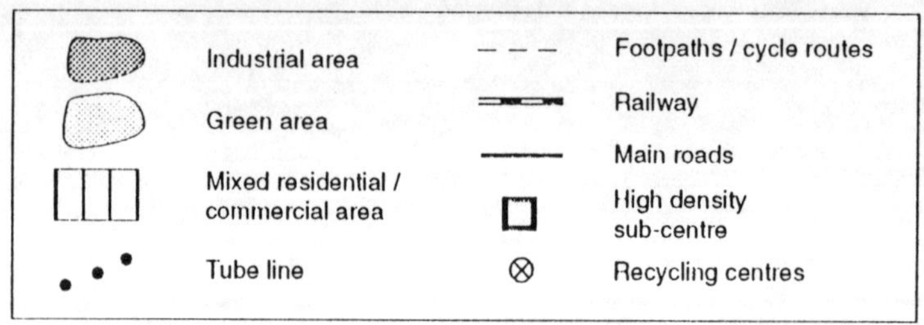

SUBURBS

Suburbs constitute one of the greatest challenges. They contain a high proportion of the population and the existing housing stock, and will continue to do so throughout the period in which the change to more sustainable forms of urban development must be accomplished. In their present form, however, they are very wasteful of energy and generate a high proportion of trips by private motor vehicle. The love of nature and the individual private home are combined par excellence in the suburb, but the lack of variety in density and land use reduces accessibility to employment and services, increasing the reliance on motorised trips and making energy conservation more difficult. The application of sustainability criteria will thus require changes in the spatial arrangements of the suburb. The introduction of these various changes, involving a gradual adaption of life-styles to new environmental and economic constraints, needs to be done with the maximum involvement of the residents if it is not to be seen as an unreasonable interference with cherished existing values.

LAND-USE AND TRANSPORT

One possible approach to creating more sustainable cities – and one that affects the suburbs directly – is that of 'decentralised concentration'. This approach promotes sub-centres in cities and larger towns to take some of the pressure from the traditional single core. This reduces congestion and facilitates the development of additional public transport systems. These centres would be people-intensive nodes – workplaces, retailing and leisure facilities – developed around rail and bus systems. Suburb-to-suburb public transport systems should be developed to cater for many trips which now take this form but which currently can only be completed conveniently by car. In the short term, such systems might be based on buses (although deregulation has made this more difficult). In the long run, rail, light rail and tram systems might contribute. There may be opportunities to increase residential densities in some areas, but care must be taken not to lower environmental standards through town cramming. Opportunities should be taken to create a greater mixing of activities. This might facilitate shorter, local trips to work and to services. Edge-of-town retail and business parks should be resisted; opportunities might be found to locate these in the enhanced suburban centres.

NATURAL RESOURCES

As well as variations in architecture, services and other facets, differences in vegetation in gardens, parks and other natural areas (biomass) can all enter the calculations of sustainability. The quantity and quality of water is increasingly becoming an issue in many areas as a result of environmentally damaging processes which must now be changed. The careful husbandry of water will become essential. Soakaways must be provided for surface water run-off, even if temporarily stored in lagoons which double as nature areas. This will require land to be set aside for the purpose. The use of permeable materials will prevent the sealing of the ground and should be part of good practice, as should the reuse of grey water. The treatment of sewerage by reed beds and other sewerage 'farms' is feasible using green belt space.

Green matter is essential for a healthy environment. A proactive management of all biomass resources, and a concern for increasing carbon dioxide absorption, will place additional importance on open spaces and their management. Areas will need to be set aside for planting to counteract the effects of building: twenty new trees for each house is suggested. Existing 'green assets', including rough ground serving as natural wildlife habitats, must not be sacrificed nor excessive infill permitted in the search for increased densities or more varied and concentrated development. The greater diversity in suburban form apparent since the Second World War needs extending. Traditional allotments should be retained for food growing purposes, as well as for their contribution in disposing of green waste and adding to total biomass. They could be used for local fish-farming where water is available, as well as bee-keeping and intensive food production of an organic nature.

ENERGY CONSERVATION

Detailed planning policies should contribute to making new build substantially more energy efficient. New forms of building with outer conservatory-like skins will seek to maximise the use of renewable energy. Opportunities should be taken wherever possible to develop CHP systems.

WASTE

Reducing the total volume of the waste stream is a prime requirement through changes in packaging habits and greatly-enlarged recycling. At the neighbourhood level, sufficient land area needs to be allocated for recycling collection centres. Careful siting will be necessary in predominantly residential suburbia for materials which generate noise in handling. Composting stations might be located at allotments to deal with that fraction of green waste which cannot be dealt with at individual homes. At a district authority level, (population of, say, 100,000) a materials recovery and processing facility will be needed for all recyclable waste, including industrial waste, where this is the appropriate scale. For some materials – such as tyres – only one or two facilities nationwide may be required. Residual waste can be incinerated for district heating.

Box 9.4 Suburbs: changes needed for future sustainability

CHECKLIST FOR MONITORING PROGRESS

1. More intensive development along public transport corridors.
2. More mixed-use zones for combined living and working.
3. Higher density mixed-use development at neighbourhood centres and public transport nodes.
4. Using redevelopment opportunities to achieve a greater variety of housing types and residential densities, with higher densities in suitable locations, especially where easily accessible to public transport and other services.
5. Growing network of safe and convenient routes for walking and cycling.
6. Reduced impact of motor vehicles on local neighbourhoods through progressive exclusion of through traffic and more extensive use of traffic-calming measures.
7. Enhancement of open spaces, improving ecological function in terms of biodiversity, wildlife habitats, urban forests and increasing total biomass to act as pollution 'sinks'.
8. Developing green corridors linking open spaces and any remaining areas of natural vegetation.
9. Greater retention of rainwater run-off, development of streams and ponds for conservation and landscape purposes.
10. Reducing water consumption, reuse of filtered grey water and increased return of used water to the ground.
11. Greater recycling of waste, reducing volume and landfill needs.
12. Increased involvement of local residents and community groups in schemes for waste recovery and other conservation measures.
13. Reduction in total energy consumption, with increasing percentage of buildings brought up to sustainability standards for conserving heat and power, and increased use of CHP and solar gain.
14. Increased share of energy obtained from renewable sources.

Planning for a Sustainable Environment

Figure 9.6   *Suburbs*

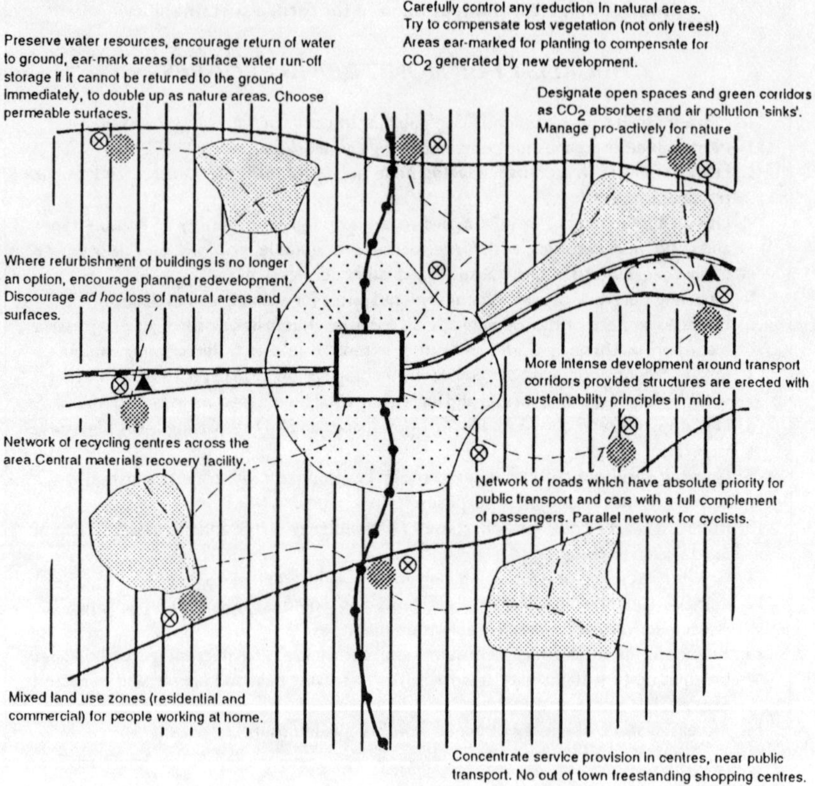

SMALL TOWNS AND NEW COMMUNITIES

The small town is one of our most successful types of community. It acts as a service centre for other towns and villages and has many of the characteristics of sustainability. At this level, however, local circumstances are likely to vary considerably. Many small towns, particularly in accessible, lowland areas, have grown rapidly in recent years. They have been seen as almost the ideal living environment: providing a semi-rural, economically buoyant, small-scale living environment, but with sufficient services to provide a high degree of self-containment. In the coming years, these towns will remain under pressure unless decentralisation from the large cities slows down considerably. Many of these towns have historic centres and other historic areas where the introduction of energy-saving measures and other changes to achieve sustainability objectives would be unacceptable unless carried out sensitively. There is no doubt, however, that many sustainability measures – such as pedestrianisation, taming the motor car, reduction of car parking, and rehabilitation instead of redevelopment in order to conserve scarce materials – would greatly assist the conservation of historic features.

LANDUSE AND TRANSPORT

As a result of their rapid growth, many small towns now have severe traffic problems. In sensitive, congested centres road pricing or severe traffic restraint measures may be appropriate, particularly in historic towns. Care must be taken, however, to ensure that the result is not simply a shift of traffic to other less restrictive towns nearby. Again, public transport has to be promoted. In some cases, an overall increase in the size of the town will facilitate improved public transport. With a single accessible node, the centre becomes particularly important, and in the case of historic towns particularly sensitive: it must carry the burden of those activities that are people intensive. Thus, the centres will have to carry those business and retailing activities that should be resisted on the edge of town. If towns are close together, then linking public transport may be important. It may be appropriate to take opportunities to achieve a greater mixing of uses. There may be circumstances in which infilling, and hence higher densities, might be appropriate in such towns. Densities should be increased near to public transport facilities, while activities, such as distribution, should be located on the edge of town near to major roads.

These positive changes will have to be complemented by strong restraints on any further edge-of-town retailing and offices together with measures such as road pricing and higher parking charges to reduce the volume of road traffic. New large-scale traffic generators should be permitted only where well served by public transport. Where nearby towns are complementary in terms of their job and leisure opportunities, accessibility by public transport should be improved so that groups of towns become more self-reliant and less dependent on more distant, bigger cities.

The building of new communities would, of course, provide the best opportunity for achieving forms of urban development that fully meet sustainability standards. Particular attention will need to be paid to:

- overall layout;
- pattern of land uses and transport;
- design of buildings;
- energy and transport systems;
- minimum generation of pollution and waste; and
- maximum provision for trees, water, wildlife and a high level of biomass.

New settlements could provide the models, demonstrating for all to see and experience what the full application of sustainability principles is like in practice; they could provide the vision towards which the gradual restructuring of existing urban areas could be directed.

NATURAL RESOURCES

The more balanced and more self-servicing urban areas which sustainability requires are already to be seen to some extent in Ebenezer Howard's Garden Cities and the later New Towns. For example, Redditch used the study of microclimate to aid environmental conditions and built separate drainage systems to create strings of lakes. In Milton Keynes, the system of open spaces planned into the structure of the town provides space for planting millions of trees, attractive routes for cycling and walking, open-air recreation close at hand, and gives ample scope for increased biomass and the further working out of ecological principles.

In older towns, there is room at the edges for developing all these ideas, together with new ones such as using the incineration of residual (non-recyclable) waste in local CHP systems for supplying greenhouses with energy for intensive horticultural production – a better alternative to paying farmers to simply set aside land. Policies for developing smallholding areas on the outskirts would encourage greater self-sufficiency in supplies of basic foods and more local employment. Local supplies of organic fertiliser could be obtained by mixing green waste with treated sewage sludge, reducing the need for expensive imports of artificial fertilisers.

ENERGY CONSUMPTION AND WASTE

Measures to reduce both of these will be needed here as much as elsewhere, and will be similar to those described for various other parts of the Social City Region. Where the overall density is high enough, there may be scope for greater self-sufficiency by combining power generation from renewables and CHP schemes with intensive area-wide heat and power conservation schemes.

> **Box 9.5 Small towns and new communities: changes needed for future sustainability**
>
> ### CHECKLIST FOR MONITORING PROGRESS
>
> 1. Reduced rate of growth in road vehicle mileage.
> 2. Increased percentage of trips by public transport.
> 3. Growth of non-motorised movement, cycling and walking; increased mileage of safe attractive routes for cycling.
> 4. Increased density of activities near public transport nodes.
> 5. Ecology centre actively promoting sustainability concepts and goals.
> 6. Urban audit published regularly, measuring air and water pollution, energy efficiency and recycling.
> 7. Business network, developing ways of promoting local use of local produce and improving the attractiveness of local markets.
> 8. Reductions in energy consumption in existing buildings.
> 9. Reduced per capita consumption of fossil fuels and increased percentage obtained from renewable sources and district CHP schemes.
> 10. Growing contribution to integrated sub-regional waste system in terms of reducing total waste stream, closed-cycle processes and recycling.
> 11. Creative management of water for conservation and landscape purposes.
> 12. Increases in tree planting and other plant life, and total biomass.
> 13. Enhancement of nature throughout all parts of the urban area.
> 14. Redevelopment normally refused permission when rehabilitation would require less use of scarce natural resources.
> 15. Conserving historic areas while improving energy efficiency.
> 16. Increasing involvement of community groups and schools in making a direct contribution to sustainability targets.

Planning for a Sustainable Environment

Figure 9.7 *Small towns and new communities*

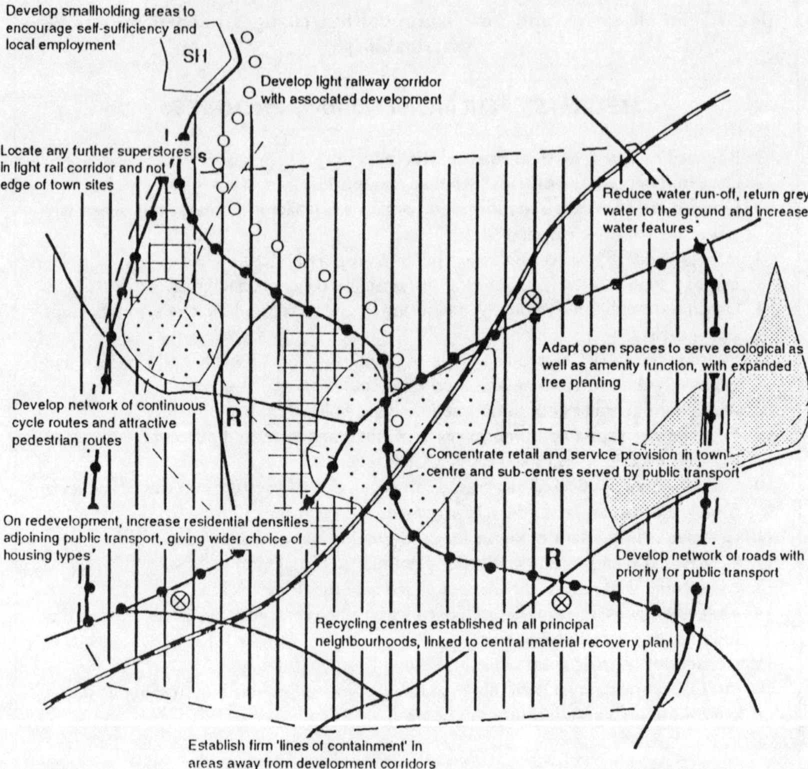

MIXED URBAN-RURAL AREAS

These areas will bear the brunt of continued economic restructuring and potential growth, particularly in South and Central England. The high rate of growth (see Table 9.1) is likely to continue as people leave the bigger urban centres seeking home environments which are less congested, less polluted, more spacious and with easier access to the countryside. This rapid growth may eventually slow down if travel costs rise steeply in the drive to cut pollution levels, and if large cities are successful in creating more attractive living conditions. However, current trends cannot be reversed quickly and substantial further growth seems inevitable, creating intense pressure on the environment but also opening useful opportunities to guide development in sustainable ways. Current set-aside policies for taking land out of agricultural production will also strongly affect these areas.

LAND USE AND TRANSPORT

Many of these areas have reasonably complete road and rail networks but have experienced major changes in accessibility with the rapid growth of private road traffic, decline in bus services and the improvement of long-distance commuter rail services at the expense of local lines. Because settlements are small with limited facilities and agricultural employment is low, many areas have increasingly changed from being mixed-use, mixed-income and relatively self-sufficient for jobs and daily needs to being dependent on more distant, large towns and cities for jobs, shopping and services, and even for affordable housing as commuters have moved in and pushed house prices out of the reach of local people. The result is more and longer trips for more purposes and greater dependency on the private motor car. Low densities and long utility runs per household add to energy inefficiencies.

New development in recent decades has exaggerated all these characteristics which are incompatible with long-term sustainability. The continued pressure for growth does provide considerable scope for correcting some of the worst deficiencies but the application of sustainability principles in these areas will require strong policies combining land use and transport objectives, applicable to all localities within an overall regional strategy.

New development should normally be to higher average densities, but much more varied to meet a wider range of household types and incomes and closely related to fixed lines of rapid public transport. There should be provision for areas or pockets of low density where there are opportunities for combining home and workplace (including smallholdings) and for more individual self-sufficiency in terms of energy supply, composting waste and on-site sewage treatment. All new development, apart from minor infilling, should be designed to achieve, first, an improved balance of homes and workplaces (to reduce long-distance work trips) and, second, an improved balance of commuter flows (to make full use of public transport capacity, giving more economical public transport and less fuel consumption).

NATURAL RESOURCES

New and existing settlements should be interspersed with community woodlands, good agricultural land protected from further urban encroachment and small holdings or market gardens for small-scale production linked to local markets, with intensive and innovative food producing areas on the best soils. As with the new community forests, the use of trees as the dominant feature in mixed areas can work wonders in assimilating development into the landscape.

These areas must continue to accommodate gravel extraction and other mineral workings in locations not requiring excessive trip lengths. Their role in the environmentally safe disposal of non-recyclable wastes will be an important part of any regional strategy for future waste disposal avoiding pollution of ground or water supplies. Quantity as well as quality of water is becoming an increasing problem, requiring both lower consumption, reduction of rainwater runoff, re-use of grey water, and redesign of drainage and sewage systems to separate out non-sewage bearing flows and using them for recharging groundwater reserves.

NEW SETTLEMENTS

Many of these objectives will be more readily achieved through the building of balanced new settlements rather than the single-use unbalanced extensions to existing settlements which have been typical of speculative development in recent decades. Given that only a fraction of future housing demand can be met within existing urban areas, there is a strong case for regional and sub-regional strategies to include the building of new settlements designed on advanced 'sustainable development' principles as an alternative to both 'town cramming' and further peripheral sprawl.

ENERGY

As elsewhere, big savings are possible through more compact new development and better designed buildings and by using all opportunities for passive solar gain and incorporating CHP systems in most projects.

Box 9.6 Mixed urban – rural areas: changes needed for future sustainability

CHECKLIST FOR MONITORING PROGRESS

1. Increased number of service sub-centres supported by higher densities and linking public transport services.
2. Better balance of homes and workplaces throughout the sub-region to achieve more even public transport loadings.
3. Improved capacity of local producers to serve local markets for daily goods and services.
4. Increased local job opportunities and social choice.
5. Increasing percentage of trips by public transport.
6. Greater diversity of new development: some achieving energy efficiency through better design; some having greater self-containment for energy and food supplies.
7. Substantial share of new development in new settlements designed to match sustainable development standards fully.
8. Integrated sub-regional waste systems to reduce waste streams; minimise landfill and maximise recycling of hard materials; compost organic waste; provide fuel for CHP plants; and improve the separation of toxic materials to prevent ground and water pollution.
9. Major increases in community forests, tree planting, and total biomass.
10. Reduction in water consumption and increasing ground-water reserves.
11. More use of passive solar gain and CHP systems.
12. Increasing percentage of existing buildings meeting full energy-efficiency standards.
13. Active landscape programmes for raising biological diversity, protecting natural features and greening urban areas.

Planning for a Sustainable Environment

Figure 9.8   *Mixed urban – rural areas*

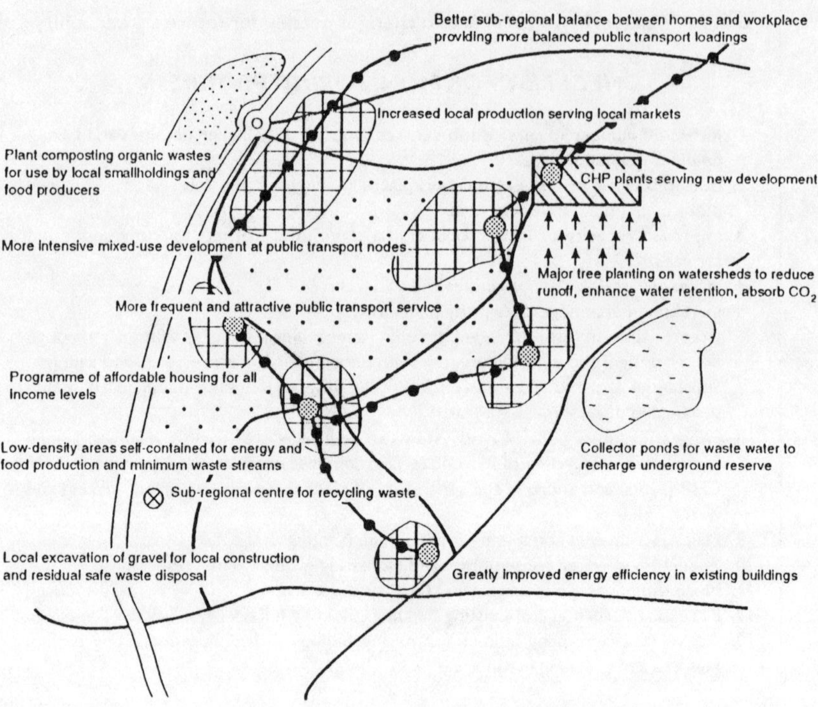

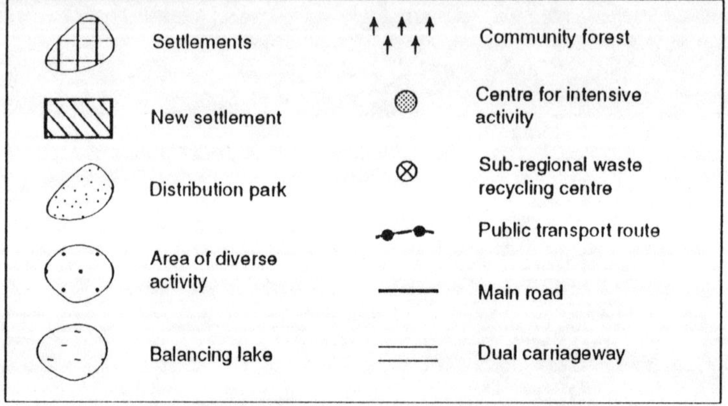

REMOTE RURAL AREAS

These areas contribute least to the total environmental damage caused by modern industrialised society, by reason of their small and scattered total populations and their predominantly non-urban and non-industrial life-styles. However, they are likely to have an increasingly important role to play in achieving sustainability targets for the region as a whole: for a greatly enlarged supply of renewable energy; for greater regional self-sufficiency in food and timber; for major increases in forest cover; for augmenting regional water supplies; and for their valuable leisure resources of natural beauty and peaceful havens well away from the rush and pressures of areas more dominated by urban demands and values. The demands for all these are bound to grow, partly as a continuation of established trends and partly as the inevitable result of the search for greater sustainability for the region as a whole.

It is likely that remoter rural areas will continue to receive in-migration – a well-established trend that general regional policies in pursuit of greater sustainability are unlikely to stop. Densities, however, are likely to remain low. There is no reason to think that any general drive for more concentrated forms of urban development would have much impact here. Other objectives will have much greater relevance, including greater reliance on local sources of energy, food and natural materials; home- and community-based employment; and better provision for energy and water conservation and for recycling of recoverable wastes. Happily, the search for greater regional sustainability will necessarily slow down or reverse the centralisation of production and employment which has until now left these remoter areas with vulnerable economies, substandard services and associated social problems. However, new institutional arrangements may be needed to promote sustainable development practices, in particular to achieve integration in land management, settlement planning, transport operations and resource development.

LAND USE AND TRANSPORT

The economic circumstances of such areas vary considerably. Some have received jobs and people as a result of decentralisation, sometimes making up for the decline in traditional employment and therefore remaining economically and socially viable. Others have suffered from job losses, increasingly inadequate public transport and obsolete public services and community facilities. With their emphasis on greater self-sufficiency in the local economy, enhanced local production to reduce unnecessary road transport, and improved public transport services, sustainability policies should provide greatly improved prospects for the future of these hitherto disadvantaged areas. However, economic viability will be partly dependent on a balanced package of measures, sensitively adapted to local conditions, including, for example: improved jobs and services in locations well served by public transport; transport improvements aimed primarily at improving sub-regional accessibility rather than long-distance commuting; wider application of the 'tele-cottage' principle to facilitate home-working or small new enterprises in more (and, indeed, in less) remote areas and for combining smallholdings with tele-linked businesses; and development of local distribution networks aimed at efficient servicing of local markets.

NATURAL RESOURCES

The UK has one of the largest potentials for wind energy in the whole of Europe and the opportunities for exploiting this are located largely in the more remote rural uplands, especially in the West. Ways will have to be found of designing and developing windfarms in these areas without causing unacceptable damage to their natural beauty. The other major sources of renewable energy (wave and tidal power) are less concentrated in remote rural areas, so it will be a function of the energy strategy for the region as a whole to determine how much wind power in remoter areas needs to be developed relative to these other sources and other locations in order to meet energy sustainability targets.

Changing agricultural policies and measures to deal with 'surplus' farmland are already creating opportunities for more varied activities, including tourism and leisure activities, and for more forestry and forestry-based products. Some of these areas are, after all, the 'rainforests' of Britain, amply provided with water and favourable conditions for plant growth and biological diversity – valuable assets in achieving a balanced and sustainable development for the region as a whole. Special audits to identify the potential for renewable resources of all kinds will be necessary.

ENERGY CONSUMPTION

If these areas are to become principal suppliers of wind- and water-generated electricity to the rest of the city region, expanded research programmes and careful detailed planning and design will be necessary to minimise any adverse effects on the local environment. To meet local demand, small-scale local power stations will help to reduce distribution losses; CHP schemes will be viable in some settlements; and – as elsewhere – making all buildings more energy efficient will be a major contributor to the important goal of reducing overall consumption.

Box 9.7 Remote rural areas: changes needed for future sustainability

CHECKLIST FOR MONITORING PROGRESS

1. Expansion of total biomass through increasing forests, tree planting along field boundaries and roadside verges, and protection of areas of natural vegetation.
2. Increasing biological diversity, including avoidance of monocultures and protection of wildlife habitats.
3. Growth of groundwater reserves, protection of watersheds.
4. Reduced pollution of streams and ground-water.
5. Increased composting of organic wastes and reduced use of artificial fertilisers.
6. Increasing production of energy from renewable sources: wind, wave, tide, geothermal.
7. Reduced consumption of fossil fuels.
8. Progressive upgrading of all buildings to meet new sustainability standards for energy efficiency.
9. Improved public transport in terms of frequency and convenience, improved accessibility, more attractive travelling conditions.
10. Reduction in long-distance commuting.
11. Growing self-sufficiency of the local economy in terms of the capacity of the sub-region to provide a greater variety of job opportunities and to supply daily goods and services from local sources.
12. Better telecommunications to aid homeworking.
13. Publication of regular audits on waste, pollution, energy and water.
14. Regularly updated plans for integrating land management, settlements, transport, and resource development.

Planning the Sustainable City Region

Figure 9.9 *Remote rural areas*

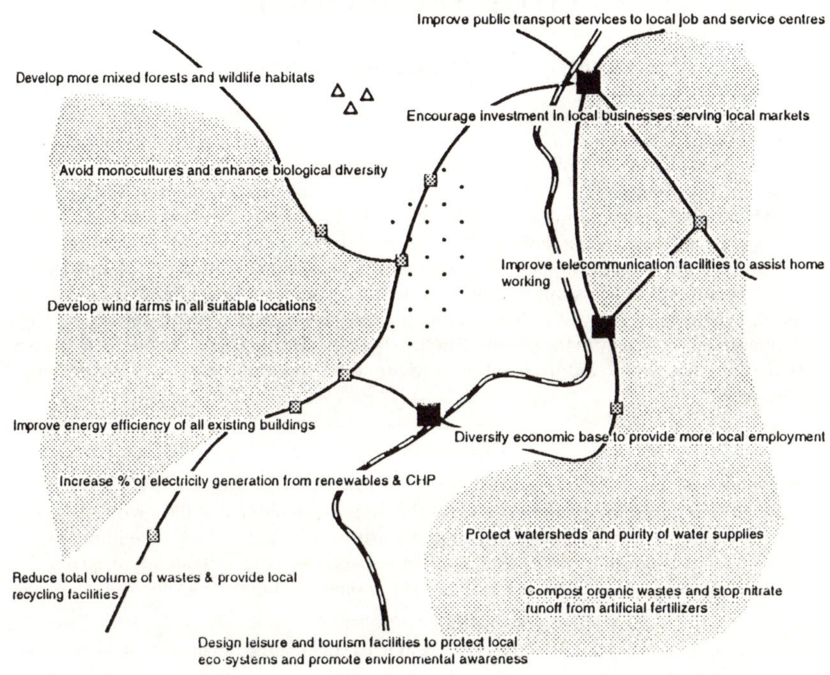

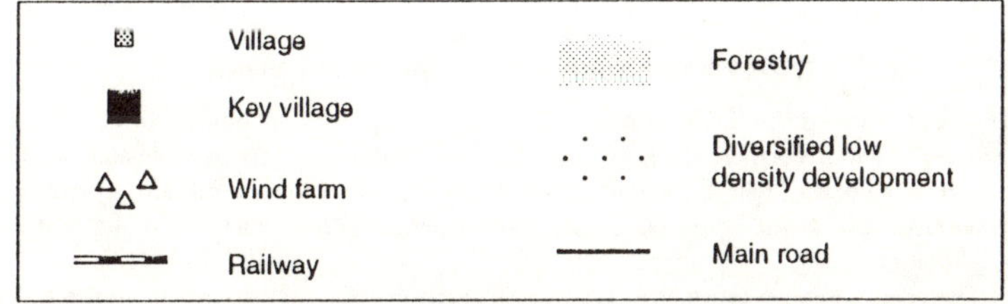

SUSTAINABLE TOWN, SUSTAINABLE COUNTRY – INSTITUTIONAL CHANGE

DELIVERING SUSTAINABLE URBAN DEVELOPMENT

The previous sections have proposed a detailed policy agenda for achieving sustainable development at local levels. The question now is how to deliver such initiatives at the regional and local level? In considering the arrangements to do this, a basic principle to be adopted is that plans at all levels should be more closely co-ordinated. The TCPA is convinced that policy initiatives should fully reflect the desires and aspirations of local communities. Thus, consistent with the aim of effective implementation (as argued in Chapter 1), we strongly support the European Commission's notion of 'subsidiarity' – which requires that decisions are made at the lowest effective level. However, it is also the case that each layer of policy making must be consistent with that above it. This applies most obviously in the planning field, where local plans should be consistent with structure plans, which in turn must be consistent with regional objectives and national guidance.

Recommendation

Policy making must encompass the twin principles of subsidiarity and plan consistency, avoiding excessive centralisation and maximising the involvement of those whose daily living environment will be affected by new development, while ensuring that there is consistency between the details of proposed development and the broader policies at regional and national levels.

If new policy vehicles are introduced to deal with sustainable development, as we have suggested in Chapter 1 and will pursue below, then these must also follow these principles.

BOX 9.8 Community involvement in Leicester

Leicester – styled the 'Environment City' – has set up eight specialist working groups with representatives from the public, private and voluntary sectors to guide and develop action around the built environment; the social environment; food and agriculture; economy and work; energy; waste and pollution; transport; and the natural environment.

The groups involve more than 120 senior decision and policy makers from the three sectors. The groups aim, within the framework of a twenty-year plan, to build on Leicester's significant achievements in moving towards greater sustainability and to achieve realistic and practical solutions to such problems as car dependency. The involvement of all sectors of the community – including business – is seen as crucial if genuine changes in the environmental field are to be accomplished.

Although the concern here is with the local scale, there are, of course, constraints imposed on local action by national governments. Thus certain desirable initiatives at the local level require changes in central government regulations and practices. A good example of this is the case of appeal decisions where local authorities have refused permission on environmental grounds. To date, the Department of the Environment has not been very sympathetic to such arguments. However, if central government is serious about achieving sustainability objectives, it must encourage local authorities to use their planning and other environmental control functions for this purpose.

Recommendation

Central government advice and appeal decisions must actively promote and support local planning authorities in their attempts to achieve environmental improvements and sustainability objectives through their local plans and development control decisions.

In the absence of elected regional governments, and pending the reorganisation of some elements of local government, it is essential that the fullest possible use is made of existing arrangements to implement environmental policy. The present and developing system of regional guidance can make a greater contribution to environmental policy. Although developed within the land-use planning field, this is the only vehicle available at present for the discussion and adoption of any regional-level policies. Because it is an informal system, albeit one that is currently being promoted strongly by central government, it has a largely advisory role, setting a context for structure plan policies. Environmental statements are now very much to the fore in regional advice being prepared by regional conferences. However, these tend to take the form of generalised statements. Regional guidance could usefully go further in considering the consequences of regional-scale settlement patterns and transport systems and in proposing changes that will improve sustainability. Debates and policy formulations at this scale need not be too constrained by the land-use origins of the system. A number of regional conferences are finding the system to be a suitable vehicle for addressing non-land-use issues.

Recommendation

Regional guidance should give more detailed advice on environmentally sustainable development patterns within regions.

Although in the short term such improvements to the treatment of environmental issues in regional guidance is highly desirable, we believe this should be viewed as an interim arrangement only. The experience to date strongly indicates that the present arrangements for dealing with major development and environmental issues of regional or national significance – in terms of both policy formation and implementation – are inadequate and will only be effectively handled by setting up a regional level of government capable of preparing and operating long-term strategies. The arguments and proposals for doing so are detailed in the TCPA report *Strategic Planning for Regional Development*.[11] These arguments apply especially strongly to policies for sustainable development and their prospects of being effectively implemented would be greatly strengthened if these strategic bodies existed at the regional level to guide and support the local action which is needed to make national policies work in practice.

Recommendation

A regional level of government should be established to prepare strategies for future development, with special reference to the need for effective implementation of national policies for environmental protection and future sustainability.

At the local level, the new system of unitary authorities – assuming regional government

– should provide an effective means of implementing environmental policy. At both elected regional and unitary authority levels, however, a new integrated approach to such policy is crucial. It is therefore suggested that it be a statutory requirement that regional and unitary authorities produce integrated environmental plans, as suggested in Chapter 1. An informal system, even if backed by central government – as, for example, with regional guidance – would be far less effective.

Recommendation

Legislation and regulations should be amended to require regional and local authorities to prepare Integrated Environment Plans (IEPs), which state environmental objectives, policies, targets and responsibilities.

In Chapter 1 it was suggested that integrated environmental planning must recognise three crucial characteristics of environmental processes: their trans-media nature, through air, land and sea; their trans-sectoral nature, as they cut across traditional policy boundaries; and their trans-boundary nature, as they cut across political frontiers. These characteristics imply an integration of analysis and policy formulation that will be novel to most agencies. But they also imply organisational arrangements that may have to be novel too. Despite efforts at 'corporate planning' in the 1970s, whereby all local government services were to be co-ordinated within a planning approach, local authority activities remain largely compartmentalised within departments. However, environmental concerns cannot be the sole preserve of a single department. It is essential that all local environmental initiatives, at regional and local levels, are co-ordinated.

Recommendation

Organisational arrangements must be devised in regional and local agencies to enable genuinely integrated environmental policies to be formulated and implemented.

Integrated Environmental Plans would probably be best co-ordinated from a chief executive's department. Contributions to the plan would come from individual departments, but within a clear co-ordinated framework. The environmental agenda to be addressed by regional and local integrated environmental plans would be determined in each case, as the discussion of settlement types earlier in this chapter has demonstrated. However, some indication can be given here of issues that might be addressed:

- new urban form and energy consumption (residential, workplace, retail and leisure locations, varieties of urban densities etc);
- existing urban form and energy consumption;
- promotion of public transport patronage;
- promotion of CHP;
- trade-offs between environmental and other criteria;
- waste disposal arrangements;
- telecommunications;
- habitat protection and creation;
- urban greening;
- recycling schemes;
- building controls;
- urban densities.

BOX 9.9 An integrated approach – the London Borough of Sutton

Starting from a short, robust policy statement in 1986, Sutton Council has gradually set out to change its attitudes and work practices to make them more environmentally relevant. Accepting that not everything can be done at once, steady progress has, nevertheless, been maintained. Where an issue has been tackled, such as recycling, it has not been seen in isolation but as part of wider issues, in this case including waste avoidance, waste collection, waste disposal and the finding of markets for recovered materials. For example, the Council uses its purchasing powers to generate a higher demand for recycled products.

Faced with limited resources, Sutton Council has achieved its results by redistributing resources and by setting up special funds, such as an energy conservation fund. Monitoring of implementation and a gradual change of attitudes and aptitudes by staff has played an important role.

Cumulatively, the effect of Sutton's work in the fields of the preservation and enhancement of nature, environmental education and recycling have all started to contribute to a more sustainable future. Of particular importance are the efforts to involve the community. The overriding principle in Sutton's work is to concentrate on the manageable, to be imaginative, and to maintain continuity. Crucially, it is accepted that, whatever the circumstances, everybody can make a contribution here and now.

The distinction between the appropriate agendas for regional and local integrated enviromental plans will depend on circumstances. However, clearly the regional level would need to establish the objectives and targets for the region as a whole and provide facilities or support beyond the resources of individual local authorities (for waste disposal and recycling, for instance). Local authorities would devise the programmes of action which would be appropriate to their local circumstances, while also contributing their share of the overall regional effort. In the absence of regional strategies, some local authorities have already taken major initiatives in promoting environmental awareness in their areas, setting up local conservation programmes and schemes for waste recovery and recycling – such as Leicester City Council's 'Environment City' scheme (see Box 9.8) and the London Borough of Sutton's council-wide programme for involving all council departments and community groups (see Box 9.9). Such initiatives need to become standard practice throughout the country – with such active government support as is necessary in terms of power and resources.

Recommendation

All local councils should take the lead in creating an awareness and understanding of environmental issues, in developing council-wide programmes for at least a number of priority issues such as energy conservation and waste recycling, and in involving local residents – with positive support, as necessary, from central government.

Effective planning for sustainable development will rely heavily on good information, both about the current state of the environment and about the various key factors which have been identified as requiring change if environmental sustainability is to be achieved. One essential source of data will be local environmental audits which will be required to measure the amount and rate of change in conditions such as the level of pollutants in air, water and soil, the degree of biodiversity, and the reserves of essential resources including water and topsoil. Equally important will be an organised programme of regular monitoring to measure progress in changing those key environment-influencing factors which are the subject of sustainability policies and for which specific targets have been set in the IEP, for example energy conservation, transport efficiency, development of renewables and proportions of waste materials recycled.

Recommendation

Local environmental audits should be carried out and published regularly by the appropriate regional and local authorities in order to establish to what extent sustainability policies are having the intended effect.

Monitoring of key environment-influencing factors and the regular publication of results should be required as an integral part of every Integrated Environment Plan in order to assess the extent and rate of progress in achieving the sustainability targets set in the plan.

Monitoring is not an end in itself, however. It has to be the basis of further action: either to take action to ensure that missed targets are achieved in future or as the basis for the amendment of policy.

RESOURCES

If more sustainable policies are to be developed for our towns and our countryside, it will be essential to have earmarked financial resources available both to fund specific projects and to assist in paying compensation where appropriate. One potential source of such resources is for government to impose a tax on the increase in land value that arises from the granting of permission for development and to use the proceeds for environmental purposes. As suggested in Chapter 2, it seems entirely appropriate to use 'betterment' in this way, as it is physical development itself that causes so many environmental problems.

Vast amounts of money change hands when land is developed. A retailer may pay as much as £10 million for 2 hectares of farmland that has planning permission for a superstore. This enhanced value reflects the profit anticipated by the retailer, but it is considered by many people to belong to the community whose collective actions brought services and population near enough to the site to justify its development. The potential value of the land is only realised with the grant of planning permission. In the past 45 years three attempts to collect this betterment have been made, each to be abandoned by following governments mainly for political reasons. However, the different schemes were repudiated before there had been sufficient research to assess their full effects and to identify the causes of apparent land shortages.

At the other end of the economic scale, land values fall when land is abandoned, as, for example, in areas of industrial decline. Grants are given to reclaim such land. Industrial rehabilitation is desirable but it seems illogical to grant in aid the recovery of lost land values in derelict land while refusing to collect the enhanced value from developing land.

The 'polluter pays' principle has become a catchphrase of the sustainability debate. The aim is to make the instigator of environmental problems pay for the remedial action required to correct these problems. There is a debate, however, as to how the polluter should pay. One possibility is that the polluter should be directly responsible for the cost of remedial action. Another possibility is that the public sector should carry out remedial action, funded by taxation on the polluter.

Where the polluter is the developer of land, one obvious way of taxation is through a betterment levy, charged as a proportion of the increase in land value arising from the granting of planning permission. An alternative would be the levying of an 'impact fee'. This idea is currently being promoted as an alternative to the current system of negotiable planning gain agreements. The planning gain or impact fee arrangement has to date been intended to provide for public infrastructure provision, rather than for remedial environmental objectives. However, in principle, it could also be used for the latter purposes. In making a choice between the use of impact fees or betterment to fund environmental rehabilitation, our preference is for betterment. It is a 'real' value tested by the price at which the land changes hands. It is thus likely to be scaled according to the scale of the potential environmental impact caused by development.

However raised, the funds should not be treated as general taxation but as a fund to meet the costs of remedial environmental work and to compensate communities adversely affected by economic restructuring. Because restructuring is national in its repercussions, and because related shifts in land value are both regional and national, the fund will need to operate nationally and regionally. Nationally it would be able to support communities in transition and suffering the more acute forms of growth or decline. Regionally, support would be available for the development of public transport, energy efficiency in buildings and renewable resources.

Recommendation

Effective implementation requires the establishment of a Sustainable Land Development Fund, to be sourced from a betterment tax on the increase in land value that arises from the granting of planning permission. The fund should be used for environmental improvements and community compensation.

Two obvious problems arise from this suggestion. One is the question of the means by which monies from this fund are distributed; the other is the likely loss of Fund income – and hence loss of environmental protection — in times of recession. Some means can be devised to resolve both problems. Both would involve equalisation; one geographical and the other temporal. In the first case, it should be possible to devise a formula to switch funds from areas of high fund income to areas of severe environmental problems. In the second case, monies can be held back in high-yielding years to compensate for low income in years of economic recession.

The authors wish to acknowledge the help of Ray Green in the preparation of this chapter. Figures 9.1 and 9.3 to 9.9 were drawn by Heather Browning and Judith Fox.

References

CHAPTER 9

1. Commission of the European Communities (1990) *Green Paper on the Urban Environment*, CEC
2. Breheny, M (1992) 'The Contradictions of the Compact City: A Review' in Breheny, M *Sustainable Development and Urban Form*, Pion, London; ECOTEC Research and Consulting Ltd (1992) *Reducing Transport Emissions Through Planning*, draft report to the DoE
3. Office of Population Censuses and Surveys (1992) 1991 Census – *Preliminary Report for England and Wales*, OPCS, London
4. Breheny, M, Gent, T, and Lock, D (1992) *Alternative Development Patterns: New Settlements*, draft report to the DoE
5. Elkin, T, McLaren, D and Hillman, M (1991) *Reviving the City: Towards Sustainable Urban Development*, Friends of the Earth, London
6. Sherlock, H (1990) *Cities are Good for Us*, Transport 2000, London   [223]
7. Green, R, & Holliday, J (1991) *Country Planning – A Time for Action*, TCPA, London
8. Robertson, J (1990) 'Alternative Futures for Cities' in Cadman, D, and Payne, G (eds) *The Living City: Towards a Sustainable Future*, Routledge, London
9. Owens, S (1991) *Energy Conscious Planning*, Campaign for the Protection of Rural England, London; Rickaby, P (1987) 'Six Settlement Patterns Compared' published in Environment and Planning Bulletin, Planning and Design, no 14
10. Rydin, Y (1992) 'Environmental Impacts and the Property Marker' in Breheny, M (ed) *Sustainable Development and Urban Form*, Pion. London
11. TCPA (1993) *Strategic Planning for Regional Development*, TCPA, London   [224]

Green Cities, Growing Cities, Just Cities?

Urban Planning and the Contradictions of Sustainable Development

Scott Campbell

Nothing inherent in the discipline steers planners either toward environmental protection or toward economic development—or toward a third goal of planning: social equity. Instead, planners work within the tension generated among these three fundamental aims, which, collectively, I call the "planner's triangle," with sustainable development located at its center. This center cannot be reached directly, but only approximately and indirectly, through a sustained period of confronting and resolving the triangle's conflicts. To do so, planners have to redefine sustainability, since its current formulation romanticizes our sustainable past and is too vaguely holistic. Planners would benefit both from integrating social theory with environmental thinking and from combining their substantive skills with techniques for community conflict resolution, to confront economic and environmental injustice.

Campbell is an assistant professor of urban planning and policy development at Rutgers University, where he teaches graduate courses in planning theory, research methods, environmental economics, and regional planning.

Journal of the American Planning Association, Vol. 62, No. 3, Summer 1996. ©American Planning Association, Chicago, IL.

In the coming years planners face tough decisions about where they stand on protecting the green city, promoting the economically growing city, and advocating social justice. Conflicts among these goals are not superficial ones arising simply from personal preferences. Nor are they merely conceptual, among the abstract notions of ecological, economic, and political logic, nor a temporary problem caused by the untimely confluence of environmental awareness and economic recession. Rather, these conflicts go to the historic core of planning, and are a leitmotif in the contemporary battles in both our cities and rural areas, whether over solid waste incinerators or growth controls, the spotted owls or nuclear power. And though sustainable development aspires to offer an alluring, holistic way of evading these conflicts, they cannot be shaken off so easily.

This paper uses a simple triangular model to understand the divergent priorities of planning. My argument is that although the differences are partly due to misunderstandings arising from the disparate languages of environmental, economic, and political thought, translating across disciplines alone is not enough to eliminate these genuine clashes of interest. The socially constructed view of nature put forward here challenges the view of these conflicts as a classic battle of "man versus nature" or its current variation, "jobs versus the environment." The triangular model is then used to question whether sustainable development, the current object of planning's fascination, is a useful model to guide planning practice. I argue that the current concept of sustainability, though a laudable holistic vision, is vulnerable to the same criticism of vague idealism made thirty years ago against comprehensive planning. In this case, the idealistic fascination often builds upon a romanticized view of pre-industrial, indigenous, sustainable cultures—inspiring visions, but also of limited modern applicability. Nevertheless, sustainability, if redefined and incorporated into a broader understanding of political conflicts in industrial society, can become a powerful and useful organizing principle for planning. In fact, the idea will be particularly effective if, instead of merely evoking a misty-eyed vision of a peaceful ecotopia, it acts as a lightening rod to focus conflicting economic, environmental, and social interests. The more it stirs up conflict and sharpens the debate, the more effective the idea of sustainability will be in the long run.

The paper concludes by considering the implications of this viewpoint for planning. The triangle shows not only the conflicts, but also the potential complementarity of interests. The former are unavoidable and require planners to act as mediators, but the latter area is where planners can be especially creative in building coalitions between once-separated interest groups, such as labor and environmentalists, or community groups and business. To this end, planners need to combine both their procedural and their substantive skills and thus become central players in the battle over growth, the environment, and social justice.

The Planner's Triangle: Three Priorities, Three Conflicts

The current environmental enthusiasm among planners and planning schools might suggest their innate predisposition to protect the natural environment. Unfortunately, the opposite is more likely to be true: our historic tendency has been to promote the development of cities at the cost of natural destruction: to build cities we have cleared forests, fouled rivers and the air, leveled mountains. That is not the complete picture, since planners also have often come to the defense of nature, through the work of conservationists, park planners, open space preservationists, the Regional Planning Association of America, greenbelt planners, and modern environmental planners. Yet along the economic-ecological spectrum, with Robert Moses, and Dave Foreman (of *Earth First!*) standing at either pole, the planner has no natural home, but can slide from one end of the spectrum to the other; moreover, the midpoint has no special claims to legitimacy or fairness.

Similarly, though planners often see themselves as the defenders of the poor and of socio-economic equality, their actions over the profession's history have often belied that self-image (Harvey 1985). Plan-

ners' efforts with downtown redevelopment, freeway planning, public-private partnerships, enterprise zones, smokestack-chasing and other economic development strategies don't easily add up to equity planning. At best, the planner has taken an ambivalent stance between the goals of economic growth and economic justice.

In short, the planner must reconcile not two, but at least three conflicting interests: to "grow" the economy, distribute this growth fairly, and in the process not degrade the ecosystem. To classify contemporary battles over environmental racism, pollution-producing jobs, growth control, etc., as simply clashes between economic growth and environmental protection misses the third issue, of social justice. The "jobs versus environment" dichotomy (e.g., the spotted owl versus Pacific Northwest timber jobs) crudely collapses under the "economy" banner the often differing interests of workers, corporations, community members, and the national public. The intent of this paper's title is to focus planning not only for "green cities and growing cities," but also for "just cities."

In an ideal world, planners would strive to achieve a balance of all three goals. In practice, however, professional and fiscal constraints drastically limit the leeway of most planners. Serving the broader public interest by holistically harmonizing growth, preservation, and equality remains the ideal; the reality of practice restricts planners to serving the narrower interests of their clients, that is, authorities and bureaucracies (Marcuse 1976), despite efforts to work outside those limitations (Hoffman 1989). In the end, planners usually represent one particular goal—planning perhaps for increased property tax revenues, or more open space preservation, or better housing for the poor—while neglecting the other two. Where each planner stands in the triangle depicted in figure 1 defines such professional bias. One may see illustrated in the figure the gap between the call for integrative, sustainable development planning (the center of the triangle) and the current fragmentation of professional practice (the edges). This point is developed later.

The Points (Corners) of the Triangle: the Economy, the Environment, and Equity

The three types of priorities lead to three perspectives on the city: The economic development planner sees the city as a location where production, consumption, distribution, and innovation take place. The city is in competition with other cities for markets and for new industries. Space is the economic space of highways, market areas, and commuter zones.

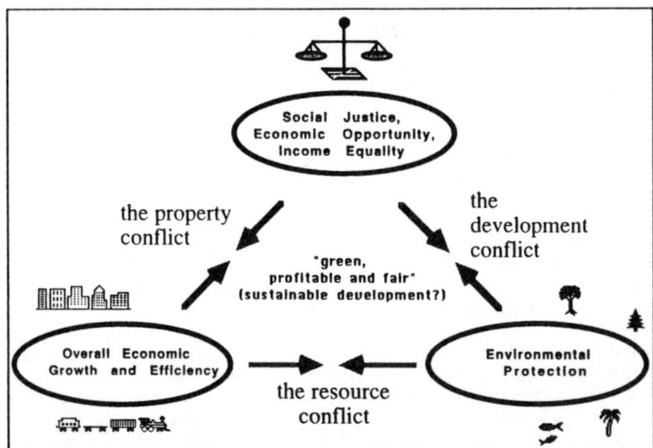

FIGURE 1.   The triangle of conflicting goals for planning, and the three associated conflicts. Planners define themselves, implicitly, by where they stand on the triangle. The elusive ideal of sustainable development leads one to the center.

The environmental planner sees the city as a consumer of resources and a producer of wastes. The city is in competition with nature for scarce resources and land, and always poses a threat to nature. Space is the ecological space of greenways, river basins, and ecological niches.

The equity planner sees the city as a location of conflict over the distribution of resources, of services, and of opportunities. The competition is within the city itself, among different social groups. Space is the social space of communities, neighborhood organizations, labor unions: the space of access and segregation.

Certainly there are other important views of the city, including the architectural, the psychological, and the circulatory (transportation); and one could conceivably construct a planner's rectangle, pentagon, or more complex polygon. The triangular shape itself is not propounded here as the underlying geometric structure of the planner's world. Rather, it is useful for its conceptual simplicity. More importantly, it emphasizes the point that a one-dimensional "man versus environment" spectrum misses the social conflicts in contemporary environmental disputes, such as loggers versus the Sierra Club, farmers versus suburban developers, or fishermen versus barge operators (Reisner 1987; Jacobs 1989; McPhee 1989; Tuason 1993).[1]

Triangle Axis 1: The Property Conflict

The three points on the triangle represent divergent interests, and therefore lead to three fundamental conflicts. The first conflict—between economic growth and equity—arises from competing claims on and uses of property, such as between management and labor, landlords and tenants, or gentrifying professionals and long-time residents. This growth-equity conflict is further complicated because each side not only resists the other, but also needs the other for its own survival. The contradictory tendency for a capitalist, democratic society to define property (such as housing or land) as a private commodity, but at the same time to rely on government intervention (e.g., zoning, or public housing for the working class) to ensure the beneficial social aspects of the same property, is what Richard Foglesong (1986) calls the "property contradiction." This tension is generated as the private sector simultaneously resists and needs social intervention, given the intrinsically contradictory nature of property. Indeed, the essence of property in our society is the tense pulling between these two forces. The conflict defines the boundary between private interest and the public good.

Triangle Axis 2: The Resource Conflict

Just as the private sector both resists regulation of property, yet needs it to keep the economy flowing, so too is society in conflict about its priorities for natural resources. Business resists the regulation of its exploitation of nature, but at the same time needs regulation to conserve those resources for present and future demands. This can be called the "resource conflict." The conceptual essence of natural resources is therefore the tension between their economic utility in industrial society and their ecological utility in the natural environment. This conflict defines the boundary between the developed city and the undeveloped wilderness, which is symbolized by the "city limits." The boundary is not fixed; it is a dynamic and contested boundary between mutually dependent forces.

Is there a single, universal economic-ecological conflict underlying all such disputes faced by planners? I searched for this essential, Platonic notion, but the diversity of examples—water politics in California, timber versus the spotted owl in the Pacific Northwest, tropical deforestation in Brazil, park planning in the Adirondacks, greenbelt planning in Britain, to name a few—suggests otherwise. Perhaps there is an *Ur-Konflikt*, rooted in the fundamental struggle between human civilization and the threatening wilderness around us, and expressed variously over the centuries. However, the decision must be left to anthropologists as to whether the essence of the spotted owl controversy can be traced back to Neolithic times. A meta-theory tying all these multifarious conflicts to an essential battle of "human versus nature" (and, once tools and weapons were developed and nature was controlled, "human versus human")—that invites skepticism. In this discussion, the triangle is used simply as a template to recognize and organize the common themes; to examine actual conflicts, individual case studies are used.[2]

The economic-ecological conflict has several instructive parallels with the growth-equity conflict. In the property conflict, industrialists must curb their profit-increasing tendency to reduce wages, in order to provide labor with enough wages to feed, house, and otherwise "reproduce" itself—that is, the subsistence wage. In the resource conflict, the industrialists must curb their profit-increasing tendency to increase timber yields, so as to ensure that enough of the forest remains to "reproduce" itself (Clawson 1975; Beltzer and Kroll 1986; Lee, Field, and Burch 1990). This practice is called "sustained yield," though timber companies and environmentalists disagree about how far the forest can be exploited and still be "sustainable." (Of course, other factors also affect wages, such as supply and demand, skill level, and discrimination, just as lumber demand, labor prices, transportation costs, tariffs, and other factors affect how much timber is harvested.) In both cases, industry must leave enough

of the exploited resource, be it human labor or nature, so that the resource will continue to deliver in the future. In both cases, how much is "enough" is also contested.

Triangle Axis 3: The Development Conflict

The third axis on the triangle is the most elusive: the "development conflict," lying between the poles of social equity and environmental preservation. If the property conflict is characterized by the economy's ambivalent interest in providing at least a subsistence existence for working people, and the resource conflict by the economy's ambivalent interest in providing sustainable conditions for the natural environment, the development conflict stems from the difficulty of doing both at once. Environment-equity disputes are coming to the fore to join the older dispute about economic growth versus equity (Paehlke 1994, 349–50). This may be the most challenging conundrum of sustainable development: how to increase social equity and protect the environment simultaneously, whether in a steady-state economy (Daly 1991) or not. How could those at the bottom of society find greater economic opportunity if environmental protection mandates diminished economic growth? On a global scale, efforts to protect the environment might lead to slowed economic growth in many countries, exacerbating the inequalities between rich and poor nations. In effect, the developed nations would be asking the poorer nations to forgo rapid development to save the world from the greenhouse effect and other global emergencies.

This development conflict also happens at the local level, as in resource-dependent communities, which commonly find themselves at the bottom of the economy's hierarchy of labor. Miners, lumberjacks, and mill workers see a grim link between environmental preservation and poverty, and commonly mistrust environmentalists as elitists. Poor urban communities are often forced to make the no-win choice between economic survival and environmental quality, as when the only economic opportunities are offered by incinerators, toxic waste sites, landfills, and other noxious land uses that most neighborhoods can afford to oppose and do without (Bryant and Mohai 1992; Bullard 1990, 1993). If, as some argue, environmental protection is a luxury of the wealthy, then environmental racism lies at the heart of the development conflict. Economic segregation leads to environmental segregation: the former occurs in the transformation of natural resources into consumer products; the latter occurs as the spoils of production are returned to nature. Inequitable development takes place at all stages of the materials cycle.

Consider this conflict from the vantage of equity planning. Norman Krumholz, as the planning director in Cleveland, faced the choice of either building regional rail lines or improving local bus lines (Krumholz et al. 1982). Regional rail lines would encourage the suburban middle class to switch from cars to mass transit; better local bus service would help the inner-city poor by reducing their travel and waiting time. One implication of this choice was the tension between reducing pollution and making transportation access more equitable, an example of how bias toward social inequity may be embedded in seemingly objective transit proposals.

Implications of the Planner's Triangle Model

Conflict and Complementarity in the Triangle

Though I use the image of the triangle to emphasize the strong conflicts among economic growth, environmental protection, and social justice, no point can exist alone. The nature of the three axial conflicts is mutual dependence based not only on opposition, but also on collaboration.

Consider the argument that the best way to distribute wealth more fairly (i.e., to resolve the property conflict) is to increase the size of the economy, so that society will have more to redistribute. Similarly, we can argue that the best way to improve environmental quality (i.e., to resolve the resource conflict) is to expand the economy, thereby having more money with which to buy environmental protection. The former is trickle-down economics; can we call the latter "trickle-down environmentalism"? One sees this logic in the conclusion of the Brundtland Report: "If large parts of the developing world are to avert economic, social, and environmental catastrophes, it is essential that global economic growth be revitalized" (World Commission on Environment and Development 1987). However, only if such economic growth is more fairly distributed will the poor be able to restore and protect their environment, whose devastation so immediately degrades their quality of life. In other words, the development conflict can be resolved only if the property conflict is resolved as well. Therefore, the challenge for planners is to deal with the conflicts between competing interests by discovering and implementing complementary uses.

The Triangle's Origins in a Social View of Nature

One of the more fruitful aspects of recent interdisciplinary thought may be its linking the traditionally separate intellectual traditions of critical social theory and environmental science/policy (e.g., Smith 1990; Wilson 1992; Ross 1994). This is also the purpose of the triangle figure presented here: to integrate the environmentalist's and social theorist's world views. On one side, an essentialist view of environmental conflicts ("man versus nature") emphasizes the resource conflict. On another side, a historical materialist view of social conflicts (e.g., capital versus labor) emphasizes the property conflict. By simultaneously considering both perspectives, one can see more clearly the social dimension of environmental conflicts, that is, the development conflict. Such a synthesis is not easy: it requires accepting the social construction of nature but avoiding the materialistic pitfall of arrogantly denying any aspects of nature beyond the labor theory of value.

Environmental conflict should not, therefore, be seen as simply one group representing the interests of nature and another group attacking nature (though it often appears that way).[3] Who is to say that the lumberjack, who spends all his or her days among trees (and whose livelihood depends on those trees), is any less close to nature than the environmentalist taking a weekend walk through the woods? Is the lumberjack able to cut down trees only because s/he is "alienated" from the "true" spirit of nature—the spirit that the hiker enjoys? In the absence of a forest mythology, neither the tree cutter nor the tree hugger—nor the third party, the owner/lessee of the forest—can claim an innate kinship to a tree. This is not to be an apologist for clear-cutting, but rather to say that the merits of cutting versus preserving trees cannot be decided according to which persons or groups have the "truest" relationship to nature.

The crucial point is that all three groups have an interactive relationship with nature: the differences lie in their conflicting *conceptions* of nature, their conflicting *uses* of nature, and how they incorporate nature into their systems of values (be they community, economic, or spiritual values). This clash of human values reveals how much the ostensibly separate domains of community development and environmental protection overlap, and suggests that planners should do better in combining social and environmental models. One sees this clash of values in many environmental battles: between the interests of urban residents and those of subsidized irrigation farmers in California water politics; between beach homeowners and coastal managers trying to control erosion; between rich and poor neighborhoods, in the siting of incinerators; between farmers and environmentalists, in restrictions by open space zoning. Even then-President George Bush weighed into such disputes during his 1992 campaign when he commented to a group of loggers that finally people should be valued more than spotted owls (his own take on the interspecies equity issue). Inequity and the imbalance of political power are often issues at the heart of economic-environmental conflicts.

Recognition that the terrain of nature is contested need not, however, cast us adrift on a sea of socially-constructed relativism where "nature" appears as an arbitrary idea of no substance (Bird 1987; Soja 1989). Rather, we are made to rethink the idea and to see the appreciation of nature as an historically evolved sensibility. I suspect that radical environmentalists would criticize this perspective as anthropocentric environmentalism, and argue instead for an ecocentric world view that puts the Earth first (Sessions 1992; Parton 1993). It is true that an anthropocentric view, if distorted, can lead to an arrogant optimism about civilization's ability to reprogram nature through technologies ranging from huge hydroelectric and nuclear plants down to genetic engineering. A rigid belief in the anthropocentric labor theory of value, Marxist or otherwise, can produce a modern-day Narcissus as a social-constructionist who sees nature as merely reflecting the beauty of the human aesthetic and the value of human labor. In this light, a tree is devoid of value until it either becomes part of a scenic area or is transformed into lumber. On the other hand, even as radical, ecocentric environmentalists claim to see "true nature" beyond the city limits, they are blind to how their own world view and their definition of nature itself are shaped by their socialization. The choice between an anthropocentric or an ecocentric world view is a false one. We are all unavoidably anthropocentric; the question is which anthropomorphic values and priorities we will apply to the natural and the social world around us.

Sustainable Development: Reaching the Elusive Center of the Triangle

If the three corners of the triangle represent key goals in planning, and the three axes represent the three resulting conflicts, then I will define the center of the triangle as representing sustainable development: the balance of these three goals. Getting to the center, however, will not be so easy. It is one thing to locate sustainability in the abstract, but quite another to reorganize society to get there.

At first glance, the widespread advocacy of sustainable development is astonishing, given its revolutionary implications for daily life (World Commission 1987; Daly and Cobb 1989; Rees 1989; World Bank 1989; Goodland 1990; Barrett and Bohlen 1991; Korten 1991; Van der Ryn and Calthorpe 1991). It is getting hard to refrain from sustainable development;

arguments against it are inevitably attached to the strawman image of a greedy, myopic industrialist. Who would now dare to speak up in opposition? Two interpretations of the bandwagon for sustainable development suggest themselves. The pessimistic thought is that sustainable development has been stripped of its transformative power and reduced to its lowest common denominator. After all, if both the World Bank and radical ecologists now believe in sustainability, the concept can have no teeth: it is so malleable as to mean many things to many people without requiring commitment to any specific policies. Actions speak louder than words, and though all endorse sustainability, few will actually practice it. Furthermore, any concept fully endorsed by all parties must surely be bypassing the heart of the conflict. Set a goal far enough into the future, and even conflicting interests will seem to converge along parallel lines. The concept certainly appears to violate the Karl Popper's requirement that propositions be falsifiable, for to reject sustainability is to embrace nonsustainability—and who dares to sketch that future? (Ironically, the nonsustainable scenario is the easiest to define: merely the extrapolation of our current way of life.)

Yet there is also an optimistic interpretation of the broad embrace given sustainability: the idea has become hegemonic, an accepted meta-narrative, a given. It has shifted from being a variable to being the parameter of the debate, almost certain to be integrated into any future scenario of development. We should therefore neither be surprised that no definition has been agreed upon, nor fear that this reveals a fundamental flaw in the concept. In the battle of big public ideas, sustainability has won: the task of the coming years is simply to work out the details, and to narrow the gap between its theory and practice.

Is Sustainable Development a Useful Concept?

Some environmentalists argue that if sustainable development is necessary, it therefore must be possible. Perhaps so, but if you are stranded at the bottom of a deep well, a ladder may be impossible even though necessary. The answer espoused may be as much an ideological as a scientific choice, depending on whether one's loyalty is to Malthus or Daly. The more practical question is whether sustainability is a useful concept for planners. The answer here is mixed. The goal may be too far away and holistic to be operational: that is, it may not easily break down into concrete, short-term steps. We also might be able to *define* sustainability yet be unable ever to actually measure it or even know, one day in the future, that we had achieved it. An old eastern proverb identifies the western confusion of believing that to name something is to know it. That may be the danger in automatically embracing sustainable development: a facile confidence that by adding the term "sustainable" to all our existing planning documents and tools (sustainable zoning, sustainable economic development, sustainable transportation planning), we are *doing* sustainable planning. Conversely, one can do much beneficial environmental work without ever devoting explicit attention to the concept of sustainability.

Yet sustainability can be a helpful concept in that it posits the long-term planning goal of a social-environmental system in balance. It is a unifying concept, enormously appealing to the imagination, that brings together many different environmental concerns under one overarching value. It defines a set of social priorities and articulates how society values the economy, the environment, and equity (Paehlke 1994, 360). In theory, it allows us not only to calculate whether we have attained sustainability, but also to determine how far away we are. (Actual measurement, though, is another, harder task.) Clearly, it can be argued that, though initially flawed and vague, the concept can be transformed and refined to be of use to planners.

History, Equity, and Sustainable Development

One obstacle to an accurate, working definition of sustainability may well be the historical perspective that sees the practice as pre-existing, either in our past or as a Platonic concept. I believe instead that our sustainable future does not yet exist, either in reality or even in strategy. We do not yet know what it will look like; it is being socially constructed through a sustained period of conflict negotiation and resolution. This is a process of innovation, not of discovery and converting the nonbelievers.

This point brings us to the practice of looking for sustainable development in pre-industrial and non-western cultures (a common though not universal practice). Searching for our future in our indigenous past is instructive at both the philosophical and the practical level (Turner 1983; Duerr 1985). Yet it is also problematical, tapping into a myth that our salvation lies in the pre-industrial sustainable culture. The international division of labor and trade, the movement of most people away from agriculture into cities, and exponential population growth lead us irrevocably down a unidirectional, not a circular path: the transformation of pre-industrial, indigenous settlements into mass urban society is irreversible. Our modern path to sustainability lies forward, not behind us.

The key difference between those indigenous, sustainable communities and ours is that they had no choice but to be sustainable. Bluntly stated, if they cut down too many trees or ruined the soil, they would die out. Modern society has the options presented by trade, long-term storage, and synthetic replacements; if we clear-cut a field, we have subsequent options that our ancestors didn't. In this situation, we must *voluntarily choose* sustainable practices, since there is no immediate survival or market imperative to do so. Although the long-term effects of a nonsustainable economy are certainly dangerous, the feedback mechanisms are too long-term to prod us in the right direction.

Why do we often romanticize the sustainable past? Some are attracted to the powerful spiritual link between humans and nature that has since been lost. Such romanticists tend, however, to overlook the more harsh and unforgiving aspects of being so dependent on the land. Two hundred years ago, Friedrich Schiller (1965, 28) noted the tendency of utopian thinkers to take their dream for the future and posit it as their past, thus giving it legitimacy as a cyclical return to the past.[4] This habit is not unique to ecotopians (Kumar 1991); some religious fundamentalists also justify their utopian urgency by drawing on the myth of a paradise lost. Though Marxists don't glorify the past in the same way, they, too, manage to anticipate a *static* system of balance and harmony, which nonetheless will require a cataclysmic, revolutionary social transformation to reach. All three ideologies posit some basic flaw in society—be it western materialism, original sin, or capitalism—whose identification and cure will free us from conflict. Each ideology sees a fundamental alienation as the danger to overcome: alienation from nature, from god, or from work. Each group is so critical of existing society that it would seem a wonder we have made it this far; but this persistence of human society despite the dire prognoses of utopians tells us something.

What is the fallout from such historical thinking? By neglecting the powerful momentum of modern industrial and postindustrial society, it both points us in the wrong direction and makes it easier to marginalize the proponents of sustainable development. It also carries an anti-urban sentiment that tends to neglect both the centrality and the plight of megacities. Modern humans are unique among species in their propensity to deal with nature's threats, not only through flight and burrowing and biological adaptation, nor simply through spiritual understanding, but also through massive population growth, complex social division of labor, and the fundamental, external transformation of their once-natural environment (the building of cities). Certainly the fixation on growth, industry, and competition has degraded the environment. Yet one cannot undo urban-industrial society. Rather, one must continue to innovate through to the other side of industrialization, to reach a more sustainable economy.

The cyclical historical view of some environmentalists also hinders a critical understanding of equity, since that view attributes to the environment a natural state of equality rudely upset by modern society. Yet nature is inherently neither equal nor unequal, and at times can be downright brutal. The human observer projects a sense of social equity onto nature, through a confusion, noted by Schiller, of the idealized future with myths about our natural past. To gain a sense of historical legitimacy, we project our socially constructed sense of equality onto the past, creating revisionist history in which nature is fair and compassionate. Society's path to equality is perceived not as an uncertain progress from barbarism to justice, but rather as a return to an original state of harmony as laid out in nature. In this thinking, belief in an ecological balance and a social balance, entwined in the pre-industrial world, conjures up an eco-Garden of Eden "lost" by modern society.[5]

It will be more useful to let go of this mythic belief in our involuntary diaspora from a pre-industrial, eco-topian Eden.[6] The conflation of ecological diasporas and utopias constrains our search for creative, urban solutions to social-environmental conflict. By relinquishing such mythic beliefs, we will understand that notions of equity were not lying patiently in wait in nature, to be first discovered by indigenous peoples, then lost by colonialists, and finally rediscovered by modern society in the late twentieth century. This is certainly not to say that nature can teach us nothing. The laws of nature are not the same thing, however, as natural law, nor does ecological equilibrium necessarily generate normative principles of equity. Though we turn to nature to understand the context, dynamics, and effects of the economic-environmental conflict, we must turn to social norms to decide what balance is fair and just.

How, then, do we define what is fair? I propose viewing social justice as the striving towards a more equal distribution of resources among social groups across the space of cities and of nations—a definition of "fair" distribution. It should be noted that societies view themselves as "fair" if the *procedures* of allocation treat people equally, even if the *substantive* outcome is unbalanced. (One would hope that equal treatment is but the first step towards narrowing material inequality.) The environmental movement expands the space for this "equity" in two ways: (1) intergenerationally (present versus future generations) and (2) across species (as in animal rights, deep ecology, and legal standing for trees). The two added dimensions of equity remain essentially abstractions, however, since no one from the future or from other species can speak up for their "fair share" of resources. Selfless advocates (or selfish ventriloquists) "speak for them."

This expansion of socio-spatial equity to include future generations and other species not only makes the concept more complex; it also creates the possibility for contradictions among the different calls for "fairness." Slowing worldwide industrial expansion may preserve more of the world's resources for the future (thereby increasing intergenerational equity), but it may also undermine the efforts of the underdeveloped world to approach the living standards of the west (thereby lowering international equity). Battles over Native American fishing practices, the spotted owl, and restrictive farmland preservation each thrust together several divergent notions of "fairness." It is through resolving the three sorts of conflicts on the planner's triangle that society iteratively forms its definition of what is fair.

The Path Towards Sustainable Development

There are two final aspects of the fuzzy definition of sustainability: its path and its outcome. The basic premise of sustainable development is one that, like the long-term goal of a balanced U.S. budget, is hard not to like. As with eliminating the national debt, however, two troubling questions about sustainable development remain: How are you going to get there? Once you get there, what are the negative consequences? Planners don't yet have adequate answers to these two questions; that is, as yet they have no concrete strategies to achieve sustainable development, nor do they know how to counter the political resistance to it.

On the *path* towards a sustainable future, the steps are often too vague, as with sweeping calls for a "spiritual transformation" as the prerequisite for environmental transformation. Sometimes the call for sustainable development seems to serve as a vehicle for sermonizing about the moral and spiritual corruption of the industrial world (undeniable). Who would not want to believe in a holistic blending of economic and ecological values in each of our planners, who would then go out into the world and, on each project, internally and seamlessly merge the interests of jobs and nature, as well as of social justice? That is, the call to planners would be to stand at every moment at the center of the triangle.

But this aim is too reminiscent of our naive belief during the 1950s and 1960s in comprehensive planning for a single "public interest," before the incrementalists and advocacy planners pulled the rug out from under us (Lindblom 1959; Altshuler 1965; Davidoff 1965; Fainstein and Fainstein 1971). I suspect that planners' criticisms of the sustainable development movement in the coming years will parallel the critique of comprehensive planning 30 years ago: The incrementalists will argue that one cannot achieve a sustainable society in a single grand leap, for it requires too much social and ecological information and is too risky. The advocacy planners will argue that no common social interest in sustainable development exists, and that bureaucratic planners will invariably create a sustainable development scheme that neglects the interests both of the poor and of nature. To both groups of critics, the prospect of integrating economic, environmental and equity interests will seem forced and artificial. States will require communities to prepare "Sustainable Development Master Plans," which will prove to be glib wish lists of goals and suspiciously vague implementation steps. To achieve consensus for the plan, language will be reduced to the lowest common denominator, and the pleasing plans will gather dust.

An alternative is to let holistic sustainable development be a long-range goal; it is a worthy one, for planners do need a vision of a more sustainable urban society. But during the coming years, planners will confront deep-seated conflicts among economic, social and environmental interests that cannot be wished away through admittedly appealing images of a community in harmony with nature. One is no more likely to abolish the economic-environmental conflict completely by achieving sustainable bliss than one is to eliminate completely the boundaries between the city and the wilderness, between the public and private spheres, between the haves and have-nots. Nevertheless, one can diffuse the conflict, and find ways to avert its more destructive fall-out.

My concern about the *ramifications* of a sustainable future is one that is often expressed: steady-state, no-growth economics would be likely to relegate much of the developing world—and the poor within the industrialized world—to a state of persistent poverty. The advocates of sustainable development rightly reject as flawed the premise of conventional economics that only a growth economy can achieve social redistribution. And growth economics has, indeed, also exacerbated the environment's degradation. However, it is wishful thinking to assume that a sustainable economy will automatically ensure a socially just distribution of resources.[7] The vision of no-growth (commonly though not universally assumed to characterize sustainable development) raises powerful fears, and planners should be savvy to such fears. Otherwise, they will understand neither the potential dangers of

steady-state economics nor the nature of the opposition to sustainable development.

Rethinking/Redefining Sustainable Development

Despite the shortcomings in the current formalation of sustainable development, the concept retains integrity and enormous potential. It simply needs to be redefined and made more precise. First, one should avoid a dichotomous, black-and-white view of sustainability. We should think of American society not as a corrupt, wholly unsustainable one that has to be made pure and wholly sustainable, but rather as a hybrid of both sorts of practices. Our purpose, then, should be to move further towards sustainable practices in an evolutionary progression.

Second, we should broaden the idea of "sustainability." If "crisis" is defined as the inability of a system to reproduce itself, then sustainability is the opposite: the long-term ability of a system to reproduce. This criterion applies not only to natural ecosystems, but to economic and political systems as well. By this definition, western society already does much to sustain itself: economic policy and corporate strategies (e.g., investment, training, monetary policy) strive to reproduce the macro- and micro-economies. Similarly, governments, parties, labor unions, and other political agents strive to reproduce their institutions and interests. Society's shortcoming is that as it strives to sustain its political and economic systems, it often neglects to sustain the ecological system. The goal for planning is therefore a broader agenda: to sustain, simultaneously and in balance, these three sometimes competing, sometimes complementary systems.[8]

Third, it will be helpful to distinguish initially between two levels of sustainability: specific versus general (or local versus global). One might fairly easily imagine and achieve sustainability in a single sector and/or locality, for example, converting a Pacific Northwest community to sustained-yield timber practices. Recycling, solar power, cogeneration, and conservation can lower consumption of nonsustainable resources. To achieve complete sustainability across all sectors and/or all places, however, requires such complex restructuring and redistribution that the only feasible path to global sustainability is likely to be a long, incremental accumulation of local and industry-specific advances.

What this incremental, iterative approach means is that planners will find their vision of a sustainable city developed best at the conclusion of contested negotiations over land use, transportation, housing, and economic development policies, not as the premise for beginning the effort. To first spend years in the hermetic isolation of universities and environmental groups, perfecting the theory of sustainable development, before testing it in community development is backwards. That approach sees sustainable development as an ideal society outside the conflicts of the planner's triangle, or as the tranquil "eye of the hurricane" at the triangle's center. As with the ideal comprehensive plan, it is presumed that the objective, technocratic merits of a perfected sustainable development scheme will ensure society's acceptance. But one cannot reach the sustainable center of the planner's triangle in a single, holistic leap to a pre-ordained balance.

The Task Ahead for Planners: Seeking Sustainable Development within the Triangle of Planning Conflicts

The role of planners is therefore to engage the current challenge of sustainable development with a dual, interactive strategy: (1) to manage and resolve conflict; and (2) to promote creative technical, architectural, and institutional solutions. Planners must both negotiate the procedures of the conflict and promote a substantive vision of sustainable development.

Procedural Paths to Sustainable Development: Conflict Negotiation

In negotiation and conflict resolution (Bingham 1986; Susskind and Cruikshank 1987; Crowfoot and Wondolleck 1990), rather than pricing externalities, common ground is established at the negotiation table, where the conflicting economic, social, and environmental interests can be brought together. The potential rewards are numerous: not only an outcome that balances all parties, but avoidance of heavy legal costs and long-lasting animosity. Negotiated conflict resolution can also lead to a better understanding of one's opponent's interests and values, and even of one's own interests. The very process of lengthy negotiation can be a powerful tool to mobilize community involvement around social and environmental issues. The greatest promise, of course, is a win-win outcome: finding innovative solutions that would not have come out of traditional, adversarial confrontation. Through skillfully led, back-and-forth discussion, the parties can separate their initial, clashing substantive demands from their underlying interests, which may be more compatible. For example, environmentalists and the timber industry could solve their initial dispute over building a logging road, through alternative road design and other mitigation measures (Crowfoot and Wondolleck 1990, 32–52).

However, conflict resolution is no panacea. Sometimes conflicting demands express fundamental conflicts of interest. The either-or nature of the technology or ecology may preclude a win-win outcome, as in an all-or-nothing dispute over a proposed hydroelectric project (Reisner 1987)—you either build it or you don't. An overwhelming imbalance of power between the opposing groups also can thwart resolution (Crowfoot and Wondolleck 1990, 4). A powerful party can simply refuse to participate. It is also hard to negotiate a comprehensive resolution for a large number of parties.

Planners are likely to have the best success in using conflict resolution when there is a specific, concise dispute (rather than an amorphous ideological clash); all interested parties agree to participate (and don't bypass the process through the courts); each party feels on equal ground; there are a variety of possible compromises and innovative solutions; both parties prefer a solution to an impasse; and a skilled third-party negotiator facilitates. The best resolution strategies seem to include two areas of compromise and balance: the procedural (each party is represented and willing to compromise); and the substantive (the solution is a compromise, such as multiple land uses or a reduced development density).

Procedural Paths to Sustainable Development: Redefining the Language of the Conflict

A second strategy is to bridge the chasms between the languages of economics, environmentalism, and social justice. Linguistic differences, which reflect separate value hierarchies, are a major obstacle to common solutions. All too often, the economists speak of incentives and marginal rates, the ecologists speak of carrying capacity and biodiversity, the advocate planners speak of housing rights, empowerment, and discrimination, and each side accuses the others of being "out of touch" (Campbell 1992).

The planner therefore needs to act as a translator, assisting each group to understand the priorities and reasoning of the others. Economic, ecological and social thought may at a certain level be incommensurable, yet a level may still be found where all three may be brought together. To offer an analogy, a Kenyan Gikuyu text cannot be fully converted into English without losing something in translation; a good translation, nevertheless, is the best possible way to bridge two systems of expression that will never be one, and it is preferable to incomprehension.

The danger of translation is that one language will

dominate the debate and thus define the terms of the solution. It is essential to exert equal effort to translate in each direction, to prevent one linguistic culture from dominating the other (as English has done in neocolonial Africa). Another lesson from the neocolonial linguistic experience is that it is crucial for each social group to express itself in its own language before any translation. The challenge for planners is to write the best translations among the languages of the economic, the ecological, and the social views, and to avoid a quasi-colonial dominance by the economic *lingua franca,* by creating equal two-way translations.[9]

For example, planners need better tools to understand their cities and regions not just as economic systems, or static inventories of natural resources, but also as *environmental systems* that are part of regional and global networks trading goods, information, resources and pollution. At the conceptual level, translating the economic vocabulary of global cities, the spatial division of labor, regional restructuring, and technoburbs/edge cities into environmental language would be a worthy start; at the same time, of course, the vocabulary of biodiversity, landscape linkages, and carrying capacity should be translated to be understandable by economic interests.

This bilingual translation should extend to the empirical level. I envision extending the concept of the "trade balance" to include an "environmental balance," which covers not just commodities, but also natural resources and pollution. Planners should improve their data collection and integration to support the environmental trade balance. They should apply economic-ecological bilingualism not only to the content of data, but also to the spatial framework of the data, by rethinking the geographic boundaries of planning and analysis. Bioregionalists advocate having the spatial scale for planning reflect the scale of *natural* phenomena (e.g., the extent of a river basin, vegetation zones, or the dispersion range of metropolitan air pollution); economic planners call for a spatial scale to match the *social* phenomena (e.g., highway networks, municipal boundaries, labor market areas, new industrial districts). The solution is to integrate these two scales and overlay the economic and ecological geographies of planning. The current merging of environmental Raster (grid-based) and infrastructural vector-based data in Geographic Information Systems (GIS) recognizes the need for multiple layers of planning boundaries (Wiggins 1993).

Translation can thus be a powerful planner's skill, and interdisciplinary planning education already provides some multilingualism. Moreover, the idea of sustainability lends itself nicely to the meeting on common ground of competing value systems. Yet translation has its limits. Linguistic differences often represent real, intractable differences in values. An environmental dispute may arise not from a misunderstanding alone; both sides may clearly understand that their vested interests fundamentally clash, no matter how expressed. At this point, translation must give way to other strategies. The difficulties are exacerbated when one party has greater power, and so shapes the language of the debate as well as prevailing in its outcome. In short, translation, like conflict negotiation, reveals both the promises and the limitations of communication-based conflict resolution.

Other Procedural Paths

Two other, more traditional approaches deserve mention. One is political pluralism: let the political arena decide conflicts, either directly (e.g., a referendum on an open space bond act, or a California state proposition on nuclear power), or indirectly (e.g., elections decided on the basis of candidates' environmental records and promised legislation). The key elements here, political debate and ultimately the vote, allow much wider participation in the decision than negotiation does. However, a binary vote cannot as easily handle complex issues, address specific land-use conflicts, or develop subtle, creative solutions. Choosing the general political process as a strategy for deciding conflict also takes the process largely out of the hands of planners.

The other traditional strategy is to develop market mechanisms to link economic and environmental priorities. Prices are made the commonality that bridges the gap between the otherwise noncommensurables of trees and timber, open space and real estate. The market place is chosen as the arena where society balances its competing values. This economistic approach to the environment reduces pollution to what the economist Edwin Mills (1978, 15) called "a problem in resource allocation." This approach can decide conflicts along the economic-environmental axis (the resource conflict), but often neglects equity. However, the market does seem to be dealing better with environmental externalities than it did ten or twenty years ago. Internalizing externalities, at the least, raises the issues of social justice and equity: e.g., who will pay for cleaning up abandoned industrial sites or compensate for the loss of fishing revenues due to oil spills. The recent establishment of a pollution credit market in the South Coast Air Quality Management District, for example, is a step in the right direction—despite criticism that the pollution credits were initially given away for free (Robinson 1993).

The role of the planner in all four of these approaches is to arrange the procedures for making decisions, not to set the substance of the actual outcomes. In some cases, the overall structure for decision-making already exists (the market and the political system). In other cases, however, the planner must help shape that structure (a mediation forum; a common language), which, done successfully, gives the process credibility. The actual environmental outcomes nevertheless remain unknowable: you don't know in advance if the environment will actually be improved. For example, environmentalists and developers heralded the Coachella Valley Fringe-Toed Lizard Habitat Conservation Plan as a model process to balance the interests of development and conservation; yet the actual outcome may not adequately protect the endangered lizard (Beatley 1992, 15–16). Similarly, although the New Jersey State Development Plan was praised for its innovative cross-acceptance procedure, the plan itself arguably has not altered the state's urban sprawl.

The final issue that arises is whether the planner should play the role of neutral moderator, or of advocate representing a single party; this has been a long-standing debate in the field. Each strategy has its virtues.

Substantive Paths to Sustainable Development: Land Use and Design

Planners have substantive knowledge of how cities, economies, and ecologies interact, and they should put forth specific, farsighted designs that promote the sustainable city. The first area is traditional planning tools of land-use design and control. The potential for balance between economic and environmental interests exists in design itself, as in a greenbelt community (Elson 1986). Sometimes the land-use solution is simply to divide a contested parcel into two parcels: a developed and a preserved. This solution can take crude forms at times, such as the "no-net-loss" policy that endorses the dubious practice of creating wetlands. A different example, Howard's turn-of-the century Garden City (1965), can be seen as a territorially symbolic design for balance between the economy and the environment, though its explicit language was that of town-country balance. It is a design's articulated balance between the built development and the unbuilt wilderness that promises the economic-environmental balance. Designs for clustered developments, higher densities, and live-work communities move toward such a balance (Rickaby 1987; Commission of the European Communities 1990; Hudson 1991; Van der Rys and Calthorpe 1991). Some dispute the inherent benefits of the compact city (Breheny 1992). A further complication is that not all economic-environmental conflicts have their roots in spatial or architectural problems. As a result, ostensible solutions may be merely symbols of ecological-economic balance, without actually solving the conflict.

Nevertheless, land-use planning arguably remains the most powerful tool available to planners, who should not worry too much if it does not manage all problems. The trick in resolving environmental conflicts through land-use planning is to reconcile the conflicting territorial logics of human and of natural habitats. Standard real estate development reduces open space to fragmented, static, green islands—exactly what the landscape ecologists deplore as unable to preserve biodiversity. Wildlife roam and migrate, and require large expanses of connected landscape (Hudson 1991). So both the ecological and the economic systems require the interconnectivity of a critical mass of land to be sustainable. Though we live in a three-dimensional world, land is a limited resource with essentially two dimensions (always excepting air and burrowing/mining spaces). The requirement of land's spatial interconnectivity is thus hard to achieve for both systems in one region: the continuity of one system invariably fragments continuity of the other.[10] So the guiding challenge for land-use planning is to achieve simultaneously spatial/territorial integrity for both systems. Furthermore, a sustainable development that aspires to social justice must also find ways to avoid the land-use manifestations of uneven development: housing segregation, unequal property-tax funding of public schools, jobs-housing imbalance, the spatial imbalance of economic opportunity, and unequal access to open space and recreation.

Substantive Paths to Sustainable Development: Bioregionalism

A comprehensive vision of sustainable land use is bioregionalism, both in its 1920s articulation by the Regional Planning Association of America (Sussman 1976) and its contemporary variation (Sale 1985; Andrus et al. 1990; Campbell 1992). The movement's essential belief is that rescaling communities and the economy according to the ecological boundaries of a physical region will encourage sustainability. The regional scale presumably stimulates greater environmental awareness: it is believed that residents of small-scale, self-sufficient regions will be aware of the causes and effects of their environmental actions, thereby reducing externalities. Regions will live within their means, and bypass the environmental problems caused by international trade and exporting pollution.

The bioregional vision certainly has its shortcomings, including the same fuzzy, utopian thinking found in other writing about sustainable development. Its ecological determinism also puts too much faith in the regional "spatial fix": no geographic scale can, in itself, eliminate all conflict, for not all conflict is geographic. Finally, the call for regional self-reliance—a common feature of sustainable development concepts (Korten 1991, 184)—might relegate the regional economy to underdevelopment in an otherwise nationally and internationally interdependent world. Yet it can be effective to visualize sustainable regions within an interdependent world full of trade, migration, information flows and capital flows, and to know the difference between *healthy interdependence* and *parasitic dependence*, that is, a dependence on other regions' resources that is equivalent to depletion. Interdependence does not always imply an imbalance of power, nor does self-sufficiency guarantee equality. Finally, the bioregional perspective can provide a foundation for understanding conflicts among a region's interconnected economic, social and ecological networks.

Other Substantive Paths

One other approach is technological improvement, such as alternative fuels, conservation mechanisms, recycling, alternative materials, and new mass transit design. Stimulated by competition, regulation, or government subsidies, such advances reduce the consumption of natural resources per unit of production and thereby promise to ameliorate conflict over their competing uses, creating a win-win solution. However, this method is not guaranteed to serve those purposes, for gains in conservation are often cancelled out by rising demand for the final products. The overall increase in demand for gasoline despite improvements in automobile fuel efficiency is one example of how market forces can undermine technologically-achieved environmental improvements. Nor, importantly, do technological improvements guarantee fairer distribution.

The role of the planner in all these substantive strategies (land use, bioregionalism, technological improvement) is to design outcomes, with less emphasis on the means of achieving them. The environmental ramifications of the solutions are known or at least estimated, but the political means to achieve legitimacy are not. There also is a trade-off between comprehensiveness (bioregions) and short-term achievability (individual technological improvements).

Merging the Substantive and Procedural

The individual shortcomings of the approaches described above suggest that combining them can achieve both political and substantive progress in the environmental-economic crisis. The most successful solutions seem to undertake several different resolution strategies at once. For example, negotiation among developers, city planners, and land-use preservationists can produce an innovative, clustered design for a housing development, plus a per-unit fee for preserving open space. Substantive vision combined with negotiating skills thus allows planners to create win-win solutions, rather than either negotiating in a zero-sum game or preparing inert, ecotopian plans. This approach is not a distant ideal for planners: they already have, from their education and experience, both this substantive knowledge and this political savvy.

In the end, however, the planner must also deal with conflicts where one or more parties have no interest in resolution. One nonresolution tactic is the NIMBY, Not In My Back Yard, response: a crude marriage of local initiative and the age-old externalizing of pollution. This "take it elsewhere" strategy makes no overall claim to resolve conflict, though it can be a productive form of resistance rather than just irrational parochialism (Lake 1993). Nor does eco-terrorism consider balance. Instead, it replaces the defensive stance of NIMBY with offensive, confrontational, symbolic action. Resolution is also avoided out of cavalier confidence that one's own side can manage the opposition through victory, not compromise ("My side will win, so why compromise?"). Finally, an "I don't care" stance avoids the conflict altogether. Unfortunately, this ostensible escapism often masks a more pernicious NIMBY or "my side will win" hostility, just below the surface.

Planners: Leaders or Followers in Resolving Economic-Environmental Conflicts?

I turn finally to the question of whether planners are likely to be leaders or followers in resolving economic-environmental conflicts. One would think that it would be natural for planners, being interdisciplinary and familiar with the three goals of balancing social equity, jobs, and environmental protection, to take the lead in resolving such conflicts. Of the conflict resolution scenarios mentioned above, those most open to planners' contributions involve the built environment and local resources: land use, soil conservation, design issues, recycling, solid waste, water treatment. Even solutions using the other approaches—environmental economic incentives, political compromise, and environmental technology innovations—that are normally undertaken at the state and federal levels could also involve planners if moved to the local or regional level.

But the planners' position at the forefront of

change is not assured, especially if the lead is taken up by other professions or at the federal, not the local, level. The lively debate on whether gasoline consumption can best be reduced through higher-density land uses (Newman and Kenworthy 1989) or through energy taxes (Gordon and Richardson 1990) not only reflected an ideological battle over interpreting research results and the merits of planning intervention, but also demonstrated how local planning can be made either central or marginal to resolving environmental-economic conflicts. To hold a central place in the debate about sustainable development, planners must exploit those areas of conflict where they have the greatest leverage and expertise.

Certainly planners already have experience with both the dispute over economic growth versus equity and that over economic growth versus environmental protection. Yet the development conflict is where the real action for planners will be: seeking to resolve both environmental and economic equity issues at once. Here is where the profession can best make its unique contribution. An obvious start would be for community development planners and environmental planners to collaborate more (an alliance that an internal Environmental Protection Agency memo found explosive enough for the agency to consider defusing it) (Higgins 1994). One possible joint task is to expand current public-private partnership efforts to improve environmental health in the inner city. This urban-based effort would help planners bypass the danger of environmental elitism that besets many suburban, white-oriented environmental organizations.

If planners move in this direction, they will join the growing environmental justice movement, which emerged in the early 1980s and combined minority community organizing with environmental concerns (Higgins 1994). The movement tries to reduce environmental hazards that directly affect poor residents, who are the least able to fight pollution, be it the direct result of discriminatory siting decisions or the indirect result of housing and employment discrimination. The poor, being the least able to move away, are especially tied to place and therefore to the assistance or neglect of local planners. Understandably, local civil rights leaders have been preoccupied for so long with seeking economic opportunity and social justice that they have paid less attention to inequities in the local environment. The challenge for poor communities is now to expand their work on the property conflict to address the development conflict as well, that is, to challenge the false choice of jobs over the environment. An urban vision of sustainable development, infused with a belief in social and environmental justice, can guide these efforts.

Yet even with the rising acceptance of sustainable development, planners will not always be able, on their own, to represent and balance social, economic, and environmental interests simultaneously. The professional allegiances, skills, and bureaucracies of the profession are too constraining to allow that. Pretending at all times to be at the center of the planner's triangle will only make sustainability a hollow term. Instead, the trick will be for individual planners to identify their specific loyalties and roles in these conflicts accurately: that is, to orient themselves in the triangle. Planners will have to decide whether they want to remain outside the conflict and act as mediators, or jump into the fray and promote their own visions of ecological-economic development, sustainable or otherwise. Both planning behaviors are needed.

AUTHOR'S NOTE

The author thanks Elizabeth Mueller, Susan Fainstein, Diane Massell, Jonathan Feldman, Karen Lowry, Jessica Sanchez, Harvey Jacobs, Michael Greenberg, Renée Sieber, Robert Higgins, the Project on Regional and Industrial Economics (PRIE) Seminar, and three anonymous reviewers for their comments.

NOTES

1. A curious comparison to this equity-environment-economy triangle is the view of Arne Naess (1993), the radical environmentalist who gave Deep Ecology its name in the 1970s, that the three crucial postwar political movements were the social justice, radical environmental, and peace movements, whose goals might overlap but could not be made identical.

2. Perhaps one can explain the lack of a universal conflict in the following way: if our ideas of the economy, equity, and the environment are socially/culturally constructed, and if cultural society is local as well as global, then our ideas are locally distinct rather than universally uniform.

3. For planners, if one is simply "planning for place," then the dispute about suburban housing versus wetlands does indeed reflect a conflict between an economic and an environmental use of a specific piece of land. But if one sees this conflict in light of "planning for people," then the decision lies between differing social groups (e.g., environmentalists, fishermen, developers) and between their competing attempts to incorporate the piece of land into their system and worldview. (This classic planning distinction between planning for people or for place begs the question: Is there a third option, "planning for nonpeople, i.e., nature"?)

4. Schiller, using Kant's logic, recognized 200 years ago this human habit of positing the future on the past: "He thus artificially retraces his childhood in his maturity, forms for himself a *state of Nature* in idea, which is not

indeed given him by experience but is the necessary result of his rationality, borrows in this ideal state an ultimate aim which he never knew in his actual state of Nature, and a choice of which he was capable, and proceeds now exactly as though he were starting afresh. . . ."

5. Some radical ecologists take this lost world a step further and see it not as a garden, but as wilderness (e.g., Parton 1993).

6. I use the term diaspora to mean the involuntary dispersal of a people from their native home, driven out by a greater power (Hall 1992). The curious nature of the diaspora implied by the environmental worldview is that it is ambiguously voluntary: western positivistic thinking is the villain that we developed, but that eventually enslaved us. Then, too, diasporas invariably combine dislocations across both time and space, but the mythic "homeland" of this environmental diaspora is only from an historical era, but from no specific place.

7. The reverse may also not be automatic. David Johns (1992, 63), in advocating a broad interspecies equity, reminds us that not all forms of equity go hand-in-hand: "The nature of the linkages between various forms of domination is certainly not settled, but deep ecology may be distinct in believing that the resolution of equity issues among humans will not automatically result in an end to human destruction of the biosphere. One can envision a society without class distinctions, without patriarchy, and with cultural autonomy, that still attempts to manage the rest of nature in utilitarian fashion with resulting deterioration of the biosphere. . . . But the end of domination in human relations is not enough to protect the larger biotic community. Only behavior shaped by a biocentric view can do that."

8. The ambiguity of the term sustainable development is therefore not coincidental, given that reasonable people differ on which corner of the triangle is to be "sustained": a fixed level of natural resources? current environmental quality? current ecosystems? a hypothetical pre-industrial environmental state? the current material standards of living? long-term economic growth? political democracy?

9. These issues of language and translation were raised by Ngũgĩ wa Thiong-o and Stuart Hall in separate distinguished lectures at the Center for the Critical Analysis of Contemporary Cultures, Rutgers University (March 31 and April 15, 1993).

10. Conservationists have in fact installed underpasses and overpasses so that vulnerable migrating species can get around highways.

REFERENCES

Altshuler, Alan. 1965. The Goals of Comprehensive Planning. *Journal of the American Institute of Planning* 31,3: 186–94.

Andrus, Van, et al., eds. 1990. *Home: A Bioregional Reader.* Philadelphia and Santa Cruz: New Catalyst/New Society.

Barrett, Gary W., and Patrick J. Bohlen. 1991. Landscape Ecology. In *Landscape Linkages and Biodiversity,* edited by Wendy E. Hudson. Washington, DC and Covelo, CA: Island Press.

Beatley, Timothy. 1992. Balancing Urban Development and Endangered Species: The Coachella Valley Habitat Conservation Plan. *Environmental Management* 16,1: 7–19.

Beatley, Timothy, and David J. Brower. 1993. Sustainability Comes to Main Street. *Planning* 59,5: 16–9.

Beltzer, Dena, and Cynthia Kroll. 1986. *New Jobs for the Timber Region: Economic Diversification for Northern California.* Berkeley: Institute of Governmental Studies, University of California.

Bingham, Gail. 1986. *Resolving Environmental Disputes: A Decade of Experience.* Washington, DC: The Conservation Foundation.

Bird, Elizabeth Ann R. 1987. The Social Construction of Nature: Theoretical Approaches to the History of Environmental Problems. *Environmental Review* 11,4: 255–64.

Bramwell, Anna. 1989. *Ecology in the Twentieth Century, A History.* New Haven: Yale University Press.

Breheny, M. J., ed. 1992. *Sustainable Development and Urban Form.* London: Pion.

Bryant, Bunyan, and Paul Mohai, eds. 1992. *Race and the Incidence of Environmental Hazards.* Boulder, CO: Westview Press.

Bullard, Robert D. 1990. *Dumping in Dixie: Race, Class, and Environmental Quality.* Boulder, CO: Westview Press.

Bullard, Robert D., ed. 1993. *Confronting Environmental Racism: Voices from the Grassroots.* Boston: South End Press.

Callenbach, Ernest. 1975. *Ecotopia: The Notebooks and Reports of William Weston.* Berkeley, CA: Banyan Tree Books.

Campbell, Scott. 1992. Integrating Economic and Environmental Planning: The Regional Perspective. Working Paper No. 43, Center for Urban Policy Research, Rutgers University.

Clawson, Marion. 1975. *Forests: For Whom and For What?* Washington, DC: Resources for the Future.

Commission of the European Communities. 1990. *Green Paper on the Urban Environment.* Brussels: EEC.

Crowfoot, James E., and Julia M. Wondolleck. 1990. *Environmental Disputes: Community Involvement in Conflict Resolution.* Washington, DC and Covelo, CA: Island Press.

Daly, Herman E. 1991. *Steady State Economics.* 2nd edition, with new essays. Washington, DC and Covelo, CA: Island Press.

Daly, Herman E., and John B. Cobb, Jr. 1989. *For the Common Good: Redirecting the Economy toward Community, the Environment, and a Sustainable Future.* Boston: Beacon Press.

Davidoff, Paul. 1965. Advocacy and Pluralism in Planning. *Journal of the American Institute of Planners* 31,4: 544–55.

Duerr, Hans Peter. 1985. *Dreamtime: Concerning the Boundary Between Wilderness and Civilization.* Oxford: Basil Blackwell.

Elson, Martin J. 1986. *Green Belts : Conflict Mediation in the Urban Fringe.* London: Heinemann.

Fainstein, Susan S., and Norman I. Fainstein. 1971. City Planning and Political Values. *Urban Affairs Quarterly* 6,3: 341–62.

Findhorn Community, The. 1975. *The Findhorn Garden: Pioneering a New Vision of Man and Nature in Cooperation.* New York: Harper and Row.

Foglesong, Richard E. 1986. *Planning the Capitalist City.* Princeton: Princeton University Press.

Friedmann, John, and Clyde Weaver. 1979. *Territory and Function: The Evolution of Regional Planning.* Berkeley and Los Angeles: University of California Press.

Goldstein, Eric A., and Mark A. Izeman. 1990. *The New York Environment Book.* Washington, DC and Covelo, CA: Island Press.

Goodland, Robert. 1990. Environmental Sustainability in Economic Development—with Emphasis on Amazonia. In *Race to Save the Tropics: Ecology and Economics for a Sustainable Future,* edited by Robert Goodland. Washington, DC and Covelo, CA: Island Press.

Gordon, Peter, and Harry Richardson. 1990. Gasoline Consumption and Cities—A Reply. *Journal of the American Planning Association.* 55,3: 342–5.

Hall, Stuart. 1992. Cultural Identity and Diaspora. *Framework 36.*

Harvey, David. 1985. *The Urbanization of Capital.* Baltimore: Johns Hopkins University Press.

Higgins, Robert R. 1994a. Race and Environmental Equity: An Overview of the Environmental Justice Issue in the Policy Process. *Polity,* forthcoming.

Higgins, Robert R. 1994b. Race, Pollution, and the Mastery of Nature. *Environmental Ethics,* forthcoming.

Hoffman, Lily. 1989. *The Politics of Knowledge: Activist Movements in Medicine and Planning.* Albany: SUNY Press.

Howard, Ebenezer. 1965. *Garden Cities of To-Morrow* (first published in 1898 as *To-Morrow: A Peaceful Path to Real Reform*). Cambridge, MA: MIT Press.

Hudson, Wendy E., ed. 1991. *Landscape Linkages and Biodiversity.* Washington, DC and Covelo, CA: Island Press.

Jacobs, Harvey. 1989. Social Equity in Agricultural Land Protection. *Landscape and Urban Planning* 17,1: 21–33.

Johns, David. 1992. The Practical Relevance of Deep Ecology. *Wild Earth* 2,2.

Korten, David C. 1991. Sustainable Development. *World Policy Journal* 9,1: 157–90.

Krumholz, Norman, et al. 1982. A Retrospective View of Equity Planning: Cleveland, 1969–1979, and Comments. *Journal of the American Planning Association* 48,2: 163–83.

Kumar, Krishan. 1991. *Utopia and Anti-Utopia in Modern Times.* Oxford and Cambridge, MA: Basil Blackwell.

Lake, Robert. 1993. Rethinking NIMBY. *Journal of the American Planning Association* 59,1: 87–93.

Lake, Robert, ed. 1987. *Resolving Locational Conflict.* New Brunswick, NJ: Center for Urban Policy Research.

Lee, Robert G., Donald R. Field, and William R. Burch, Jr., eds. 1990. *Community and Forestry: Continuities in the Sociology of Natural Resources.* Boulder, CO: Westview Press.

Lindblom, C. E. 1959. The Science of Muddling Through. *Public Administration Review* 19 (Spring): 79–88.

MacKaye, Benton. 1962 (first published in 1928 by Harcourt, Brace and Co.). *The New Exploration: A Philosophy of Regional Planning.* Urbana: University of Illinois Press.

Marcuse, Peter. 1976. Professional Ethics and Beyond: Values in Planning. *Journal of the American Institute of Planning* 42, 3: 264–74.

McPhee, John. 1989. *The Control of Nature.* New York: Farrar, Straus, Giroux.

Mills, Edwin S. 1978. *The Economics of Environmental Quality.* New York: Norton.

Naess, Arne. 1993. The Breadth and the Limits of the Deep Ecology Movement. *Wild Earth* 3, 1: 74–5.

Newman, Peter W. G., and Jeffrey R. Kenworthy. 1989. Gasoline Consumption and Cities—A Comparison of U.S. Cities with a Global Survey. *Journal of the American Planning Association* 55, 1: 24–37.

Paehlke, Robert C. 1994. Environmental Values and Public Policy. In *Environmental Policy in the 1990s,* 2nd edition, edited by Norman J. Vig and Michael E. Kraft. Washington, DC: Congressional Quarterly Press.

Parton, Glenn. 1993. Why I am a Primitivist. *Wild Earth* 3, 1: 12–4.

Rees, William. 1989. *Planning for Sustainable Development.* Vancouver, B.C.: UBC Centre for Human Settlements.

Reisner, Marc. 1987. *Cadillac Desert: The American West and its Disappearing Water.* New York: Penguin Books.

Rickaby, P A. 1987. Six Settlement Patterns Compared. *Environment and Planning B: Planning and Design* 14: 193–223.

Robinson, Kelly. 1993. The Regional Economic Impacts of Marketable Permit Programs: The Case of Los Angeles. In *Cost Effective Control of Urban Smog,* Federal Reserve Bank of Chicago (November): 166–88.

Ross, Andrew. 1994. *The Chicago Gangster Theory of Life: Ecology, Culture, and Society.* London and New York: Verso.

Sale, Kirkpatrick. 1985. *Dwellers in the Land: The Bioregional Vision.* San Francisco: Sierra Club Books.

Schiller, Friedrich. 1965. *On the Aesthetic Education of Man* [translated by Reginald Snell]. Originally published in 1795 as *Über die Äesthetische Erziehung des Menschen in einer Reihe von Briefen.* New York: Friedrich Unger.

Sessions, George. 1992. Radical Environmentalism in the 90s. *Wild Earth* 2,3: 64–7.

Smith, Neil. 1990. *Uneven Development: Nature, Capital and the Production of Space.* Oxford, U.K.: Blackwell.

Soja, Edward. 1989. *Postmodern Geographies: The Resurrection of Space in Critical Social Theory.* London and New York: Verso.

Susskind, Lawrence, and Jeffrey Cruikshank. 1987. Mediated Negotiation in the Public Sector: The Planner as Mediator. *Journal of Planning Education and Research* 4: 5–15.

Sussman, Carl, ed. 1976. *Planning the Fourth Migration: The Neglected Vision of the Regional Planning Association of America.* Cambridge, MA: MIT Press.

Tuason, Julie A. 1993. Economic/Environmental Conflicts in 19th-Century New York: Central Park, Adirondack State Park, and the Social Construction of Nature. Unpublished manuscript, Dept. of Geography, Rutgers University.

Turner, Frederick W. 1983. *Beyond Geography: The Western Spirit Against the Wilderness.* New Brunswick, NJ: Rutgers University Press.

Van der Ryn, Sim, and Peter Calthorpe. 1991. *Sustainable*

Communities: A New Design Synthesis for Cities, Suburbs and Towns. San Francisco: Sierra Club Books.

Wiggins, Lyna. 1993. Geographic Information Systems. Lecture at the Center for Urban Policy Research, Rutgers University, April 5.

Wilson, Alexander. 1992. *The Culture of Nature: North American Landscape from Disney to the Exxon Valdez.* Cambridge, MA and Oxford, UK: Blackwell.

World Bank. 1989. *Striking a Balance: The Environmental Challenge of Development.* Washington, DC.

World Commission on Environment and Development (The Brundtland Commission). 1987. *Our Common Future.* Oxford: Oxford University Press.

[25]

Rail Transit and Joint Development
Land Market Impacts in Washington, D. C. and Atlanta

Robert Cervero

Land around urban rail transit stations can be valuable because it is so accessible. Joint development of transit stations and nearby office buildings occurs because both the public and private sectors recognize its financial rewards. This article examines how transit investments and joint development in particular affect five indicators of office market conditions: average rents; vacancy rates; absorption rates; densities; and shares of new and total office and commercial construction near the stations. Data are examined for five rail stations in the Washington, D. C. and Atlanta areas over the 1978–89 period. Average office rents near stations rose with systemwide ridership; joint development projects added more than three dollars per gross square foot to annual office rents. Office vacancy rates were lower, average building densities higher, and shares of regional growth larger in station areas with joint development projects. Where regional market conditions are favorable, rail transit appears capable of positive impacts on station area office markets. Combining transit investments with private real estate projects appears to strengthen these effects. The findings suggest that the rationale behind value recapture and other benefit-sharing programs is economically sound for conditions similar to those of the case study areas.

Cervero is Professor of City and Regional Planning at the University of California, Berkeley.

Journal of the American Planning Association, Vol. 60, No. 1, Winter 1994. © American Planning Association, Chicago, IL.

Joint development is based on the premise that transit investments significantly improve regional accessibility, and thus lead to higher land values around stations. Higher values, in turn, should give rise to higher commercial rents, densification, and a fairly rapid absorption of building space. Through programs like air rights leasing, benefit assessment financing, and fees for connecting adjacent commercial buildings to stations, transit agencies can expect to share in these benefits.

In the United States, comprehensive studies have been conducted on the land use impacts of San Francisco's BART (Gannon and Dear 1975; Webber 1976), San Diego's trolley (San Diego Association of Governments 1984) and Washington's Metrorail (Lerman et al. 1978), and also on the impact of combinations of systems (Knight and Trygg 1978; Cervero 1984). In general, the conclusions of these studies have been similar: urban rail transit will significantly benefit land use and site rents only if a region's economy is growing and a number of supportive programs are in place, for example permissive zoning to allow higher densities, and infrastructure such as pedestrian plazas and street improvements. Transit guides rather than creates growth, and by itself rarely effects significant land use changes.

This paper aims to extend our knowledge of how both urban transit investments and joint development programs affect site rents and other land use characteristics, using data from two new-generation, heavy-rail transit systems in the United States: Washington's Metrorail and Atlanta's MARTA. Since both systems, which began service in the mid-to-late 1970s, have now operated for well over a decade, enough time has elapsed to permit assessment of land use impacts. This analysis concentrates on office and commercial land uses around suburban stations, in part because almost all joint-development programs to date have involved these uses, and also because often the value of the commercial tracts around suburban stations shows the greatest rise. Since both the Washington and Atlanta areas had healthy regional growth during the 1980s, the analysis admittedly examines "best case" examples of what is possible when conditions are ripe for transit-linked changes in land use. (Between 1980 and 1990, metropolitan Washington's population grew 28.2 percent and its employment increased 35.3 percent; over the same period, metropolitan Atlanta's population grew 39.6 percent and its employment rose 57.3 percent.) To the extent that rail transit can be shown to benefit commercial rents, absorption rates, and other measures of real estate performance, joint development gains legitimacy as a mechanism to recapture some of the value that transit investments create.

Rail-Transit Joint Development in the United States

Joint development can be defined as:

any formal, legally binding arrangement between a public entity and a private individual or organization that involves either private-sector payments to the public entity or private-sector sharing of capital or operating costs, in mutual recognition of the enhanced real estate development potential or higher land values created by the siting of a public transit facility.

Thus the three trademarks of joint development are: (1) a legally binding agreement between two or more parties; (2) some form of remuneration by the private to the public sector, either revenue payments or cost-sharing; and (3) voluntary agreement to all terms and conditions.

By this definition, around 115 transit joint-development projects had been constructed in more than two dozen U. S. cities as of 1990; eighty-five percent of these were completed between 1980 and 1989.[1] Several factors spurred joint development in the 1980s: the completion of ten new U. S. urban rail systems; rapid suburban office growth in many rail corridors; the resurgence of downtown real estate markets in several large cities with established rail systems; deep cuts in federal transit assistance, pressuring local authorities to seek other ways to finance transit; and the emergence of public-private partnerships for redeveloping cities and building infrastructure.

Of the 115 joint-development projects completed by 1990, around two-fifths involved cost sharing—public-private sharing of such costs as those for excavation, construction staging sites, labor and heavy equipment, heating/ventilating/air-conditioning systems, and parking lots. Rail operators in New York City (MTA) and Philadelphia (SEPTA) have entered into by far the most cost-sharing agreements to date. New York uses zoning incentives such as density bonuses to encourage developers to renovate subway stations and relocate passageways; Philadelphia leases commercial space in suburban rail stations at favorable rates, and in return the developers upgrade and maintain public concourses and passageways. As of 1990, Philadelphia transit officials estimated they had attracted $2.4 million in private investments for station rehabilitation.

Approximately one out of four joint-development projects in the United States have used revenue-sharing in the form of air rights and property leasing, connection fees (for physically linking a retail store to a station) or benefit-assessment financing. Washington's Metrorail is the national leader in striking revenue-sharing deals, having entered into nine separate station leases and eleven station connection agreements to date. Atlanta ranks second; to date, MARTA has received revenues from three air-rights leases (IBM Tower, Southern Bell Tower, and Georgia State Office Building) and three station connection projects (Atlantic Plaza, Resurgens Plaza, and Rich's Department Store). Nationally, other joint-development projects have taken multiple forms, usually joint leases of station space along with cost sharing for station rehabilitation.

To date, joint-development schemes have brought only modest benefits to United States transit agencies. Although between 1979 and 1989 New York's MTA received over $63 million in capital contributions (in 1989 dollars), when these funds are amortized over the typical 30-year bond period for transit projects at an interest rate of 12.5 percent, they amount to only about four percent of MTA capital expenditures over the period. Examined this way, capital contributions from joint-development projects accounted for, respec-

tively, only 0.7 percent and 0.2 percent of rail capital expenditures in Washington, D. C. and in Atlanta over the same period. Leasing and fee revenues have generally been a smaller percentage of each rail system's annual operating budget. Over the 1979–89 period, Washington's WMATA received over $20 million in joint-development revenues, but these payments have never amounted to more than 0.7 percent of annual income. One explanation for these meager results may be that most United States transit agencies, with the possible exception of WMATA, have had limited experience in appraising the potential market value of joint-development sites and in negotiating favorable real estate deals. The modest earnings may also reflect the reluctance of most transit boards to engage in real estate transactions and other entrepreneurial pursuits; in fact, legal restrictions often bar transit authorities in the United States from land banking and from recapturing transit-induced rises in land value by acquiring more land.

Besides the lease income, joint development projects generate more fare revenues to the extent that they stimulate more transit trips. In a 1983 study of nine transit joint-development projects in the U. S., Keefer found that every 1,000 square feet of new commercial floorspace near a rail station generated an additional six transit trips per day. For the nine projects, this yielded an additional $11.4 million (in 1982 dollars) in annual farebox receipts—ranging from $56,000 for Santa Ana, California's bus-transit joint-development venture to a high of $5 million for Philadelphia's Gallery I and II retail redevelopment projects. Washington's Metrorail may have been the most successful among United States new-generation rail systems at winning over motorists to rail transit. Metrorail officials calculate that the annual worth of an easement and private construction of a passageway to the Fashion Center mall near the Pentagon City station is more than $250,000, but that the annual gains in farebox revenues from being near the mall have been easily twice that amount. In all, 4.2 million Washington Metrorail riders annually have as their destinations buildings directly connected to Metro stations.

Study Cases

To study the land-use impacts of rail transit and joint development, data were pooled across five station areas in metropolitan Washington, D. C. and Atlanta where commercial development grew significantly over the 1978–1989 period. Data availability and reliability determined the choice of three station areas on the Washington Metrorail system—Ballston, Bethesda, and Silver Spring, and two stations on the Atlanta MARTA system—Arts Center and Lenox. (See Figures 1 and 2.) At each station area at least one joint-development project had begun some time between 1978 and 1989. Tables 1 and 2 summarize office market characteristics, and transit ridership and service characteristics for the five station areas.

Ballston

When Metrorail service began there in 1979, Ballston was a small commercial district in Arlington, Virginia, sur-

RAIL TRANSIT AND JOINT DEVELOPMENT

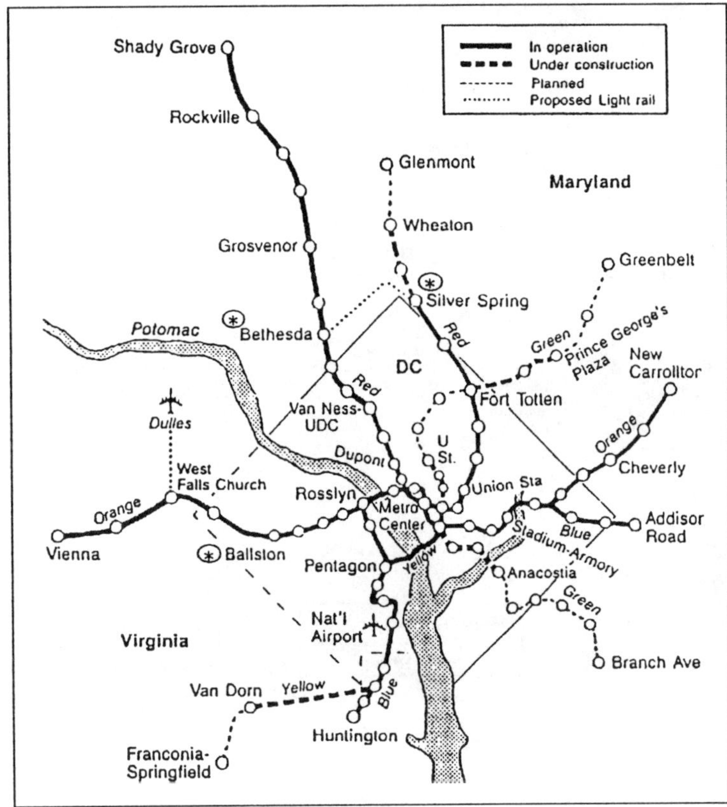

FIGURE 1:
Washington,
D.C.
Metrorail
System, 1991.

(✻) **Case Study Station Areas**

rounded by single-family homes and garden apartments. Since then, Ballston has blossomed into one of the city's "new downtowns," surrounded by high-rise commercial towers and a massive shopping mall. Ballston's major joint-development project is the Metro Centre, located above the Metrorail station on what had been a major bus transfer lot. In addition to office space, this twenty-eight-story tower contains 200 hotel rooms, 284 condominium units, retail shops, and a health club. Washington's transit authority, WMATA, receives approximately $200,000 in annual revenues, in the form of base rent plus a percentage of the rents from a tract that WMATA owns and leases to the developer.

Bethesda and Silver Spring

Both Bethesda and Silver Spring lie just north of Washington, D. C. on Metrorail's Red line; they form two of the largest commercial centers in Montgomery County, Maryland. Bethesda has long been a suburban center in its own right, but the density there has increased considerably since 1980. Bethesda Metro Center, located above the Bethesda Metrorail station, is a massive joint-development project with mixed uses (office, hotel, retail) that yields over $1.6 million from annual leases, the highest revenue for any single project in the United States. Silver Spring, a much smaller suburban center, has not experienced quite the boom seen at Bethesda; local residents have resisted efforts to develop the area. The only form that joint development takes in Silver Spring is some small concession fees paid by retail vendors and nearby shops.

Arts Center and Lenox Square

Located midway between central Atlanta and the booming Buckhead retail area along MARTA's north line, the Arts

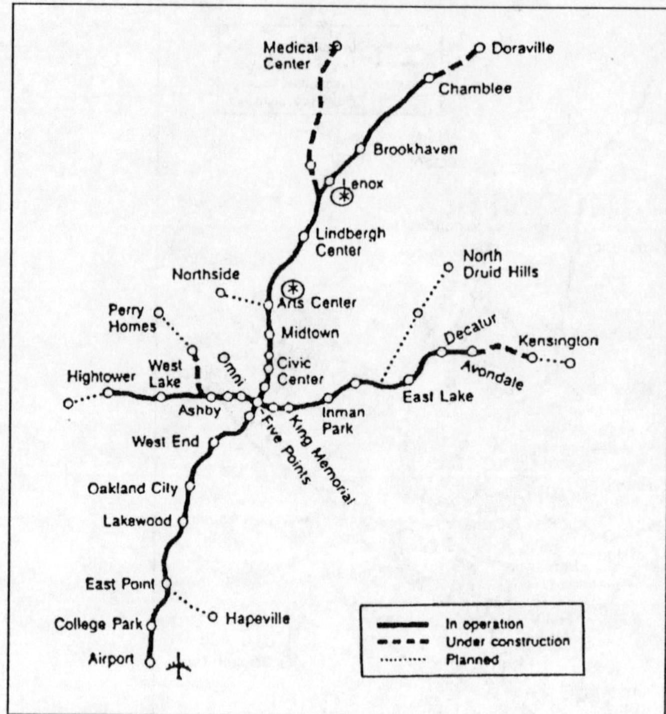

FIGURE 2: Atlanta MARTA System, 1991.

(✱) **Case Study Station Areas**

Center area was until recently a major cultural center, not a major office address. In 1985, the fifty-story IBM Tower was built adjacent to the MARTA station, sparking the construction of several smaller office complexes. By 1991, the IBM Tower had generated over $1.5 million in lease revenues to MARTA. Lenox Square lies several miles north of the Arts Center station, in an area known for its super-regional shopping mall. Since MARTA's 1984 opening, the Lenox Square area has acquired over three million square feet of office space, which is now nearly ten percent of greater Atlanta's total office inventory. Owners of Resurgens Plaza, a luxurious office building adjacent to MARTA's Lenox station, pay MARTA over $100,000 in lease revenues annually.

Study Approach

Multiple regression analysis was used to isolate the effects of rail transit from other factors that also influence property values and local real estate market conditions, such as the opening of a new freeway nearby or overall regional growth. Stepwise procedures determined the best-fitting, most parsimonious models. In all, sixty data points were obtained by pooling data for the five station areas across twelve years (1978–89).[2] For most models, first-order auto-regressive estimation was used to correct for serial correlation of error terms.[3]

In compiling data, land-use impacts were measured for all commercial and office properties having over 100,000 square feet of floorspace and sited within a one-quarter-mile radius of one of the five transit station areas. (The one-quarter-mile radius was defined as the land-use impact zone.) For each time point, station-area averages of land use and transportation variables were measured. Variables broke down into four sets: (1) *Station-area real estate market performance variables:* office rents, vacancy rates, absorption rates, and total square footage of commercial floorspace. These were the policy, or dependent, variables. (2) *Transit service variables:* ridership, frequency of train services, average fares, and other

RAIL TRANSIT AND JOINT DEVELOPMENT

TABLE 1: 1989 office market characteristics for five selected transit stations

	Date of Station Opening	Total Commercial Floorspace (SQFT)	Average Vacancy Rate (%)	Average Office Rent (S/SQFT)	Average Absorption Rate (%)
ATLANTA MARTA STATIONS					
Arts Center	1983	4,302,612	7.7	$19.61	14.9
Lenox	1985	4,918,736	22.4	$23.35	8.9
WASHINGTON METRORAIL STATIONS					
Ballston	1980	2,268,179	29.6	$26.62	21.1
Bethesda	1984	9,438,187	19.4	$22.86	3.0
Silver Spring	Pre-1978	3,846,048	32.4	$19.91	−1.9

Sources: Atlanta: *Black's Guide* and Frank Carter & Associates
Washington: *Black's Guide* and Smithy Braedon

characteristics of rail services. These were the chief explanatory variables. (3) *Regional economic and growth factors:* metropolitan employment totals as well as regional averages for commercial rents, absorption rates, new office construction, and vacancy rates. These were control variables. (4) *Station-area transportation, infrastructure, and development characteristics:* lane miles of nearby freeway facilities, average daily traffic volumes on nearby roads, maximum allowable floor area ratios, zoning requirements, and the existence of joint development initiatives. These also were control variables. Land use data came from local real estate leasing guides; transportation and other data were obtained from local transportation and planning agencies.[4]

The following sections present the research results. Included are separate regression models to explain: station-area office rents, vacancy rates, average office building size (a proxity for density), and the shares of total and of new regional office space that were located in the five station areas studied.

Office Rents

Average annual office rents at the five station areas drifted steadily upwards during the 1980s, as shown in Figure 3. In the cases of Bethesda and Lenox, office rents appeared to increase most sharply in anticipation of, rather than after, rail service—i.e. during the year before the station opened.

Table 3 presents the model that best predicted average office rents for the five Washington Metrorail and Atlanta MARTA stations between 1978 and 1989. Controlling for other factors, office rents near stations tended to increase as systemwide transit ridership increased—rising by nearly four dollars per square foot for every 100,000 additional daily riders. The fact that "systemwide ridership" instead of "station ridership" entered the equation is important. It suggests that transit's influence on office rents was not related to ridership activity at specific stations so much as it was to overall system demand. (This variable probably also served as a proxy for secular growth, reflecting the parallel trends of rising rents and rising systemwide ridership during the 1980s.) The next most significant variable in Table 3 is a dummy variable signifying whether or not a station is a terminus, which for this data set was the case for Silver Spring and Ballston (until 1986). Offices near terminal stations rented for around $3.35 less per square foot than offices near non-terminal stations did, *ceteris paribus*. These lower average rents probably reflect not only the fact that terminal stations tend to lie farthest from the city center, but also the

TABLE 2: Ridership and other summary statistics for five selected transit stations

	Date of Station Opening	Average One-Way Fare to Downtown Station (1989)	Average Weekday Passengers Entering Station (1989)	Freeway Directional Miles Within a 3-Mile Radius*
ATLANTA MARTA STATIONS				
Arts Center	1983	$0.85	10,596	17
Lenox	1985	$0.85	6,766	12
WASHINGTON METRORAIL STATIONS				
Ballston	1980	$1.12	8,902	20
Bethesda	1984	$1.58	7,305	12
Silver Spring	Pre-1978	$1.64	15,729	10

*Miles of freeway (one direction only) within a three-mile radius of station, not adjusted for number of freeway lanes.
Sources: Metropolitan Atlanta Regional Transit Authority
Washington Metropolitan Area Transportation Authority

ROBERT CERVERO

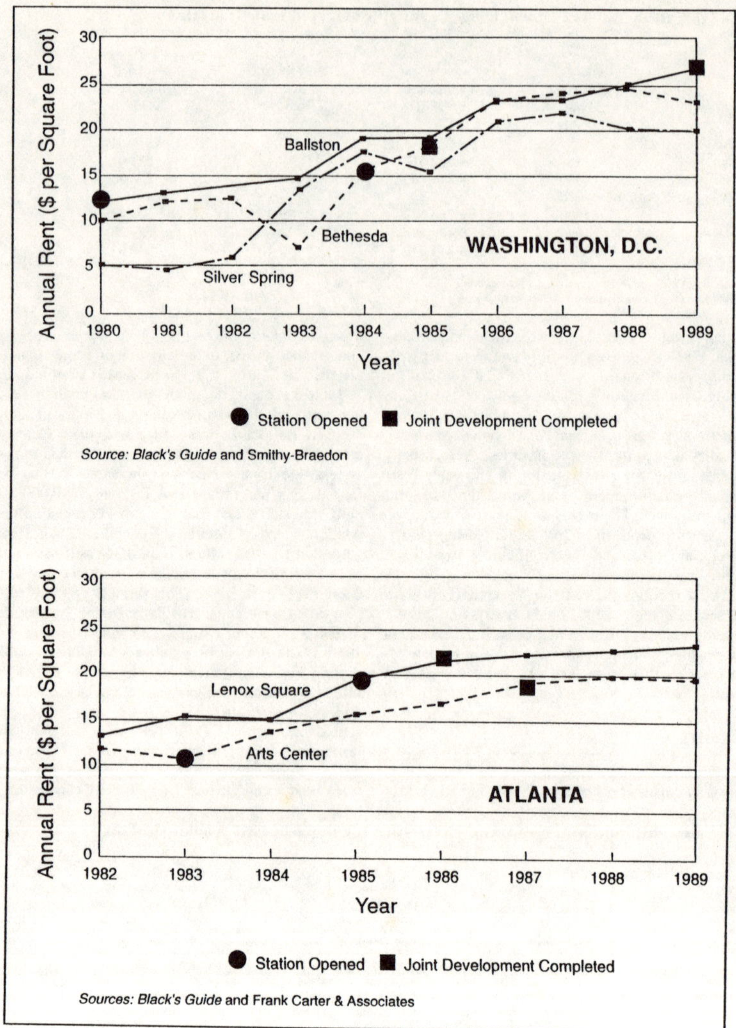

FIGURE 3: Trends in station-area office rents, in 1990 dollars per square foot.

function of terminal stations as major bus transfer points and park-and-ride lots, since bus and parking activity near stations may somewhat depress rents.

Table 3 also reveals that the presence of joint-development projects at stations raises rents. All else being equal, it appears that annual office rents are about three dollars per square foot higher at station areas with joint-development projects. Of course, the relationship between joint develop-

RAIL TRANSIT AND JOINT DEVELOPMENT

TABLE 3: Predictors of average office rent for five urban rail transit stations in Washington, D.C. and Atlanta, 1978–89

	Dependent Variable: Average Annual Office Rent per Square Foot, in Current Dollars		
	Coefficient	t statistic	Significance
SYSTEM RIDERSHIP	0.0396	3.72	.001
TERMINAL STATION	−3.3543	−2.53	.016
JOINT DEVELOPMENT	3.1718	2.46	.019
UNEMPLOYMENT RATE	−1.3755	−2.16	.038
Constant	15.2250	3.31	.002

Summary Statistics
  R^2 = .823
  F = 31.61
  Prob(F) = .000
  Durban Watson Statistic = 2.223

Variable Definitions:

SYSTEM RIDERSHIP = daily systemwide rail ridership, paid passengers, in 1,000s.

TERMINAL STATION = dummy variable designating a terminal station at the end of a line. Equals 1 if a terminal station and 0 otherwise.

JOINT DEVELOPMENT = dummy variable designating the existence of a joint development program, involving some form of either revenue sharing or cost sharing. Equals 1 if a joint development program exists and 0 otherwise.

UNEMPLOYMENT RATE = regional unemployment rate, expressed as a percentage.

ment and rents is both indirect and simultaneous. Joint-development projects induce more building activity, promote higher densities and agglomeration economies, and improve station environments by linking a station concourse directly with an adjoining building and by coordinating the building designs; operating together, these factors are likely to make higher rents possible.

The inclusion of a variable measuring regional unemployment rate adds an important macroeconomic dimension to the model. Over time, every one percent increase in the regional unemployment rate, *ceteris paribus*, is associated with a drop in annual office rents of $1.37 per square foot. Clearly, recession and high unemployment, which occurred in the early 1980s, reduce the demand for office space, and rents decline.

Several other analyses were conducted to probe the influences of rail transit and joint development on office rents. Another regression model, not shown here, related station area office rents to regional averages, finding that joint-development projects provided about a 15 percent office-rent premium above the regional average, controlling for factors like ridership and the quality of nearby infrastructure. Convenient freeway access was also a significant and positive predictor of higher rents, suggesting that rail transit and freeway services can complement rather than work against one another in shaping suburban growth.

Office rents were also compared between each of the five case-study station areas and a nearby competitive office market served only by freeways and not by rail (i.e. matched-pairs testing). From 1978 to 1989, for instance, Ballston averaged an annual office rent premium of over three dollars per square foot (in nominal terms) over Tysons Corner, a massive "suburban downtown" that lies six miles to the southwest. Similarly, Bethesda, Arts Center, and Lenox all enjoyed more than a two-dollars-per-square-foot annual office rent premium over their nearest suburban competitors served by freeways. Overall, office projects immediately adjacent to Washington Metrorail stations commanded up to ten percent more in rents than did similar buildings two blocks away (Sedway Cooke Associates 1984). Part of the difference is due to the fact that joint-development projects usually feature more retail space than highway-served office projects do; retail space typically leases for twice as much as office space. In the past few years, moreover, mixed-use projects have outperformed single-use office buildings, leasing new space more quickly and at higher rents (Urban Land Institute 1991). Then, too, the net leasable space can often be greater for a joint-development project because on-site tenants require less parking space, and mixed-use projects make shared parking possible. A reflection of the fact that joint development projects command rent premiums is the favorable treatment they often receive in securing permanent financing. Long- term real estate lenders now assign credit in their loan evaluations for joint developments because of their proven ability to generate top rents over long periods (Cervero et al. 1992).

Office Vacancy and Absorption Rates

Rail-linked development should increase not only rents, but also the demand for office space, thus reducing vacancy rates. Table 4, which presents the best-fitting model for predicting office vacancy rates, confirms what every office leasing agent knows: vacancy rates tend to be higher for larger buildings with high rents. Controlling for rents and building size, however, Table 4 also shows that vacancy rates tend to be lower in station areas or at time points with joint-

ROBERT CERVERO

TABLE 4: Predictors of relative vacancy rate for five urban rail transit stations in Washington, D.C. and Atlanta, 1978–89

	Dependent Variable: Average Annual Office Vacancy Rate in Station Area minus Average Annual Office Vacancy Rate for the Region, expressed as a percentage		
	Coefficient	t statistic	Significance
AVERAGE OFFICE SIZE	0.0187	8.18	.000
JOINT DEVELOPMENT	−5.5726	−2.36	.024
OFFICE GROWTH SHARE	−300.0708	−5.69	.000
Constant	5.5374	2.68	.011

Summary Statistics
R^2 = .720
F = 30.81
Prob(F) = .000
Durban Watson Statistic = 1.734

Variable Definitions:

AVERAGE OFFICE SIZE = average square footage office space per plot, in 1,000s.

JOINT DEVELOPMENT = dummy variable designating the existence of a joint development program, involving some form of either revenue sharing or cost sharing. Equals 1 if a joint development program exists and 0 otherwise.

OFFICE GROWTH SHARE = square feet of new office space in the station area divided by square feet of new office space in the region, expressed as a proportion. This measures the share of new regional office space in the station area.

development projects—on average, eleven percent lower than vacancy rates at comparable stations without joint-development projects. When compared to the regional averages of the two metropolitan areas over the 1978–89 period, office vacancy rates for comparable joint-development properties were found to be 5.5 percent lower. Stations with joint-development projects also tended to lease new offices faster. A separate regression analysis, not shown here, found that for every ten percent of new regional office space that was located in the five station areas, there was a statistical association with a 6.5 percent rise in the absorption rate above the metropolitan averages (Cervero et al. 1992).

Match-pair comparisons further confirm the attractiveness of joint-development sites, especially in Atlanta. From 1980 to 1989, the inventory of leased office space at the Arts Center station increased by ten percent per year. By contrast, office growth along the Northwest Interstate-75 Freeway corridor submarket, a collection of campus-style business parks some two miles to the west, was fairly sluggish over the same period, increasing by only about one percent per year.

Overall, these findings probably reflect two market dynamics. First, joint-development projects are usually built at precisely those station areas with low vacancy rates—that is, in office submarkets that are expanding and profitable. The second and more important dynamic is that joint-development projects, by virtue of their proximity to transit stations, are easier to lease. In other words, although large speculative office buildings near transit have higher-than-average vacancy rates, large office buildings developed as coordinated joint projects tend to have lower-than-average vacancy rates.

Office Density

As land around rail transit stations increases in value, building heights too can be expected to rise. Indeed, one of the strongest arguments in favor of building rail transit systems is that they may encourage greater urban density (Pushkarev and Zupan 1977; Smith 1984). Data on such common density measures as the number of employees per 1,000 square feet of building space, or average floor area ratios (FARs) were not available for the five stations for the twelve-year study period; however, average building size was easily estimated from available time series data on each station's total number of office buildings and their square footage. While this figure does not directly indicate land use intensity (since it is not indexed to land area), it does provide some indication of relative density.

Table 5 shows that average office building size tended to increase with systemwide ridership in the previous year and with joint-development activity. The model suggests that the effect of ridership on building density was not instantaneous, but rather lagged. It may take a while before the advantages of accessible transit service are capitalized into the increased land values that encourage higher densities. Even when developers anticipate the benefits, it still takes several years to design a structure, secure financing, get necessary government approvals, and construct the building. The model further indicates that the presence of a joint-development project was associated with buildings that were around 350,000 square feet bigger than the typical office building in the five study areas during the years 1978–89. This is a huge difference; it no doubt reflects the fact that all the air rights lease programs in this sample involved high-rise towers, including Atlantic Center at the Arts Center station, Resurgens Plaza at Lenox Station, and Metro Centre above the Ballston station.

In sum, these results support previous research findings that transit investments—and the ridership and coordinated joint development that they stimulate—encourage dense development. While that usually benefits both developers and transit agencies directly, society at large also benefits to some extent if more compact growth increases transit modal splits, and if that conserves energy, reduces pollution, and improves regional mobility. Recent evidence from Washington, D.C. suggests that rail has had a significant influence on modal split even outside the District. Around one-quarter of those working in office buildings within one-half mile of the Silver Spring Metrorail station and fifteen percent of those working near Ballston's downtown station arrived to work each day by transit, which is above the regional work-trip average of twelve percent (JHK & Associates 1989). Moreover, seventy-three percent of residents at a 315-unit apartment complex near the Silver Spring station, and sixty-nine percent of those residing at a 500-unit complex near the Ballston station took the train to work.

Regional Office Space and Growth Share

A final model explored whether the existence of a joint-development project increased a station area's relative attractiveness in the office marketplace. Table 6 suggests the answer is only slightly, adding about two percentage points to the share of regional office space at a particular station area. Being at the end of a transit line, on the other hand, lowered the share of regional growth by 1.3 percentage points. For new regional office inventories, it was also found that a joint development project added about five percentage points to any station's share of the annual metropolitan growth in office space. Thus, joint-development activities not only were correlated with high rents, low vacancy rates, and tall nearby buildings; they also characterized station areas undergoing a building boom. Certainly, the causality was working both ways. While joint development induced new construction, growth itself probably encouraged interest in coordinated development from both the public and private sectors.

Summary and Conclusion

The basic proposition that transit investments in general, and joint-development projects in particular, create measurable land value and associated benefits appears for the most part to be borne out by empirical evidence, at least during the 1980s in the case of the five non-CBD Washington, D.C. and Atlanta station areas studied. The numerous positive effects build a compelling case for expanding joint development, particularly where commercial real estate conditions are similar to those found in the Washington, D.C. and Atlanta regions during the 1980s.

Table 7 summarizes the findings of this research by presenting the elasticities between various office-market performance measures and the key explanatory variables that emerged from the stepwise analyses. All figures shown are midpoint elasticities. Among the dependent variables, the "average office rent" variable was the most closely correlated with the most transit factors (e.g., ridership, joint development). The strongest relationship was between office rents and ridership. Of particular note is the finding that office rents were more strongly influenced by transit ridership than by nearby freeway traffic volumes. The existence of joint development appeared to add a significant rent premium. At terminal stations, however, the presence of transit had a fairly weak influence on rents.

In station areas with joint-development activities, vacancy rates tended to be low. Joint development was also positively associated with project size and a healthy local real estate market. Stations with joint development tended to capture a larger share of regional office and commercial growth than stations with no such programs did.

The outlook for joint development in the United States during the 1990s is mixed. Hampering such initiatives is the fact that while many new fixed-guideway transit systems are now discussed, few have actual funding commitments. Thus joint

---

TABLE 5: Predictors of average size of office project for five urban rail transit stations in Washington, D.C. and Atlanta, 1978-89

	Dependent Variable: Average Square Footage of Office Buildings on Individual Plots in Station Area		
	Coefficient	t statistic	Significance
SYSTEMWIDE RIDERSHIP (-1)	5.0352	5.52	.000
JOINT DEVELOPMENT	345,381.49	3.31	.002
Constant	$-586,012.29$	3.21	.004

Summary Statistics:
  $R^2 = .603$
  $F = 25.82$
  Prob(F) $= .000$
  Durban Watson Statistic $= 2.083$

Variable Definitions:

SYSTEMWIDE RIDERSHIP (-1) = annual systemwide rail ridership, paid passengers, in 1,000s, lagged by one year.

JOINT DEVELOPMENT = dummy variable designating the existence of a joint development program, involving some form of either revenue sharing or cost sharing. Equals 1 if a joint development program exists and 0 otherwise.

ROBERT CERVERO

TABLE 6: Predictors of share of regional office and commercial space in the station area for rail stations in Washington, D.C. and Atlanta, 1978–89

	Coefficient	t statistic	Significance
	Dependent Variable: Average Square Footage of Office and Commercial Buildings in Station Area, divided by Total Regional Office and Commercial Square Footage		
JOINT DEVELOPMENT	0.0195	3.11	.003
TERMINAL STATION	−0.0133	−2.21	.034
Constant	0.0338	6.86	.000

Summary Statistics:
$R^2 = .539$
$F = 19.91$
Prob(F) = .000
Durban Watson Statistic = 1.935

Variable Definitions:

JOINT DEVELOPMENT = dummy variable designating the existence of a joint development program, involving some form of either revenue sharing or cost sharing. Equals 1 if a joint development program exists and 0 otherwise.

TERMINAL STATION = dummy variable designating a terminal station at the end of a line. Equals 1 if a terminal station and 0 otherwise.

development in the immediate future is likely to be limited to existing station areas or new rail extensions. A second limiting factor is that most commercial real estate markets in the United States are vastly over-built. Both office and retail vacancy rates are high and are likely to remain so; credit is tight. Residential development remains the one real estate bright spot, and, depending on the city, there may be opportunities and pressures for high-density residential development within walking distance of transit stations. Joint residential development around transit stations is largely untested, but has promise. In the San Francisco Bay Area, the regional rail transit authority, BART, has recently negotiated several joint development deals to build mid-rise housing complexes on existing parking lots at the El Cerrito, Pleasant Hill, and Hayward stations. Rising land values and pressures for affordable housing have prompted BART to seriously consider leasing parts of its vast inventory of park-and-ride lots to housing developers.

New housing projects may eventually lead to mini-communities mushrooming around dozens of BART stations, as was envisaged when BART was originally conceived over 40 years ago. A recent survey found that ten of the thirty-six northern California jurisdictions with rail transit stations have introduced an array of development incentives around stations (including higher allowable densities, lower minimum parking requirements, tax-increment financing, and industrial development bonds), and several have made transit-based housing the centerpieces of their community development programs (Bernick et al. 1993).

The experiences of rail cities like Toronto, Stockholm, and Singapore make clear that clustered residential growth is essential for transit to capture significant shares of inter-suburban work trips and to achieve bi-directional ridership flows. Transit-based housing will yield important environmental benefits if it encourages infill development and con-

TABLE 7: Land market-transit elasticities

Independent Variables	Dependent Variables				
	Average Rents	Vacancy Rate	Absorption Rate	Average Building Size	Share of Regional Growth
Transit Factors					
Ridership	0.496	—	—	0.210	—
Joint Development	0.063	−0.164	—	0.146	0.125
Terminal Station	−0.095	—	−0.382	—	−0.189
Other Factors					
Unemployment Rate	−0.389	—	—	—	—
Freeway Traffic or Miles	0.370	—	.142	—	—

Dashes indicate that the explanatory variables were not siginificant predictors of the dependent variables.

verts former park-and-ride trips to walk-and-ride trips.[5] Since transit systems like Washington's WMATA and Atlanta's MARTA have moved "up the learning curve" from their years of joint office development, they should consider capitalizing on their experience by negotiating leases of land, for example of park-and-ride lots, to residential home builders for constructing garden apartments, condominiums, and mixed-use projects. To the extent that society gains from such transit-linked development, home-builders should be rewarded with such paybacks as credits against taxes, impact fees, affordable housing quotas, or emission reduction requirements. In the 1990s, the conditions seem ripe for forging new partnerships between public and private interests to create more transit-based housing. The rewards could very well exceed those of the most successful commercial-office joint-development programs of the 1980s.

AUTHOR'S NOTE

The Office of Policy and Budget of the Federal Transit Administration (formerly the Urban Mass Transportation Administration) provided financial support for this work. I thank John Landis and Peter Hall for their collaboration and assistance on this research project. I alone, however, am responsible for any errors or omissions contained in this article.

NOTES

1. See Cervero et al. (1992) for more detailed discussions of the statistics in this section.
2. Merging station-area data across two metropolitan areas and twelve time points allowed a pooled longitudinal/cross-sectional framework for studying the land market impacts of joint development. The use of data across two metropolitan areas created greater variation in the policy variables of interest, while the use of regional statistical controls, e. g., unemployment rate, removed the influence of cross-metropolitan variation.

   In theory, if regression coefficients are constant over time and over cross-section units, more efficient parameter estimates can be obtained by combining all data and applying ordinary least squares (OLS) estimation. If the intercept terms of the regression equations vary systematically over time or over cross-section units, that information can be incorporated by creating dummy variables and producing covariance models. While creating dummy variables for each cross-sectional case (less one) and time series case (less one) can improve overall model fit, at the same time each new variable entrant causes the loss of a degree of freedom in the estimate of regression parameters. For small data sets, that can cause serious problems (Pindyck and Rubinfeld 1991).

   In the analyses which follow, covariance models were estimated and their error sums of squares were compared to the error sums of squares of OLS models to see if they significantly improved fit. In none of the analyses was the model fit enhanced through a covariance model; thus OLS estimation was used instead. Error-components models were also used to test whether error terms were correlated across time and simultaneously across cross-section units. Again, fit was not improved by these specifications. From these results, the pooling of data across time points and cross-section units appeared to be statistically justified and did not require any significant alterations in how the models were specified.
3. Both lagged and non-lagged versions of explanatory variables were tried initially in estimating best-fitting models. Lagged variables were selected only when they outperformed their non-lagged counterparts.
4. In Washington, D. C., data for specific buildings within each market area were obtained from *Black's Office Leasing Guide* and records provided by the Smithy-Braden Company. Data were aggregated by station area, by year, for 1978 to 1989. In calculating station area average rents and vacancy rates, building size was used to weight the contribution of each individual parcel. For Atlanta, the primary data source was summary reports for office submarkets provided by Frank Carter and Associates, a major commercial developer. For most stations, these data were supplemented by proprietary information made available from brokers, leasing agents, and real estate firms interviewed.
5. For the typical five-mile drive to a park-and-ride lot, eighty percent of hydrocarbon emissions are due to cold starts and hot evaporative soaks (Cameron 1991). Thus, rail transit trips that rely on short-distance automobile access contribute little to reducing tailpipe emissions. Converting some park-and-ride trips to walk-and-ride trips, however, would yield real improvement in air quality.

REFERENCES

Bernick, M., P. Hall, and R. Schaevitz. 1993. Planning Strategies for High-Density Housing Near Rail Transit Stations in Northern California. *CPS Brief* 5, 2: 1–5.

Cameron, M. 1991. *Transportation Efficiency: Tackling Southern California's Air Pollution and Congestion.* Oakland, California: Environmental Defense Fund.

Cervero, R. 1984. Light Rail Transit and Urban Development. *Journal of the American Planning Association* 50, 2:133–47.

Cervero, R., P. Hall and J. Landis. 1992. *Transit Joint Development in the United States: A Review of Recent Experiences and an Assessment of Future Potential.* Washington, D.C.: Urban Mass Transportation Administration, U. S. Department of Transportation.

Gannon, C. and M. Dear. 1975. Rapid Transit and Office Development. *Traffic Quarterly* 29, 2: 223–42.

JHK & Associates. 1989. *Development-Related Ridership Survey.* Washington, D.C.: Washington Metropolitan Area Transit Authority.

Keefer, L. 1983. *A Review of Nine UMTA-Assisted Joint Development Projects.* Washington, D.C.: Urban Mass Transportation Administration.

Knight, R. and J. Trygg. 1978. Urban Mass Transit and Land Use Impacts. *Transportation* 5, 1: 12–24.

Lerman, S., D. Damm, E. Lam, and J. Young. 1978. *The Effects*

ROBERT CERVERO

of the Washington Metro on Urban Property Values. Washington, D.C.: Urban Mass Transportation Administration.

Pindyck, R. and D. Rubinfeld. 1991. *Econometric Models & Economic Forecasts.* New York: McGraw-Hill, Third Edition.

Pushkarev, B. and J. Zupan. 1977. *Public Transportation and Land Use Policy.* Bloomington: Indiana Press University.

San Diego Association of Governments. 1984. *San Diego Trolley: The First Three Years.* San Diego: San Diego Association of Governments.

Sedway Cooke Associates. 1984. Joint Development. *Urban Land* 43, 7: 16–20.

Smith, W. 1984. Mass Transit for High-Rise, High-Density Living. *Journal of Transportation Engineering* 100, 6: 521–35.

Urban Land Institute. 1991. *Market Profiles: 1990.* Washington, D.C.: Urban Land Institute.

Webber, M. 1976. The BART Experience—What Have We Learned? *The Public Interest* 12, 3: 79–108.

[26]

Pergamon

Transpn Res.-A, Vol. 31, No. 4, pp 309–333, 1997
© 1997 Elsevier Science Ltd
All rights reserved. Printed in Great Britain
0965-8564/97 $17.00 + 0.00

TWENTY YEARS OF THE BAY AREA RAPID TRANSIT SYSTEM: LAND USE AND DEVELOPMENT IMPACTS

ROBERT CERVERO and JOHN LANDIS

Department of City and Regional Planning, Institute of Urban and Regional Development, University of California, Berkeley CA 9472, U.S.A.

(Received 10 September 1995; in revised form 10 July 1996)

Abstract—Planners of the Bay Area Rapid Transit (BART) system, the first large-scale urban rail project built in the U.S. since the early part of this century, hoped BART would encourage compact and orderly growth, and spawn a multi-centered settlement pattern. The initial BART impact study, conducted a few years following the system's 1973 opening, concluded that BART played a fairly modest, though not inconsequential, role in shaping metropolitan growth and land-use patterns. This paper summarizes findings from an update of the original BART impact study, examining BART's influences on urban development patterns 20 years after services started. In general, our findings are similar to those of the original impact study. Over the past 20 years, land-use changes associated with BART have been largely localized, limited to downtown San Francisco and Oakland and a handful of suburban stations. Elsewhere, few land-use changes have occurred, either because of neighborhood opposition or a lackluster local real estate market. While BART appears to have helped bring about a more multi-centered regional settlement pattern, such as inducing mid-rise office development near the Walnut Creek and Concord stations, it has done little to stem the tide of freeway-oriented suburban employment growth over the past two decades. Indeed, recent office additions near East Bay stations pale in comparison to the amount of floorspace built in non-BART freeway corridors. Near several suburban stations, the most notable change has been the addition of multi-family housing. In most instances, local redevelopment authorities helped leverage these projects by providing various financial incentives and assistance with land assemblege. Statistical analyses reveal that the availability of vacant and developable land is an important predictor of whether land-use changes occurred near stations. BART, in and of itself, has clearly not been able to induce large-scale land-use changes, though under the right circumstances, it appears to have been an important contributor. If the Bay Area is to achieve the compact, multi-centered built form that was originally envisaged, we conclude that stronger public policy initiatives will be needed to channel future regional growth to BART corridors. © 1997 Elsevier Science Ltd

INTRODUCTION

America has a rich history of rail transit investments shaping the form and character of cities and regions. Classic works by Warner (1962), Vance (1964), and Fogelson (1967) chronicled how the extension of electric streetcar lines around the turn-of-the-century led to massive decentralization and the emergence of 'streetcar suburbs' in Boston, the San Francisco Bay Area, and Southern California. Many east coast U.S. cities today stand as testaments to rail transit's city-shaping abilities.

The Bay Area Rapid Transit (BART) system was planned to very much continue this American tradition. BART's planners hoped a modern era rail system would guide future population and employment growth in the region. By providing one of the largest incremental additions to regional accessibility in the post-WWII era, BART was expected to strengthen the Bay Area's urban centers while guiding suburban growth along radial corridors, leading to a star-shaped, multi-centered metropolitan form. The entire BART project was premised on the basis that it would eventually lead to minicommunities mushrooming around suburban rail stations (Johnston and Tracy, 1983). A 1956 planning document, *Regional Rapid Transit*, contained the first regional land-use plan ever prepared for the Bay Area. The plan called for the Bay Area to become a 'subcentered metropolis' — "something between the tightly nucleated clusters which form the typical metropolitan areas of the East Coast and the vast low-density sprawl of the West Coast's Los Angeles" (Parsons, Brinckerhoff, Hall and MacDonald, Inc., 1956, p. 10). Merewitz (1972) maintains that a tacit reason for building BART was to differentiate the region from its freeway-oriented sibling to the south, Los Angeles. Proponents felt that BART would help catapult San Francisco into the position of 'Manhattan of the West'. A 1962 alternatives analysis report often and ominously referred to the likely consequences of not building BART:"The outward thrust of our urban area is characterized by scatter and dispersion of land development activities throughout the peripheries...(and) this uncoordinated process of land development imposes added costs on the home owner which could be avoided if land development were orderly and compact" (Parsons, Brinckerhoff, Tudor and Bechtel, Inc., 1962, p. 83).

In view of these expectations, the original BART impact studies placed a strong emphasis on gauging the land use impacts of BART. These studies, carried out in the mid-1970s only a few years after the 1973 opening of the 72-mile BART system, concluded that BART had a modest, though not inconsequential, influence on land uses and urban development in the Bay Area, both directly by improving accessibility and indirectly by inducing various policies supportive of compact development, such as incentive zoning and redevelopment financing. BART did not create new growth, but rather acted to redistribute growth that would have taken place even without a rail investment. The initial study also found that BART's primary land use impacts occurred at the local rather than regional level. BART, for instance, was credited with focusing much of San Francisco's downtown office construction south of Market Street and rejuvenating inner-city Oakland (Dyett *et al.*, 1979). BART, however, was only part of the reason. A redevelopment authority was formed at the same time BART was built to encourage development in the south of Market (SoMa) area. New zoning significantly increased allowable floor area ratios within 700 ft of stations and provided density bonuses for buildings adjacent to downtown stations. A $15 million beautification program, complete with new street furniture and landscaping and funded through tax increment financing, helped lure new development to the Market Street corridor. In downtown Oakland and at the Lake Merritt station, significant public efforts to assemble land and site new public buildings around BART stations were critical to redeveloping these areas. Without these public initiatives, far less development would have occurred.

Outside of downtown, the original study found BART's land-use influences to be fairly modest, save for several East Bay station areas. Local opposition to growth, downzoning, and freeway medians suppressed station-area development outside of downtown. BART largely failed to attract high-density housing around stations. Webber (1976) argued that BART's poor land-use performance outside of downtowns was mainly because it was only marginally faster than buses and was markedly slower than its chief competitor, the private automobile. Critics argued that fixed guideway rail was the wrong technology for the Bay Area given the rapid growth in automobile and home ownership, and freeway building, during postwar years. Noted sociologist Homer Hoyt (1939) observed over half a century ago that urban form is largely a product of the dominant transportation technology during a city's prevailing period of growth. The Bay Area grew most rapidly during the 1950s and 60s, a period of massive freeway construction and the automobile's ascendency. BART, critics charged, was too little, too late.

The original BART impact study concluded that BART affected land uses only where supportive conditions — such as incentive zoning, local citizen backing, and a buoyant local economy — were present. In the absence of these factors, BART was found to have little influence on where growth occurred and in what form (Knight and Trygg, 1977). Because BART's board did not have the authority or entrepreneurial leanings to assemble extra land and leverage private real estate investments (unlike in Toronto and other cities abroad), it could not exploit the development potential it had created.

While the original BART Impact Study found few instances of significant land-use changes, it did suggest that "BART's impacts on the Bay Area land uses may become more widespread in the future" (Metropolitan Transportation Commission, 1979, p. 25). A criticism of the original impact studies was that they were premature — it was perhaps unrealistic to expect any significant and measurable land use changes over the short 3–5 yr time span in which post-BART evaluations were carried out. Large-scale land use changes often occur slowly, in fits and starts. While transportation investments always have some degree of short-term impacts on travel behavior, only over the long run do demonstrable changes in urban form take place.

This article summarizes findings on the land-use and development impacts of BART over the past twenty years as part of the larger BART@ 20 update study*. It examines historical changes in residential and non-residential (e.g. commercial, industrial) development for a sample of stations on the BART system (see Fig. 1). Differences in land-use changes around BART stations and

---

*The interested reader is referred to Cervero (1995a) and Landis *et al.* (1995) for more details on the methods and findings of these studies.

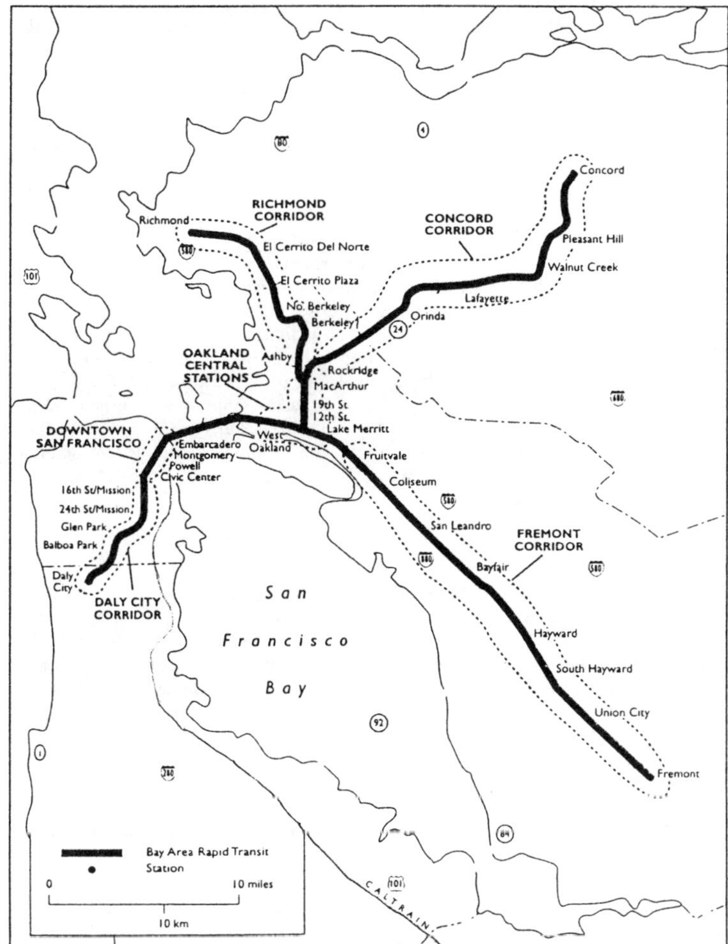

Fig. 1. BART stations and corridors.

matched pairs of nearby freeway interchanges are compared. Models are also presented that identify factors associated with station-area land-use changes. The article concludes with a discussion of the research finding's policy implications.

We should note that, like all other studies to date, our work does not, nor did it attempt to, disentangle the influences of market forces (e.g. improvements in accessibility) from planning interventions (e.g. incentive zoning) in inducing recorded land-use changes — a far richer, more comprehensive, and more dynamic data base would have been required than we, or anyone else to date, had available. We, like others, have been forced to draw inferences by looking at a handful of time slices using less-than-complete data, thus the results of our work should be interpreted accordingly. The conventional wisdom (e.g. Knight and Trygg, 1977; Cervero, 1984) holds that both market and institutional forces work together, in a complementary and mutually reinforcing way, to shape transit-land use outcomes. Our research provides 'snapshots' that, we believe, lend credence to this proposition. However, the purpose of our work was less on proving such propositions and more on probing the degree to which the original land-use objectives of BART have been attained as well as providing a more intermediate to longer term perspective into the land-use impacts of a modern regional rail transit investment, in one particular metropolitan area, during the past quarter century of high auto-freeway accessibility. Nevertheless, through a balance of statistical comparisons and qualitative case reviews (involving informant interviews), we believe plausible inferences can be drawn on the association between BART's presence and land-use changes over the past 20 years.

Another necessary caveat pertains to the scales of analyses. We start with simple comparisons of rates of population and employment changes for 'superdistricts' (amalgams of census tracts) to obtain 'first-cut' insights into BART's association with subregional land-use changes. Since research shows suburban BART stations draw commuters from an average catchment area of 6 miles in radius (Cervero, 1995b), suburban superdistricts, which also average a radius of around 6 miles, generally reflect the spatial extent of access trips to suburban BART stations. Superdistrict comparisons are followed by more disaggregate-scale analyses using census tracts, zipcodes, and hectare grid cells. Thus, this paper starts out with fairly coarse data, and proceeds to a more refined, disaggregate scale of analysis. By triangulating the research design to probe multiple dimensions of BART's relationship to land-use changes, to examine relationships at different geographic scales, and to embellish statistical inquiries with narrative case summaries, this paper attempts to uncover patterns of consistent and reinforcing findings, as well as provide broad perspectives into the link between BART and land-use changes over the past two decades.

POPULATION AND EMPLOYMENT CHANGES IN BART AND NON-BART AREAS

Population changes

Since BART's 1973 opening, population has grown relatively faster away from BART than near BART. To provide some order-of-magnitude insights, we began by looking at differences in growth within subareas, or 'superdistricts'*, that contain BART stations vs those that do not. Over the 1970–90 period, population grew 35.2% in the 25 Bay Area superdistricts not served by BART compared to 17.1% in the 9 BART-served superdistricts, shown in Fig. 2 by the shaded areas. Breaking data down by counties reveals that population grew three to five times faster, in percentage terms, in the suburban and exurban parts of Alameda and Contra Costa counties with no BART services than in the BART-served portions (Table 1). Only in San Francisco was the pattern different — population grew in the BART-served part of the city while the western half of the city lost some 4000 residents. It should be noted that percentage changes mask the fact that BART superdistricts attracted over 140,000 more residents from 1970 to 1990 than did non-BART superdistricts.

Table 1. Comparison of 1970/80/90 population growth in BART-served and non-BART superdistricts, by three counties

County				Absolute change			% change		
Super-district	1970	1980	1990	1970–80	1980–90	1970–90	1970–80	1980–90	1970–90
San Francisco									
BART	387,180	368,137	402,538	−19,043	34,401	15,358	−5.0	9.4	4.0
Non-BART	325,729	310,837	321,421	−14,892	10,584	−4308	−4.6	3.4	−1.3
Alameda									
BART	990,497	1,000,973	1,143,347	10,476	142,374	152,850	1.1	14.2	15.4
Non-BART	77,637	104,406	135,835	26,769	31,429	58,198	34.5	30.1	75.0
Contra Costa									
BART	410,288	484,763	547,470	74,475	62,707	137,180	18.2	12.9	33.4
Non-BART	146,301	171,617	256,259	25,316	84,642	109,958	17.3	49.3	75.2
Three-county total									
BART	1,787,965	1,853,873	2,093,355	65,908	239,482	305,390	3.7	12.9	17.1
Non-BART	549,667	586,860	713,515	37,193	126,655	163,848	6.8	21.6	29.8

*Superdistricts represent aggregations of census tracts, defined by the Metropolitan Transportation Commission (the region's regional transportation planning authority) to examine travel patterns at the subregional level (Purvis, 1994). Giuliano (1996), in her comprehensive review of transportation and land-use relationships, similarly relies on superdistrict comparisons in probing BART's influences on urban form.

Fig. 2. Nine county Bay Area superdistricts, including BART-served superdistricts.

At a corridor-specific level, non-BART areas also grew relatively faster. Along Interstate-680 from Concord to Pleasanton, a stretch that experienced explosive growth during the 1970-90 period, population along the non-BART-served southern section of Interstate-680 grew twice as fast as along the BART-served northern section — 61.9 vs 30.1% for subareas of comparable size. Moreover, population along the southern flank of Interstate-880 that is unserved by BART (Milipitas) grew more than seven times faster than did population in BART-served sections (Hayward-Fremont).

Employment changes

Relative employment gains in non-BART superdistricts were even greater than population gains. During the 1970–90 period, employment grew 84.5% in the non-BART (mostly outlying) superdistricts compared to 38.9% in the BART-served ones, mirroring the trend of job decentralization that occurred throughout the U.S. Table 2 shows that, at the county level, employment grew seven times faster in non-BART portions of Alameda County (e.g. such as Pleasanton, where many back-office jobs located in large-scale office parks). Still, 153,000 more jobs were created in BART-served superdistricts of Alameda and Contra Costa counties than non-BART superdistricts. At the corridor level, employment grew more than twice as fast from 1970 to 1990 in the 'BART-less' San Ramon–Pleasanton–Livermore triangle than the BART-served northern I-680

Table 2. Comparison of 1970/80/90 employment growth in BART-served and non-BART superdistricts, by three counties

County: Super-district	1970	1980	1990	Absolute change			% change		
				1970–80	1980–90	1970–90	1970–80	1980–90	1970–90
San Francisco									
BART	357,761	409,940	442,370	52,179	32,430	84,609	14.6	7.9	23.6
Non-BART	94,436	98,703	113,037	4267	14,334	18,601	4.5	14.5	19.7
Alameda									
BART	393,755	461,198	532,872	67,443	71,674	139,117	17.1	15.5	35.3
Non-BART	19,908	36,332	71,817	16,424	35,485	51,909	82.5	97.7	260.7
Contra Costa									
BART	120,406	173,366	236,174	52,960	162,808	119,768	44.0	36.2	96.1
Non-BART	27,817	39,732	77,390	11,915	37,658	49,573	42.8	94.8	178.2
Three-county total									
BART	871,922	1,044,504	1,211,416	172,582	166,912	339,494	19.8	16.0	38.9
Non-BART	142,161	174,767	262,244	32,606	87,477	120,083	22.9	50.0	84.5

corridor (Walnut Creek–Pleasant Hill–Concord) — 347.9 vs 141.1%, although in absolute terms it gained 13,000 fewer jobs.

A second analysis of employment growth was carried out using the U.S. Department of Commerce's *County Business Patterns* data disaggregated at the zipcode level for the 1981–90 period*. Shift-share analysis was used to measure employment growth differentials between the 35 zipcodes with BART stations and the remaining 117 zipcodes without BART stations in the three BART-served counties (Alameda, Contra Costa, and San Francisco). The BART zipcodes gained 139,400 jobs from 1981 to 1990, growing by 30.3% and accounting for 57.1% of the employment growth in the three counties. Employment in the non-BART zipcodes increased by 110,300, or 19%. Almost all of the BART-related employment growth, however, occurred in downtown San Francisco; jobs in the East Bay's zipcodes, by comparison, increased just 1.1%. Among employment sectors, Finance–Insurance–Real Estate (FIRE) experienced the greatest absolute job growth and the fastest job growth rate (+ 108.2%) in the BART zipcodes, followed by non-business services (+ 52.9%), and business services (+ 46.2%).

Using data from Part II of the 1990 Census Transportation Planning Package (CTPP), we were further able to examine employment differentials by occupation. These data reveal that businesses near BART hire high shares of executive, professional, and technical workers (consistent with the finding that BART's primary locational influence was in the FIRE and consumer services sectors). Along the Fremont–Richmond corridors, census tracts with BART stations were found to consistently average around 15–20 percentage points more of professional and technical workers than do businesses in census tracts in the parallel Interstate-80 and Interstate-880 corridors. These findings suggest businesses and occupations that benefit from the face-to-face contact and access to specialized labor provided by urban agglomerations have been attracted to BART station areas, consistent with urban economic theory.

Overall, job growth has been consistently higher around BART stations than elsewhere in the region, though this was mainly attributable to gains in downtown San Francisco. In the East Bay, job growth has generally been faster away from BART, especially along the I-680 corridor. In the context of both national and regional trends toward office decentralization, these findings suggest that BART might have played a role in slowing the exodus of jobs from downtown San Francisco. This inference is supported by a 1980–1990 comparison of the CBD's share of regional regional employment in the Bay Area vs California's other megametropolis, greater Los Angeles, which had no urban rail system in 1990. From 1980 to 1990, the share of regional jobs in San Francisco's CBD fell from 17.4 to 16.3%, a 1.1 percentage point drop (Cervero and Wu, 1996). Over the same period, the share of Southern California jobs[†] fell from 7.6 to 5.7%, a 1.9 percentage point decline (Gordon and Richardson, 1996). However, since Los Angeles' percentage base was much lower, the relative loss of regional employment in downtown Los Angeles has been much more substantial. To the degree that maintaining a dominant, primary commercial and employment center has

---

*Data from *County Business Patterns* are reported only at the zipcode level. Zipcodes represent a geographic scale that falls roughly in between superdistricts and census tracts.

[†]Measured for the five counties of Los Angeles, Orange, San Bernadino, Riverside, and Ventura.

increased economic productivity in the region (e.g. accruing from agglomeration economies), BART has likely produced real, though immeasurable, economic benefits.

Urban densities

BART's presence is spatially correlated with population and employment densities. In 1990, over 85% of Bay Area census tracts with population densities above 7.5 persons per acre contained a BART station or some segment of a BART line. Figure 3 shows that BART's alignment was also highly correlated with 1980 and 1990 employment densities, and that the employment density gradient steepened during the 1980s in downtown San Francisco as well as several East Bay nodes served by BART. The map also shows, however, that outside of downtown San Francisco, significantly more regional employment growth occurred away from BART (especially in the Silicon Valley in the South Bay) than close to BART. Over the postwar era, the Bay Area has transformed from a predominantly single-centered metropolis to one with multiple, hierarchical

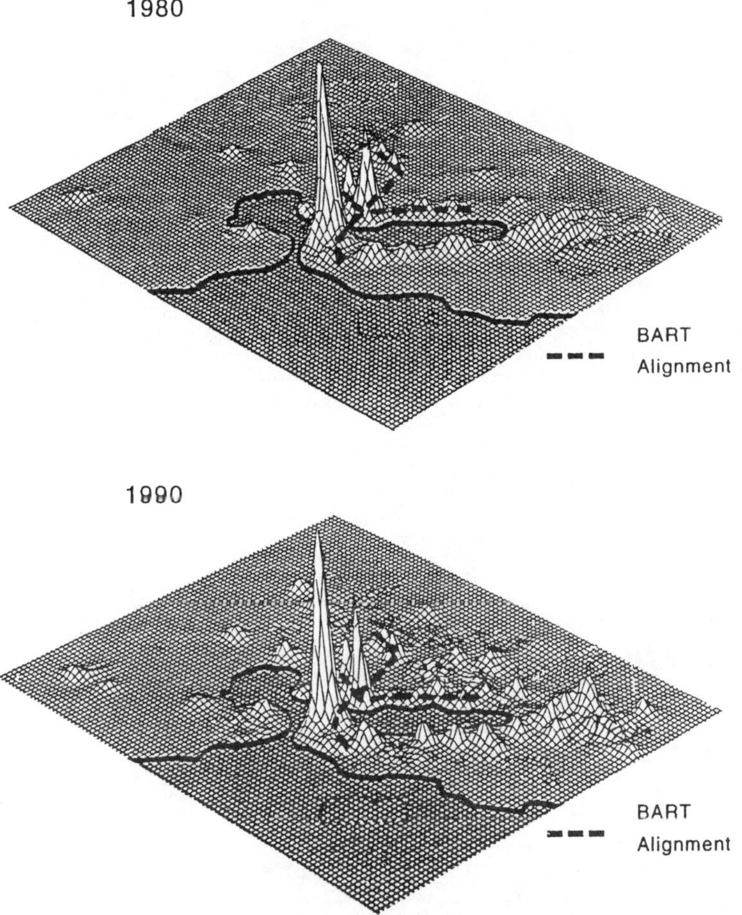

Fig. 3. Three-dimensional maps of employment densities and BART alignment for the San Francisco Bay Area, 1980 and 1990. Adapted from Wu (1994).

centers, many strongly oriented to BART. While measuring BART's precise role in bringing about this built form is difficult, based on employment growth differentials we believe its role has been significant.

Using census data on employment by place of work (i.e. the 1980 Urban Transportation Planning Package and the 1990 CTPP), we computed net employment densities (workers per net commercial–industrial–institutional acre) for 1980 and 1990 for stations on the Richmond–Fremont corridor. Figure 4 plots the employment density gradient from the downtown Berkeley station southward to the Fremont terminal station. Densities rose slightly over the 1980–90 period around all stations except Lake Merritt, a station surrounded by predominantly governmental offices, institutional uses, and light manufacturing. The loss of manufacturing jobs in the area largely accounted for Lake Merritt's density decline.

Overall, there has been a slight trend toward employment densification on BART's Richmond–Fremont corridor. Though not shown here, employment also tended to be more densely concentrated around BART stations than around nearby freeway interchanges. Commercial-office floor area ratios have also generally increased along all BART corridors, notably in downtown San Francisco and the outer segments of the Concord line. Collectively, these trend statistics reinforce the inference that BART has functioned, to some degree, as a growth magnet, helping to organize office employment growth into nodes, a topic which we probe in more detail later in the paper.

LAND-USE TRENDS

This section summarizes the findings of vintage models constructed for land-use changes around 25 of the 34 BART stations — all of the downtown stations, all of the fast-growing stations, and a sample of the remaining stations. The primary data input was the TRW-REDI data base which provides on-line digitized property tax records (square footage, lot area, year of construction) for privately owned parcels within local taxing jurisdictions. From these data, we tracked the accumulation of total square footage of residential and non-residential development within a quarter-mile ring of downtown stations and half-mile ring of other stations. This was done by maintaining a running account of the square footage added to each station area each year, based on the recorded year of construction. Overall, complete records were available for 88.7% of residential parcels (27,879 in all) and 59.9% of non-residential parcels (5412 in all). From field checks, we found buildings on most of the parcels without recorded construction dates were fairly old, consistently predating BART. The omission of these cases, we believe, did not seriously bias the estimates of square footage added since BART opened. Moreover, the most complete records were for the largest and fastest growing station areas — e.g. complete records were available for 100% of residential parcels and 95.8% of parcels with non-residential buildings within a quarter mile of the four downtown San Francisco BART stations.

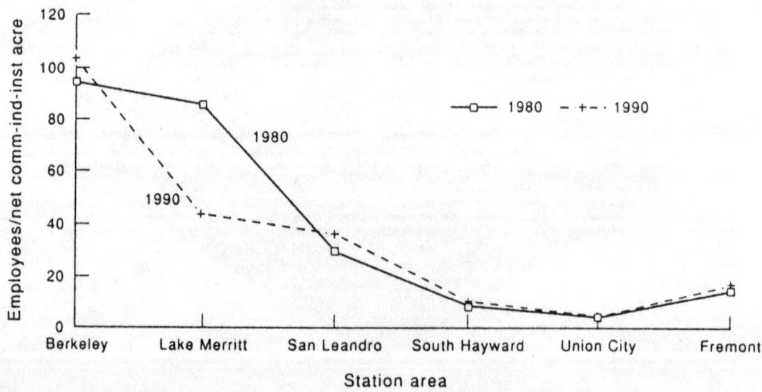

Fig. 4. Changes in net employment densities along the Berkeley–Fremont BART axis, 1980–1990.

Figure 5 presents trend lines of building area for all parcels within the rings of the 25 stations studied. Data are shown for the pre-BART (1965–1973), early-BART (1973–1979), and recent-BART (1979–93) periods. Among the parcels studied, non-residential uses (commercial, office, industrial) accounted for most station-area development; they increased from around 45 million ft^2 to nearly 100 million ft^2 from 1965 to 1993. Commercial and office development grew fastest during the pre- and later- BART eras. Among residential development, multi-family housing grew most rapidly in the vicinity of BART stations. Single-family home construction, by comparison, was fairly stagnant.

Among the 33,291 privately owned station-area parcels studied, the distributions of land uses, in terms of building square footage, for 1965, 1973, and 1993 are shown in Fig. 6. Most prominent has been the growth in office space — from 27.9% of all station-area square footage in 1965 to 45.4% in 1993. While multi-family housing in station areas increased by nearly 8 million ft^2 from 1965 to 1993 (as shown in Fig. 5), its share of total building space fell from 22.6 to 17.9%. Shares

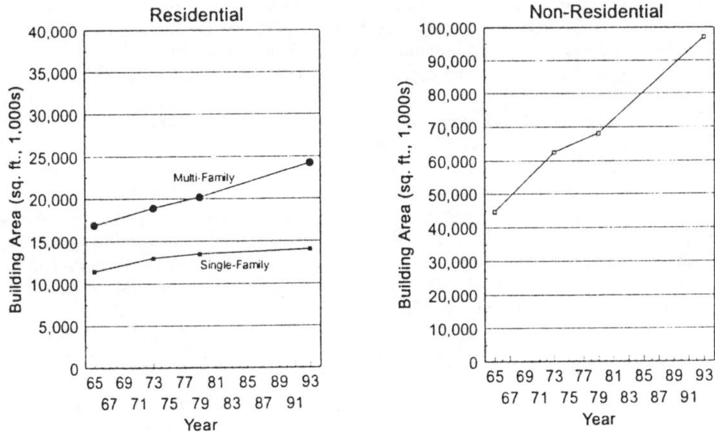

Fig. 5 Changes in residential and nonresidential building floorspace around 24 BART station areas, 1965-1993.

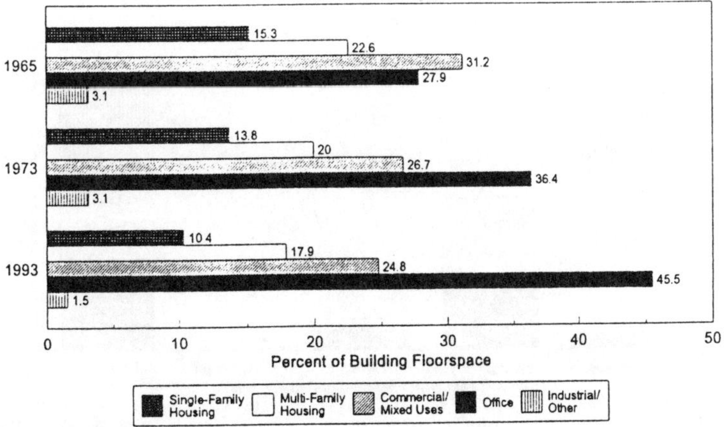

Fig. 6. Land use composition around 25 BART stations, 1965, 1979, and 1993.

of other land uses also fell. Around the four downtown San Francisco stations (Embarcadero, Montgomery, Powell, and Civic Center), the share of building space devoted to offices increased 32.4% in 1965, to 40.6% in 1973, and to 49.8% in 1993.

A more complete source for tracking office growth is the *Black's Guide to Office Leasing* (McGraw-Hill, 1993). Prior to 1962 (the year the bond issue authorizing the construction of BART was approved), around 9 million ft^2 of office space was within a quarter mile of the four downtown San Francisco stations (Fig. 7). During the 12 years of BART construction, from 1963 to 1974, the city of San Francisco's office inventory expanded by 16 million ft^2, and more than two-thirds of this new space was within a quarter-mile of downtown stations. During the next 18 years, between 1975 and 1992, another 40 million ft^2 of office space was built in San Francisco, and nearly three-quarters of this was in the immediate station areas. Figure 8 shows most of the major new building additions from 1977 to 1994 were within 1–2 blocks of the Embarcadero and Montgomery Street stations in the heart of downtown San Francisco.

In contrast to San Francisco, BART's influence on office development in the East Bay appears to have been been weak (Fig. 9). The major changes have been in downtown Oakland, where around 4.6 million ft^2 of office space was added between 1975 and 1992; a significant share of this was for public buildings. The largest amount of office development in the suburbs has been around the Walnut Creek station, which added nearly 3 million ft^2 of office space since 1975. However, this amount pales in comparison to over 50 million ft^2 of office space built in Alameda and Contra Costa Counties away from BART from 1975–1992, much of it in the form office parks and stand-alone spec-buildings sited near freeway interchanges. Nearly 22 million ft^2 of the office additions from 1975 to 1992 occurred along the southern Interstate-680 corridor, home to the 875-acre Hacienda Business Park in Pleasanton and the 585-acre Bishop Ranch Business Park in San Ramon. All of this 22 million ft^2 of office additions was within a half mile of an I-680 interchange; this compares to just 10 million ft^2 of East Bay office space that was added within a half mile of BART stations. Overall, of the 60 million ft^2 of office inventory added to Alameda and Contra Costa Counties from 1975 to 1992, 37% was within a half mile of Interstate-680 interchanges compared to 17% within a half-mile of BART stations.

RAIL MODAL SPLITS FOR OFFICE DEVELOPMENT NEAR BART

The vintage models presented in the previous section suggested that BART functioned as a stronger magnet of office development in downtown San Francisco than in the East Bay's suburbs,

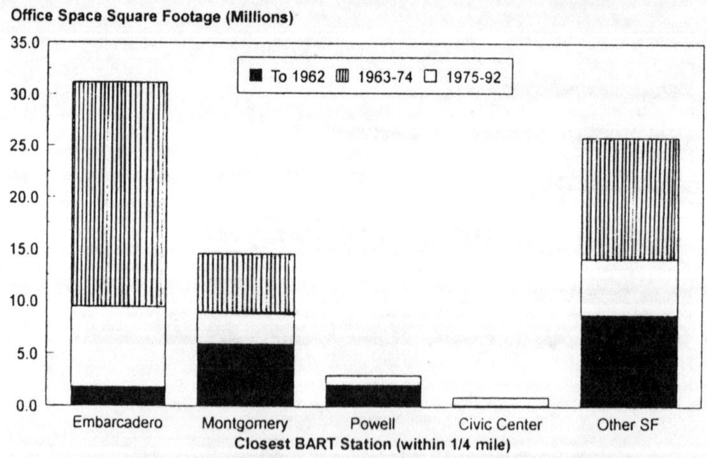

Fig. 7. San Francisco office space construction by period: prior to 1963, 1963–1974, and 1975–1992.

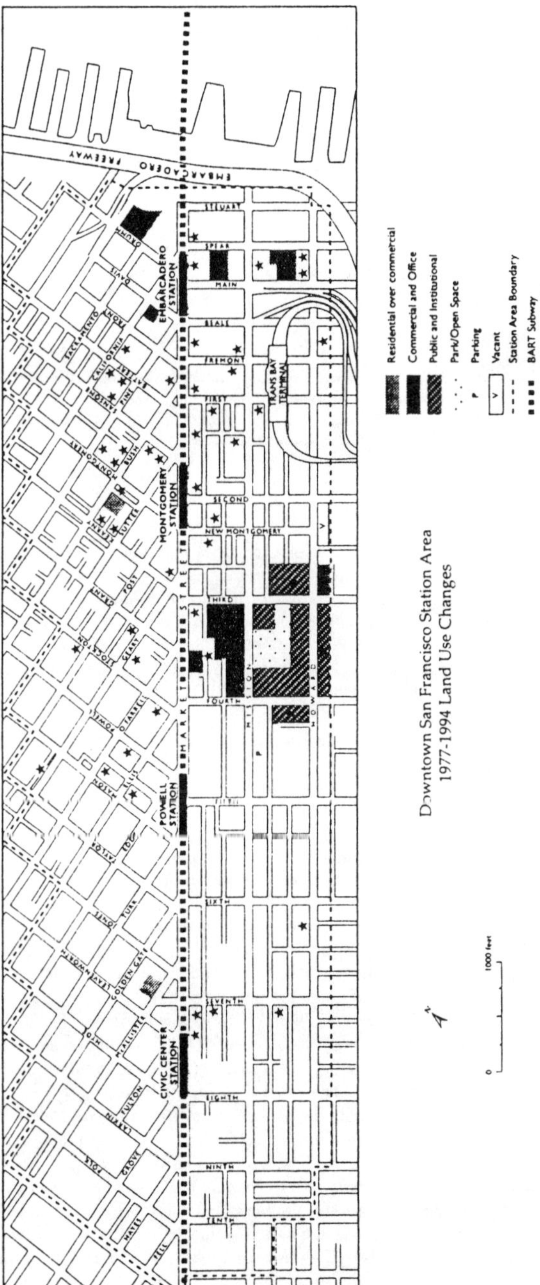

Fig. 8. Downtown San Francisco station-area land use changes, 1977–1994.

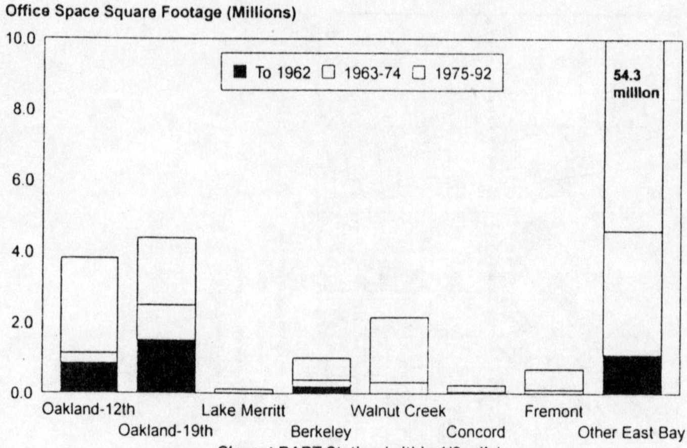

Fig. 9. East Bay office space construction by period: prior to 1963, 1963–1974, and 1975–1992.

though without sufficient statistical controls (e.g. over changes in zoning regulations, changes in roadway access, etc.) one is hard-pressed to attribute these differences to BART. Perhaps a better indicator of BART's functional influence on station-area development are statistics on the degree to which office workers in different settings rely upon BART as a commute mode. To the degree that significantly higher shares of office workers in downtown San Francisco commute via BART than their counterparts working near East Bay stations, one can surmise that BART's functional influence on station-area office development was substantially stronger in downtown San Francisco, thus buttressing the inferences from the previous section.

Travel diary data collected from a sample of employees working in office buildings near downtown San Francisco and East Bay BART stations in February–March 1993 allowed modal split comparisons to be drawn. (For details on the survey methodology and sampling frame, see: Cervero, 1993, 1994.) Table 3 shows work-trip modal splits for workers at office buildings that lie within a quarter mile of a BART station — 1 office building each near the Montgomery and Embarcadero stations in downtown San Francisco, 1 office building each near the Berkeley and Pleasant Hill stations, and 2 office buildings near the Fremont terminal station. While the surveyed office buildings stood varying distances from BART faregates (with the ones in more outlying Fremont and Pleasant Hill situated the farthest away), all were within a quarter mile walking catchment. Research suggests a quarter mile can be traversed within 5 min at a normal pace, a walking time that is acceptable to most Americans and for which walkers are generally indifferent to precise distances (Stringham, 1982; Untermann, 1984).

Table 3 reveals nearly half of the surveyed office workers near downtown San Francisco stations commuted via BART, substantially higher than the share of BART commuters among surveyed office workers in downtown Berkeley (where few land-use changes have occurred since BART's introduction), in the relatively compact suburban node of Pleasant Hill, or in the relatively low-density Fremont station area. In an earlier analysis of these survey data, it was found that people working near BART stations were about 4 times more likely to travel to work than the typical Bay Area employee (Cervero, 1994). Moreover, a logit analysis showed that the propensity of station-area workers to commute by BART rose sharply in situations where workers: lived near BART; commuted long distances; owned one or no automobiles; and had to pay for parking at their workplace (Cervero, 1993, 1994). Overall, the substantially higher tendency for downtown San Francisco office workers to commute via BART than their East Bay counterparts arguably lends the most compelling support to the proposition that BART has had a stronger functional influence on development in downtown San Francisco than elsewhere in the region.

Table 3. Comparison of commute trip modal splits between samples of office workers near BART stations in downtown San Francisco vs the East Bay, 1993

	% of surveyed workers commuting by:		Distance of office to BART station (ft)†	No. of office workers sampled
	BART	SOV*		
San Francisco CDB BART stations				
Montgomery	47.8	15.2	490	54
Embarcadero	46.4	14.0	450	81
East Bay BART Stations				
Berkeley	17.8	48.9	110	55
Pleasant Hill	9.1	77.3	650	114
Fremont (office 1)	8.1	80.6	1300	124
Fremont (office 2)	1.8	94.5	1000	79

*Single-occupant vehicle.
†Measured as shortest sidewalk walking distance from station faregate to the office building's main entrance.
Source: Cervero (1993, 1994).

MATCHED-PAIR COMPARISON OF LAND-USE CHANGES

This section addresses the question: 'has there been relatively more development and different types of land-use changes around regional rail nodes versus nearby freeway nodes?' Since BART stations are access points to the regional rail system and interchanges are the access points to the regional freeway system, this analysis allows land-use changes around BART to be compared to those of its chief competitor, nearby freeways. At minimum, we would expect relatively more apartment and condominium construction and denser office-commercial development near BART since rail, in theory, depends on concentrations of nearby urban activities to attract riders.

A matched-pair analysis was conducted for parts of the Fremont and Richmond corridors since suitable freeway pairs were only available for this stretch. (Most of the Concord line lies in the median of a freeway, meaning freeway interchanges and BART stations are in near-identical locations; major arterials flank stations along the Daly corridor, moreover, providing few suitable freeway matches.) The chief matching criteria were that the station and freeway interchange be within 1 to 2-1/2 miles of each other and be connected by the same arterial roadway*. Invoking this basic pairing criteria produced nine suitable pairs, five on the Fremont line (San Leandro, Hayward, South Hayward, Union City, and Fremont stations and their nearby I-880 interchanges) and four on the Richmond line (Ashby, Berkeley, North Berkeley, and Richmond stations and their closest I-80 interchanges). (See Fig. 1 for these station locations.)

Figure 10 reveals little difference in the growth of single-family housing between BART stations and freeway pairs over the post-BART era. BART stations, however, outperformed their freeway counterparts in terms of multi-family housing construction, especially during the 1980s. The inventory of commercial–office–industrial floorspace increased only slightly faster around stations (Fig. 11). In absolute terms, BART stations gained 403,000 more ft^2 of single-family space, 1.58 million more ft^2 of multi-family housing, and 553,000 more ft^2 of non-residential inventory from 1973 to 1993 than their freeway counterparts.

The Fremont station, the terminus of the Fremont line, is one of the best examples of moderately dense, transit-based housing built after BART. Its nearby development also stands in contrast to the exclusively single-family housing around the nearest freeway interchange, Mowry Avenue/I-88. Figure 12 shows that considerable land-use changes occurred within a half-mile ring of the Fremont station since 1965, including over 150,000 ft^2 of retail shops, over 400,000 ft^2 of office space, and over 800 condominium and apartment units. The most prominent housing addition was the three-story, 392-unit Mission Wells apartment complex, located around one-quarter mile from the station. To encourage a transit-oriented project, the city of Fremont zoned the Mission Wells site for 30 dwelling units per acre in the first phase and 50 units per acre in the second, and reduced parking standards from 2.0 to 1.65 spaces per unit. These initiatives appear to

---

*We note that these comparisons do not control for other factors that might have accounted for land-use changes in station areas and near interchanges, like differences in zoning, in the amount of vacant and buildable land, in crime rates, and so on. If such additional controls were introduced, all potential matched-pairs would have been eliminated. Thus, the findings in this section should be interpretted in this light.

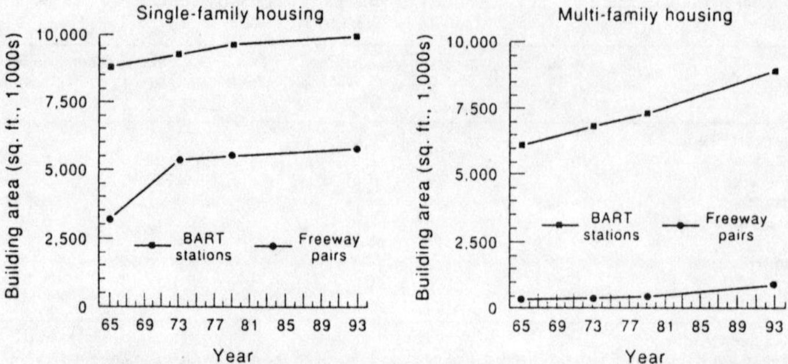

Fig. 10. Trends in residential building area for BART stations vs freeway pairs, 1965–1993.

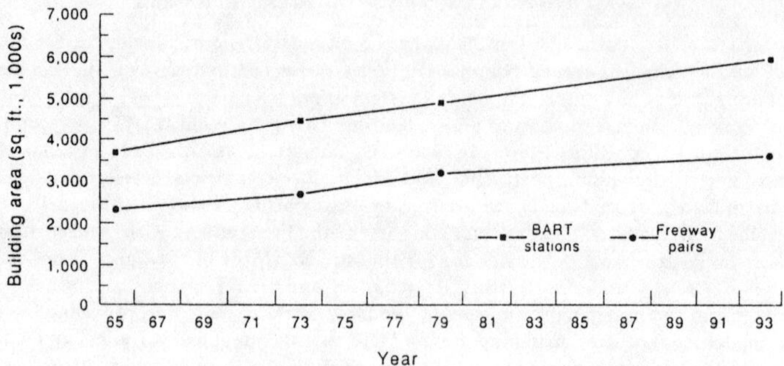

Fig. 11. Trends in non–residential building area for BART stations vs freeway pairs, 1965–1993.

be paying off financially. Mission Well's average rent per ft^2 is around 12% higher than that of comparable apartment projects in Fremont that are of similar age and have a similar amenity package, reflecting the rent premium associated with being close to rail (Bernick *et al.*, 1994). Research also shows that 17% of Mission Wells' employed tenants commute by BART, compared to just 2.4% of all Fremont employed residents in 1990 (Cervero, 1993). This lends support to the hypothesis of residential sorting (Voith, 1991) — many tenants of transit-based housing appear to choose these locations in order to economize on commuting.

Overall, there has been more land-use action around BART stations than nearby freeway nodes along the Fremont–Richmond corridor over the past 20 years, especially in terms of apartment and condominium construction. Since rail transit depends on concentrations of urban activities within reasonable walking distances of stations, these findings confirm expectations.

CORRIDOR AND AREA SUMMARIES

BART's influences on development patterns over the past 20 years have been highly uneven, certainly more so that BART's planners had envisioned. Some areas, notably downtown San Francisco and the outer portions of the Concord and Fremont lines, have witnessed significant land-use changes, while others, such as the Daly City and Richmond corridors, have experienced little new development. This section summarizes differences in land-use changes among corridors with an eye toward identifying the role of policy instruments in influencing these outcomes.

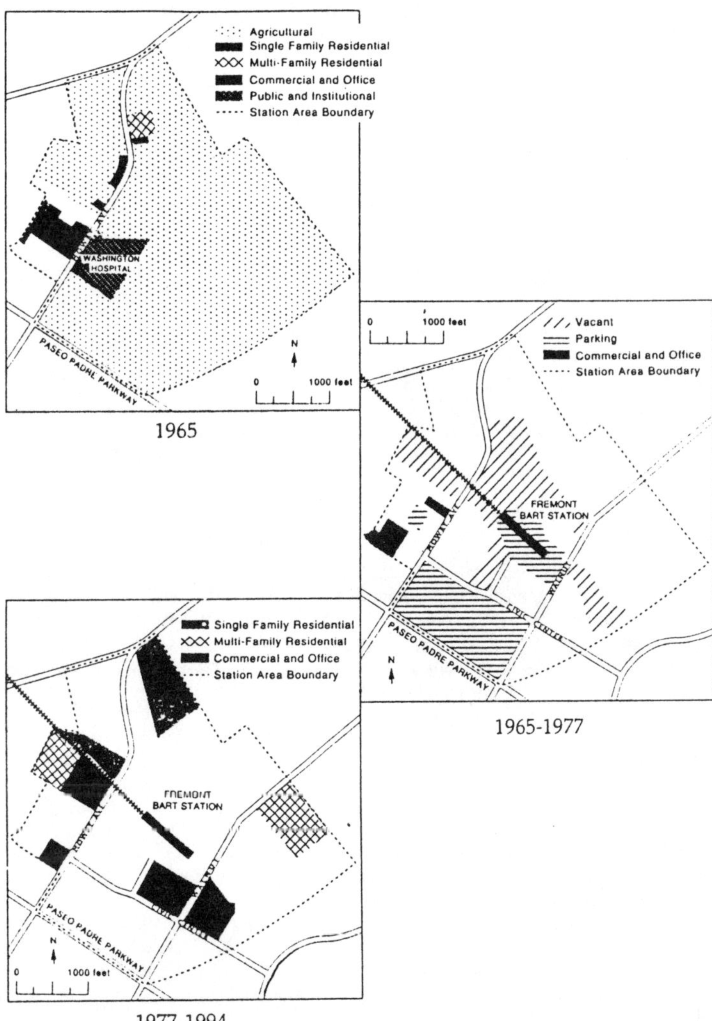

Fig. 12. Land use in Fremont station area. 1965–1994.

Downtown San Francisco

Since 1973, more than twice as much office space was added to the four downtown BART stations — Embarcadero, Montgomery, Powell, and Civic Center — than all other BART stations put together. Between 1973 and 1993, around 28 million ft^2 of office floorspace was built (Fig. 13). Net non-residential floor area ratios increased from 4.2 in 1965 to 7.0 in the early-1990s. The exact role BART played in attracting this development is unknown, however it was likely one of many factors that helped downtown San Francisco maintain its pre-eminence as the region's office and financial center over the past 20 years; other contributing factors include San Francisco's

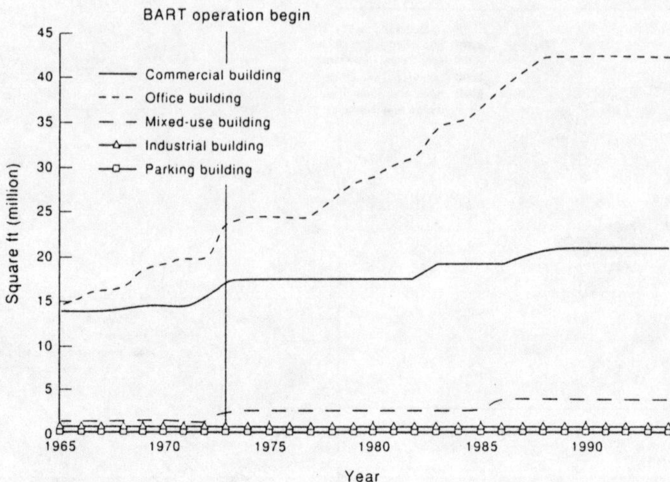

Fig. 13. Vintage model plot of changes in non-residential building area near downtown San Francisco BART stations.

emergence as an international financial center, agglomeration and urbanization economies, cultural attractions, and supportive public policies (e.g. tax increment financing, density bonuses). Regardless, it is unlikely that the 28 million ft^2 of office space built since BART's 1973 opening could have been accommodated without a regional rail network. Because the San Francisco–Oakland Bay Bridge is filled to capacity during rush hours, the estimated 80,000 jobs added to downtown San Francisco since 1970 could not have been accommodated without the high-capacity access provided by BART*. According to the 1990 journey-to-work census (CTPP — Part II), 46% of workers with jobs in census tracts surrounding the Embarcadero and Montgomery Street stations commuted by rail transit. If three-quarters of the new workers added to downtown San Francisco who currently ride BART drove instead, this would have added over 28,000 automobiles to the already saturated bridges and highways leading into downtown San Francisco. During rush hours, these facilities would struggle to accommodate even a fraction of this additional traffic. More likely, nowhere near the amount of employment growth that took place would have been possible without BART. Of course, the dynamics of workplace–residential locations are complex and the absence of BART would no doubt have induced other regional shifts, such as deflecting more residential locations to the north Bay (e.g. Marin County) and peninsula (e.g., San Mateo County) as well as modal adjustments (e.g. expansion of express bus services). While BART might not have been the decisive factor influencing downtown office and retail construction over the past 20 years, BART's presence was likely a vital and necessary pre-condition for much of the growth that did occur.

Daly City corridor

To date, the Daly City corridor, from Mission 16th Street to the Daly City terminus, has been largely unaffected by BART's presence. From 1973 to 1993, the square footage of non-residential floorspace within one-half mile of the corridor's stations rose merely 0.8%. The absence of significant land-use impacts along this corridor is attributable to two main factors: one, the BART line was sited in a fairly mature, built-out area with relatively little vacant land and little development potential; and two, neighborhood opposition to densification led to downzoning in the Mission District and around the Glen Park and Balboa Park stations.

---

*These job additions are for the four census tracts encompassing the Market Street corridor, an area which is roughly three times the size of the quarter-mile catchment zone used in this analysis.

Downtown Oakland

Downtown Oakland has experienced a healthy expansion of office and commercial space since the opening of BART, though much less than in downtown San Francisco and the outer Concord line. New office towers did not spring up in BART's early years, but rather a good decade or more after 1973 when services began. Figure 14 shows the land-use changes that occurred in downtown Oakland from 1977 to 1993; considerable commercial development occurred immediately adjacent to the 12th Street station. The centerpiece has been the Oakland City Center, a mixed retail-office

Downtown Oakland Station Area
1977-1994 Land Use Changes

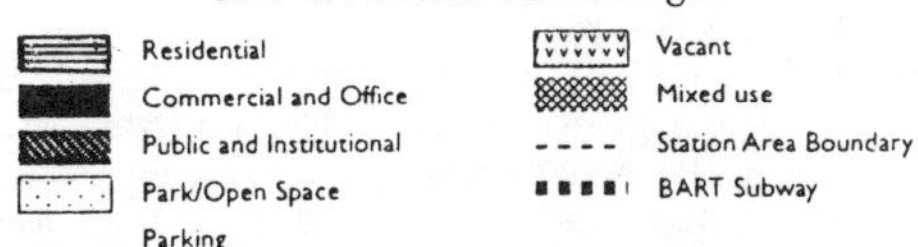

Fig. 14. Land use changes in downtown Oakland, 1977-1994.

complex that is architecturally integrated with the station and has received several design awards (including the coveted Urban Land Institute's Design Excellence award).

By far, downtown Oakland has attracted more institutional and public-sector office development, 1.6 million ft^2 in all (or 29% of the downtown total), over the past 20 years than any other area served by BART. Government agencies have been drawn by Oakland's attractive rents, pro-development policies, and good transportation services. Unlike downtown San Francisco, where the bulk of commercial-office development was market-driven, in Oakland the city redevelopment authority played a vital role in orchestrating new development. The city leveraged much of the private and public office construction through a combination of assistance with land assemblage, tax increment financing of public infrastructure, securing federal urban renewal grants, subordination of loans, and equity participation (including majority ownership of a downtown convention hotel). During informant interviews, professional staff with Oakland's redevelopment office strongly believed that siting public buildings near BART helped to leverage private office development by creating agglomeration and urbanization economies that could sustain more downtown services and ancilliary business-related functions.

Fremont corridor

The Fremont corridor, an elevated stretch from Fruitvale to Fremont, experienced the fastest growth in multi-family housing development during the post-BART era, accounting for one-third of all apartments and condominiums built within a half mile of the BART system. Residential development has been uneven, however. Virtually no housing additions have come on line around the Coliseum, Fruitvale, and Hayward stations, though in the case of the latter two stations, plans to transform nearby areas into transit villages aim to reverse this (Knack, 1995). In contrast, since 1965, 96% of the current 1180 multi-family units near Union City BART and 99% of the 940 units near Fremont BART have been built. Surveys show that between 20 and 30% of employed tenants living in apartment complexes near the Union City station ride BART to work, considerably above the citywide average of 6% of employed-residents who commute by rail (Cervero, 1993). With the exception of the Fremont station, public policies, outside of normal zoning practices, have played little role in shaping development patterns along the Fremont corridor. Rather, most land-use changes appear to have been market-driven.

Concord line

The Concord line has received among the least and the most commercial-office development within a half-mile ring of stations. In the affluent communities of Rockridge, Orinda, and Lafayette, stiff neighborhood opposition to proposed apartment and commercial development near rail, followed by building moratoria and downzoning, all but eliminated any possibility of large-scale development along the inner Concord line. In contrast the pro-development attitude of local officials, coupled with community acquiescence, have produced fairly dense suburban centers at the three outermost stations — Walnut Creek, Pleasant Hill, and Concord. The fact that the three innermost stations lie in a freeway median while the three outermost ones do not might have also had some bearing on land-use outcomes.

Walnut Creek has emerged as one of the Bay Area's premier edge cities. Nearly 4 million ft^2 of modern, class-A office space has been built within a half-mile ring of the station since BART opened, more than any non-downtown station (Fig. 15). While this development would likely have occurred in the suburbs without BART, it more than likely would have been freeway-oriented, in the form of executive parks and stand-alone structures. Walnut Creek's office boom leveled off in the late 1980s, partly due to a community backlash against escalating traffic congestion (which led to the passage of a growth moratorium in the mid-1980s) as well as an oversupply of local office inventory.

The Pleasant Hill BART station area is one of the best example of suburban transit-oriented development in the U.S. Between 1988 and 1993, over 1800 housing units and 1.5 million ft^2 of prime office space was built within a quarter mile of the Pleasant Hill station. This development occurred despite the fact that during BART's first twenty years, the Pleasant Hill station was surrounded by BART's largest parking lot (3245 spaces) and lies in an unincorporated part of Contra Costa County, which in many situations might have suppressed land development. Although average densities of nearby apartments are around 30–45 dwelling units per gross acre,

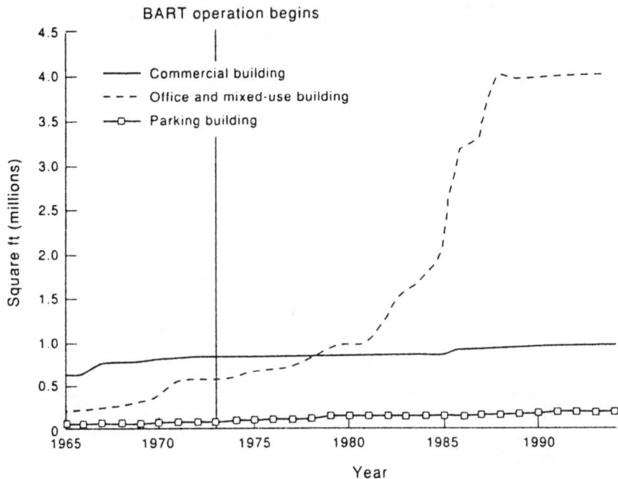

Fig. 15. Vintage model plot of changes in non-residential building area in Walnut Creek Station area, 1965–1993.

very high by suburban standards, they nonetheless cater to a fairly upscale market, with most featuring swimming pools, spas, and recreational facilities. Half of occupants in the Park Regency complex (892 units at 70 units per acre) earn over $40,000 annually, well above the regional average (Cervero and Menotti, 1994). An estimated one-half of employed-residents living near the Pleasant Hill station work in downtown San Francisco or Oakland, compared to a citywide average of just 10%. Many take BART to work — surveys show 36 to 55% commute via BART, compared to 16% of all Pleasant Hill employed-residents (Cervero, 1993). The strong demand for apartments has also produced a rent premium — two-bedroom/two-bathroom apartments near the station leased for around $1.09 per ft^2 in 1994 compared to around $0.94 per ft^2 for comparable units (in terms of size, age, and amenities) within the city that lie away from BART (Bernick *et al.*, 1994).

Pleasant Hill's success in attracting housing and office development can be credited to three key factors: one, the creation of a specific plan in the early 1980s that served as a blueprint for guiding growth near the rail station over the ensuing 15 years; second, the existence of a proactive redevelopment authority whose staff aggressively sought to implement the plan by assembling irregular parcels into developable tracts, seeking out private co-ventures, and investing in public infrastructure; and third, having a local elected official who became the project's 'political champion', working tirelessly and participating in numerous public hearings to shephard the project through to implementation (Cervero *et al.*, 1993).

Relative to the Walnut Creek and Pleasant Hill stations, the Concord station was a late bloomer in attracting office development. Commercial-office floorspace remained fairly constant at around 0.5 million ft^2 until 1985; over the next three years, inventory increased fourfold. As in Pleasant Hill, the local redevelopment agency spearheaded much of the station-area development in Concord by helping with land assemblage and financing complementary public infrastructure improvements.

As noted earlier, much of the Interstate-680 corridor without BART services also experienced an office building boom during the 1980s. This suggests that the outer Concord line's surge in office development was part of a much larger dynamic of employment decentralization. Corporate relocations from San Francisco have been a major contributor to the I-680 corridor's growth (Sedway and Associates, 1993). Without BART, however, it is unlikely that office development in Walnut Creek, Pleasant Hill, and Concord would have been nearly as concentrated. Office densities around the three BART stations are around 0.80–0.90 F.A.R., considerably above the 0.10–0.15 F.A.R. found at large-scale office parks nearly I-680, like Bishop Ranch and Hacienda, that are unserved by BART. Surveys show relatively higher shares of workers with jobs near the Pleasant Hill station commute by transit — 12% (10.4% by rail) vs only 1.6% (all by bus) of workers at Hacienda Business Park (Cervero, 1993; City of Pleasanton, 1993). Thus, while it is unlikely BART had much influence on the number of jobs that ended up along the Walnut Creek-to-Concord axis, it appears to have had a strong influence on the built form that the development took — namely, concentrated, mixed-use development.

Richmond corridor

Among all suburban East Bay BART corridors, the Richmond line has witnessed the fewest land-use changes. The one notable exception is the El Cerrito del Norte Station, which in the past few years has attracted a large mixed apartment-retail project and several large retailers nearby. Elsewhere, the real estate market has been flat. Community opposition to apartment proposals has suppressed development around the Ashby and North Berkeley stations. Interestingly, the largest inventory of dense housing, offices, and retail-commercial floorspace to come on line along this corridor has been in Emeryville — one of the few East Bay shoreline cities without a BART station.

As in the cases of Fremont and Pleasant Hill, local policies have been instrumental in leveraging land-use changes near El Cerrito's del Norte station. Over the past decade, the city's redevelopment authority used tax-exempt financing to underwrite some of the costs of assembling land and financing nearly $10 million of the $14 million in infrastructure improvements necessary to support several housing projects near the del Norte station. The city worked closely with a developer to create Del Norte Place, a 135-unit apartment complex with 19,000 square feet of ground-floor retail; 27 of the units are priced below market as set asides for low- and moderate-income families. The redevelopment authority became an equity partner, leasing land to the developer for $1 per year and 15–20% of cash flow. To date, Del Norte Place has leased rapidly. It opened in mid-1992 and by mid-1993, 97% of its apartments were occupied. The project developers aggressively put in a bid to the El Cerrito redevelopment authority to build on the site because they believed that living near rail stations will become increasingly attractive as regional traffic congestion worsens (McCloud, 1992). A recent survey of employed residents of Del Norte Place found that 29% commuted to work by BART, considerably above the 8% of all El Cerrito working residents (Menotti and Cervero, 1995).

The greatest disappointment along the Richmond corridor has been at the Richmond station itself. When BART arrived, city officials had high hopes it would trigger a building boom because of the area's intermodal facilities and large inventory of vacant land. Besides the addition of a large public office building and a few small apartment complexes, little has changed around the Richmond station over the past 20 years, despite efforts by the city's redevelopment authority to entice new investment through various incentive programs. A depressed local economy, urban blight, and increased crime have suppressed development. Richmond's experiences underscore the fact that opening a rail station, in and of itself, will not stimulate major land-use changes unless there are reasonably favorable local market conditions.

FACTORS INFLUENCING LAND-USE CHANGES

In light of the varying degrees of land-use changes around BART stations, models were constructed that sought to identify factors that were statistically significant predictors. The first analysis presents a logit model that predicts the likelihood of a land-use conversion, while the second analysis presents regression models that estimate the rate of building construction during the post-BART era.

Land use changes and proximity to BART

This first model tests whether proximity to BART affected the likelihood of a significant land use change. Nine BART stations were studied: Concord, Daly City, El Cerrito del Norte, Fremont, Hayward, Pleasant Hill, Rockridge, Union City, and Walnut Creek. Two primary data inputs for this analysis were: a regionwide 1990 digital inventory of dominant land uses (across 24 categories) for hectare grid cells (100×100m), published by the Association of Bay Area Governments (ABAG); and estimates of dominant land uses near BART stations in 1965 made from aerial photographs.

For half-mile rings around these nine stations, vacant land fell sharply as the dominant land use — from 27.6% of total area in 1965 to just 4.2% of area in 1990. Of the 1557 hectares of vacant land that had been developed by 1990, the shares that were converted to different dominant uses were: 41% to residential, 21% to commercial, 16% to public, 15% to industrial, and 7% to roads or parking lots. Overall, residential uses increased from 47.4% of station-area (dominant) land uses in 1965 to 51.3% in 1990.

Table 4 presents a binomial logit model that predicts the probability of each hectare grid-cell changing dominant land uses from 1965 to 1990 as a function of distance to the nearest BART station, whether the land was undeveloped in 1965, and several other predictors. This model correctly predicts 82.3% of the grid-cell land-use changes that occurred within a half-mile of these nine stations over the 25 year study period. All predictor variables were statistically significant at the 0.05 level. All else being equal, sites (i.e. grid-cells) closer to BART stations were more likely to have changed dominant uses than more distant sites. Additionally, sites which were originally undeveloped or residentially developed were more likely to have changed use than commercially developed sites. Land-use conversions were also more likely if grid-cells were surrounded by dissimilar uses — i.e. in a more mixed-use setting. Having vacant land close to BART stations also induced land-use changes. Relative to El Cerrito, the suppressed station-area dummy variable, land in all of the other station areas, except Fremont, had a higher likelihood of changing land uses, controlling for other factors like distance to BART.

Overall, this analysis suggests three variables that local officials maintain some control over have influenced land-use changes in station areas: proximity to BART; amount of developable land; and levels of land-use mixture. Overall, vacant parcels near BART in mixed-use settings were most likely to have undergone a land-use conversion.

Predictors of station-area development rates

A second set of models was produced that estimate the percentage increases in building square footage during 1973–93 within the catchments of the 25 stations for which building permit data were compiled. Table 5 identifies four variables that, in combination, were the strongest predictors of the percentage change in multi-family building floorspace (among 18 candidate variables that measured characteristics of land uses in station areas, designs of station sites, ridership profiles, the existence of various supportive public policies, and neighborhood incomes). The models predict growth rates in residential and non-residential floorspace as functions of parking supplies,

Table 4. Binomial logit model for predicting land-use changes for grid cells near selected BART stations, 1965–1990

Dependent variable: land use change in hectare grid-cell (0 = no, 1 = yes)

Variable	Coefficient	Probability
Distance to the nearest BART station, in straightline meters	−0.002	0.002
Initial (1965) use was undeveloped (1 = yes, 0 = no)	7.177	0.000
Initial (1965) use was residential (1 = yes, = no)	7.113	0.013
Similarity index: proportion of the same land use type in the surrounding eight grid cells	−0.036	0.023
Relative vacant land available: proportion of undeveloped land within half-mile ring that is closer to a BART station than to the grid-cell case	0.012	0.001
Concord dummy (1 = yes, 0 = no)	1.123	0.002
Fremont dummy (1 = yes, 0 = no)	−1.191	0.000
Hayward dummy (1 = yes, 0 = no)	1.040	0.003
Rockridge dummy (1 = yes, 0 = no)	0.833	0.039
Union City dummy (1 = yes, 0 = no)	1.334	0.000
Walnut Creek dummy (1 = yes, 0 = no)	0.959	0.000
Daly City dummy (1 = yes, 0 = no)	0.220	0.002
Constant	−1.375	0.005

Summary statistics
Observations = 2423
Percent of land use changes predicted correctly = 82.3
Percent of non-changes predicted correctly = 93.3
Overall prediction accuracy = 89.9%
p-squared (pseudo R^2) = 0.654

Table 5. Regression model for predicting multi-family residential growth rates around BART stations, 1973–1993

Dependent variable: % change in multi-family residential building floorspace withing BART station catchments,* 1973–1993

Variable	Coefficient	Standard error	Probabilitiy
Dwelling units per acre within station catchment, 1990	9.049	6.938	0.194
Park-and-ride spaces at station, 1993	0.172	0.049	0.003
Distance of the nearest freeway to the station: 1 = 0–0.05 miles, 2 = 0.5–1.0 miles, 3 = 1.0–2.0 miles, 4 = > 2.0 miles.	97.557	31.203	0.007
Entropy index of land–use mixture within station catchment†	667.928	287.786	0.035
Constant	−828.309	255.739	0.006

Summary Statistics
$R^2 = 0.600$
$F = 5.62, p = 0.006$
No. of cases = 25

*Catchment area equals a one-half mile radius from stations except for downtown San Francisco, Oakland, and Berkeley stations. For these downtown stations, catchments are one-quarter mile radius.

†Entropy = $\{ \Sigma_i [p_i * \ln(p_i)] \} \ln(k)$ where p_i = proportion of land area in land-use category i, and k = number of land-use categories. Ranges between 0 and 1, where 0 signifies land devoted to a single use and 1 signifies land area evenly spread among all uses.

proximity to freeways*, land-use mixture (for the residential model), vacant land† (for the residential model), and (for the non-residential model) whether a station is at or near the end of a line, controlling for 1990 densities‡.

The model in Table 5 indicates that multi-family housing additions tended to occur in settings with relatively high residential densities (as recorded in 1990). This could reflect the tendency for apartment and condominium builders to concentrate construction in station areas that were already moderately dense because of more receptive zoning and the greater likelihood of community acceptance. Multi-housing housing also tended to expand most rapidly in settings with more mixed land uses. The availability of park-and-ride lots is positively associated with housing development, possibly suggesting that station areas where land is more readibly available (and land values are potentially lower) tend to have more plentiful parking and more multi-family development. Pleasant Hill, for example, has both the most surface parking spaces and largest stock of apartments within a quarter mile ring of BART than any other station. Freeway proximity, on the other hand, was associated with lower rates of multi-family housing construction. Overall, apartments and condomiums were typically built in relatively dense, mixed-use station areas with large parking supplies and away from a freeway. Put another way, attached housing was generally built in station areas that were not established and exclusively single-family neighborhoods.

A second model predicted growth rates in non-residential (office, commercial, industrial, and institutional) floorspace near BART stations (Table 6). Non-residential construction was most active in station areas with relatively large supplies of vacant land and park-and-ride spaces. Park-and-ride supplies could have attracted office and commercial development by creating buffer spaces (as well as overflow parking opportunities). More likely, however, parking supplies serve as a proxy for low-density residential environments, settings where some of the greatest percentage increases in office and commercial floorspace have been registered (e.g. Walnut Creek, Pleasant Hill). The table also reveals that non-residential growth was healthiest in settings with relatively high employment densities (in 1990) and non-terminal stations. Having high employment densities could reflect more permissive zoning and a receptive local attitude to office additions; however, the relationship could also be tautological (e.g. rapid office growth created higher employment densities). Terminal stations might be less attractive for office development because of the heavy traffic

---

*Distance was expressed in ordinal terms because distances to the nearest freeway(s) varied according to direction from the stations, and could thus be better represented in ordinal increments. Additionally, studies show that proximity to access points is generally perceived in terms of distance increments vs precise metrics (Untermann, 1984; Landis et al., 1995; Cervero, 1995b).

†Because vacant land was not inventoried in the TRW-REDI data base, the amount of vacant land could not be precisely determined. Instead, for each station area, the share of total land area around stations that is vacant was estimated from field surveys using the ordinal categories shown in Table 6.

‡The use of density control variables measured at a time point (i.e. 1990) to predict rates of land-use changes (from 1973–90) allowed the influences of current land-use intensities on growth rates to be controlled and reduced possible estimation problems related to endogeneity.

Table 6. Regression model for predicting non-residential growth rates around BART stations, 1973–1993

Dependent variable: % change in non-residential building floorspace within BART station catchments,* 1973–1993

Variable	Coefficient	Standard error	Probabilitiy
Employees per acre within station catchment, 1990	5.644	2.853	0.067
Vacant land as a share of total area within station catchment, 1990: 1 = < 10%, 2 = 10–25%,3 = > 25%	243.585	87.618	0.014
Park-and-ride spaces at station, 1993	0.312	0.085	0.003
Terminal or near-terminal station (0 = no, 1 = yes)†	−335.596	165.727	0.062
Distance of the nearest freeway to the station:1 = 0–0.5 miles, 2 = 0.5–1 miles, 3 = 1–2 miles, 4 = > 2 miles	75.871	46.733	0.126
Constant	−684.009	187.466	0.002

Summary statistics
$R^2 = 0.600$
$F = 5.62$, $p = 0.006$
No. of cases = 25
*Catchment area equals a one-half mile radius from stations except for downtown San Francisco, Oakland, and Berkeley stations. For these downtown stations, catchments are one-quarter mile radius.
†Near-terminal represents stations toward the end of the line that function like terminals because they are closer to freeways than actual terminals and thus serve a larger catchment area. BART's near-terminal stations, El Cerrito del Norte and Pleasant Hill, have larger supplies of parking than terminal stations since they are easier to reach by freeway.

accessing and egressing park-and-ride lots during peak hours. The lower rate of non-residential growth for BART stations near freeways likely reflected the tendency for these areas to be already built out.

It should be pointed out that many policy-related variables that were considered for this analysis did not emerged as statistically significant predictors. For example, the siting of a station in a freeway median was not associated with a lower rate of building activities around stations, as some analysts have postulated (Knight and Trygg, 1977; Dingemans, 1978). Variables indicating whether or not any form of incentive zoning (e.g. density bonuses) or restrictive zoning (e.g. downzoning of densities) was enacted around stations also failed to enter equations.

CONCLUSION

We conclude that the findings of the original BART Impact Study have not been altered much by the passage of two decades. We too have found that in a larger regional context, BART has played a fairly modest, though not inconsequential, role in shaping metropolitan growth in the San Francisco Bay Area. Its impacts have been highly localized and uneven, far from the uniform pattern of subcentering that planners had hoped for. Evidence suggests that BART has allowed downtown San Francisco to continue to grow and maintain its primacy in the urban hierarchy. Downtown Oakland has lured both public and private investment, ostensibly in part because of the excellent regional accessibility provided by BART. BART seems to have also played a role in the emergence of a multi-centered metropolitan form, as was called for in the original 1956 plan. Today, Walnut Creek boasts a moderately dense concentration of offices, Pleasant Hill features 1800 apartment and condominium units within a quarter-mile ring of the station, and Fremont has a mix of transit-oriented developments. Around most other stations, however, few significant land-use changes have occurred, often for market reasons though in some instances because of neighborhood opposition.

Among all BART corridors, downtown San Francisco captured the lion's share of office growth — accounting for over three-quarters of all office construction within a half-mile of all BART stations since 1973. Thus, BART appears to have helped accomplish the original objective of maintaining downtown San Francisco's pre-eminence as the region's employment and commercial hub. Outside of downtown San Francisco, Oakland, and several suburban stations, however, most employment and office growth over the past two decades has turned its back on BART, oriented toward freeway corridors instead. Far more office construction has occurred in freeway-oriented suburbs like Pleasanton and San Ramon than in BART-served ones like Hayward or Lafayette.

Perhaps the biggest difference in station-area land uses since the original BART Impact Studies has been the addition of a considerable amount of multi-family housing within a quarter-mile ring of suburban BART stations. Much of this is attributable to aggressive actions on the part of local redevelopment authorities to entice housing development by underwriting infrastructure investments, assisting with land assemblage, and, in several instances, becoming equity partners in building transit-based housing. Many people residing in these projects consciously sought out housing near transit in order to economize on commuting. Research shows they are three to five times more likely to rail commute than others living in the same city but away from BART. Many apartments near rail are also commanding rent premiums. Transit-based housing, however, will only draw commuters to trains if there is continued growth in transit-based office development. Cities like Toronto and Stockholm have proven this to be the case (Pill, 1988; Cervero, 1995c). In the Bay Area, the greatest job growth has occurred outside of BART corridors. For BART to be able to effectively compete with the private automobile for commute trips in coming years, its station areas will need to capture even larger shares of future employment growth in addition to housing.

The essential role of local government in promoting station-area development is clearly underscored by BART's experiences. BART has created opportunities for attracting new development and reinvigorating stagnant areas that some communities have successfully capitalized upon. However, the mere presence of BART has been unable to turn around flat or declining local real estate markets — for example, around the Richmond or Fruitvale stations. BART is clearly not a sufficient condition to significant land development around stations, however under the right circumstances, it has proven to be an important contributor.

The finding that BART's land-use impacts have largely been localized reflects the fact that land uses are largely locally controlled. In the absence of any regional forum to manage and guide growth, these outcomes were predictable. Over the past forty years, the Bay Area has flirted with the idea of strengthening the role of regional government, however political opposition at the local and state levels has stonewalled these efforts, as it has elsewhere in the U.S. (Porter, 1992). In recent years, market-based strategies, such as road pricing and 'cashing out' free parking (Shoup, 1995), have gained greater acceptance as policy instruments for shaping transportation-land use outcomes. BART is presently embarking on the largest expansion program in its history, with some 25 miles of suburban extensions at various stages of planning and implementation. The degree to which the Bay Area embraces stronger regional planning, turns to market-based approaches, or continues with the status quo will, we believe, largely determine the land-use impacts of both existing and future corridors in coming years. We hope there will be a BART@40 study to see if we are right.

Acknowledgements—This research was supported by a grant from the Federal Transit Administration and the California Department of Transportation. We thank our research assistants for their contributions to this work — Carlos Castellanos, Wicak Sarosa, Kenneth Rich, Ming Zhang, Kang-Li Wu, Bruce Fukuji, and David Loutzenheister. We alone are responsible for any errors that might be contained in this paper.

REFERENCES

Bernick, M., Cervero, R. and Menotti, V. (1994) Comparison of rents at transit-based housing projects in northern California. Working paper 624. Institute of Urban and Regional Development, Berkeley.

Cervero, R. (1984) Light rail transit and urban development. *Journal of the American Planning Association* **50**(2), 133–147.

Cervero, R. (1993) Ridership impacts of transit-focused development in California. Monograph 45. Institute of Urban and Regional Development, Berkeley.

Cervero, R. (1994) Rail-oriented office development in California: how successful? *Transportation Quarterly* **48**(1), 33–44.

Cervero, R. (1995a) BART @ 20: land use and development impacts. Monograph 49. Institute of Urban and Regional Development, Berkeley.

Cervero, R. (1995b) Rail access modes and catchment areas for the BART system. Monograph 50. Institute of Urban and Regional Development, Berkeley.

Cervero, R. (1995c) Sustainable new towns: Stockholm's rail-served satellites. *Cities* **12**(1), 41–51.

Cervero, R. and Menotti, V. (1994) Market profiles of rail-based housing projects in California. Working paper 622. Institute of Urban and Regional Development, Berkeley.

Cervero, R. and Wu, K. L. (1996) Subcentering and commuting: evidence from the San Francisco Bay Area, 1980–1990. Working paper 668. Institute of Urban and and Regional Development, Berkeley.

Cervero, R., Bernick, M. and Gilbert, J. (1993) Market opportunities and barriers to transit-based development in California. Working paper 621. Institute of Urban and Regional Development, Berkeley.

City of Pleasanton (1993) *Pleasanton Employer Travel Survey*. Pleasanton, California: mimeo.

Dingemans, D. (1978) Rapid transit and suburban residential land use. *Traffic Quarterly* **32**(3), 289–306.

Dyett, M., Dornbusch, D., Fajans, M., Falcke, C., Gussman, V. and Merchant, J. (1979) *Land Use and Urban Development Impacts of BART: Final Report*. John Blayney Associates/David M. Dornbusch and Co. Inc., San Francisco.

Fogelson, R. (1967) *The Fragmented Metropolis: Los Angeles from 1850 to 1930.* Harvard University Press, Cambridge.

Giuliano, G. (1996) Land use impacts of transportation investments: highway and transit. In *The Geography of Urban Transportation,* ed. S. Hanson. Guilford Press, New York.

Gordon, P. and Richardson, H. (1996) Beyond polycentricity: the dispersed metropolis, Los Angeles, 1970-1990. *Journal of the American Planning Association* 62(3), 289-295.

Hoyt, H. (1939) *The Structure of Growth of Regional Neighborhoods in American Cities.* U.S. Government Printing Office, Washington D.C.

Johnston, R. and Tracy, S. (1983) Suburban resistance to density near transit stations in the San Francisco Bay Area. In *The Social Constraints on Energy—Policy Implementation,* eds. N. Neiman and B. Burt. Heath and Company, Lexington MA.

Knack, R. (1995) BART's village vision. *Planning* 61(1), 18-21.

Knight, R. and Trygg, L. (1977) Evidence of land use impacts of rapid transit systems. *Transportation* 6, 231-247.

Landis, J., Guhathakurta, S., Huang, W. and Zhang, M. (1995) Rail transit investments, real estate values, and land use change: a comparative analysis of five California rail transit systems. Monograph 48. Institute of Urban and Regional Development,Berkeley.

McCloud, J. (1992) High-density housing near San Francisco: builder betting proximity to commute line. *New York Times,* Vol. 141, Section 1, July 5, p. 23.

McGraw Hill (1993) *Black's Guide to Office Leasing: 1993 San Francisco Bay Area Edition.* McGraw Hill, San Mateo, California.

Menotti, V. and Cervero, R. (1995) Transit-based housing in California: profiles. Working Paper 638. Institute of Urban and Regional Development, Berkeley.

Merewitz, L. (1972) Public transportation: wish fulfillment and reality in the San Francisco Bay Area. *The American Economic Review* 62(2), 78-86.

Metropolitan Transportation Commission (1979) *BART in the San Francisco Bay Area,* p. 25. Metropolitan Transportation Commission, Berkeley.

Parsons, Brinckerhoff, Hall and MacDonald Inc. (1956) *Regional Rapid Transit: A Report to the San Francisco Bay Area Rapid Transit Commission.* Parsons, Brinckerhoff, Hall, and MacDonald, New York.

Parsons, Brinckerhoff, Tudor and Bechtel Inc. (1962) *The Composite Report: Bay Area Rapid Transit.* Parsons, Brinckerhoff, Tudor, and Bechtel, New York.

Pill, J. (1988) Toronto: thirty years of development. In *Transit, Land Use, and Urban Form,* ed. W. Attoe, pp. 57-62. Center for the Study of American Architecture, Austin .

Porter, D. (1992) Tough choices: regional governance for San Francisco. *Urban Land* 51(3), 36–39.

Purvis, C. (1994) Detailed commute characteristics in the San Francisco Bay Area: 1990 census transportation planning package, urban element. Working paper 7. Metropolitan Transportation Commission, Oakland.

Sedway and Associates (1993) *Urban Land* 52(7), 16–22.

Shoup, D. (1995) An opportunity to reduce minimum parking requirements. *Journal of the American Planning Association* 61(1), 14–28.

Stringham, M. (1982) Travel behavior associated with land uses adjacent to rapid transit stations. *ITE Journal* 52(4), 18–22.

Untermann, R. (1984) *Accommodating the Pedestrian: Adapting Towns and Neighborhoods for Walking and Bicycling.* Van Nostrand Reinhold, New York.

Vance, J. E. (1964) *Geography and Urban Evolution in the San Francisco Bay Area.* Institute of Governmental Studies, Berkeley.

Voith, R. (1991) Transportation, sorting, and house values. *Journal of the American Real Estate and Urban Economics Association* 19(2), 117–137.

Warner, S. B. (1962) *Streetcar Suburbs.* Harvard University Press, Cambridge.

Webber, M. (1976) The BART experience: what have we learned?. *Public Interest* 12(3), 79-108.

Wu, K. L. (1994) A study of th spatial relationship between jobs and housing in the San Francisco Bay Area in 1990: Improving the jobs housing balance to improve regional mobility. Masters thesis, University of California, Berkeley.

[27]

Are Compact Cities a Desirable Planning Goal?

Peter Gordon and Harry W. Richardson

This paper considers some key issues that help to evaluate whether or not the promotion of compact cities is a worthwhile planning goal. These are: the pressures on prime agricultural land; residential density preferences; energy resource savings; the potential for expanding transit use and promoting TODs (transit-oriented developments); the costs and benefits of suburbanization; the efficiency gains from compactness; the impact of telecommunications on the density of development; the prospects for downtowns; the influence of rent-seeking on the promotion of downtown projects; the social equity of compactness; and the effects of competition among cities. Our evaluation of these issues does not support the case for promoting compact cities.

Gordon and Richardson are both professors of Planning and Economics in the School of Urban Planning and Development and the Department of Economics at the University of Southern California.

Journal of the American Planning Association, Vol. 63, No. 1, Winter 1997. ©American Planning Association, Chicago, IL.

The revolution in information processing and telecommunications is accelerating the growth and dispersion of both economic activities and population, possibly moving towards the point where "geography is irrelevant." Yet, at the same time, many planners (and policymakers) advocate "compact cities" as an ideal, in contrast to the reality of increasingly spread-out metropolitan development. The term "compact cities" is in increasingly common use in planning discussions, conferences and other similar venues. It can take on different meanings, each with different planning implications. To mention merely three possibilities: (1) a macro approach, based on high average densities at the city-wide or even metropolitan level, but more likely to be applied to a freestanding small town;[1] (2) a micro approach, reflecting high densities at the neighborhood or community level; and (3) a spatial structure approach, emphasizing a pattern oriented to downtown or the central city versus a polycentric (or dispersed) spatial pattern, with obvious density consequences. All three meanings are touched upon in this paper, although the micro approach is the one that has received most attention in the literature. An alternative classification is to distinguish among low-density, strip, scattered, and leapfrog development as forms of "sprawl," sometimes used as an antonym for "compactness" (Ewing 1995).

In this paper, we revisit several issues relevant to the compact cities discussion. Although the analysis is probably general enough to apply to most of the developed world's major cities, we restrict our remarks to United States cases. However, most of the differences between the United States and other developed countries are probably explained by a moderate time lag (e.g., in decentralization trends) rather than by significant differences in spatial structure. For example, Mieskowski and Mills (1993) sum up the results of another study by Goldberg and Mercer (1986): "Goldberg and Mercer set out to demonstrate that Canadian metropolitan areas are relatively compact and more centralized than those in the U.S. However, the authors conclude ... that Canada and U.S. metropolitan areas were decentralizing *at the same rate*" [emphasis added].

PETER GORDON AND HARRY W. RICHARDSON

Open Space and Agricultural Land

America is not running out of open space, nor in any danger of having cities encroach on reserves of "prime" agricultural land.

Compact city studies frequently refer to the savings in prime agricultural land. However, the favorite analytical model of cities (and their hinterlands) uses bid-rent curves that show how the highest and best use of land is determined and how policies to "contain" cities in order to preserve suburban farmlands force land into lower valued uses. The welfare losses show up in higher prices for urban space. High urban land prices in Japan, especially in the 1980s, resulting from government restrictions on the marketability of agricultural land, are an example (Miyao 1991).

Moreover, the United States has a major problem of agricultural surpluses. Fischel (1985) showed that if the entire United States population lived at "suburban sprawl" densities of one acre per household (all of them made up of four people), just three percent of the total land area of the forty-eight contiguous states would be utilized. He also cited Frey's 1979 land use data for the contiguous mainland states, which show that almost ninety percent of the total area is in forest, range, pasture, and cropland uses. The cropland proportion could *expand* substantially if crop prices were to rise.[2]

The rural land preservation argument is sometimes extended to the global level. United States agricultural land must be preserved now, it is argued, because at some date in the future the growth in world population will result in insufficient food. Although this is a common argument, the evidence for it is weak. World food production per capita has increased modestly in the past decade and a half, while food production per capita in Asia has increased by about 23 percent; in the developing world, only in Africa did food production per capita decline (by six percent), and that reflects primarily structural development problems rather than an intrinsic shortage of fertile land (Sen 1994, 66). Of course, malnutrition is rampant (perhaps 700 million people are undernourished), but that is the result of poverty and an unequal distribution of food, not of food scarcity. In the words of Per Pinstrup-Andersen, Director-General of the International Food Policy Research Institute: "The world is perfectly capable of feeding 12 billion people 100 years from now" (quoted in *The Economist,* June 10, 1995, 39).

Density Preferences

Low-density settlement is the overwhelming choice for residential living.

Some observers have argued that this is not an unconstrained choice, but influenced by instruments promoting suburbanization, policies such as the preferential income tax treatment of home mortgage interest, subsidies to automobile use, and the ubiquitous interstate highway system. United States-Canadian differences (or similarities) may be a good test of these objections; for example, there is no home mortgage deductibility in Canada. Goldberg and Mercer (1986) marshalled considerable evidence to emphasize the differences. Yet, even their comparisons of the United States and Canada are subject to multiple interpretations, including the hypothesis of a simple time lag in decentralization trends. For example, both countries' cities are shown to have declining (and converging) population density gradients, although central city densities in Canada remain higher than those in the United States.

The policy explanations of United States suburbanization often emphasize the argument that more subsidies are given to auto travel than to public transit. The opposite is true. Federal, state and local expenditures for highways (and parking) were $66.5 billion in 1991; revenues were $53.8 billion (81 percent recovery); federal, state and local expenditures for transit were $20.8 billion, while revenues were $8.8 billion (42 percent recovery). On a per-passenger-mile basis, the auto subsidy was 0.54 cents; the transit subsidy was 54 times as large, 29.42 cents. Moreover, the transit subsidies have been growing faster: the same calculations for 1981 show that the transit subsidy per passenger-mile was then "only" 33 times the auto subsidy (U.S. Department of Transportation 1994).

The absence of congestion pricing and emissions fees is a widely acknowledged problem; it constitutes an implicit subsidy to auto users. While estimates of these costs cover a wide range, the Environmental Defense Fund (Cameron 1994) suggested that air pollution costs per passenger mile in Southern California in 1991 were 3.6 cents and congestion costs were 7.5 cents. Donald Shoup (1995) suggested that there may be up to an additional 11 cents per passenger mile of parking subsidies for Los Angeles automobile commuters. In any event, even with these adjustments (and making the extreme assumption that these "costs" are "subsidies"), the full auto subsidy adds up to little more than 22 cents per passenger mile and still falls short of the transit subsidy.

Many consumer surveys have shown strong preferences for suburban living (see, for example, the Federal Home Mortgage Association's National Housing Survey: FHMA 1992, 1993, 1994), and the link between household preferences and preferred spatial patterns is clear: "[in] evaluating the desirability of existing spatial patterns, revealed preferences of consumers, especially when they have persisted as long as they have in the U.S., must be given some weight" (Dyckman 1976, A-2).

Has the decentralized residential spatial structure that reflects these preferences been influenced by government intervention? Salins (1994) argued that zoning has inhibited high-density development and mixed residential and commercial land uses, that core preservation strategies have undermined the recycling of obsolete central city land uses, and that the absence of market-driven strategies (such as school vouchers and the privatization of infrastructure provision and services) has contributed to the deterioration of the central city. It remains questionable whether such reforms would have more than a negligible impact on densities and spatial patterns.[3]

Of course, in a world of heterogeneous tastes, there are people who prefer alternatives to the dominant decentralized lifestyle. As an example, Handy (1994) laments the consequences of moving from Berkeley, California, to Austin, Texas. In her words: "I miss having my favorite restaurants, a copy shop, a bike shop, a pet store, a bookstore, and a supermarket, all within a short and pleasant walk from home" (Handy 1994, 3). She longs for the application of principles of what she calls "coordinated transportation and land use planning" of the kind adopted in Portland, Oregon, "where state-level mandates have pushed coordination: an urban-growth boundary was adopted at the same time that policies shifted away from freeway expansion, and land use plans are now being created for development of areas around current and future light-rail stations" (6). The interesting point about this statement is that what is happening in Portland (which is highly controversial, by the way) is as a result of top-down command-and-control planning rather than the expression of individual preferences.

A related argument is that developers are prevented by land-use regulations, zoning, and building standards from building at higher densities that would be more profitable and perhaps, if available at much lower cost, more attractive to consumers. The problem with this argument is that such regulations are not ubiquitous, so that we can find locations where high-density construction is feasible, and in some cases has been undertaken. In most instances sales have been slow. In an industry as cyclical as residential construction, developers are very market-conscious. The risks of building an unacceptable product are very high, and builders are well aware of the strong consumer preference for the single-family detached home (a preference that has probably been reinforced by the

increased publicity about legal, insurance, and other problems with condominium and townhouse associations and other common-wall developments). We have no objection to developers promoting pilot, or demonstration, higher-density projects to test consumer acceptance. However, even under the wildest, most optimistic scenarios, we would expect such projects to have a less than negligible effect on the prevailing average densities in any type of settlement. The compact settlement projects may have a boutique appeal; and the essence of consumer sovereignty is the ability of the market to cater to the wide variety of consumer tastes. We are in favor of compact developments being subjected to a market test; we oppose attempts to impose these through command-and-control zoning and design regulations, and we reject the argument that enough projects of this kind will be implemented to have any discernible impact on overall land use patterns.

The Energy Glut

Energy is one of many scarce resources; markets are required to husband scarce resources; government interventions are the real sources of energy "crises."

It is now well established that there has been a global energy glut, and it continues. The queues of the 1970s at gasoline stations were a uniquely U.S. phenomenon, predictably linked to United States price controls prevalent at the time. Ever since the controls were lifted, the OPEC cartel has lost clout and markets have performed exactly as expected. Controling for the effects of inflation and taxes, the September 1996 price per gallon of gasoline in the United States is *below* the 1974 price; consequently, the relative price of gasoline compared with other goods and services has fallen dramatically. Paradoxically, in California and probably in other states, the fall in the price of gasoline relative to the price of housing has encouraged households to substitute housing for transportation costs by living farther out, thus contributing to suburbanization. Furthermore, per capita energy consumption in the United States is now below its 1973 level, in spite of the relative price change (Bohi and Darmstadter 1994). Energy resource constraints are a weak argument for promoting compactness; in any event, as suggested below, the link between high-density development and reduced VMT (vehicle miles traveled), and hence reduced energy consumption, is by no means clear.

The Scope for Transit

Low densities make high-capacity transit systems unattractive and therefore wasteful (of all resources utilized, including energy).

Because the spreading out of cities reduces markets for conventional public transit (especially fixed rail, which is spatially inflexible and usually oriented to downtown), it should surprise no one that the United States transit industry has been in decline for most of the twentieth century. Massive subsidies have not helped; they may have made matters worse. The Congressional Budget Office concluded that "despite more than 25 years of federal assistance, mass transit carries only about 5 percent of people who commute to work. The other 95 percent mostly use automobiles.... New federally assisted transit systems have not added to mass transit; instead, they have replaced flexible bus routes with costly fixed-route services to a few downtown areas, while the growth in jobs and population has been in the suburbs and in the smaller cities. At the same time, transit costs are rising: transit fleets in general are greatly underused, and the new transit systems have for the most part added to costs and to unused capacity without attracting riders from cars" (Congressional Budget Office 1988). A large (and still growing) number of studies echo this finding (from Meyer, Kain and Wohl 1965 up to recent years, e.g., Pickrell 1989).[4]

It appears that "neotraditional" neighborhoods, pedestrian pockets, mixed land use developments and other features of the New Urbanism do not make much of a difference. Cervero (1994b) reports: "Overall, focusing development near transit and designing communities to be more transit-friendly, by themselves, will have little bearing on people's travel choices." Moreover, Crane (1996) has suggested it is possible that neotraditional neighborhoods may increase rather than reduce automobile use, depending on case-by-case empirical considerations, because shorter origin destination distances reduce the average cost per trip. Cheaper trips mean more *vehicle* trips, and it is conceivable, perhaps more probable than not, that total VMT (vehicle miles traveled) may increase. Thus, neotraditional neighborhoods may neither increase transit use nor reduce auto travel.

Meanwhile, Downs (1994), in a recent attack on what he calls the "dominant vision" of decentralized development and low-density growth, has nevertheless criticized the effectiveness of Calthorpe's (1993) idea of transit-oriented development (TOD) as a basis for the next American metropolis (Downs 1994, Appendix C). Downs attempts to simulate whether Calthorpe's approach could have accommodated all the suburban growth (about 237,000 people) in the average MSA (Metropolitan Statistical Area) during the 1980s. He assumes, generously, that a TOD might be 288.5 acres (a circle with a radius of 2,000 feet around

a transit station), and that 35 percent would be devoted to residential use developed at a density of 15 units per acre. Accommodating the average MSA's suburban growth would require 63 TODs. At intervals of 1.5 miles, this would require 96 miles of a transit system. In cases of faster growth, the number of TODs might rise to 140, and the transit system mileage might rise to 210 miles. Even in the first case, the required system would be larger than BART (the Bay Area Rapid Transit System in San Francisco), larger even than the Washington, DC Metro. Given the numbers of people served, construction of the needed system would not have been feasible, in terms of either financing or passengers served. Nor is there any evidence that such a system would divert significant proportions of travelers from private cars to transit, judging by experience in other United States metropolitan areas. Substituting buses for rail would not work, either, because most of the trips would be too long to attract much patronage.

Suburbanization and Congestion?

The traffic consequences of suburbanization are benign.

Industry moves to the suburbs, following the labor force, which allows many workers to enjoy a shorter worktrip in time if not in distance and reduces congestion pressures in traditional centers. Although this type of adjustment is not instantaneous, and there are inevitable short-term disequilibria, the important point is that the self-corrections are relatively fast. Orange County was Los Angeles' quintessential "bedroom community," with a local workers-to-jobs ratio of 1.4 in 1974. By 1993, the ratio had fallen below 1.1, almost identical to that of the core county of Los Angeles.

Suburbanization has been the dominant and successful mechanism for reducing congestion. It has shifted road and highway demand to less congested routes and away from core areas. All of the available recent data from national surveys on self-reported trip lengths and/or durations corroborate this view. The findings from *all seven* recent large-scale national household surveys present a consistent story of the containment of metropolitan area commuting times (Gordon and Richardson 1994b). Evidence from NPTS (Nationwide Personal Transportation Study) reports (1977, 1983, 1990), a commuting questionnaire included in the American Housing Surveys (1985, 1989), and the two decennial Census reports (1980 and 1990) all help to make the same point. The 1990 data indicate some increase in average commuting distances, which is accounted for largely by changes in the two tails of the trip distribution (i.e. fewer very short trips and more very long trips). However, that increase was offset by faster travel speeds. As a result, commuting times remained more or less the same.

The Efficiency of Compactness?

The economic and resource "efficiency" of compact development has never been adequately demonstrated.

The debate touched off by publication of the Real Estate Research Corporation's (RERC's) *The Costs of Urban Sprawl* (1974) revealed the complexity of the issue. Altshuler (1977, 1979) and Windsor (1979) have summarized the many errors that weaken the RERC report and its sweeping conclusions beyond repair, although it continues to be quoted approvingly, especially in nonacademic circles (e.g., Bank of America et al. 1995).

Recent NPTS data give some idea of the range of RERC's errors. RERC assumed that auto daily travel time (for "head of household") living in "low density sprawl" (i.e. a housing density of 1,360 units per square mile[5]) was 61.2 minutes per day, and that the same individual living in "high density planned" development (i.e. 4,102 units per square mile) traveled only 37.8 minutes per day; hence, sprawl living patterns induced more than 60 percent more travel. But in the real world, central city residents and suburban residents incur similar trip times. 1990 NPTS files (Vincent et al. 1994) show that average commuting times were 18.2 minutes (one-way, all modes) for central city residents in urbanized areas, and 20.8 minutes for urbanized area residents living outside central cities. RERC also assumed that clustered development would generate considerable travel savings in shorter *nonwork* trips. The 1990 NPTS showed that auto users' average shopping trip time in the New York CMSA (Consolidated Metropolitan Statistical Area) was 12.4 minutes for central city residents and 11.8 minutes for suburban residents; the comparable numbers for the Los Angeles CMSA were 11.0 and 9.9 minutes (Gordon and Richardson 1994a, 1994b, 1995). The L.A. suburbanite had a 20 percent *shorter* shopping trip time than the New York center city resident. RERC, on the other hand, assumed that total annual travel for the average household in high-density communities would be 9,900 miles, but 19,700 miles in low densities.

It is now well known that the still frequently quoted RERC's report is badly flawed; for example, it focuses on on-site servicing costs at the expense of more general public service costs, such as roads to provide access to jobs, shopping and recreation, and does not allow for quality differences (e.g., the value of a private yard) in the cost comparisons. Yet advocates of compact cities have used similar techniques to offer more recent empirical corroboration for their claims. Newman and Kenworthy are a notable example, and they also made a number of serious errors (Gomez-Ibanez 1991; Brindle 1994). Another example is the CUPR (Center for Urban Policy Research) group (e.g., Burchell et al. 1992a, 1992b; Burchell and Listokin 1995), which used an approach similar to that of RERC, that is, a prospective view of the comparative costs of alternative types of development under sets of very precise assumptions. Their conclusion was that "the state of New Jersey could save $1.3 billion [a 10 percent saving] in infrastructure costs for roads, utilities, and schools over a twenty-year period if a state plan managing growth were followed, as opposed to the sprawl patterns of development" (Burchell and Listokin 1995). Government-sponsored studies (e.g., Duncan et al. 1989; Resource Management Consultants 1989) also have argued in favor of low cost/high density development. Furthermore, Frank (1989) reviewed several decades of studies and found that for streets, utilities and schools, capital costs tended to be higher at lower densities and at increasing distances from the central core. In addition, as pointed out much earlier by Downing (1977), costs may increase with distance from central facilities such as sewage treatment plants and water sources (but, of course, these may not be *centrally* located, so the relationship with density is obscure). On the other side, Ladd (1992) argued that, except within a range of very low densities, public service costs for traffic management, waste collection and disposal, and crime control increase with higher densities. Peiser (1984, 1989) estimated that infrastructure cost savings in "planned" as opposed to "unplanned" developments were very small. Altshuler and Gomez-Ibanez (1993, chapter 5) concluded that none of this research has given convincing support to the fears of sprawl.

A final problem in discussions of the compact city is the pejorative use of the term "urban sprawl." It conjures up connotations of the general meaning of "sprawl" as an unaesthetic, lazy and undisciplined form of body expression. The original application of this term in a planning context was to describe predominantly commercial "ribbon" development along both sides of highways over considerable distances, sometimes called "retailscape." Now the term has been generalized to include almost any kind of low-density suburban development and "leapfrog" development (Altshuler and Gomez-Ibanez 1993). But that suburbanization itself should be an object of attack is amazing, given the expressed preferences of the majority of Americans for suburban lifestyles and the supposed sanctity of consumer sovereignty.

Technology and Agglomeration-Congestion Trade-Offs

High-rise or concentrated settlement is costly and only worthwhile if transport or communications costs are high; yet these have been falling for many years, and communication costs, at least, are likely to continue to fall steeply in the mid-term future.

High density settlement involves trade-offs between inevitable costs (congestion) and prospective benefits (agglomeration). High-rise buildings exist where they do only because the high costs of erecting and maintaining them were considered to be worth the economies realized through increased accessibility, communication and interaction, and the ease of face-to-face transactions.

These trade-offs help to explain how, over the past century, numerous innovations in technology and organization have changed cities, first by extending the "effective radius" from the center to the periphery, and subsequently by modifying the congestion-agglomeration trade-offs. These advances include the streetcar, the substitution of electric power for other energy resources, the rise of trucking, and the construction of interstate and intra-metropolitan highway systems. Major innovations in transportation and communications have made the benefits of agglomeration available over areas of increasingly greater spatial extent, allowing many of the costs of congestion to be avoided.

For most of the twentieth century, the highway system has been the major force for continued low-density settlement and suburbanization. The barriers of distance continue to "dissolve" (Webber 1993); factories and offices continue to move to where employees want to live. Most commuting is now suburb-to-suburb, taking congestion pressures off traditional downtowns and allowing many to drive faster on less congested suburban highways. Suburb-to-central-city commuting continues to diminish. City forms continue to evolve beyond polycentricity to patterns of generalized dispersion. Recent research on the Los Angeles CMSA that compares employment concentrations in the three census years, 1970, 1980, and 1990, shows that all places qualifying as "centers" (based on trip generation densities) accounted for 19 percent of regional employment in 1970, 17 percent in 1980 and only 12 percent in 1990. Also, the number of places qualifying as centers declined from 20 (in 1970) to 12 (in 1990) during a period when the region's employment base grew from 3.6 million to 6.3 million jobs (Gordon and Richardson 1996a). This dispersion of economic activities, clear-cut in Los Angeles and perhaps evident in other metropolitan areas once the research has been done, is much more radical than implied by the adoption of concepts such as "edge cities," "satellite cities," "polycentricity," and "urban villages."

Rapid advances in telecommunications are now accelerating the decentralization trends set in motion by the advent of the automobile. In 1890, the "effective radius" of U.S. cities was said to be about 2 miles, based largely on pedestrian access. Dyckman (1976) reported that this had grown to 8 miles by 1920 because of the development of public transit, to 11 miles by 1950 (the diffusion of automobile ownership), and to 20–24 miles by the 1970s (the construction of urban freeways systems). The centrifrugal trends have now accelerated because telecommunications access cannot be measured in terms of geographical distance. The locational choices open to both households and firms have expanded accordingly. In the extreme case, geography might become irrelevant. Peter Drucker suggests that "[o]ffice work, rather than office workers, will do the traveling" (Drucker 1989, 38). Proximity is becoming redundant. Rural (as well as "exurban" and outer suburb) workplaces are growing the fastest of all. The revolution in telecommunications has been neatly summarized in "Moore's Law": information processing capabilities double about every 18 months. Intense global competition ensures that the newest technologies are quickly adopted.

Entertainment already is, and instruction is more likely to be, transmitted over broad-band radio frequencies rather than seen in traditional theaters or lecture halls. Today's cities continue to become less compact; the city of the future will be anything but compact.

Those who misread these trends do so at considerable cost. For example, Asian real estate investors lost approximately one-half of their $77 billion investment in American cities over the last decade or so by focusing on downtown locations. Americans should not feel too smug, however, because their elected representatives have squandered, in total, even larger sums on dubious downtown renewal schemes.

Downtowns in Eclipse

Small-area employment data analysis show that the decentralization and dispersion of most activities continues, and that downtown renewal efforts have failed.

When we compare decennial population census files or quinquennnial economic census data, or examine cross-sectional data from sources such as the Wharton Decentralization Project (Linnemann and Summers 1991), the same conclusion emerges: most job growth, regardless of economic sector, is in the *outer* suburbs far away from downtowns and transit stations, even in the more transit-oriented metropolitan areas. The Wharton data also show that in the 1980s (the period of greatest downtown investment), CBD job growth was slow, negligible, or negative. Together, CBDs in the top ten cities (New York, Los Angeles, Chicago, Philadelphia, Dallas, San Francisco, Boston, Detroit, Washington, DC, and Houston) grew at barely over one percent per year in the period 1980–1986. It may be merely coincidental that the Census Bureau abandoned CBD tabulations in their 1990 reports. Although the compact city advocates focus primarily on increasing densities in suburban, exurban and free-standing settlements, they are invariably sympathetic to downtown and transit-oriented development. They are also supportive of central city revival efforts (Porter 1995); however, recent central-city employment performance (1988–1994), as reflected in central county data, has been as bleak as that of the CBDs (Gordon, Richardson, and Yu 1996).

Rent-Seeking and Politics

Declining sectors turn to political support for remedies. For cities, this leads to a rejection of market processes and creates coalitions for policies that attempt to offset them. However, these efforts are likely to fail; they waste taxpayers' funds and misallocate scarce public sector resources. As a result, the plight of cities worsens.

Generally, rent-seeking activities are facilitated by the actions of dirigiste governments, which in turn feed off rent-seekers. This augments the possibilities for waste: not only are there consumer surplus losses from the "welfare triangles" of elementary microeconomics diagrams (the inefficient use of resources), but resources are also diverted to the politics of seeking or avoiding favorable or unfavorable regulation. Dynamic analysis is even more disturbing: rent-seeking deters the "creative destruction" of buoyant economic growth; as pointed out by Mancur Olson thirty years ago (Olson 1965), the market losers are often the most politically connected, as well as the most economically motivated to resist change.

In United States cities, downtown interests have managed a broad spectrum of often creative political efforts on their own behalf. These have included downtown renewal projects that were hailed as breakthrough public-private partnerships by some planners, but seldom evaluated for efficiency or the incidence of their costs and benefits. (See Sawicki's review [1990] of Frieden and Sagalyn's [1989] celebration of *Downtown Inc.*). Among other efforts are downtown-focused rail transit systems, downtown-sited convention centers, and the revitalization of architecturally significant core neighborhoods as entertainment centers, stadiums, theaters, etc. The proof

of the political nature of many of these investments has been their across-the-board failure to reverse the decline of downtowns. In Los Angeles, the Community Redevelopment Agency has spent $2.5 billion (in terms of constant 1992 dollars) on downtown renewal over the past 25 years. The results have been disappointing. Currently, the agency is unable to continue its attempts to revitalize downtown because of declining tax increment revenues from commercial properties within its development area. That was not the plan.

Despite expensive revitalization, downtowns compete poorly as public gathering spaces against suburban malls and "invented streets," such as MCA's $100 million City Walk at Universal City in Los Angeles, where the street performers do not panhandle and where the graffiti is public art commissioned by architects. Throughout the United States, downtowns continue to decline, rail transit systems continue to lose passengers, and convention centers continue to claim large subsidies (Mills 1991). Many of the new downtown projects might pass Hall's (1980) criteria to qualify as "planning disasters"; although their implementation can easily be explained by the victories of interest groups, that does not justify them. Their main effect has been a fiscal drain, further weakening the central cities they are supposed to save.

Keating and Krumholz (1991) examined six recent downtown plans and criticized them for not adequately addressing "social equity concerns." Their call for analysis cannot be faulted, but it may be naive to expect such plans to be resistant to the rent-seeking agendas of powerful interests. Serious evaluation with a careful consideration of costs, benefits and incidence might show an unwelcome combination of inefficiencies and regressivity.

The oldest and the largest United States cities often have the most entrenched interests and the most intrusive governments. They are prone to higher taxes, more mandates on businesses and landlords, and more burdensome regulations, often along with deteriorating public services. The effect is to drive more and more economic activities out from central cities. At the same time that bureaucracies are strengthened, the cities increasingly become the haven of the poor and the unemployed. A vicious cycle sets in that further weakens traditional city centers.

Compactness and Equity

The equity case for compact cities is weak.

Some reviewers of an earlier draft of this paper complained about its preoccupation with economic efficiency arguments and its neglect of social equity concerns, with the implication that compact cities are more equitable. For example, "market processes might produce socially unacceptable results ... and ... market processes in urban areas are hugely affected by political forces controlled by upper-income rent-seekers who favor socio-economic segregation" (Anthony Downs, letter to the Editors of *JAPA*). Or, in the words of one of our colleagues: "A second rationale for attempting to change land use and transportation patterns is to increase social equity." Suburbanization is "the result of the affluent population escaping the fiscal and social problems of central cities. ... Once they establish such communities, they can exercise land use controls to exclude households with different housing needs or preferences. This process results in spatial segmentation of the population on the basis of income, ethnicity, and race; ... intervention is justified because suburban residents are actively preventing a spontaneous mixing of population, thus denying less affluent and minority populations access to suburban jobs and suburban amenities" (Giuliano 1995, 10–11).

Such arguments involve several separate, but interrelated, strands: existing suburban land-use patterns are inequitable; suburban areas are racially segregated; measures to increase compactness would improve equity; and, more generally, land use policies *should* be designed so as to increase social equity.

First, in the United States, 30.3 percent of urban households living in suburban areas have annual incomes below $25,000, a significant proportion although lower than the central city share (46.8 percent; U.S. Bureau of the Census 1990). Second, in many suburban communities the nonwhite population share is high, sometimes in the majority.[6] Of course, this does not apply to all types of suburbs, especially high-income locations. But the absence of significant numbers of minorities in such communities is the result of their lower incomes, not their race. Third, the link between interventions to increase compactness by promoting higher densities and improvements in equity is obscure at best. The more highly publicized compact communities (e.g. Laguna West, Seaside, Kentlands) are much less affordable relative to statewide average house prices than are many more typical suburban communities such as Moreno Valley in Riverside County, California, one of the fastest growing communities in the country during the 1980s. Fourth, poor people are excluded from buying into expensive residential neighborhoods not because of exclusionary zoning, but in exactly the same way that they are excluded from buying Lexus or Mercedes automobiles; they cannot afford them. If this is regarded as inequitable, the remedy is to press for direct income redistribution, not for changes in land use policies. The latter are a feeble approach to social equity issues.

Competition Among Cities

The major countervailing force to these trends derives from the fact that in an age of increasingly mobile capital, cities (and their governments) must compete to survive.

As capital becomes more mobile, crossing both state and even international frontiers with ease, policy errors are quickly punished by capital markets, inflicting considerable damage on the offending localities in terms of lost jobs and investment. Cities that are the most captive to special interests are the least likely to adopt growth-oriented policies. Enlightened administrations such as Indianapolis' mayor, Stephen Goldsmith, and Jersey City's mayor, Bret Shundler, understand this, and are pursuing reforms that resist rent-seekers. The differing responses to policy errors are one of the best answers to the old question of why some regions prosper while others decline. That answer induces skepticism about the desirability of the reduced competition that would surely result if the advocates of metropolitan and regional government had their way.

Conclusion

Bourne (1992) directs attention to "more compact and humane" urban forms. He does not recommend New York City as his model, but rather Toronto and its published plans that offer "the possibility of achieving new agglomeration economies for firms, lower automobile dependency for households, reduced environmental destruction, lower pollution levels and higher quality of service" (512). However, Bourne provides little empirical evidence for his position, citing only Newman and Kenworthy's (1989) and Nowlan and Stewart's (1991) findings.

Suburban life is often dismissed by visionaries for its alleged "moral minimalism," evidenced by lack of involvement in community affairs or "social control" (Baumgartner 1988). However, the moral superiority of core-city programs that forcibly divert huge resources towards downtown projects that enrich favored developers and their political allies is highly dubious. Not surprisingly, advocates usually link downtown capital projects to inner city revitalization and redistributive agendas. However, such projects' "porkbarrel" aspects and their regressive financing via sales taxes are well established. Los Angeles' downtown-focused rail transit projects account for more lobbying activity than does the entire California State government!

This paper has reviewed some of the findings that must be refuted before Bourne's proposals can be taken seriously. Citing the problems of the compact city ideal does not imply, however, an endorsement of the status quo. There are inevitable problems with *how we manage* the highway system, negative externalities and urban service delivery systems. Approaches to some of these shortcomings, such as time-of-day road pricing, tradable development rights, and fully portable education vouchers, have been discussed elsewhere (Richardson and Gordon 1993). Spelling out the details of why such policies are cost-effective remains a research challenge; but the alternative of attempting a *reversal* of existing urban development trends is neither feasible nor desirable.

POSTSCRIPT

The first draft of this paper was written in 1994. The controversy about compact cities and sprawl has raged on. It is infeasible here to review all the new literature, but an overview can be obtained from two Lincoln Institute of Land Policy publications (Lincoln Institute of Land Policy 1995; Diamond and Noonan 1996) and from a review paper on the relationship between energy use and urban form (Anderson, Kanaroglou, and Miller 1996).

AUTHORS' NOTE

We are grateful to our referees, both anonymous and named, and mostly critical, for helping us to clarify our arguments, if not to change our minds.

NOTES

1. According to the 1990 Census of Population, gross population densities per square mile in the United States as a whole were 3,320 in "central places inside urbanized areas," 2,813 in central cities, 2,149 in suburban areas and 1,498 in "central places of 10,000 population or more outside urbanized areas." These data indicate relatively low densities overall and moderate differentials among different types of urban settlement. Eight cities (New York, San Francisco, Jersey City, Chicago, Boston, Philadelphia, Newark, and Miami) have densities in excess of 10,000 per square mile (Downs 1994, Table 8–3). In addition, higher suburban densities can be found at specific locations; for example, Downs (1994, Table 8–1) estimates that of all suburban residents in Los Angeles County, 31.9 percent live at densities of more than 10,000 per square mile. (The equivalent numbers are 10.3 percent in Dade County, Florida and 10.5 percent in the suburbs of New York City.) Thus, there is considerable scope for increasing densities in an abstract sense. The real issue is whether this could be stimulated on a sufficient scale to influence overall average densities.

2. A more recent study by Frey (1995) increases the urban land share to about 15 percent by 1987. The contradiction between this and Fischel's conclusion is partly explained by the difference between gross and net residential densities and the proportion of urban land devoted to nonresidential use.

3. In a widely quoted article, *Newsweek* magazine lists "15 ways to fix the suburbs," namely: (1) smaller lots (especially front yards); (2) promote stores within walking distance; (3) narrower streets; (4) abolish cul-de-sacs; (5) establish urban growth boundaries; (6) hide the garage; (7) mix housing types; (8) plant trees on sidewalks; (9) redevelop or revitalize old shopping malls; (10) promote mass transit; (11) build mixed-use developments that link work to home; (12) develop town centers; (13) shrink parking lots; (14) less garish streetlighting; and (15) preserve rural green areas (Adler 1995). Many of these proposals refer more to design elements than to the broader issue of density.

4. Not only academics, but also politicians are joining the chorus. For example, in California, State Senator Tom Hayden, a radical in terms of California politics and, incidentally, a driver of an alternative fuel vehicle, wrote an op-ed piece in the *Los Angeles Times* (Hayden 1995) arguing vehemently for pulling the plug on the Los Angeles rail transit project. We agree with his arguments 100 percent. In view of our notoriety as the libertarians of the planning profession, we can only marvel that logic makes such strange bedfellows.

5. In fact, prevailing suburban gross housing densities in 1990 were 780 units per square mile; even central city housing densities were only 1,060 units per square mile, while equivalent "central places inside urbanized areas" densities were 1,261 units per square mile. The implication of the RERC data is that in national average terms all the United States is "low density sprawl." The compact city proponents argue in favor of densities of 5–6 units per acre, or up to 3,840 units per square mile, not very different from the RERC's high-density standard.

6. To illustrate this point, consider the following examples from Southern California. Starting alphabetically and stopping with the letter C, the nonwhite household share in 1990 was 50.8 percent in Alhambra, 31.5 percent in Anaheim, 35.9 percent in Artesia, 41.0 percent in Baldwin Park, 49.3 percent in Bell, 56.0 percent in Bell Gardens, 57.8 percent in Carson, 51.1 percent in Cerritos, 35.9 percent in Colton, 90.8 percent in Compton, and 61.5 percent in Cudahy. We would not argue that Southern California is typical, but it is clear that the wholly white suburb assumption requires drastic qualification.

REFERENCES

Adler, Jerry. 1995. Bye-Bye, Suburban Dream. *Newsweek*, May 15: 40–53.

Altshuler, Alan A. 1977. Review of *The Costs of Sprawl*. *Journal of the American Planning Association* 43, 2: 207–9.

Altshuler, Alan A. 1979. *The Urban Transportation System: Policies and Policy Innovation*. Cambridge: MIT Press.

Altshuler, Alan A., and Jose A. Gomez-Ibanez. 1993. *Regulation for Revenue: The Political Economy of Land Use Exactions*. Washington, DC: Brookings Institution.

Anderson, William P., Pavlos S. Kanaroglou, and Eric J.

Miller. 1996. Urban Form, Energy and the Environment: A Review of Issues, Evidence and Policy. *Urban Studies* 33,1: 7–35.

Bank of America et al. 1995. *Beyond Sprawl: New Patterns of Growth to Fit the New California.* San Francisco: Bank of America.

Baumgartner, Michael P. 1988. *The Moral Order of the Suburb.* New York: Oxford University Press.

Bohi, Douglas R., and Joel Darmstadter. 1994. Twenty Years after the Energy Crisis: What Lessons Were Learned? *Resources* 116,1: 16–20.

Bourne, Larry S. 1992. Self-Fulfilling Prophecies? Decentralization, Inner City Decline, and the Quality of Urban Life. *Journal of the American Planning Association* 58,4: 509–13.

Brindle, Ray. 1994. Lies, Damned Lies and 'Automobile Dependence.' *Australasian Transport Research Forum* 19 (Papers): 117–31.

Burchell, Robert W., and David Listokin. 1995. Land, Infrastructure, Housing Costs, and Fiscal Impacts Associated with Growth: The Literature on the Impacts of Traditional Versus Managed Growth. Paper prepared for "Alternatives to Sprawl" Conference, The Brookings Institution, Washington, DC, March 22.

Burchell, Robert W., et al. 1992a. *Impact Assessment of the New Jersey Interim State Development and Redevelopment Plan, Report II: Research Findings.* Trenton: New Jersey Office of State Planning.

Burchell, Robert W., et al. 1992b. *Impact Assessment of the New Jersey Interim State Development and Redevelopment Plan, Report III: Supplemental AIPLAN Assessment.* Trenton: New Jersey Office of State Planning.

Calthorpe, Peter G. 1993. *The Next American Metropolis.* Princeton: Princeton University Press.

Cameron, Michael W. 1994. *Efficiency and Fairness on the Road: Strategies for Unsnarling Traffic in Southern California..* New York: Environmental Defense Fund.

Cervero, Robert. 1994a. Transit-Focused Development. Does it Draw People into Transit and Buses? *IURD Universe* 4: 3–5.

Cervero, Robert. 1994b. Transit Villages: From Idea to Implementation. *Access* 5: 8–13.

Congressional Budget Office. 1988. *New Directions for the Nation's Public Works.* Washington, DC: U.S. Government Printing Office.

Crane, Randall. 1996. Cars and Drivers in the New Suburbs: Linking Access to Travel in Neotraditional Planning. *Journal of the American Planning Association* 62,1: 51–65.

Diamond, Henry L., and Patrick F. Noonan. 1996. *Land Use in America.* Washington, DC: Island Press for the Lincoln Institute of Land Policy.

Downing, Paul B., ed. 1977. *Local Service Pricing and Their Effect on Urban Spatial Structure.* Vancouver: University of British Columbia Press.

Downs, Anthony. 1994. *New Visions for Metropolitan America.* Washington, DC: The Brookings Institution; Cambridge: Lincoln Institute of Land Policy.

Drucker, Peter F. 1989. Information and the Future of the City. *Urban Land* 48: 38–9.

Duncan, James E., et al. 1989. *The Search for Efficient Urban Growth Patterns.* Tallahassee: Florida Department of Community Affairs.

Dyckman, John W. 1976. Speculations on Future Urban Form. Working paper. Baltimore: Johns Hopkins University, Center for Metropolitan Planning and Research.

The Economist. 1995. Will the World Starve? June 10, 39–40.

Ewing, Reid H. 1995. Characteristics, Causes, and Effects of Sprawl: A Literature Review. *Environmental and Urban Issues* (Spring): 1–15.

Federal Home Mortgage Association. 1992, 1993, 1994. *National Housing Survey.* Washington, DC: FHMA.

Fischel, William A. 1985. *The Economics of Zoning Laws: A Property Rights Approach to American Land Use Controls.* Baltimore: The Johns Hopkins University Press.

Frank, James E. 1989. *The Costs of Alternative Development Patterns: A Review of the Literature.* Washington, DC: Urban Land Institute.

Frey, Thomas A. 1995. Trends in Land Use in the U.S. In *The State of Humanity,* edited by Julian L. Simon. Cambridge: Basil Blackwell.

Frieden, Bernard, and Lynne B. Sagalyn. 1989. *Downtown, Inc.: How America Rebuilds Cities.* Cambridge: MIT Press.

Giuliano, Genevieve. 1995. The Weakening Transportation-Land Use Connection. *Access* 6: 3–11.

Goldberg, Michael A., and John Mercer. 1986. *The Myth of the North American City.* Vancouver: University of British Columbia Press.

Gomez-Ibanez, Jose A. 1991. A Global View of Automobile Dependence. *Journal of the American Planning Association* 57,3: 376–9.

Gordon, Peter, and Harry W. Richardson. 1989a. Gasoline Consumption and Cities: A Reply. *Journal of the American Planning Association* 55,3: 342–6.

Gordon, Peter, and Harry W. Richardson. 1989b. Notes from the Underground: The Failure of Urban Mass Transit. *The Public Interest* 94. 77–86.

Gordon, Peter, and Harry W. Richardson. 1994a. Geographic Factors Explaining Worktrip Length Changes. Prepared for the U.S. Department of Transportation, Federal Highway Administration.

Gordon, Peter, and Harry W. Richardson. 1994b. Congestion Trends in Metropolitan Areas. In *Curbing Gridlock: Peak-Period Fees to Relieve Traffic Congestion.* National Research Council. Washington, DC: National Academy Press. 1–31.

Gordon, Peter, and Harry W. Richardson. 1995. Sustainable Congestion. In *Cities in Competition: The Emergence of Productive and Sustainable Cities for the 21st Century,* edited by J. Brotchie et al. Sydney: Longham Cheshire. 348–58.

Gordon, Peter, and Harry W. Richardson. 1996a. Beyond Polycentricity: The Dispersed Metropolis, Los Angeles, 1970–90. *Journal of the American Planning Association* 62,3: 289–95.

Gordon, Peter, and Harry W. Richardson. 1996b. Los Angeles Among Other CMSAs: Outlier or the Norm? *Environment and Planning A* 23: forthcoming.

Gordon, Peter, Harry W. Richardson, and Y. Choi. 1992.

Tests of the Standard Urban Model: A Micro (Trade-off) Alternative. *Review of Urban and Regional Development Studies* 4,1: 50–66.

Gordon, Peter, Harry W. Richardson, and Myung-Jin Jun. 1991. The Commuting Paradox: Evidence from the Top Twenty. *Journal of the American Planning Association* 57,4: 416–20.

Gordon, Peter, Harry W. Richardson, and Gang Yu. 1996. Settlement Patterns in the U.S.: Recent Evidence and Implications. Paper presented at the 1996 TRED Conference on Transportation and Land Use, Lincoln Institute of Land Policy, Cambridge, Massachusetts, October 11–12.

Hall, Peter. 1980. *Great Planning Disasters.* Berkeley: University of California Press.

Handy, Susan. 1994. Highway Blues: Nothing a Little Accessibility Can't Cure. *Access* 5: 3–7.

Hayden, Tom. 1995. Stop the Train Before We Crash. *Los Angeles Times,* July 14, B9.

Hilton, George W. 1974. *Federal Transit Subsidies.* Washington, DC: American Enterprise Institute.

Kain, John. 1988. Choosing the Wrong Technology: Or How to Spend Billions and Reduce Transit Use. *Journal of Advanced Transportation* 21: 197–213.

Kain, John. 1990. Deception in Dallas: Strategic Misrepresentation in Rail Transit Promotion and Evaluation. *Journal of the American Planning Association* 56, 2: 184–96.

Kain, John. 1991. Trends in Urban Spatial Structure, Demographic Change, Auto and Transit Use, and the Role of Pricing. Statement prepared for the United States Senate, Committee on Environment and Public Works.

Keating, W. Dennis, and Norman Krumholtz. 1991. Downtown Plans for the 1980s: The Case for More Equity in the 1990s. *Journal of the American Planning Association* 57, 2: 136–52.

Ladd, Helen F. 1992. Population Growth, Density and the Costs of Providing Public Services. *Urban Studies* 29,2: 273–96.

Lincoln Institute of Land Policy. 1995. *Alternatives to Sprawl.* Cambridge, MA: Lincoln Institute of Land Policy and The Brookings Institution.

Linnemann, Peter D., and Anita A. Summers. 1991. Patterns and Processes of Employment and Population Decentralization in the U.S., 1970-86. New Orleans: 38th North American Meeting of the Regional Science Association.

Maher, Ian. 1992. Commuting Calculations. *Journal of the American Planning Association* 58,3: 386–7.

Meyer, John R., John F. Kain, and Martin Wohl. 1965. *The Urban Transportation Problem.* Cambridge: Harvard University Press.

Mieskowski, Peter, and Edwin S. Mills. 1993. The Causes of Metropolitan Suburbanization. *Journal of Economic Perspectives* 7,3: 135–47.

Mills, Edwin S. 1991. Should Governments Own Convention Centers? Palatine, IL: Heartland Institute Study #33.

Miyao, Takahiro. 1991. Japan's Urban Economy and Land Policy. *The Annals of the American Academy of Political and Social Science* 513: 130–38.

Newman, Peter W. G., and Jeffrey R. Kenworthy. 1989. Gasoline Consumption and Cities: A Comparison of U.S. Cities with a Global Survey. *Journal of the American Planning Association* 55,1: 24–37.

Nowlan, David, and Greg Stewart. 1991. Downtown Population Growth and Commuting Trips: Recent Experience in Toronto. *Journal of the American Planning Association* 52,2: 165–82.

Olson, Mancur. 1965. *The Logic of Collective Action: Public Goods and the Theory of Groups.* Cambridge, MA: Harvard University Press.

O'Toole, Randal. 1995. The Battle of Oak Grove. *Liberty* 9,1: 22–4, 68.

Peiser, Richard B. 1984. Does It Pay to Plan Suburban Growth? *Journal of the American Planning Association* 50,4: 419–33.

Peiser, Richard B. 1989. Density and Urban Sprawl. *Land Economics* 65,3: 193–204.

Pickrell, Donald H. 1989. *Urban Rail Transit Projects: Forecast vs. Actual Ridership and Costs.* Urban Mass Transportation Administration Report, United States Department of Transportation. Washington, DC: United States Government Printing Office.

Pisarski, Alan E. 1987. *Commuting in America: A National Report on Commuting Patterns and Trends.* Westport, CT: Eno Foundation for Transportation.

Porter, Michael E. 1995. The Competitive Advantage of the Inner City. *Harvard Business Review* (May-June): 55–71.

Real Estate Research Corporation. 1974. *The Costs of Urban Sprawl: Detailed Cost Analysis.* Washington, DC: U.S. Government Printing Office.

Resource Management Consultants, Inc. 1989. *Development in Wright County, Minnesota: Cost-Revenue Relationship.* Minneapolis: RMC.

Richardson, Harry W., and Peter Gordon. 1993. Market Planning: Oxymoron or Common Sense? *Journal of the American Planning Association* 59,3: 347–52.

Salins, Peter D. 1994. Metropolitan Visions. *Reason* (December): 60–3.

Sawicki, David. 1990. Review of *Downtown, Inc. Journal of the American Planning Association* 56,2: 244–6.

Sen, Amartya K. 1994. The Population Delusion. *New York Review of Books,* September 22.

Shoup, Donald C. 1995. An Opportunity to Reduce Minimum Parking Requirements. *Journal of the American Planning Association* 61,1: 14–28.

U.S. Bureau of the Census. 1990. *1990 Census of Population: Social and Economic Characteristics.* Washington, DC.: U.S. Government Printing Office.

U.S. Department of Transportation, Bureau of Transportation Statistics. 1994. *Transportation Statistics Annual Report 1994.* Washington, DC: United States Department of Transportation.

Vincent, Mary Jayne, et al. 1994. *NPTS Urban Travel Patterns: 1990 NPTS.* Washington, DC: Office of Highway Information Management, Federal Highway Administration, United States Department of Transportation.

Wachs, Martin. 1989. United States Transit Subsidy Policy: In Need of Reform. *Science* 244 (June): 1545–9.

Webber, Melvin M. 1976. The BART Experience—What Have We Learned? *The Public Interest* 45 (Fall): 79–108.

Webber, Melvin M. 1993. The Marriage of Autos and Transit: How to Make Transit Popular Again. Presented to the Fourth International Research Conference, Center for Transportation Studies, University of Minnesota.

Windsor, Duane. 1979. A Critique of The Costs of Sprawl. *Journal of the American Planning Association* 45,2: 279–92.

Wohl, Martin. 1976. The Case for Rapid Transit; Before and After the Fact. *Transportation Alternatives in Southern California*. Los Angeles: University of Southern California, The Institute for Public Policy Research, Center for Public Affairs.

[28]

Transport and urban form in thirty-two of the
world's principal cities

By Peter W. G. Newman

Associate Professor in Environmental Science, Murdoch University,
Murdoch, Western Australia

and Jeffrey R. Kenworthy

Research Fellow, Institute for Science and Technology Policy,
Murdoch University, Murdoch, Western Australia

A study of 32 major world cities shows that there are very clear relationships between transport and urban form. Economic factors such as income and petrol price are less important than the direct policy instruments of the transport planner and urban planner, such as the relative provision of infrastructure for automobiles and rapid transit, or the density of population and jobs. Transport and urban planning policies are developed with quantitative guidelines that can help cities ease their dependence on the automobile, for example, by increasing population densities where these are under 30 per hectare.

1. Introduction

This paper presents some of the findings from an Australian Government funded study of transport and land use in 32 of the world's principal cities. The major purpose of the study was to establish policies at the urban level for reducing transport energy use. However, there are so many social, economic and environmental implications in the relationships between transport and urban form, that the project has significance for many aspects of urban and transport policy. Thus for this paper it is possible at the outset to suggest that the following aims are considered to be desirable outcomes from improving transport and urban form:

lessening the vulnerability of a city to oil supply disruptions thus improving its sustainability in energy terms;

minimizing the effect of transport-related inflation and the national balance of payments due to imported oil;

reducing the level of dependence on the private car;

improving the balance between public and private transport, thus reducing the public transport deficit;

increasing the amount of non-motorized transport i.e. walking and bicycling;

improving the level of accessibility to the transport disadvantaged i.e. the elderly, children, poor people and handicapped, who cannot use a car;

reducing the quantity of emissions including those that contribute to the 'greenhouse effect' and to smog;

250   P. W. G. Newman and J. R. Kenworthy

lessening the possibilities of road accidents; and

enhancing several less quantifiable variables concerning the 'human' aspects of a
city, especially the attraction of the central city.

The full list of parameters chosen for this study are summarized in table 1. The data
covering 1960, 1970 and 1980 were collected over a five-year period, principally by
personal visits to each city in 1983 and 1986, and a long series of letters and telephone
calls. The utmost care was taken to ensure the data were supported by relevant
transport and planning authorities in each city, and numerous internal consistency
tests were carried out to check the reliability of the data.

Considerable work was done to ensure the parameters were defined in a
comparable way in each city and in particular, urban land-use data were defined to
exclude all rural land uses such as farms, forests, undeveloped land and large bodies of
water. The raw data and standardized data (reduced to transport planning parameters)
amounting to over 100 data items per city is now available complete with detailed
comments on source material, assumptions and computations in a book (Newman and
Kenworthy 1989).

It should be stressed that the great majority of parameters collected are not readily
available from published sources but must be sought out and compiled from detailed
documents within government agencies. A major part of this work is often the
definition of the relevant area of the city (e.g. inner area) and the compilation of data
such as population and employment to match the definition. The book discusses these
issues in detail and provides clear descriptions of how the data on each city were drawn
together from many diffuse and unrelated sources.

This paper will review the main transport and land-use patterns in the 32 cities for
1980. For many of the parameters Moscow is not available and hence the total is
generally made up of 12 European, 10 American, 1 Canadian, 5 Australian and 3 Asian
cities. An analysis of the patterns in the ten US cities has been published (Newman and
Kenworthy 1988 a). The major questions being assessed by the study which will be
examined here are:

How much variation is there in the transport and land use of the world's major
cities?

How closely does transport relate to land use in these cities?

Table 1.   Parameters collected in world cities study for 1960, 1970 and 1980.

Population, urbanized area and employment for central business district (CBD), inner area and
  total city
Parking (on-street and off-street) in CBD
Length of road network in whole city
Passenger cars and total vehicles on register
Total annual VKT (vehicle kilometres of travel) by passenger cars and other vehicles
Average vehicle occupancy
Average speed of travel in the road traffic network
Total annual gasoline consumption and diesel consumption for whole city
Journey to work modal split (%) and other modal split data where available
Average trip lengths (km) for the journey to work and other trips
Annual vehicle kilometres, passengers carried, average travel distance of passengers, average
  speed of travel and annual energy consumption for all bus, train, tram and ferry operations
  (including publicly and privately operated transit services)

How does automobile usage relate to the provision of infrastructure for automobiles?

Are economic factors such as income and petrol price so dominant in determining transport patterns that transport infrastructure and urban form cannot be addressed directly for urban policy?

What are the direct policy implications from the study?

These questions have been the subject of many academic debates as well as soul-searching within transport and planning authorities. This study is able to throw some light on the issues as it is probably the first time there has been a reliable set of urban data for this number of cities with such an international cross-section.

2. Results and discussion

Table 2 presents the main transport variables emphasizing the modal split. Passenger km of private car use and public transport use enable a real comparison of the relative importance of these modes and the percentage of workers bicycling and walking to work gives some idea of the relative priority of these non-motorized modes. Petrol use gives an overall feel for the transport system in each city by acting as a kind of barometer which rises with increasing automobile emphasis.

Table 3 sets out the parameters which relate to the provision of infrastructure for automobile usage i.e. how many roads and car parking spaces are provided, the level of congestion, and the relative speed of the public transport options that are available.

Table 4 provides the main urban form parameters: population and job densities in the city as a whole and then by central city, inner city and outer area.

3. Transport patterns

3.1. *Petrol use*

US cities use on average twice as much petrol per capita as in Australian cities, four times as much as in European cities and ten times as much as in Asian cities. Moscow which has almost no private car use, manages on a mere 380 MJ per capita which is nearly two-hundred times less than some US cities.

Toronto uses more than Australian cities but this raises the question about the role of car size as Toronto private car use is some 8% less than in Australian cities and it has more than double the public transport usage. Hence if the cities are adjusted for vehicle efficiency as in table 5 the comparisons are a little more meaningful in purely transport terms.

The table shows that if all cities had vehicles like US cities then Toronto's petrol use is less than Australian cities and the variation from US cities to Asian cities would be reduced from a factor of ten to a factor of seven, and US to European cities reduces from four times to three times. Thus this technological factor is a relevant parameter but clearly is not the dominant factor often described in energy conservation literature (see, for example, La Belle and Moses 1982, Chandler 1985). Other economic factors will be discussed shortly to see their contribution to this variation in petrol usage.

3.2. *Modal split*

The highly automobile-oriented US cities at the top of the list in table 2 have virtually no public transport as a percentage of their total passenger km of travel e.g. Houston 0·8%, Phoenix 0·5%, Detroit 0·8%; even in a city like Denver where there is a

252

P. W. G. Newman and J. R. Kenworthy

Table 2. Transport patterns in the world's major cities (1980).

City	Petrol use (MJ per capita)	Total vehicles (per 1000 people)	Car ownership (per 1000 people)	Private car (passenger km per capita)	Public transport (passenger km per capita)	Private car/public transport balance (% of total passenger km on public transport)
US cities						
Houston	74 510	797	603	15 968	128	0·8
Phoenix	69 908	689	499	13 170	66	0·5
Detroit	65 978	691	594	14 017	112	0·8
Denver	63 466	853	666	11 630	218	1·8
Los Angeles	58 474	667	542	13 865	384	2·7
San Francisco	55 365	681	543	13 200	926	6·6
Boston	54 185	557	465	12 570	518	4·0
Washington	51 241	645	561	11 670	616	5·0
Chicago	48 246	518	445	11 122	971	8·0
New York	44 033	459	412	7 856	1 285	14·1
Average	58 541	656	533	12 507	522	4·4
Australian cities						
Perth	32 610	614	475	11 477	592	4·9
Brisbane	30 653	595	458	11 721	745	6·0
Melbourne	29 104	528	446	10 128	779	7·1
Adelaide	28 791	568	475	10 625	655	5·8
Sydney	27 986	489	412	9 450	1 511	13·8
Average	29 829	559	453	10 680	856	7·5
Canadian city						
Toronto	34 813	554	463	9 850	1 976	16·7
European cities						
Hamburg	16 671	382	344	7 470	1 516	17·0
Frankfurt	16 093	427	387	6 810	1 713	20·1
Zürich	15 709	432	375	7 254	2 157	22·9
Stockholm	15 574	390	347	6 570	2 124	24·4
Brussels	14 744	408	361	5 706	1 396	19·7
Paris	14 091	383	338	4 199	1 827	30·3
London	12 426	356	288	4 452	1 717	27·8
Munich	12 372	398	360	5 235	1 592	23·3
West Berlin	11 331	306	269	4 572	2 159	32·1
Copenhagen	11 106	296	246	6 231	1 657	21·0
Vienna	10 074	374	311	4 262	1 828	30·0
Amsterdam	9 171	342	308	4 441	1 801	28·9
Average	13 280	375	328	5 595	1 791	24·8
Asian cities						
Tokyo	8 488	267	156	2 993	5 191	63·4
Singapore	6 003	155	65	1 789	1 942	52·1
Hong Kong	1 987	66	42	615	2 043	76·9
Average	5 493	163	88	1 799	3 059	64·1
USSR city						
Moscow	380	40	20	230	>4 262†	>95

† Moscow commuter rail data are missing.

continued overleaf

Table 2 (*concluded*)

City	Public transport vehicle km of service per person	Public transport passenger trips per person	Proportion of public transport passenger km on trains (%)	Proportion of workers using public transport (%)	Proportion of workers using private transport (%)	Proportion of workers using foot or bicycle (%)
US cities						
Houston	9	15	0·0	3·3	93·9	2·8
Phoenix	7	9	0·0	2·2	94·6	3·2
Detroit	17	26	2·7	4·1	93·1	2·8
Denver	25	27	0·0	6·5	88·1	5·3
Los Angeles	27	59	0·0	7·7	88·0	4·2
San Francisco	50	115	33·9	17·0	77·5	5·5
Boston	26	80	52·3	16·1	74·1	9·8
Washington	40	91	37·2	14·1	80·7	5·2
Chicago	42	115	66·7	18·3	75·5	6·2
New York	58	122	78·0	28·3	63·6	8·1
Average	30	66	27·1	11·8	82·9	5·3
Australian cities						
Perth	53	71	14·4	12·0	84·0	4·0
Brisbane	48	79	55·8	16·6	78·1	5·3
Melbourne	53	95	63·1	20·6	73·7	5·7
Adelaide	51	83	33·5	16·5	77·7	5·8
Sydney	77	142	69·9	29·5	65·1	5·4
Average	56	94	47·3	19·0	75·7	5·2
Canadian city						
Toronto	81	178	40·2	31·2	63·0	5·8
European cities						
Hamburg	80	248	64·4	41·0	43·9	15·3
Frankfurt	55	306	51·3	19·0	54·0	27·0
Zürich	62	363	55·6	34·0	45·0	21·0
Stockholm	119	302	60·4	46·0	34·0	20·0
Brussels	54	266	43·2	26·7	57·7	15·6
Paris	47	259	83·8	39·8	36·4	23·8
London	120	284	63·7	39·0	38·0	23·0
Munich	75	307	61·1	42·0	38·0	20·0
West Berlin	83	395	58·3	37·0	48·0	15·0
Copenhagen	110	201	48·0	31·0	36·8	32·2
Vienna	69	313	26·6	44·9	40·4	14·7
Amsterdam	74	345	45·5	14·0	58·0	28·0
Average	79	299	55·1	34·5	44·2	21·3
Asian cities						
Tokyo	94	472	94·9	59·0	16·1	24·9
Singapore	98	353	0·0	59·6	24·6	15·8
Hong Kong	116	466	17·1	62·2	3·3	34·5
Average	103	430	37·3	60·3	14·7	25·1
USSR city						
Moscow	>131	>678	>75	74·0	2·0	24·0

P. W. G. Newman and J. R. Kenworthy

Table 3. Provision for the automobile in the world's major cities (1980).

City	Road supply (m/person)	Parking spaces (per 1000 CBD workers)	Average speed of traffic (km/h)	Total vehicles per km of road	Car kilometres per km of road	Average speed of public transport (km/h)				
						Bus	Train	Tram	Ferry	Total system
US cities										
Houston	10·6	370	51	76	939 428	22	—	—	—	22
Phoenix	10·4	1 033	42	66	818 455	23	—	—	—	23
Detroit	5·8	473	44	119	1 714 024	21	42	—	—	22
Denver	9·4	498	45	107	1 002 509	21	—	—	—	21
Los Angeles	4·5	524	45	158	1 989 979	21	—	—	—	21
San Francisco	4·9	145	46	140	1 923 096	22	45	15	25	29
Boston	5·2	322	39	112	1 586 674	18	45	20	—	30
Washington	5·1	264	39	127	1 562 228	18	40	—	—	26
Chicago	5·0	91	41	103	1 505 631	18	47	—	—	37
New York	4·7	75	35	99	1 267 248	15	35	—	20	31
Average	6·6	380	43	111	1 430 927	20	42	18	23	26
Australian cities										
Perth	13·3	562	43	46	497 392	22	35	—	14	24
Brisbane	6·9	268	48	94	930 096	23	37	—	—	31
Melbourne	7·9	270	48	67	740 564	21	33	18	—	28
Adelaide	9·1	380	43	64	658 970	21	45	28	—	29
Sydney	6·2	156	39	82	870 836	20	45	—	23	37
Average	8·7	327	44	71	739 572	21	39	23	19	30
Canadian city										
Toronto	2·7	198	?	204	2 262 597	20	34	16	—	25
European cities										
Hamburg	2·2	149	30	171	1 974 143	22	36	—	12	31
Frankfurt	2·0	242	30	214	2 136 111	22	44	17	—	37
Zürich	2·6	140	36	165	1 647 922	20	46	15	?	33
Stockholm	2·3	153	30	171	2 128 378	25	36	26	—	32
Brussels	1·7	186	?	246	2 376 794	20	38	17	—	27
Paris	0·9	201	28	410	2 997 666	13	45	—	—	40
London	1·9	130	31	186	1 321 401	18	38	—	—	31
Munich	1·7	285	35	238	1 961 237	20	55	17	—	44
West Berlin	1·5	438	28	208	1 850 153	20	32	—	11	27
Copenhagen	4·3	212	45	69	810 087	24	54	—	—	38
Vienna	1·7	190	30	216	1 539 623	19	38	17	—	23
Amsterdam	2·1	208	39	161	1 378 489	18	57	15	—	36
Average	2·1	211	30	205	1 843 500	20	43	18	12	33
Asian cities										
Tokyo	1·9	66	21	140	1 122 092	12	40	13	—	38
Singapore	1·0	97	30	158	727 886	19	—	—	—	19
Hong Kong	0·2	37	21	290	1 518 142	15	31	10	14	17
Average	1·0	67	24	196	1 122 707	15	36	12	14	25
USSR city										
Moscow	0·4	?	45	93	281 895	21	41	18	—	> 37

Table 4. Urban form in the world's major cities (1980).

City	Whole city density		Central city density		Inner area density		Outer area density		Proportion of population in CBD (%)	Proportion of jobs in CBD (%)	Proportion of population in inner area (%)	Proportion of jobs in inner area (%)
	Population	Jobs	Population	Jobs	Population	Jobs	Population	Jobs				
US cities												
Houston	9	6	6	443	21	26	8	4	0·1	11·6	16·6	41·1
Phoenix	9	4	17	67	19	24	8	4	0·5	3·9	3·7	10·6
Detroit	14	6	11	306	48	20	11	5	0·1	6·6	31·6	29·6
Denver	12	8	19	263	19	17	10	5	0·4	11·6	30·9	49·7
Los Angeles	20	11	29	472	30	14	18	9	0·1	4·8	31·3	43·3
San Francisco	16	8	90	713	59	48	13	5	1·1	17·0	21·3	34·4
Boston	12	6	126	383	45	33	10	4	2·7	15·9	24·3	34·6
Washington	13	8	8	584	44	38	11	6	0·1	16·1	21·4	32·5
Chicago	18	8	16	938	54	26	11	5	0·1	12·3	42·3	44·9
New York	20	9	217	828	107	53	13	6	2·8	22·9	39·5	41·9
Average	14	7	54	500	45	30	11	5	0·8	12·3	26·3	36·3
Australian cities												
Perth	11	5	8	121	16	15	10	3	0·7	24·1	22·9	51·0
Brisbane	10	4	15	346	19	16	9	3	0·3	13·9	21·7	45·7
Melbourne	16	6	25	647	29	40	16	4	0·2	15·2	9·0	33·2
Adelaide	13	5	8	251	19	25	12	4	0·2	14·4	11·6	37·3
Sydney	18	8	11	434	39	39	16	5	0·1	13·2	16·7	39·3
Average	14	6	13	360	24	27	13	4	0·3	16·2	16·4	41·3
Canadian city												
Toronto	40	20	25	757	57	38	34	14	0·2	13·4	35·7	47·9
European cities												
Hamburg	42	24	26	407	88	106	35	12	0·7	20·0	26·8	56·0
Frankfurt	54	43	65	389	63	74	49	25	2·5	18·4	43·3	64·2
Zürich	54	33	44	422	79	66	42	17	0·9	13·6	47·4	65·2
Stockholm	51	34	97	280	58	62	46	16	6·4	26·3	49·3	74·7
Brussels	67	42	74	592	101	85	50	16	1·9	24·6	51·8	75·9
Paris	48	22	235	400	106	60	26	8	5·4	20·2	60·9	75·1
London	56	30	66	397	78	62	48	19	2·7	29·7	37·2	55·1
Munich	57	34	111	231	159	192	48	21	5·9	20·5	21·4	42·9
West Berlin	64	27	133	333	84	46	57	20	0·8	4·8	31·8	41·8
Copenhagen	30	16	85	325	59	38	24	11	2·2	16·0	37·3	44·8
Vienna	72	38	65	403	133	113	59	23	1·3	14·9	31·9	50·8
Amsterdam	51	23	108	153	83	46	32	10	9·7	29·9	59·2	71·7
Average	54	31	92	361	91	79	43	17	3·4	19·9	41·5	59·9
Asian cities												
Tokyo	105	66	82	477	153	114	58	20	1·3	26·6	32·3	84·8
Singapore	83	37	204	339	202	?	63	?	6·6	24·3	35·2	?
Hong Kong	293	110	160	1 259	1 037	478	224	66	0·4	7·3	30·0	45·3
Average	160	71	149	692	464	296	115	43	2·8	19·4	32·5	65·1
USSR city												
Moscow	139	?	155	?	?	?	?	?	3·7	?	?	?

Table 5. Adjusted average 1980 petrol use per capita in cities by region to account for vehicle efficiency (relative to US vehicle efficiencies, using national values and adjusted for average speed in cities).

City	Unadjusted petrol use per capita (MJ)	Average vehicle efficiency (national values) (l/100 km)	Adjusted for average speed in cities (l/100 km)	Petrol use per capita with US vehicle efficiency (MJ) National values	Adjusted for average speed
US cities	58 541	15·35	19·33	58 541	58 541
Australian cities	29 829	12·50	15·33	33 446	37 612
Toronto	34 813	16·30	21·72	32 784	30 982
European cities	13 280	10·66	16·38	19 123	15 727
Asian cities	5 493	7·63	15·05	11 051	7 248

Note 1: Adjustments for average speed are made by using $y = 1·0174x + 37·4291$, where y = fuel consumption in ml/km and x is the inverse of average speed in s/km (Kenworthy and Newman 1982) and national fuel efficiencies are assumed to be at an average speed of 60 km/h.

Note 2: Detailed data on vehicle efficiencies are contained in table 4.1 of Newman and Kenworthy (1989).

strong policy to encourage bus usage due to the smog, only 1·8% of total passenger travel is by public transport. It is only in the US cities with rail systems that any significant proportion of transport is by non-automobile modes e.g. San Francisco 7%, Chicago 8%, New York 14%, (the proportion of total transit passenger km by trains in these cities is San Francisco 34%, Chicago 67% and New York 78%). At the same time the bicycling/walking proportion for journey to work trips rises (up to 10% in Boston, 6 to 8% in others).

Australian cities overall are a little less automobile oriented, though Perth (5% transit, 4% bicycle/walking) is virtually an average US city. Sydney with 14% public transport use is the most non-car oriented Australian city with once again a high proportion on rail (70% of transit). Toronto is significantly different to its North American neighbours with 17% transit use (in particular the comparison with its nearest neighbour Detroit at 0·8% is quite stunning).

European cities on average have 25% public transport use for the total passenger transport task (passenger km) and for the work journey 21% of trips are by bicycling/walking. This ranges from 17% public transport in Hamburg to 32% in West Berlin and 30% in Paris and Vienna; for bicycling/walking to work Copenhagen at 32% and 28% in Amsterdam are the best. In the European cities 55% of public transport passenger km are on trains. On average, people in US cities travel nearly 7000 km further by car and nearly 1200 km less by public transport than in European cities. Among other things this suggests urban travel distances are shorter in Europe and in fact work journey average distances are 30 to 40% shorter in European cities (8 km) compared with US (13 km) and Australian cities (12 km).

All these comparisons are even more striking when the Asian cities are examined where 64% of the transport task is by public transport and 25% of people go to work by walking or biking (35% in Hong Kong). In the modern metropolis of Tokyo only 16% of the people use a car to go to work and in the public transport system 95% of passenger km are by train.

3.3. *Congestion and public transport speeds*

The very clear pattern distinguishing automobile dominated cities from those with significant public transport use (particularly rail) can be related in purely transport terms to how easy it is to travel by car and how the transit option competes in time. The data in table 3 show the automobile based cities to have average traffic speeds of 43 km/h (US) and 44 km/h (Australia) compared with European cities 30 km/h and Asian cities 24 km/h. On the other hand, the bus-only cities of the US provide little competition for cars with 21 to 23 km/h transit speeds. Only the rail option can compete with cars as the average speed of urban trains is 42 km/h in the US, 45 km/h in Sydney, 43 km/h in Europe and 40 km/h in Tokyo (compared with 21 km/h for cars). Tram speeds are much lower but they act usually as distributors in central areas linking in to the major train stations (Vuchic 1981), and typically operate with very high passenger loadings especially compared with buses. It is also interesting that the average speed of buses in US, Australian and European cities as well as Toronto and Moscow is 20 to 21 km/h, a remarkably constant figure considering the enormous diversity in urban conditions in these cities. In the very much denser and congested Asian cities it drops to 15 km/h. It would thus appear that, in general, bus-based public transport systems seem to have an in-built limit on operating speed of no more than 25 km/h, and thus cannot be considered genuine competitors in speed to the car in any city. It could be concluded that any city seriously wishing to change the private car/public transport equilibrium in favour of public transport, must move in the direction of rail-based systems.

3.4. *Road supply and parking*

Table 3 also looks at how cities provide for their transport modes in terms of road supply and central city parking. Here again the automobile cities of the US and Australia provide around three to four times as much road per capita as in European cities and nearly seven to nine times as much as in Asian cities. Central city parking does not have quite such a large variation with the US cities having some 80% more spaces per 1000 workers than European cities and six times that provided in the three Asian cities. Perth is the outstanding city in the sample as far as automobile provision is concerned with by far the highest road supply per capita and a central city parking provision second only to Phoenix which does not in fact have a true central city area.

4.   Urban form patterns

4.1. *Total density*

The main parameter describing the form of a city is its density which has significant effects on travel distances and modal split (e.g. Pushkarev and Zupan 1977). The overall shape of the US and Australian automobile city is of low density in population and jobs with European cities generally being three to four times more dense. Newer cities like Houston, Phoenix, Perth and Brisbane have densities around half that of the older cities like Chicago, New York and Sydney. Toronto tends to be more like a European city in its overall urban form. The Asian cities are again even more extreme with densities some ten times those of the US and Australian cities. Hong Kong is by far the highest density city in the sample and probably in the world.

258   P. W. G. Newman and J. R. Kenworthy

4.2. *Central city density*

One of the significant differences between the US/Australian automobile cities and the more transport balanced European and Asian cities is that the former have central cities which have become areas of very high job concentration with generally few residents and the latter have a much better balance between central city jobs and residences. The central city high rise office block is a characteristic mainly of the automobile city and it gives to US cities much higher average central city job concentrations than in Europe. In fact, the average job density profile of the US city is extremely sharp going from 500 per ha in the central city to 30 per ha in the inner city and 5 per ha in the outer areas, compared with European cities which have 361 per ha, 79 per ha and 17 per ha. On the other hand the residential density of US and Australian central cities is generally less than 20 per ha (except for New York, Boston and San Francisco), whilst in Europe they average around 90 per ha and in Asia about 150 per ha. One of the questions to examine in the correlations between transport and urban form is whether this extreme pattern of job densities in US and Australian cities has any significant effect on balancing automobile use patterns as public transport is favoured by strong central cities (Thomson 1977) or whether the residential density pattern is more dominant.

4.3. *Inner city and outer area density*

As well as being different in overall density there are clear differences in urban form between US/Australian cities and European/Asian cities in terms of their inner cities and their outer areas.

The US/Australian inner city is generally two to three times less dense than in European, and ten times less than that in Asian cities. However, the old inner cities of San Francisco, Washington, Boston, Chicago, Sydney and particularly New York are similar to many European cities (as is Toronto), while the inner cities of newer US and Australian cities are generally little more than their overall density. This confirms the generally accepted picture of older cities as having steeper population density gradients (e.g. Clark 1982).

The outer area densities of US and Australian cities are amazingly uniform in all cases with very low land-use intensity. European cities are marked by much more intensively utilized outer areas—some four times more on average than in US and Australian cities. Toronto is again more like a European city in its outer area; from observation it appears to develop its density partly through a number of intensively utilized sub-centres linked by rapid transit to the city centre. Tokyo's outer areas are similar to European outer areas although Hong Kong is once again at the extreme in land-use intensity with an overall outer area density greater than the central cities of some US and Australian cities.

The variations in total density and in inner/outer area patterns suggest that these may be highly significant in determining the overall transport patterns. Thus the next section examines the correlations between transport and urban form as revealed by our data.

5.   Transport and urban form correlations

Table 6 provides the linear correlations between the transport and urban form variables and table 7 provides the linear correlations between the transport variables so that the question of petrol use and private car dependence can be linked to the degree of provision for the automobile. More sophisticated statistical analysis of the data is

Table 6. Transport and urban form correlations.

	Urban density	Job density	CBD population density	CBD job density	Inner area population density	Inner area job density	Outer area population density	Outer area job density	Proportion of population in CBD (%)	Proportion of jobs in CBD (%)	Proportion of population in inner area (%)	Proportion of jobs in inner area (%)
Petrol use (MJ per capita)	−0·6099 s=0·000	−0·6627 s=0·000	−0·4827 s=0·003	−0·0301 s=0·436	−0·3914 s=0·015	−0·4849 s=0·003	−0·5752 s=0·000	−0·5913 s=0·000	−0·4810 s=0·003	−0·5067 s=0·002	−0·4561 s=0·005	−0·6412 s=0·000
Total vehicles (per 1000 people)	−0·7619 s=0·000	−0·7649 s=0·000	−0·6523 s=0·000	−0·2325 s=0·104	−0·5930 s=0·000	−0·6524 s=0·000	−0·7177 s=0·000	−0·7322 s=0·000	−0·4726 s=0·003	−0·3864 s=0·016	−0·4349 s=0·007	−0·5031 s=0·002
Car ownership (per 1000 people)	−0·7801 s=0·000	−0·7792 s=0·000	−0·6350 s=0·000	−0·2000 s=0·140	−0·6129 s=0·000	−0·6758 s=0·000	−0·7305 s=0·000	−0·7501 s=0·000	−0·4395 s=0·006	−0·3637 s=0·022	−0·3503 s=0·027	−0·4879 s=0·003
Private car (passenger km per capita)	−0·7438 s=0·000	−0·7793 s=0·000	−0·6698 s=0·000	−0·1360 s=0·233	−0·5409 s=0·001	−0·6204 s=0·000	−0·6931 s=0·000	−0·7164 s=0·000	−0·5379 s=0·001	−0·4694 s=0·004	−0·5186 s=0·001	−0·6214 s=0·000
Public transport (passenger km per capita)	+0·5234 s=0·001	+0·6773 s=0·000	+0·3959 s=0·014	+0·1452 s=0·218	+0·2927 s=0·055	+0·3675 s=0·023	+0·4602 s=0·005	+0·4897 s=0·003	+0·2981 s=0·052	+0·4500 s=0·006	+0·4185 s=0·010	+0·6935 s=0·000
Private car/public transport balance (% of total passenger km on public transport)	+0·8537 s=0·000	+0·9077 s=0·000	+0·5948 s=0·000	+0·3155 s=0·042	+0·7405 s=0·000	+0·7810 s=0·000	+0·8402 s=0·000	+0·8458 s=0·000	+0·3549 s=0·023	+0·2902 s=0·057	+0·3639 s=0·022	+0·5352 s=0·001
Public transport vehicle km of service per person	+0·5785 s=0·000	+0·6205 s=0·000	+0·3879 s=0·015	+0·1762 s=0·172	+0·4365 s=0·007	+0·4850 s=0·003	+0·5893 s=0·000	+0·5975 s=0·000	+0·3772 s=0·018	+0·4813 s=0·003	+0·3333 s=0·033	+0·4660 s=0·005
Public transport passenger trips per person	+0·7390 s=0·000	+0·8414 s=0·000	+0·5314 s=0·001	+0·1574 s=0·199	+0·5289 s=0·001	+0·6151 s=0·000	+0·7185 s=0·000	+0·7564 s=0·000	+0·4515 s=0·005	+0·3893 s=0·015	+0·5179 s=0·001	+0·6653 s=0·000
Proportion of public transport passenger km on trains (%)	+0·0863 s=0·319	+0·1287 s=0·245	+0·3275 s=0·034	+0·1683 s=0·183	−0·0921 s=0·311	+0·0257 s=0·446	−0·0277 s=0·441	+0·0295 s=0·439	+0·2317 s=0·101	+0·4543 s=0·005	+0·3186 s=0·04	+0·4788 s=0·004
Proportion of workers using public transport (%)	+0·7143 s=0·000	+0·7835 s=0·000	+0·5725 s=0·000	+0·2989 s=0·051	+0·5582 s=0·001	+0·6661 s=0·000	+0·6941 s=0·000	+0·7044 s=0·000	+0·3244 s=0·037	+0·4000 s=0·013	+0·3554 s=0·025	+0·5667 s=0·001
Proportion of workers using private transport (%)	−0·7615 s=0·000	−0·8395 s=0·000	−0·6114 s=0·000	−0·2378 s=0·099	−0·5963 s=0·000	−0·6883 s=0·000	−0·7387 s=0·000	−0·7606 s=0·000	−0·4359 s=0·007	−0·4334 s=0·007	−0·4685 s=0·004	−0·6239 s=0·000
Proportion of workers using foot or bicycle (%)	+0·6636 s=0·000	+0·7387 s=0·000	+0·5349 s=0·001	+0·0725 s=0·349	+0·5218 s=0·001	+0·5767 s=0·000	+0·6417 s=0·000	+0·6900 s=0·000	+0·5306 s=0·001	+0·3898 s=0·015	+0·5577 s=0·001	+0·5843 s=0·000

260 P. W. G. Newman and J. R. Kenworthy

Table 7. Intercorrelations between the transport variables.

	Petrol use	Total vehicle ownership	Car ownership	Private car (pass. km per capita)	Public trans. (pass. km per capita)	Private car/ public trans. balance	Public trans. vehicle km per person	Public trans. pass. trips per person	Prop. of public trans. pass. km on trains	Prop. of workers using public trans.	Prop. of workers using private trans.
Petrol use											
Total vehicle ownership	+0·8950 s=0·000										
Car ownership	+0·8555 s=0·000	+0·9813 s=0·000									
Private car (pass. km per capita)	+0·9185 s=0·000	+0·9437 s=0·000	+0·9258 s=0·000								
Public trans. (pass. km per capita)	−0·7328 s=0·000	−0·7328 s=0·000	−0·7450 s=0·000	−0·7633 s=0·000							
Private car/public trans. balance	−0·7340 s=0·000	−0·8889 s=0·000	−0·9205 s=0·000	−0·8746 s=0·000	+0·8046 s=0·000						
Public trans. vehicle km per person	−0·8305 s=0·000	−0·8256 s=0·000	−0·8082 s=0·000	−0·7981 s=0·000	+0·7026 s=0·000	+0·7347 s=0·000					
Public trans. pass. trips per person	−0·8750 s=0·000	−0·8908 s=0·000	−0·8712 s=0·000	−0·9234 s=0·000	+0·8551 s=0·000	+0·8995 s=0·000	+0·7635 s=0·000				
Prop. of public trans. pass. km on trains	−0·5169 s=0·001	−0·4633 s=0·004	−0·3828 s=0·015	−0·4452 s=0·005	+0·5858 s=0·000	+0·3312 s=0·032	+0·4101 s=0·011	+0·4043 s=0·012			
Prop. of workers using public trans.	−0·8216 s=0·000	−0·8775 s=0·000	−0·8775 s=0·000	−0·8835 s=0·000	+0·7906 s=0·000	+0·8721 s=0·000	+0·8098 s=0·000	+0·8547 s=0·000	+0·4153 s=0·010		
Prop. of workers using private trans.	+0·8831 s=0·000	+0·9339 s=0·000	+0·9218 s=0·000	+0·9430 s=0·000	−0·8148 s=0·000	−0·9120 s=0·000	−0·8459 s=0·000	−0·9244 s=0·000	−0·4336 s=0·007	−0·9536 s=0·000	
Prop. of workers using foot or bicycle	−0·7822 s=0·000	−0·8117 s=0·000	−0·7809 s=0·000	−0·8241 s=0·000	+0·6635 s=0·000	+0·7654 s=0·000	+0·7083 s=0·000	+0·8279 s=0·000	+0·3634 s=0·022	+0·6434 s=0·000	−0·8441 s=0·000
Road supply	+0·7081 s=0·000	+0·7737 s=0·000	+0·7026 s=0·000	+0·7854 s=0·000	−0·6621 s=0·000	−0·6744 s=0·000	−0·6257 s=0·000	−0·8205 s=0·000	−0·4563 s=0·004	−0·7559 s=0·000	+0·8033 s=0·000
Central city parking	+0·5775 s=0·000	+0·5935 0·0000	+0·5271 s=0·001	+0·5574 s=0·001	−0·5795 s=0·000	−0·5394 s=0·001	−0·6238 s=0·000	−0·5694 s=0·000	−0·5699 s=0·000	−0·6546 s=0·000	+0·6472 s=0·000
Average speed of traffic	+0·6340 s=0·000	+0·6502 s=0·000	+0·6232 s=0·000	+0·7212 s=0·000	−0·7737 s=0·000	−0·5660 s=0·001	−0·6472 s=0·000	−0·8601 s=0·000	−0·3465 s=0·030	−0·8438 s=0·000	+0·8510 s=0·000
Total vehicles per km of road	−0·4661 s=0·004	−0·4093 s=0·010	−0·3437 s=0·027	−0·5317 s=0·001	+0·4038 s=0·012	+0·3547 s=0·023	+0·3143 s=0·042	+0·6219 s=0·000	+0·2006 s=0·135	+0·5736 s=0·000	−0·6173 s=0·000
Car km per km of road	−0·0733 s=0·345	+0·0059 s=0·487	+0·1145 s=0·266	−0·0675 s=0·357	+0·1951 s=0·146	−0·1138 s=0·268	+0·0508 s=0·393	+0·3098 s=0·045	+0·1739 s=0·170	+0·2436 s=0·093	−0·2667 s=0·073
Average speed of buses	+0·2362 s=0·096	+0·3437 s=0·027	+0·3402 s=0·028	+0·4156 s=0·009	−0·5043 s=0·002	−0·4005 s=0·011	−0·1553 s=0·202	−0·4244 s=0·009	−0·3508 s=0·024	−0·4298 s=0·008	+0·4304 s=0·008
Average speed of trains	−0·0636 s=0·376	+0·0174 s=0·466	+0·0557 s=0·391	−0·0163 s=0·468	−0·0108 s=0·479	−0·0997 s=0·310	−0·0767 s=0·355	+0·0153 s=0·470	+0·0849 s=0·337	−0·2367 s=0·122	+0·0317 s=0·439
Average speed of trams	+0·2533 s=0·181	+0·3386 s=0·076	+0·4255 s=0·056	+0·4145 s=0·062	−0·4124 s=0·071	−0·4417 s=0·049	−0·1964 s=0·250	−0·5527 s=0·020	+0·0290 s=0·459	−0·3562 s=0·015	+0·4550 s=0·051
Average speed of ferries	+0·7962 s=0·014	+0·6123 s=0·069	+0·6095 s=0·070	+0·6297 s=0·062	−0·4504 s=0·153	−0·4483 s=0·154	−0·5159 s=0·115	−0·6257 s=0·064	+0·1908 s=0·340	−0·4915 s=0·129	+0·5196 s=0·113
Average speed overall	−0·3708 s=0·020	−0·2481 s=0·091	−0·1594 s=0·196	−0·2503 s=0·087	+0·4083 s=0·011	+0·0521 s=0·0390	+0·2428 s=0·094	+0·2633 s=0·076	+0·8079 s=0·000	+0·1623 s=0·191	−0·2698 s=0·071

continued overleaf

Table 7 (concluded)

	Prop. of workers using foot or bicycle	Road supply	Central city parking	Average speed of traffic	Total vehicles per km of road	Car km per km of road	Average speed of buses	Average speed of trains	Average speed of trams	Average speed of ferries	Average speed overall
Road supply	−0·6960 $s=0·000$										
Central city parking	−0·4800 $s=0·003$	+0·6489 $s=0·000$									
Average speed of traffic	−0·6797 $s=0·000$	+0·6983 $s=0·000$	+0·4555 $s=0·006$								
Total vehicles per km of road	+0·5474 $s=0·001$	−0·7127 $s=0·000$	−0·3537 $s=0·025$	−0·6975 $s=0·000$							
Car km per km of road	+0·2438 $s=0·093$	−0·5166 $s=0·001$	−0·2498 $s=0·088$	−0·4479 $s=0·006$	+0·7941 $s=0·000$						
Average speed of buses	−0·3287 $s=0·035$	+0·4005 $s=0·012$	+0·4331 $s=0·007$	+0·5686 $s=0·001$	−0·4814 $s=0·003$	−0·2210 $s=0·112$					
Average speed of trains	+0·2913 $s=0·074$	−0·0773 $s=0·351$	−0·0417 $s=0·120$	+0·2740 $s=0·092$	−0·0245 $s=0·452$	+0·0031 $s=0·494$	+0·0632 $s=0·377$				
Average speed of trams	−0·4638 $s=0·047$	+0·5586 $s=0·015$	+0·6753 $s=0·004$	+0·3702 $s=0·106$	−0·4890 $s=0·032$	−0·1230 $s=0·331$	+0·6368 $s=0·005$	+0·0436 $s=0·439$			
Average speed of ferries	−0·5458 $s=0·100$	+0·2380 $s=0·303$	−0·3846 $s=0·195$	+0·6853 $s=0·042$	−0·4678 $s=0·143$	−0·1532 $s=0·371$	+0·0236 $s=0·480$	+0·8810 $s=0·004$			
Average speed overall	+0·3974 $s=0·013$	−0·2795 $s=0·064$	−0·3509 $s=0·026$	−0·1560 $s=0·209$	+0·1453 $s=0·218$	+0·2206 $s=0·116$	−0·1467 $s=0·215$	+0·6980 $s=0·000$	+0·1302 $s=0·0328$	+0·5392 $s=0·103$	

                    P. W. G. Newman and J. R. Kenworthy

currently underway but these correlations provide sufficient basis for clarifying and
confirming the patterns already discussed.

5.1. *Urban form*

The correlations suggest that strong negative relationships exist between petrol use
or private vehicle use and all the density variables, except central city job densities. This
highlights the question of the US and Australian cities with their central city high rise
office blocks. There is no correlation between central city job density and any of the
transport variables (including public transport use) suggesting that this factor has little
overall effect on transport patterns despite the apparent importance of peak hour CBD
oriented public transport activity in these cities. It would appear to be more important
to have higher residential densities mixed in with the employment activity if there is to
be much less dependence on the automobile. Residential density in the central city does

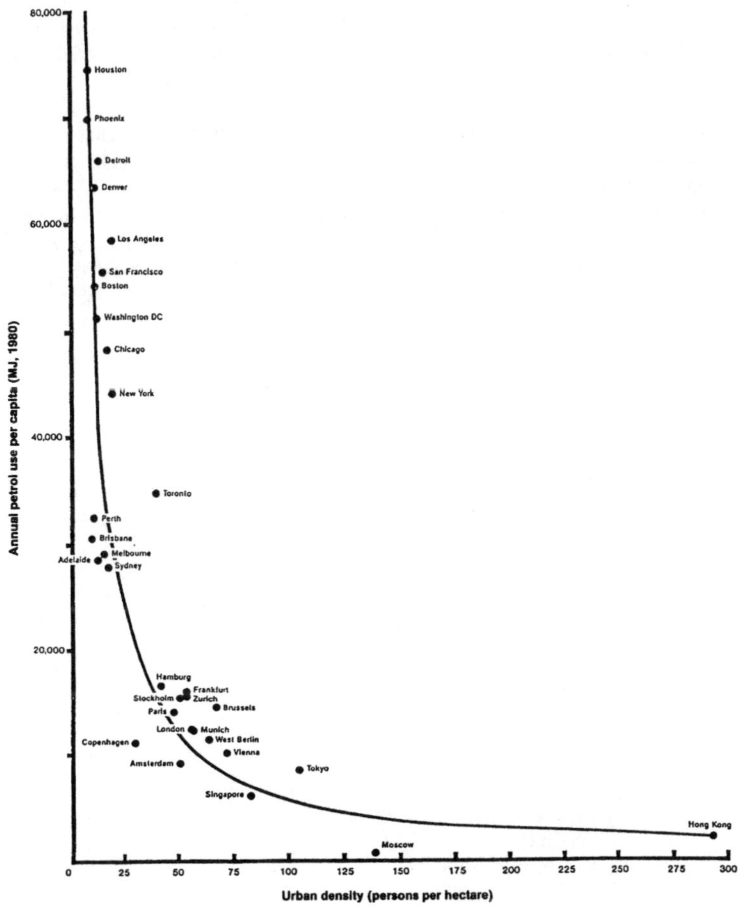

Figure 1.   Petrol use per capita versus urban density (1980).

correlate strongly with all the transport patterns, including the amount of walking/bicycling. The case of Boston highlights this as it is the highest US city for bicycling/walking to work (10%) and it has for its 72 000 central city residents the highest population to jobs ratio (0·33) for US CBDs, thus it is more like a European city in this regard. It is not hard to see that city centres with plenty of employment activity that also have high residential densities (e.g. Paris 235 per ha) would have a significantly higher proportion of people walking and having little need for a car.

The relationship between density and petrol use may be more complex than a purely linear linkage. Figure 1 suggests that it may in fact be closer to an exponential relationship particularly under 30 or so people per hectare. This is conceptually quite possible as a city with density in the less than 30 per ha range does not just have longer distances for all types of journey, it is ensuring that modes other than the automobile are not feasible because of the sheer lack of people living near a transit line and the time required for walking and biking. Thus the effects of lowering density are multiplicative. This cut off around 30 per ha we have also found to be significant for transport within different parts of urban areas (Newman and Hogan 1987). It means that in terms of transport energy saved or private car use curtailed the effects of increasing density can be considerable if they move urban areas into at least the 30 per ha density range i.e. more like the old inner area densities.

The significance of the inner area (with its mixture of jobs and residences at medium densities) as a model for directing policy in transport and urban form is highlighted by transport data collected in a few US cities on an inner/outer area basis. Table 8 shows that the New York Tri State region petrol usage per person is 44 030 MJ, however for the inner area residents (City of New York) this reduces to 20 120 MJ and for the 1·4 million residents of Manhattan, their average petrol consumption drops to an extraordinary 11 860 MJ. The average outer area New Yorker consumes 59 590 MJ and in Denver it is possible to distinguish the 240 000 ex urban residents who live on the fringe of the city and consume some 137 000 MJ on average. The linkage to density would appear to be very strong.

5.2. *Provision for the automobile*

There is a strong correlation between petrol consumption and provision for the automobile in terms of road supply and parking. Also the significant positive correlation between average speed and petrol use highlights one of the traffic management controversies.

Table 8.   Petrol use and urban density by city region in the New York Tri State Metropolitan Area, 1980.

Area	Petrol use (MJ per capita)	Urban density (persons per hectare)
Outer area New York	59590	13
Whole city (New York Tri State Metro Area)	44033	20
Inner area (City of New York)	20120	107
Central city (New York County including Manhattan)	11860	251

Table 9. Average value for per capita petrol use in cities by region 1980, compared with adjusted values (for US petrol prices, incomes and vehicle efficiency).

Cities	Actual petrol use (MJ per capita)	Adjusted petrol use for US petrol prices, incomes and vehicle efficiency (MJ per capita)		% Difference between US petrol use and adjusted petrol use by other cities	
		Short-term elasticities	Long-term elasticities	Short-term elasticities	Long-term elasticities
US cities	58 541	58 541	58 541	—	—
Australian cities	29 829	38 488	43 680	51%	25%
Toronto	34 813	29 995	26 090	49%	55%
European cities	13 280	17 082	31 080	71%	47%
Asian cities	5 493	7 676	12 340	87%	79%
Average for non-US cities	17 133	21 450	31 160	63%	47%

Note 1: Petrol consumption elasticities used were: petrol price -0.20 short-term, -1.0 long-term; incomes $+0.11$ short-term, $+0.6$ long-term.

Note 2: As petrol consumption elasticities include a component due to vehicle efficiency, it is necessary to subtract this when adjusting other cities for US vehicle efficiencies otherwise it would be accounted for twice.

Vehicle efficiency elasticities used were: petrol price $+0.11$ short-term, $+1.0$ long-term; incomes -0.11 short-term, -1.0 long-term.

Vehicle efficiencies used were national values adjusted for average speed in each city (table 5). In all cases vehicle efficiencies in the long-term became more than equivalent to US levels and hence the vehicle efficiency factor in the long-term is cancelled out.

Source: Pindyck (1979), Dahl (1982), Archibald and Gillingham (1981) and Wheaton (1982).

There is clearly less petrol use in cities with low average speeds which contradicts those traffic planners who suggest freeing up congestion to increase average speeds will save petrol (see Newman and Kenworthy 1984, 1988 b, c). Although free flowing traffic may improve individual vehicle efficiencies, the evidence suggests that it also causes overall fuel consumption increases presumably due to greater private vehicle use.

Before examining the policy implications of these relationships it is necessary to show to what degree the patterns are explained by economic parameters.

6. Economic factors versus physical planning factors

The ten US cities in which petrol use per capita varies some 40% were examined first to see if there were any direct economic relationships. No significant correlation was found with per capita income (-0.1219) or petrol price (-0.1765) which varies a little across the nation. Thus transport patterns appear to be clearly related to other non-economic factors in this US sample. In the global sample there are significant correlations between petrol use and price (-0.8500), income per capita (0.7477) and average vehicle fuel efficiency (1/100 km) (0.5906). The question is thus how much do these economic factors influence transport.

To compare across the international sample requires the use of accepted price and income elasticities for petrol consumption together with vehicle efficiencies which also vary with petrol price. Table 9 sets out the expected petrol consumption if US incomes, US petrol price and US vehicle efficiency were found in all the 31 cities (excluding Moscow), i.e. if these economic factors were the sole or primary factors then all the cities should have the same petrol use. They clearly do not. On average, the economic factors explain at the most around half the petrol use. It can be argued that these long-term elasticities are overestimates as they incorporate some degree of anticipated urban form change but even they do not adequately explain the variations in petrol use in the sample. What is suggested by these results is that a purely economic approach to transport matters will be inadequate, that matters of urban form and provision for the automobile have direct and independent influence on transport patterns. Thus planners who provide the transport infrastructure or who set out the physical plan of a city are directly and actively influencing transport patterns, they are not just responding to economic factors.

7. Policy implications

As outlined in the introduction, if a city is to move towards less transport energy use, this will almost certainly imply less use of the private car and more use of public transport, bicycling and walking; it will more than likely also mean greater accessibility by the transport disadvantaged, less emissions and road accidents and most probably a more 'human' city especially in the central city (Schaeffer and Sclar 1975, Newman and Hogan 1981, Kenworthy 1986). The analysis followed so far will be further developed in terms of what transport planners and urban planners can do to assist cities to move in this direction. In particular, the assumption will be how to shift the automobile dependent cities of the US and Australia into something more like the transport balance found in European cities (and Asian cities), though the notional numbers suggested in the policies tend to be less extreme than those in European cities and are more like those found in Toronto (and in other Canadian cities).

266　　　　　　　　**P. W. G. Newman and J. R. Kenworthy**

7.1. *Transport infrastructure policies*

As the data suggest, the provision of transport infrastructure has a direct effect on the balance of transport modes and travel distances, thus it would seem appropriate to directly address the provision of transport infrastructure.

It would appear from the data presented that the transport patterns (and urban form) of a city would be shifted more in the direction outlined above if the following were adopted.

A policy to restrict the amount of road supply within a city to something around 2 m to 3 m per capita. This would essentially mean curtailing new road projects that pass through the city. It would depend also on urban form policies outlined below. In particular, since roughly three quarters of the road kilometrage in a city is comprised of minor and local streets this would imply a move away from the single family house with a typical wide street frontage, towards innovative family housing which shares road access more intensively (and which also has less need of roads because of its public transport and walking/bicycling orientation). For example, in Toronto single family housing is around 60% and road provision is 2·7 m per person. According to the Real Estate Research Corporation (1974), single family housing requires around seven times as much road length as that for high rise apartments. The money generated from road project savings and from the selling of major road reserves through cities could be put into traffic management and some of the other transport projects listed below.

A policy to restrict central city parking to a level around 200 spaces or less per 1000 CBD workers. This would require a concurrent policy that provides good public transport access and a series of central city policies on housing, cultural attractions, urban design, pedestrianization and commercial activity that allows a central city to compete strongly with suburban centres where easy parking is available (McNulty, Penne and Jacobson 1986).

A policy accepting that average speeds in a city of around 30 km/h are adequate. This means rejecting the notion that fuel is saved by increasing average speeds.

A policy that provides a rapid transit option (most likely to be rail) which is substantially faster than the average traffic speed in the city and together with other improvements slowly builds up public transport in stages so that it provides something more like 20 to 30% of total passenger km. This would be a considerable change for many cities where the present situation has public transport at less than 10% and in some cities less than 1%. However, in almost every city examined by us public transport utilization went up between 1970 and 1980 after decades of decline, and the indications are that it is on a continued trend upward.

A policy that encourages pedestrianization, traffic-calming treatment of streets and bicycle facilities so that the proportion of work journeys by bicycling and walking rises to something more like 20% rather than its present 5% in automobile cities. This policy like the others is not really very contentious, however such policies are unlikely to be successful unless they are wedded to the following land use policies.

7.2. *Urban form policies*

Each of the transport infrastructure policies outlined will have an influence on urban form and should not be seen as separate. In the same way, the following major urban form policy directions are a necessary adjunct to the transport infrastructure policies as outlined.

The primary urban form policy theme is *Reurbanization*, a policy emphasized mainly in Europe but with even greater application to US and Australian cities (e.g. van den Berg *et al.* 1982, 1987). This policy is pictured in the two diagrams (figure 2 and 3) and in the following detailed policies.

A policy to increase by stages the intensity of urban activity overall so that population densities of around 30 per ha to 40 per ha and job densities of around 20 per ha are obtained. This will mean an immediate policy of restricting or at least slowing urban development at the urban fringe and concentrating on redevelopment; this consolidation generally has the added benefit of considerable capital savings due to the better use of present urban infrastructure rather than requiring new infrastructure at the fringes (Wilmoth 1982, Bunker 1983).

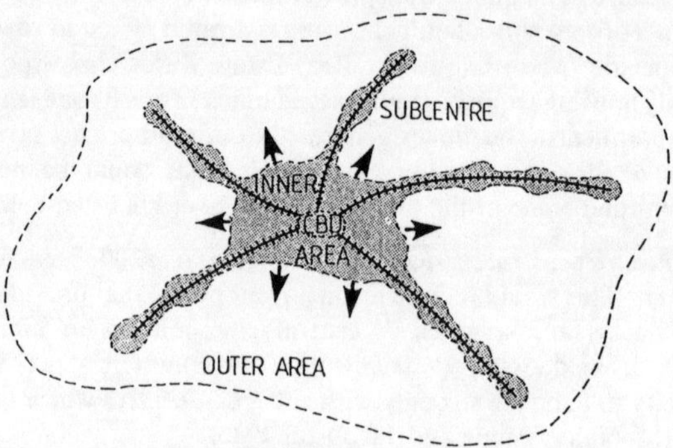

Figure 2.   Conceptual plan for re-urbanization.

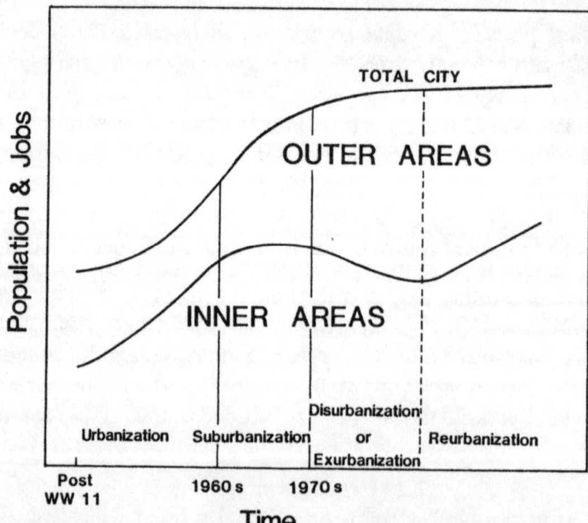

Figure 3.   Stages of urban development (after van den Berg *et al.* 1982).

268   P. W. G. Newman and J. R. Kenworthy

A policy to build up the central city activity intensity so that job densities are maintained at more than 300 per ha and population densities are built up to over 50 to 60 per ha. The provision of housing in central city areas of automobile cities seems to be harder than providing for jobs though some outstanding successes have been achieved in recent years in places like Boston, Toronto and San Francisco.

A policy to build up or maintain the inner area at population densities of 40 to 50 per ha and job densities of similar levels. Most of the older automobile cities have inner cities with these densities, however in many cases, particularly in the US, these have been declining in recent decades. Policies to contain inner city decline appear to have been relatively successful in Sydney, Melbourne and Toronto. In newer automobile cities like Houston, Denver, Brisbane, Adelaide and Perth there is enormous development potential in their inner areas.

A policy to build up outer area urban activity to population densities of around 20 to 30 per ha and job densities of around 15 per ha. As outlined in figures 2 and 3 the way that this is most likely to be effective in transport and land use terms is (*a*) to slowly expand the present inner area type of development (i.e. mixed and more intensive) into the outer area, and (*b*) building up densities around rapid transit routes. For low density cities like Brisbane and Adelaide with present rail systems, and in cities like Los Angeles and Perth which are building new lines, this policy would appear to be of primary importance. Washington and Toronto are good examples where this policy has made major changes in transport and urban form in less than a decade.

8. Conclusion

A range of transport infrastructure and urban planning policies have been developed for those cities with an excessive dependence on the automobile. This paper does not attempt to outline the implementation of such policies, it merely attempts to suggest what are feasible goals for automobile-oriented cities. The time scale for such changes could possibly be gauged from cities like Detroit and Los Angeles which over a 30 to 40 year period were transformed from being compact rail-oriented cities to dispersed automobile-oriented cities. The re-urbanization process could arguably be even faster with modern technology and more rapid turnover of buildings. The forces of dispersal and greater automobile reliance are obviously very powerful and to overcome them cities must first begin by recognizing what is possible (Newman 1988). This study has attempted to set out the patterns of transport and urban form which currently exist in more balanced cities and which could thus be emulated in substance, but in style and manner fitting to the social, cultural and environmental conditions peculiar to each city.

Acknowledgments

This work was partially funded by the Australian Department of Primary Industry and Energy through the National Energy Research Development and Demonstration Council. Their support is gratefully acknowledged.

Transport of the world's principal cities   269

Foreign summaries

L'examen de trente deux villes parmi les plus importantes de la planète révèle la relation étroite entre l'organisation du transport et la morphologie de la ville. Des facteurs économiques tels que les niveaux de revenus et le prix des carburants marquent moins l'espace que les instruments de l'urbaniste et de l'organisateur de transport, tels que la création d'infrastructures routières ou ferroviaires, ou la densité d'emploi et de résidence. Les politiques de planification urbaine et de transport ont leur propres règles quantifiées qui peuvent soulager les villes de leur dépendance à l'égard de l'automobile, par example, en accroissant la densité là où l'habitat est inférieur à trente par hectare.

Eine Studie über 32 Hauptstädte der Welt zeigt, daß es sehr deutliche Zusammenhänge zwischen dem Verkehr und der Stadtform gibt. Wirtschaftliche Faktoren wie Einkommen und Kraftstoffpreise sind weniger bedeutend als die direkten Maßnahmen der Verkehrs- und Stadtplaner wie z.B. das relative Infrastrukturangebot im individuellen Personen- und Schienenschnellverkehr oder die Dichte von Einwohnern und Arbeitsplätzen. Verkehrs- und Stadtplanung handen nach quantitativen Maßstäben, die dazu beitragen können, daß die Städte sich von der Abhängigkeit vom Auto lösen, indem sie beispielsweise die Einwohnerdichten dort anhaben, wo sie unter 30 Einwohner je Hektar liegen.

Un estudio de las treinta y dos ciudades más importantes del mundo muestra que existen relaciones muy claras entre el transporte y la forma urbana. Factores económicos, tales como el ingreso y el precio del petróleo, tienen menor importancia que los instrumentos directos de política de los planificadores de transporte y urbanistas, tales como la provisión relativa de infraestructura vial y de transporte público, o la densidad de población y empleo. Las políticas de planifiación de transporte y urbanismo se desarrollan en base a direccionamientos cuantitativos que pueden ayudar a aliviar la dependencia en el automóvil de las ciudades, por ejemplo, mediante el incremento de las densidades poblacionales en sitios en que éstas sean menores a 30 habitantes por hectárea.

References

ARCHIBALD, R., and GILLINGHAM. R., 1981, Decomposition of the price and income elasticities of the consumer demand for gasoline. *Southern Economic Journal*, **47** (4), 1021–1031.

BUNKER, R., 1983, *Urban Consolidation: the experience of Sydney, Melbourne and Adelaide*, Australian Institute of Urban Studies, Publication No. 111, Canberra.

CHANDLER, W. U., 1985, Energy Productivity: Key to Environmental Protection and Economic Progress, *Worldwatch Paper 63*, Worldwatch Institute, Washington DC.

CLARK, C., 1982, *Regional and Urban Location*, University of Queensland Press, St Lucia, Australia.

DAHL, C. A., 1982, Does gasoline demand elasticities vary? *Land Economics*, **58** (3), 373–382.

KENWORTHY, J. R., 1986, Transport Energy Conservation through Urban Planning and Lifestyle Changes: some fundamental choices for Perth, edited by C. McDavitt. *Towards a State Conservation Strategy:* Invited Review Papers, Department of Conservation and Environment, Western Australia, Bulletin 251, pp. 69–99.

KENWORTHY, J. R., and NEWMAN, P. W. G., 1982, *A Driving Cycle for Perth: Methodology and Preliminary Results.* Presented to Joint SAEA/ARRB Second Conference on Traffic, Energy and Emissions, Melbourne, May 19–21, Paper 82149.

LA BELLE, S. J., and MOSES, D. O., 1982, *Technology Assessment of Productive Conservation in Urban Transportation* (ANL/ES-130), Energy and Environmental Systems Division, Argonne National Laboratory.

MCNULTY, R. H., PENNE, R. L., JACOBSON, D. R., and Partners for Livable Places, 1986, *The Return of the Livable City* (Washington DC: Acropolis Books).

NEWMAN, P. W. G., 1988, Australian Cities at the Crossroads. *Current Affairs Bulletin*, December, 4–15.

NEWMAN, P. W. G., and HOGAN, T. L. F., 1981, A Review of Urban Density Models. *Human Ecology*, **9** (3), 269–302.

270   P. W. G. Newman and J. R. Kenworthy

NEWMAN, P. W. G., and HOGAN, T. L. F., 1987, Urban Density and Transport: A simple model based on 3 city types. *Transport Research Paper* 1/87 pp. 36, Environmental Science Murdoch University.

NEWMAN, P. W. G., and KENWORTHY, J. R., 1984, The Use and Abuse of Driving Cycle Research: Clarifying the Relationship between Traffic Congestion, Energy and Emissions. *Transportation Quarterly*, **38**, (4), 615–635.

NEWMAN, P. W. G., and KENWORTHY, J. R., 1988 a, Gasoline Consumption and Cities: A comparison of US Cities with a Global Survey. *Journal of the American Planning Association*, **55** (1), 24–37.

NEWMAN, P. W. G., and KENWORTHY, J. R., 1988 b, The Transport Energy Trade-Off: Fuel-Efficient Traffic versus Fuel-Efficient cities. *Transportation Research*, A, **22** (3), 163–174.

NEWMAN, P. W. G., and KENWORTHY, J. R., 1988 c, Does Free Flowing Traffic Save Energy and Reduce Emissions in Cities? *Search*, **19** (5/6), 267–272.

NEWMAN, P. W. G., and KENWORTHY, J. R., 1989, *Cities and Automobile Dependence: An International Sourcebook* (Aldershot, UK: Gower).

PINDYCK, R. S., 1979, *The Structure of World Energy Demand* (Massachussetts, Cambridge: MIT Press).

PUSHKAREV, B. S., and ZUPAN, J. M., 1977, *Public Transportation and Land Use Policy* (Bloomington and London: Indiana University Press).

REAL ESTATE RESEARCH CORPORATION, 1974, *The Costs of Sprawl, Detailed Cost Analysis*, US Goverment Printing Office, Washington, DC.

SCHAEFFER, K. H., and SCLAR, E., 1975, *Access for All* (Harmondsworth: Penguin).

THOMSON, J. M., 1977, *Great Cities and their Traffic* (England: Penguin).

VAN DEN BERG, L., DREWETT, R., KLAASSEN, L. H., ROSSI, A., and VIJVERBERG, C. H. T., 1982, *Urban Europe: a Study of Growth and Decline* (Oxford: Pergamon Press).

VAN DEN BERG, L., BURNS, L. S., and KLAASSEN, L. H., 1987, *Spatial Cycles* (England, Aldershot: Gower).

VUCHIC, V. R., 1981, *Urban Public Transportation Systems and Technology* (New Jersey, Englewood Cliffs: Prentice Hall).

WHEATON, W. C., 1982, The long-run structure of transportation and gasoline demand. *Bell Journal of Economics*, **13** (2), 439–454.

WILMOTH, D., 1982, Urban Consolidation Policy and Social Equity, in Conference on *Urban Consolidation and Equity*, Centre for Environmental Studies, Macquarie University.

[29]

Urban Studies, Vol. 34, No. 10, 1667–1691, 1997

Sustainable Cities or Cities that Contribute to Sustainable Development?

David Satterthwaite

[Paper received in final form, April 1997]

Summary. This paper outlines a framework for assessing the environmental performance of cities in regard to the meeting of sustainable development goals. It also considers how the environmental goals fit with the social, economic and political goals of sustainable development and the kinds of national framework and international context needed to encourage city-based consumers, enterprises and governments to progress towards their achievement. In a final section, it considers the extent to which the recommendations of the Habitat II Conference helped to encourage national governments and city and municipal authorities in this direction.

Introduction

The past ten years have brought examples of considerable innovation among city and municipal authorities in most parts of the world in regard to sustainable development. In Europe and North America, many cities have put in place long-term programmes to improve their environment, reduce resource use and reduce waste (Mega, 1996a; UNCHS, 1996; European Commission, 1994). A growing number of cities have local authorities who have committed themselves to sustainable development goals—as in the European Campaign of Sustainable Cities and Towns—and have shown a greater willingness to share knowledge and experiences with other city authorities (Mega, 1996a; UNCHS, 1996). Certain cities in Latin America have also put in place long-term programmes to address environmental prob-

lems—for example, Curitiba in Brazil (Rabinovitch, 1992) and Ilo in Peru (Díaz *et al.*, 1996)—while in many cities in all regions of the world, there has been considerable innovation by city authorities in addressing environmental problems. There is also a worldwide movement of 'Healthy cities' in which local authorities in more than 1000 cities have sought new ways to work with the many different actors and interests within their boundaries in the promotion of health and prevention of disease (WHO, 1996).

The discussion of sustainable development in regard to cities has also gained greater official recognition. For instance, the terms 'sustainable cities' and 'sustainable human settlements' were much in evidence at Habitat II, the second UN Conference on Human

David Satterthwaite is director of the Human Settlements Programme in the International Institute for Environment and Development, 3 Endsleigh Street, London, WC1H 0DD, UK. Fax: 0171 388 2826. E-mail: david@iied.org. This paper draws on the work that the author has undertaken with the World Health Organization in preparing two documents whose findings are used in this paper—WHO, 1992 and WHO, 1996—and on the work he undertook in preparing UNCHS, 1996. He is particularly grateful to Sam Ozolins, Greg Goldstein and Wilfrid Kreisel at WHO and Donatus Okpala at UNCHS for their help. Thanks are also due to Cedric Pugh, Diana Mitlin, Nick Robins and Koy Thomson for their comments on an earlier draft.

Settlements (also known as the City Summit) held in Istanbul in June 1996. Despite the disagreements between the different groups represented at the Conference—for instance, between the European Union, the Group of 77 and the US—all government delegations appeared to support the idea of 'sustainable human settlements' or 'sustainable urban development'.

But this apparent unanimity is misleading because there was no clear, agreed definition as to what the terms 'sustainable cities' and 'sustainable human settlements' mean. Such a diverse range of environmental, economic, social, political, demographic, institutional and cultural goals have been said to be part of 'sustainable development' that most governments or international agencies can characterise some of what they do as contributing towards sustainable development. This can include goals whose achievement in one sector or location implies a move away from the achievement of sustainable development goals in another sector or location. For instance, one reason why the environmental quality of wealthy cities can improve is because the consumers and producers they concentrate can import all the goods whose production requires high levels of resource use and usually includes high levels of waste (including serious problems with hazardous wastes), pollution and environmental risk for their workforce (Satterthwaite, 1997).

Governments in the world's wealthiest nations can also support the notion of 'sustainable cities' without admitting that it is consumers and enterprises in their cities that need to make the largest reductions in resource use and waste generation. Most governments in the North also continue to view economic growth as the main means by which unemployment is to be reduced and incomes increased and it is difficult if not impossible to combine these with significant falls in the use of non-renewable resources and the generation of greenhouse gases, unless there is an explicit linking of employment generation with such goals. The simultaneous achievement of the social and environmental goals inherent in the Brundt-

land Commission's definition of sustainable development (meeting the needs of the present without compromising the ability of future generations to meet their own needs) implies very different policies to reduce unemployment and increase incomes among those with inadequate incomes—that address more directly the problem than 'trickle-down' from economic growth and that support reduced resource use and waste. And while many national governments may claim that they are promoting sustainable development, few have begun to put in place the fiscal and institutional framework that supports a move towards the achievement of the complete set of sustainable development goals in the urban (and rural) areas within their boundaries (see for instance O'Riordan, 1989; Haughton and Hunter, 1994).

This lack of progress among the nations in 'the North' discourages progress among nations in 'the South'. The fact that 'the South' includes three-quarters of the world's population and a large and growing share of its economic activity and high-level consumers also means a large and growing share in global resource use, waste generation and greenhouse gas emissions. But despite the diversity of nations within 'the South', they can collectively point not only to higher levels of resource use, waste and greenhouse gas emissions per person in the North, but also to much higher historical contributions to these problems. Without a strong commitment by governments in the North to reduce resource use, waste and greenhouse gas emissions, and to support the achievement of sustainable development goals in the South, the governments in the South are reluctant to act. This delays the actions that could make the (often) rapidly urbanising nations' settlement patterns and transport systems less dependent on high levels of private automobile use and their buildings less dependent on high levels of energy for lighting and heating or cooling. As will be discussed in more detail later, it is difficult to adjust buildings, settlement patterns and transport systems that developed during a long period of cheap oil and (generally) growing prosperity to much lower levels of fossil fuel use. However, in nations which are urbanising rapidly, putting in place the institutional and regulatory framework that encourages energy conservation in all sectors, minimises the need for heating or cooling in buildings and encourages settlement patterns that limit the need for high levels of private automobile use can ensure the development of cities that are more compatible with some of the main sustainable development goals. A framework encouraging efficient use of water within all sectors and promoting the re-use of waste water where appropriate can also considerably reduce the prospect of water scarcity.

The ambiguity as to what 'sustainable cities' or 'sustainable human settlements' means also allows many of the large international agencies to claim that they are the leaders in promoting sustainable cities when, in reality, they have contributed much to the growth of cities where sustainable development goals are not met. For instance, most international agencies give a low priority to meeting directly human needs—for example, in supporting provision of safe and sufficient supplies of water and provision for sanitation, primary education and health care. Most also give a low priority (or allocate nothing) to improving garbage collection and disposal, energy conservation and public transport in cities, despite their importance for the achievement of sustainable development goals.[1]

This paper contends that to progress towards the achievement of sustainable development goals, the environmental performance of cities has to improve not only in terms of improved environmental quality within their boundaries, but also in terms of reducing the transfer of environmental costs to other people, other ecosystems or into the future. This presents considerable institutional difficulties for city and municipal authorities whose official responsibilities are to the citizens within their boundaries. Within a competitive world market, it is difficult for city authorities to reconcile the need to attract or retain new investment with a commitment to the full range of sustainable development goals, especially those sustainable development goals that raise costs within the city to reduce environmental costs for people outside these cities. This is a subject to which this paper will return, after describing a framework for assessing the environmental performance of cities.

A Framework for Considering the Environmental Performance of Cities

The Difficulties of Comparing Environmental Performance between Diverse Urban Centres

Perhaps the main difficulty facing any researcher or institution intent on comparing the environmental performance of different cities (including those in the North and in the South) is the range of problems that are 'environmental'. For instance, from the perspective of environmental health, cities in the North perform much better for their inhabitants than most cities in the South, as can be seen in the much smaller role of environmental hazards in illness, injury and premature death (WHO, 1996; UNCHS, 1996). But from the perspective of average levels of resource use or waste or greenhouse gas emissions per person, most cities in the South have much lower levels than cities in the North (Hardoy *et al.*, 1992; UNCHS, 1996).

There is also the difficulty of knowing how to judge the environmental performance of cities when the achievement of a high-quality environment in many cities is in part achieved by transferring environmental problems to other people or locations. For instance, sewage and drainage systems that take the sewage and waste water out of the city bring major environmental advantages to city-dwellers and city businesses. However, the disposal of untreated waste water in nearby water bodies usually brings serious environmental and economic costs to others—for instance, through damage to local fisheries or to water bodies that are then unfit for use by communities downstream. The transfer of environmental costs can also be

1670   DAVID SATTERTHWAITE

over much greater distances or into the future.

This suggests the need to distinguish between different kinds of environmental problem when making comparisons between cities, so that like can be compared with like. But there is a danger that this reduces inter-city comparisons on environmental performance to those indicators that are easily measured. For instance, it is easier to get information on the concentration of certain air pollutants such as sulphur dioxide in major cities in the South than the proportion of their population with adequate provision for piped water and sanitation or the contribution of motor vehicle accidents to injury and premature death. This means that discussions of sulphur dioxide concentrations probably get more prominence than they deserve within the discussions of environmental hazards in cities, while the inadequacies in provision for water and sanitation and in limiting traffic accidents get insufficient attention. In assessing the environmental performance of cities, there is a need both to distinguish between different environmental problems and to seek a more comprehensive coverage of all environmental problems including those for which there are often few data. There is also a need to ensure that improved environmental performance in one area is not at the expense of improved performance in another.

Within a commitment to sustainable development, there are five broad categories of environmental action within which the performance of all cities should be assessed. These are:

1. Controlling infectious and parasitic diseases and the health burden they take on urban populations, including reducing the urban population's vulnerability to them. This is often termed the 'brown agenda' or the sanitary agenda as it includes the need to ensure adequate provision for water, sanitation, drainage and garbage collection for all city-dwellers and businesses. It should include more than this—for instance, in controlling the infectious and parasitic diseases that are not associated with inadequate water and sanitation, including acute respiratory infections (the single largest cause of death worldwide) and tuberculosis (the single largest cause of adult death worldwide) and the many diseases that are transmitted by insect or animal vectors.

2. Reducing chemical and physical hazards within the home, the workplace and the wider city.

3. Achieving a high-quality urban environment for all urban inhabitants—for instance, in terms of the amount and quality of open space per person (parks, public squares/plazas, provision for sport, provision for children's play) and the protection of the natural and cultural heritage.

4. Minimising the transfer of environmental costs to the inhabitants and ecosystems surrounding the city.

5. Ensuring progress towards what is often termed 'sustainable consumption'—i.e. ensuring that the goods and services required to meet everyone's consumption needs are delivered without undermining the environmental capital of nations and the world. This implies a use of resources, a consumption of goods imported into the city and a generation and disposal of wastes by city enterprises and city-dwellers that are compatible with the limits of natural capital and are not transferring environmental costs on to other people (including future generations).

The first three categories can be considered as the environmental aspects of meeting city-dwellers' needs. These fit within the conventional mandate of local authorities—although there is great variety in the ways in which local authorities promote their achievement. The fourth and fifth are more problematic since they are concerned with environmental impacts that generally occur outside the jurisdiction of the local authorities with responsibility for environmental management in cities.

Separating a consideration of the environmental performance of cities into these five categories allows a consideration of the common elements that all cities share within an understanding of how priorities must differ. For instance, perhaps the main environmental priority in most cities in the North is to reduce levels of resource use, wastes and greenhouse gas emissions while also maintaining or improving the quality of the urban environment. But this does not mean neglecting the other aspects—for instance, in most cities, much remains to be done to reduce physical hazards (such as those caused by motor vehicles) and chemical pollutants—and, as outlined below, there are also new threats to be confronted in the control of infectious diseases. In addition, in most cities in the North, there are still a proportion of the population that live or work with unacceptable levels of environmental risk. By contrast, the environmental priorities in most small cities in the lower-income countries of the South will centre on the first two categories—although building into their urban plans a concern for a high-quality urban environment, efficient resource use, good management of liquid and solid wastes and a minimising of greenhouse gas emissions will bring many long-term advantages. Considering cities' environmental performance across the five categories also helps to clarify how environmental problems change for cities that become increasingly large and/or wealthy (see Bartone *et al.*, 1994; Satterthwaite, 1997).

Controlling Infectious and Parasitic Diseases

By concentrating people and economic activities, cities have many advantages over a more dispersed settlement pattern for the control of infectious and parasitic diseases—especially the concentration of people which lowers the unit costs of most forms of infrastructure (including piped water, drainage and most kinds of sanitation) and services (including health care, emergency services and garbage collection). With good manage-

ment in public health and environmental health and with all sectors of a city's society contributing to health, cities can be among the most healthy places to live in, work and visit (WHO, 1996).

However, in the absence of such management, there are many infectious and parasitic diseases that thrive when provision for water, sanitation, drainage, garbage collection and health care is inadequate or where it breaks down. As a result, cities can become among the most health-threatening of all human environments as disease-causing agents and disease vectors multiply, as the large concentration of people living in close proximity to each other increases the risk of disease transmission, and as health care systems become unable to respond rapidly and effectively. If provision for sanitation, drainage and garbage collection breaks down or fails to keep up with a city's expanding population, this greatly increases health hazards, especially from the many diarrhoeal and other diseases spread by human excreta and from diseases spread by vectors that breed or feed on uncollected garbage or breed in standing water (for instance malaria, filariasis, yellow fever and dengue fever, in the climates where the mosquito species that are their vectors can survive). At any one time, close to half of the urban population in the South is suffering from one or more of the main diseases associated with inadequate provision for water and sanitation (WHO, 1996). If health care systems break down, or fail to keep up with the growth in population, the health problems of those who catch diseases are much magnified—for instance, acute respiratory infections as among the main causes of infant and child death, although they are easily cured if diagnosed and treated appropriately. In addition, if health care systems cannot implement immunisation programmes, diseases such as measles and diphtheria can become major causes of death.

Most cities also concentrate large numbers of people who are particularly vulnerable to infection. For instance, most cities in the South have high proportions of infants within their populations and these have immune systems that have not developed to protect them from common infectious diseases. In many such cities, a large proportion of infants and young children (and adults) have immune systems that are compromised by undernutrition and worm infections. Many cities or particular city districts in the North and some in the South also have a high concentration of older people who are more vulnerable to many infectious diseases. Most cities also have a constant movement of people in and out of them which can mean the arrival of newcomers who bring new infections to which the city population has no immunity (WHO, 1996).

There are also two further problems. The first is the growing number of what are usually termed 'new' or 'emerging' diseases, of which AIDS is the best known and one of the most widespread. These are new in the sense that they only recently became a significant public health problem, but in most instances it is their incidence and geographical range that is new, as they previously existed either in nature or in isolated communities (WHO, 1996). The second is the re-emergence of well-known infectious diseases that until recently were considered under control. For instance, cholera and yellow fever are now striking in regions that were once thought to be safe from them. Malaria and dengue fever have become among the most serious health problems in many urban centres. Tuberculosis remains the single largest cause of adult death in the world—and its incidence has been increasing rapidly over the last decade, in the North as well as in the South. The main reason why emerging and re-emerging diseases have become such a serious problem is the low priority given by most governments and international agencies to public health and health care. But part of the reason is also the greater difficulties in preventing and controlling infectious diseases as societies urbanise and as population movements increase (including the very rapid growth in the number of people crossing international borders), and as disease-causing agents develop resistance to public health measures or adapt to changing ecological circumstances

in ways that increase the risks of infection for human populations. For instance, the control of malaria has become more difficult in many places as the *Anopheles* mosquitoes can no longer be killed by many insecticides and many of the drugs used to provide immunity or to treat malaria are no longer effective. Various species of the anophelines have also proved able to adapt to urban environments (WHO, 1992, 1996). Similarly, many bacterial disease-causing agents including those that cause pneumonia, tuberculosis and typhoid fevers and some diarrhoeal diseases and forms of food poisoning have become resistant to many antibiotic drugs (WHO, 1996). Meanwhile, the development and distribution of new antibiotics cannot keep up with the speed at which many disease-causing agents develop a resistance to them, especially in the lower-income countries in the South (Leduc and Tikhomirov, 1994).

Urbanisation can also create foci for disease vectors and new ecological niches for animals which harbour a disease agent or vector. This may be the result of the expansion of built-up areas, the construction of roads, water reservoirs and drains and land clearance and deforestation (WHO, 1992) or, the result of increased volumes of human excreta, garbage or waste water that are not cleared away. In addition, as cities expand, it is common for low-income groups to develop settlements on land subject to flooding or on or beside wetlands, as this land has less commercial value and the inhabitants have more chance of being permitted to stay there. But this may also mean close proximity to places where various insect vectors can breed and so putting their inhabitants at risk from, for instance, malaria or dengue fever or yellow fever (from *Aedes* mosquitoes).

The means enormously to reduce these problems are well known and have long been applied in cities in the North and in some cities in the South. In such cities, although some of the emerging or re-emerging diseases are causing serious difficulties for public authorities, the contribution of infectious and parasitic diseases to ill-health and premature death has been enormously diminished. The speed of this transformation in the health of urban populations is often forgotten. It is only in the last 100 years or so that societies have developed the knowledge, capacity and competence to protect against diseases that formerly thrived, especially in cities. This can be seen in the infant mortality rates that existed only 100 years ago in the world's most prosperous cities. Today, infant mortality rates in healthy, well-served cities are around 10 per 1000 live births and it is very rare for an infant or child to die from an infectious or parasitic disease. Most prosperous European cities 100 years ago still had infant mortality rates that exceeded 100 per 1000 live births; in Vienna, Berlin, Leipzig, Naples, St Petersburg and many of the large industrial towns in England, the figure exceeded 200 and in Moscow exceeded 300 (Bairoch, 1988; Wohl, 1983).

In most of the South, much remains to be done. Infant mortality rates of 100 or more per 1000 live births still remain common in cities in the South or in the urban areas where low-income groups live. Even higher infant mortality rates are common in the informal or illegal settlements where there is inadequate provision for water, sanitation and health care. A 1990 estimate suggested that 600 million urban dwellers in the South lived in shelters and neighbourhoods where their lives and health were continually threatened because of the inadequate provision of safe, sufficient water supplies, sanitation, removal of solid and liquid wastes, and health care and emergency services (Cairncross *et al.*, 1990; WHO, 1992).

Reducing Chemical and Physical Hazards within the Home, Workplace and Wider City

The scale and severity of many chemical and physical hazards increase rapidly with increasing industrial production and with the growth in road traffic. While controlling infectious and parasitic diseases or reducing the urban population's vulnerability to them centres on provision of infrastructure and services to the populations of entire cities (whether through public, private, NGO or community organisation provision), achieving progress in this second category is largely achieved by regulating the activities of enterprises and individuals. Probably the most important factor in terms of improving health is controlling occupational hazards—including people's exposure to dangerous concentrations of chemicals and dust, inadequate lighting, ventilation and space and a lack of protection from machinery and noise. Action is needed in these areas from the large factories down to small 'backstreet' workshops (WHO, 1996).

One of the most serious chemical hazards in many cities is indoor air pollution from smoke or fumes from open fires or inefficient stoves (WHO, 1992). This is especially so when coal and biomass fuels are used as domestic fuels. High levels of indoor air pollution can cause inflammation of the respiratory tract which, in turn, reduces resistance to acute respiratory infections while these infections in turn enhance susceptibility to the inflammatory effects of smoke and fumes. There are also many other health problems associated with high levels of indoor air pollution (WHO, 1992).

There is also a need to reduce to a minimum the risk from accidents within the home and its immediate surrounds. Accidents in the home are often among the most serious causes of injury and premature death, especially in cities in the South where it is common for a high proportion of the population to live in accommodation with three or more persons to each room in a shelter made from temporary (and inflammable) materials and with open fires or stoves used for cooking and (where needed) heating. It is almost impossible to protect occupants (especially young children) from burns and scalds in such circumstances.

There are also tens of millions of urban-dwellers in the South who are at high risk from floods, mudslides or landslides. In most cities in the South, a considerable proportion

1674 DAVID SATTERTHWAITE

of the population live on land sites that are subject to floods, mudslides or rockfalls. Low-income households choose such hazardous sites because they are often the only sites within easy reach of employment that are available to them. Safer sites are too expensive and any attempt to occupy these illegally and develop housing on them would result in eviction.

As in the control of infectious and parasitic diseases, a good primary health care system and provision for emergency services are also important so that those who are injured or poisoned can rapidly get appropriate treatment. There is also a need for traffic management which minimises the risk of motor vehicle accidents and which protects pedestrians and for ensuring an adequate provision for play and recreation for the entire urban population. Clean, safe and stimulating playgrounds for children are needed most in the poorest residential areas where there is the least space within and around homes in which children can play. City-wide, there is an urgent need for a full range of measures to promote healthy and safe working practices in all forms of employment and to penalise employers who contravene them.

There is also a need to control air and water pollution. As cities become larger, more industrialised and wealthier, so there is a growing need for more comprehensive and effective control of emissions and wastes from industries and motor vehicles. Worldwide, more than 1.5 billion urban-dwellers are exposed to levels of ambient air pollution that are above the recommended maximum levels and an estimated 400 000 additional deaths each year are attributable to ambient air pollution (WHO, 1996). Once problems of indoor air pollution are greatly reduced by the use of cleaner fuels and better stoves and ventilation, and occupational hazards are greatly reduced by effective enforcement of health and safety regulations, governments usually have to turn their attention to reducing ambient air pollution. If industrial pollution has been much reduced, it is usually motor vehicles that become the main source of urban air pollution.

Achieving a High-quality Urban Environment

Action in the two above categories is essentially to reduce or remove the health problems that arise from the concentration of people, enterprises and motorised transport systems within a city. Their focus is on prevention and on rapid and effective treatment for any illness or injury. This third category is qualitatively different in that it centres on ensuring provision of those facilities that make urban environments more pleasant, safe and valued by their inhabitants. It includes ensuring sufficient area and quality of open space per person (for instance, in terms of parks, public squares/plazas, provision for sport and provision for children's play) and a concern that all city-dwellers have access to such provision. Integrated into this would also be a concern to protect natural landscapes with important ecological and/or aesthetic value—for instance, wetland areas, river banks or coasts. It includes a concern to preserve a city's cultural heritage There are obvious links between this and the first two categories. For instance, ensuring adequate provision for children's play in each neighbourhood of a city that is safe, well-maintained, accessible and managed in ways to serve the needs of different income groups and age groups can greatly reduce accidents as fewer children play on roads, on garbage tips or in other unsafe areas. Such provision can also contribute much to children's physical, mental and social development (Hart, 1997). Such provision is particularly important in the lower-income areas of cities in the South which lack adequate provision for water, sanitation and drainage and where housing is generally overcrowded—as it allows children to play without exposing them to the risk of faecal contamination or garbage or infection from disease vectors (Satterthwaite *et al.*, 1996).

There are also many other ways in which improving the urban environment can be combined with reducing environmental hazards. For instance, provision for water bodies in parks and the protection of wetlands can be integrated into systems for treating stormwater and for reducing the risk of flooding or limiting flood damage when it occurs. Planting trees in cities and suburbs can not only be justified for their aesthetic value, but also for their contribution to, among other things, reducing cooling costs, absorbing pollutants and acting as windbreaks and noise barriers. Support for urban agriculture can be integrated into provision for open space and the re-use of waste waters—and can prove particularly important for improving the diets and livelihoods of low-income groups in most urban centres in the South (Smit *et al.*, 1996).

Ensuring provision for public space within each neighbourhood in ways which respond to the diverse needs and priorities of the different groups within the population is rarely given much attention in rapidly growing cities in the South. As a result, little or no provision for public space becomes built into the urban fabric and as all land sites are developed for urban activities, it becomes almost impossible to remedy this deficiency. In addition, pressure from middle- and upper-income groups for public action to address this may be much lessened as their purchasing power allows them exclusive access to such resources—through purchasing or renting homes with gardens or homes in areas with good provision for open space or through membership of clubs which allow members access to open space or beaches or provision for sports. The capacity of middle- and upper-income groups to pay for such provision may not only reduce the pressure from such groups for more public provision, but the country clubs, sports clubs, golf courses and private beaches may also preempt land and natural resources that had previously been open to use by all the city's inhabitants.

Minimising the Transfer of Environmental Costs to the Inhabitants and Ecosystems Surrounding the City

The fourth and fifth categories for environmental action are both about minimising the transfer of environmental costs to the ecology and the people living outside the city. The fourth category concentrates on the transfer of costs to the 'city-region' while the fifth concentrates on the transfer to more distant peoples and ecosystems (including those in different nations) and to the future. The distinction between the two is important in that improved performance in the former is often achieved at the expense of the latter.

The ecology of the regions around large and prosperous cities has generally been much changed by the demand for resources and the generation of wastes concentrated within the cities. As Ian Douglas has described, the development of cities transforms the ecology of their regions as land surfaces are reshaped, valleys and swamps filled, large volumes of clay, sand, gravel and crushed rock extracted and moved and water sources tapped—and rivers and streams channelled (Douglas, 1983, 1986). This rearrangement of water, materials and stresses on the land surface combined with the natural tendency of city-dwellers and urban businesses to dispose of their wastes in the region around the city brings damaging consequences. Changes brought to the hydrological cycle by the city's construction and its system for water, sanitation and drainage usually bring damaging consequences 'downstream'. In addition, as provision for sewers and drains improves in the city, the impact of the waste water on the wider region increases, as it is disposed of untreated into a river, estuary or sea, close to the city. Solid wastes (including toxic and hazardous wastes) are often disposed of on land sites around the city, often with little or no provision to prevent these from contaminating local water resources. Air pollution from city-based industries, space heating, thermal power stations and motor vehicles often results in acid precipitation that damages terrestrial and aquatic ecosystems outside the city. Tall smokestacks for thermal power stations and city enterprises can also simply transfer environmental costs from in and around the power station and enterprise to 'downwind' of the city, although the impact may be pushed far beyond the city-region. There is also the damage to vegetation arising from ozone generated by the complex photochemical reactions involving urban air pollutants and sunlight—with ozone concentrations often higher downwind of large and wealthy cities than over the city itself (Conway and Pretty, 1991).

It was only in the 1960s that this aspect of the environmental impact of cities began to be addressed in the North. The growth in environmentalism from the 1960s onwards pressed for major reductions in air pollution, for large investments in the treatment of liquid wastes and in the management of solid wastes (with special provision for hazardous wastes) and in more controls on the extraction of building materials in the city surrounds. In the world's wealthier nations, this has considerably reduced the environmental impact of city-based production and consumption on the region around cities. It has also begun to set limits on the environmental impact that city-based demand for fresh water can inflict on local or increasingly distant watersheds. However, in most major cities in the South, much remains to be done to lessen the transfer of environmental costs to the region surrounding the city. In addition, at least part of this problem has been solved by transferring the environmental costs to more distant peoples and ecosystems.

Sustainable Consumption

The fifth category for environmental action in any city is reducing or eliminating the transfer of environmental costs to people and ecosystems beyond the city-region, including their transfer into the future. This could be considered as ensuring that the environmental performance of the people and businesses the city concentrates becomes compatible with the goals of sustainable development at national and global levels.

For the largest and wealthiest cities, a large part of the transfer of environmental costs to their region has now been transferred to other region and to global systems. The demands they concentrate for food, fuel and raw materials are largely met by imports from distant ecosystems with much less demand placed on the surrounding region—which makes it easier to maintain high environmental standards in this region and, for instance, to preserve forests and natural landscapes. In addition, the goods whose fabrication involves high levels of fossil fuel consumption, water use and other natural resource use, and dirty industrial processes (including the generation of hazardous wastes) and hazardous conditions for the workforce can be imported. The possibilities for enterprises and consumers to import such goods is much helped by the low price of oil.

Other cost transfers are into the future. For instance, air pollution may have been cut in many of the world's wealthiest cities, but emissions of carbon dioxide (the main greenhouse gas) remain very high and in most cities may continue to rise—for instance, because of increasing private automobile ownership and use. This is transferring costs to the future through the human and ecological costs of atmospheric warming. The generation of hazardous non-biodegradable wastes (including radioactive wastes) and non-biodegradable wastes whose rising concentrations within the biosphere are having worrying ecological consequences are also transferring costs to the future. Current levels of consumption for the products of agriculture and forestry are also a concern where the soils and forests are being destroyed or degraded and biodiversity reduced.

While there is disagreement as to where the limits are for the use of non-renewable resources, the exploitation of soils and forests, and the use of the global sink for greenhouse gases, it is clear that the level of waste and greenhouse gas emissions per capita created by the lifestyles of most middle- and upper-income households in the North could not be sustained if most of the world's population were to have comparable levels. Wealthy households in the South may have comparable levels of consumption, but it is the concentration of the world's high-consumption households in the North and the much greater historical contribution of the population in the North to existing global environmental problems that makes this a North–South issue.

When judged only in terms of resource use and waste generation, most urban centres in the lower-income nations of the South perform well in that the low levels of economic activity and limited consumption levels of most of the population ensure that figures for resource use per person are very low. So too are per capita levels of greenhouse gas emissions and stratospheric ozone-depleting chemical emissions. Low-income urban citizens are also models of 'sustainable consumption' in that they use very few non-renewable resources and generate very little waste. They are also among the most assiduous collectors and users of recycled or reclaimed materials. But these are also generally the people who face the most serious poverty and have the most serious environmental problems in terms of exposure to infectious and parasitic diseases and to chemical and physical hazards. This is a reminder of the need to assess the environmental performance of cities in all five of the above categories.

Assessing Cities' Regional and Global Ecological and Human Footprints

It is difficult to estimate the ecological costs that arise from producing the large and diverse range of raw materials, intermediate goods and final goods that meet the demands of urban producers and consumers. Certain concepts have helped to map out and to begin to quantify the scale and nature of these inter-regional or international transfers of environmental costs. One is the calculation of cities' 'ecological footprints' developed by William Rees (Rees, 1992; Wackernagel and Rees, 1996) which makes evident the large land area on whose production the inhabitants and businesses of any city depend for food, other renewable resources and the absorption of carbon to compensate for the carbon dioxide emitted from fossil fuel use. Rees calculated that the lower Fraser valley of British Columbia (Canada)

in which Vancouver is located has an ecological footprint of about 20 times as much land as it occupies—to produce the food and forestry products its inhabitants and businesses use and to grow vegetation to absorb the carbon dioxide they produce (Rees, 1992). London's ecological footprint is estimated to be 125 times its actual size, based on similar criteria (Jopling and Giradet, 1996). However, care is needed in comparing the size of different cities' ecological footprints. One reason is that the size of the footprint as a multiple of the city area will vary considerably, depending on where the city boundary is drawn—and this is the main reason why London's inhabitants appear to have a much larger individual ecological footprint than the inhabitants of the Fraser valley.[2] A second reason is differences between cities in the quality and range of statistics from which a city's ecological footprint is calculated. Finally, the calculation of ecological footprints for cities should not obscure the fact that particular enterprises and richer income groups contribute disproportionately to these footprints. For example, Wackernagel and Rees (1996) calculate that the average ecological footprint for the poorest 20 per cent of Canada's population is less than one-quarter that of the wealthiest 20 per cent.

The concept of ecological footprints can also be applied to particular activities—for instance, Wackernagel and Rees (1996) consider the ecological footprint of different kinds of housing, different commuting patterns, road bridges and different goods (including tomato production and newspapers). Another concept that helps to reveal the reliance of wealthy cities on non-renewable resources is the 'material intensity' of the goods consumed in that city (or what is sometimes termed the 'ecological rucksack' of the goods) The material intensity of any good can be calculated, relative to the service it provides, as a way of providing a quick and rough estimate of its environmental impact (Schmidt-Bleek, 1993). This calculation can include all the energy and material inputs into any good—from the extraction or fabrication of materials used to make it, through its use, to its final disposal. It can also include consideration of how much service that good provides, including how long it lasts—so, for instance, a fridge or car that lasted 20 years would have less material intensity than one that lasted 10 years. It has been calculated that a home fridge designed to lower its 'material input: intensity of service ratio' could be constructed with available technologies and materials to achieve a resource productivity of roughly six times that of currently available models (Tischner and Schmidt-Bleek, 1993). There is also the long-established practice of calculating the energy-intensity of different goods which can take into account the energy used in their fabrication, transport, preparation for sale, sale, use and disposal. Since, in most instances, most or all of the energy input comes from fossil fuels, this allows an idea of how the use of this good contributes to the use of fossil fuels and the generation of carbon dioxide (the largest contributor to atmospheric warming)—and perhaps also some idea of the air pollution implications of its fabrication, use and disposal.

While these concepts have helped to make apparent the extent to which modern cities generate environmental costs far from their boundaries, it is difficult to quantify all such transfers. For instance, the long-term health and ecological consequences of many chemical wastes are unknown—including those arising from the accumulation of certain persistent chemicals. It is also difficult to estimate the scale of the health risks faced by the workers and their families who make the goods which the consumers and enterprises within wealthy cities use. It is also difficult to adjust the calculations for a city's 'ecological footprint' to take account of the goods and services that its enterprises produce for those living outside its boundaries. To take an extreme example, a city which produced high-fuel-efficiency buses or solar panels would have the fossil fuel inputs into their fabrication taken as part of the city's ecological footprint, but no allowance made for these goods' contribution to reducing the ecological footprint in other locations.

Constraints on Action in the Five Categories

The distinction between the five categories for environmental action outlined above is reflected in the historical evolution of government intervention in the urban environment—as the first category became a major concern during the second half of the 19th century (and is often referred to as the sanitary revolution) with the second and third following soon after, although progress on many aspects of these had to wait until citizen pressure helped to ensure that safeguarding environmental quality became an accepted part of governments' responsibilities. The fourth and fifth are more recent in terms of their widespread discussion among governments and international agencies, although there is a literature dating back at least 20 years on the need to move in this direction (see, for instance, Ward, 1976, and the discussions about a 'conserver society' within Canada during the mid 1970s).[3] This should not be taken to imply that environmental action in cities has to go through these five categories sequentially—and there are many long-term advantages for city authorities in recognising the validity of all five, as long as their priorities do not become distorted (as in a concern for 'sustainable consumption' detracting from more pressing and immediate needs for improved environmental health).

This distinction between these five categories is also useful in considering the political economy of environmental problems since there are differences between the categories in terms of who is responsible for the problems; who is most affected by them; the possibilities for those who are affected to get the problems addressed; how the problems are addressed; and by whom. Addressing the environmental problems in the first category has long been understood as the responsibility of public authorities—in public health and environmental health—even if many of the actions may be delegated or contracted to private enterprises, non-government organisations or community-based organisations. In category 2, it is again recognised as the role of public authorities to set standards and to enforce them—with unions and other worker organisations having a major role in promoting solutions for occupational health and safety and consumer groups and democratic political structures having importance in getting action on other chemical and physical hazards. Democratic political structures also have great importance in category 3, in ensuring that the environmental priorities of all the urban population are addressed.

There are obvious vested interests that oppose public action in each of these categories as they imply higher costs for certain enterprises or citizens or controls over what they can do within their enterprise or on land that they purchase or with the wastes they generate. But in categories 1–3, at least city authorities can seek compromises between those involved; it is one of their central functions to do so. In most cities, there are areas of broad agreement among diverse groups for the promotion of health, prevention of disease and achievement of environmental quality—and it is developing and promoting this common agenda that is at the core of Healthy City programmes (WHO, 1996).

One important institutional difficulty arises if environmental problems or costs are being transferred from one area to another and the local authority structure is made up of different, largely autonomous local authorities with no mechanisms to manage inter-municipality disputes and resource transfers. The transfer of environmental costs from richer to poorer areas within nations or regions is what underlies what is often termed 'environmental racism' as polluting industries or wastes are systematically located in lower-income areas. There is also the institutional difficulty in addressing environmental problems in category 4, where urban authorities have no jurisdiction in the wider region and where the power of the city-based vested interests to use resources or sinks in the region around the city in environmentally damaging ways is generally greater than is that of its inhabitants to prevent such uses.

The institutional difficulties in categories 1–4 have greater possibilities of being resolved since they fall within the boundaries of one nation. For category 5, most do not and it is difficult to foresee how to prevent such transfers. There has been some progress on this front in recent years, mostly through pressure brought on governments and business by consumer groups or NGOs (see, for instance, Harrison, 1997). For example, what is termed 'green consumerism' (where purchasers choose goods whose fabrication or use has less damaging environmental consequences), and which is supported by 'eco-labelling' by environmental groups, has put pressure on many manufacturers to address the environmental implications of their products' fabrication, use and disposal. 'Fair-trade' campaigns and the sale of 'fair-trade' goods have helped to raise issues such as the wages and/or working conditions of those who make the goods or the human rights records of their governments. These have also put pressure on producers and retailers to take what is usually termed 'ethical sourcing' more seriously—for instance, to avoid the use of goods produced in countries or by companies with poor human rights or environmental records. Many companies' unethical investments or products or poor environmental performance have been exposed by campaigns—for instance, to promote consumer boycotts of their products—or by environmental or human rights campaigners purchasing some shares and bringing pressure on the company at shareholder meetings. There are examples of companies (including multinational corporations) who have made explicit commitments to improving environmental performance or better wages and working conditions for their workforce or for those working in major sub-contractors—and even a few that allow independent audits to check on their claims. There are examples of governments who have promoted or supported eco-labelling and the control of certain imports for ethical or environmental reasons. But the people who are affected by the international transfer of environmental costs have no direct political influence on the governments of the nations into which the goods they helped to produce are imported.

There is some international action to prevent the most obvious and blatant international transfer of environmental costs—as in the controls on the export of hazardous wastes and on the trade of endangered species or products derived from them. But the basis of international trade would be threatened if action extended to address all such transfers—for instance, through governments in the North only permitting imports from countries in the South where good standards of occupational health and safety were maintained. Or where the import of goods produced by multinational corporations was only permitted if the corporation and its main sub-contractors met agreed standards for good environmental practice in the use of resources and generation and management of wastes in all its operations in different countries—with independent groups allowed to monitor their performance. Such controls appear at odds with the process of globalisation, but it is difficult to foresee how to prevent this transfer of environmental costs to other people or ecosystems without such measures (see Goodland, 1995, and Redclift, 1996). The initiatives to promote green consumerism and fair trade can only have limited impact if the goods they promote have to compete with those whose lower price reflects the inadequate wages and poor working conditions of those who made them and the avoidance of costs through no attention to pollution control and waste management.

Integrating Improved Environmental Performance into the Social, Economic and Political Goals of Sustainable Development

One of the more contentious issues in discussions of 'sustainable development' is what the 'sustainable' refers to. A review of the literature on sustainable development found that much of it was almost exclusively concerned with ecological sustainability, with little or no mention of 'development' in the sense of the meeting of human needs (Mitlin,

1992). Perhaps partly in reaction to this, there are also discussions of sustainable development that focus almost exclusively on meeting human needs with little consideration of ecological sustainability—as in, for instance, the Habitat II documents, as will be discussed later. There is also a third set of literature, most of it coming from international agencies, where the term 'sustainable development' is used in discussions about whether the projects of international agencies will continue to function, after the removal of foreign aid; here, too, little or no consideration is generally given to ecological sustainability. Perhaps what makes the Brundtland Commission's statement so important is its insistence that meeting human needs must be combined with ecological sustainability—to meet 'the needs of the present without compromising the ability of future generations to meet their own needs' (World Commission on Environment and Development, 1987, p. 8).

In previous work with Jorge Hardoy and Diana Mitlin, we suggested that the 'sustainable' part of sustainable development be considered as avoiding the depletion of environmental capital (or concentrating on ecological sustainability) while the 'development' part of sustainable development be considered the meeting of human needs (see, for instance, Hardoy *et al.*, 1992; Mitlin and Satterthwaite, 1996). This led to an elaboration of the social, economic and political goals, based on the Brundtland Commission's statement given above—within a commitment to limit or stop the depletion of the four kinds of environmental capital (see Table 1). The upper part of this table summarises the social, economic and political goals inherent in meeting human needs; these will not be elaborated here, since the purpose of this paper is to concentrate on the environmental aspects of sustainable development.[4]

However, some mention should be made of the issue of population growth since this affects both the 'sustainable' and the 'development' components—and the issue of population growth is rarely given much attention within the discussions of sustainable devel-

Table 1. The multiple goals of sustainable development as applied to cities

---

Meeting the needs of the present....

Economic needs—includes access to an adequate livelihood or productive assets; also economic
security when unemployed, ill, disabled or otherwise unable to secure a livelihood.

Social, cultural and health needs—includes a shelter which is healthy, safe, affordable and secure,
within a neighbourhood with provision for piped water, sanitation, drainage, transport, health
care, education and child development. Also, a home, workplace and living environment
protected from environmental hazards, including chemical pollution. Also important are needs
related to people's choice and control—including homes and neighbourhoods which they value
and where their social and cultural priorities are met. Shelters and services must meet the
specific needs of children and of adults responsible for most child-rearing (usually women).
Achieving this implies a more equitable distribution of income between nations and, in most,
within nations.

Political needs—includes freedom to participate in national and local politics and in decisions
regarding management and development of one's home and neighbourhood—within a broader
framework which ensures respect for civil and political rights and the implementation of
environmental legislation.

.... without compromising the ability of future generations to meet their own needs

Minimising use or waste of non-renewable resources—includes minimising the consumption of fossil
fuels in housing, commerce, industry and transport plus substituting renewable sources where
feasible. Also, minimising waste of scarce mineral resources (reduce use, re-use, recycle,
reclaim). There are also cultural, historical and natural assets within cities that are irreplaceable
and thus non-renewable—for instance, historical districts and parks and natural landscapes which
provide space for play, recreation and access to nature.

Sustainable use of finite renewable resources—cities drawing on fresh-water resources at levels
which can be sustained (with recycling and re-use promoted). Keeping to a sustainable
ecological footprint in terms of land area on which city-based producers and consumers draw for
agricultural and forest products and biomass fuels.

Biodegradable wastes not overtaxing capacities of renewable sinks (e.g. capacity of a river to break
down biodegradable wastes without ecological degradation).

*Non-biodegradable wastes/emissions not overtaxing (finite) capacity of local and global sinks to
absorb or dilute them without adverse effects* (e.g. persistent pesticides, greenhouse gases and
stratospheric ozone-depleting chemicals).

Source: Developed from Mitlin and Satterthwaite (1994).

opment and cities (Drakakis-Smith, 1996).
Discussing population growth is complicated
by the scale of the differentials between the
largest and the smallest consumers in terms
of their contribution to the depletion of natural capital. There is a tendency to assume that
the size of a city's, nation's or region's population is the main influence on its depletion
of natural capital and that the rate of population growth is the main influence on the
rate of change in this depletion. But a
significant proportion of the urban population
in the South (including many of the people in
cities which have had rapid population
growth rates in recent decades) have consumption levels that are so low that they
contribute little or nothing to the use of
non-renewable resources and the generation
of wastes, including the generation of greenhouse gases. Worldwide, most resource use
and waste generation arise from the consumption patterns of middle- and upper-income households (most with very low
fertility rates) and the enterprises which produce the goods they consume. In addition,
countries in the South which have had the
fastest growing economies in recent decades
are also likely to be the countries with the
most rapid growth in the use of natural capital and generally the largest decreases in
population growth.[5] In regard to sustainable
development, perhaps the most important issue to stress is that meeting human needs as
outlined in Table 1, which includes meeting

the sexual and reproductive health needs of men and women, also supports a rapid decrease in fertility rates in countries with high population growth rates (see, for instance Sen *et al.*, 1994). But it may also provide the basis for far more people to choose high-consumption lifestyles—which is why the meeting of human needs has to be combined with considerations of how to minimise the depletion of environmental capital.

This distinction between the 'ecological sustainability' and the 'development' components of sustainable development has the advantage of avoiding the ambiguities inherent in such terms as 'economic sustainability', 'social sustainability' and 'cultural sustainability' where it is not certain what is to be sustained and how sustaining it would affect environmental capital. For instance, the concept of social sustainability might be taken to mean the sustaining of current societies and their social structures when the meeting of human needs without depleting environmental capital implies major changes to existing social structures. If social sustainability is taken to mean the social measures needed to prevent social disruption or conflict—and the reduction of poverty justified by this— as McGranahan *et al.* (1996) point out, the legitimate objection to poverty is not because it undermines 'social sustainability' as the poor protest, but the suffering the poverty causes.

Phrases such as 'sustainable cities', 'sustainable human settlements' and 'sustainable urbanisation' are also unclear for similar reasons.[6] It is not cities or urbanisation that sustainable development seeks to sustain, but to meet human needs in settlements of all sizes without depleting environmental capital. This means seeking the institutional and regulatory framework in which democratic and accountable urban and municipal authorities ensure that the needs of the people within their boundaries are addressed while minimising the transferring of environmental costs to other people or ecosystems or into the future. This in turn requires consideration of the kinds of national policies and legal and institutional frameworks and the kinds of international agreements that encourage urban and municipal authorities in this direction.

The Local, National and International Frameworks for Promoting Sustainable Development and Cities

The beginning of this paper noted the many examples of progress by urban and municipal authorities in different regions of the world towards sustainable development goals. There are examples of innovations by such authorities in all five of the categories of environmental action described above. This highlights the relevance for all cities of the point made by the European Commission's report on *European Sustainable Cities* (European Commission, 1994) that local governments with their many and varied roles are in a strong position to advance the goals of sustainable development as direct or indirect providers of services, regulator, leader by example, community informer, advocate, adviser, partner, mobiliser of community resources and initiator of dialogue and debate. There are also examples of how what might be termed a 'sustainable consumption' logic can be institutionalised in building codes and zoning and sub-division regulations, in planning for transport, water supply and waste water disposal, recreation and urban expansion, in local revenue-raising (through environmental taxes, charges and levies) and through local authorities bringing in environmental considerations when budgeting, purchasing and tendering.

But there are also the limits on the capacities of urban and municipal authorities to act. This is especially so in most of Africa, Asia and Latin America where their powers and the resources at their disposal severely limit their capacity to act on the five categories outlined above. Although there has been some decentralisation of decision-making power and considerable progress in more democratic and transparent urban authorities in many nations in the South over the past 10–15 years, most urban authorities have very limited funds for capital investment at their disposal (UNCHS, 1996). They depend on higher levels of government or international development assistance (negotiated through higher levels of government) for this and it is obviously difficult to develop a long-term programme to improve their environmental performance without an assured source of funding. Privatising public services can draw on another source of capital for investment, although private enterprises are generally only interested in those aspects of environmental improvement for which the beneficiaries can be charged and can pay. In addition, the extent to which privatisation is able to compensate for weak and ineffective local authorities in the South has been exaggerated (see, for instance, Sivaramakrishnan, 1997). Ironically, although privatisation was seen as a solution to weak and ineffective city authorities, privatisation is likely to work best where the local authorities are able to set appropriate terms for private-sector enterprises and monitor the cost and the quality of any services they provide—and, where needed, to enforce compliance with agreed standards and prices.

In the North, urban and local authorities generally have far more resources, better-trained staff and a more assured source of capital investment, although urban and municipal authorities in the poorest urban areas face particular problems. But all urban and municipal authorities are limited in what they can achieve in regard to the fifth category, 'sustainable consumption', although sustainable development cannot be achieved if there is not progress in this category. The reviews of recent experiences in European cities point to a large range of environmental innovations—for instance, expanding the pedestrianisation of streets, in public transport, in waste management (including recycling and waste reduction) and urban 'greening' (European Commission, 1994; Mega, 1996a, 1996b). They point to many examples of good governance as urban authorities become more explicit in their goals to improve health and environmental performance, more transparent and co-operative in the ways they work and with a greater commitment to en-

vironmental auditing. However, much of what is being done is only local and regional in scope and thus covering only the first four categories in which action is needed. Improving each city's environment and protecting its cultural heritage (and by doing so increasing its attraction to new investment and tourism) and reducing the environmental damage done to the surrounding region do not necessarily reduce greenhouse gas emissions (although some of the initiatives can do so by reducing fossil fuel use).

This implies the need for international agreements that set enforceable limits on each national society's consumption of scarce resources (or resources whose use implies unacceptable ecological costs) and their use of the global sink for wastes. But it is also clear that most action to achieve sustainable development has to be formulated and implemented locally. The fact that each village, province or city and its insertion within local and regional ecosystems is unique implies the need for optimal use of local resources, knowledge and skills for the achievement of development goals within a detailed knowledge of the local and regional ecological carrying capacity (see, for instance, Drakakis-Smith, 1996). As Pugh notes,

> At all levels of policy and programme application (for government agencies), there are situational complexities in endeavouring to balance economic efficiency, the operation of markets, regard to the public goods and economic externality aspects of the environment, and attention to issues affecting poverty and social justice (Pugh, 1996, pp. 234–235).

This requires a considerable degree of local self-determination, since centralised decision-making structures have difficulty in implementing decisions which respond appropriately to such diversity. Nevertheless, national and international frameworks are needed to ensure that individual cities or countries do not take advantage of others' restraint. Cities where businesses, consumers and local authorities improve their environmental performance, including reducing their

1684   DAVID SATTERTHWAITE

transfer of environmental costs to other locations, need to be rewarded, not penalised as enterprises and consumers who want to avoid good environmental performance move elsewhere.

There is the danger that Redclift (1996) highlights—that the 'solution' to what are perceived as global problems may be forms of global environmental management. But these global problems are caused by the aggregation of production and consumption, much of it concentrated within the world's urban centres. Redclift suggests that we cannot 'manage' the environment successfully at the global level without first achieving progress towards sustainability at the local level.

> We are in effect inventing new institutional structures for managing the environment which bear little or no relation to the processes through which the environment is being transformed (Redclift, 1996, p. 1).

But it is also difficult to see how local decisions will incorporate global responsibilities without international agreements among governments to take responsibility for addressing global problems within their boundaries. If the governments of nations within the North commit themselves to reduced levels of greenhouse gas emissions, they will have to develop the incentives and regulations that support reduced greenhouse gas emissions within each locality—but with local decisions about how best to achieve this. And as Redclift (1996) also points out, this must be done in ways that incorporate a knowledge of the consequences of our behaviour into the behaviour itself rather than seeking to invent management techniques to combat the contradictions of development (Redclift, 1996). We need to recover control over consumption rather than set up new institutions to manage its consequences.

National governments have the main responsibility for ensuring that local authorities address categories 4 and 5, as well as the first three. Internationally, they have the responsibility for reaching agreements to limit the call that consumers and businesses within their country make on the world's environ-

mental capital. But there is little evidence of national governments setting up the regulatory and incentive structure to ensure that the aggregate impact of the economic activities within their boundaries and their citizens' consumption is not transferring environmental costs to other nations or to the future—although a few governments in Europe have taken some tentative steps towards some aspects (see European Commission, 1994; UNCHS, 1996; Mega, 1996b). What is also noticeable is the extent to which urban issues are given little attention in most national sustainable development strategies, despite the prominent role of city-based production and consumption in most nations' resource use, waste generation and greenhouse gas emissions and despite the great potential for cities and for urban policies to contribute to addressing sustainable consumption (Mitlin and Satterthwaite, 1996; UNCHS, 1996). Much of the general literature on national environmental and sustainable development plans also ignores or gives very little attention to urban issues—see, for example, Carew-Reid *et al.*, 1994, and Dalal-Clayton, 1996.

The kind of incentive and regulatory structure that is needed to promote the achievement of sustainable development goals in cities is relatively easy to conceive, as an abstract exercise. Certainly, human needs can be met and poverty greatly reduced without an expansion in resource use and waste generation which threatens ecological sustainability. It is also possible to envisage a considerable reduction in resource use and waste generation by middle-and upper-income households, without diminishing their quality of life and in some aspects enhancing it (see, for instance, the many studies showing how fossil fuel use in the North can be cut considerably without reducing living standards—as in Leach *et al.*, 1979). The work of the Rocky Mountain Institute in the US (among other groups) has highlighted the extent to which resource use and waste can be cut within prosperous economies, without compromising living standards (for example, Lovins and Lovins, 1991). There is also considerable potential for employment creation in a shift to lower levels of resource use and waste, although some employment in certain businesses or sectors will suffer (see Mitlin and Satterthwaite, 1996; and, for Europe, Wikima Consulting, 1993).

It is also possible to envisage the poorer nations achieving the prosperity and economic stability they need to underpin secure livelihoods and decent living conditions for their populations and the needed enhancement in the competence and accountability of their government without a much increased call on environmental capital. The knowledge exists on how to develop more productive and sustainable agriculture (see, for instance, Pretty *et al.*, 1992), forestry management (see, for instance, Sargent and Bass, 1992), industrial production (Robins and Trisoglio, 1992) and settlement patterns (Breheny, 1992; Haughton and Hunter, 1994; Blowers, 1993; UNCHS, 1996). But the prospects for translating what is possible into the needed national frameworks and international agreements remain much less certain. Powerful vested interests oppose most if not all the needed policies and priorities. Richer groups will oppose what they see as controls on their right to consume or higher costs that arise from changed pricing structures to encourage conservation and waste reduction. Technological change can help resolve this—for instance, moderating the impact of rising gasoline prices through the relatively rapid introduction of increasingly fuel-efficient automobiles and the introduction of alternative fuels derived from renewable energy sources. But if combatting atmospheric warming does demand the scale of reduction in greenhouse gas emissions that the IPCC's most recent assessment suggests, this will imply changes in people's right to use private automobiles which cannot be met by new technologies and alternative ('renewable') fuels—at least at costs which at present would prove politically acceptable. As Professor O'Riordan recently commented, 'as the scientific case to curb global warming has strengthened, so the politicians have retreated' (quoted in Pearce, 1997, p. 12).

There are also the difficulties in converting buildings, settlement patterns, urban systems and energy, transport and waste disposal systems that developed during the last 40 years of low oil prices which are not easily modified for much-reduced fossil fuel use. So many existing commercial, industrial and residential buildings and urban forms (for instance, low-density suburban developments and out-of-town shopping malls) have high levels of energy use built into them and these are not easily or rapidly changed (Gore, 1991). This means a number of critical consumption areas that are not determined by consumer preference, as individuals are locked into relatively high consumption patterns by physical infrastructure over which they have little or no control—energy, housing, transport and waste collection systems are prime examples (Robins and Roberts, 1996). It is difficult for urban households to maintain a commitment to recycling if it is difficult for them to take the separated materials to recycling points. In many cities in the North, it is difficult for households to avoid purchasing a car, as urban forms have changed to serve car users and not pedestrians, bicyclists and public transport users. Many of the lowest-income households in the North have the worst-insulated housing and the least capacity to pay for addressing this. Many also rent their accommodation and are reluctant to invest in improvements from which the landlord will draw most benefits. There are also consumption habits that have developed among the world's middle- and upper-income groups that are probably incompatible with sustainable development, if extended to more than a small minority of the world's population— for instance, the much-increased use of air transport and the widespread use of private automobiles for leisure.

An Initial Assessment of the Outcome of Habitat II for Promoting Sustainable Development and Cities

In light of the above discussion, the two key documents that came out of the Habitat II

Conference (the Istanbul Declaration on Human Settlements and the Habitat Agenda) can be assessed for the extent to which they addressed the two central points of sustainable development in regard to cities: a strong priority to meeting human needs within a strong commitment to minimise the depletion of the four different kinds of environmental capital listed in the bottom half of Table 1.

In making this assessment, it must be remembered that these large global conferences seek a consensus among the representatives of all governments present. Both the Declaration and the Habitat Agenda had to be acceptable to the representatives of some 150 government delegations and with considerable pressure being brought to bear on government delegations from groups as diverse as the Catholic Church, the US government's delegation (and their strong opposition to housing being considered a human right through much of the preparatory process) and feminist and human rights coalitions. It is easy to point to a lack of precision in some of the language used, the repetition and the tendency to have long lists of 'problems' with little consideration of their linkages (and often their underlying causes). But these are to be expected in a document that had to cover such a large subject area, including many issues which are controversial, *and* to be endorsed by representatives of so many different governments with diverse positions *and* in which so many groups demanded or promoted additional text or changes to the draft text. Where the wording of a paragraph on some controversial issue appears unclear or imprecise, this may be because greater clarity or precision prevented agreement by some government representative or representative of some group of countries. One of the persons involved in drafting the document admitted that on the first day of the Conference itself, nearly seven hours were spent in deciding whether sustainable settlements 'promote' or 'should promote' human rights and this is a reminder of how complex it can be to reach agreement among so many interested parties (Kakakhel, 1996).

A first impression of the treatment of sustainable development and cities within the two key documents could be favourable. Both the Istanbul Declaration on Human Settlements and the Habitat Agenda make frequent mention of 'sustainable human settlements' or 'sustainable human settlements development'; sustainable urban development is also mentioned several times. Sustainable human settlements development is one of the two major themes for the conference, the other being 'adequate shelter for all'. In addition, both documents give a high priority to the meeting of human needs in cities (and other human settlements) including the need for a strong priority for poverty reduction. They also stress the need to address environmental problems and acknowledge the important health components in doing so. There is also a strong stress on the need to strengthen city and municipal authorities.

However, the documents are weakest where they needed to be strongest—in agreeing on the kind of national and international frameworks that would ensure sustainable development goals are addressed in cities (and other settlements). As one of the World Bank's most experienced urban specialists noted:

> The biggest gap in the Istanbul discussions was the lack of progress in operationalizing the notion of environmentally sustainable development ... While the term 'sustainable development' was mentioned repeatedly, little progress was made in suggesting how it could be operationally applied to urban areas (Cohen, 1996, p. 4).

The Habitat II documents make little mention of the kinds of framework needed to achieve significant reductions in the depletion of environmental capital from the people and enterprises who at present contribute most to these (a high proportion of which are concentrated in cities in the North). It also made little mention of the new resources that need to be directed to the meeting of human needs in the nations where there are insufficient resources to achieve this.

There is also considerable confusion within the Habitat II documents as to what sustainable development is meant to sustain—whether it is settlements or settlement policies or particular activities within settlements. This was not a confusion that arose from the search for consensus at the Conference itself, for it was present in earlier drafts of what became the Habitat Agenda. Within the text, sometimes, it is human settlements that are to be sustainable—for instance, 'sustainable human settlements' or 'sustainable urban centres' or 'sustainable communities'—or aggregates of human settlements, as in sustainable spatial development patterns. In other instances, it is society in general or living conditions that are to be 'sustainable'. In others, it is particular activities within urban areas that are to be sustainable—as in sustainable shelter markets and land development or sustainable transport, sustainable agriculture, sustainable livelihoods, sustainable resource use, sustainable water supply or sustainable energy use. 'Sustained economic growth and equity' are also mentioned as part of sustainable development; clearly, 'sustained economic growth' is not part of sustainable development, although one suspects that what the delegates meant was that the promotion of sustainable development should not inhibit lower-income countries achieving higher incomes and greater economic prosperity and stability.

The worry of government delegates from the South that environmental measures might be the means by which the North inhibits their economic development is still strong in these global meetings—after surfacing as long ago as the 1972 UN Conference on the Human Environment in Stockholm which initiated the cycle of global UN conferences on environment and development issues. The closest the Habitat II documents come to addressing the loss of environmental capital arising from high-consumption lifestyles is several references to 'unsustainable consumption and production patterns, particularly in industrialized countries' (Istanbul Declaration, para. 4), but these are not addressed in the recommendations. And despite the length of the Habitat II documents, there is no mention of the dangers posed to settlements by global warming or of the need to curb greenhouse gas emissions. Perhaps the delegates felt that this was unnecessary, since the Habitat II documentation endorsed the recommendations of previous conferences, and that this was an issue covered by Agenda 21, coming out of the Earth Summit (the UN Conference on Environment and Development in 1992).

The Habitat II documents also have many examples of where it is not human settlements or activities in human settlements, but the development of human settlements that should be sustainable—or particular human settlements policies as in sustainable land-use policies or more sustainable population policies. Sometimes it is broader than this as in sustainable economic development and social development activities. In regard to what constitutes sustainable development, the documents often refer to this being a combination of economic development, social development and environmental protection.[7] These are mentioned as 'interdependent and mutually reinforcing components of sustainable development'.[8] This highlights another flaw in the documents—the assumption that a concern for environmental quality within cities is all that is needed to achieve the environmental component of sustainable development goals. What this misses is the many means by which enterprises and those with high-consumption lifestyles transfer some of their environmental costs to other people, other regions or into the future, as outlined in earlier sections.

Although much of the literature on sustainable development can be criticised for emphasising the sustaining of environmental capital to the virtual exclusion of any consideration of human needs, the Habitat II documents do the opposite. Two factors help explain this. The first, already noted, is the way in which many development agencies came to use the term sustainable development as the label given to ensuring that their development projects continued to operate when these agencies' external support was cut off at the 'end of the project'. Although this is a problem that was recognised before the term sustainable development became widely used, many international agencies borrowed the new terminology, without taking on board its original meaning. The second is the desire of the United Nations Centre for Human Settlements which was responsible for organising the Habitat II Conference and the government ministries which deal with this UN agency—mainly ministries of housing (Sivaramakrishnan, 1997)—to put human needs at the centre of 'sustainable development'—partly in reaction to the failure of so much of the sustainable development literature to do so. But in doing so, they gave little attention to the fact that sustainable development is also about addressing the depletion of environmental capital (and not just promoting environmental quality in settlements). Perhaps the avoidance of clear positions and specific recommendations that address the more contentious issues within sustainable development is the cost that had to be paid for achieving consensus. But this means that the Habitat II documents include no recommendations on many of the key points in regard to what needs to be done to ensure that sustainable development goals are met in cities (and other settlements).

Conclusions

This paper has outlined a framework for a more comprehensive accounting of cities' environmental performance, within a commitment to other sustainable development goals. It has stressed the importance of taking account of the environmental costs generated or imposed by city-based activities on people or ecological resources outside city boundaries or displaced into the future. It has also stressed the importance of integrating the discussions about cities and sustainable development with the general discussions about sustainable development and ensuring that urban issues are fully considered within national environmental plans and national sustainable development strategies.

Given the tendency for many environmentalists to view cities only as places which generate environmental costs, a greater attention to cities' environmental problems might also ignore the benefits that city-based enterprises and consumers provide (or can provide) for people, natural resources and ecosystems outside their boundaries. Of course, these include the goods purchased by city businesses, governments and consumers which provide incomes from those living outside the city and the goods and services provided by city-enterprises to those living outside the city. Also, care must be taken in ascribing blame to 'cities' for environmental costs transferred from within cities to other ecosystems or people, in that it is particular groups in cities (mostly the higher-income groups) and particular enterprises who are responsible for most such costs.

In addition, the inherent advantages that cities have or can have for combining high-quality living conditions with low levels of resource use, waste and greenhouse gas emissions per person should not be forgotten (Mitlin and Satterthwaite, 1996; UNCHS, 1996). Nor must we forget the fact that wealthy rural or suburban households generally have higher levels of resource use and waste generation than their counterparts living in cities—they own more automobiles, use them more often and have higher levels of energy use within their homes. What this paper has sought to stress is the areas where improved environmental performance is needed in cities and how this should also be integrated with the social, economic and political goals of sustainable development. This is not achieved by focusing on sustainable cities, but on how city consumers, enterprises and governments can contribute more to sustainable development.

Notes

1. IIED monitors the priority given by international agencies to addressing basic needs and to urban development. A summary of the findings of its work in this regard was published in UNCHS (1996).

2. The calculation for London was based on an area of 1580 sq km (virtually all of which is built-up area) with a population of 7 million. The calculation for the lower Fraser valley was for an urban-agricultural region of 4000 sq km with 1.8 million inhabitants.

3. These were published in a quarterly publication *Conserver Society Notes* by the Science Council of Canada in Ottawa.

4. The social, economic and political aspects are described in more detail in Mitlin and Satterthwaite (1996).

5. This association masks the many factors that influence fertility. It also obscures the fact that rapidly increasing or high per capita incomes are not necessary to bring down population growth rates or to have low population growth rates—as can be seen in, for instance, the state of Kerala in India where high priority to education and health care helped to achieve low population growth rates at a low per capita income and without co-ercive population control policies (Sen, 1994; Sen *et al.*, 1994).

6. The justification for avoiding this is discussed in more detail in Mitlin and Satterthwaite (1996).

7. See paragraph 3 of the Istanbul Declaration; also paragraph 4 and paragraph 43(b) of the Habitat Agenda. Paragraph 29 talks of sustainable human settlements development ensuring 'economic development, employment opportunities and social progress, in harmony with the environment'.

8. Paragraph 3 of the Istanbul Declaration; this is also repeated in paragraph 1 of the Habitat Agenda, then again in paragraph 8 and paragraph 43(b); paragraph 21 talks of 'economic development, social development and environmental protection' being 'indispensable and mutually reinforcing components of sustainable development'.

References

BAIROCH, P. (1988) *Cities and Economic Development: From the Dawn of History to the Present*. London: Mansell.

BARTONE, C., BERNSTEIN, J., LEITMANN, J. and EIGEN, J. (1994) *Towards Environmental Strategies for Cities: Policy Considerations for Urban Environmental Management in Developing Countries*. UNDP/UNCHS/World Bank Urban Management Program No. 18, World Bank, Washington, DC.

BLOWERS, A. (Ed.) (1993) *Planning for a Sustainable Environment*. London: Earthscan Publications.

BREHENY, M. J. (Ed.) (1992) *Sustainable Develop-ment and Urban Form*. European Research in Regional Science 2. London: Pion.

CAIRNCROSS, S., HARDOY, J. E. and SATTERTHWAITE, D. (1990) The urban context, in: J. E. HARDOY, S. CAIRNCROSS and D. SATTERTHWAITE (Eds) *The Poor Die Young: Housing and Health in Third World Cities*, pp. 1–24. London: Earthscan.

CAREW-READ, J., PRESCOTT-ALLEN, R., BASS, S. and DALAL-CLAYTON, B. (1994) *Strategies for National Sustainable Development: A Handbook for their Planning and Implementation*. London: Earthscan Publications.

COHEN, M. (1996) *Reflections on Habitat II*. Working Group on Habitat II of the Woodrow Wilson Center, Washington, DC.

CONWAY, G. R. and PRETTY, J. N. (1991) *Unwelcome Harvest*. London: Earthscan.

DALAL-CLAYTON, B. (1996) *Getting to Grips with Green Plans: National-level Experiences in Industrial Countries*. London: Earthscan Publications.

DÍAZ, D. B., LÓPEZ FOLLEGATTI, J. L. and HORDIJK, M. (1996) Innovative urban environmental management in Ilo, Peru, *Environment and Urbanization*, 8(1), pp. 21–34.

DOUGLAS, I. (1983) *The Urban Environment*. London: Edward Arnold.

DOUGLAS, I. (1986) Urban geomorphology, in: P. G. FOOKES and P. R. VAUGHAN (Eds) *A Handbook of Engineering Geomorphology*, pp. 270–283. Glasgow: Blackie and Son.

DRAKAKIS-SMITH, D. (1996) Third world cities: sustainable urban development, II—population, labour and poverty, *Urban Studies*, 33, pp. 673–701.

EUROPEAN COMMISSION EXPERT GROUP ON THE URBAN ENVIRONMENT (1994) *European Sustainable Cities, Part 1*. Brussels: European Commission, X1/95/502-en, October.

GOODLAND, R. (1995) The concept of environmental sustainability, *Annual Review of Ecological Systems*, 26, pp. 1–24.

GORE, C. (1991) *Policies and Mechanisms for Sustainable Development: The Transport Sector* (mimeograph).

HARDOY, J. E., MITLIN, D. and SATTERTHWAITE, D. (1992) *Environmental Problems in Third World Cities*. London: Earthscan.

HARRISON, R. (1997) Ethical consumption: barefaced check, *New Internationalist*, 289, April, pp. 26–27.

HART, R. (1997) *Children's Participation: The Theory and Practice of Involving Young Citizens in Community Development and Environmental Care*. London: Earthscan Publications.

HAUGHTON, G. and HUNTER, C. (1994) *Sustainable Cities*. Regional Policy and Development series. London: Jessica Kingsley.

JOPLING, J. and GIRADET, H. (1996) *Creating a*

Sustainable London. London: Sustainable London Trust.

KAKAKHEL, B. S. (1996) To bracket or not to bracket: negotiating the Habitat Agenda, *Habitat Debate*, 2(3/4), p. 15.

LEACH, G., LEWIS, C., ROMIG, F. *ET AL.* (1979) *A Low Energy Strategy for the United Kingdom.* London: Science Reviews Ltd.

LEDUC, J. W. and TIKHOMIROV, E. (1994) Global surveillance for recognition and response to emerging diseases, *Annals of the New York Academy of Sciences*, December, pp. 341–345.

LOVINS, A. B. and HUNTER LOVINS, L. (1991) Least-cost climatic stabilization, *Annual Review of Energy and Environment*, 16, pp. 433–531.

McGRANAHAN, G., SONGSORE J. and KJELLÉN, M. (1996) Sustainability, poverty and urban environmental transitions, in: C. PUGH (Ed.) *Sustainability, the Environment and Urbanization*, pp. 103–133. London: Earthscan.

MEGA, V. (1996a) Our city, our future: towards sustainable development in European cities, *Environment and Urbanization*, 8(1), pp. 133–154.

MEGA, V. (1996b) *Innovations for the Improvement of the Urban Environment: Austria, Finland, Sweden.* European Foundation for the Improvement of Living and Working Conditions Office for Official Publications of the European Communities, Luxembourg.

MITLIN, D. (1992) Sustainable development: a guide to the literature, *Environment and Urbanization*, 4(1), pp. 111–124.

MITLIN, D. and SATTERTHWAITE, D. (1994) *Cities and sustainable development.* Background paper for Global Forum '94, Manchester City Council.

MITLIN, D. and SATTERTHWAITE, D. (1996) Sustainable development and cities, in: C. PUGH (Ed.) *Sustainability, the Environment and Urbanization*, pp. 23–61. London: Earthscan Publications.

O'RIORDAN, T. (1989) The challenge of environmentalism, in: R. PEET and N. THRIFT (Eds) *New Models of Geography, Vol. 1*, pp. 77–102. London: Unwin Hyman.

PEARCE, F. (1997) Chill winds at the summit, *New Scientist*, No. 2071, pp. 12–13.

PRETTY, J., GUIJT, I., SCOONES, I. and THOMPSON, J. (1992) Regenerating agriculture; the agroecology of low-external input and community-based development, in: J. HOLMBERG (Ed.) *Policies for a Small Planet*, pp. 91–123. London: Earthscan Publications.

PUGH, C. (1996) Conclusions, in: C. PUGH (Ed.) *Sustainability, the Environment and Urbanization*, pp. 229–243. London: Earthscan.

RABINOVITCH, J. (1992) Curitiba: towards sustainable urban development, *Environment and Urbanization*, 4(2), pp. 62–77.

REDCLIFT, M. (1996) *Wasted: Counting the Costs of Global Consumption.* London: Earthscan.

REES, W. E. (1992) Ecological footprints and appropriated carrying capacity, *Environment and Urbanization*, 4(2), pp. 121–130.

ROBINS, N. and ROBERTS, S. (1996) *Sustainable Consumption, Inequality and Poverty.* London: IIED. (Mimeograph).

ROBINS, N. and TRISOGLIO, A. (1992) Restructuring industry for sustainable development, in: J. HOLMBERG (Ed.) *Policies for a Small Planet*, pp. 157–194. London: Earthscan Publications.

SARGENT, C. and BASS, S. (1992) The future shape of forests, in: J. HOLMBERG (Ed.) *Policies for a Small Planet*, pp. 195–224. London: Earthscan Publications.

SATTERTHWAITE, D. (1997) Environmental transformations in cities as they get larger, wealthier and better managed, *The Geographical Journal*, 163(2), pp. 216–224, July.

SATTERTHWAITE, D., HART, R., LEVY, C. *ET AL.* (1996) *The Environment for Children.* London: Earthscan and UNICEF.

SCHMIDT-BLEEK, F. (1993) MIPS revisited, *Fresenius Environmental Bulletin*, 2(8), pp. 407–412.

SEN, A. (1994) *Beyond Liberalization: Social Opportunity and Human Capability.* Development Economics Research Programme DEP No. 58, London School of Economics.

SEN, G., GERMAIN, A. and CHEN, L. C. (Eds) (1994) *Population Policies Reconsidered.* Boston: Harvard University Press.

SIVARAMAKRISHNAN, K. C. (1997) *The legacy of Habitat II: issues of governance*, Paper presented at the meeting of the Woodrow Wilson Centre, February.

SMIT, J., RATTU, A. and NASR, J. (1996) *Urban Agriculture: Food, Jobs and Sustainable Cities.* Publication Series for Habitat II, Vol. 1, New York: UNDP.

TISCHNER, U. and SCHMIDT-BLEEK, F. (1993) Designing goods with MIPS, *Fresenius Environmental Bulletin*, 2(8), pp. 479–484.

UNCHS (1996) *An Urbanizing World: Global Report on Human Settlements 1996.* Oxford: Oxford University Press.

WACKERNAGEL, M. and REES, W. (1996) *Our Ecological Footprint: Reducing Human Impact on the Earth.* Gabriola (Canada): New Society Publishers.

WARD, B. (1976) *The inner and the outer limits*, The Clifford Clark Memorial Lectures 1976, *Canadian Public Administration*, 19(3), Autumn, pp. 385–416.

WHO (1992) *Our Planet, Our Health.* Report of the Commission on Health and the Environment, Geneva.

WHO (1996) *Creating Healthy Cities in the 21st*

Century. Background paper prepared for the Dialogue on Health in Human Settlements for Habitat II, World Health Organization, Geneva.

WIKIMA CONSULTING (1993) *The Employment Implications of Environmental Action*. Report prepared for the Commission of the European Communities, Directorate-General on Employ-ment, Industrial Relations and Social Affairs, London.

WOHL, A. S. (1983) *Endangered Lives: Public Health in Victorian Britain*. London: Methuen.

WORLD COMMISSION ON ENVIRONMENT AND DEVELOPMENT (1987) *Our Common Future*. Oxford: Oxford University Press.